Creating Economic Space for Social Innovation

Creating Economic Space for Social Innovation

Edited by
ALEX NICHOLLS
and
RAFAEL ZIEGLER

OXFORD
UNIVERSITY PRESS

OXFORD
UNIVERSITY PRESS

Great Clarendon Street, Oxford, OX2 6DP,
United Kingdom

Oxford University Press is a department of the University of Oxford.
It furthers the University's objective of excellence in research, scholarship,
and education by publishing worldwide. Oxford is a registered trade mark of
Oxford University Press in the UK and in certain other countries

First Edition published in 2019

Impression: 1

Published in the United States of America by Oxford University Press
198 Madison Avenue, New York, NY 10016, United States of America

British Library Cataloguing in Publication Data
Data available

Library of Congress Control Number: 2019946151

ISBN 978–0–19–883051–1

DOI: 10.1093/oso/9780198830511.003.0001

Printed and bound in Great Britain by
Clays Ltd, Elcograf S.p.A.

Preface

This book aims at a comprehensive discussion of economic space for social innovation, addressing especially marginalized groups and the long-term projects, programmes, and policies that have emerged and evolved within and across European states for more equitable, inclusive, and sustainable societies.

Our book approaches the explanatory and normative questions raised by this goal via a novel approach: the Extended Social Grid Model (ESGM). The model takes inspiration from three major sources in the social sciences and ethics. It analyses social change as well as the reproduction of marginalization and exclusion within an interrelated grid of social networks, institutions, and cognitive frames, drawing on Jens Beckert's Social Grid model of social change in markets. Moving beyond market exchange, however, it situates social innovations not only within economic power dynamics but also within the interplay of economic, political, cultural, artefactual, environmental, and security-related power. It thereby situates the trajectory of social innovations in the redistributions of distributive and collective power in historical context, as pioneered by Michael Mann's work on the social sources of power. Finally, it analyses the plural ends of social innovation drawing on the capability approach, as pioneered by Amartya Sen and Martha Nussbaum. The focus on people's capabilities—their real opportunities to do and be what they have reason to value—provides an entry for the ethical evaluation of the ends and outcomes of social innovation, and also of the way people, and especially marginalized groups, are included in the formulation of ends and means. We suggest that such processes are structural and require change in power relations, if marginalization is to be effectively dealt with, rather than reproduced, via social innovation.

Part I of the book sets out the Extended Social Grid Model. It includes an exposition of the model along with background chapters on innovation, power, and marginalization, on ethics and social innovation, and on the qualitative and quantitative methods employed for the use of the model in social innovation research.

Part II of the book explores the model with a focus on social innovation trajectories and social innovation policy. Chapters on social housing, drinking-water provision, employment, education, and food provision track the emergence and development of social innovations in relation to central capabilities. They take a long-term perspective, sometimes going back to the nineteenth century or earlier. In addition to these qualitative comprehensive cases, there is a report on the quantitative results of the operationalization of the model with a view to agency and empowerment across three social innovations in Europe. This shows how a mixed-method approach can use the qualitative information of the model to tackle the difficult task of tracking agency, here modelled as self-perceived autonomy. Part II concludes with one chapter on social innovation policy in the European Union and across its member states, and a chapter on a tool that has received much attention for financing social innovation: Social Impact Bonds.

Part III revisits the Extended Social Grid Model in the light of this qualitative and quantitative research. Chapters consider the explanatory adequacy and fruitfulness of the model for innovation research and for theorizing social innovation. They draw lessons regarding the power dynamics that have to be dealt with for overcoming rather than reproducing marginalization and exclusion. Key questions include: What is the role as well as the limitation of participation in social innovation for the marginalized (chapter 13)? What is the role of capital for creating economic space for capabilities (chapter 14)? How can we approach the social impact of social innovation (chapter 15)? The part concludes with a discussion of implications for social innovation policy (chapter 16).

As this brief outline shows, this books aims to be more than yet another collection of chapters on social innovation. Rather, it aims to reflect a collaboration of many diverse scholars across Europe. Inevitably this has caused some contestation—with chapter authors from economics, sociology, and philosophy agreement on concepts and methods takes time and, even then, is not always possible. Therefore, this collection aims at a comprehensive and heterogeneous approach—one that includes many different perspectives and some unresolved theoretical tensions. The hope is that this offers the reader a rich range of perspectives on understanding and addressing the key issue of marginalization.

The material possibility for such a collective effort is due to the funding we received from the European Union's Seventh Framework Programme for research, technological development, and demonstration under grant agreement no. 613261 for the project CrESSI—Creating Economic Space for Social Innovation. It provided the possibility for discussion and joint work from 2014 until 2018. The book is a result of this joint-working possibility. Particularly, we would like to acknowledge the support and guidance of Marianne Paasi within the European Commission.

It is also a result of discussion with colleagues who were part of CrESSI but are not among the authors of this final product. We would like to thank Léa Bigot, Toa Giroletti, Gunnar Glänzel, Christopher Houghton Budd, Justus Lodemann, Sabrina Schulz, and Thomas Scheuerle for their support, as well as Ilse Oosterlaken who early on supported the project application. Their work, as well as further work of the authors of the present book, can be found on the project homepage https://www.sbs.ox.ac.uk/creating-economic-space-social-innovation, which documents the numerous working papers, two special issues, articles, and book chapters that have resulted from this book, along with practice-oriented workshops, a documentary, and a social innovation youth campaign. For such documentation as well as the practical organisation of the project, we would much like to thank the CrESSI project managers Breanne Svehla, Penny Farrar and Alexandra Robasto for their professionalism, expertise, and good spirited support throughout. Finally, the empirical part of this research projects—over a hundred interviews and a quantitative survey with more than 3,400 participants would not have been possible without the participation of innovators and beneficiaries from various social innovation networks. We hope that this book provides a way of giving something back.

We would also like to express our gratitude to the Oxford University Press editorial and production team, especially Catherine Owen and Jenny King. Most of the chapters of this book were discussed at CrESSI workshops in Berlin, Budapest, and Heidelberg and at conferences, such as notably the annual International Social Innovation Research Conference. This book has much benefitted from the discussions within this emerging social innovation research community. We hope that our book will contribute to the further development of a resilient social innovation research and practice sector across Europe that, unfazed by political obstacles (old and new), can contribute to overcoming social marginalization and exclusion via an improved understanding of these long-term challenges.

As editors we would like to dedicate this book to our children Sam, Harriet, and Juliette, as well as Aljoscha and Abigail.

Contents

List of Figures

List of Tables

List of Contributors

Jari Aro is a university researcher at Tampere University, Finland. He completed his holds a PhD in sociology, and has worked as a university lecturer in sociology and researcher in various research projects on science and technology studies. His research interests include political sociology, social studies of technology, theory and history of sociology. His most recent publication is a co-edited book with Risto Heiskala: *Policy Design in the European Union—An Empire of Shopkeepers in the Making?* (2018).

Cees van Beers is an economist and professor of economics and management of technological innovations in the Department of Technology, Policy, and Management at Delft University of Technology. He has published extensively on determinants and management of innovations and how they contribute to organizational and societal performance in international journals such as *Energy Economics, Industrial and Corporate Change, Journal of Innovation Product Management, Research Policy, Small Business Economics,* and *Technological Forecasting and Social Change.* He is co-founder of the Centre for Frugal Innovation in Africa, a joint initiative of Leiden University, Delft University of Technology, and Erasmus University Rotterdam, established to tackle complex innovation and socio-economic development challenges facing society. He has also been involved in many research projects on the impact of hidden government subsidies to fossil fuel use resulting in, among others, a monograph and studies for the World Bank.

Enrica Chiappero-Martinetti is professor of economics at the Department of Political and Social Sciences at the University of Pavia (Italy) and extraordinary professor of economics, Faculty of Economic and Management Sciences, University of Free State, South Africa. She served as vice-president of the Human Development and Capability Association (in 2004–8 and 2010–11) and she is currently editor of the *Journal of Human Development and Capabilities.* Her research interests are in the field of poverty and inequality measurement, the operationalization of the Capability Approach, agency and empowerment measures, and social innovation.

Daniel Edmiston is a lecturer in sociology and social policy at the University of Leeds. He holds a PhD in sociology and social policy and has previously worked for the Economic and Social Research Council, Prime Minister's Strategy Unit, and the Centre for Analysis of Social Exclusion, LSE. His research interests include poverty and inequality, comparative welfare reform, social innovation, and the political economy of social citizenship.

Susanne Giesecke is a political scientist by training and got her PhD from the Free University of Berlin. For more than twenty-five years she has been working on qualitative innovation research and Grand Challenges, technology assessment, governance of research and development, and evaluation of research programmes in Germany, Austria, the United States, and Brazil. She has been engaged in several national and European research projects and foresights as well as foresight networks, and many sectoral studies. As well as research projects, Susanne Giesecke's work is dedicated to a broad participatory approach, involving stakeholders and other experts into the problem solving of future societal challenges. Susanne Giesecke has also been working as an advisor and evaluator for the European Commission and for several scientific journals and research organizations. She has also worked on social innovation, organizational development, and social transformation.

Attila Havas is a senior research fellow at the Institute of Economics, Hungarian Academy of Sciences, regional editor of *International Journal of Foresight and Innovation Policy*, and member of the editorial board of *Foresight and STI Governance*. His academic interests are in economics of innovation, national and sectoral innovation systems, theory and practice of innovation policy, (technology) foresight as a policy tool, and social innovation.

Risto Heiskala is professor and director of the Institute for Advanced Social Research (IASR) at the University of Tampere Tampere University, Finland. His publications include books *Policy Design in the European Union: An Empire of Shopkeepers in the Making?* (Palgrave 2018; edited jointly with Jari Aro), *Social Innovations, Institutional Change and Economic Performanc: Making Sense of Structural Adjustment Processes in Industrial Sectors, Regions and Societies* (Edward Elgar 2007; edited jointly with Timo Hämäläinen) and *Society as Semiosis: Neostructuralist Theory of Culture and Society* (Peter Lang 2003) as well as articles in several journals.

Nadia von Jacobi is post-doctoral researcher and adjunct professor in international cooperation and development policies at the Department of Political and Social Sciences at the University of Pavia (Italy), previously post-doctoral researcher at the Saïd Business School, University of Oxford. She is member of the editorial board of the *Journal of Social Entrepreneurship*. Her research interests are in the field of institutional interconnections, institutional change and its effects on society, poverty and inequality measurement, agency and empowerment processes through social innovation.

Klaus Kubeczko is senior expert advisor and scientist at the Center for Innovation Systems and Policy at AIT—Austrian Institute of Technology. He holds a doctoral degree in socio-economics and his expertise covers innovation policy, innovation studies, and strategic foresight with a thematic focus on grand societal challenges and the transition of socio-technical systems. He has been advising policy-makers at global, European, national, and city level on these topics for more than fifteen years. His research focus lies on developing and applying heuristics to design RTI-policies such as functional innovation systems approach, system innovation, and complex innovation systems. Klaus publishes in academic books and journals, often with colleagues from SSH and natural sciences, and has been on the executive boards of the European Association for Evolutionary Political Economy and the European Society for Ecological Economics. Former research posts include IIASA, IFF Social Ecology, and other Austrian universities.

Lara Maestripieri holds a PhD in sociology and social research. She is a Marie Skłodowska-Curie fellow at the Institute of Government and Public Policies (IGOP) at the Universitat Autònoma de Barcelona, studying gender and social vulnerability from an intersectional perspective. She has previously worked on the EU-funded projects FLOWS (2011–14),

WILCO (2011–14) and CrESSI (2015–16). In 2015, she was a fellow at the Giangiacomo Feltrinelli Foundation. Her main interests of research are labour transformation in the post-industrial society, in particular: marginalized groups in labour markets (women and young people), social innovation, and emerging professions.

Georg Mildenberger manages the research department of the Center for Social Investment and Innovation of Heidelberg University. He has been working at CSI since 2007, and has been leader of different project teams working on social innovation in a European context. In the last years Georg worked not only in research on social innovation and impact measurement but also cooperated and counselled NPOs in developing and growing social innovations and building supporting structures for innovative ideas. He holds a doctoral degree of Darmstadt University, and a master's degree in philosophy and political science from Tübingen University.

György Molnár is a senior research fellow and head of the public economics and public policy research unit at the Centre for Economic and Regional Studies, Hungarian Academy of Sciences. His research interest covers welfare economics, labour economics, subjective well-being, poverty, social innovation, and social microcredit. As a volunteer, he is an expert and board member of a Hungarian social microfinance initiative, Kiútprogram, working mainly in poor Roma neighbourhoods.

C. W. M. (Ro) Naastepad is a macroeconomist with expertise in the analysis of productivity growth, work, and monetary policy, associated with the Section Economics of Innovation at Delft University of Technology as a senior lecturer. Her current focus is on how to shape technological progress and how the 'productivity dividend' could be used to fund the further development of human capacities and capabilities. Two recent publications on this topic are 'Robots and Us: Towards an Economics of the "Good Life"', *Review of Social Economy* 76(3): 302–34 (with Jesse Mulder) and 'Preventing Technological Unemployment by Widening our Understanding of Capital and Progress: Making Robots Work for Us', *Ethics and Social Welfare* 13(2): 115–32 (with Christopher Houghton Budd).

Alex Nicholls is the first tenured professor in social entrepreneurship appointed at the University of Oxford. Alex is also a tutorial fellow and member of the governing body at Harris Manchester College, University of Oxford. He was also the first staff member of the Skoll Centre for Social Entrepreneurship in 2004 for which he helped raise the funding. Alex's research interests range across several key areas within social entrepreneurship and social innovation, including: social and impact investment; the nexus of relationships between accounting, accountability, and governance; public and social policy contexts including impact bonds; and Fair Trade. To date, Alex has published more than one hundred papers, working papers, book chapters, and articles and six books. Most appear in a wide range of peer-reviewed journals and books, including seven papers in Financial Times Top 30 journals. His 2009 paper on social investment won the Best Paper Award (Entrepreneurship) at the British Academy of Management. In 2010, Nicholls edited a Special Edition of *Entrepreneurship, Theory and Practice* on social entrepreneurship—the first time a top-tier management journal had recognized the topic in this way. He has been the general editor of the Skoll Working Papers Series and is the editor in chief of the *Journal of Social Entrepreneurship*. Alex is the co-author of a major research book on Fair Trade (with Charlotte Opal, Sage, 2005) and the editor of the first scholarly collection of papers on social entrepreneurship (Oxford University Press, 2006, 2008). In 2011, he published a co-edited volume on social innovation—again, the first scholarly book on the subject. In 2015, he published a further co-edited volume on social finance and a new book on social innovation with NESTA.

Gudrun-Christine Schimpf works as research associate at the Center for Social Investment and Innovation of Heidelberg University. She has been employed at CSI since 2014, and has participated in international and interdisciplinary project teams on social innovation. Gudrun holds a doctoral degree of Heidelberg University and a master's degree in history and political science. Her main research interests include social innovation, civic engagement, urban history, and gender studies.

Martijn Jeroen van der Linden is a PhD researcher in the Department of Technology, Policy and Management at Delft University of Technology and since October 2018 professor in new finance at the Hague University of Applied Sciences (the Netherlands). Previously he worked in the financial sector. In his PhD research he applies design science to investigate how digital technologies can be used to overcome some of the shortcomings of the current design of the monetary-financial system. Moreover, he is a board member of two NGOs and an art institute in The Netherlands.

Rafael Ziegler's work is inspired by social innovations not only as a source of empirical materials but also as a spring of new ideas and concepts. His focus is on social innovation in relation to water, justice, and sustainability. After studies in philosophy and economics, Ziegler co-founded in 2009 the social-ecological research group GETIDOS (www.getidos.net) based in Greifswald and Berlin. The group jointly published *Social Entrepreneurship in the Water Sector—Getting Things Done Sustainably* (2014). After ten years of directing GETIDOS, he recently moved to Montreal, Canada, where he is Professeur associé à l' Institut national de la recherche scientifique. He remains a GETIDOS fellow, and in pursuit of the important yet elusive GETIDOS maxim: getting things done sustainably.

PART I

APPROACH: THE EXTENDED SOCIAL GRID MODEL

1
The Extended Social Grid Model

Alex Nicholls and Rafael Ziegler

Introduction

Social innovation is not a new phenomenon, but it does appear to be entering a new phase—a phase in which it is seen by a range of actors as potentially offering solutions not just to localized problems but to more systemic and structural issues. Policy-makers, particularly, have been increasingly engaging with the *idea* (if not always the *practice*) of social innovation in the context of intractable policy problems. In this context, the European Union (EU) has provided significant funding for research into the policy implications of social innovation, notably via the Framework 7 and Horizon 2020 research protocols. Indeed, the former provided the funding for the research that informs this book via the CrESSI (Creating Economic Space for Social Innovation) project.[1]

However, despite increasing interest in the subject, the growing set of examples of and attendant discourses for social innovation have not yet coalesced around a common definition, a set of standard performance measures, or an established policy agenda. Thus, there is, as yet, no established paradigm of social innovation (Nicholls 2010). Rather, there is considerable malleability in terms of the conceptualization and enactment of social innovation. Perhaps counter-intuitively, this fluidity of meaning and interpretation can be seen as a strength of social innovation in terms of its flexibility in addressing complex social problems and challenges in practice. In this way, 'fuzzy' social innovation can provide 'clumsy solutions' to so-called 'wicked' problems. These problems are characterized by multiple—and sometimes contradictory—analyses and diagnoses (Rittel and Webber 1973) creating a space for a diversity of inter- and trans-disciplinary collaborations in practice (Ziegler 2017a). In this context, theorizing social innovation remains an intriguing research challenge (Grimm et al. 2013). Partly to address this lacuna, the following chapter introduces a novel, theoretical approach to social innovation drawing mainly from economic and historical sociology as well as ethics.

[1] This chapter has benefitted from a discussion of an earlier draft at the CrESSI-Berlin Workshop, January 2017, and written comments by Christopher Houghton Budd, György Molnár, Georg Mildenberger and Gudrun-Christine Schimpf.

Alex Nicholls and Rafael Ziegler, *The Extended Social Grid Model*. In: *Creating Economic Space for Social Innovation*. Edited by: Alex Nicholls and Rafael Ziegler, Oxford University Press (2019). © Oxford University Press.
DOI: 10.1093/oso/9780198830511.003.0001

But first, some further remarks on 'social innovation' as a construct. The rise of social innovation is, in some ways, indicative of a wider collapse in trust in the status quo—as established models and social relations have increasingly failed to deliver well-being for the many rather than the few. Intractable problems highlight the failure of conventional solutions and established paradigms, entrenched in longstanding institutional settings across government, business, and civil society. This is evident through private sector market failures, public sector 'siloed-thinking' and a lack of scale in—and fragmentation across––civil society. As Moulaert and his colleagues (2013: 2) noted:

> Socially innovative actions, strategies, practices, and processes arise whenever problems of poverty, exclusion, segregation, and deprivation or opportunities for improving living conditions cannot find satisfactory solutions in the 'institutionalized field' of public or private action.

As such, the growth of interest in social innovation reflects the failure of established institutional arrangements (in technology, markets, policy agendas, governance structures, and so on) to deliver well-being and economic prosperity to all parts of society. Fundamentally, this centres upon structural, distribution, and equity problems. Social innovation can be seen, therefore, as a response to patterns of modernity that have marginalized certain populations by representing the individual citizen as either an economic actor or as a welfare recipient, but not as an active participant in collective decision-making. As a consequence, social innovation can offer a response both to the inequalities produced in the capitalist markets of late modern states and to the limitations and unintended consequences of the 'social' or 'welfare' state in carrying out large-scale social change. In this context, civic or democratic 'experimentalism' (Sabel 2012) serves to highlight this political, as well as contextual, aspect of social innovation as a process in late modern societies (Unger 2015, Evers and Brandsen 2016: 178)—a point that is discussed further below.

Defining Social Innovation

In the light of this chapter's focus on creating *economic* space for social innovation, it seems logical initially to approach social innovation from a business studies perspective, where foundational work has already been done on social entrepreneurship (Dees 1998; Nicholls 2006) and social enterprise (Alter 2006; Nyssens 2006). In this setting, social innovation can be seen as the macro-level field of action encompassing any new idea, discourse, inspiration, cognitive frame of reference (of which more later), or model that aims to address a complex, structural, social (or environmental) need. Social entrepreneurship can, then, be seen as a *subset* of social innovation—as the organizational enactment of social innovation ideas and models. However, social entrepreneurship itself also represents a spectrum of organizational types and models from charities and voluntary or community-based not-for-profits to cooperatives and mutually owned ventures to fully commercial 'profit with purpose' businesses and, even, corporate collaborations or joint ventures. In this wide spectrum, 'social enterprises' represent the subset of social entrepreneurship that are for-profit or, at least, break-even social businesses (Nicholls 2006).

Yet, while this set of inter-relationships helps to locate social innovation in terms of two important connected fields of action, it does not serve to deliver a clear definition or delineate strong boundaries. An analysis of the existing social innovation literature provides some better guidance. Drawing from a bibliometric analysis of the 'coming to be' of social innovation (Ayob, Teasdale, and Fagan 2016, see also Nicholls, Simon, and Gabriel 2015: 2ff.; Nicholls and Murdock 2012), two, initial streams of social innovation research can be distinguished. The first has a focus on *outcomes* and social value production. For example, Mulgan and colleagues described social innovation as 'new ideas that address unmet social needs—and that work' (Mulgan et al. 2007: 2). The second has a focus on structural changes in power relations that emphasize new social *processes* and *relations* aiming at rebalancing power disparities and economic inequalities in society (see Moulaert et al. 2013). However, Ayob and her colleagues' (2016) analysis also suggests that, in the second decade of the new millennium, there appears to be some 'decontestation' in the sense that both the outcome and process dimensions now tend to be accepted as common elements of social innovation definitions together.

Within the EU, an influential report by the Bureau of European Policy Advisors defined social innovation as:

> Innovations that are social in both their ends and their means. Specifically, we define social innovations as new ideas (products, services, and models) that simultaneously meet social needs (more effectively than alternatives) and create new social relationships or collaborations. (BEPA 2010: 9)

This is an example of a social innovation definition that acknowledges process and change in social relations, and not just welfarist outcome objectives. Following on from this, the working definition of social innovation used in this book is:

> The development and delivery of new ideas and solutions (products, services, models, modes of provision, processes) at different socio-structural levels that intentionally seek to change power relations and improve human capabilities, as well as the processes via which these solutions are carried out.

This definition, with its emphasis on changes in power relations and human capabilities, is situated in a socio-structural conceptualization of social innovation and its economic underpinnings that we will discuss further in the next section. It also acknowledges the political aspect of social innovation, and the challenges of change rather than reproduction of the status quo, especially if issues of marginalization are to be addressed.

While there is a need to better 'theorize' social innovation, much can be learnt from prior social innovation research. A review of the social innovation literature (Nicholls and Murdock, 2012; van der Have and Rubalcaba 2016: 1928f.) points to four scholarly communities:

- Community psychology focused on experimental social innovation (Fairweather 1967) for social and behavioural change
- Creativity research examining the process of social innovation and its changes to or creation of social relationships and organizations (Mumford 2002)
- Sustainability transitions and grassroots innovation research concerned with socio-technical challenges of dealing with climate change, energy provision, and further sustainability challenges (Seyfang and Smith 2007)
- Local development focused on communities, cities, and regions frequently with a focus on governance, power, and participation (Moulaert et al. 2005).

The approach taken here seeks to learn from all of these traditions of research—especially the last two. But as is set out below, social innovation is primarily located here at the intersection of economic sociology and ethics due to the specific focus on social innovation and marginalization of this research.

In addition to these social innovation research streams, the 'older' tradition of innovation studies with its primary focus on business innovation and markets is also relevant—in particular with respect to the more transformative or disruptive claims associated with social innovation (cf. Schumpeter 1942). In a review of the business innovation literature, Havas (2016) distinguished the subject of change (goods, processes, organizations, markets, technological systems, and techno-economic paradigms) and the degree of change (incremental, radical). Beyond a focus on goods, processes, and organizations, social innovation research also extends its analysis from capitalist markets to civil society and government and, especially, to the reconfiguration of these different sectors for the provision of social or welfare goods and services. Likewise, the scope of technological systems and techno-economic paradigms can be extended by a focus on social movements and their 'social technologies' for change. Thus, there is overlap, but also some differentiation, between business and social innovation studies.

Of particular importance in social innovation are a set of defined social goals and clear social process specifications that in business innovation tend to be only implied (i.e. innovation is 'good for' economic performance, which is 'good for' society). Accordingly, politics and ethics are more visible in social innovation and this, necessarily, also changes the conceptualization of notions such as 'scaling', 'spreading', or 'diffusion' of social innovations. If marginalized groups are not only the 'object' but also the 'subject' of change, non-economic conditions such as political legitimacy and democratic process become important variables to be studied.

Once these differences in the 'subject of change' in social innovation are defined, a 'degree of novelty' distinction also becomes relevant. For example, there is good evidence of *incremental innovation* in social goods and services to address social needs more effectively or efficiently. This is the focus of many successful charities and not-for-profits, as well as some so-called 'Bottom of the Pyramid' (Prahalad 2006) commercial market models. Moreover, there are innovations that harness or retool existing social and economic structures to generate new social value and outcomes. Examples such as Fair Trade (Nicholls and Opal 2005) or mobile-phone-based banking systems typically exploit or modify existing market structures in order to deliver new or additional social value. This points to a type of *institutional innovation* located 'between' incremental and more radical degrees of change. Beyond efficiency and effectiveness considerations, it also includes social goal and process aspects—for example, not only the 'extension' of a micro-credit market for 'the poor' but also a rethinking of 'the poor' as equal participants in production, distribution, and consumption. Finally, there is a place for radical change in social innovation, be it in terms of entirely new products and services or social movements and self-consciously political actors, groups and networks that aim to change entrenched power-relations, alter social hierarchies, or reframe issues to the benefit of otherwise disenfranchised groups. With such radical innovation in mind, Moulaert and his co-authors spoke of the importance of focusing 'on the role of SI [social innovation] in developing alternative socio-political discourses and on its potential for change in particular contexts' (2013: 13). This framing of social innovation is particularly significant for the research presented in this collection focusing, as it does, on addressing marginalization and how societal power relations continually reproduce it.

The social movements' literature suggests that truly systemic change only comes about through a reframing (often by civil struggle) of the dominant cognitive frames that shape society's perception of social issues. Such activity typically comes up against strong vested interests and can encounter (sometimes violent) resistance. As a consequence, recognizing the political dimension of social innovation is a research opportunity that raises significant practical questions and challenges. First, political action often prompts a reaction and can lead to institutional confrontation or even danger. Second, when social innovation addresses public welfare issues or aims to drive political change, it often does so as private action that lacks formal democratic legitimacy. This is particularly problematic in cases where social innovation acts as a 'shadow state' substituting for what would otherwise be the welfare responsibilities of the elected government. Such a democratic deficit may challenge rights-based models of citizens' relationship to their government. Third, there is the more general issue of who is included in, and who is excluded from, social innovation impacts and who decides. This issue is particularly relevant for a focus on marginalization.

As a consequence, social innovation can have a negative social impact for some populations by excluding them from the focus of its provision of social goods and services or its campaigns for social change. Importantly, within a marginalized group, the *most* marginalized might be further excluded or marginalized by social change processes, since 'improvements' may be more easily achieved with the *least* marginalized within this group.

Another set of consequences can arise from different framings or perceptions of social innovation. A well-known example is the hybrid nature of those social innovations that blend social and financial objectives. From one point of view such activities can be seen as inherently exploitative and representing the 'privatization' of the social, as critiques of the high interest rates offered by many micro-finance organizations have pointed out. Likewise, priority given to financial return and break-even points can tip the balance to cost savings rather than dealing with the most marginalized causing mission drift. More generally, it is important to distinguish the self-actualization of any marginalized group (including personal and collective self-esteem, learned helplessness, further differences within the group) from the image(s) of this group in the eyes of other groups in its field—this may lead to potentially divergent views on what constitutes 'effective' social innovation. Indeed, there is no clear determinism or guaranteed *telos* of social innovation. Social innovation can be 'hijacked' for socially divisive or destructive objectives and intentions—for example by secret societies or extreme political parties or simply by mainstream parties that feel little responsibility to address the marginalization of groups outside of their core constituency or support base.

Furthermore, social innovation can result in perverse effects in cases of operational failure (e.g. Tracey and Jarvis 2006). Since social innovation is often expressed organizationally in the form of innovative initiatives in weak institutional spaces with disempowered service users, it is inherently risky. As a result, it is reasonable to expect that some social innovations will fail or create perverse externalities with potentially damaging effects for vulnerable populations.

A further critical issue concerns the public legitimacy of social innovation. Alternative solutions developed by social innovation actors intended to address socio-structural problems may lack legitimacy for many stakeholders since they often take the form of interventions that combine otherwise distinct institutional logics and models of action in innovative forms to challenge normative notions of the roles and responsibilities of government, business, or civil society. Such hybrid forms of action typically blend the logics and rationales of two or more established sectors to build new organizational structures (i.e. 'social' business), processes (i.e. work integration models), or goods and services (i.e. user-led welfare models) that seek to meet complex sets of needs and demands in late modern societies better than conventional interventions can. However, crossing normative boundaries can generate public legitimacy issues too, since the logics and rationales of action of each conventional sector are quite different and even contradictory at the normative level. As a consequence, the public legitimacy of social innovation (at both normative and cognitive levels, see Suchman 1995) can often be compromised (Nicholls and Cho 2006). This, in turn, has lead to public criticism of some social enterprise/social business hybrid models within social innovation since they challenge many fundamental principles of the state and civil society as not-for-profit sectors across countries. Such a loss of public legitimacy can have serious consequences in terms of access to resources, market competitiveness, policy support, and staff recruitment. Prima facie, a focus on marginalization reinforces the challenge: the groups at issue are likely to be already stigmatized or subject to prejudices and these, in turn, can be used to question the legitimacy or, even, the need for such interventions.

The Extended Social Grid Model

Next this chapter sets out the Extended Social Grid Model (ESGM) that will be used throughout this book both to explore the structural issues that cause and reproduce marginalization and to set out the role of social innovation in overcoming or stabilizing these structures. The ESGM served as a theoretical orientation for the CrESSI project as a whole and provides the core analytic orientation for this book project. The overall aim of the ESGM is to develop a novel set of research lenses well suited to the empirical examination of the key themes in the overall project that were:[2]

- How can issues of social marginalization be conceptualized within a structural model of socio-economic change?
- What are the long-term drivers of, and barriers to, structural social innovation for marginalized groups across various modes in which these goods and services are provided?
- What are the roles of public policy instruments and of finance in driving structural social innovation?

[2] See also the background papers to the project: https://www.sbs.ox.ac.uk/research/centres-and-initiatives/skoll-centre-social-entrepreneurship/creating-economic-space.

The ESGM engages with a variety of sociological, economic, and philosophical sources in an attempt to provide a suitably sophisticated model for the exploration of these complex processes. Specifically, the model draws upon three key theoretical elements: the Social Grid analysis proposed by Beckert (2010); the social sources of power analysis developed by Mann (Mann 1986); the capabilities approach pioneered by Sen and Nussbaum (Sen 1999; Nussbaum 2000). Each of these elements will be outlined in the following sections. However, it needs to be stressed at the outset that the intention of the ESGM is to suggest a mode of thinking that informs subsequent analysis and policy development rather than to represent a thorough commentary on these individual thinkers and their schools of thought.

The Social Grid

The first stream of work in economic sociology underpinning the ESGM draws upon Beckert's (2010) work on exchange theory in markets. Beckert noted that, across a range of literatures, common analyses of markets as social structures failed to integrate different approaches. Such analyses tended to focus exclusively on one explanatory theory alone. In terms of our research, this reductionist thinking fails to give a full account of the social enactment of economic structures and social exchange relationships[3] and, as a consequence, typically does not acknowledge socio-economic exclusion as a *product* of market arrangements. Beckert identified three schools of theory in socio-economic analyses of market exchange relationships based upon: social networks; institutions; cognitive frames. Drawing on these literatures, Beckert defined each element as follows:

- *Social networks* are the structures of social relations and relational patterns in society, particularly at the field level. Fields are comprised of the specific structures of social networks that create power differences between actors and status hierarchies.
- *Institutions* are the constraining and enabling rules and norms of a society
- *Cognitive frames* are the shared meanings and interpretations which make sense of society and its functionings.

Taken together, these three social 'forces' constitute a Social Grid that, in Beckert's analysis, shapes the formation of market fields. Critically, the three forces are held together by a set of dynamic relationships that are constantly in

[3] In a Social Grid analysis, 'social exchange relationships' are determined by structural factors that enact and socially reproduce hierarchical power relations. The role of social innovation is, therefore, to disrupt and reconfigure such relationships with a view to increasing equity and inclusion.

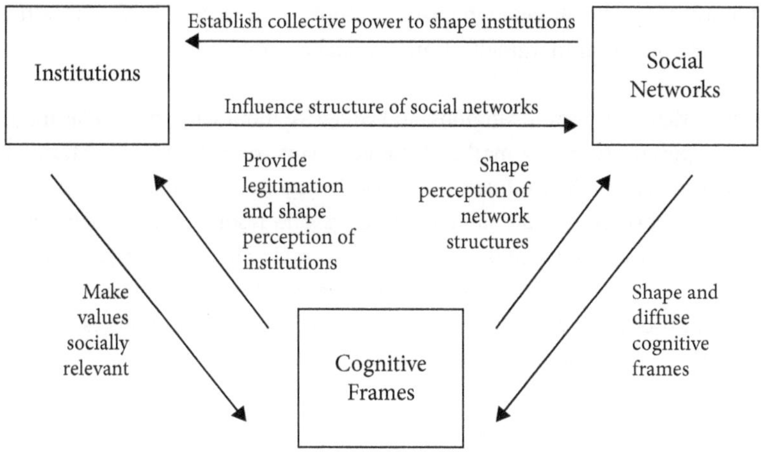

1.1 Beckert's Social Grid
Source: Beckert (2010).

flux. Thus, the Social Grid is not static, though it may be self-reinforcing in a particular mode (see Figure 1.1).

In conventional economic terms, the economic underpinnings of social innovation would be approached via the question of how different actors gain access to the resources needed to innovate in a general context of scarcity. However, economic sociology has stressed the need to analyse innovation in terms of the formal and informal rules and institutional structures governing access to, and use of 'scarce' resources, as well as the networks within which innovators are located and the cognitive frames that define and legitimize innovation in a social context. Beckert's Social Grid framework captures all these dimensions and calls attention to their relationships and interactions. It highlights the dynamic relationships between each of the three elements in a model that allows for continual change and innovation.

Our rationale for using this schematic model is its emphasis on explanatory pluralism: approaches based on a single explanatory theory typically fail to give a full account of the social enactment of economic structures and social exchange relationships and, by implication, of social innovation as a contested process. Following Beckert, the working assumption here is that there is important analytic value in an investigation of the relationships between social networks, institutions, and cognitive frames that, first, understands the structures of marginalization and, second, explores social innovation as a set of interventions across the dynamic relationships of the Social Grid that change such structures and, so, reduce the marginalization of certain populations. Such an analysis will, therefore, allow the identification of the key dimensions and leverage points within the Social Grid that may, then, be targeted by social innovation to best address systems of economic and social marginalization. As Beckert noted:

> I argue that networks, institutions, and cognitive frames are irreducible and that one important source of market dynamics stems from their interrelations. The structures lead to the stratification of fields by positioning actors in more or less powerful positions. At the same time, actors gain resources from their position which they can use to influence institutions, network structures, and cognitive frames. To simultaneously consider all three social forces in market fields and their reciprocal influences allows us to consider their interrelations as sources of field dynamics. (Beckert 2010: 606).

From this perspective, (economic) agency (or lack of it) in social exchange markets is a *product* of the social forces and ties that enable or dis-empower key actors within the Social Grid. Moreover, the three analytic elements (or 'forces') of the model are closely connected through multiple interactions and feedback loops. Following Beckert's model this research conceptualizes social innovation as a *response* to a Social Grid that has marginalized certain populations historically. Thus, social innovation here refers to a process change in social relations across these three forces.

However, the model developed here also *extends* Beckert's framework in two significant ways. First, this research applies Beckert's Social Grid to contexts outside of the market. Second, it connects a macro- and meso-level Social Grid analysis to a micro-level focus on individuals who receive benefits or harm, who are affected by and reproduce a status quo, but who also provide the seeds for change by seeking to co-determine their own socio-structural positions.

It is acknowledged here that applying Beckert's Social Grid model to non-market settings goes beyond Beckert's original intention. Two reasons justify this extension—one theoretical, one empirical. First, Beckert himself acknowledges that his Social Grid is based upon principles drawn from general field theory—and that these foundations are not specific to market contexts:

> Such a more comprehensive understanding needs to be based on a general framework that can encompass the notions of networks, institutions, and cognitions. I suggest that the notion of fields (DiMaggio and Powell 1991; Bourdieu 2005; Fligstein 2001a: 67ff.) makes it possible to bring simultaneous attention to the different types of social structures relevant in markets and at the same time shift the theoretical focus on the relationship between structures and agency processes. Fields are understood here as local social orders or social arenas where 'actors gather and frame their actions vis-à-vis one another' (Fligstein 2001: 108). Based on the field concept I discuss the interrelationships

> between the three types of structures identified and their role in the change of market fields. (Beckert 2010: 606)

So, this research uses Beckert's model in the context of its more general grounding in field theory, rather than narrowly exploring market issues alone (though these, of course, will often be relevant to the analysis carried out in this book).

Second, it is apparent that, in practice, marginalization is not only a matter of markets. Marginalization also includes many non-market variables such as cultural effects, as well as access to non-market goods, such as education or healthcare. It is, therefore, important to consider non-market factors within the overall model in order to provide effective analyses and policy recommendations with respect to social innovation. Indeed, the extension of Beckert's model to an analysis of the conversion factors that affect individual capabilities (to use Sen's language—see below) via a power framework[4] plays exactly to Fligstein's definition of a field as: a population of actors that constitute a social arena by orienting their actions toward each other (Fligstein 2001: 108).

Social Change and Power

As has already been noted, social change, in general, and social innovation, more specifically, only partly focus on markets and the economy.[5] Rather, specific instances of social change typically involve economic drivers as well as other political, cultural, and environmental forces. Therefore—and this is in line with the rejection of reductionism that motivates the Social Grid approach—there is a need to endorse explanatory pluralism.

Drawing on a multi-volume study of world history, Mann argued for four irreducible social sources of power as ideal types for the analysis of 'messy' reality: ideological; economic; military; and political (known as IEMP: Mann 1986: 22).[6] In his approach, power is understood as the ability to pursue and attain goals through mastery of one's environment. Power is social when it is exercised over other people: it is 'the capacity to get others to do things that otherwise they would not do' (Mann 2013: 1). Such power has two intertwined aspects: its distributive aspect refers to one party's power over another and its collective aspect lies in the ability of all parties involved to enhance joint power over third parties or over nature. Both types of power have increased considerably throughout history and particularly during the past two or three hundred years.

[4] See following discussion of the work of Michael Mann.

[5] To put it differently, it is assumed here that economic determinism—as, for example, attributed to orthodox Marxism—cannot adequately explain social change processes.

[6] The brief exposition here is complemented by an in-depth exposition in chapter 2 by Risto Heiskala. See also Heiskala (2014) and Lodemann (2014).

Mann introduced the four social sources of power in the IEMP approach in the following terms:

> Ideological power derives from the human need to find ultimate meaning in life, to share norms and values, and to participate in aesthetic and ritual practices with others . . . economic power derives from the human need to extract, transform, distribute, and consume the produce of nature . . . I define military power as the social organization of concentrated and lethal violence . . . political power is the centralized and territorial regulation of social life. (Mann 2013: 1–2)

Drawing on and developing the theory of social forces of power, this research extends Beckert's Social Grid model in a way that aims to avoid market reductionism's inability to do justice to the complex and messy world of social innovation. As the following paragraphs will outline, it does so in two ways: by understanding 'economic' power as itself not only a matter of markets and by considering further sources of power.

Following Mann, this book understands economic power broadly in terms of the transformation, distribution, and consumption of the products of nature, and the various modes of provision associated with this. Exchange relations in markets are one especially dynamic part of this power, but they do not exhaust economic power. Self-provision, informal provision in families and communities, as well as public provision by government are further examples of providing and distributing 'the produce of nature'. These further modes are needed for a comprehensive analysis of the economic underpinnings of social innovation and they are especially relevant for a focus on social innovation and marginalization. This is because self, communal, and even public forms of provision tend to be under enormous pressure from capitalist markets.[7] This point is evidenced by the fact that a major approach to political power and the state, namely, class theories inspired by Marx, tend to reduce the state to economic power linked to the interests of a dominating economic class.

This point was noted above in terms of some contestation over the 'hybrid' logics associated with introducing the market in social or welfare provision: for example, reducing social issues to a matter of financial impact investing, even if there is no short- or medium-term prospect of financial returns. The ESGM does not downplay this dynamic, but aims to go beyond an analysis of this issue alone. Following Mann, the ESGM draws upon plural social sources of power for an in-depth analysis of the complex dynamics of social innovation.

A further type of power is political. While class and economic interests no doubt influence government (and their relations), and, sometimes, entirely set the

[7] See chapter 3 for an exploration of this point as well as the modes of provision terminology.

societal agenda, there is still a distinct set of institutions and personnel in modern states that wield authoritative power from the political and administrative centres across their respective state territories (Mann 2013: 55). A well-known candidate is the 'rational-legal domination' with which state administrations exercise power, as Weber famously pointed out in his analysis of the modern state and bureaucracy (Weber 1978). If the political aspect of social innovation is to be taken seriously, this source of power cannot be ignored. In fact, the 'democratic experimentalism' mentioned above originates with a brighter vision of political power (in American pragmatism). A key idea here is that while central political and administrative powers set targets and standards, there should be some freedom at the local level in the implementation of targets and standards. In fact, there should be a 'transformative' freedom that, if need be, can propose revisions or changes to targets and standards. Thus, a closer focus on political power reveals space for social innovation, and the political aspect of social innovation. Or, as Mann remarked:

> Infrastructural power [as] the institutional capacity of a central state to penetrate its territories and logistically implement decisions . . . is a two-way street: it also enables civil society to control the state. (Mann 2013: 59)

Accordingly, it is an important analytical question in terms of social innovation for the marginalized just how, and in what ways, such 'enabling' is possible.[8] Indeed, given that it likely also has a role in the reproduction of marginalization, can the state act as a social innovator or only as a promoter of social innovation outside the state? Do multi-level entities such as the EU offer opportunities to tackle this issue (Ziegler et al. 2017)?

The ESGM adopts a plural focus on power, but it also modifies and extends Mann's account. The modifications are twofold. First, in terms of the IEMP model, Heiskala has pointed out that 'ideology' is a narrow term for such phenomena as Christianity, gender relations, patriarchy, or racism (Heiskala 2016). The term 'culture' appears to capture this ideal-type better. This point holds in particular once it is noted that here the analysis complements notions of power within Beckert's Social Grid so as to pay attention to cognitive frames in culture as a key element of 'ideology'. Second, Mann used the term 'military' in relation to organized, lethal violence. Following Heiskala (2016), we adopt the wider term 'security' to capture 'all organized violence capacities' (see also Heiskala, chapter 2). With these modifications we aver culture over ideology, switching from IEMP to CESP.

The ESGM further *extends* Mann's IEMP (now CESP) model by including nature and artefacts. As Mann noted, in terms of climate change, the modernist idea of a 'conquest of nature' is put into question, and may even prove self-

[8] It is for this reason also interesting to note that for Weber, a 'party' is any group collectively organized for the acquisition of power (Mann 2013: 59).

destructive (Mann 2013: 395). This suggests the addition of *nature* as a further source of power to our CESP model (Heiskala 2016). There are two ways, in which this addition adds analytic value. First, nature has the capacity to get others to do things that otherwise they would not do—for example, via floods and droughts caused by global warming. Moreover, this power has distributive consequences: the enactment of individual human capabilities will be heavily influenced by whether one lives in a cold or hot climate, in an arid or humid region, under conditions of stable or unpredictable weather. Thus, the concept of nature makes a case for including physical force and natural structures as potentialities of power in the CESP model. At the same time, natural power is different from the other power dimension as it cannot be attributed responsibility and, hence, be made to change in response to reason and argument, even though discussions of climate change are motivated strongly by precisely this point. More generally, 'the climate' does not act according to cognitive frames, follow rules, or have social networks.

Second, nature can also be interpreted in terms of a social category. 'Being able to live with concern for and in relation to animals, plants, and the world of nature' (Nussbaum 2006: 77) is a central human capability. In times of global ecological crisis, it has given rise to global 'environmental' power: climate change activists seek to reconfigure human relations to nature, for example calling for major reforestation programmes worldwide. More generally, all over the world nature conservationists have pushed for national parks, biosphere reserves, and other schemes and regulations that control, with distributive consequences, humanity's relationship to the natural environment. They have also co-shaped political consumerism and self-governance in terms of lifestyles. Transnational NGOs such as Greenpeace—with an estimated membership base of 3 million people worldwide—have helped co-structure this power. In this second sense, the addition of 'nature' is, therefore, consistent with the approach taken to the other social sources of power above, so that now we can speak of CESPN.

Moreover, climate change science illustrates the need to consider yet a further source of power: scientists who advise government agencies dealing with the environment and provide an inner channel of concern for politicians. Schröder has argued that in the modern period the enormous growth of the institutions of science and technology has converted them into another source of social power (cited in Mann 2013: 363).[9] As science has a practical power impact mainly via technology, this can be called a source of *artifactual* power that includes 'science as an institution but also tools, technologies, and other artefacts as well as infrastructures' (Heiskala 2016). This source of power also responds to a central human capability: 'being able to use the senses, to imagine, think, and reasons . . . informed and cultivated by an adequate education, including, but by no means

[9] Mann has first refused to make this addition but in the light of climate change (science) acknowledged that he 'wavers' (Mann 2013, 363).

limited to, literacy and basic mathematical and scientific training' (Nussbaum 2006: 76). In turn—and as in the case of environmental power—it is, therefore, not surprising to see this source of power evolve across different cultures throughout history. Thus, the IEMP can be extended further as the CESPNA.

The CESPNA model has important methodological implications for the ESGM as follows:

- It offers a non-reductive source of social power model that rests on the assumption that 'society' is not a unitary or total phenomenon (Mann 1986: 1f.). Rather, when society is studied, it is in terms of specific social aspects of history, present or future: the nation state, capitalism, and so on.
- The methodological implications of the CESPNA model for the study of social innovation are a focus on specific historical patterns or ways of life: for it is here that power 'congeals' (i.e. not in three or *n*-dimensional models of society and its dimensions etc.). In this book, this is the contemporary European nation state and its membership of the EU as a supra-national entity.[10] Social change and social innovation happens through these historical forms that are neither purely political nor purely economic, but 'multiple overlapping and intersecting socio-spatial networks of power' (Mann 1986: 1). In this spirit, later chapters in this book will consider social innovations such as social housing or freshwater supply as internally complex, dynamic patterns.
- In the light of the last point, what Mann calls 'promiscuity' is a further methodological implication that is important for the study of social innovation (Mann 1986: 17). For example, the administration of a nation state is not purely focused on policy preparation/implementation, nor is the administration of a corporation purely focused on business. Rather they are likely to embody a variety of ends and means: political, economic, cultural, and so on. Mann—with a whiff of modernist purism—calls this the 'functional promiscuity' of organized power networks. At the conceptual level this introduces a phenomenon of social entrepreneurship and social innovation: the hybrid nature of organizations, networks and approaches, and the ethical and political questions to which this gives rise.

In summary, the ESGM draws on multiple, entwined social sources of power to study change processes. It analyses these multi-faceted processes with the help of Beckert's Social Grid model—in terms of institutions, social networks, and cognitive frames. It also considers historical contexts (see further below), where

[10] For an early discussion of social innovation in EU nation states and their regions see Hämäläinen and Heiskala (2007).

possibilities congeal in an organized and promiscuous way and where new possibilities and alternatives emerge.

Power, Capabilities, and Marginalization

A particular vision of human nature lies at the core of Mann's theory of social power:

> Human evolution has differed from the evolution of other species by the very fact that it has retained its unity. Speciation has not occurred. (Mann 1986: 35)

Human beings are:

> Restless, purposive, and rational, striving to increase their enjoyment of the good things of life and capable of choosing and pursuing appropriate means for doing so... These human characteristics are the original source of power.
> (Mann 1986: 4)

However, due to his specific focus on power issues, Mann did not pay much attention to human ends or to their evaluation. As purposive beings, we can choose and create means. From these means new needs may emerge. For the study of power, it is the means that matter: what is effective, what succeeds and why in a specific context? From this point of view, the primary needs, as well as the emergent needs associated with means, are of secondary importance. As Mann commented: 'we leave the area of goals and needs altogether' (Mann 1986: 6).

Yet, in order to evaluate the processes and impacts of social innovation, there is a need to uncover anthropology and the *ends* of human beings. The formation and structure of the Social Grid is not a neutral process, but, rather, reflects particular power relations and pre-existing social structures. The ESGM draws on the Capability Approach (CA) to human development (Sen 1999; Nussbaum 2006; Robeyns 2016) to explore the evaluative, ethical aspect of social innovation and marginalization in an explicit way. The ethical individualism of the CA adds a focus with which to render explicit the evaluative aspect of social innovation processes and ends that are often found in social innovation discourses but rarely explicitly analysed.

Capabilities are themselves a form of power: the real opportunity to do and to be what one has reason to value.[11] They represent—as noted above—a 'power to'

[11] The discussion of impact in social innovation is usually anthropocentric. From an ethical perspective, however, questions concerning the scope of the 'community of impact' arise: human beings only (anthropocentrism), sentient beings (sentientism), living beings (biocentrism) etc. Conceptually the capabilities approach is open to variations of all these approaches (Ziegler 2017). Moving beyond anthropocentricism is another conceptual frontier that needs to be taken seriously when

that, in practice, depends on other patterns of distributive and collective power. Capabilities as freedom 'to do' and 'to be' refer to heterogeneous 'functionings' such as 'participating in decision-making' or 'being in good health'. This heterogeneity of the good is important for understanding marginalization and social innovation, as we will see.

Disempowerment, lack of recognition, and material poverty all refer to deprivations that detract from a 'dignified' or even 'good' life. There are some absences or disfunctionalities of capabilities and functionings that imply great harm and disadvantage to individuals. An example is insufficient nutrition, a disadvantage that is much more serious than, for example, the missed opportunity to fly four times a year on holiday. Marginalization in the ethical sense has a plural content, reflecting heterogeneous ends and goods. However, the specification of disadvantage (Wolff and De-Shalit 2007) and related central capabilities (Nussbaum 2006)[12] are, in practice, contested—not least due to the redistributive policy implications for the better off or competing others.

Marginalization, from a CA perspective, results from social processes through which personal, social, or environmental traits are transformed into actual or potential factors of disadvantage (von Jacobi et al. 2017): for example, when physical difference (skin colour, gender, handicap) becomes associated with humiliation or differential treatment at home, at work, or in public, or with a lack of access to infrastructure mobility. Similarly, if a location in a rural setting is associated with a way of infrastructure management that is unnecessarily expensive or politically unwanted in this setting this has negative effects on capabilities—for example, when a government plan to connect a hamlet to a central wastewater system contradicts the preference of the hamlet to avoid the costs of connecting to such a system and using its own constructed wetland instead.

Furthermore, disadvantage is frequently associated with exclusion from political decision-making as well as from economic systems. The marginalized are not only disadvantaged in terms of income, health, and education, they are also marginalized in terms of political decision-making. Therefore, empowerment in the sense of including and strengthening marginalized voices in decision-making plays an important role in policies and social innovation projects that seek to understand what marginalization means for those affected by it and that seek to overcome its structural elements.

seeking to analyse and understand social innovation processes that need not only be about and for human beings. A well-known historical example is national parks, an innovation attributed in part to John Muir and the Sierra Club. As will be seen in chapter 3, this seemingly 'exotic' environmental theme, is also relevant for thinking about moral subjects in more established social settings.

[12] In the capabilities approach, central capabilities usually refer to those capabilities required for leading a life in dignity and are, therefore, politically closely associated with human rights (see Lodemann and Ziegler 2014: section 3).

An important analytical tool within the CA that explores these issues is that of a 'conversion factor' (Robeyns 2016: 406ff.). The basic insight here is that, with respect to any good or service, the ability of people to use the good and benefit from it differs affecting the ultimate functioning outcomes. The difference can be in part explained by different traits. A physically handicapped person will find it more difficult to convert a mobility good (bike, public transport, etc.) into mobility functioning; women are blocked from using cars in patriarchal societies; and for the Finish colleagues in our research project, it might simply be too cold to use a bike in the winter months. In short, there are personal, social, and environmental conversion factors that need to be taken into account when studying the goods and services at issue in social innovation processes.[13]

Thus, the ESGM suggests that, for the study of the social structures that drive marginalization processes, there is a need to pay attention to the social powers that structure the position of those involved in the process in a historical context. The ESGM fine-tunes this with a focus on the social networks, institutions, and cognitive frames that reproduce and enact marginalization processes. For the evaluation of these processes, the emphasis is on disadvantage associated with personal, social, or environmental traits and on how individual capabilities can flourish or be blocked. The three key conceptual elements of the ESGM set out above are summarized in Figure 1.2. This figure aims to show their interrelationships, albeit presented as a static model. Dynamism and change across the

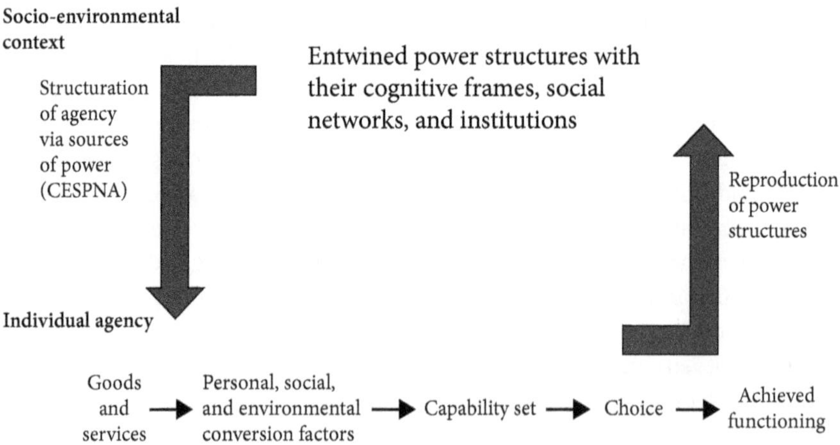

1.2 The Extended Grid Model (static version)
Source: Authors' own.

[13] For an in depth discussion of the intricacies of 'conversion factors' specifically in relation to technology design see Oosterlaken (2015: 84ff).

ESGM—the primary purpose of social innovation as construed here—is considered further below.

Social Innovation, Marginalization, and the ESGM

At first sight the ESGM might seem to suggest a variety of 'spheres' of innovation: cultural, economic, security-related, political, natural, and artefactual that need to be understood in terms of the dynamics of social networks, institutions, and cognitive frames. This suggestion is helpful in the sense that it situates an often business-focused perspective on innovation in a broader conceptual framework of social power.

This suggestion is, however, problematic if it reproduces the 'siloed' or 'sectoral' thinking that social innovation seeks to address. Social innovations, conceived as power processes themselves can be expected to be 'promiscuous'. It can be hypothesized that social innovations are not purely economic, or purely political, and so on. Rather, they will impact on and involve social power in different, interrelated ways. As a feature of social change, this point has also been noted in the CA. Sen (1999) argued that human development depends on the complementarity and mutual strengthening of various societal- and individual-level objectives. Further, he suggested that the purist argument of 'economic growth first, everything else later' is conceptually and empirically false, because it ignores the interrelations between various societal objectives and their corresponding human capabilities. Social innovation can facilitate and strengthen such interrelations of capabilities (Ziegler 2010). This point is particularly important for understanding marginalization: if disadvantages cluster, reversing the process and promoting 'fertile' rather than 'corrosive' capabilities/functionings (Wolff and de-Shalit 2007) is both important and challenging. As noted by Molnár (2016), there is a danger of focusing on the 'least marginalized' of the marginalized, where success is relatively 'easy' and less costly for social innovators (but not for the least marginalized who might, in fact, bear the costs of further exclusion (see also chapter 7). Therefore, analysing the real effects of a social innovation on marginalized or even socially excluded groups is an important issue.

Another entry point to dynamism in the ESGM is a focus on agency in changing the relationships between cognitive frames, social networks, and institutions (see Scheuerle, Schimpf, and Mildenberger 2014). There are six such dynamic relationships in the ESGM (see Table 1.1). Between institutions and social networks: the former can influence the structure of social networks, while the latter can establish collective power to shape institutions. Between institutions and cognitive frames: the former can make values socially relevant for the latter, while the latter provides legitimation and can shape the wider perceptions of institutions. Between social networks and cognitive frames: the former can shape

Table 1.1. Social innovation dynamics in the Social Grid model

Social Force	Dynamic Effect	Social Innovation (Example)
Institutions	Influences the structure of social networks	Builds bridging social capital
	Makes values socially relevant for cognitive frames	Influences regulatory norms
Social Networks	Establishes collective power to shape institutions	Increases political mobilization
	Shapes and diffuses cognitive frames	Deepens focused activism
Cognitive Frames	Provides legitimation and shapes the wider perceptions of institutions	Builds a social movement for change
	Shapes perceptions of network structures	Changes value perceptions of cultural material

Source: Authors' own.

and diffuse cognitive frames while the latter can shape perceptions of network structures. Table 1.1 shows some analytical options.

Again, however, it is important to stress the special challenges of understanding marginalization. An important explanatory hypothesis of Becker's Social Grid model is that the dynamics of change depend on the '*simultaneous* [our italics] consideration of all three structural forces' (Beckert 2010: 606). Put differently, the reproduction of marginalization depends on: cognitive frames that represent the marginalized as beyond help; institutions that constrain their capabilities; and social networks that successfully prevent change from happening. Molnár (2016) showed—with the example of the Roma communities in Central Europe—how their continued marginalization and social exclusion depended on the interplay of all three social forces, rather than the influence of only one of them. Therefore, social innovation processes that seek to overcome marginalization and exclusion are complex and challenging. As Beckert noted:

> Agents must synthesize in their responses the demands stemming from different social forces. The demands are multifaceted and may stand in contradiction to each other, thereby opening up a variety of ways to respond to the situation . . . an agency-cantered approach of this kind to the analysis of the role of social structures demands that the focus is shifted to the interaction of social structures and agency processes. (Beckert 2010: 611)

In keeping with the general insights of the Social Grid approach, overcoming marginalization calls for tackling all three social forces at once and as a unified whole. For example, in one of the cases explored in this book (see chapter 6) that is focused on decentralized freshwater supply as a marginalized practice in modern

European nation states (Ziegler 2017b), social innovators faced a triple task. First, they needed to work on cognitive frames in a context where the idea of using house water fountains or local wells was perceived by mainstream water suppliers variously as romantic, ridiculous, or simply too risky for health reasons. Second, even if they managed to organize their own network, they also faced a well-established network of water professionals, water authorities, and politicians that were used to, and in part directly benefitted from, the mainstream approach to drinking-water provision. Finally, a central task of their network was to advocate for legislation—and for the implementation of legislation—in such a way that a decentralized solution had a real opportunity to happen and/or to sustain itself. In short, cognitive frames, social networks, and institutions were each relevant for such a social innovation to overcome marginalization and effectively develop a voice in local water management.

The example also suggests that there are a variety of ways whereby social innovations grow and mature. Social innovators might aim at entirely reconfiguring a solutions-based approach and establish their solution as the new mainstream. Alternatively, social innovators might aim at diversifying an existing solutions-based approach by adding their solution as a new element in the existing mix of solution possibilities (Smith and Raven 2012). Finally, social innovators might aim to restore the option of a solutions-based approach that has already existed but has become marginalized by the mainstream and now needs to be restored (Ziegler 2017b).

The term 'solutions-based approach' is used as a placeholder for something very messy and complex in social reality. The lesson from Mann's study of the social sources of power is that it would be ill conceived to think of solutions-based approaches as exclusively products and services for markets. Rather, multiple-sources of power are likely to be involved and the respective changes to cognitive frames, institutions, and social networks will cut across political, economic, and cultural power depending, in each case, on the nature of the issue at hand. Yet, there is, of course, no 'issue' simply waiting out there to be discovered and studied. Rather, the very nature of a social issue is often a contested and interpretative matter.

This observation leads to a final important point about social innovation and the ESGM. Social innovation discourses have typically focused primarily on innovation not just 'for', but also 'with' citizens (BEPA 2010). In terms of our observations here, this focus is justified and important, as only in this way will a joint 'problem' *and* 'solution' discussion of the social issue be possible. In terms of an evaluative focus on human capabilities, this implies that there is a need to think of people not just as 'objects' that are empowered by a social innovation but, rather, as 'agents' who can co-create a social innovation process. Participation, therefore, plays a crucial role in effective social innovation or, in Nussbaum's formulation, participation 'in decision-making that governs one's life' (Nussbaum

2006: 77) plays a central architectonic role as it co-creates the way capabilities (health, education) are perceived, discussed, and enacted. This raises two, interrelated sets of questions (each considered further below) for the study of social innovation via the ESGM:

- How are citizens involved in social innovation processes and policymaking (von Jacobi et al. 2017)? Is this role changing over time? What are effective ways to involve citizens directly or indirectly?
- Why should citizens be involved in social innovation processes as a normative question of democracy? What are the reasons for this, and when is such inclusion justified, given that there is also a concern that social innovation might be a way of cutting costs or increasing processes of privatization of state functions in times of austerity (Evers, Ewert, and Brandsen 2014)?

This conceptualization of agency *as* social innovation corresponds to the individual focus of the CA—with its account of human agency and its heterogeneous goods—and intersects with the Social Grid within the ESGM. Accordingly, Figure 1.3 adds these dynamic elements. Power structures not only influence the individual conversion factors of actors, but the enactment of capabilities by agents includes a moment of choice and possible change that social innovators—as individuals and groups—draw on to initiate changes in networks, institutions, and cognitive frames across cultural, economic, security-related, political, natural, and artefactual power. Marginalized populations can

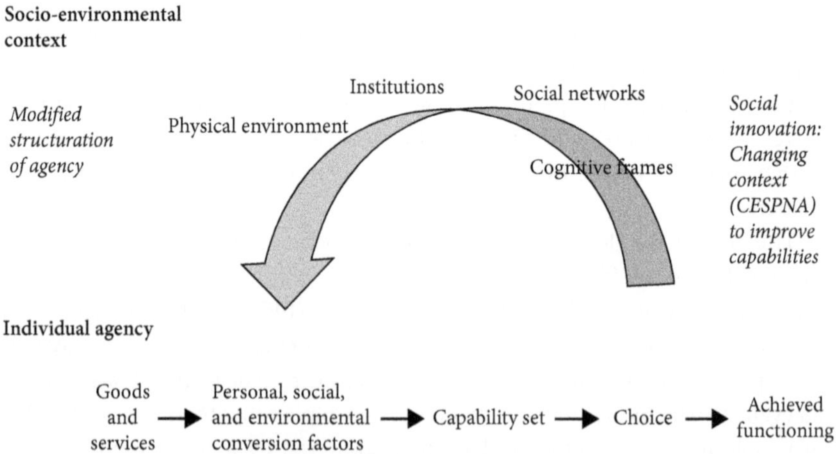

1.3 The Extended Grid Model (dynamic version)
Source: Authors' own.

co-create social innovation processes via the choices they make (or are allowed to make) in their social networks, institutional positioning, and interpretations of normative cognitive frames, but they face formidable challenges too due to the dominant reproduction of existing cognitive frames, social networks, and institutions (see Figure 1.3).

Conclusion

In summary, for the analysis and explanation of social innovation and marginalization processes, the ESGM proposes a plural focus on the social sources of power—cultural, economic, security-related, political, natural, and artefactual—and how these come together and link to the cognitive frames, social networks, and institutions in a specific time and place. Drawing on lessons from historical sociology, the ESGM suggests that effective social innovation will be functionally promiscuous—it will not be purely economic or political. Rather, effective social innovation has to reconfigure the Social Grid across multiple sources of social power and their enactment via cognitive frames, institutions, and social networks. It will be a matter of empirical investigation whether this model and its constituent elements prove to be adequate for the analysis of social innovation trajectories. This is considered further in Part II of the book.

Social innovation processes are neither good nor bad but rather contested and linked to cognitive frames that are contingent and shifting. As a normative vocabulary of analysing such contestation, the ESGM draws upon the CA to explore the processes and impacts of social innovation with a specific focus on marginalized groups. This is a difficult challenge in practice, as disadvantage tends to cluster, making the reversal of marginalization process particularly hard. Our approach here suggests that at the level of individual impact evaluation, we should focus on the plural spaces of actual or potential disadvantage that marginalized groups face and on the evidenced effects of any social innovation on such disadvantage for and within the group. For a focus on marginalization, it is important to distinguish the cognitive frames of the marginalized themselves from the cognitive frames that other groups supporting or opposing them have in terms of social innovation. In addition, a CA focus on the marginalized as 'subjects' of social change makes their participation in the processes of social innovation a particularly important part of its success in both an analytical and evaluative way (Evers, Ewert, and Brandsen 2014). Finally, the ESGM helps us considers how far the state can act as a social innovator given that it is likely also to have been implicit in the reproduction of marginalization over time.

The remainder of the book is structured as follows. Part I offers a further in-depth exploration of the overarching theoretical framework set out in the

ESGM. Chapter 2 devotes special attention to the concept of power. It situates Mann's work in historical sociology and provides the background for the revision and extension of the social sources of power in the ESGM. It also discusses the links between Mann's work and social innovation. Chapter 3 turns to the capabilities approach and the ethical aspects of social innovation. As social innovation is not limited to innovation in markets, this chapter, first, proposes a typology of modes of provision, capturing goods and services also provided informally, publicly, or by professional service organizations. The typology serves as an analytical tool for the ethical issues arising with social innovation and its reconfigurations of these modes. It also considers what are the central issues for analysing and creating economic space for social innovation if social innovation is about improving capabilities (as outcomes and processes). Chapter 4 turns to methodologies and explores how the ESGM can be used in empirical analyses. The chapter presents the qualitative and quantitative approach pursued in this book and its implications for analysing social innovation.

Part II of this book explores the explanatory utility of the ESGM in more detail. Chapters 5 to 9 examine the ESGM in terms of long-term historical case-study analysis. These chapters focus on social housing (chapter 5), urban drinking-water supply (chapter 6), micro-credit and employment creation for marginalized groups (chapter 7), education reforms (chapter 8) and, finally, solidarity purchasing groups (chapter 9). The approach taken throughout these chapters is qualitative: the ESGM is explored from a long-term historical perspective and with a view to the respective social innovation agendas identified in examples of housing, water and food provision, and employment creation. By contrast, chapter 10 takes on some of these themes—solidarity purchasing, drinking-water provision, and the provision of a local currency—to present results from a quantitative survey to explore the issue of agency in social innovation in Italy, Germany, and the Netherlands. Finally, chapters 11 and 12 apply the model to policy analysis. Chapter 11 surveys EU and member-state social innovation policies in terms of the ESGM lens, while chapter 12 specifically focuses on public policy *as* social innovation exploring the example of Social Impact Bonds in the United Kingdom as a novel but controversial, outcome-based instrument for improved outcomes for marginalized populations.

Part III of the book returns to the ESGM in the light of the empirical explorations of Part II. Chapter 13 revisits the model with a view to further theory building.

Chapter 14 considers the wider implications of the ESGM in terms of the relationship between capital and capacities. Chapter 15 considers the key issue of measuring the impact of social innovation. Finally, chapter 16 concludes with a set of social policy recommendations at the EU and member-state levels.

This book proceeds from the assumption that social innovation is a multi-level set of processes that can address key social problems—notably marginalization—in a systemic way. Policy and practice recommendations derive from the key insights of the ESGM that marginalization and social exclusion are the result of socio-economic structural issues that can best be addressed by targeting change across the Social Grid. This approach builds on existing work in social innovation theory but extends it further by integrating its insights with other bodies of relevant work in examining power and human capabilities. This complex, multi-dimensional model aims to capture the sophistication of empirical reality in a way that is both explanatory and policy-relevant.

References

Alter, Sutia Kim. 2006. 'Social Enterprise Models and their Mission and Money Relationships'. In *Social Entrepreneurship: New Models of Sustainable Social Change*, edited by A. Nicholls, pp. 205–32. Oxford: Oxford University Press.

Ayob, Noorshea, Simon Teasdale, and Kylie Fagan. 2016. 'How Social Innovation "Came to Be": Tracing the Evolution of a Contested Concept'. *Journal of Social Policy* 45(4): 635–53.

Beckert, Jens. 2010. 'How Do Fields Change? The Interrelations of Institutions, Networks, and Cognition in the Dynamics of Markets'. *Organization Studies* 31 (5): 605–27.

Bourdieu, Pierre. 2005. 'Principles of an Economic Anthropology'. In *The Handbook of Economic Sociology*, edited by Neil. J. Smelser and Richard Swedberg, pp. 75–89. Princeton, NJ: Princeton University Press.

BEPA (Bureau of European Policy Advisers). 2010. 'Empowering People, Driving Change: Social Innovation in the European Union.' https://ec.europa.eu/migrant-integration/librarydoc/empowering-people-driving-change-social-innovation-in-the-european-union, accessed 17 June 2019.

Di Maggio, Paul, and WalterPowell. 1991. 'Introduction'. In *The New Institutionalism in Organizational Analysis*, edited by Paul DiMaggio and Walter Powell, pp. 1–38. Chicago, IL: Chicago University Press.

Dees, Gregory. 1998. 'The Meaning of "Social Entrepreneurship"'. https://entrepreneurship.duke.edu/news-item/the-meaning-of-social-entrepreneurship/, accessed 17 June 2019.

Evers, Adalbert, and Taco Brandsen. 2016. 'Social Innovations as Messages: Democratic Experimentation in Local Welfare Systems'. In *Social Innovations in the Urban Context*, edited by Taco Brandsen, Sandro Cattacin, Adalbert Evers, and Annette Zimmer, pp. 161–80. Dordrecht: Springer Open.

Evers, Adalbert, Benjamin Ewers, and Taco Brandsen. 2014. *Social Innovations for Social Cohesion: Transnational Patterns and Approaches from 20 European Cities.* Liege: EMES European Research Network.

Fairweather, George. 1967. *Methods for Experimental Social Innovation.* New York: Wiley.

Fligstein, Neil. 2001. 'Social Skill and the Theory of Fields'. *Sociological Theory* 19: 105–25.

Grimm, Robert, Christopher Fox, Susan Baines, and Kevin Albertson. 2013. 'Social Innovation, an Answer to Contemporary Societal Challenges? Locating the Concept in Theory and Practice'. *Innovation: The European Journal of Social Science Research* 26(4): 436–55.

Hämäläinen, Timo, and Risto Heiskala (eds). 2007. *Social Innovations, Institutional Change, and Economic Performance: Making Sense of Structural Adjustment Processes in Industrial Sectors, Regions, and Societies.* Cheltenham: Edward Elgar.

Havas, Attila. 2016. 'Recent Economic Theorising on Innovation: Lessons for Analysing Social Innovation'. CrESSI Working Paper No. 27. Brussels: European Commission, DG Research.

Heiskala, Risto. 2014. 'Forms of Power, European Empires and Globalizations: Michael Mann's *The Sources of Social Power* and Beyond'. In 'Report on Institutions, Social Innovation and System Dynamics from the Perspective of the Marginalised', edited by Christopher Houghton Budd, C.W.M. Naastepad, and Cees van Beers, pp. 93–112. Oxford: CrESSI.

Heiskala, Risto. 2016. 'The Evolution of the Sources of Social Power, and Some Extensions'. In *Global Powers: Michael Mann's Anatomy of the Twentieth Century and Beyond*, edited by Ralph Schroeder, pp. 11–37. Cambridge: Cambridge University Press.

Jacobi, Nadia v., Daniel Edmiston, and Rafael Ziegler. 2017. 'Tackling Marginalisation through Social Innovation? Examining the EU Social Innovation Policy Agenda from a Capabilities Perspective'. *Journal of Human Development and Capabilities* 18 (2): 148–62.

Lodemann, Justus. 2014. 'How Does the Analysis of Mann Enrich the Capabilities Approach to Social Innovation?' In 'Report on Institutions, Social Innovation and System Dynamics from the Perspective of the Marginalised', edited by Christopher Houghton Budd, C.W.M. Naastepad, and Cees van Beers, pp. 113–21. Oxford: CrESSI.

Lodemann, Justus, and Rafael Ziegler. 2014. 'How Can Resilience Theory Inform Social Innovation for the Marginalised?' CrESSI Working Paper No. 6. Brussels: European Commission, DG Research.

Mann, Michael. 1986/2012. *The Sources of Social Power, Vol. 1: A History of Power from the Beginning to AD 1760.* New edition. Cambridge: Cambridge University Press.

Mann, Michael. 2013. *The Sources of Social Power, Vol. 4: Globalizations, 1945–2011.* Cambridge: Cambridge University Press.

Molnár, György. 2016. 'Analysis of Individual Case Kiút Program for Microcredit and Self-employment Using the Extended Social Grid Model'. In 'Report on Relevant Actors in Historic Examples and an Empirically Driven Typology of Types of Social Innovation', edited by Scheuerle et al., pp. 300–34. CrESSI Working Paper No. 29. Brussels: European Commission, DG Research.

Moulaert, Frank, Diane MacCallum, Abdid Mehmood, and Abdelillah Hamdouch, (eds). 2013. *The International Handbook on Social Innovation: Collective Action, Social Learning and Transdisciplinary Research.* Cheltenham: Edward Elgar.

Moulaert, Frank, Flavia Martinelli, Eric Swyngedouw, and Sara Gonzalez. 2005. 'Towards Alternative Model(s) of Local Innovation'. *Urban Studies* 42: 1969–90.

Mulgan, Geoff, Simon Tucker, Rushanara Ali, and Ben Sanders. 2007. 'Social Innovation: What It Is, Why It Matters and How It Can Be Accelerated'. Oxford: Skoll Centre for Social Entrepreneurship.

Mumford, Michael D. 2002. 'Social Innovation: Ten Cases from Benjamin Franklin'. *Creativity Research Journal* 14(2): 253–66.

Nicholls, A. 2010. 'The Legitimacy of Social Entrepreneurship: Reflexive Isomorphism in a Pre-Paradigmatic Field'. *Entrepreneurship Theory and Practice* 34(4): 611–33.

Nicholls, Alex (ed.). 2006. *Social Entrepreneurship: New Models of Sustainable Social Change.* Oxford: Oxford University Press.

Nicholls, Alex, Julie Caulier-Grice, and Madeleine Gabriel (eds). 2015. 'Introduction'. In *New Frontiers in Social Innovation Research*, edited by Alex Nicholls, Julie Simon, and Madeleine Gabriel, pp. 1–28. Basingstoke: Palgrave Macmillan.

Nicholls, Alex, and Albert Cho. 2006. 'Social Enterpreneurship: The Structuration of a Field.' In *Social Entrepreneurship: New Models of Sustainable Social Change*, edited by Alex Nicholls, pp. 99–118. Oxford: Oxford University Press.

Nicholls, Alex, and Alexander Murdock (eds). 2012. *Social Innovation: Blurring Boundaries to Reconfigure Markets.* Basingstoke: Palgrave Macmillan.

Nicholls, Alex, and Charlotte Opal. 2005. *Fair Trade: Market-driven Ethical Consumption.* London: Sage.

Nussbaum, Martha. 2000. *Women and Human Development: The Capabilities Approach.* Cambridge: Cambridge University Press.

Nussbaum, Martha. 2006. *Frontiers of Justice: Disability, Nationality, Species Membership.* Cambridge, MA: Harvard University Press.

Nyssens, Marthe (ed.). 2006. *Social Enterprise.* Basingstoke: Palgrave Macmillan.

Oosterlaken, Ilse. 2015. *Technology and Human Development.* London: Routledge.

Prahalad, C. K. 2006. *The Fortune at the Bottom of the Pyramid.* Upper Saddle River, NJ: Pearson Prentice Hall.

Rittel, Horst W. J., and Melvin M. Webber. 1973. 'Dilemmas in a General Theory of Planning'. *Policy Sciences* 4(2): 155–69.

Robeyns, Ingrid. 2016. 'Capabilitarianism'. *Journal of Human Development and Capabilities* 17(3): 397–414.

Sabel, Charles. 2012. 'Dewey, Democracy, and Democratic Experimentalism'. *Contemporary Pragmatism* 9(2): 35–55.

Scheuerle, Thomas, Gudrun-Christine Schimpf, Gunnar Gänzel, and Georg Mildenberger. 2014. 'How Does Economic Sociology Enrich the Capability Approach to Social Innovation?' In 'Report on Institutions, Social Innovation and System Dynamics from the Perspective of the Marginalised', edited by Christopher Houghton Budd, C.W.M. Naastepad, and Cees van Beers, pp. 109–14. Oxford: CrESSI.

Schumpeter, Joseph. 1942/1975. *Capitalism, Socialism, and Democracy.* New York: Harper Collins Publishers.

Sen, Amartya. 1999. *Development as Freedom.* Oxford: Oxford University Press.

Seyfang, Gill, and Adrian Smith. 2007. 'Grassroots Innovations for Sustainable Development: Towards a New Research and Policy Agenda.' *Environmental Politics* 16(4): 584–603.

Smith, Adrian, and Rob Raven. 2012. 'What Is Protective Space? Reconsidering Niches in Transitions to Sustainability'. *Research Policy* 41(6): 1025–36.

Suchman, M. C. 1995. 'Managing Legitimacy: Strategic and Institutional Approaches'. *Academy of Management Review* 20(3): 571–610.

Tracey, Paul, and Owen Jarvis. 2006. 'An Enterprising Failure: Why a Promising Social Franchise Collapsed'. *Stanford Social Innovation Review*, Spring issue: 6–70.

Unger, Roberto. 2015. 'Conclusion: The Task of the Social Innovation Movement.' In *New Frontiers in Social Innovation Research*, edited by Alex Nicholls, Julie Caulier-Grice, and Madeleine Gabriel, pp. 233–51. Basingstoke: Palgrave Macmillan.

van der Have, Robert, and Luis Rubalcaba. 2016. 'Social Innovation Research: An Emerging Area of Innovation Studies?' *Research Policy* 45(9): 1923–35.

Weber, Max. 1978. *Economy and Society*, 2 vols. Berkeley, CA: University of California Press.

Wolff, Jonathan, and Avner de-Shalit. 2007. *Disadvantage.* Oxford Political Theory. Oxford: Oxford University Press.

Ziegler, Rafael. 2010. 'Innovations in Doing and Being: Capability Innovations at the Intersection of Schumpeterian Political Economy and Human Development'. *Journal of Social Entrepreneurship* 1(2): 255–72.

Ziegler, Rafael. 2017a. 'Social Innovation as a Collaborative Concept'. *Innovation: The European Journal of Social Science Research* 30(4): 388–405.

Ziegler, Rafael. 2017b. 'Citizen Innovation as Niche Restoration: A Type of Social Innovation and its Relevance for Political Participation and Sustainability'. *Journal of Social Entrepreneurship* 8(3): 338–53.

Ziegler, Rafael. 2017c. 'Innovation and Justice: Contributions of the Capabilities Approach to a Twenty-First-Century Transformative Perspective on Innovation.' In *Human Development in Times of Crisis: Renegotiating Social Justice,* edited by Hans-Uwe Otto, Spyridon Pantazis, Holger Ziegler, and Anotanneta Potsi, pp. 327–46. Basingstoke: Palgrave Macmillan.

Ziegler, Rafael, György Molnár, Enrica Chiappero-Martinetti, and Nadia von Jacobi. 2017. 'Creating (Economic) Space for Social Innovation'. *Journal of Human Development and Capabilities* 18(2): 293–298.

2

Social Innovation, Power, and Marginalization

Risto Heiskala

Introduction

This book considers how to tackle the many forms of marginalization with social innovation. In addition, it explores how to create research-based policy and practice advice to politicians, administrators, companies, non-governmental organizations, and citizens to achieve this goal. This chapter aims to contribute to this larger task by developing a social theory of power. The structure of the chapter goes as follows.[1]

In his *The Sources of Social Power*, historical sociologist Michael Mann outlines a four-fold theoretical model for the study of society (Mann 1986, 1993, 2012, and 2013). The model reduces the multitude of relations of interaction in social networks to ideological, economic, military, and political (IEMP) sources of social power. This chapter takes Mann's IEMP model as its point of departure for an attempt to develop such an approach in the theory of innovation, that goes beyond a crude dichotomy between technological and social innovation, recognizing instead that there are several types of innovation and there is a social aspect to all of them. The chapter then introduces the Social Grid model—that synthesizes different approaches in the field of economic sociology (Beckert 2010: see chapter 1) to supplement Mann's analysis of the economic sources of power. In that analysis, it turns out that a similar approach can also be used in the analysis of the three other power sources developed by Mann and Beckert's model can, thus, be extended to work within all of the four power sources. The analytical power of this synthesis is, then, further enhanced by adjusting it to take account of two additional approaches: Heiskala's extension of the IEMP model to a 'NACEMP model' that also includes nature (N), artefacts (A), and the whole culture (C) as

[1] I would like to thank everybody who participated in the CrESSI meeting in Berlin in January 2016 and the Institute for Advanced Social Research meeting at the University of Tampere in March 2016 for their comments on a draft of this chapter. In addition, I have got useful written comments from Jari Aro, Enrica Chiappero-Martinetti, Christopher Houghton Budd, Nadia von Jacobi, Klaus Kubeczko, György Molnár, Alex Nicholls, Pirjo Nikander, Gudrun-Christine Schimpf and Rafael Ziegler and am extremely grateful for that too.

Risto Heiskala, *Social Innovation, Power, and Marginalization*. In: *Creating Economic Space for Social Innovation*. Edited by: Alex Nicholls and Rafael Ziegler, Oxford University Press (2019). © Oxford University Press.
DOI: 10.1093/oso/9780198830511.003.0002

sources of power (Heiskala 2016a); Sen and Nussbaum's Capability Approach to well-being (Sen 1999; Nussbaum 2000). After these additions, an enhanced theory of innovation is presented that aims to make it more versatile and more sensitive to the forms of suffering that follow from a lack of development of human capabilities. This section's core contribution outlines the benefits of such an approach to the analysis of different types of marginalization and how innovation can help to tackle it—the main focus of the CrESSI project. The section also shows that even if the storyline of the chapter with its several variations and unexpected combinations somewhat resembles improvisation in jazz, not all of the music in it is played by the Ornette Coleman Orchestra—that would never have been comfortable in the still waters of synthesis sought here. For those interested in theoretical jazz there is still one more section discussing different interpretations of the theoretical schema presented here.

Mann's IEMP Model and Innovation Theory

According to Mann, human beings are purposeful creatures who strive to attain various ends. To reach their ends they need power to make social networks work for them. There are countless forms of causation in the assemblage of social networks. Four, however, are above the others and suffice for telling informative stories about societies and comparing different times and places. These four are: ideological; economic; military; and political power. Mann calls his analytical scheme the IEMP model after these four power sources. All four power sources can be found institutionalized into contingent forms in all societies since the birth of the state some five millennia ago, even if their relative significance and causal relationships vary in different societies creating different configurations. As forms of power, all four have both a *distributive* and a *collective* dimension. Distributive power has to do with the relative standing and gains of actors. It is most visible in situations of a zero-sum game in which all the gains of actor A are losses of actor B and vice versa. Collective power is an additive and cumulative form of power. It refers to the fact that by acting together, A and B can enhance their joint power in regard to C, whether C is a third party in human society or nature. It is possible to find pure cases of distributive or collective power in the social process, but in most real-life situations both dimensions come together in various combinations.[2]

For Mann, *ideological power* refers to 'the human need to find ultimate meaning in life, to share norms and values, and to participate in aesthetic and ritual

[2] The introduction to Mann's power analysis is here kept as concise as possible. For a more extensive, yet still parsimonious, summary see Heiskala (2016a). For a broader account see Mann (1986, 1993, 2012, and 2013). For the relationship of Mann's power analysis to some other conceptions of power see Heiskala (2001) and for an empirical application of the simultaneous analysis of a change in the distributive and collective power relations see Heiskala and Hämäläinen (2007).

practices ... Religions provide most examples ... with secular ideologies like liberalism, socialism and nationalism.' Diffusion of ideological power takes two principal forms: 'it may be sociopathically "transcendent". That is, an ideology may diffuse through the boundaries of economic, military, and political organizations, as Christianity did in the European Middle Ages and human rights do today. Ideological power may solidify an existing power organization, developing its "immanent morale"' (Mann 1993: 7), as happened within that narrow segment of the male military aristocracy, who were interpreted as citizens in ancient Athens and as happens within the top administrative personnel of every state or, in a slightly different way, within a motorbike gang today. To be effective in social networks, ideological power must be institutionalized in organizations such as churches, schools, and the media and transferred through some carrier strata such as priests, educators, or journalists.

Economic power derives 'from the need to extract, transform, distribute, and consume resources of nature' that characterize the human condition (Mann 1993: 7). It includes market exchange but is not restricted to it because as Polanyi (1944), Marx (1867) and many other political economists (starting with Smith 1776) have claimed, the 'economy' in the widest sense of the word is about the ways human beings secure their living in a productive relationship with nature, and this may well happen in some societies completely without markets and in all societies to some extent outside markets (see Polanyi 1968 and 1977; Dale 2010).

Military power is the social organization of physical force. Recently, Mann has emphasized its lethal nature and says that its message everywhere is 'if you resist, you die' (Mann 2012: 11). Previously, however, he was quite ready to follow Herbert Spencer and include all forms of *corvée* labour (enforced labour based on tradition, from that which built the pyramids or the Roman network of highways to that which provided the European nobility with its affluence compared to the populace) under the heading of 'organized physical force' (see especially Mann 1986).

Political power 'derives from the usefulness of territorial and centralised regulation ... Domestically, it is "territorially centralised"; externally, it involves geopolitics' (Mann 1993: 9). In both these senses, Mann restricts the use of the term 'political power' to the sphere of states. Here he departs from many other sociologists, including Weber (1922)—whose lead he otherwise often follows in his historical sociology—because they would also consider as 'political' many other kinds of institutional organizations. Mann makes the restriction to avoid unnecessary complexity in his narration stretching over five millennia, but for other purposes, such as the chapters within this book, it is possible and useful to extend his definition of political power to what is more normal in political sociology and, in this way, use it to cover also other public authorities than the central government.

If we now ask how to make Mann's conception useful for the study of innovations, two considerations immediately emerge. First, Mann does not speak about 'innovations' but the perspective itself is not alien to him. What he does speak about is 'leading edges' in the development of new forms of power. Especially in the first volume of his book series (Mann 1986), the emergence of new technological and socio-technological 'leading edges' (inventions in the field of navigation, military, or production technology as well as new forms of governance, for example) have a role in which they act as the 'switchmen of history' (as Weber's famous expression concerning religious ideas put it). Therefore, it is fitting to apply Mann's concepts to the theory of innovation. Second, what we learn when we apply his conception is that the ordinary way to make a distinction between technological and social innovations is insufficient. Instead of a dichotomy, there are at least four types of innovation—ideological, economic, military, and political—and all of these have both technological and social aspects.

This division provides a versatile classification of innovations to work on. Later on in this chapter, I will try to extend Mann's model in several respects to build up an even more versatile model. Before that, however, the next section seeks to mediate between Mann's conception of power and Beckert's Social Grid approach.

Extending the Social Grid Model

Beckert's research on the Social Grid was discussed in chapter 1. Therefore, it suffices here just briefly to outline its main characteristics as follows. Economic sociology was born to give a more realistic account of the workings of markets than pure economics by supplementing the economist's account with a sociological description of the societal conditions that make markets possible and enable their reproduction. In the field of economic sociology, three traditions can be recognized: the traditions of institutionalism; network analysis; and cultural analysis. They have all developed important, if one-sided, viewpoints but they have rarely interacted with each other in any genuine way. Beckert (2010) suggested that a more extensive research programme than any of these single traditions could be built by interpreting markets as *fields* (following Lewin 1951; Bourdieu 2005; DiMaggio and Powell 1983; and Fligstein 2001) and describing those fields as a triangle, the apexes of which are the central concepts of the three traditions (institutions, social networks, and cognitive frames). As shown in Figure 1.1 in chapter 1, the relationships of the three elements of the Social Grid work in the following way. Institutions establish the rules of the game, while in the process making certain values socially relevant and influencing the structure of social networks. Social networks link actors together, establishing collective power to shape institutions, as well as shaping and diffusing cognitive frames. Finally, cognitive frames give actors a worldview that tells them how social reality 'works' by defining what is legitimate and shaping perceptions of institutions as well as network structures. To analyse the economic field effectively is to pay attention to all the three apexes and all their six relationships.

Beckert's synthetic programme—the Social Grid—is an important achievement in itself because it provides the building blocks of a new research programme for economic sociology that shows that a productive division of intellectual labour can replace the struggle between the three competing traditions. In addition, it can also be interpreted as a contribution to Mann's power source analysis in two senses. First, Mann spoke about social networks on an abstract level when he presented his IEMP model, but he seldom conducted detailed analyses of the networks. The same is true with institutions: the model has it that, to be effective, power sources must be institutionalized into organizations in social processes. Indeed, Mann often describes such organizations but not systematically. Finally, the analysis of cognitive frames is weakly developed in Mann's conception because in his analysis of culture he stuck to the concept of ideology that made him omit the wider concept of culture as the frame of reference guiding the interpretation of reality. The interplay between the three apexes is sometimes touched upon in Mann's empirical descriptions but not in such a systematic way as suggested by the Social Grid. Beckert's way of describing the economic field, thus, provides a whole toolbox for describing the actual workings of economic power as envisaged in Mann's conception.

Once the above discovery has been made, it also opens a perspective onto an even wider application of the Social Grid within the IEMP model. Why not apply it in regard to the three other power sources as well? This would mean that in the analysis of ideological, military, and political power, attention should also be paid to the three elements of the Social Grid (institutions, social networks, and cognitive frames), making it possible to establish and maintain ideological, military, and political power. The six interrelationships of the three elements should also be covered to get a relatively complete picture of what is going on in a certain society at a certain time. It would also be good to keep in mind Mann's warning that the four power sources should not be understood as four distinct entities. Rather, they are four perspectives on the same reality and should, therefore, be analysed together, paying attention to their contingently changing configurations in time and place.

This is how we get a relatively complex typology of innovations and quite a complex apparatus for describing the processes of emergence or halting of innovations. Before we go any deeper into the explication of this approach, I would still like to add some other theoretical elements. I start with an attempt to extend the IEMP model a little in the next section. From there I move to the way of interpreting well-being in the so-called Capabilities Approach. Armed with these supplementary resources I am ready to move to the section on the classification of innovations and the relationship of that classification to the analysis of different types of marginalization as well as ways of tackling them. That will be the core of the chapter, even though it will be followed by discussion in the closing section of alternative possibilities for adjusting the scheme for the purposes of different end-users.

The IEMP Model, the NACEMP Model, and the CESPNA Model

Mann and Beckert are both sociologists. It is, therefore, no surprise that they follow the lead of the sociological classics and maintain that sociologists should concentrate their attention on social action (Weber 1922) and that social facts should be explained only with other social facts (Durkheim 1895). This emphasis on social causation is often valid but it also obscures that other aspect of the human condition which has to do with the human species' relationship to nature, as studied in the tradition going from political economy to historical materialism (Therborn 1976; Castoriadis 1975). The almost complete and, to a high degree, politically motivated split between these two perspectives in social research was most unfortunate and led to one-sided interpretations in both traditions (Clarke 1991). There were some attempts at mediation in the 1970s and 1980s (Habermas 1975; Eder 1980; Giddens 1981), but they soon went out of fashion as unintended and mostly unnecessary casualties of the cultural turn and the postmodernity debate (Heiskala 2011). Today, when the political landscape has once again changed and we are facing problems such as a potential global environmental crisis, we cannot afford to maintain this partition any more. What is needed, instead, is the combined analytical force of both traditions. That is the motivation behind my attempt below to develop the IEMP model further and extend it into a wider model to be used in addition to—and sometimes instead of—the original model.

To be accurate, Mann is only partly guilty of the above omission because, especially in the first volume of his series where he deals with the long historical durée of five millennia. Here he presented a list of historical innovations, many of which were technological in nature, spoke about infrastructural power, and outlined a conception of the economy that clearly goes beyond neoclassical market economics and more resembles that of political economy (Mann 1986). Even in that volume, however, he often omitted the material side of human existence and, in the more recent volumes, it has been marginalized almost completely as he admitted himself (Mann 2016: 289). Something must, therefore, be done if we want to introduce nature and human interaction into the model. Here is my suggestion, presented in Heiskala (2016a).

We could extend the concept of power from social power so that it would, in addition to causation radiating from human agents, broadly cover other kinds of causation that emerge from nature and techno-structures. That is not often done in the field of studies of power (see e.g. Clegg and Haugaard 2009), but we actually already do something of the kind when we speak about 'electric power', for example. With that expression we admit that natural processes and infrastructures too can have directive force on human behaviour (as has also recently been emphasized by the Actor Network Theorists, albeit with a more culturally constructionist tone than mine here; see Latour 1987 and 2005). That is certainly a different form of power than the one represented by intentional, conscious, and goal-directed human action, but, then again, that form of power is a special case because much of the power of human agents is actually transmitted through unwitting agency (Giddens 1976). We can, therefore, adopt a theoretical model for the broad concept of power that is a continuum extending from fully conscious and self-reflexive goal-oriented social action through half or completely unconscious agency (whether social or not) to artefactual or natural causation.

This thinking can be introduced into the IEMP model if we transform it into a NACEMP model, with the letter N referring to 'nature'. The natural power resources of human actors vary according to their genotype (women are but men are not capable of giving birth to new human beings, intelligent people are in many situations privileged over less intelligent, etc.), environment (some areas are better suited for agriculture, fishing, mining, or industrial production than others) and the density of population in their community (sometimes the population is too small for certain activities to emerge and sometimes the contrary is true and there are so many people that their sheer density prevents some desirable activities). Throughout history, the breakdown of natural power resources has been largely outside human control, although that has, especially since the first industrial revolution and its aftermaths, been changing to some extent.

Moreover, the development of different technologies has brought about ways to intervene humanly in the workings of natural causation. That is what civilization is all about, and the whole of that technological intervention can be called 'artefactual power', represented in the NACEMP model by the letter A. Especially in today's scientific-technological culture, artefactual power can intervene in almost any area of the human relation to nature (Schroeder 2007). We thus learn how to prevent births with contraception, how to create new human beings in laboratories outside the female body, how to go beyond obstacles for agriculture, fishing, mining, and production in certain environments and how to adjust the size of whole populations. We are not gods though, and both external and internal nature will always impose limits on us that we cannot overstep.

In addition to enabling new things, techno-structures themselves also set limits on our agency in the form of historically developed infrastructures and artefacts. Mann's strategy would be to analyse those under the four dimensions of the IEMP model, and he maintains that a separate artefactual power source is, therefore, not needed at all (Mann 2016: 289 commenting on Heiskala 2016a). This is convincing to the extent that we deal with specific infrastructures and artefacts such as churches or schools (I), the productive machinery and the mall (E), the military–industrial complex (M), or the houses of parliament and ministries (P). However, much of the infrastructure and the whole of artefacts are not designed in this sectorially purposeful way. Instead, they are just there. Think of a fork, for example. It does not serve anybody's interest in particular and its existence is not part of any actor's ongoing project. Yet it has directive force to our universe of choice when we dine. A fork, of course, may be a trivial example but it is important to realize that it is just one example of a vast universe of similar things. Jean-Paul Sartre (1960) had the expression 'frozen praxis' (*pratico-inerte*) for such forms of social materiality, the existence of which is not part of anybody's project but which still possesses the quality of 'facticity' for any social actor. It is for the analysis of frozen praxis that we need the concept of artefactual power (A) as a concept on the same level of abstraction as the concept of natural power (N), even if we accept Mann's sectorial idea of studying specific technologies, infrastructures, and artefacts in the context of the other four power sources whenever that can be sensibly done.

Now that we have started to tinker with the IEMP model let us make one more adjustment. Mann's original concept of ideological power with its two aspects (transcending power and immanent morale) was useful because it provides precise tools to study the transmission and reproduction of ritually affirmed value commitments and norms. The more critical assessment is that it represents a rather narrow take on culture that was obvious when he analysed phenomena such as the role of Christianity as a shared worldview of medieval Europe. These analyses clearly demanded that he extend the limitations of his narrowly defined concept of ideological power (see Mann 1986). The same was even more obvious when, in the third volume of his book series, he introduced a third aspect to his conception of ideological power in order to analyse changing gender relations and ethnicity. That third element was 'institutionalized ideologies' such as patriarchy or racism (Mann 2012). This change of conception brought him quite close to the concept of cultural power. Yet, he did not want to adopt the new term because he thought that 'culture' was a too loosely defined concept and could mean almost anything (Mann 2016: 289).

The obvious alternative to 'ideology' is, of course the concept of 'cognitive frames', which Beckert used within the Social Grid. I would personally prefer the concept of 'semiosis' that refers to the study of signs and the transmission of meanings through signs (Heiskala 2003), but I understand that that may be a little technical for this context.[3] Yet, the reference to semiosis shows that 'cognitive

[3] The two main traditions are the North American current of 'semiotics' emerging from the work of C. S. Peirce (1839–1914) and other pragmatist philosophers such as James (1842–1910) and

frames' too is somewhat inadequate because it is a particular way of conceptualizing culture (drawing more from phenomenology and cognitive science than pragmatism or neo-structuralism) and easily directs attention to conscious and preconscious cultural schemes that obscure the relations of meaning that their carriers reproduce unwittingly and are not able to reflect (Heiskala 2003; Gronow 2008). In the following I will replace the term 'ideological power' (I) with that of 'cultural power' (C). The implication of the change is that all signifying material is included, while, in a similar vein to 'frozen praxis' in the case of artefactual power, part of it is understood such that it is not reproduced as result of anybody's communicative project to transmit meanings but persists just by the weight of tradition.[4]

We have now transformed the IEMP model into a more extensive NACEMP model with implications for the classification of innovations. The simplest way to turn the model into such a classification would be to follow the pattern used above when turning the IEMP model into a classification of innovations by linking one type of innovation to each of the power sources, and that, indeed, is the basic idea of the classification presented here. However, three adjustments are needed. First, as argued above, nature is a source of power, yet there cannot be anything called 'natural innovation' because some form of conscious thinking must be present whenever we speak about innovations, and that is not so in the case of nature. Nature too develops but that happens in the form of evolution, not by means of innovations.[5] Second, to anticipate the use of the model for the purposes of innovation studies in the CrESSI project and similar contexts I would like to extend the definition of military power source a little and speak about security-related innovations, thus including, in addition to lethal power, all organized violence in its field. Third, also to anticipate the use in the CrESSI project and in the empirical analyses included in Part II of this book, I will for the purpose of this book and as specially requested by the authors of the empirical case studies change the order of the letters referring to the different forms of power so that the

G. H. Mead (1863–1931) and the French tradition of 'semiology' rooted in the work of linguist Ferdinand de Saussure (1857–1913), developing later to structuralism, post-structuralism, and neo-structuralism (see Short 2007; Culler 1986). In my *Society as Semiosis* I have tried to show that, contrary to a widely held belief, these traditions are not contradictory and can, thus, both contribute to a synthetic conception of semiotics and make that tradition useful again in the field of social theory (see Heiskala 2003).

[4] An alternative to this tradition is chance or the mechanism of 'cultural chiasma'. In this case we are dealing with an unintentional, yet significant, conflation of two or more messages typically taking place in multicultural urban centres or in media that are intersections of vast flows of information (see Heiskala 1993).

[5] This book deals with innovations in human societies. I will, therefore, exclude problems having to do with the consciousness of developed animals such as apes, dolphins, and pigs and so on that may all be able to learn and come up with some limited forms of innovations. It is obvious that this topic merits careful study in some other context.

new power sources do not come first but last. This is how we get the CESPNA model of power analysis and the CESPA model of innovation studies covering the following pure forms of innovation:

- Cultural innovations (Ci)
- Economic innovations (Ei)
- Security-related innovations (Si)
- Political innovations (Pi)
- Artefactual innovations (Ai).

Finally, it needs to be noted that this typology, as well as other typologies presented in this chapter, is one of ideal types in the Weberian sense. That means that some empirical cases may be perfect matches with one of the types but many of the chapters of this volume—including the case analyses—combine more than one of the theoretical types. That is a phenomenon to which the authors of chapter 1 refer with Mann's concept of 'functional promiscuity'. To see what can be done with the CESPNA model in the study of innovations and forms of marginalization, we will discuss well-being in the next section.

Capabilities

One of the most powerful interpretations of human well-being is the Capabilities Approach. Its basic idea is that it is not enough for people's well-being to provide them with material resources and formal rights to use resources. What is needed in addition is the possibility for everybody to actually realize some basic human 'capabilities'.

However, there are a number of open questions in the interpretation of the exact nature and theoretical status of capabilities. Sen outlined the Capabilities Approach by referring to five distinctive types of freedom that must all be present—at least to some extent—for people to be able to realize their capabilities. These freedoms include: '(1) political freedoms, (2) economic facilities, (3) social opportunities, (4) transparency guarantees, and (5) protective security' (Sen 1999: 10). According to Sen, this is one possible list among others, and it is always a context-specific task relative to local standards and objectives of the developmental project at hand to specify those capabilities that are central to each context. Nussbaum is more ambitious. In the tradition of human rights and a Rawlsian theory of justice (Rawls 1971), she presented a list of ten 'basic capabilities', which every political system should honour. The list includes: life; bodily health; bodily integrity; senses, imagination, and thought; emotions; practical reason; affiliation; other species; play; control over one's environment in political and material senses (Nussbaum 2000: 78–80). Nussbaum understood her list as an abstract frame that can have various different context-specific local applications. She also emphasized that the list is open to debate. Yet, she thought that it is a universal measure of human dignity and should, therefore, be obeyed in all contexts and political constitutions. Here she departed from Sen, who thought that it is better to work with a more open set of context-specific lists without an abstract 'basic' frame on which these local lists should always be somehow grounded. Debate about the controversy between Sen and Nussbaum on the nature and status of the Capability Approach still continues and there is no easy solution in sight.[6]

Personally, I am more inclined toward Sen's position because it is difficult to see exactly upon what lists of basic capabilities such as Nussbaum's are grounded. The list itself is a sympathetic one, but because it very much resembles a new version of the UN Declaration of Human Rights, one immediately starts to search for an authority such as the UN General Assembly behind it. As such an authority cannot be found, it remains an intervention made by a single scholar. That again means irrespective of what Nussbaum said, the status of the list is the same as Sen's—namely, it is a context-specific interpretation tailored for the purposes at hand. This encourages me to provide a third list based on the transformed version of Mann's power sources—the CESPNA model. This is the list of capabilities of relevance to the discussion here:

- Cultural capabilities (Cc)
- Economic capabilities (Ec)
- Security-related capabilities (Sc)
- Political capabilities (Pc)
- Natural capabilities (Nc)
- Artefactual capabilities (Ac).

The status of the list is the same as Sen's: the instructions for use read simply: 'Use in cases of need, otherwise tailor an alternative list of your own.'

Contributions

Now, finally, it is the time to wrap things up. In line with what has been said above, I propose that there are six forms of marginalization:

[6] For an overview of the debate see Robeyns (2005 and 2016); however, see also Qizilbash (2002) who suggests that the controversy has been exaggerated and on a more abstract level both parties share an almost identical set of values.

- Cultural marginalization (Cm), such as lack of cultural capital (as happens in the case of marginalization of the Roma in Hungary analysed in chapter 7)
- Economic marginalization (Em), such as lack of economic resources (as happens in cases analysed in chapter 7 in which micro-credit is a viable solution as well as most of the other cases analysed in this volume)
- Security-related marginalization (Sm), such as lack of physical protection (as happens in the lack of housing analysed in chapter 5)
- Political marginalization (Pm), such as limited access to public discourse or centres of political power (which characterizes the situation of most social groups analysed in this volume)
- Natural marginalization (Nm), such as physical disability
- Artefactual marginalization (Am), such as lack of technical means for the use of the Internet, the network of highways, or the water-management system (as happens in the case analysed in chapter 6).

Five types of innovation can refine these forms of marginalization. There are five instead of six because there is no such thing as natural innovation—even if 'natural' marginalization can be tackled by other types of innovation, especially artefactual:

- Cultural innovations (Ci), such as new forms of education or new conceptualizations of citizenship rights
- Economic innovations (Ei), such as new forms of credit
- Security-related innovations (Si), such as prevention programmes of intimate violence or political terror
- Political innovations (Pi), such as new forms of mobilization or new institutional patters for decision-making
- Artefactual innovations (Ai), such as new auxiliary devices for disabled people.

Sometimes, one innovation is not enough to tackle marginalization. Let us say that a person has a disease that has so far proved to be incurable (Nm), but a new medicine capable of healing her is invented (Ai). However, nothing much is changed if the medication is so expensive that it is out of the person's reach. Other kinds of innovations are, therefore, needed to provide the resources for the medication (Ei) and to spread the resources evenly among the patients in need (Pi or Si). This is how innovations must sometimes come in chains if they are to have an impact. Chapter 6 presents one case in which exactly that happens and shows that social innovations are often complex and mixed. Therefore, theoretical typologies consisting of pure types must be used with caution: in most cases they do not provide a one-to-one match with reality but, rather, offer a theoretical toolbox with which to describe a reality. As noted above, this can be characterized by 'functional promiscuity'.

In addition, marginalization can also be prevented or eased in ways that are quite traditional and not innovative at all, such as improving social security or enhancing the coverage of health benefits among the population. This is also important to remember when tailoring policy advice. Old recipes can work well too!

Conclusion: Enigma Variations

The above discussion concludes the building of the theoretical model presented in this chapter. Practically minded readers can, therefore, move to chapter 3. However, for lovers of theoretical 'jazz' I would still like to add some further considerations. First, the last remark in the previous section about old recipes potentially opens a broad field of analysis, which can only be touched on here but remains worthy of mention. The lack, or insufficiency, of effective policies for addressing marginalization is not always based on lack of learning, innovation, or knowledge of how to proceed. Sometimes the old recipes are well known but their effective use is a matter of political struggle. Here we enter into the field of distributive power games pure and simple. Examples of this kind of situation are many: in this volume, we might point to the discussion of the Roma people in Hungary (see chapter 7). The lack of effective policies to improve their situation is not so much a matter of not knowing the way. Instead, it is a straightforward matter of politically lacking will, and that, of course, is not a matter of innovation and learning but of political struggle.[7]

Furthermore, Beckert's Social Grid approach is based on the concept of a 'field'. This is why the suggestion to build a mediation between the Grid and Mann's IEMP model goes against Mann's explicitly stated intention *not* to consider the elements of his model as 'subsystems', 'levels', 'dimensions', or any other of the geometric terms favoured by social theorists. Rather, they should simply be understood as 'an analytical point of entry for dealing with mess' (Mann 1993: 10). This commitment to a radical interpretation of the Weberian ideal-type method sets Mann apart from many social theorists and is a sensible warning, especially if one is operating with a timespan of five millennia. Yet, the issue can also be considered a contingent and empirical question. That leads us to a less radical interpretation of the ideal-type method according to which it is a contingent question to be studied empirically—when and where ideal types are not just theoretical constructions but also to some degree 'real types' describing adequately

[7] For more on this aspect see Heiskala (2007) and Heiskala and Hämäläinen (2007).

actually existing social relations. Following such a less radical interpretation, we can say that in some societies, at some times, power sources are organized as fields and in others they are not. The vital question to ask is whether it is possible to detect specified institutions, social networks, and cognitive frames that define the fields of ideological, economic, military, and political power—including some actors and projects and excluding others. I expect that in the case of all modern societies, possibly excluding certain radical transition periods such as revolutions, it is safe to expect that this is the case. The Social Grid model, therefore, should work well in the societies analysed in this compilation.

Moreover, there are different ways to use the terms 'nature' and 'infrastructure', and the differences may cause needless confusion if not briefly discussed here. In the context of commenting on the limitations of authoritarian power in the Middle East and Africa, Mann wrote about infrastructures:

> I define infrastructural powers as those that enable regimes to penetrate their territories. But I stress that these powers are not confined to . . . 'literal infrastructures'--like roads and telecommunications. These are the technological side of infrastructural power that Schroeder and Heiskala would both fit within their categories of, respectively, scientific/technological and artefactual power. But I want to add social infrastructures too, like a ruling party, security police, clans, and tribes related to ruling families, supportive religious sects, plus, in some cases, the provision of social benefits such as social citizenship financed by oil revenues. All these are used to try to undercut opposition.
>
> (Mann 2016: 314)

Here we have obviously two different uses for the term 'infrastructure'. In Mann's use in the quotation and in Mann (1986), he included both 'literal infrastructures' and all social organizations that a ruling political power can use as means of its political power. That is a definition that works well for the purposes Mann wanted to use it. Yet here, and elsewhere, I have been using the term in a different and more conventional meaning, referring only to the technological and artefactual dimension of human existence, which Mann above called 'literal infrastructures'.

A similar polysemy is present in the use of the term 'nature'. This time Mann is not part of the debate, which has been going on in the CrESSI project as well as in the social scientific community more widely, about the use of concepts such as nature. One party to the debate has taken the radically constructionist view according to which 'nature' is a word in human language and, as with any other term, gets its meaning within the human linguistic community through a social process. The other party, often called *realists*, find the constructionist view futile because it does not give sufficient emphasis to the existence of extra-linguistic entities as referents of expressions such as 'nature'. In Heiskala (2000), I have defended a mediating position called 'moderate constructionism'. That approach admits that constructionists are right when they say that, as human beings, we cannot conceptualize objects such as 'nature' without the means of language. Yet it also understands realists when they emphasize that with the term 'nature' our language refers to a reality, that is largely independent of our conceptualizations, and it is exactly for this reason that the concept is useful. In other words, it is because 'nature' is also something more than and above a socially constructed concept that we can use the term in referring to phenomena such as climate change, that includes the possibility that if it eradicates all of humankind it does this whether or not some human beings have seen the catastrophe coming and whether or not they called it 'climate change'. The systematic theoretical and empirical methods used to create an increasingly effective understanding of the ways of nature in modern science make science a huge institutional arrangement and constantly ongoing process that, through the practice of trial and error, attempts to reach a better and better understanding of its workings (Niiniluoto 2000). The possibility to ground successful technologies in science and, thus, create affluence such as never before seen in the history of humankind, again gives us a strong reason to believe that modern science actually works (Schroeder 2007; Marks 2015; Heiskala 2016b). I still believe that when moving in the deep waters of the epistemology of science, we should adopt this moderate constructionist view mediating between the two extremes.[8] In the CrESSI project, however, we have not been digging that deep. References to nature in the case analyses in this volume are often restricted to socially constructed conceptualizations of nature, but that is not meant to express an epistemological commitment. Instead, it is a working solution having to do with the nature of the cases and our level of analysis.

Finally, how exactly should the model be used? What has been developed in this chapter is quite a complex conceptual approach. It is open to further theoretical discussion but it is also ready for use in empirical analysis as it is. In its complete form it includes six power sources, five of which can be analysed by means of the Social Grid (once again, natural power defies such analysis because there are no social networks, institutions, or cultural frames in nature), six forms of marginalization, and five modes of innovation to tackle marginalization. However, the potential user is by no means faced with a 'take it or leave it' situation because the overall conceptualization can also be understood as a toolkit from which each user can pick up the tools she needs and use only those, adjusted as seems fit for the analytic task at hand. That is exactly what happens in some of the empirical chapters later in this volume, and is exactly as it should be. Concepts are not coined to be worshipped but, rather, to serve some purpose.

[8] That also has implications for the interpretation of the natural power source because the commitment to moderate constructionism sets its interpretation apart from the radical constructionist views of the Actor Network Theorists such as Latour and others.

References

Beckert, Jens. 2010. 'How Do Fields Change? The Interrelations of Institutions, Networks, and Cognition in the Dynamics of Markets'. *Organization Studies* 31(5): 605–27.

Bourdieu, Pierre 2005. 'Principles of an Economic Anthropology'. In *Handbook of Economic Sociology*, edited by Neil J. Smelser and Richard Swedberg, pp. 75–89. Princeton, NJ: Princeton University Press.

Castoriadis, Cornelius. 1975. *L'Institution imaginaire de la société*. Paris: Editions du Seuil.

Clarke, Simon. 1991. *Marx, Marginalism and Modern Sociology: From Adam Smith to Max Weber.* Basingstoke: Palgrave.

Clegg, Stewart R. and Mark Haugaard. 2009. *The Sage Handbook of Power.* London: Sage.

Culler, Jonathan. 1986. *Ferdinand de Saussure.* Revised edition. Ithaca, NY: Cornell University Press.

Dale, Gareth. 2010. *Karl Polanyi: The Limits of the Market.* Cambridge: Polity.

DiMaggio, Paul, and Walter Powell. 1983. 'The Iron Cage Revisited: Institutional Isomorphism and Collective Rationality in Organizational Fields'. *American Sociological Review* 48(2): 147–60.

Durkheim, Émile. 1895. *The Rules of Sociological Method.* New York: The Free Press, 1982.

Eder, Klaus. 1980. *Die Entstehung staatlich organisierter Gesellschaften. Ein Betrag zu einer Theorie sozialer Evolution.* Frankfurt am Main: Suhrkamp.

Fligstein, Neil. 2001. *The Architecture of Markets.* Princeton, NJ: Princeton University Press.

Giddens, Anthony. 1976. *New Rules of Sociological Method: A Positive Critique of Interpretative Sociologies.* London: Hutchinson.

Giddens, Anthony. 1981. *A Contemporary Critique of Historical Materialism, Volume 1: Power, Property, and the State.* London: Macmillan.

Gronow, Antti. 2008. 'Not by Rules or Choice Alone: A Pragmatist Critique of Institution Theories in Economics and Sociology'. *Journal of Institutional Economics* 4(3): 351–73.

Habermas, Jürgen. 1975. 'Towards a Reconstruction of Historical Materialism'. *Theory and Society* 2(3): 287–300.

Heiskala, Risto. 1993. 'Modernity and the Intersemiotic Condition'. *Social Science Information* 32(4): 581–604.

Heiskala, Risto. 2000. *Toiminta, tapa ja rakenne. Kohti konstruktionististista synteesiä yhteiskuntateoriassa.* Helsinki: Gaudeamus. ['Action, Habit and Structure: Toward a Constructionist Synthesis in Social Theory'].

Heiskala, Risto. 2001. 'Theorizing Power: Weber, Parsons, Foucault and Neostructuralism'. *Social Science Information* 40(2): 241–64.

Heiskala, Risto. 2003. *Society as Semiosis: Neostructuralist Theory of Culture and Society*. Frankfurt am Main: Peter Lang.

Heiskala, Risto. 2007. 'Social Innovations: Structural and Power Perspectives'. In *Social Innovations, Institutional Change and Economic Performance: Making Sense of Structural Adjustment Processes in Industrial Sectors, Regions and Societies*, edited by Timo Hämäläinen and Risto Heiskala, pp. 52–79. Cheltenham: Edward Elgar.

Heiskala, Risto. 2011. 'From Modernity through Postmodernity to Reflexive Modernization: Did We Learn Anything?' *International Review of Sociology* 21(1): 3–19.

Heiskala, Risto. 2016a. 'The Evolution of the Sources of Social Power, and Some Extensions'. In *Global Powers: Mann's Anatomy of the Twentieth Century and Beyond*, edited by Ralph Schroeder, pp. 11–37. Cambridge: Cambridge University Press.

Heiskala, Risto. 2016b. 'Have We Ever Been Modern?' *European Sociologist* 39(1): 4–7.

Heiskala, Risto and Hämäläinen, Timo. 2007. 'Social Innovation or Hegemonic Change? Paradigm Change in Finland in the 1980s and 1990s'. In *Social Innovations, Institutional Change and Economic Performance: Making Sense of Structural Adjustment Processes in Industrial Sectors, Regions and Societies*, edited by Timo Hämäläinen and Risto Heiskala, pp. 80–94. Cheltenham: Edward Elgar.

Latour, Bruno. 1987. *Science in Action: How to Follow Scientists and Engineers through Society*. Cambridge, MA: Harvard University Press.

Latour, Bruno. 2005. *Reassembling the Social: An Introduction to the Actor-Network Theory*. Oxford: Oxford University Press.

Lewin, Kurt. 1951. *Resolving Social Conflicts and Field Theory in the Social Science*. Washington, DC: American Psychological Association, 1997.

Mann, Michael. 1986. *The Sources of Social Power, Volume 1: A History of Power from the Beginning to A.D. 1760*. Cambridge: Cambridge University Press.

Mann, Michael. 1993. *The Sources of Social Power, Volume 2: The Rise of Classes and Nation-States, 1760–1914*. Cambridge: Cambridge University Press.

Mann, Michael. 2012. *The Sources of Social Power, Volume 3: Global Empires and Revolution, 1890–1945*. Cambridge: Cambridge University Press.

Mann, Michael. 2013. *The Sources of Social Power, Volume 4: Globalizations, 1945–2011*. Cambridge: Cambridge University Press.

Mann, Michael. 2016. 'Response to the Critics'. In *Global Powers: Mann's Anatomy of the Twentieth Century and Beyond*, edited by Ralph Schroeder, pp. 281–322. Cambridge: Cambridge University Press.

Marx, Karl. 1867. *Capital: A Critique of Political Economy, Volume 1*. London: Penguin Books and New Left Review, 1976.

Marks, Rovert B. 2015. *The Origins of the Modern World: A Global and Environmental Narrative from the Fifteenth to the Twenty-First Century.* Lanham: Rowman and Littlefield.

Niiniluoto, Ilkka. 2000. *Critical Scientific Realism.* Oxford: Oxford University Press.

Nussbaum, Martha C. 2000. *Women and Human Development: The Capabilities Approach.* Cambridge: Cambridge University Press.

Polanyi, Karl. 1944. *The Great Transformation: The Political and Economic Origins of Our Time.* Boston: Beacon Press, 1971.

Polanyi, Karl. 1968. *Primitive, Archaic and Modern Economies: Essays of Karl Polanyi,* edited by George Dalton. New York: Anchor Books.

Polanyi, Karl. 1977. *The Livelihood of Man,* edited by Harry W. Person. New York: Academic Press.

Qizilbash, Mozaffar. 2002. 'Development, Common Foes and Shared Values'. *Review of Political Economy* 14(4): 463–80.

Rawls, John. 1971. *A Theory of Justice.* Cambridge, MA: Belknap.

Robeyns, Ingrid. 2005. 'The Capability Approach: A Theoretical Survey'. *Journal of Human Development* 6(1): 93–114.

Robeyns, Ingrid. 2016. 'Capabilitarianism'. *Journal of Human Development* 17(3): 397–414.

Sartre, Jean-Paul. 1960. *Critique of Dialectical Reason, Volume 1.* London: Verso, 1991.

Schroeder, Ralph. 2007. *Rethinking Science, Technology and Social Change.* Stanford, CA: Stanford University Press.

Sen, Amartya. 1999. *Development as Freedom.* Oxford: Oxford University Press.

Short, T. L. 2007. *Peirce's Theory of Signs.* Cambridge: Cambridge University Press.

Smith, Adam. 1776. *An Inquiry into the Nature and Causes of the Wealth of Nations, Volumes 1 and 2.* Indianapolis, IN: Liberty Fund, 1981.

Therborn, Göran. 1976. *Class, Science and Society: On the Formation of Sociology and Historical Materialism.* London: NLB.

Weber, Max. 1922. *Economy and Society: An Outline of Interpretative Sociology,* edited by Guenther Root and Claus Wittich. Berkeley, CA: University of California Press, 1978.

3

Creating Fair (Economic) Space for Social Innovation? A Capabilities Perspective

Rafael Ziegler and Nadia von Jacobi

Introduction

Social innovation is not limited to innovation in markets. Accordingly, the 'economic space' in our analysis is not confined to standard markets and exchange based on prices alone. In fact, there is frequently a tension between the search for profits and saving costs and the search for social solutions. For example, helping the least well-off is likely, often, to cost more than helping the better-off in a marginalized group (see chapter 7) and, either way, there might not be a 'market' product or service available that is suitable for the social intervention. How, then, to think about and analyse the economic space for social innovation?[1]

This chapter draws on a typology of *modes of provision*, i.e. the plural ways in which a service or good is provided to users and beneficiaries, to investigate 'economic space' of social innovation with an analytical tool suitable for the plurality of economic practices. Based on work at the intersection of economics and ethics (Anderson 1993; Claassen 2009), this typology provides a tool for analysing social innovation and its reconfigurations beyond the market/non-market dichotomy. This approach helps us to avoid the tendency in some strands of social innovation research to reduce social innovation to 'social business' only focused on the integration of organizations and individuals into markets.[2] In addition to a focus on market provision, this typology adds modes of self, informal, public, and professional provision. We introduce the term *collaborative pluralism* to highlight these varieties of modes of provision, as well as their reconfigurations in social innovation. We propose that collaborative pluralism captures a central dynamic of social innovation and related policy, and with it a series of distinct *ethical* questions worthy of further consideration.

[1] This text has benefitted from written comments by Taco Brandsen, Rutger Claassen, Daniel Edmiston, Adalbert Evers, and Christopher Houghton Budd, discussions at the Berlin CrESSI workshop in January 2017 and at the CRÉ Montreal in December 2017, and from Amelia Pope's and Alex Nicholls' editorial work.

[2] For a critical discussion of this point see Jessop et al. (2013: 110f.).

Rafael Ziegler and Nadia von Jacobi, *Creating Fair (Economic) Space for Social Innovation? A Capabilities Perspective*. In: *Creating Economic Space for Social Innovation*. Edited by: Alex Nicholls and Rafael Ziegler,
Oxford University Press (2019). © Oxford University Press.
DOI: 10.1093/oso/9780198830511.003.0003

For this ethical analysis, we draw on the capabilities approach, as one contemporary ethical approach to justice and development (Nussbaum 2006; Sen 2009). If social innovation is about improving and securing human capabilities, what ethical issues arise with respect to modes of provision and their reconfigurations in social innovation processes? We suggest that due to the diversity of people involved in these processes and their social and environmental contexts, a variety of modes of provision will, in principle, improve choice and outcomes. This point especially holds for disempowered service users—those who cannot effectively choose their own 'beings and doings' and whose well-being is unlikely to be met via one model of provision only. Societies, however, are in a constant process of change. Drawing from the social innovation literature (Evers and Brandsen 2016), we, therefore, propose that for fostering and securing an effective economic space for social innovation, it is useful to think of social innovation as 'messages' that point to potential changes in modes of provision and their configurations. We use the formulation 'fair space for social innovation' to highlight the evaluative aspect behind our discussions of the economic underpinnings of social innovation. This term introduces a general ethical or social perspective on social innovation and its role in society.

The next section introduces our typology of modes of provision. After this, the chapter considers a capabilities approach to various modes of provision in the economic space for social innovation. The chapter offers a refinement of the Extended Social Grid Model (ESGM) based on our new typology, as well as the lessons of the latter for the issues discussed here.

Modes of Provision

Mann (see chapter 2) defined economic power as deriving 'from the human need to extract, transform, distribute, and consume the produce of nature' (Mann 2013: 1–2). This wide framing of economic issues beyond markets is useful for social innovation, but calls for further elaboration as an analytical tool. Anderson (1993) identified four modes of production, distribution, and consumption of goods and services: markets; gift-exchange in private relations; public-good provision via the state; and professional standards used in the sphere of civil society. Refining her typology, Claassen defined five modes of provision; 'each provides a specific way of integrating the economic phases of production, exchange and consumption of goods' (2009: 423–5):

- *Self-provision*. The producer of the good consumes it herself. There is no exchange with others, no money involved. A well-known example, *avant la lettre* of current social innovation discourse, is Henry Thoreau's *Walden* self-sufficiency experiment (Thoreau 1854). A social variation of this experiment is communal gardening, which takes us to the next mode.

- *Informal provision.* The exchange of goods is governed by social norms, for example in reciprocal gift-giving. No money is involved in such exchanges and there is no expectation that the respective giving is of equal value—such reciprocity is 'open to discretion as to value and time' (Offer 1997: 457). If a neighbour helps you fix something in your flat, you 'owe' her. This usually means she can ask you a favour at some point in the future and this might simply be something you can provide, no matter if it has the same value. Social innovation examples include sharing-platforms such as 'free-cycle', where people offer and request goods from others for free. Notoriously, such platforms are easily taken over by market forces, which takes us to a third mode.
- *Market provision.* Exchanges are based on price signals and based on individual wants, preferences, and purchasing power. If producers and consumers are willing to include other-regarding considerations in their consumer choices, there is room for social innovation within markets (e.g. Fair Trade goods). Often, however, markets find it difficult to achieve such a dynamic without state regulation.
- *Public provision.* Resources are pooled (e.g. via taxes or mandatory labour) so as to provide goods to the respective group's members, be it public goods such as public radio or military defence or the provision of specific welfare goods linked to individual entitlements (e.g. public infrastructure for wheelchair accessibility). The provisioning process is organized via a political process of decision-making. Drinking water and social housing (see chapters 5 and 6) are examples of social innovations frequently provided by the state.
- *Professional provision.* The good or service is based on the expert knowledge of the provider (e.g. doctors). Professionals are either paid directly by their clients or indirectly via public schemes (such as health insurance), private initiatives (such as philanthropic activities), or some combination thereof.

This typology shows how the human need to extract, transform, distribute, and consume the produce of nature (see chapter 1) can be provided by more than market provision. It allows us better to specify the typically vague and rather unsatisfactory category of the 'non-market' for analysing the economic space for social innovation. It also corrects an often-skewed image of economic space as essentially a matter of markets. As Offer noted, while price-driven market exchange has been at the centre of economics ever since Adam Smith, there is a 'less noted ... persistence of non-market exchange into modern times' (Offer 1997: 450 and 458). For example, household production in Australia, the United Kingdom and the United States, as estimated by extended national accounts, fluctuate around one quarter to one third of the total gross national product.

However, these modes are ideal-types, identifying the main modes of provision rather than the more messy reality. For example, market provision in practice includes corporations that are often highly 'political' structures not so different from the bureaucracy of the state—this is one reason for Schumpeter's (1942) claim that the growth of corporations in capitalism leads to a necessary development towards socialism. Moreover, the list itself may be controversial. Consider what is likely the most controversial mode on the list: professional provision. We see professionals working in public, market, and even informal provision—is professional provision, then, a transversal phenomenon across state, business, civil society, and family? As a matter of funding, this is, no doubt, correct. Professionals can be funded by the state, via market mechanisms or supported informally. Still, Anderson has a point when she observed that professional norms would be compromised if the market determined them exclusively (Anderson 1993: 156)—for example, the provision of health. Or, as another example, if the state exclusively decided what and how educators teach (see chapter 8). Education and health are prominent examples of the provision of goods and services that are of primary societal importance, yet sufficiently complex to support the idea that provision should be strongly informed by professionals so as to ensure quality. Offer suggested that an important mechanism in professional provision is the support of a professional peer group as a 'gift' to be 'repaid' later with considerable discretion (Offer 1997: 463).

The fact that these modes of provision are blurry in practice—and that hybrid goods and services are identifiable across all the modes—is taken up later on in this chapter in our discussion of collaborative pluralism. Here we only note one further question relevant for our discussions: should we add theft and robbery as a mode of provision?[3] This question points to the large 'shadow market' in the grey zone of market provision, where there are numerous issues of marginalization, exclusion, and deprivation relevant for social innovation.

In our view, this addition is of interest for social innovation chiefly as a transitional phenomenon. It highlights a central point: social innovation is about changing modes of provision and their reconfiguration. 'Ordinary' theft and robbery is associated with widespread aspects of informal provision—for example, in mafia-organized robbery for the benefit of their immediate community. Such shadow market activity—as in much of the market for drugs, weapons, and prostitution—also connects with varieties of corruption in public and professional provision. But consider by contrast a famous inspiration for social entrepreneurs and innovators: the social action of Gandhi (Tiwari 2011). At the end of his salt march in 1930, in violation of British rule, Gandhi collected salt. For Gandhi this public act of civil disobedience was a call for change in the wider (unjust) imperial law (Ziegler, Schulz et al. 2014). Gandhi aimed for a change in the mode of provision. The example suggests two insights: there are borderline

[3] We owe this suggestion of a sixth mode to Rutger Claassen (personal communication to Rafael Ziegler, 13 October 2017).

cases that challenge a prevailing mode of provision; civil disobedience is arguably one form this challenge can take for social innovation. The point of this example is not to introduce a new mode of 'robbery and theft' but rather to point to the importance of social dynamics in understanding the economic space for social innovation. In our Gandhi example, these dynamics were expressed in the campaign for a different taxation system that would drive an end to colonial rule (see also 'the war on drugs': Kahane 2013). We return to this dynamic later in the discussion of social innovation as message.

We suggest this typology usefully highlights a diversity of provision within economic space, beyond a reductive focus on markets (Table 3.1, column 1, lists these five modes). We can draw on this typology to investigate:

- The values, norms and institutional logics governing the respective modes of provision
- The ability of the respective modes to deliver goods and services, especially for marginalized groups
- The ethical desirability of the modes and their (re)combinations.

While the first two points mostly call for empirical research, the third point calls for further conceptual analysis. It is hence central in the following sections of this chapter.

Simple, Complex, and Collaborative Pluralism

Communitarian pluralists, following Walzer (1983), distinguish different social spheres and associated goods such as education, political power, and security. From their perspective, liberal theorizing in the tradition of Rawls (1999) mistakenly investigates distributive principles for society as a whole: instead, we should look for appropriate principles within each sphere. Claassen (2009) called such theorizing *simple pluralism*: for each good there is one appropriate mode of provision and associated rule of distribution. As Miller put it:

> The relationship between the meaning of a good and the distributive principle is not here a conceptual one; it is rather that once we have seen what kind of good medicine is, this immediately triggers a particular distributive principle which we see as applying to all goods of this sort. (quoted in Claassen 2009: 429)

Claassen made the case for *complex pluralism* that suggests that there can be various modes of provision for a good and that diversity might even be normatively preferable. Consider health: we might value the choice offered by a society that pursues good health for everyone simultaneously as a good provided publicly,

Table 3.1. Modes of provision, associated norms, beneficiaries as agent and as patient perspective, and collaborative strategies

Mode of provision	Main actors involved	Associated values and norms	Examples beneficiary as patient	Examples beneficiary as agent	Capabilities	Examples for collaborative strategies
Self	Individuals	Autarky	Lack of choice in self-provision	Individuals self-provide based on values and norms they have reason to value	*For all modes* *Process*: a) consideration, reflection and voice of marginalized groups in process (also relative to others); b) specific capabilities required for agency *Output and outcome*: a) capabilities fostered by mode of provision, also relative to other people's capabilities b) capabilities harmed by mode of provision, also relative to other people's capabilities	Market or public finance for informal/self-provision
Informal	Family, community	Solidarity, community	Beneficiary as passive community member, part of a 'target group'	Beneficiary as active community member, using her agency to contribute to collective achievements		Public delegation of provision to informal/self-provision Public regulation of collective goods, e.g. property or user rights Informal solutions informing public decision-making
Market	Enterprises	Self-interest, profit-maximization, efficiency	Beneficiary as customer	Beneficiary as producer or as political/responsible consumer		Public finance/fiscal arrangements for market provision such as subsidies/tax cuts Public delegation of provision (without finance) to market provision Public regulation of production

(Continued)

Table 3.1. Continued

Mode of provision	Main actors involved	Associated values and norms	Examples beneficiary as patient	Examples beneficiary as agent	Capabilities	Examples for collaborative strategies
						processes, e.g. *certification* procedures Informal groupings that act as collective consumer on the market
Public	State: government, administration, and associated authorities	Representative and direct democracy, legal justice and basic rights	Beneficiary as welfare-recipient	Beneficiary as citizen, involved in set-up and/or controlling provision of services (for example participatory budgeting)		Involvement of civil society and markets in the definition of targets and regulations Public–Private partnerships in delivery of goods or services
Profes-sional	Experts, professional associations/networks	Expertise and knowledge, professional codes	Beneficiary as service recipient	Beneficiary as layperson in position to control experts (for example, via participatory councils)		Public–Private Partnerships in delivery of goods or services Public regulation of professional associations and of service access Informal gathering to request and acquire professional services

Source: Authors' own.

informally, and through the market. In view of the empirical reality of variety of contexts as well as populations in practice, complex pluralism is justified where it improves overall choices and outcomes.

This distinction between simple and complex pluralism is helpful for what we call the *collaborative pluralism of social innovation*. Social innovation includes innovations in goods and services that go beyond market provision. Thus, it welcomes the 'simple pluralist' emphasis on a variety of social spheres and goods. However, it does not follow that each sphere is 'distinct' with unique goods, actors, and distributive principles. In social innovation, actors from politics, business, and civil society tend to be involved in various reconfigurations of provision—for example, a move from pure public provision to provision by other sectors such as business and civil society. This observation takes us into the direction of complex pluralism and a variety of modes of provision for a public good or service. However, 'reconfigurations' in social innovation refer not only, and not necessarily, to modes of provision existing alongside each other but also to more complex hybrids—thereby offering more choice, potentially greater innovation, and improved outcomes (as compared to complex pluralism). This complexity typically involves actors from different modes working together towards innovations in provision. We use the term 'collaborative pluralism' to emphasize not just the plurality of modes, associated actors and their values, but also to their social relations and re-combinations in social innovation.[4]

In social innovation research, the collaborative dynamic is frequently framed as a matter of social ontology (Ziegler 2017a), for example the three-sector framing of society as comprised of civil society, market and state (Nicholls et al. 2015).[5] 'Multi-sector collaboration' (Nicholls et al. 2015: 9) refers to various hybrid

[4] We are not aware of any prior usage of this term in social innovation research. However, there are three related uses we would like to point out:

1. In environmental thought, 'collaborative pluralism' is used in the discussion of environmental pluralism and the claim that there is no one (monetized) value framework for analysing and dealing with environmental problems. Accordingly, environmental pluralists call 'negotiators to accept the legitimacy of alternative frames and look for outcomes that maximize the preference of diverse stakeholders that collectively have the ability and will to affect change' (Hull 2008: 386). This use of collaborative pluralism draws from pragmatist philosophy.
2. In political science, specifically the study of transition processes in Central and Eastern Europe, Bernard (1992: 4f.) contrasted individualist pluralism and collaborative pluralism. Both oppose the idea of an imposed 'unity', but the latter draws from solidarism to search for a pluralism of social entities so as to achieve abstract ideals such as socialism. Just like the Gandhi example above, this use emphasizes the political nature of pluralism and the variety of options that become visible once pluralism is acknowledged.
3. In psychology, McLeod (2013: 393) used 'collaborative pluralism' to refer to therapist–patient relations, where the patient is seen as a participant making valuable contributions (conceptual, methods, cultural etc.) to therapy as a process.

While we cannot discuss these uses further here, it does seem that the questioning and breaking of hierarchies and dominance of conceptual schemes, of political regimes, of interpersonal relations, is a commonality throughout these uses and, in this sense, resonates well with our use here.

[5] Or, alternatively, the quadruple welfare diamond proposed by Jenson (2015).

relationships across the three sectors: public–private for state–market collaboration; social enterprise for market–civil society collaboration; and the 'shadow state' for state–civil society collaborations. The focus is on the 'blurring of the boundaries' (Nicholls and Murdock 2012), on hybrid modes of provision and on hybrid organizations (Jay 2013).

Jenson (2015: 99) provided the example of an increasingly collaborative form of childcare provisioning in the United Kingdom after 1997. While public funding increased as part of the 'social investment state', service provision could be via public, private, or civil society actors, and coordination and cooperation across these sectors was encouraged. According to Lyon and Fernandez (2012: 4, quoted in Jenson 2015), by 2009, 73 per cent of full-time day-care centres were in the private sector, 15 per cent in the voluntary sector of civil society, and 12 per cent in the public sector. A variety of modes of provision were on offer; moreover, this variety was a result of actors and institutions from these different modes collaborating deliberatively. Finally, the high percentage of private sector involvement here underscores the importance of *evaluative* analysis. For example, does the market mode dominate the other modes, possibly reducing choice and encouraging mission-drift and perverse service-user selection incentives, especially if access to private day-care centres is not affordable for all?

Another example is Vickers' et al. (2017: 3) analysis of a recent change in the British health sector: from a traditionally tax-funded universal National Health Service provided largely by public organizations to a new model with more civil society and business involvement. According to their analysis, this reconfiguration and its 'hybrid cultures' created, on the one hand, 'space for innovation' partly due to reduced 'bureaucratic disincentives' providing staff with more space to experiment (Vickers et al. 2017: 11). However, on the other hand, they reported a tension between the norms associated with the respective modes in the new configurations of provision. For example, while government claimed that private sector involvement would increase 'efficiency' and 'effectiveness' (Vickers et al. 2017: 3), the internal business logic of the private sector clashed with ideas of knowledge-sharing (Vickers et al. 2017: 11). Extrapolating from these examples, such reconfigurations in education and health point both to normative advantages (more choice, more space for experimentation) and risks (a business logic erodes the ethos of universal health care and creates unequal access to provision). Moreover, both cases point to the fundamental role of the state as regulator and significant funder of new welfare configurations.

The state, however, is not necessarily the initiator of such reconfigurations. In a discussion of the 'Québec model', Klein et al. (2013: 372) noted that: responding to a crisis in the province regarding its social and economic policies, citizens' associations—together with health and social service professionals—developed 'public medical clinics implemented in several Montreal working-class neighbourhoods' (Klein et al. 2013: 375). The Québec government later adopted and expanded this bottom-up innovation in the form of local community centres (Klein et al. 2013: 376). They also reported that the women's movement in Québec introduced public day-care centres that were also institutionalized by the government—though this also reduced local autonomy (Klein et al. 2013: 376). These examples suggest that social innovation initiatives sometimes emerge from the grassroots. There is no specific 'direction' as far as the initiative for collaboration is concerned, rather historical context and the respective social regimes are of great importance.

Moving from these examples back to the conceptual level of collaborative pluralism, it is noteworthy that Anderson anticipated its potential:

> Hybrid social practices that combine features of different spheres of life may help break through currently sterile debates which suppose that there is no 'third way' between laissez-faire capitalism and comprehensive state planning of the economy. (1993: 167)

The qualifier 'collaborative' broadens the focus on a pluralism of *various* modes of provision and the *interrelations* this implies amongst various sectors and actors. We refer to these collectively as 'collaborative strategies' (see Table 3.1, column 7).

The choice of modes of provision and their reconfigurations raises further questions. We tend to associate modes of provision with evaluative concepts and norms[6] that, in turn, are frequently invoked to legitimatize reconfiguration. In the above example, the UK government brought in private actors to increase 'efficiency' and 'effectiveness'. Table 3.1, column 3 lists values commonly associated with the respective modes. We need to be cautious, however, regarding the empirical accuracy of such associations, not least due to their role for the legitimation of policies. These associations merit further scrutiny:

- What are the values and norms associated with each respective mode and who holds them?
- Can the values and norms of one mode be transferred to another mode or effectively orient new reconfigurations? What about the resulting tensions or institutional resistance?
- What evaluative considerations should be taken into account for an ethical discussion of the economic space of social innovation?

In our discussion here, we will focus on the last question since it is a conceptual, whereas the other two strongly depend on empirical research and social

[6] 'Evaluative' includes value concepts and predicates such as good or bad, better or worse, desirable or undesirable; 'normative' includes operators such as right or wrong, ought and may (List and Valentini 2016). Social innovation includes both evaluative issues of the 'good' and normative issue of the 'right'. For simplicity, we use 'evaluative' as shorthand for 'evaluative and normative'.

innovation case studies. Next we draw from the capabilities approach as an entry point to the contemporary discussion of justice and equality.

Capabilities and Economic Space for Social Innovation

The capabilities approach derives its values and principles from a general reflection on human beings, rather than from specific norms governing a mode of provision. It is, in Sen's vision, an 'agent-oriented view' (Sen 1999: 11) emphasizing the intrinsic and instrumental value of agency for justice and development. However, this focus on agency is incomplete if *patiency* is not part of the analysis, especially when marginalized groups are concerned. Accordingly, this section introduces both concepts and links them to our discussion of the economic space for social innovation.

According to the capabilities approach, agency is primarily a question of individuals.[7] Sen defines agency as the ability to pursue goals one values and has reason to value—an agent is 'someone who acts and brings about change, and whose achievement can be judged in terms of her own values and objectives, whether or not we assess them in terms of some external criteria as well' (Sen 1999: 18). Agency involves a moment of reflection, placing the capabilities approach in the tradition of political philosophy that emphasizes the intrinsic importance of individual choice and reflection (Nussbaum 2006: 184f.). Agency, in addition, includes action—the 'bringing about'—thereby situating the capabilities approach within traditions of political philosophy that emphasize the need not just to look at formal rights and entitlements but also at the individual opportunities to exercise and enjoy them. 'Beings and doings', or 'functionings' as the capabilities approach calls them, are very important. This focus on an individual's capabilities and functionings emerges from, and is closely tied to, an extended philosophical discussion of the appropriate category (or 'currency') for evaluating equality and justice: capabilities, resources, primary goods, utility... (Cohen 1993). In this book, we assume that the capabilities approach offers a valuable and justified approach and we do not discuss its strengths and weakness vis-à-vis other approaches.[8]

Yet, the capabilities approach raises further questions:

- Which capabilities?
- For whom?
- Decided by whom?

[7] This evaluative focus notwithstanding, social or collective agency is also important for understanding social change processes in relation to social innovation (see Ibrahim 2017, on collective capabilities and social innovation).

[8] But see the conclusion below for some hints in this direction.

Within the capabilities approach, we can distinguish between *democratic* and *philosophical* ways of dealing with these questions. Sen and Nussbaum exemplify these two positions (Byskov 2016; Claassen 2010; Sen 2009; Nussbaum 2000). According to the democratic approach, capabilities should be determined via a public, democratic deliberation (Sen 2009). By contrast, the philosophical approach proposes a more substantive interpretation of capabilities. Nussbaum proposed a list of ten central capabilities as a threshold requirement for social justice (Nussbaum 2011: 17–45). She suggested that, whatever the subjective ways may be that bring about social change there is a threshold of central human capabilities required for living in dignity. Her list of central capabilities is probably the most well-known account of capabilities *as* social justice.[9] The threshold idea can be spelled out differently—Nussbaum sees her account as open to corrections and improvements—and, in practice, there is much overlap between the democratic and philosophical positions in the domain of social justice. Sen (2009) proposed a focus on 'manifest injustices' that overlaps with Nussbaum's focus on basic justice.

A commonality across capability theorizing is a focus on the diversity of individuals and groups. Unlike economists and philosophers theorizing about justice and the economy in terms of 'representative agents', the capabilities approach emphasizes heterogeneity as a key consideration for analysis: differences in personal traits and in social and environmental contexts make a difference for the real freedom of individuals. 'Conversion factors' are the differential ability of individuals to convert a good or service into an achieved functioning for themselves. Differences in the distribution of conversion factors can explain the unequal distribution of capabilities across a population, even where access to resources is the same. This suggests a normative reason to focus on the distribution of capabilities, rather than on resources alone.

An illustrative example can be seen in Germany. This country requires prison staff to pass on all information obtained from prisoners. Prisoners, accordingly, cannot trust prison staff to keep their information confidential. The Violence Prevention Network responded to this problem via the creation of an outside organization that visits prisoners without this constraint and, thus, creates room for confidential discussions as an opportunity to build trust, create social ties, and ultimately reduce recidivism (Korn 2009). For simplicity, we can imagine two agents, prison and NGO staff, both seeking to reduce crime. The prison staff cannot fully 'convert' their work into achieved functioning due to government regulations. While this example focuses on a conversion problem with others as the beneficiaries, it is straightforward to imagine *self-regarding* conversion problems. Standard examples include riding a bike, which depends on personal traits, social norms, infrastructure, and the environment, or the example of a woman's

[9] For a recent account that focuses on agency, see Claassen (2016).

difficulty of exercising of her formal right to vote in a society with strong patriarchal norms.

Differences in conversion factors can also lead to the marginalization of individuals and groups. Due to the enormous diversity of society—its individuals, norms, and institutional structures—there will likely always be some populations in danger of marginalization from a good or service. Take the 'capability' of eating ice cream. People with lactose intolerance cannot eat ice cream; in the past, religious norms blocked the public eating of ice cream as too frivolous; in extremely hot places, your ice cream simply melts away before you can enjoy it and so on. In short, the category of capability and its associated conversion factor differences are general concepts not specific to justice, marginalization, and exclusion. Therefore, an evaluative focus on important ethical matters requires further specification.

We propose an understanding of marginalization as the result of a social process through which personal, social, or environmental traits are transformed (or blocked) into actual or potential factors of disadvantage (von Jacobi et al. 2017). The term *trait* puts the focus on the relative immovability of this aspect of marginalization. Personal traits comprise individual characteristics that cannot be modified by choice in the short term. Personal traits are variously distributed and it is a matter of much controversy whether this distribution is 'earned', 'deserved', 'contingent', or a 'brute fact'. Overall in this book, we take a socio-structural perspective. Personal traits do not *cause* marginalization in isolation—rather, social processes transform these traits into actual or potential factors of disadvantage. Likewise, social and environmental traits are (potential) factors of marginalization. Group membership or environmental characteristics are examples of such traits that can be transformed into factors of disadvantage. For example, location in the countryside is a trait that can become a disadvantageous conversion factor when urban infrastructure (e.g. water supply, grid energy, and so on) is 'extended' (or not) to the countryside. From the philosophical perspective (in the sense introduced above), the *disadvantaged* are deprived of (sufficient) access to basic aspects of living in dignity.[10] From the democratic perspective, the *disadvantaged* are identified via the determination of capability deprivation in the public discussion. Philosophical reflection and democratic discussion are interrelated in dynamic equilibrium of public discourse, where substantive philosophical proposals (such as Nussbaum's) are put to public scrutiny and, then, revised if need be (Wolff and De-Shalit 2007).

[10] This point can be further spelled out via Nussbaum's threshold list of central capabilities for living in dignity, yielding a, roughly speaking, *sufficientarian* position for the evaluation of social justice. However, there are also other ways of spelling this out but, at this point, it is not an essential part of our discussion. So, we only want to highlight that there are various ways to do this (see Wolff and De-Shalit 2007). Anticipating the discussion further below, it is noteworthy that especially for marginalization and social exclusion the 'philosophical' starting point and, thus, the proposal of capabilities is important as such groups typically are in no position to voice their own perspective.

Patiency

A focus on human beings as agents is incomplete if humans as *patients* are not considered.[11] We posit the agency–patiency dynamic as two poles of a multi-dimensional spectrum, rather than a dichotomy. For example, a social housing programme might improve the social aspects of agency and the well-being of formerly homeless people—by providing a secure and safe shelter—while not improving their political agency as citizens involved in the decision-making around their social housing programme (see Edmiston and Aro 2016).

'Patients' are individuals who cannot effectively choose their functionings. For example, in a patriarchal context, women might not exercise learning opportunities, perhaps sometimes not even 'wanting' to exercise them due to their upbringing and the attendant social norms. A social innovation focused on the empowerment of such a group is likely to encounter psychological and social resistance by a variety of people, including those it seeks to empower. 'Learned helplessness' might be a personal, psychological trait blocking agency even in the presence of resources and rights (see chapter 7).

Another variant of the issue is 'passive empowerment' (Bonvin 2017: 19f.). In our social housing case (see chapter 5), well-being—and possibly some aspects of agency—improved. However, the homeless people did not define or control the conditions of their programme. As Bonvin noted, passive empowerment is typically ambivalent. It can improve well-being and agency to some extent, yet it sets the conditions. These conditions, and their material and symbolic implementation, determine eligibility and uptake. While a homeless person who does not accept the housing programme 'emancipates' herself from this institutional constraint,[12] the functioning possibilities provided via the policy (such as safe shelter) then need to be provided in an alternative way (Bonvin 2017: 29) or else the person remains disadvantaged in a fundamental respect. With a view to the diversity of individuals and contexts, this point about conditionality and alternatives suggests an argument for a variety of modes of provision, assuming that such variety increases the suitable options for individuals. Evers and Brandsen (2016: 165f.) found that, in urban social innovations across Europe, the innovators they studied tended to relax the conditionality of admission into welfare programmes, including what counted as 'giving something back' in return. This finding reflects the more discretionary understanding of reciprocity in informal provision discussed above. In practice, however, the dominant trend in social policy is quite

[11] We would like to emphasize that the term 'patient' in this discussion carries no negative connotations. Rather, it aims to provide an ethical framework for the discussion that comprehensively includes the 'target groups' of social innovations as 'ends'.

[12] 'Emancipate' is in quotes here because non-acceptance might be an active 'I would not prefer not to', but it might also be a simple 'mess-up' where conditions are such that potential beneficiaries fail to meet up on time, have the right papers etc.

different—resource provision is based on conditions mainly aimed at improving employability in markets (Bonvin 2017: 25).[13] These examples point to the complexity and intricacy of the agency–patiency dynamic. We are all patients in some contexts.

A well-known point from environmental ethics further shows the extent of the challenge. 'Moral patient' refers to the important and difficult question of who ought to be considered as a member of the community (Ott 2010), as a subject of *consideration* and not only as an object of *use*. If moral patients are considered, the community conception includes a sub-group of beings with functionings making up their well- or ill-being but without a capability of choosing functionings in a reflective way—at least not if such choice includes joint deliberation and decision-making on policies and programmes. Moral patients might be in their situation contingently or permanently. While the boundaries of this community are controversial (Nussbaum 2006), it is evident that practically any ethical theory will include moral patients. Moral patients in this sense include babies and to some extent, children, persons with disabilities, animals and plants, ecosystems, the planet (with increasing contestation as we move along this list) and all of us in certain contexts.

Social innovation aimed at empowerment typically deals with patients, individuals without (or with reduced) agency and voice. Accordingly, the dynamics that drive patients into agents, and encourage agents to support patients are of central importance here. It follows that an issue for social innovation in many contexts is paternalism. We return to this important topic in chapter 13, after the empirical studies presented in Part II of this book.

Capabilities and Modes of Provision

Evaluating social innovations and their (mixed) modes of provision requires investigating if, how, and whose agency is promoted; if, how, and whose patiency are morally considered; and, for both patients and agents, which capabilities are

[13] Bonvin distinguished two approaches with respect to 'activation' for employability: workfare strategies mainly aimed at putting pressure on people to take up available jobs; human capital strategies (often associated with the 'social investment state') that seek to improve on employability by providing employers with adequate education and training. While there are important differences between these approaches, the 'final objective in both is the independent man characteristic of liberal and social contract approaches… [rather than] recognizing that *all* human beings without exception are both vulnerable and autonomous' (Bonvin 2017: 26, italics added). Moreover, the objective is primarily understood in relation to the primary labour market, bracketing both the question of quality of work in this market as well as other varieties of work and life (Bonvin 2017: 27–8). This social policy observation also holds, by and large, for social innovation policy in Europe, or as the European Commission simply puts it: 'The European Commission's objective is to encourage market uptake of innovative solutions and stimulate employment' (http://ec.europa.eu/growth/industry/innovation/policy/social_de, accessed 26 October 2017, see also von Jacobi et al. 2017: section 3).

promoted/hindered. This goes beyond modes of provision, actors, and associated values. Table 3.1 lists the beneficiaries of social innovation as patients in social innovation processes (in column 4), as agents in such processes (in column 5), as well as the cross-cutting capability questions (in column 6). We use the term 'beneficiary' as a general term to refer to the target group of a social innovation, be it as agents, patients, or both. Three other aspects of Table 3.1 need further elaboration:

- *Agency*: As social innovation emphasizes agency as end and as mean,[14] there is the question of the role of beneficiaries as agents of change in the various modes of provision. What is the form and the degree of active involvement of beneficiaries in social innovation processes? What is the outcome of a social innovation in terms of improved agency of beneficiaries? Both questions are needed, because a beneficiary as patient in the process might be a beneficiary as agent in the outcome.
- *Patiency*: Column four of the table provides examples of beneficiaries as patients, i.e. those permanently or contingently lacking capacities for reflection, voice, and participation in social innovation processes. To paraphrase Bonvin, they might be 'passively empowered' in the sense of improved outcomes, but they have no say in the conditions of this process. In this context, we need to distinguish between *permanent* and *contingent* patients. For permanent patients the lack of choice and agency is not problematic as such. It is only problematic if their well-being is not considered, hence there is a question of appropriate 'advocates' or 'spokespersons' to ensure that the entitlements of patients are considered. For those who are only contingently in a position of being a patient, advocates and spokespersons might still be required driving the familiar social innovation telos of *empowering* by bringing individuals into a position of choice and self-determination.[15]
- *Capabilities*: As noted above, a patient in the process might be an agent in the outcome. This dynamic illustrates that considered over time—say, during the whole implementation of a project—beneficiaries might be both patients and agent and the two roles are, therefore, not mutually exclusive options for a

[14] For example, a widely referred to social innovation definition in the EU says that 'social innovation is social in both its ends and its means. This kind of innovation not only serves society but also enhances society's capacity to act' (BEPA 2010). Likewise, albeit with a greater emphasis on the power questions thereby raised, the CrESSI definition used in this book includes a focus on agency as outcome and as a means (see chapter 1).

[15] In keeping with the capabilities approach, we need to emphasize that a position of choice does not mean that people have to get actively involved in decision-making (for example as homeless people in a social housing programme), but they have to be in a position to do so, if they so wish. This is the 'liberal' aspect of the capabilities approach. In practice, however, it is a matter of judgement to what extent choice remains a real opportunity, and if those subjected to the respective policy or programme do exercise some control (the 'republican' concern that liberty might turn into domination (Pettit 2014; see also chapter 13)).

social innovation, as far as contingent moral patients are concerned. Column 6 of Table 3.1 sets out all modes of provision and looks at capabilities in terms of two categories: process (are beneficiaries morally considered in the process as patients, is their voice heard and do they have a say as agents); outcomes (what capabilities are improved, what capabilities are harmed as a result of the social innovation). Column six adds as a further, relational, point that there is a danger of failure if beneficiaries are considered in isolation. Marginalization is a relational phenomenon: some are at 'the margin' (in terms of health, educational, and economic opportunity) as compared to others. Where this position is dependent on those 'in the centre'—say, if one group's wealth is based on the exploitation of another—then overall equality and relative standing is important for dealing with the disadvantage.

Fair Space for Social Innovation

This last point about distribution makes it clear that, beyond specific evaluative questions, a more general question arises due to the prevailing focus on innovation in markets:

Is public regulation and finance of social innovation biased towards provisioning in markets, neglecting other modes of innovation in an ethically problematic way?

This is a very difficult and complex question. Still, our discussion so far suggests some approaches to thinking about it. Economic space for social innovation is de facto a matter of various modes. While one mode might be stronger than another depending on the respective welfare regime and socio-economic system, all modes of provision seem generally present. For example, while the Soviet Union had a state-organized system of production, there were, already in the 1930s, Kolkhoz markets of artisanal production that were publicly tolerated (Fitzpatrick 1999: 57).[16] As noted above, while market provision has significantly grown in capitalist regimes, household production continues to be a very significant part of GNP. While, for any specific context, one mode of production might be preferable to another, as a starting point a presumption of equality seems warranted: no mode seems preferable to any other. Rather, each mode has its own advantages and disadvantages. In terms of marginalization (as opposed to, say, profit maximizing returns to capital), it is a question of the right 'mix of modes' to improve agency possibilities and functioning outcomes. Any exclusive focus on

[16] Along with a 'black' or 'second economy' that always existed alongside state production.

one mode is problematic for creating a fair and versatile economic space for social innovation. The EU-social innovation objective of increased market-uptake and job creation exhibits such problematic one-sidedness. One mode appears to *dominate* the others (to adopt a term used by Michael Walzer).

Furthermore, this starting point can be juxtaposed against the complexity of the modes of provision in context, following a basic analytic insight of the innovation system research (Lundvall and Borrás 2005: 611–14): focus on the specific characteristics of a system and its emergence in a region, state or supra-national entity. In context, many questions arise, such as:

- Do the eligibility criteria of public finance, fiscal policy, and regulatory systems favour some modes of provision and collaborative strategies over others?
- Are relevant policies directly or indirectly aimed at creating space for social innovation also backed up with sufficient resources for implementation (for example, not only a commitment to multi-level governance according to the principle of subsidiarity from the EU, but also resources to include new civil society actors at the local level; see Miquel et al. 2013: 158)?
- Do they also take into account that social innovation produces losers as well as winners (for example, that moving away from commodification is against the interest of the respective market actors—the trend towards social business as social innovation can be interpreted as market actors using their cultural capital to 're-commodify' as far as possible)?

For such questions in context, a general presumption of equality seems insufficient. Where to start in such necessarily complex contexts? Recalling the Gandhi example above, we can think of social innovations as 'messages'.[17] In markets, prices signal information to producers and consumers. An increase in energy prices can signal to producers that it is worthwhile to invest in innovation: such as new technologies for producing and storing energy. For social innovation, money as a universal currency does not apply across all modes. However, we can think of social innovations as 'messages' that there is an issue to be dealt with. In the European context, such messages typically originate from civil society and, hence, also highlight the role of informal provision. However, in keeping with our comprehensive approach to creating economic space, we stress that such 'messages' can originate with actors from all modes of provision. Though one

[17] See Evers and Brandsen (2016: 162f.), who, in the context of urban development, discussed social innovation as 'messages'. While their discussion is situated in a specific empirical context, we suggest that the 'message' idea is conceptually also relevant for the evaluative questions discussed here. The language of 'thin' price signals is appropriate for exchange relations; whereas the language of 'messages' seems appropriate to social innovation that requires (often complex) communication across a diversity of modes.

exception might be organizations that are structurally required to maximize profits, as this introduces a clear tension with a primary pursuit of social goals.[18]

This 'message'—and its frequent origin in civil society—has implications for the 'scaling' and 'diffusion' discussion of *social* innovation since there is frequently no motive to attract further 'customers'. Rather, the 'message' sends a signal to the respective public sphere that there is an issue worthy of public attention. As the profit motive for 'scaling' or 'diffusion' in social innovation is much weaker than in business (or simply absent) and those from whom the message originates may well have few resources for 'effective' signalling, the role of intermediaries becomes important (Evers and Brandsen 2016: 174). Anticipating the discussion in later sections of this book, the role of social networks that can take on and distribute 'messages' is, therefore, very important. As these networks might also have few resources, the utility of applied social science and action research in interpreting the messages in their complexity emerges (Howaldt and Kropp 2017; Weaver and Kemp 2017; Nicholls 2015; Jessop et al. 2013). This task is not least one of legitimacy research—'messages', as such, are neither good or bad. Rather, they have to be publicly discussed in terms of their relevance in indicating and dealing with disadvantage of agents and patients. If such a discussion is enabled—if there is listening and discussion with practical consequences—a fair and versatile space for social innovation is fostered.

There is some evidence that social innovation enhances stakeholder voice in social and environmental policy and surfaces new ways of empowering its beneficiaries (Evers and Brandsen 2016: 167; Ziegler, Partzsch et al. 2014: 196f.). Still, our discussion of the agency–patiency dynamic above suggests caution at this point. The 'fairness' of a social system depends on the consideration of all its members, and especially of those who are most disadvantaged (Rawls 1999). Yet patients are unlikely to have much capacity to message, or simply to organize themselves collectively to get their voice heard. Moreover, the complex tasks of many working in social innovation along with their diverse and insecure funding implies that there is frequently not much time to 'message': for example, via regular and comprehensive reporting, let alone own research into the issue. These points suggest that for fostering a fair and versatile space for social innovation at least two issues have to be further considered: the capability to associate, especially of the marginalized; and the role of the state in creating and sustaining the infrastructure for people to engage in such tasks (education, economic security, etc.). These two issues will be considered in Part III of this book.

[18] We leave it at this cautious formulation as even within such, frequently large, organizations there might be space for 'intrapreneurs' or, perhaps as a result of a spin-out, 'extrapreneurs' that trigger social change within and between organizations (Tracey and Stott 2017: 55f.).

Finally, 'listening' takes places across various modes of provision. This can be, on the one hand, important to improve effectiveness and impact (Scheuerle et al. 2016). On the other hand, it introduces the possibility of messages getting captured, for better or worse, by more powerful actors (Pel and Bauler 2014). This tension seems unavoidable in a complex economic space. It underlines, however, the importance of strengthening the voice and the associative capability of the most marginalized. This dynamic takes us back to an important insight from 'simple pluralism' to which we will now turn.

Blocked Modes and Blocked Collaborations

Are there modes of provision that should be 'blocked'? In his defence of pluralism, Walzer came up with an impressive list when he argued that some elements of the social world should be blocked from exchange in the market, for example: human beings; political power; criminal justice; basic liberties such as free speech, marriage, and procreation rights; membership in the polis; exemptions from public service (military, juries, and so on); political office; unequal exchange; prizes and honours; divine grace; love and friendship; and criminal action (Walzer 1983: 100–3). The list makes an important point about the economic space for social innovation: not all possible modes of provision are ethically desirable for the provision of a good.

Thus, identifying 'blocked exchange' is a central concern for defining the economic space for social innovation. For example, a concern with an overly economistic framing of social innovation is frequently linked with critiques concerning the more general commodification of public and welfare goods (health, education) via marketization.

Our typology of modes of provision invites a generalization of Walzer's question moving from 'blocked exchange' to 'blocked mode of provision'. Market exchange is a central bone of contention. But we can also ask, under what conditions, is a good better provided informally, publicly, and/or professionally. For example, in Greece, Germany, and the Netherlands home schooling (informal provision) is 'blocked' by law, whereas it is legal in Hungary, France, and the United Kingdom. In many countries, the state provides education, but some argue it should only regulate it (see further chapter 8). Health professionals often want to block the provision of health services by providers who have not obtained the respective certificates and training and so on (see further Abbott 2014).

In addition, the collaborative pluralism of social innovation reveals a further set of issues: blocked collaborations across modes of provision. For example, there are numerous controversies around public–private partnerships—where market actors provide (in part or entirely) public goods (see further chapter 6). One concern is that for goods and services linked to entitlements—such as freshwater provision and the human right to water—market provision encourages profit maximization contra universal entitlement. Moreover, such models create a 'black box' hindering democratic accountability, as it can be difficult for public regulators to hold private organizations accountable regarding pricing, investment, and staff policy.[19] Many critiques of the 'neo-liberal' turn in social innovation focus on such reconfigurations under conditions of government 'austerity' and public budget cuts.

Except for extreme examples, our perspective does not automatically generate answers as to what should (not) be blocked. Rather, it provides two guidelines in terms of thinking about it:

- Do not just focus on the market, but on the whole variety of modes of provision.
- When considering arguments for or against blocked modes or blocked collaborations, consider beneficiaries of the provision as patients and agents, and the disadvantage(s) overcome (or created) via the respective provision.

Taken together, blocked modes and blocked collaborations foster an important desideratum of an ethical focus on social innovation: to avoid a pro-innovation bias. Rather than focusing only on social innovation and their diffusion, there is value in focusing also on the need to remove, or prevent in the first place, innovations that have ethically negative consequences.

The Extended Social Grid Model Revisited

The typology introduced here aims to provide a further refinement of the ESGM introduced in chapter 1. Inversely, the typology benefits from the model too in terms of a more refined analysis of its (mixed) modes of provision.

With respect to economic power, our typology of modes of provision (and of their combination) deepens the analysis of economic space for social innovation and of the goods and services provided. In addition to market provision, four further modes of provision come into view. We are not saying market provision plays no role in social innovation. Rather, the modes of provision lens offers a way to move beyond the frequently used, but analytically unsatisfactory, category of 'non-market provision' or 'non-market social innovation' by replacing it with a richer typology. We also stress that our point is not just about *additional* modes. Rather, much of the dynamism in social innovation comes from the interrelation

[19] For these and the related objections of the water justice movement, see Barlow (2008).

of these various modes. We introduce the term collaborative pluralism to make this point.

A richer analysis of economic space and its various modes of provision also enhances the capability analysis within the ESGM. This extension asks us to explore how modes of provision foster or prevent the agency of heterogeneous participants and groups in social innovation processes. While much of this depends on the details of the respective good and service, a variety of modes analysis increases the participation opportunities and the benefits of offering and using goods and services. One reason is due to diversity: one mode of providing a good is more appropriate for a specific group and its relation between providers and beneficiaries, whereas another mode is more suitable for another group. Take the example of public provisioning for job placement services only available to citizens registered for more than five years in a particular residence. The individual trait of having lived in the same place over the last five years becomes a discriminatory characteristic: those who arrived more recently are excluded from the service and are, therefore, more disadvantaged. If provision expands to a private or civil society provider, the selection criteria are likely to change and the 'duration of residence' issue ceases to be as relevant. Other traits will then gain importance, such as access to resources (if the service has a cost), membership in a community (if the provider is based in, say, a religious charity), or availability of information (if the main promotion mechanism relies on word-of-mouth). There is, thus, a reshuffling of traits that define who assumes a (dis)advantaged position with respect to the conversion process. Inversely, the imposition or domination of one mode of provision reduces agency and choice. For example, the extension of centrally provided freshwater supplies puts considerable pressure on decentralized informal water providers in rural areas, sometimes forcing them to change their mode of provision against their will (Ziegler 2017b). Collaborative pluralism calls for a careful examination of such social innovation and marginalization cases.

A related issue is the consideration of *patiency*. Social innovation discourse, at least in the EU, emphasizes the active involvement of citizens in social innovation processes. Closer consideration of agency in social innovation for marginalized groups suggests two points. First, marginalized groups are likely to have limited agency precisely due to their marginalized position. Second, some groups that ought morally to be considered are permanent patients (such as animals for political agency). Both points raise key questions as to which mode(s) or reconfiguration(s) may be the most appropriate to foster, respectively, agency and the empowerment and integration of key beneficiaries.

Happily, the ESGM supports a refined analysis of the economic space for social innovation and its (mixed) modes of provision. Beckert's Social Grid analysis and its analytical separation of cognitive frames, institutions, and social networks (Beckert 2010) helpfully refines the analysis of modes of provision and collaborative pluralism, as it shows the complexity of reconfigurations across modes of provision. Several points emerge:

- *Values associated with one cognitive frame can be transferred to others:* A value such as reciprocity associated with the solidarity-economy cognitive frame in informal provision can transfer to market provision if social enterprises include them in their missions. Conversely, values such as self-interest and profit-maximization associated with neo-liberalism as a cognitive frame can transfer to informal or public provision. In practice, such questions of transfer imply tensions between different 'institutional logics' (Vickers et al. 2017; Thornton et al. 2012) that require negotiation within the new hybrid collaboration.
- *Formal or informal rules originating within one mode can influence other modes*: In public-private partnerships, there is a public regulation of market provision. For example, when water is 'privatized', the state and municipalities still can determine the rules according to which private operations can provide water. Conversely, when water is re-nationalized, business rules relating to profits and organizational structures might prevail even under public provision (Härlin 2017).
- *Social networks advocating a mode of provision or its reconfiguration can draw in actors associated with other modes*: The cases in the later empirical chapters here (chapters 5 to 9) repeatedly show that effective networks are often able to organize support and coalitions with actors from other modes. Social activists can benefit from support by professionals, public administrators, or businessmen (and women). Again, networks are ambivalent: as coalitions they can strengthen a social case, but they can also capture, reduce, or change the social mission.

As far as basic needs and human capabilities are concerned, the state is likely to regulate statutory entitlement. Put differently, it is not helpful to think of the various modes as separate worlds or sectors. They are, to use a term of Mann, 'entwined', and we would expect state and public sectors to play a particularly important role in this 'entwining'. The ESGM not only takes into account economic sources of power, but also political, cultural, environmental, artefactual, and other security-related ones (Mann 2013; Heiskala 2016: see chapter 2). While the analysis of economic power centrally focuses on the production and use of goods and services, this extension serves as a helpful reminder that the social world includes more than goods and services.

Finally, the ESGM encourages a more reflexive use of the capabilities approach—which is itself a cognitive frame advanced by a network of social scientists and policy-makers with a view to institutional change, especially in relation to development, poverty, and basic justice (for example Human

Development Reports since 1990). It is not itself neutral. Social innovation research is typically value laden both in theory and practice. This is no disadvantage; rather, our perspective should be seen as one ethical approach amongst others making the topic available for analysis (Ziegler 2017a).

Conclusion

This chapter draws from the capabilities approach and a typology of modes of provision for the analysis of the economic space for social innovation. The typology enables a move beyond markets without lapsing into the black-box thinking of 'non-markets'. It shows that multiple modes comprise economic space. While market provision is important, it is only one mode. An exclusive focus on the market uptake of social innovation and job creation is like removing all but one wheel from a vehicle, and then wanting to drive on.

In a nutshell, the case for the collaborative pluralism of social innovation is based on five main points:

- A focus on modes of provision and their interrelation improve the empirical grasp of 'economic space': instead of markets and non-markets it offers a typology that can be fully empirically explored.
- Due to the diversity of people and their social and environmental contexts, a variety of modes of provision—in principle—improves choice and outcomes. This is especially true for patients, whose well-being is unlikely to be met via one mode only.
- Societies are in a constant process of change; social innovation as a 'message' points to changes in modes of provision and their reconfiguration that prima facie need to be reconfigured for fostering and securing a fair space for social innovation.
- There is nothing automatic about this 'message' process. Rather, much depends on societies capacity to 'message' as well as to 'listen', where taking a balanced perspective includes paying attention to blocked modes and blocked reconfigurations.
- There is no unitary 'pricing'-mechanism that communicates social innovation messages. That is why we have proposed that, rather than exploring the contours of an ideal economic space for social innovation in isolation, we should start from social innovation as messages emerging from issues around modes of provision in the real world and the capacity to 'listen'—and act—on those linked to the capacity, especially of those marginalized, to 'message' themselves.

Investigating these issues further raises many questions: from the identification of social innovation to the requirements of 'listening' and drawing the practical consequences. While these are, in part, questions for social science, it is also a call for reflection on the role of value (and legitimacy) research in the analysis of social innovation. Can researchers offer a test for 'good' and 'bad' social innovations (as Mulgan (2015: xvi), demands)? There is no unitary good securing legitimacy; no ethical expert can offer a litmus test for social innovation policies and projects, as some versions of welfarist or utilitarian approaches to social innovation might lead one to expect.[20] Rather, there is a heterogeneous, interrelated set of ends in social innovation processes. The ethical task is to ensure that these ends are present in the discussion of social innovation reconfigurations, so we can consider which ends are involved, whose ends are they, and how are they distributed. Perhaps, sometimes there are genuine 'win–win' cases where everyone gains, or Pareto cases where no one is made worse off. More likely, reconfigurations imply distributive consequences where some are made better off and some worse, where some capabilities improve and others are reduced or blocked. Thus, a normatively explicit approach to social innovation research is unlikely to yield social innovation evaluations in terms of 'good' or 'bad', but rather some gains in some capabilities for some groups, and some losses in others. Such results can contribute to an enriched discussion and judgement formation. The role of ethical research on the economic space for social innovation is neither prescriptive—in the sense of yielding imperatives of what policy-makers or social innovators should do—nor relativist—in the sense of delegating all value judgements to social innovators and policy-makers. Researchers are, themselves, participants amongst others in the process. In this role, they can draw on a range of discussions within ethics to draw attention to what they propose as ethically relevant issues.

While we have proposed here a capabilities approach to these issues, there are, partly complementary, partly conflicting, ethical perspectives for the investigation of the economic space for social innovation. As far as we know, there is no extant ethics literature on this topic. Hence we can only cautiously sketch out the differences of our approach vis-à-vis other ethical positions. We already noted some scepticism with respect to a utilitarian perspective on our topic. While a workable focus on maximizing utility might yield a decision tool for determining 'good' or 'bad' social innovations in terms of their respective overall positive or negative contribution to social impact, such a decision tool would risk undermining any focused attention on the most marginalized groups and individuals in the name of the greater overall utility. This classic liberal objection to utilitarianism takes us to liberal resourcist perspectives (Rawls 1999). Due to the clustering of negative effects among marginalized groups, Rawls' focus on the least-advantaged

[20] Ayob et al. (2016: 645) classify Mulgan within a utilitarian tradition of thinking about value in social innovation research.

in terms of income and wealth may overlap with a focus on the marginalized identified by their disadvantages in relation to their human capabilities. However, a Rawlsian analysis puts more emphasis on the relational impact of those better-off on those worse-off. It also adds a long-term focus on the stability of just institutions via discussions of a 'just-savings' principle, especially relevant to the state as a large-scale investor in innovation (Ziegler 2015). However, a singular focus on resources risks overlooking conversion differences due to personal, social, and environmental heterogeneity. In fact, the focus on income and wealth as main indicators of economic inequality seems precisely to risk a reductive focus in terms of defining what is the economic space for social innovation, as noted above. Finally, a republican focus on the control of power (Pettit 2014) highlights that innovation produces winners and losers, encounters resistance and hence raises important questions of power and domination. But is the republican focus on civic control equipped to deal with permanent patients? Its singular focus on freedom might be problematic regarding the non-agency concerns relevant for ethical evaluation. So much for some hints at the many further, partly complementary research possibilities. In our view, the rich, internally heterogeneous, open, framework of the capabilities approach offers a fruitful invitation for further discussion.[21]

References

Abbott, Andrew. 2014. *The System of Professions: An Essay on the Division of Expert Labor*. Chicago, IL: University of Chicago Press.

Anderson, Elizabeth. 1993. *Value in Ethics and Economics*. Cambridge, MA: Harvard University Press.

Ayob, Noorshea, Simon Teasdale, and Kylie Fagan. 2016. 'How Social Innovation "Came to Be": Tracing the Evolution of a Contested Concept'. *Journal of Social Policy* 45(4): 635–53.

Barlow, Maude. 2008. *Blue Covenant: The Global Water Crisis and the Coming Battle for the Right to Water*. New York: The New Press.

Beckert, Jens. 2010. 'How Do Fields Change? The Interrelations of Institutions, Networks, and Cognition in the Dynamics of Markets'. *Organization Studies* 31 (5): 605–27.

Bernard, Fredrick. 1992. *Pluralism, Socialism and Legitimacy: Reflections on Opening up Communism*. Cambridge: Cambridge University Press.

Bonvin, Jean. 2017. 'The Ambivalence of Social Policies and the Challenge of Human Development: A Proposal for Assessing their Impact against the Capability

[21] See Robeyns (2016) for a methodological proposal as to how the capabilities approach can be fruitfully linked to both other social science research and to a variety of other normative theories.

Approach'. In *Human Development in Times of Crisis: Renegotiating Social Justice*, edited by Hans-Uwe Otto, Spyridon Pantazis, Holger Ziegler, and Antoanneta Potsi, pp. 27–38. London: Palgrave Macmillan.

BEPA (Bureau of European Policy Advisers). 2010. *Empowering People, Driving Change: Social Innovation in the European Union*. Brussels: European Commission.

Byskov, Morten F. 2016. 'Democracy, Philosophy, and the Selection of Capabilities'. *Journal of Human Development and Capabilities* 18(1): 1–16.

Claassen, Rutger. 2009. 'Institutional Pluralism and the Limits of the Market'. *Politics Philosophy Economics* 8(4): 420–47.

Claassen, Rutger. 2010. 'Making Capability Lists: Philosophy versus Democracy'. *Political Studies* 59(3): 491–508.

Claassen, Rutger. 2016. 'An Agency-Based Capability Theory of Justice'. *European Journal of Philosophy* 25(4): 1279–304.

Cohen, G. A. 1993. 'Equality of What? On Welfare, Goods, and Capabilities'. In *The Quality of Life: A Study Prepared for the World Institute for Development Economics Research (WIDER) of the United Nations University*, edited by Martha Nussbaum and Amartya Sen, pp. 9–29. Oxford: Clarendon Press.

Edmiston, Daniel, and Jari Aro. 2016. 'Public Policy, Social Innovation and Marginalisation in Europe: A Comparative Analysis of Three Cases'. CrESSI Working Paper No. 33. Brussels: European Commission, DG Research.

Evers, Adalbert, and Taco Brandsen. 2016. 'Social Innovations as Messages: Democratic Experimentation in Local Welfare Systems'. In *Social Innovations in the Urban Context*, edited by Taco Brandsen, Sandro Cattacin, Adalbert Evers, and Annette Zimmer, pp. 161–80. Dordrecht: Springer Open.

Fitzpatrick, Sheila. 1999. *Everyday Stalinism: Ordinary Life in Extraordinary Times: Soviet Russia in the 1930s*. Oxford: Oxford University Press.

Härlin, Dorothea. 2017. 'The Berlin Water Charter: Water Ethics from an Activist's Viewpoint'. In *Global Water Ethics: Towards a Global Ethics Charter*, edited by Rafael Ziegler and David Groenfeldt, pp. 267–80. Abingdon: Routledge.

Heiskala, Risto. 2016. 'The Evolution of the Sources of Social Power and Some Extensions'. In *Global Powers: Michael Mann's Anatomy of the Twentieth Century and Beyond*, edited by Ralph Schroeder, pp. 11–37. Cambridge: Cambridge University Press.

Hull, Bruce. 2008. 'Environmental Pluralism'. In *Encyclopedia of Environmental Ethics and Philosophy*, edited by J. Bair Callicott and Robert Frodeman, pp. 384–7. New York: Macmillan Reference.

Ibrahim, Solava. 2017. 'How to Build Collective Capabilities: The 3C-Model for Grassroots-Led Development'. *Journal of Human Development and Capabilities* 22(2): 1–26.

Jacobi, Nadia von, Daniel Edmiston, and Rafael Ziegler. 2017. 'Tackling Marginalisation through Social Innovation? Examining the EU Social Innovation Policy Agenda from a Capabilities Perspective'. *Journal of Human Development and Capabilities* 18 (2): 148–62.

Jay, Jason. 2013. 'Navigating Paradox as a Mechanism of Change and Innovation in Hybrid Organizations'. *Academy of Management Journal* 56(1): 137–59.

Jenson, Jane. 2015. 'Social Innovation: Redesigning the Welfare Diamond'. In *New Frontiers in Social Innovation Research*, edited by Alex Nicholls, Julie Simon, and Madeleine Gabriel, pp. 89–106. London: Palgrave Macmillan.

Jessop, Bob, Frank Moulaert, Lars Hulgard, and Abdelillah Hamdouch. 2013. 'Social Innovation Research: A New State in Innovation Research?' In *The International Handbook on Social Innovation: Collective Action, Social Learning and Transdisciplinary Research*, edited by Frank Moulaert, Diane Maccallum, Abdid Mehmood, and Abdelillah Hamdouch, pp. 110–30. Cheltenham: Edward Elgar.

Kahane, Adam. 2013. 'Exploring Alternatives to the War on Drugs'. Stanford Social Innovation Review Blog, 20 November 2013.

Klein, Juan-Luis, Jean-Marc Fontan, Denis Harrisson, and Benoît Lévesque. 2013. 'The Québec Model: A Social Innovation System Founded on Cooperation and Consensus Building'. In *The International Handbook on Social Innovation: Collective Action, Social Learning and Transdisciplinary Research*, edited by Frank Moulaert, Diane Maccallum, Abdid Mehmood, and Abdelillah Hamdouch, pp. 371–83. Cheltenham: Edward Elgar.

Korn, Judith. 2009. 'Taking Responsibility: Breaking Away from Hate and Violence'. In *An Introduction to Social Entrepreneurship: Voices, Preconditions, Contexts*, edited by Rafael Ziegler, pp. 33–52. Cheltenham: Edward Elgar.

Howaldt, Jürgen, and Cordula Kropp. 2017. 'Transformative Forschung'. In *Innovationen für die Gesellschaft. Neue Wege und Methoden zur Entfaltung des Potenzials sozialer Innovationen*, edited by Jürgen Howaldt and Ralf Kopp, pp. 53–8. Dortmund: SfS TU Dortmund.

List, Christian, and Laura Valentini. 2016. 'The Methodology of Political Theory'. In *The Oxford Handbook of Philosophical Methodology*, edited by Herman Cappelen, Tamar Szabó Gendler, and John Hawthorne, pp. 525–31. Oxford: Oxford University Press.

Lundvall, Bengt-Åke, and Susanna Borrás. 2005. 'Science, Technology, and Innovation Policy'. In *The Oxford Handbook of Innovation*, edited by Jan Fagerberg, David C. Mowery, and Richard R. Nelson, pp. 599–633. Oxford: Oxford University Press.

Mann, Michael. 2013. *Globalizations, 1945–2011*. Cambridge: Cambridge University Press.

McLeod, John. 2013. *Introduction to Counselling*. 5th edition. Maidenhead: McGraw Hill Education.

Miquel, Marc, Marisol Cabeza, and Santiago Anglada. 2013. 'Therorizing Multi-Level Governance in Social Innovation Dynamics'. In *The International Handbook on Social Innovation: Collective Action, Social Learning and Transdisciplinary Research*, edited by Frank Moulaert, Diane Maccallum, Abdid Mehmood, and Abdelillah Hamdouch, pp. 142–53. Cheltenham: Edward Elgar.

Mulgan, Geoff. 2015. 'The Study of Social Innovation: Theory, Practice and Progress'. In *New Frontiers in Social Innovation Research*, edited by Alex Nicholls, Julie Simon, and Madeleine Gabriel, pp. x–xxi. London: Palgrave Macmillan.

Nicholls, Alex. 2015. 'Synthetic Grid: A Critical Framework to Inform the Development of Social Innovation Metrics'. CrESSI Working Paper No. 14. Brussels: European Commission, DG Research.

Nicholls, Alex, and Alexander Murdock (eds). 2012. *Social Innovation: Blurring Boundaries to Reconfigure Markets*. Basingstoke: Palgrave Macmillan.

Nicholls, Alex, Julie Simon, and Madeleine Gabriel (eds). 2015. *New Frontiers in Social Innovation Research*. London: Palgrave Macmillan.

Nussbaum, Martha. 2000. *Women and Human Development: The Capabilities Approach*. Cambridge: Cambridge University Press.

Nussbaum, Martha. 2006. *Frontiers of Justice: Disability, Nationality, Species Membership*. Cambridge, MA: Harvard University Press.

Nussbaum, Martha. 2011. *Creating Capabilities: The Human Development Approach*. Cambridge, MA: Belknap Press.

Offer, Avner. 1997.'Between the Gift and the Market: The Economy of Regard.' *The Economic History Review* 50(3): 450–76.

Ott, Konrad. 2010. *Umweltethik zur Einführung*. Hamburg: Junius.

Pel, Bono and Tom Bauler. 2014. 'The Institutionalization of Social Innovation: Between Transformation and Capture'. Transit Working Paper No. 2, Rotterdam.

Pettit, Philip. 2014. *Just Freedom: A Moral Compass for a Complex World*. New York: W. W. Norton.

Rawls, John. 1999. *A Theory of Justice*. Revised edition. Oxford: Oxford University Press.

Robeyns, Ingrid. 2016. 'Capabilitarianism.' *Journal of Human Development and Capabilities* 17(3): 397–414.

Scheuerle, Thomas, Gudrun-Christine Schimpf, Gunnar Gänzel, and Georg Mildenberger. 2016. 'Report on Relevant Actors in Historic Examples and an Empirically Driven Typology of Types of Social Innovation'. CrESSI Working Paper No. 29. Brussels: European Commission, DG Research.

Schumpeter, Joseph. 1942/1975. *Capitalism, Socialism, and Democracy*. New York: Harper Collins Publishers.

Sen, Amartya. 1999. *Development as Freedom*. Oxford: Oxford University Press.

Sen, Amartya. 2009. *The Idea of Justice*. London: Penguin.

Thoreau, Henry. 1854/1993. *Walden and Resistance to Civil Government*. New York: W. W. Norton.

Tiwari, Meera. 2011. 'Exploring the Role of Capabilities in Social Innovation.' Paper presented at the 8th annual conference of the HDCA, The Hague. https://ethicsandtechnology.eu/news/hdca-conference-2011/.

Thornton, Patricia, William Ocasio, and Michael Lounsbury. 2012. *The Institutional Logics Perspective: A New Approach to Culture, Structure, and Process*. Oxford: Oxford University Press.

Tracey, Paul, and Neill Stott. 2017. 'Social Innovation: A Window on Alternative Ways of Organizing and Innovating'. *Innovation—Organisation and Management* 19(1): 51–60.

Vickers, Ian, Fergus Lyon, Leandro Sepulveda, and Caitlin McMullin. 2017. 'Public Service Innovation and Multiple Institutional Logics: The Case of Hybrid Social Enterprise Providers of Health and Wellbeing'. *Research Policy* 46(10): 1755–68.

Walzer, Michael. 1983. *Spheres of Justice: A Defense of Pluralism and Equality*. New York: Basic Books.

Weaver, Paul, and René Kemp. 2017. 'A Review of Evaluation Methods Relevant for Social Innovation: With Suggestions for their Use and Development'. Transit Working Paper No. 14, Rotterdam.

Wolff, Jonathan, and Avner de-Shalit. 2007. *Disadvantage*. Oxford: Oxford University Press.

Ziegler, Rafael. 2015. 'Justice and Innovation--towards Principles for Creating a Fair Space for Innovation'. *Journal of Responsible Innovation* 2(2): 184–200.

Ziegler, Rafael. 2017a. 'Social Innovation as a Collaborative Concept'. *Innovation: The European Journal of Social Science Research* 30(4): 388–405.

Ziegler, Rafael. 2017b. 'Citizen Innovation as Niche Restoration–A Type of Social Innovation and its Relevance for Political Participation and Sustainability'. *Journal of Social Entrepreneurship* 8(3): 338–53.

Ziegler, Rafael, Sabrina Schulz, Lukas Richter, and Martin Schreck. 2014. 'Following Gandhi: Social Entrepreneurship as a Non-Violent Way of Communicating Sustainability Challenges'. *Sustainability* 6(2): 1018–36.

Ziegler, Rafael, Lena Partzsch, Jana Gebauer, Marianne Henkel, Justus Lodemann, and Franziska Mohaupt. 2014. *Social Entrepreneurship in the Water Sector: Getting Things Done Sustainably*. Cheltenham: Edward Elgar.

4

Empirical Approaches to Social Innovation

Georg Mildenberger, Gudrun-Christine Schimpf, Enrica Chiappero-Martinetti, and Nadia von Jacobi

Introduction

This book focuses on the economic underpinnings of marginalization in EU countries and considers how social innovation can address them. It does so with a clear commitment to a theoretical framework—the Extended Social Grid Model (ESGM) (see chapter 1)—that explores the social forces that hinder, enable, and drive social innovation, without neglecting the role individuals and collective agency can play in bringing about change. The empirical contribution of this research is the development of a theoretical approach to study social innovation on different levels and for different time periods through both qualitative and quantitative analysis. This chapter describes two empirical approaches with which social innovation and its potentially transformative role can be studied: an analysis of long-term comprehensive case studies; a mixed-method approach inspired by the capabilities approach for evaluating the impact of social innovations.[1]

The field of social innovation research remains at an early stage of development (Domanski and Kaletka 2017:13). While its roots reach back to the late nineteenth century, the concept itself was not widely used before the early twenty-first century (Ayob et al. 2016: 637). Currently, it still remains unclear what types of empirical phenomena are at the core of social innovation research and consequently, which methodologies are most apt for its investigation. Much of the research to date place social innovation close to phenomena like social entrepreneurship (Moulaert et al. 2017: annex 3, 80–105) and, to a lesser extent, the new developments stemming from the rise of ICT and social media (Millard and Carpenter 2014). The attention such new phenomena and the connected research have received (and the attendant funding opportunities) has led to a research focus on cutting-edge 'newness' that tries to follow the fast-paced developments

[1] We would like to thank Amelia Pope. The chapter has gained a lot by her editing and suggestions. Parts of this chapter were presented earlier at several workshops and conferences. We considered the valuable feedback we received there and incorporated the input where possible.

Georg Mildenberger, Gudrun-Christine Schimpf, Enrica Chiappero-Martinetti, and Nadia von Jacobi, *Empirical Approaches to Social Innovation*. In: *Creating Economic Space for Social Innovation*. Edited by: Alex Nicholls and Rafael Ziegler, Oxford University Press (2019). © Oxford University Press.
DOI: 10.1093/oso/9780198830511.003.0004

and trends in the field. The assumed newness and disruptive nature of social innovation, however, seems to tempt many researchers to neglect more established types of explanations and examples, often demanding an approach to research that is equally completely new.

Social innovation research resembles a discipline in a pre-paradigmatic phase (Kuhn 1996). Such a phase is typically marked by the collection of examples, new taxonomic endeavours and the development of innovative concepts and theories that do not necessarily build on previous research traditions or theory. Thus, social innovation lacks a clear and agreed definition, a shared theoretical frame, or a consensus on basic empirical methodologies for research.

By developing and applying the ESGM, the book aims to present 'a novel but appropriate set of research lenses well suited to the empirical examination' of different themes by building on complementary theoretical strands in socio-economics (Nicholls and Ziegler 2015: 2). The ESGM is not a research *method* per se, but rather it is an abstract schema that can be used as a heuristic tool to orient empirical research. This chapter explores such approaches and links them to a series of theoretical arguments, intended to transform the ESGM's basic categories and their interconnections into more concrete concepts related to types of social phenomena. These concepts can then support empirical work and collection of evidence that can be used to examine social innovation more deeply.

This exercise of translating the ESGM into empirical methodologies presented here was carried out in two different ways. While a first strand of research collected data to observe and analyse social innovation in its historical context over time, a second strand empirically measured the impact of social innovation on the life of beneficiaries. As a useful by-product, the latter also contributes to the emergent field of social-impact measurement.

This chapter is structured as follows. The next section offers a review of current approaches to social innovation research based upon a survey of the existing literature. After this, the chapter outlines our approach to exploring social innovation from a long-term, historical perspective in the form of extended case studies.[2] Following on from this, we offer an explanation of our approach to capture the impact of social innovation at the individual level, based on the human capabilities approach embedded within the ESGM. Finally, the chapter summarizes the lessons learnt from developing and implementing these novel methodologies.

Heterogeneity in Social Innovation Research

Social innovation research addresses a relatively new and hybrid field, to which researchers from different disciplines have aimed to contribute. Just as their

[2] The other CrESSI case studies dealing with more recent social innovations are not the subject of this chapter. More information can be found in Scheuerle et al. (2016) and Schimpf (2017).

scientific backgrounds vary, so do their methods. In an overview article, Pelka and Terstriep stated that there are a 'variety of objects, means and results' (Pelka and Terstriep 2016: 12) within social innovation research. Moulaert et al. offered similar conclusions (2017: 34): the common denominator of much of social innovation research is its trans-disciplinary approach (though this is often more suggested than enacted). Moreover, the research methods employed vary across a broad spectrum of approaches.

While this heterogeneity can be fruitful and enriching, it also hampers the comparability of results. The research field not only lacks an integrated concept of social innovation covering all sectors (Domanski and Kaletka 2017: 7), but it also lacks a basic theory guiding the research methods and epistemology. In this regard, the ESGM offers a useful starting point, showing how networks, social forces, and cognitive frames interact across various dimensions of social power, and how this affects the capabilities of people and co-shapes patterns of marginalization.

Although important and pioneering work has been done in terms of developing integrated theories of social innovation (Howaldt et al. 2014; Haxeltine et al. 2016), there has yet to be a systematic academic discussion over the best methods for capturing social innovation data. Workshops on methods for social innovation research have taken place and a special issue of the *European Public and Social Innovation Review* has been published (Wittmayer et al. 2017). However, a broad and structured discussion has yet to happen and an established canon of methods for social innovation research is still not in sight. As a result, one has to look at the concepts and reports of many different projects to get a picture of what is going on.[3]

Since the turn of the twenty-first century the number of publications on social innovation has increased (Ayob et al. 2016: 638). The overwhelming majority offer data from isolated qualitative cases. Thus, at face value, it may seem as if there is a common approach emerging focused on case studies (Domanski and Kaletka 2017: 23). But it is not clear that this has come about as a consequence of any deliberative process of methodological discussion or analysis—rather it may simply reflect the empirical biases of the early researchers in the field. Nevertheless, the result has been a wealth of rich *examples* of social innovations. Given the diverse disciplinary backgrounds of researchers, these case studies follow various designs. The resulting material is very heterogeneous and fragmented. Additionally, many researchers and projects concentrate on recent cases (Hamdouch 2013: 259). Hence, many of the social innovations under study are at an 'early stage' and no information can be gathered on adaptation efforts or changes in the social innovation, with the result that hardly anything can be told

[3] Even the *International Handbook on Social Innovation* (Moulaert et al. 2013: part IV) discusses in its chapter on methodologies only research approaches suited for new and recent social innovations (co-production, cross-learning, (participatory) action research, and partnership-based research).

or learned about breakpoints and failures for example. Furthermore, early-stage cases may not be able to demonstrate the systemic impact at which many social innovations aim.

Some research projects follow a mapping approach, collecting social innovations in a certain geographic area according to defined criteria (Howaldt et al. 2016). Given the prevalence of the case-study approach, many projects deal with qualitative data of different kinds, mostly derived from interviews (phone or face-to-face, semi-structured or narrative) (Davies 2014; Pel et al. 2017; Terstriep et al. 2015). Others apply an ethnographic approach using participant observation as part of their methodology (Robinson 2012).

This book offers several different empirical approaches, all referring to the ESGM. The core empirical advantages of focusing on the ESGM are threefold: a certain comparability of the cases as they are analysed in terms of the same theoretical categories; the possibility of a long-term approach; and a (normative) impact assessment by detecting the changes in the capabilities of the people involved. Conversely, the empirical work allowed the theoretical robustness of ESGM to be tested via real case studies, thereby gaining valuable insights to further enhance the model. In the following two sections, we will set out our two main methodologies: a long-term case-study method inspired by social history; a micro-level, mixed-method model based upon Sen's capabilities approach.

Long-Term Case Study Research

Social innovation may be a new phenomenon for research, yet it is an open question whether its nature is completely different to other forms of innovation. Business innovation, for instance, has been studied for decades and has generated a well-equipped toolbox for researchers. Is a new methodology to study social innovation even necessary? Could the existing tools used to study innovation be already fit for purpose? To give at least a preliminary answer to these questions, a brief overview of approaches that focus on different units of analysis and pursue different paradigms (quantitative, qualitative) in social innovation research now follows.[4]

Surveying Social Innovation Research

An initial survey of social innovation research methods reveals various attempts to build on existing methods of measuring innovation at the macro-level. So, one

[4] The research approach described in this part of the chapter was developed together with Thomas Scheuerle and Gunnar Glänzel. Both left the research team of the CSI before the end of the project. Template development and data collection gained a lot from their ideas.

approach would simply be to enlarge on these with specific, new indicators of social innovation impact and thus provide a usable data collection framework (Krlev et al. 2014; Bund et al. 2013b, 2013a). An alternative has been to use community innovation surveys with the additional inclusion of social innovation variables to study it at the organizational level (Innobasque and Sinnergiak Social Innovation 2013; Wintjes et al. 2016; Huysentruyt and Stephan 2017). However, these approaches have tended to focus on the conditions and status of social innovation in a single country at a very general level and only at a single point in time. While these are interesting questions relevant for better understanding innovation with a view on enabling and hampering conditions, they are not so apt to grasp the trajectories of given social innovations and their diffusion.

Another way to get insights into the trajectories of social innovation is via biographies that add a dynamic perspective to such research (Butzin et al. 2012: 11–12; Rehfeld et al. 2015: 46). This method is also drawn from established innovation research but has been adjusted to fit better with social innovation. Through narrative interviewing methods and triangulation, the biography of a social innovation is reconstructed thereby showing how the innovation evolved (Terstriep 2016: 7–8). However, interviewing methods limit the target social innovation to be studied, as they are bound to the lifespans of the relevant social innovators and their contemporaries. Conversely, in technological innovation research 'innovation biography' is not necessarily restricted to the action of one organization, but can be used to describe the formation of a new concept and how it becomes an established technology (Bruns et al. 2008).

Another approach is historic research. The most interesting recent research approaches to social innovations in their historical context have been longitudinal ones, in which the main object of observation is how social innovations develop over time. Several such case studies are discussed in chapters 5 to 9—some successful, some less so.[5]

Murray and the research team at the Young Foundation developed a metaphorical picture of social innovation as a spiral with six stages to explain how social innovations evolved over time (Murray et al. 2010: 11).[6] This model was later slightly modified: 'many of these stages overlap and may be undertaken in a different order . . . feedback loops exist between every stage, which makes the process iterative rather than linear' (The Young Foundation 2012: 34). Yet, the underlying assumption that the main agent of social innovation has to be a single individual or organization remains contested. One might also wonder if scaling can be considered a stage or if every social innovation can (and intends to) lead to systemic change. Besides that the spiral metaphor offers an uneasy synthesis of disparate concepts.

[5] The case studies have been published in two working papers: Scheuerle et al. (2016) and Schimpf (2017). Examples for recent social innovations studied in CrESSI can be found in chapters 7 and 9.

[6] The stages were: prompts, proposals, prototyping, sustaining, scaling, and systemic change.

In the original Schumpeterian understanding of innovation, it is seen as a part of a bigger process within the 'business cycle'—one piece of the invention–innovation–diffusion chain. In the spiral metaphor, 'innovation' refers to the whole process and, at the same time, refers to one stage of it. Other scholars on social innovation processes have pointed out that the path from idea to diffusion is not predictable or deterministic, as presented by the model, and might contain backward steps and adjustments (Howaldt et al. 2014: 61). It also remains unclear how this model explains social innovation originating from the conjunction of different sectors and if it is able to reflect dynamic adjustments in the aims, meanings, and instruments of a social innovation. An advanced version of the spiral model includes concepts such as 'growing and spreading' instead of scaling. This acknowledges that the assumption of a single actor might not be of core importance when explaining social innovation (Davies 2014; Davies and Simon 2013)—it may, instead, be a plurality of actors that push a social innovation forward.

An alternative approach is provided by the 'adaptive cycle' of innovation (Westley 2008: fig. 1). Building upon the work of Holling (e.g. Walker et al. 2004), Gunderson and others (Gunderson and Holling 2002; Westley et al. 2007: 66–67), it consists of four phases (release, reorganization, exploitation, and conservation). The conception here is that every idea or organization has to renew itself when it reaches the 'conservation' phase in order to stay resilient. Resources are needed for new explorations to maintain the loop (Westley 2008: 3). This model brings resilience theory into social innovation research (Westley 2013). However, again, an underlying analytic assumption concerning the precedence of single actors can be detected. However, it is also acknowledged that the unit of analysis could be an idea rather than an individual/organization.

However, it has also been argued that 'resilience' as a heuristic concept should be used with caution when analysing social-ecological systems. Its implicit normativity should be made transparent from the beginning (what is the desirable state or process that should be maintained?). Also, one should keep in mind at which socio-structural level social innovation strategies are aimed—successful change on one level might produce (unintended and undesirable) stability on another (Lodemann and Ziegler 2014: 7).

McGowan and Westley explored the 'roots and developments of social innovations through comparative historical case studies' (2015: 52; Westley et al. 2017). They were particularly interested in key trends and dynamics: new ideas that created space for new combinations, various agents and agents' activities, and the importance of obstacles and opportunities at different societal levels (McGowan and Westley 2015: 55). Their aim was to better understand the conditions supporting disruptive change as well as the lifecycle of social innovation. Westley and McGowan use elements of discourse analysis and network theory to analyse concepts, reinterpretations, and transformations of social innovation. This useful approach suggested that a deeper understanding of social innovation might stem from a perspective that does not concentrate on the point in time where something new emerges, but, rather, follows its evolution in society through time to better understand its development, how these occurred, and what influenced them. One of their examples shows how the IQ test initially evolved as a means to prove white supremacy, but later was a tool to foster equal opportunities in the education system (McGowan and Westley 2015: 60–4).

Blundel and Lyon examined 'how historically informed research might enhance our understanding of growth processes' (2015: 80). They analysed the long-term growth process of two British social ventures with regards to opportunity recognition, entrepreneurial adjustment, and institutional structure. This work offered some interesting insights on periodization and continuity. Perhaps even more interesting was the use of a long analytic perspective backwards that uncovered some profound discontinuities resulting in strategic realignments. Taken together, all these approaches acknowledge the value of a historical perspective, but are either focused on a single actor/organization or use a simplistic theoretical background. But there are other strands of thought too.

Some approaches have broadened the concept of (social) innovation by perceiving it as independent of organizations. In these approaches, organizations are seen, rather, as contributors, carriers, and/or implementers of ideas. A similar idea is the notion of a Social Innovation Stream (Anheier et al. 2017: 7).

Starting in the 1980s, scholars of the history of technology and social scientists combined social history, sociology of science and technology, sociology of knowledge, and philosophy of science and technology into what is commonly called science and technology studies (STS). One main insight from this collaboration has been that technology and technological innovation cannot be properly understood without understanding their given social contexts. The Social Construction of Technology (SCOT) is one prominent school of STS (Bijker et al. 1987; Bijker and Law 1992; Bijker 1995) offering a productive method to reconstruct technological evolution (Heßler 2001: 20). The approach consists of four elements: artefacts; actors and social groups; meanings; closure and stabilization. Artefacts are always a matter of interpretation instead of being understood as firmly established entities. It is assumed they change in time, develop new meanings and may have different meanings for different actors at a given time. While stabilization depends on a consensus on the meaning of an artefact within a social group, closure is reached when different social groups agree upon a form and a meaning of an artefact (Degele 2002: 101).

One of SCOT's benefits is that it recognizes the importance of interaction amongst social groups as part of the (social) innovation process. Other important points are its interpretative flexibility and a focus on the social capacity to drive technology and give it meaning, especially during the early stages of development (Degele 2002: 99). Moreover, SCOT argues that social processes deriving from the influence and interests of social groups drive and shape technology (Heßler 2001: 25). Critics argue, however, that its strong focus on artefacts leads to a neglect of social structures and power relationships (Kline and Pinch 1999: 114).

The long-term case studies set out in chapters 5 to 7 transfer the SCOT approach from technology studies to social innovation research. In combination with the ESGM, and its focus on social forces and different sources of power, the SCOT approach is respected but further developed.

One important research focus of this book is to analyse key social innovations over a long time period. In making a longitudinal section through the phases of a social innovation's trajectory for a period of more than 150 years, the intention has been to find relevant constellations and dynamics around social innovation in the long run and to draw lessons about the boundaries of social innovation ecosystems. Investigating and analysing crucial developments and critical points of their trajectory up to the present helps reveal the interrelations and interactions of different drivers, institutions, and actors. Furthermore, social innovation's adaptation to new contexts, often overlooked, becomes more evident.

While the SCOT approach supports our longitudinal analysis of social innovation, we further enriched it with historical methods developed in social and cultural history. Common historical methods such as discourse analysis helped us to distinguish relevant actors and networks, to analyse narratives and discourses concerning social issues, to explore their sources and relevance to marginalized groups, and to examine how people perceive changes in these fields caused by social innovation processes. Cognitive frames, as conceived of in the ESGM, underlie these narratives, as they reflect attitudes of people at various points in time.

The long-term nature of this approach offers three key analytic advantages:

1. Looking back into history provides insights on the nature and comprehensive benefits of social innovation that are not available if one concentrates only on the often still-immature social innovations of today.
2. The historical perspective uncovers the interplay between different inventions that are not accounted for if one concentrates on case studies of recent social innovations alone.
3. Through longer-term analysis, a case is also more likely to describe and examine potentially negative outcomes of social innovations that have not been in the centre of social innovation research or innovation research in general so far (cf. Havas 2016).

However, it is also important to state the limitations of such an approach. It is beyond the scope of such an analysis to provide a detailed account of the development factors behind a social innovation from a single actor's perspective—as in Van de Ven et al.'s seminal work on the innovation journeys of enterprises (2008). Nevertheless, long-term analysis can complement more aggregated macro-perspectives with a closer analysis of specific innovations in towns or countries, or during specific periods of time in order to zoom in on crucial aspects of a social innovation's history. Such a perspective is helpful to uncover important influences from socio-economic structures on social innovation processes that cannot be seen from an actor-centric perspective in shorter timeframes.

The historic approach also questions the appropriate unit of analysis, as it refrains from a focus on single individuals, organizations, or social movements. Deviating from common approaches to social innovation (Westley et al. 2007; Murray et al. 2010; Mulgan et al. 2007; Rüede and Lurtz 2012), the historic approach investigates social innovations as a joint endeavour of a variety of actors in an aggregated perspective over time. Accordingly, it is not only organizations that are the point of focus of a social innovation, but, rather, society as a whole. To provide a comprehensive picture and to understand how the social innovations have become mainstream over time, our research implemented comprehensive case studies from various European countries, covering more than 150 years, from the nineteenth century until today. They confirmed that social innovations emerge from the interplay of various actors in various places across time and are episodic. Only looking back can these actions and dynamic phases of change be perceived as one single social innovation.

The areas covered in the comprehensive case studies set out in chapters 5 to 7 are:

- *Social housing*: this social innovation initially addressed the urban poor during industrialization. It has undergone several phases on its way to becoming mainstream after the Second World War, often drawing on market-based solutions with public subsidies and being provided by a variety of societal actors. Due to recent EU legislation, in many countries in Europe social housing is only accessible for (more or less) marginalized populations.
- *Freshwater supply*: starting more or less under the same circumstances as social housing, this social innovation developed into a very centralized and often solely municipally provided good, mostly due to the strong path-dependency in one of its core elements, the physical infrastructure. This also means almost everybody in society is linked to the supply system, including most of the marginalized.
- *Financing access to education*: this social innovation affects the whole of society, which simultaneously shapes it. Different countries, in line with their respective historical developments, displayed distinct approaches, but a common set of circumstances clearly emerged. There has been a difficult choice between either the generalization of access to education allowed by state funding that brings with it a state curriculum, or a more flexible and pluralistic curriculum that is connected to marketization, with the threat of prohibited access for some, especially marginalized people.

Chapters 8 and 9 present further case studies done in the CrESSI project. They use the ESGM to structure the material in a similar way but covered shorter time periods and do not recur to the SCOT approach:

- *The marginalization of the Roma population in Hungary*: the Roma have faced social exclusion in many European countries for a long time. This remains an unresolved problem. Various government strategies launched over the years have not tackled the root of the problem. This case examines the Kiútprogram, a non-profit corporation, which provides unsecured loans and mentoring primarily to socially excluded Roma in Hungary to alleviate their marginalization enabling them to set up their own business or to become self-employed vegetable producers.
- *Solidarity purchasing groups*: Solidarity Purchasing Groups (SPGs) are groups of individuals that decide to organize themselves together to buy food collectively, selecting suppliers on the basis of solidarity and critical consumption. The main goal of their activities is to put their purchasing practices in line with ethical principles of critical consumption: fair prices for producers, preference for local products, and sustainability in production and transportation of goods. Like Fair Trade organizations, SPGs volunteer to distribute goods among members. Unlike Fair Trade organizations, their activities happen mostly in informal groups or associations, not in shops open to the public.

All five case studies look at European examples but offer findings that have wider significance around the world.

Research Design

In the research design for these cases, the ESGM is used as theoretical framework combined with historical methods. To get a broad picture of the trajectory of social innovation at several levels, a qualitative case-study approach was applied, following the logic of an *embedded single case study* (Yin 2003: 39 ff.).[7] This means it is possible to focus on a single phenomenon (here the social innovation), while also giving attention to specific subunits of this phenomenon (different country or city contexts, different models used). Accordingly, from an ecosystem perspective there is a wide overlap between our approach and other innovation system methods, such as national, regional, sectoral, or technical systems analysis. All these methods, to different extents, refer to a variety of actors, relevant knowledge

[7] Embedded single case studies are suitable for research questions on *causal* explanations ('how' or 'why'), particularly when there is little opportunity to influence or control the context (Yin 2003: 1).

bases, technological paradigms and trajectories, institutions, and sub-systems such as policy-makers, financial services, and so on (cf. Havas 2016). Moreover, they all emphasize the co-evolution of these elements and their relevance for system dynamics. While these approaches have tended to be centred on innovative companies, here it is assumed they are also relevant in terms of agency in the general development of a social innovation.

Furthermore, the case studies aim to understand the neuralgic points and crucial components in the diffusion processes of a social innovation, including varieties of adaptation across different contexts and backgrounds such as different welfare regimes or economic and political systems and dynamics. Such a perspective is oriented towards dynamic, non-linear, lifecycle analyses (cf. Havas 2016)—social innovation activities for a given town, organization, or social movement, serve to illustrate specific aspects of more general developments.

A Common Template

The data collection for the case studies was conducted following a common template. This ensured that all ESGM categories were taken into account, that there was sufficient material for each comprehensive case study, and that some comparison across different social innovations would be possible.[8] Data collection was purposefully descriptive, but the design of the research templates clearly reflected the different elements of the ESGM ('actors and networks' for social networks, 'narratives and discourses' for cognitive frames, 'rules, norms, and policies' for information on institutions). The ESGM helped us to explore the interplay of different social dimensions in the formation of social innovation. The template took into account different solution approaches, different marginalized groups and actor constellations, various phases of a social innovation and its impact, different laws and norms, a range of information on resources, and relevant technological developments. Background and contextual data was derived from secondary sources (historical literature, statistical data), or from desktop research about key policy agendas and provider organizations. Beyond the major narrative of the respective social innovation, analytic 'spotlights' were used to zoom into specific individual trajectories along the course of the social innovation. In each comprehensive case study this was done for several EU countries. Moreover, the researchers prepared their own country-specific reports to create further illustrative material for the embedded single case studies. This helped capture not only a societal perspective, but also other information on more

[8] Special thanks go to our CrESSI partners Jari Aro, Daniel Edmiston, Margherita Fabbri, Susanne Giesecke, Attila Havas, Christopher Houghton Budd, Justus Lodemann, György Molnár, and Martijn van der Linden for their cooperation and contribution.

specific developments in certain towns, countries, or over periods of time that provided extra insights into local processes of innovation. Given the breadth and complexity of the social innovations chosen, this data collection could not be exhaustive. However, this approach served to surface a range of specific local developments, complementing the societal perspective of the overall narrative and enriching the analysis.

Data Analysis

According to the different research interests pursued, the data analysis was conducted in several steps. The material of each case study was first arranged by phases derived through analysis and it was then structured in line with a set of key issues:

- *Societal responsibility and governance of the solution*: Which roles were assigned to different societal actors (public, market, civil society) in the provision of solutions to the problem? Who took the initiative, and what constellations of actors emerged?
- *Design of the solution*: How were the solutions shaped regarding quality standards, applied technological solutions, extent of integrated or linked services, business models, organizational models, involvement of beneficiaries etc.?
- *Targeted beneficiaries*: Who were accepted as people in need and were able to enjoy the benefits of the solutions?

During this process, the forces within the Social Grid (cognitive frames, social networks, and institutions) and their attendant power dimensions served as a heuristic structure for analysing all the material. The role of the Social Grid was critically reflected upon and special attention was paid to the interrelations of its three forces in line with Beckert's research (2010: 606). The economic underpinnings of marginalization were also examined as crosscutting topics, not analysed separately. By comparing the developments in different countries, different periods, and different constellations, it was possible to acquire more general insights.

In the next analytic step—aimed at testing the ESGM's consistency and explanatory power—each phase of a given case study was analysed separately through the lens of the model.

Where feasible, the effects on beneficiaries' capabilities were also discussed. As far as possible, different types of power sources were used for data triangulation. However, given the holistic nature of case studies and the relatively limited available data, this part of the analysis was only indicative and illustrative.

The previous steps made it possible inductively to derive a synopsis of relevant social innovation dimensions and a list of propositions on key ecosystems and lifecycles, as well as the agency and impact of social innovations. Finally, the ESGM was critically reflected upon with reference to its fit with our empirical data.

This complexity-inspired approach surfaced several important factors. For example, it shed light on the dynamic relationship between the social forces: social networks and institutions, institutions and cognitive frames, or cognitive frames and social networks. This fitted well with the idea of interpretative flexibility in the SCOT model: actors either fall back on existing institutions or create and shape new ones.

Another important finding was that many actors were typically involved in the trajectory of a social innovation—in its development as well as its implementation. They acted in various contexts, under various conditions, and with various motivations. These divergent initial conditions could be described as a specific ecosystem. On different levels, different groups and social networks were active and tried—in a constant interplay with institutions and dominant cognitive frames—to best advance their respective social innovation agenda. Recognizing the plurality of actors that co-shape innovation processes seems to be key for future investigations of social innovation.

In addition, it became obvious that each social innovation experienced different developmental steps or phases. These can be framed as the *lifecycle* of a social innovation. Starting from a social need and initial random set of ideas as to how to address it, discourses and different approaches typically developed. By implementing, and later scaling, a social innovation, the social need was moderated or even eliminated (at least for a certain time). This was not a linear process and it was not always a success story. Many social problems seem to never be entirely solved—according to changing social needs, they re-emerge in different contexts and manifestations. Consequently, there is a constant need for adaptation and improvement in social innovation, for continuous innovation by various actors. In cases where a solution had already been reached in the past, expectations might be even higher.

The analysis did not find any evidence for a consistent lifecycle pattern of social innovation. Social innovations appear to develop and adapt to their context-specific Social Grid at a given point in time. They are dynamic and constantly renew to survive. Their specific ecosystem is decisive for the way this happens.

The ESGM proved to be a helpful heuristic tool in recognizing the social forces that shaped or influenced social innovations. We also found that these social forces can damage the integrity of an underlying idea behind a social innovation, often by altering its meaning or the target group (see chapters 11 and 16 for such 'institutional capture'). Also, relevant incidents, some quite random and unintended, were detected as decisive for the ongoing trajectory of the social innovation.

The addition of sources of power from Mann proved to be analytically helpful. It allowed us to examine the data from different perspectives. Also, it brought some new dynamic factors into the Social Grid. Changes in sources of power were identified as important factors in the social innovation trajectories. As a result, a series of different (context- and time-specific) Social Grids for each social innovation was compiled, which provided information on the interactions of institutions, social networks, and cognitive frames at different points in time and in different places. Nevertheless, it is not possible to explain all the dynamics across a Social Grid by the ESGM alone. The ESGM provided a useful structure for data collection and analysis. However, it is inherently a static model, so it failed to explain why social innovations emerge or develop over time.

Mixed Methods in Primary-Data Collection

In addition to investigating social innovation processes in their historical context, this research also applied the ESGM in order to analyse ongoing examples of social innovation in context. A key goal of this second strand of empirical investigation was to test our central theoretical model, this time coupled with the aim of evaluating its social impact on society, especially for marginalized individuals. Unlike the historical analysis, our analysis of current social innovations incorporated the voice of key beneficiaries as a part of the analysis of human capabilities and how social innovation may enlarge or affect them. An important additional challenge here was to develop a quantitative analysis of the ESGM's key concepts. Measuring social innovation in quantitative ways raised several methodological challenges linked to the complex and multifaceted nature of this phenomenon. It was also demanding in terms of information needs, data requirements, and methodological design. Consequently, the empirical evidence that emerged was somewhat patchy and difficult to interpret.

The ESGM perspective on social innovation made its operationalization rather challenging, requiring the identification of a complex empirical strategy aimed at preserving the complexity and multi-layered nature of the model on one hand, and the specificity of the social innovation case studies under investigation on the other. The following sections summarize the methodological requirements for a primary-data collection method that sought to reflect the ESGM. Three recent European social innovations were investigated (see chapter 10 for details and results). Although the empirical strategy described here is tailored to the ESGM and rooted in our case studies, some general prescriptions on how to implement empirical analysis on social innovations will also be presented.

Multiple Units of Analysis and Agency

Due to its systemic approach, social innovation might be expected to engage a plurality of actors. First, it typically involves the promoters of social innovation such as single individuals or, more often, a formal or informal network of people intending to activate initiatives that address some sort of social need in their community. Second, it includes a target group—the intended beneficiaries of the social innovation itself. Third, it can involve actors not directly engaged or affected by the social innovation, who are worth considering either because they indirectly benefit (e.g. household members of the beneficiaries) or because, as non-beneficiaries, they can be considered as a control group and juxtaposed with beneficiaries to measure the social innovation impact on individuals' capabilities within that given society or community. Moreover other groups may be (unintentionally) affected negatively and, hence, may oppose the social innovation: social innovation focused on political decentralization, for example, may encounter political resistance at different levels (see chapter 10).

A full-fledged empirical account of social innovation must, therefore, consider the plurality of agents involved and their roles within the ecosystem. This process includes: paying attention to their objective living and social conditions and their relative position within the overall ecosystem; gathering the perceptions, expectations, and motivations of individuals; capturing the engagement of social innovators as well as the social inclusion or exclusion of the key beneficiaries.

Along with considering a plurality of potential actors, the ESGM conceptual framework also requires the investigation of complex social forces—cognitive frames, actor networks, and institutions (Beckert 2010). These are typically macro-level or meso-level variables that may vary across social innovation contexts. The methodological strategy described below aimed to encompass such factors, connecting to and complying with or opposing existing rules, preferably without reducing the complexity these elements enshrine within each context.

Inspired by the capabilities approach, people's voices and their agency and empowerment are a major dimension of the ESGM. Therefore, the necessity to identify methods of investigation that can give voice to the individuals engaged in social innovation initiatives is both intrinsically and instrumentally important in order to measure people's active participation in social innovation processes. It is relevant for the beneficiaries, who are often at the margins of the public debates or do not have enough capacity or the competences to have their voices heard. It is also important for the social innovators to have a better understanding of beneficiaries' motivations and expectations regarding the social innovation promoted. These issues underpinned the approach of integrating quantitative information aimed at describing individual living conditions with interviews designed to hear social innovators' voices.[9]

[9] Social innovators often assume the role of 'spokespersons' that defend the rights and interests of marginalized individuals (Schmitz 2015).

Context Matters

In the research framework developed here, the key role played by social innovation initiatives is located at multiple levels or contexts. It originates at the micro-level, where single individuals, households, and enterprises live, relate, and interact with each other. It is affected by the meso-level that is the context where groups such as neighbourhoods, local communities, or grass-root organizations operate and where local administrations, municipal or regional, determine or affect the formal and informal socio-economic settings within which individuals are embedded. A key role is also played by the macro-level (national or global), where the general conditions and societal 'rules of the game' are institutionalized. These micro-, meso-, macro-levels represent a continuum of analysis: each of them can play an important role in promoting or constraining social innovation initiatives through different social forces that are active and activated. To analyse the heterogeneity of these contexts requires gathering a plurality of information at each level in order to identify which pre-conditions, if any, exist that can foster social innovation or which constraints can inhibit such initiatives. Of particular analytic interest for the ESGM are the linkages between the micro- and the meso-levels, where social networks and cognitive frames take shape and exert their influence back on individual behaviours and choices.

The methodological design pursued here has led to a hierarchical—or nested—data collection approach in which each individual, whether belonging to the treatment or the control group, is attributable to a specific context in which the social innovation is being implemented.

A Mixed-Method Approach

The interdisciplinary approach characterizing our research, the articulation and complexity of the theoretical model developed, the specificity of the case studies chosen, and the heterogeneity of contexts where they took place, did not allow us to make use of pre-existing secondary data nor to replicate consolidated statistical or econometric strategies applied in economics nor to rely on purely qualitative methodologies. Therefore, a new combination of quantitative and qualitative methods (and integrated data collection) was needed in order to reflect the richness of the ESGM framework, to capture the context-dependent dimensions of social innovation, and to give the people involved in the process as much voice as possible.

According to Bulsara (2015):

> Mixed methods research is a methodology for conducting research that involves collecting, analysing, and integrating (or mixing) quantitative and qualitative research (and data) in a single study or a longitudinal program of inquiry. The

> purpose of this form of research is that both qualitative and quantitative research, in combination, provide a better understanding of a research problem or issue than either research approach alone. (cf. Tashakkori and Teddlie 2003)

While quantitative methods generate data that can be easily aggregated and analysed in order to describe and predict relationships, qualitative research can help us to investigate and explain those relationships and the contextual differences that can determine them. There are several good reasons for using a mixed-methods approach. First, it triangulates data to improve validity; second, it allows us to address the research questions from different perspectives; third, it reduces the risk of pre-existing assumptions associated with a chosen method.

Different ways of combining quantitative and qualitative methods have been suggested in the literature (Carvalho and White 1997; Tashakkori and Teddlie 2003), which can involve either concurrent or sequential use of these two classes of methods. They include, among others, instrument design, triangulation design, data transformation design, and explanatory models (see Bulsara 2015).

The method adopted in our empirical approach is largely inspired by the instrument design method (Bulsara 2015), where qualitative methods—based on focus groups and interviews—are applied before moving on to the quantitative design, piloting, and testing phase. In a first explorative phase, a series of interviews with the social innovators enables a deeper understanding of the social innovation process, a *thick description* of it (Geertz 1973), and the identification of the conditions under which such a process is happening. A subsequent step, based on a questionnaire addressing the treatment group (i.e. the beneficiaries) and the control group (i.e. individuals in similar situations and with similar traits that were not beneficiaries of the social innovation), helps to get a broader and statistically more significant picture of what mechanisms are behind the phenomenon of social innovation. Figure 4.1 summarizes the steps composing the mixed-methods strategy adopted here in terms of primary-data collection.

All data were—from the start—conceived as being nested: each beneficiary belongs to a particular social innovation *context*. Interviews with social innovators provided information on the emergence and contextual difficulties, challenges and types of support experienced, allowing a better understanding of:

- The goals pursued by the specific social innovation
- The implementation processes chosen
- The drivers of the marginalization that the social innovation was trying to address
- The mechanisms through which network formation was being mediated
- The institutions that played a role for the activation, implementation and success of the social innovation process
- The cognitive frames that the social innovators defended and promoted, often in juxtaposition to ways of thinking they seek to overcome or substitute.

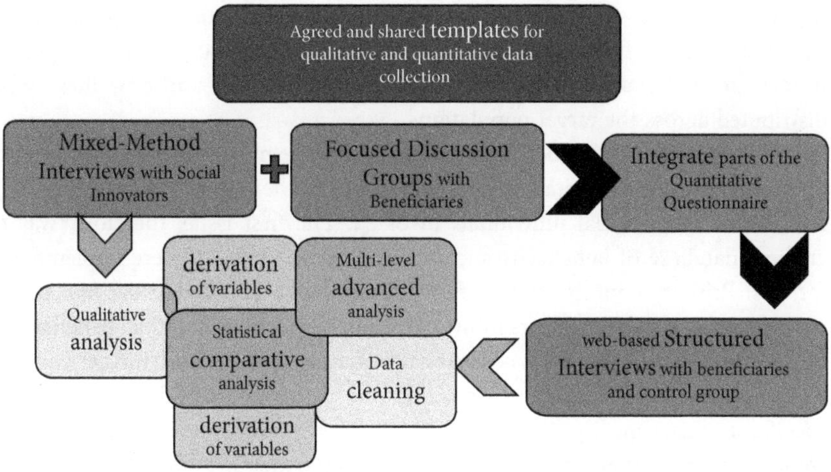

4.1 Research design for primary-data collection mixing qualitative and quantitative approaches

Source: Elaboration by the authors.

The collection of information from social innovators was implemented through the use of two different tools: semi-structured interviews that served as guidelines to gather specific information on the social innovation context; a 'pre-qualitative questionnaire', comprising several pre-determined standard questions about the social innovation organization that was sent to the interviewees beforehand in order to reduce interview duration.[10]

For the selection of social innovation contexts—namely, the single local experiences of the investigated social innovation within each country—a stratified sampling model was constructed. First, all potential social innovation contexts (defined at the municipality level) were listed for each country and categorized according to their degree of vulnerability,[11] identified in terms of high vulnerability (highest quartile), medium vulnerability (two middle quartiles), and lowest vulnerability (lowest quartile).[12] Subsequently, ten social innovation contexts for each vulnerability group were randomly chosen, providing roughly thirty comparable social innovation experiences for each country case.

Following on from this, more detailed and more structured questions were developed in a questionnaire submitted to beneficiaries and their respective control groups. The goal of such an approach was a 'cascade' effect, through which it was possible to verify the rich data gathered from social innovators within a

[10] In total, ninety-three semi-structured interviews and their corresponding pre-qualitative questionnaire with social innovators were implemented in three different countries.

[11] A composite index was constructed as a harmonic mean of three indicators: the at-risk-of-poverty rate (NUTS2 level), the employment rate (NUTS3 level), and the GDP (NUTS3 level). Indicators came from Eurostat databases for at-risk-of-poverty rate and GDP and from national sources for employment rate information.

[12] Quartiles refer to national distributions of contexts.

wider-ranging data collection. The aim was to provide a statistical representativeness that allowed for a better understanding of the heterogeneity of cognitive frames, perceptions of institutions, and actual behaviours and how these were distributed across the target populations.

With phenomena like social innovation, one of the most important obstacles to overcome during quantitative data collection is the missing availability of a reliable list of potential individuals involved. The first issue, therefore, was to create a database of beneficiaries' contacts. Several strategies were implemented for this. Primary contacts to beneficiaries were collected during the first phase, meaning that social innovators informed us about actual or potential beneficiaries of their own social innovation context whenever possible. Second, further contacts to beneficiaries and the control groups were gathered by additional, country-specific strategies mostly via networking with relevant associations that facilitated contact with potential interviewees. For the sample identification of beneficiaries, the contacts provided by social innovators were used in order to identify beneficiaries in the randomly selected contexts. Where the amount of contacts was insufficient, a step-wise inclusion of other beneficiaries—also from other contexts—was implemented in order to increase the survey sample size.

Measuring the Impact of Social Innovation

Apart from effectively reaching the niche populations of social innovation processes, a second methodological challenge concerns the assessment of the potential impact of the social innovation (see chapter 15). In order to address this, our research design included data collection that explicitly distinguished actual beneficiaries from potential ones (as a 'control group'). The latter were similar to the focus beneficiaries in terms of a series of characteristics, but had not participated in the social innovation at the time of interview. Within our primary-data collection, attempts to measure impacts concentrated on what could be isolated as effects solely on beneficiaries.

To facilitate the evaluation of social impact, the data collection strategy among beneficiaries also made use of focus groups.[13] For each country case, beneficiaries were engaged via one qualitative tool (a focus group), and one quantitative (a survey). The focus groups gathered between six and ten beneficiaries of the country-specific type of social innovation. The aim of the discussion was to identify possible ways in which exposure to the social innovation process affected

[13] Specifically, the technique used is called the 'brainstorming technique' (Bezzi and Baldini 2006); this is a group interview aimed at producing knowledge by using a bottom-up approach in which the knowledge is co-constructed in a group discussion directly with interviewees. This technique is usually employed for bottom-up definitions of indicators for assessing a specific process or outcome. For reasons of simplicity, here it is described as 'focus groups' and not 'brainstorming' (for further information, see Chiappero-Martinetti et al. 2017).

their autonomy (Deci 1971)—in line with the capabilities approach. The focus group began by exploring the six power dimensions enshrined in the ESGM with which social innovation processes can potentially deploy empowerment effects (see Heiskala 2015). The focus group then verified whether these dimensions were significant for beneficiaries in their definition of autonomy and what their pragmatic impacts were within the different cases. Focus groups invited beneficiaries to concentrate on actual benefits they had experienced from participating in the social innovation. Suggestions were gathered in the first phase of the discussion and then—with the help of a moderator—subsequently attributed to the six power dimensions. The practical everyday aspects of life mentioned by the beneficiaries constituted the main source for specifying the self-assessment questions that measured the perceived autonomy of all beneficiaries subsequently involved in the survey stage.

The second step involved a questionnaire implemented via an online platform that combined a standardized core set of questions with others adapted to the case-specificities based on information gathered in the first phase of qualitative interviews. Where the online tool was deemed inadequate to capture the entire population of beneficiaries (e.g. due to insufficient ICT capacity) or where response rates were low due to other reasons, additional data collection strategies were used. In some cases, a paper version of the questionnaire was sent out by post (in Germany and Italy, for example) or additional call-ups via phone (Italy) increased the total number of completed surveys.

Overall, it has to be acknowledged that this mixed methodological strategy was very demanding, expensive, and challenging with high transaction costs. Nonetheless, the mixed-method approach adopted here seemed to be able to address the empirical needs of the ESGM. Qualitative methods proved to be adequate for identifying the relevant context- and time-specific social forces at play in each example, as well as the features of the social innovation process. Our quantitative methods were appropriate for the statistically significant collection of the subjective perceptions of beneficiaries. Throughout the process, attempts were focused on validating the qualitative data by means of partial re-categorization and combination with quantitative results. In many cases, elements gathered during the qualitative phases of the data collection provided guidance for the precise formulation of questions inserted in the quantitative (survey) phase. None of these efforts alone could address in a satisfying manner the methodological requirements of the ESGM, but combined as a mixed-method they yielded some interesting findings (see chapter 10).

Conclusion

The two empirical approaches for studying social innovation described here are clearly different, yet both represent effective methods of applying the ESGM to concrete cases in which social innovation plays a role in reducing marginalization. In these concluding remarks—based on our methodological work—some critical reflections on the usefulness of the ESGM are outlined.

During the development of the long-term case studies, it became clear that the ESGM could not explain how and why change happened from one Social Grid to another. As a result, in an additional step, a multi-level perspective (MLP) was used as a further tool of analysis.[14] The MLP offers a 'middle-range framework for analysing socio-technical transitions to sustainability' (Geels 2011: 24). The MLP helps to show that different societal levels are important when a social innovation moves from a *niche* to an institutionalized *regime*. This model suggests that Social Grids are linked with one another and exist at all levels of the MLP: landscape (the general societal context—such as in the mid-nineteenth century); regime (the context of, say, a freshwater supply); niche (new ideas by committed actors on how to establish or improve, say, a freshwater supply). Our research also confirmed that action at all levels (micro-, meso-, macro- or landscape, regime, niche) had to be considered in the long-term analysis of social innovations.

The applied methodology building upon approaches from (social) innovation studies, SCOT and historical methods proved to be apt in both grasping the historical perspective and in offering generalizable insights. It went beyond the analysis of single projects and, because of its long-time perspective, allowed the study of changes, displacements, or negative results.

Historical analysis shows clearly that social innovation has always happened. We find social innovators too, though they have different personae. Some of them act as philanthropists, realizing pilot projects funded by their personal wealth. Others act as political reformers, creating support for new ideas and legislation. Still others act as revolutionaries or, less dramatically, as leaders of social movements, operating at the fringes of legality. Finally, we can identify a group of people that look like technical or academic experts who effectively promote new ideas and methods that in the end bring dramatic changes.

Thus, we can identify key actors, but for their plans to succeed other additional factors often need to come together—for example, coalitions of sometimes differing interests that lead to new waves of innovation. Moreover, it is often the case that such coalitions can best realize their ambitions for systemic change when there is a window of opportunity such as an external shock: economic crises; wider socio-structural or political upheaval; wars and so on. Often radical social innovation succeeds best and fastest when the status quo loses its legitimacy with a majority of people. Thus, genuinely systemic social innovation is not something that can be realized easily. Social innovators need the will and ability to coalesce with others. They need flexibility of thought and a pragmatic attitude to

[14] For further examples of the use of the MLP for the analysis of social innovations, see Thümler (2014) and Giesecke (2016).

sometimes only partial implement their ambitions. In these regards, our findings fit nicely with Westley et al. (2017).

In the primary-data collection of currently ongoing cases, several difficulties were met (see further chapter 10). Particular difficulties were encountered in constructing an appropriate sample: the identification of the beneficiaries of social innovation is not always obvious as many initiatives maintain an informal nature or simply do not keep exact records of the people involved. This makes it challenging to adopt an experimental design in which a neat boundary can be drawn between the treatment and control groups. While control groups were constructed for each case, it remains difficult to assess to what degree they were really comparable, and to what extent spill-over effects between beneficiaries and control groups were fully excluded.

Despite the difficulties encountered, the approach adopted here proved capable of comparing different social innovations implemented in different contexts. Moreover, a focus on agency proved to be a promising methodological perspective to evaluate and compare the impact of social innovations. The capabilities approach also offered an important conceptual model with which to empirically investigate social innovation and its transformative effects on individuals in society. An open issue remains the clarification of self-selection sample bias: do more engaged and active people self-select into participating in a social innovation? Such potential bias is reflected in the operational difficulty to construct reliable control groups and remains a challenge for future empirical investigation of social innovation and its impact (see chapter 15). Another constraint was revealed by our findings obtained (see further in chapter 10). Participants in social innovation reported mainly intangible benefits in terms of new knowledge and the opportunity to develop and reinforce social relations (they also acknowledged their own perceptions of improved agency). These elements link closely to key elements of the Social Grid and represent a mechanism with which marginalized individuals may acquire more advantageous positions in society (see chapter 3). They may also gradually modify key social structures within the Social Grid—at the interplay of institutions, cognitive frames, and social networks—that drive their marginalization. The data collection was able to capture some of the effects of social innovation on these cognitive frames and networks, though more detailed analysis remains necessary. The use of specific power dimensions (see chapter 2) via which social innovation can promote the agency of participants represents an important finding derived from our primary-data collection, in as much as it reflects the multidimensional nature of human capabilities and helps identify and specify the aspects that should be considered when gathering information on subjective perceptions. Despite the various limitations noted in this chapter, our innovative methodologies allowed us to make empirical observations concerning the systemic nature of marginalization and how social innovation may be able to address it that were both robust and novel.

References

Anheier, H. K., G. Krlev, C. Behrendt, and G. Mildenberger. 2017. 'Findings: The Who, What and How of Social Innovation'. For 'Impact of the Third Sector as Social Innovation' (ITSSOIN). Brussels: European Commission, DG Research.

Ayob, N., S. Teasdale, and K. Fagan. 2016. 'How Social Innovation 'Came to Be': Tracing the Evolution of a Contested Concept'. *Journal of Social Policy* 45(4): 635–53.

Beckert, J. 2010. 'How Do Fields Change? The Interrelations of Institutions, Networks, and Cognition in the Dynamics of Markets'. *Organization Studies* 31(5): 605–27.

Bezzi, C., and I. Baldini. 2006. *Il brainstorming. Pratica e teoria*. Milano: Franco Angeli Editore.

Bijker, W. E. 1995. *Of Bicycles, Bakelites, and Bulbs: Towards a Theory of Sociotechnical Change*. Cambridge, MA: MIT Press.

Bijker, W. E., T. P. Hughes, and T. J. Pinch (eds). 1987. *The Social Construction of Technological Systems: New Directions in the Sociology and History of Technology*. Cambridge, MA: MIT Press.

Bijker, W. E., and J. Law (eds). 1992. *Shaping Technology—Building Society: Studies in Sociotechnical Change*. Cambridge, MA: MIT Press.

Blundel, R. K., and F. Lyon. 2015. 'Towards a "Long View": Historical Perspectives on the Scaling and Replication of Social Ventures'. *Journal of Social Entrepreneurship* 6(1): 80–102.

Bruns, E., J. Köppel, D. Ohlhorst, and S. Schön (eds). 2008. *Die Innovationsbiographie der Windenergie. Absichten und Wirkungen von Steuerungsimpulsen*. Projekt im Schwerpunkt 'Innovationsprozesse in Wirtschaft und Gesellschaft' der Volkswagen-Stiftung, Hannover: Lit.

Bulsara, C. 2015. 'Using a Mixed Methods Approach to Enhance and Validate your Research'. Notre Dame University.

Bund, E., D.-K. Hubrich, B. Schmitz, G. Mildenberger, and G. Krlev. 2013a. 'Blueprint of Social Innovation Metrics: Contributions to an Understanding of the Opportunities and Challenges of Social Innovation Measurement'. For 'The Theoretical, Empirical and Policy Foundations for Building Social Innovation in Europe' (TEPSIE). Brussels: European Commission, DG Research.

Bund, E., D.-K. Hubrich, B. Schmitz, G. Mildenberger, and G. Krlev. 2013b. 'Report on Innovation Metrics: Capturing Theoretical, Conceptual and Operational Insights for the Measurement of Social Innovation'. For 'The Theoretical, Empirical and Policy Foundations for Building Social Innovation in Europe' (TEPSIE). Brussels: European Commission, DG Research.

Butzin, A., D. Rehfeld, and B. Widmaier (eds). 2012. *Innovationsbiographien. Räumliche und sektorale Dynamik*, Baden-Baden: Nomos-Verlag.

Carvalho, S., and H. White. 1997. 'Combining the Quantitative and Qualitative Approaches to Poverty Measurement and Analysis: The Practice and the Potential'. World Bank Technical Paper No. WTP 366. Washington, DC: World Bank.

Chiappero-Martinetti, E., N. v. Jacobi, L. Maestripieri, R. Ziegler, M. van der Linden, and C. P. van Beers. 2017. 'Comparison of Four Cases of Social Innovation in Europe: A Statistical Report'. CrESSI Working Paper No. 34. Brussels: European Commission.

Davies, A. 2014. 'Spreading Social Innovations: A Case Study Report'. For 'The Theoretical, Empirical and Policy Foundations for Building Social Innovation in Europe' (TEPSIE). Brussels: European Commission, DG Research.

Davies, A., and J. Simon. 2013. 'Growing Social Innovation: A Literature Review'. For 'The Theoretical, Empirical and Policy Foundations for Building Social Innovation in Europe' (TEPSIE). Brussels: European Commission, DG Research.

Deci, E. L. 1971. 'Effects of Externally Mediated Rewards on Intrinsic Motivation'. *Personality and Social Psychology* 18(1): 105–15.

Degele, N. 2002. *Einführung in die Techniksoziologie*. München: Fink.

Domanski, D., and C. Kaletka (eds). 2017. 'Exploring the Research Landscape of Social Innovation'. For Social Innovation Community (SIC). Dortmund: TU Dortmund University, Sozialforschungsstelle.

Geels, F. W. 2011. 'The Multi-Level Perspective on Sustainability Transitions: Responses to Seven Criticisms'. *Environmental Innovation and Societal Transitions* 1(1): 24–40.

Geertz, C. 1973. *The Interpretation of Cultures: Selected Essays*. New York: Basic Books.

Giesecke, S. 2016. 'Community Housing in the City of Vienna––100 Years of Social Transformation: A Case Study for the Social Grid Approach'. In 'Report on Relevant Actors in Historic Examples and an Empirically Driven Typology on Types of Social Innovation'. For 'Creating Economic Space for Social Innovation' (CrESSI), edited by T. Scheuerle, G.-C. Schimpf, G. Glänzel, and G. Mildenberger, pp. 225–99. Brussels: European Commission.

Gunderson, L. H., and C. S. Holling (eds). 2002. *Panarchy: Understanding Transformations in Human and Natural Systems*. Washington, DC: Island Press.

Hamdouch, A. 2013. 'Introduction: "Reality" as a Guide for SI Research Methods?'. In *The International Handbook on Social Innovation: Collective Action, Social Learning and Transdisciplinary Research*, edited by F. Moulaert, D. MacCallum, A. Mehmood, and A. Hamdouch, pp. 259–63. Cheltenham: Edward Elgar.

Havas, A. 2016. 'Recent Economic Theorising on Innovation: Lessons for Analysing Social Innovation'. For 'Creating Economic Space for Social Innovation' (CrESSI). CrESSI Working Paper No. 27. Brussels: European Commission, DG Research.

Haxeltine, A., F. Avelino, B. Pel, A. Dumitru, R. Kemp, N. Longhurst, J. Chilvers, and J. M. Wittmayer. 2016. 'A Framework for Transformative Social Innovation'. TRANSIT Working Paper No. 5. http://www.transitsocialinnovation.eu/resource-hub/a-framework-for-transformative-social-innovation-transit-working-paper-5, accessed 19 Dec 2017.

Heiskala, R. 2015. 'Relating Mann's Conception to CrESSI'. In 'Report on Institutions, Social Innovation and System Dynamics from the Perspective of the

Marginalised'. CrESSI Working Paper No. 9. Brussels: European Commission, DG Research.

Heßler, M. 2001. 'Mrs. Modern Woman'. *Zur Sozial- und Kulturgeschichte der Haushaltstechnisierung* (Campus Forschung, 827). Frankfurt: Campus.

Howaldt, J., A. Butzin, D. Domanski, and C. Kaletka. 2014. 'Theoretical Approaches to Social Innovation: A Critical Literature Review'. For 'Social Innovation: Driving Force of Social Change' (SI-DRIVE). Dortmund: Sozialforschungsstelle.

Howaldt, J., C. Kaletka, A. Schröder, D. Rehfeld, and J. Terstriep. 2016. 'Mapping the World of Social Innovation: Key Results of a Comparative Analysis of 1.005 Social Innovation Initiatives at a Glance' (SI-DRIVE). Brussels: European Commission, DG Research.

Huysentruyt, M., and U. Stephan. 2017. 'European Policy Brief: Social Enterprises, an Economic Force for Building More Inclusive Societies?: Evidence from the SEFORIS Study'. Brussels: European Commission, DG Research.

Innobasque and Sinnergiak Social Innovation. 2013. 'Resindex. Regional Social Innovation Index: A Regional Index to Measure Social Innovation'. Bilbao: Basque Innovation Agency.

Kline, R., and T. J. Pinch. 1999. 'The Social Construction of Technology'. In *The Social Shaping of Technology*, edited by D. A. MacKenzie and J. Wajcman, pp. 113–15. Buckingham: Open University Press.

Krlev, G., E. Bund, and G. Mildenberger. 2014. 'Measuring What Matters: Indicators of Social Innovativeness on the National Level'. *Information Systems Management* 31(3): 200–24.

Kuhn, T. S. 1996. *The Structure of Scientific Revolutions*, 3rd edition. Chicago, IL: University of Chicago Press.

Lodemann, J., and R. Ziegler. 2014. 'How Can Resilience Theory Inform Social Innovation for the Marginalized?' In 'Report on Institutions, Social Innovation and System Dynamics from the Perspective of the Marginalised'. CrESSI Working Paper No. 6. Brussels: European Commission, DG Research.

McGowan, K., and F. Westley. 2015. 'At the Root of Change: The History of Social Innovation'. In *New Frontiers in Social Innovation Research*, edited by A. Nicholls, J. Simon, and M. Gabriel, pp. 52–68. Basingstoke: Palgrave Macmillan.

Millard, J., and G. Carpenter. 2014. 'Digital Technology in Social Innovation: A Synopsis'. For 'The Theoretical, Empirical and Policy Foundations for Building Social Innovation in Europe' (TEPSIE). http://tepsie.eu/images/documents/synopsisdigitaltechnologyinsocialinnovation.pdf, accessed 11 Jul 2017.

Moulaert, F., D. MacCallum, A. Mehmood, and A. Hamdouch (eds). 2013. *The International Handbook on Social Innovation: Collective Action, Social Learning and Transdisciplinary Research*. Cheltenham: Edward Elgar.

Moulaert, F., A. Mehmood, D. MacCallum, and B. Leubolt. 2017. 'Social Innovation as a Trigger for Transformations: The Role of Research'. Brussels: European Commission, DG Research and Innovation.

Mulgan, G., S. Tucker, R. Ali, and B. Sanders. 2007. 'Social Innovation: What It Is, Why It Matters and How It Can Be Accelerated'. Working Paper, Oxford: Saïd Business School.

Murray, R., J. Caulier-Crice, and G. Mulgan. 2010. *The Open Book of Social Innovation.* Social Innovator Series: Ways to Design, Develop and Grow Social Innovation. http://youngfoundation.org/wp-content/uploads/2012/10/The-Open-Book-of-Social-Innovationg.pdf.

Nicholls, A., and R. Ziegler. 2015. 'An Extended Social Grid Model for the Study of Marginalization Processes and Social Innovation'. In 'Report on Institutions, Social Innovation and System Dynamics from the Perspective of the Marginalised'. CrESSI Working Paper No. 2. Brussels: European Commission, DG Research.

Pel, B. et al. 2017. The Critical Turning Points Database: Concept, Methodology and Dataset of an International Transfomative Social Innovation Comparison'. TRANSIT Working Paper No. 10. Brussels: European Commission, DG Research.

Pelka, B., and J. Terstriep. 2016. 'Mapping Social Innovation Maps: The State of Research Practice across Europe'. *European Public and Social Innovation Review* 1(1): 3–16.

Rehfeld, D., J. Terstriep, J. Welschhoff, and S. Alijani. 2015. 'Comparative Report on Social Innovation Framework'. Brussels: European Commission, DG Research.

Robinson, J. (ed.). 2012. 'Combating Inequalities through Innovative Social Practices of and for Young People in Cities across Europe' (CITISPYCE). Working Paper No. 8. Brussels: European Commission, DG Research. http://www.citispyce.eu/sites/default/files/CITISPYCE%20Final%20Report%20Part%20I%2022%20Feb16%20JR%20proofed.pdf, accessed 12 Dec 2017.

Rüede, D., and K. Lurtz. 2012. 'Mapping the Various Meanings of Social Innovation: Towards a Differentiated understanding of an Emerging Concept'. Research Paper Series, 12-03. Oestrich-Winkel: EBS Business School.

Scheuerle, T., G.-C. Schimpf, G. Glänzel, and G. Mildenberger (eds). 2016. 'Report on Relevant Actors in Historic Examples and an Empirically Driven Typology on Types of Social Innovation'.. CrESSI Working Paper No. 29. Brussels: European Commission, DG Research.

Schimpf, G.-C. (ed.). 2017. 'Comparative Report on Historic Examples and Similar Recent Social Innovations in an Early Stage'. CrESSI Working Paper No. 35. Brussels: European Commission, DG Research.

Schmitz, B. 2015. 'Social Entrepreneurship, Social Innovation, and Social Mission Organizations: Toward a Conceptualization'. In *Cases in Innovative Nonprofits: Organizations That Make a Difference*, edited by R. A. Cnaan and D. Vinokur-Kaplan, pp. 17–42. Los Angeles, CA: Sage.

Tashakkori, A., and C. Teddlie. 2003. *Handbook of Mixed Methods in Social and Behavioral Research.* Thousand Oaks, CA: Sage.

Terstriep, J. (ed.). 2016. 'Boosting SI's Social and Economic Impact: From Roots to Results'. Gelsenkirchen: Institut Arbeit und Technik. http://www.simpact-project.eu/publications/overview.htm, accessed 7 Feb 2017.

Terstriep, J., M. Kleverbeck, A. Deserti, and F. Rizzo. 2015. 'Comparative Report on Social Innovation across Europe'. Brussels: European Commission.

The Young Foundation. 2012. 'Social Innovation Overview'. Brussels: E0075ropean Commission, DG Research.

Thümler, E. 2014. 'Islands of Success Revisited: Which Role for Philanthropy?' In *Philanthropy and Education: Strategies for Impact*, edited by H. K. Anheier, E. Thümler, N. Bögelein, and A. Beller, pp. 236–45. New York: Palgrave Macmillan.

Van de Ven, A. H., D. E. Polley, R. Garud, and S. Venkataraman. 2008. *The Innovation Journey*. New York: Oxford University Press.

Walker, B., C. S. Holling, S. R. Carpenter, and A. Kinzig. 2004. 'Resilience, Adaptability and Transformability in Social–Ecological Systems'. *Ecology and Society* 8(2): 5–13.

Westley, F. 2008. 'The Social Innovation Dynamic'. University of Waterloo, Canada. http://sig.uwaterloo.ca/highlight/the-social-innovation-dynamic.

Westley, F. 2013. 'Social Innovation and Resilience: How One Enhances the Other'. *Stanford Social Innovation Review* (Summer): 6–8.

Westley, F., K. McGowan, and O. Tjörnbo (eds). 2017. *The Evolution of Social Innovation: Building Resilience through Transitions*. Cheltenham: Edward Elgar.

Westley, F., B. Zimmermann, and M. Q. Patton. 2007. *Getting to Maybe: How the World Is Changed*. Toronto: Vintage Canada.

Wintjes, R., N. Es-Sadki, R. Glott, and A. Notten. 2016. 'Improved Measurement of the Economics of Social Innovation'. Simpact Project Report No. D5.1. Gelsenkirchen: Institute for Work and Technology/University of Applied Science Gelsenkirchen. http://www.simpact-project.eu/publications/reports/SIMPACT_D51.pdf, accessed 11 Jul 2017.

Wittmayer, J. M., B. Pel, T. Bauler, and F. Avelino. 2017. 'Editorial Synthesis: Methodological Challenges in Social Innovation Research'. *European Public and Social Innovation Review* 2(1): 1–16.

Yin, R. K. 2003. *Case Study Research: Design and Method*, 3rd edition. Los Angeles, CA: Sage.

PART II
DATA: EXPLORING THE MODEL

5

Trajectories of Social Innovation

Housing for All?

Gudrun-Christine Schimpf, Georg Mildenberger, Susanne Giesecke, and Attila Havas

Introduction

Social housing aims to supply decent shelter for every marginalized citizen, irrespective of her personal resources. This innovation originated in the nineteenth century as a response to the strong population growth and increased migration that posed severe problems for the infrastructure of European cities. During this period, Europe's industrialized centres became very overpopulated and there was insufficient housing stock to accommodate this challenge. As a consequence, several serious problems arose. Quickly and cheaply built houses offering poor living standards were rented out at very high prices. The working population could only afford their rent by subletting rooms, individual beds, or even time slots in beds (creating 'bed lodgers'). This not only deprived the working class of most of their meagre wages, but also contributed to the spread of chronic infections and a dramatic increase in premature deaths—especially among children. Furthermore, such slum housing was perceived as having a bad influence on the overall morals over a town by spreading bad habits. Informal and illegal settlements sprung up widely, ignoring all building regulations.

This situation was common in many European countries and cities in the nineteenth century. As a result, various models evolved in order to tackle the housing crisis. However, there was no widely accepted solution to this problem: each country, region, or individual city developed their own approach. Many different models were developed, each with distinct features, including: what type of buildings was thought best; what standards for buildings were established; which groups of the population were entitled or not entitled to benefit from social housing; who owned these buildings; how the housing was financed; who was thought to be the best actor to provide and run these houses. Despite these differences, the solutions shared enough common traits to make it possible to discern certain typologies of social housing. Several types of social housing models emerged in the more-than-one-hundred-year timespan covered by this case study. The perceptions and expected problem-solving capacities related to social housing

Gudrun-Christine Schimpf, Georg Mildenberger, Susanne Giesecke, and Attila Havas,
Trajectories of Social Innovation: Housing for All? In: *Creating Economic Space for Social Innovation.*
Edited by: Alex Nicholls and Rafael Ziegler, Oxford University Press (2019). © Oxford University Press.
DOI: 10.1093/oso/9780198830511.003.0005

differed over time, as did the target groups and the guiding principles connected to this specific social innovation.

This chapter reflects on these models and then gives a brief overview of the history of social housing in Europe and the motives behind it.[1,2] This section is followed by a digression dedicated to the special case of the city of Vienna. Idiosyncrasies notwithstanding, this analysis reflects and illustrates well the wider developments across Europe. The chapter then turns to the diffusion of social housing in Europe, focusing on the important role of coalitions and social movements. This part also relates the analysis to the Extended Social Grid Model (ESGM) introduced in chapter 1. The concluding section highlights the main lessons learnt from our historical analysis.

Social Housing in Europe: Historical Phases

While social housing was perceived in a variety of ways across EU countries, there are some common elements:

- A *social mission* focused on public welfare
- An *objective* to increase the supply of affordable housing by constructing, managing, or purchasing social housing
- *Target groups* defined in terms of socio-economic status and/or the presence of vulnerability (IZA—Institute for the Study of Labor 2013: 9).

However, to achieve even this elementary consensus has required some time. The development of social housing from the mid-nineteenth century until today was by no means linear. A variety of factors and incidents influenced this evolutionary process. Certain elements of path dependence can be identified, but the most important developments often represented a complete break from historical tradition (Lévy-Vroelant et al. 2008). New developments were not necessarily superior to the previous ones and changes were often driven by political decisions (Adam 2004). The literature distinguishes five historical phases of social housing,[3] at least for countries with a capitalism that was undisturbed by any period of a

[1] We would like to thank Amelia Pope. The chapter has gained a lot by her editing and suggestions. Parts of this chapter were presented earlier at several workshops and conferences. We considered the valuable feedback we received there and incorporated the inputs where possible. The research described in this chapter was conducted collaboratively with Thomas Scheuerle and Gunnar Glänzel. Both left the research team before the end of the project. Yet, our data collection and analysis approaches gained much from their contributions.

[2] The relevance of historical case studies is explained and justified in chapter 4, together with the other main research methods chosen by the CrESSI project.

[3] Some authors only mention four phases (e.g. Harloe 1995)—they do not view the beginning stage as a distinct phase.

centrally planned economy—such as Austria, Britain, Denmark, France, (the former West) Germany, and the Netherlands. Delayed industrialization (Finland)[4] or communist/central planning (present in most Eastern European countries until 1990)[5] caused the major deviations from these key phases. A new phase of social housing might be dawning in more recent times, resulting from the financial and economic crisis of 2008–9 and the structural changes of capitalist societies in the Post-Fordist era. This has also being accelerated by the migration crisis in Europe.

The main phases of social housing (building on Lévy-Vroelant et al. 2008) are as follows:

- Early industrialization and the beginning of the 'social question' (early to the second half of the nineteenth century)
- The origins of social housing shaped by utopian thinking, the rise of philanthropy, and increased industrialization (mid-nineteenth century to the beginning of the First World War)
- A period of municipal commitment to social housing (the end of the First World War to the Great Depression in 1929)
- The Great Depression's effects on social housing (1929 until the Second World War)
- Mainstreaming social housing (post the Second World War until the 1970s)
- Individualization and social fragmentation (mid-1970s until 2008)
- Global financial crisis and migration crisis (2008 onwards).

A detailed account of these periods will not be given here. However, the ESGM is applied to consider these development phases and to analyse the discourses (*cognitive frames*), normative changes (*institutions*), and main actors (*social networks*) that fostered or inhibited the development of social housing in the EU across time. Changes in power relations and access to power—as defined in the ESGM—are particularly highlighted. A tentative evaluation of the micro-level gains and losses over the periods is offered by looking at relevant changes in beneficiaries' capabilities. The aim here is to provide a sketch of these phases, enriched by observations from different regions and times.[6]

[4] In the case of Finland, there was delayed migration, and urbanization did not begin until the 1960s. Therefore, until the 1950s social housing concerned both rural and urban populations. The so-called *agrarian question*—a conflict between tenant farmers and landowners who wanted to increase productivity and, therefore, tried to change rent agreements—became a major political issue in Finland at the turn of the twentieth century (Peltonen 1992).

[5] The Eastern European Housing Model (Hegedüs and Tosics 1996) did not correspond at all to Western social housing models (Scheuerle et al. 2016b: 23).

[6] If the reader is interested in more material and richer descriptions, further material can be found in Scheuerle et al. (2016a).

The Problem Situation: Early Industrialization: The Beginning of the 'Social Question'

The beginning of the Industrial Revolution was marked by the dramatic changes that came with the development of early modern capitalism. It unleashed many forces in society. New knowledge and, particularly, scientific knowledge developed incredibly fast in a short time. A new stratum of society emerged—the rising bourgeoisie—representing a significant wave of social mobility. The bourgeois lifestyle emphasized status and privacy—leading to the separation of living and working spaces.

At the same time, many people migrated from the countryside into the cities where new industries were growing. The old feudal model combining working and housing—given in rural areas that depended heavily on agricultural production—ceased to exist. Furthermore, the new industrial capitalists did not feel responsible for the living conditions of their workers and existing models of urban housing failed to accommodate this agrarian migration.

Consequently, existing houses became densely populated. Inhabitants shared beds by sleeping in shifts. The market came to dominate social life and the state or municipality was marginalized. Investor landlords aimed to maximize their profits by providing very small flats with the lowest possible standards. The importance of hygiene and good sanitation was ignored. Poor housing in overcrowded dwellings resulted not only in stress and low moral standards for the tenants, but also caused diseases to spread easily. The largest group of those affected was migrants, who had no ties to the political or economic elites in the city and had very weak political representation.

The result was a politically, economically, and socially deprived labour force with few rights, no access to power, and poor living conditions. Around 1830, the term 'social question' was used to refer to the increasingly destitute situation of the emerging working class.

Phase 1: The Origins of Social Housing: Utopia, Philanthropy, and Industry

The very bad living conditions of workers and their families were soon perceived as an important societal issue to be addressed. However, it was not just an issue for the political classes. Many of the new wealthy industrialists identified the problem and sought solutions. Proactive bourgeois individuals took the initiative and provided houses for their workers. Some of them were industrialists who understood the necessity of providing accommodation for getting and keeping skilled employees (Viehhauser 2016: 245) (see Box 5.1).

Box 5.1: Notable industrial philanthropists

Amongst the most prominent industrialists that built settlements, even entire communities, were Jean Dollfus (1800–87; Société Mulhousienne des Cités Ouvrières, Mulhouse, France), Alfred Krupp (1812–87; company for steel production, railways, and armaments, Essen, Germany), and Jean-Baptiste André Godin (1817–88; Familistère, Guise, France). Alfred Krupp, for example, built and rented small houses in his workers' settlements to (non-unionized) workers. The paternalistic 'care' for 'his' workers was a constant motivator for Krupp, driven by economic and social considerations (Kieß 1991; Krämer 2013: 3–11).

Others were driven by purely philanthropic motives, these included: Octavia Hill, George Peabody, and Sydney Waterlow, who started unconventional firms that were not fully profit-maximizing.[7] Some of these pioneers were (seemingly) driven by humanitarian motives, while others saw that the poor housing not only had severe consequences for the poor, but that it also risked creating social unrest. The political climate was also changing: even with strong opposition against state action, the fear of socialist thought spreading and riots endangering the establishment led to the first legislation on social housing. These institutional arrangements accepted the need for action, but favoured privately driven solutions to the housing problem. At the same time, groups of poor workers began to form cooperatives.

These first projects brought great improvements for poor people, but not for all. The so-called 'undeserving poor'[8] were excluded from most opportunities. Moreover, a widespread, 'standard' solution was still far away. The first social housing projects often combined housing provision with a strong idea of controlling the lifestyles of the tenants by 'educating' them, promoting a bourgeois family life, not admitting unionized tenants, and so on (Scheuerle et al. 2016b: 39–40). Thus, poor tenants 'paid' for their housing with their freedom of choice.

Phase 2: Municipal Commitment to Social Housing

After the First World War there was significant political change that drove a new phase of social housing in many countries. The disruption caused by the war and

[7] On this approach—called 'five per cent philanthropy'—see Scheuerle and Glänzel (2016).

[8] People in the nineteenth century made a distinction between individuals who were poor because of bad luck, such as accidents, diseases, and so on—the 'deserving' poor—and others who were poor by their own 'fault' such as bad morals, bad characters, bad habits—the 'undeserving' poor.

the need to restart the economy under conditions of peace weakened the liberal-capitalist paradigm, at least temporarily. The close interaction of the state with industry—a necessary element of corporatism in wartime economies—encouraged more co-ordinated interventions by the state. The temporary inclusion of workers in corporatist cooperation stopped soon after the war, so workers began organizing themselves. Welfare state regimes were also set up in many European countries. In some, like the United Kingdom or Germany, the right to housing was enshrined in laws or constitutions (Scheuerle et al. 2016b: 46). Yet, there was widespread scepticism about the public provision of housing. Social housing was generally seen, at best, as a temporarily necessary intervention in reaction to the war and its aftermath: for example, the French Caisse des Dépôts was obliged to give loans at interest rates below market level but refused to do so (Scheuerle et al. 2016b: 45), while the Dutch Woonscholen were started to teach people how properly to use their accommodation (Scheuerle et al. 2016b: 48).

Nevertheless, social housing became more widespread and more often funded or supported by the state or municipality. Social housing experts emerged as a distinct group and became part of organized committees. Private or civil society-driven housing companies or cooperatives emerged that were non-profit or limited dividend driven. Many of these were not content with only providing housing, they also tried to influence inhabitants' lifestyles by 'educating' them. Although more people enjoyed the benefits of social housing than in the pre-war period, solutions were still partial and restricted to members of certain groups, depending on providers' preferences. Criteria included things like faith or union membership. A universal solution was still far away.

Phase 3: The Great Depression

The Great Depression and its aftermath brought further changes. States confronted with mass unemployment and the pauperization of much of society generally accepted the need for action. But the new acceptance of responsibility bringing with it organizational changes in administration, had downsides too. Many public bureaucracies integrated social housing into an increasingly centralized welfare state and started using strict criteria for access to social housing. However, the critical situation of many public budgets also led to spending cuts on social housing and drove a more low-cost model of social housing (e.g. in Germany). Moreover, private investors in the housing market reduced their construction activities due to their own economic difficulties. Thus, a differentiation between different groups of beneficiaries emerged and publicly provided social housing became a means of last resort that many still had to use. In many states this led to social segregation and stigmatization for inhabitants of such dwellings. This 'residual' approach to social housing provided by public authorities was combined with strict housing management schemes designed to coerce normatively acceptable behaviour (e.g. locking up the house at 11 p.m. Denby 1938: 117; Harloe 1995: 169; Scheuerle et al. 2016b: 56). Moreover, in several countries—such as the Netherlands and the United Kingdom—social housing was perceived as a chance for slum clearance (Harloe 1995: 34 f., 171; Malpass 1986).

Phase 4: Mainstreaming of Social Housing

Similar changes can be observed after the Second World War, but this time the bombings and widespread destruction of infrastructure and houses were much more severe. All over Europe there was massive post-war migration. Homecoming soldiers and other displaced persons were desperately in need of housing. The 'Iron Curtain' also divided Europe and many prisoners of war wished to stay in the West. Additionally, refugees from Eastern European countries came to the West, putting more pressure on the overloaded housing stock there. It seemed quite natural, therefore, that public reconstruction programmes should include new provision of social housing for all strata of the population, not only the poorest. As a result, in the United Kingdom for example, the share of beneficiaries living in council housing grew from 21.5 per cent in 1954 to 58.9 per cent in 1976 (Scheuerle et al. 2016b: 58).

At this stage, a universalistic approach to social housing became the dominant cognitive frame: primarily seen as a public responsibility to provide the whole population with affordable housing of decent quality (IZA—Institute for the Study of Labor 2013: 6). Social housing was offered directly by public authorities, by public–private partnerships, or by means of substantial subsidies for private investors. In Germany, there were subsidies and tax cuts for individual families in the post-war era to encourage private ownership of property. Across much of Europe a new mode of housing provision was emerging.

In this period, access to decent and affordable housing for all became the prevalent cognitive frame (Scheuerle et al. 2016b: 61 f.). In some countries (e.g. the Netherlands and Italy) state subsidies aimed to stimulate the building activities of individuals and investors and earlier attempts to control tenants' lifestyles ceased. But a new segregation started. Many of the newly built social housing flats were placed in multi-storey buildings that became more and more profitable for investors with the development of construction technology. Techno-structures emerged as new social networks, including investors, construction companies, architects, and urban planners. Building with precast concrete slab—a technology developed in the 1920s—became fashionable all over Europe, allowing the construction of suburbs—where the lower strata of society was concentrated—that quickly becoming deprived areas (Harloe 1995: 367). Although the late 1960s and

1970s saw a tendency to switch from (object-related) subsidies for housing providers to (subject-related) income-based consumption subsidies, a new segregation took place thwarting the universalistic cognitive frame of the period.

During this time, the 'golden age of social housing' ended and social building activities declined. The widespread economic upturn, the increase in peoples' income and living standards seemed to diminish the need for social housing. Towards the end of this period more and more buildings marked for social housing fell out of regulation and were brought to the unregulated market or even sold to tenants or investors. Gentrification of urban areas started.

Phase 5: Individualization and Fragmentation

The 1970s brought an abrupt stop to the dream of perpetual economic growth in Europe. Economic decline combined with high inflation and growing unemployment began as a consequence of the oil crisis. But it was also an effect of structural changes in old industries that lost their markets or were under heavy pressure to cut costs and rationalize production. State budgets were under pressure and severe cuts were discussed in many parliaments. The heavily subsidized social housing sector seemed a good candidate for cuts in many states. State activity declined and so did public expenditure for social housing. Massive privatization of public housing estates was conducted, especially in the formerly centrally planned Eastern European countries after 1989 (see Box 5.2).

Tax privileges for social housing companies were cut or abolished. Important demographic changes also took place: growth in the number of small households, elderly people, and single parents happened at the same time as the market with

Box 5.2: Changes in provision

In France the output of social housing construction halved between the mid-1970s and the early 1980s. The same can be seen with regard to the annual quota for non-profit housing in Denmark between the early 1970s and 1980. In the Netherlands it was even worse: rented social housing decreased from more than 60,000 to 23,000 homes from the mid-1970s to 1979 (Scheuerle et al. 2016b: 67 f.).

In Hungary the government withdrew from the housing sector after 1990. Former municipally owned dwellings were privatized in huge numbers. Subsidies for new public and private construction were cut, the industries for building and building materials were privatized, as were public housing and the banking sector (Hegedüs 2008: 145).

double-income households grew. The latter could afford to pay higher rents, which brought momentum to the process of gentrification. A new focus on the individualism and quality of life of the middle class emerged.

Overall, however, the picture is somewhat contradictory. Despite the growing demand for housing from small households, construction activity declined, social housing flats were privatized and city centres gentrified. A new era began of public–private partnerships with well-defined roles (Scheuerle et al. 2016b: 71). Tensions, even severe conflicts, arose in some countries around squats and in derelict suburbs (e.g. in the United Kingdom) (Morgan 1984: 165; Harloe 1995: 265).

Phase 6: Economic Collapse and Migration Crisis

Today, there remains a large stock of social housing in many countries, but it is often derelict and in need of modernization. This not only means adapting floor plans, but also meeting new standards of ecological efficiency. Both put pressure on construction costs. Furthermore, new needs have also arisen. In many big cities the costs of housing have reached a level that puts even middle-class families under pressure, forcing them to move to the outskirts and commute. Cooperative solutions are re-emerging to find new arrangements.

Recent EU policies have fostered a residual approach to social housing. Broadly structured social housing policies—as in the Netherlands, Sweden, or Austria—are sometimes perceived as infringements of EU Competition Law (Giesecke 2016: 35 f.). The question remains if the EC ruling in related cases constitutes a transgression of the competences of EU authorities and a breach of the subsidiarity principle.

Increasing migration has put additional pressure on the housing market, as asylum seekers need housing too. The downsides of past policies—subsidies for temporary social housing and privatization—have been increasingly felt. As a result, many municipalities finally began investing in social housing again. In many EU countries, this was made expensive by very high building standards and high prices for land—as a result, states had to devise innovative policies. In the Dutch cities of Amsterdam, Eindhoven, and Den Bosch, municipalities responsible for housing licensees set up an action plan together with housing associations and other stakeholders to create housing both for refugees and for people on the waiting list (Schimpf 2017: 8 f.).

The Special Case of Vienna

Having sketched the trajectory of social housing in European countries in general, we now take a closer look at Vienna. Many of the developments observed in the case studies for other countries can be perceived in Vienna, but in a more concentrated form. In some ways, therefore, the city can be seen as a Petri dish of this social innovation. Vienna is an example of how a unique set of conditions can influence a social innovation, establishing a pathway that dominates for a long time. For a little over a decade after the First World War, a window of opportunity opened providing the necessary conditions for establishing a new form and understanding of social housing. Vienna also demonstrates an example of social housing uniting the interests of policy-makers and the working class in the Red Vienna period starting around 1920.

Population figures in Vienna continued to rise rapidly during this period, largely as a result of the large-scale migration from across the Austro-Hungarian Empire. In 1880, the city had 726,000 inhabitants; by 1890, the number had grown to 1,365,000 thanks to the incorporations. By 1910 the city reached the highest figure in its history with a population of 2,031,000.

During the second half of the nineteenth century, the construction sector enjoyed a boom. Housing construction—and housing in general—was a sector entirely controlled by private enterprise. The turn to the twentieth century saw a new era of industrialization across Europe as the bourgeois class became more established economically and politically. These developments formed, in part, the cognitive frame of the era. At the other end of the social scale, social tenants were very dependent on private landlords. This resulted in major housing inadequacies and severe shortcomings. A typical feature of the period was the flat shaped like a corridor divided by walls into rooms, whose kitchen was entered directly from the hallway. It did not have a water tap of its own, a bathroom, or toilet. Running water had to be fetched from a communal tap in the corridor outside the flat. As much as the ruling class had the networks, institutions, and cognitive frames to maintain their control of the Social Grid, the working class lacked such structures, which in turn contributed to sustaining their misery and disempowerment. This housing situation was particularly widespread in the suburbs that had been incorporated into Vienna in 1850.

The urban area and the outskirts that formed part of the province of Lower Austria at the time converged more and more. Many of the housing problems that emerged as a result were difficult to solve for communities because their revenue was too little. This situation was perceived as increasingly harmful by society. The result was a wave of incorporations of communities south of the Danube from 1890 to 1892. In 1904 Floridsdorf, north of the Danube, became part of Vienna. It had seen a terrific economic upswing thanks to the growth of machine manufacturing industries.

At the same time, the influence of unions and their degree of organization was low. For a long time it had been forbidden by law to form labour-representing organizations, so poor workers had almost no voice to speak out for their interests. The situation was different for the ruling class, who showed a high degree of organization, for example in chambers of commerce and guilds. Before 1918, roughly 300,000 people were homeless in Vienna. During these times, the living situation for the working class was one of the worst in Europe. It is no surprise that many tenants suffered from infections such as lung disease or tuberculosis. Prior to 1914, the Vienna Social Democrats demanded the construction of municipal housing but failed due to the resistance and dominance of the Christian Social municipal government (Wiener Wohnen 2015).

The roots of community housing in Vienna can be found in company-owned residencies, the Garden City Movement, and the Kaiser Franz Joseph Stiftung. The first steps date back to the late nineteenth century. In 1883 the Association of Workers' Dwellings was initiated in order to find solutions to the housing shortage. However, only eighteen family homes were built. As a successor of this association, the Kaiser Franz Joseph I. Jubiläums Stiftung (Anniversary Foundation) for peoples' dwellings and charitable organizations was founded in 1898. A further organization for housing reform in Austria was founded in 1907 to assess the housing situation statistically and suggest legal measures. One outcome of this was a law passed by the Austrian government in 1910, according to which a share of the city's annual tax income was used for housing construction. That same year in Vienna, a share of the housing tax was earmarked for a new housing charity fund. Despite these innovations, tenants and homeless people began organizing mass demonstrations against housing shortages and over-priced rents for the first time in 1910/11. These demonstrations were suppressed bloodily.

In the pre-war years and during the First World War, further steps were taken. In 1912, the first workers' home designed by Hubert Gessner opened. This was a forerunner for the later *superblocks* of the Red Vienna period. In 1913, the Housing Policy Committee—originally founded in 1910—was transferred into an independent municipal housing agency for the city of Vienna. To fight rent speculation because of the war, the Emperor issued a housing rent decree in 1917. That same year, Jakob Reumann was appointed as first Social Democratic city councillor of Vienna, as the municipality was trying to broaden its political basis during wartime.

The population increase in pre-war Vienna went hand in hand with mounting demands on the urban infrastructure.[9] Now the city government set about operating the most important technical services and utilities itself, 'de-privatizing' many hitherto private enterprises (e.g. the transport sector, electricity and gas utilities). These programmes, which had been intended, amongst others, as sources of municipal revenue, in fact, triggered a rapid increase in expenditures. Most of the budget was spent (in this order) on education, debt service, roads and

[9] A similar demand had been met before, around the turn of the century, after the construction of the metro railway system and of the Second Vienna Spring Water Main.

streets, general administration, welfare, and water supply (Wiener Magistrat 2015). All these programmes reflected the profound changes taking place in terms of increased political participation by more of the population. The early twentieth century saw a major extension of the right to vote when 'decoupled' from tax payments (1907: men's suffrage, 1919: women's suffrage). Mass parties emerged and grew, in particular the Christian Socialist movement—the strongest party until the end of the monarchy in 1918—and the Social Democrats, whose rise began with the end of the First World War (Wiener Magistrat 2015).

After the First World War, the city of Vienna—which used to be at the geopolitical centre of the Austrian-Hungarian Empire—found itself at the periphery of the new Austrian Republic. Many civil servants and high-ranking military personnel, who had served in the former Crown Lands, returned to Vienna, as did many war veterans (Kernbauer and Weber 1984: 6; Zimmerl 1998: 62). Vienna was cut off from its former agrarian and resource hinterland. It also lost its imperial markets (in Bohemia, Moravia, Hungary, and Galicia). Consequently, the food supply situation became very constrained—an additional burden for marginalized groups, many of whom were homeless (Weber 1981: 593–5).

The cooperative movement—active in different fields like agriculture and banking[10]—was also active in social housing at this time. This is illustrated well in the Vienna case, with the Settler's Movement that started to build houses on their own outside the city. Some fifty cooperatives emerged, representing more than eighty local groups (Kampffmeyer 1926: 131). They also took charge of the organization of the housing construction and infrastructure usually been done by the municipality—that later supported the movement (Frei 1991: 172; Novy and Förster 1991: 90). This Settlement Movement was born out of the suffering of the poor. The disastrous housing shortage was, to some extent, attributable to the huge influx of people flocking to the imperial capital from all corners of the former Habsburg Empire. However, it was also partly due to the fact that private landlords owned most housing and they typically let their property with an eye to maximizing their own returns (Wiener Wohnen 2015). The Settlement Movement was essentially a grassroots phenomenon, where deprived people took action to build their own shelters and engaged in some rudimental urban farming.

In May 1919, the first democratic municipal elections with general, equal (including women), direct, and secret, voting rights took place. The Social Democrats won the election; Jakob Reumann was elected as first Social Democratic mayor of the city. The city of Vienna adopted some of the most progressive laws regarding social housing. A right to housing was formulated and a tenant protection law (1922) was implemented that became central for all municipal housing programmes (Pirhofer 1982: 30; Förster 1980: 105). Building regulations were

[10] This represents an interesting forerunner of today's micro-credit models.

revised to reduce costs for housing in the settlers' areas. This marked an epoch of self-help that was eventually supported financially and legally by the municipalities (Förster 1980: 124). A tax earmarked for building was implemented in 1924 to finance *superblocks*, after an initial phase with more Garden City-style construction. By the end of 1924, the city had acquired 7,300,000 square meters of construction land for public housing activities. By 1930, the city owned more than one-quarter of Vienna's land property (Brahams 1987: 35).

After the First World War, several mass demonstrations took place in Vienna. The first mass demonstration of the settlers was held on 26 September 1920, including representatives of all political parties—some 50,000 participants demanded the expropriation of speculative property and full land reform. At the next mass demonstration, on 3 April 1921, more than 80,000 settlers followed the call of the 'main association for settlement and allotment garden affairs' (Hauptverband für Siedlungs- und Kleingartenwesen) (Novy and Förster 1991: 29; Novy 1981: 31). The third and biggest march took place on 12 March 1922, when settlers, tenants, and construction workers demonstrated for the continuation of the tenant protection laws and for measures against homelessness and unemployment that supported the settlement movement. The demonstration included some 100,000 participants (Frei 1991: 136).

Among the European cities implementing municipal housing in the inter-war period, Vienna occupies a prominent position. The Austro-Marxism practiced at the time not only included social housing, municipal schools, and hygiene improvements, but also an emancipatory set of objectives aimed at building a new cultural mass movement focused on a shared notion of 'belonging' for the working class and for the marginalized (Reinprecht 2012: 209). To better understand the context of the municipal housing innovation, it is important to realize that this was a period of extreme political tension between the well-organized working class, active in the industrialized towns, and the, mostly rural, lower middle class. The city of Vienna developed as an Austro-Marxist municipality, based on a new type of tax policy and innovative social policies in areas such as health, education, and housing. These reformist policies were closely linked with the struggle for cultural and political hegemony. Compared to the earlier period, the Austro-Marxist city government often acted paternalistically, overruling the autonomous Settlers' Movement (Reinprecht 2012: 209). The *superblocks* were designed to prepare for a 'new society'. Housing was not just defined as giving shelter, but as a social practice and new form of culture—a contribution to the constitution and reproduction of the working class family, its collective resilience and identity. This emerging social class was to be the antidote to the conservative-reactionary Catholic social policy and its idealization of family, class, and patriotic territorialism (Pirhofer and Sieder 1982: 326).

Vienna's Social-Democratic local government, after the First World War, created a local welfare state whose aim was to promote better housing and living conditions, as well as better health and education for working-class people. As Reinprecht (2007) pointed out, among the various programmes developed in the Red Vienna period, the construction of municipal housing was the most ambitious and most prestigious undertaking. The Vienna municipality played a key role as both developer and owner. By building social housing throughout the city, it achieved a long-term anti-segregation effect.

After 1931, construction activities rapidly declined. With the end of the civil war in 1934, Red Vienna was defeated. The Austro-Fascist regime deprived the parliament of its power, inaugurated an authoritarian feudal state, and dissolved the municipal constitution of Vienna, making the capital dependent on national legislation, as it was before 1923. Under the Nazi regime (1938–45) many gigantic infrastructure projects were planned for Vienna including housing. Most of them, however, were not realized. The major established housing programmes tried to create dwellings for unemployed people on the outskirts of the city. They resembled the settlements of the first period more than the building schemes of Red Vienna. Construction activity ceased in 1942 and the Nazi regime's incapability of dealing with the continuous housing shortage was offset by the inhumane Aryanization policy of deportation and killing of the Jewish inhabitants, thus making room for the migration movement caused by the war (Eigner et al. 1999: 16).

The need for new housing programmes became apparent again after 1945. The end of the Second World War brought an end to the Nazi regime in Austria. Of all housing units in Vienna, 20 per cent (some 87,000) were destroyed and 35,000 people were made homeless. The civic context, especially the welfare state, changed dramatically compared to the period after the First World War. Instead of the Austro-Marxist Red Vienna, the new model was based on a corporatist consensus, arranged and negotiated by the elite. It was characterized by a national welfare state, legitimized by its stabilizing and paternalistic function that guaranteed social cohesion in the post-war era and an improvement in general living conditions. The welfare model also implied full employment, standardized labour relations, and a patriarchic model of the nuclear family. Financially, it was based on an employment-centred society with social insurance and a subsidiary system of social benefits, complemented by social housing (Reinprecht 2012: 210).

The reconstruction era was marked by a general increase in wealth and welfare. This collective economic and social rise was also accompanied by a catch-up in urban modernization. This development slowed down in the late 1970s due to the global economic crisis, the end of full employment, and the increasing flexibility of production systems and life styles. At the same time a socio-cultural and socio-political diversification led to the deterioration of traditional values such as the nuclear family. Social groups found new forms of identification. Employment and private life underwent changes towards more pluralization and individualization. This was reflected in a change in the dominant cognitive frame and, in a more material way, the changes imposed on Viennese municipal housing policies.

Changes ushered in a neo-liberal model that culminated in the end of Vienna-style municipal housing in the new millennium.

Starting in 1981 tenant protection for newly built dwellings was loosened. Furnishing standards increased and several new housing blocks were built reacting to individual needs instead of standardized construction. The increase of single households and the emergence of extended family structures, paired with increasing demands for more comfort and bigger spaces, called for more flexible construction approaches. This also brought about higher rents. Thematic, innovative approaches and experiments (e.g. energy-efficient houses) were also attempted. Private actors were brought in via processes of market competition for construction contractors, spreading the burden of financial and technical risks (Reinprecht 2012: 213). The share of better-off middle-class families in municipal housing decreased compared to the two prior decades and municipal housing was increasingly associated with marginalized citizens. Some observers even spoke of 'inner segmentation', as social housing was left more and more to the private sector and the state had to retreat partially from this traditional field of corporatist politics (Reinprecht 2012: 214). In the post-corporatist era the objective of municipal housing was no longer to realize collective advancement. Instead, municipal housing policies were transformed into the management and refinement of housing for a more and more diversified and fragmented society. Some of these drivers are still active today, though somewhat diluted. Whether social housing is only for the poorest strata of society or whether it is a public good remains contested (Giesecke 2016).

Social Forces, Powers, and Capabilities

The previous sections have shown that social housing is a complex model that found distinct expressions across different periods of time. Next, we offer a structured analysis of these developments using the ESGM. This section starts with a diachronic analysis of the three forces within the Social Grid. Next, there is a short reflection on the co-evolution of challenge-driven innovations that introduces a discussion of power dynamics. Finally, applying the capabilities approach, we characterize the different phases of development in terms of their impacts on the lives of marginalized groups.[11]

[11] Our analysis here concentrates on the major developments only, without offering a complete picture. For a more detailed account, see the extensive report (Scheuerle et al. 2016a) and further material of the larger CrESSI project: https://www.sbs.ox.ac.uk/research/centres-and-initiatives/skoll-centre-social-entrepreneurship/creating-economic-space, accessed 27 June 2019.

Cognitive Frames

The European Parliament adopted a generally accepted definition of social housing (IZA—Institute for the Study of Labor 2013) based on four core dimensions that help characterize and differentiate social housing models and policies (the *tenure*, the *provider* of the housing service, the *beneficiaries*, and the *funding arrangements* (Pittini and Laino 2011: 22; IZA—Institute for the Study of Labor 2013: 10 ff.). Moreover, this definition offered a general distinction between *universalistic* and *targeted* social housing models[12] (IZA—Institute for the Study of Labor 2013; Ghékière 2007), set out as follows (IZA—Institute for the Study of Labor 2013: 12 f.):

- The *universalistic approach*, that presents social housing as public utility, proposes that there is a public responsibility to provide the entire population with decent quality housing at an affordable price. Providers are typically municipal housing companies or non-profit organizations. Social housing assumes a market-regulating role (e.g. rent control) with resource allocation mechanisms such as waiting lists—sometimes with reserved vacancies for pre-identified types of households with urgent housing needs or other priority allocation criteria. While most housing rents are cost-based, housing allowances and rent-guarantees are also available for disadvantaged households. The housing provision aims to ensure a social mix (in terms of ethnicity and income) to avoid ghettoization within urban areas and to enhance overall social cohesion.
- The *targeted approach* addresses individuals and households whose demand for housing with decent quality at an affordable price is not satisfied by the free market. Two sub-models can be distinguished here. The *generalist* model allocates housing to households with an income below a pre-identified income ceiling. Generalist social housing rents are determined by a fixed ceiling, with certain households benefitting from income-based housing allowances covering part of their rents. This represents a natural evolution of traditional social housing in Western Europe that has generally been directed at workers and middle-income groups. The *residual* model allocates housing to the most vulnerable groups and focuses on a minimal standard provision for the least well-off as a safety net. Housing is provided on the basis of need. Social housing rents are either cost- or income-based. The criteria for potential beneficiaries are much more restricted and typically

[12] Regarding such models, Harloe stated: 'such models are analytical constructs of a meta-theoretical nature. They are aids to the analysis of, and theorizing about, social housing development, not a substitute for empirically grounded analysis and explanation... It follows that there can be no 'correct' specification of such models, only ones which are more or less useful for advancing our understanding of the phenomena under investigation' (1995: 71).

correspond to extremely vulnerable households relying on a variety of welfare state benefits (e.g. unemployment, disability, elderly, single parents).

These two short paragraphs present two cognitive frames for social housing. But key questions remain such as: what exactly is the responsibility of the state and does housing have characteristics of a public good the state should provide for everybody or is it a typical measure of poor relief meant only for people in need?

Interestingly, recent EU regulations can be understood in terms of wider debates concerning social housing since the nineteenth century (see Box 5.3).

Other typical questions that arose in different periods were:

- Does the state, civil society, or private investment best provide social housing?
- Does social housing only aim at providing shelter (of lower or higher standards) or does it include measures to improve individual morals or social behaviour?
- How does social housing connect to urban development and city planning?
- What types of houses are best suited for social housing?

However, it is not possible to discuss all aspects of these issues and their related cognitive frames here. Hence, we will focus on one central issue, namely the discussion on providing shelter versus improving morals and behaviour. Given the interconnections that run between the ESGM dimensions, other aspects will emerge in our subsequent discussion of networks, institutions, and powers.

Box 5.3: Housing debates

Countries with a universalistic tradition of social housing are increasingly coming into conflict with EU rulings on the permissibility of state subsidies. For example, in 2005 the EU defined social housing as 'housing for disadvantaged citizens or socially less advantaged groups who, for financial reasons, cannot access market housing' (Boccardo 2008; Ghékière 2008). Also, according to EU law, only Services of a General Economic Interest (SGEI) may receive such subsidies. Universalistic approaches that seek to achieve a social mix and foster heterogeneity within urban regions—simultaneously supporting middle and higher income groups—do not qualify as an SGEI (Whitehead and Scanlon 2007). Generally, this leads to an increase of targeting at the most vulnerable population (Schimpf et al. 2017: 6).

Social Housing and Morality

In the early phase of social housing the actors—largely philanthropists and utopians—not only aimed to provide better living conditions (by copying bourgeois or rural dwellings), but also wanted to influence the lifestyles of the inhabitants via architecture. Differences in focus can also be identified depending on the motives and worldviews of the actors.

Utopians like Robert Owen and Jean-Baptiste André Godin proposed new ways of living together. They planned their houses with rooms for families, but central functions were located in rooms used by all inhabitants. Their houses were designed for communal living. The thinking was that workers cooperating in the factories should work together in the domestic 'sphere of reproduction' too. Hence, they had a shared kitchen, laundry facilities, and the like. Other actors were motivated more so by efficiency, seen in the shared use of facilities. Krupp and other like-minded entrepreneurs wanted to educate workers about bourgeois lifestyles by providing small houses with self-contained units and no community facilities. Octavia Hills' approach as a social reformer was based on early social work done by 'friendly rent collecting': upper-class women were trained to establish friendly relations with tenants and educate them on the side. All those approaches had in common that they saw social housing as a means to 'educate' the poor and influence their lifestyles. This idea never got lost over time.[13]

Others thought of blueprints that foresaw each party living in separate quarters built together around a staircase. A first prototype was realized by Henry Roberts for the World Exhibition of 1851. The so-called 'Prince Albert House' became a model for many other settlements in the nineteenth century (Eger 2010; Frampton 2002; Roberts 1850, 1859, 1862). In another example, in 1863, Waterlow's Industrial Dwelling Company erected five-storey buildings with self-contained units around a single staircase. The idea followed bourgeois ideas of family life (Adam 2002).

Thus, one can see that diverging ideas existed from the very beginning of social housing, often expressed in novel buildings. This shows that the question of how dwellings for the masses should be designed was not only a matter of efficiency and function, but was also deeply rooted in normative opinions and cognitive frames concerning lifestyles, morals, and individual politics.[14]

Another manifestation of alternative cognitive frames was made manifest in social protest and uprising. The three mass demonstrations that occurred between 1920 and 1922 increased working class consciousness and drove social change during the Red Vienna period—they also show the dynamic interdependence of

[13] An example of the many recent reincarnations of this idea can be found in Haindlmaier (2017).

[14] Viehhauser showed that these ideas did not stop at social housing but ran like a golden thread through urban planning more generally (2016).

cognitive frames, networks, and institutions. These demonstrations made it clear that there was strong support in society for social reforms to improve the housing situation that could mobilize sufficient political pressure to provoke a political response. This example offers one of the rare examples of beneficiaries becoming politically relevant actors and innovators themselves. As a result, municipal and national policy started supporting the Vienna settlement movement—without this support the movement would not have been successful (Novy and Förster 1991: 29). While the mass demonstrations, especially the associations organizing them, marked the rise of important new social networks, they also demonstrated the formation of new cognitive frames. The Settlers' Movement gave the working class the idea of a cultural and legal identity: the strong popularity this movement gained—reflected in the mass demonstrations and in the press—contributed to the movement's strength and the settlers' unprecedented self-esteem. In turn, these developments helped stabilize political networks and their corresponding cognitive frames. This can be seen in the example of social housing in the city of Vienna during the 1920s when the Social Democrats came to power and provided shelter primarily for their clientele, propagating social-democratic values such as community life, education for the working class and its children, pre-school child care, medical provision, and supply of everyday goods through organized cooperative distribution networks circumventing free market forces (Giesecke 2015).

Architects

Social housing is often an expression of contemporary architectural thinking and a field to test new ideas of living. This was the case at the turn of the nineteenth century, despite the dominant trend of the time being to build cheaply and functionally. Architectural movements contributed to changing cognitive frames, often accompanied by the formation of new networks, in turn, influencing the formation of new institutions (see Box 5.4).

For example, Amsterdam was a city with particularly bad living conditions for the marginalized during the Industrial Revolution. The Housing Act of 1901 addressed the quality as well as the quantity of social housing. Under the guidance of national government policies, the municipality was obliged to make plans for the expansion of the city, including plans for roads, canals, squares, and sewerage (Acker et al. 2008: 7). Also, the Act organized the establishment of housing associations and allowed the government to grant advances and subsidies to these private, not-for-profit organizations so that they could build housing that met key quality standards as a public good. Other examples included the Familistère in Guise in France, where Godin adhered to the principles of social utopias and invented early resident ownership schemes (Scheuerle et al. 2016b).

Box 5.4: Architectural trends

During this time, the Amsterdam School of Architecture evolved in the Netherlands. Later on, well-known architects and planners such as Michel de Klerk (1884–1923), Hendrik Petrus Berlage (1856–1934), and Piet Kramer (1881–1961) embraced social housing in their work. They cooperated with housing associations to receive funding for their aesthetically artful buildings. Some of the most prominent examples of social housing of this time (such as Het Schip, a complex of houses for industry workers in the Spaarndammer-buurt quarter of Amsterdam) can still be visited today.

Elsewhere, the German '*Neues Bauen*' movement proposed a new architectural approach in the early decades of the twentieth century. The architects concentrated on functional and healthy buildings and settlements (with good access to air and plenty of light) and avoided purely decorative elements not only for the sake of efficiency, but for aesthetic reasons too. Technically, they combined a rationalized way of building with standard types and the use of modern technologies first tried in industrial buildings. The modern style was, however, not only a matter of technology, but the layout of the living quarters was radically redesigned too.

Remarkable in this context was the changing role of the kitchen. The so-called Frankfurt Kitchen, designed by Margarete Schütte-Lihotzky and first installed in the Frankfurt settlement programme that created a large amount of new settlements between 1926 and 1932, reinterpreted the kitchen from the central space for the family to the realm of the housewife. This meant a new layout not only for flats but also for the division of labour and the style of living. The traditional kitchen-diner, in which wood or coal-burning stoves functioned as both cooker and living room hearth became an anachronism, since stoves in the new settlements were gas fired and could be turned off when not in use for cooking. The double use of the kitchen, therefore, no longer helped drive a fuel intensive economy. Since modern apartments were centrally heated, there was no need for the kitchen to open up to the bedroom or living room. The most efficient use of space was to separate the cooking area from the living area and to make the kitchen and living room into discrete though interconnected spaces, divided by a sliding door. The new kitchen was a 'working kitchen' for meal preparation and related tasks only, but not for eating or other domestic or recreational purposes. In the development of the new kitchen design, Schütte-Lihotzky had, in fact, built upon Taylorist methods of time-and-motion studies, calculating the distances between the sink, the stove, the dining table, and so on (Blau 1999: 198; Ottillinger 2015: 52–7). This innovation in design reflected the cognitive framing of the rationalization of work, the acknowledgement of the housewife as a working woman with her own working space, similar to workshops and factories of the (mostly) male proletariat, as well as bourgeois ideas that household chores should be done more efficiently meaning that the housewife could spend more time with her family.

Vienna

During the Red Vienna period, the Vienna type of social housing was developed, symbolized especially by the first generation of housing complexes (built between 1923 and 1926). In contrast to the later layout in Frankfurt, the design of the floor plan offered an apartment with a kitchen, the main room, connected to a bedroom for all members of the family (usually consisting of five to six people). In addition, the installation of gas pipes, stoves, and portable showers in the kitchens was planned, driven by technological advances in the energy and infrastructure sectors. As a reaction to criticism by delegates at the International Town Planning and Housing Congress in 1926, who had considered these apartments too small, larger apartments were designed (Blau 1999: 198).

The floor plan design of the first- and second-generation housing units in the Red Vienna superblocks is only understandable when compared to dwellings of the 'Gründerzeit' era. The working-class dwellings before the period of Red Vienna had been little more than a corridor, divided by walls into rooms. In the usual Viennese tenement apartment, consisting of a kitchen and one room, the kitchen was the room where the family actually spent time. The other room was reserved for sleeping and representation, i.e. welcoming and meeting friends and other visitors (Blau 1999: 200). There was no direct light, thus the opening up of the apartments in the 1920s either toward the street or toward a light and spacious yard with trees and fresh air not only marked an important innovation but also an elevation of the proletariat at that time, contributing to the formation of a new cognitive frame: stronger self-esteem for the working class.

In the Vienna-type house, and in the Western modernized version of it, one still entered a room by going through another room or several other rooms, except for the kitchen and toilet.[15] Thus, instead of being channelled by means of a corridor, traffic within the apartment was organized through spaces that were as flexible, multipurpose, and multidirectional as possible. The traditional kitchen-diner was a place for cooking, eating, and attending to household chores—it was also a place for study, play, and leisure (Blau 1999: 200, Blau 2012: 182). This design of movement from room to room resembled the bourgeois Ringstraßen palace architecture and similar well-to-do family homes of the nineteenth century,

[15] The typical entry model of the first apartment type led from the front door to a small entrance hall, to the kitchen-diner, to the bedroom, and to the bathroom (if any).

which, in turn, followed the design of the emperor's palace (e.g. Schönbrunn). The Westernized version of the Vienna-type apartment was considered an 'embourgeoisement' of proletarian living spaces—causing lots of discussion of the proletarian identity.

Additional innovations in Vienna, during the Red Vienna period, concerned the interior design of the houses. In almost all big settlements of the 1920s, architects designed model furniture (Novy and Förster 1991: 76–80). As part of a changing cognitive frame, cultural identity was not only formed in various common social activities—for example, new cooperatives and educative institutions—but also through cultural artefacts and a new style in housing, furniture, and ornaments.

With the increasing construction activities in European countries after the First World War, a more differentiated market emerged. It consisted often of regional organizations that provided technical support and pooled the supply of materials (Schwan 1935). To make social housing more affordable, new materials (e.g. glass, iron, and concrete) were developed and used. The same held true for new processes and building techniques (e.g. steel casting, iron trellis construction, glass columns) (Baaser 1960; Koch 1987: 5; Novy and Förster 1991: 155). This was especially reflected in Viennese developments.

Social Networks

In the very beginning, social housing had been mostly initiated and provided for by philanthropic individuals. However, subsequently, local, national, and international networks evolved, connecting people thinking about social housing from different perspectives. Members of these networks included social reformers, people concerned about the low morals of the working class, social hygienists, architects, and others (Lévy-Vroelant et al. 2008; Adam 2002).

In the mid-nineteenth century, supporting social housing was primarily a philanthropic activity of wealthy individuals. The charitable motives of creating better living conditions were often combined with more pedagogic motives of enhancing working class morals. Others were inspired by utopian ideas of a new way of living and working together.

Another driver was the more self-interested motives of employers (like Krupp, as mentioned above) and public authorities. Better housing for labourers and their families kept workers loyal to the companies and society at large and made them more productive. The logic was that if social cohesion, security, and hygiene conditions were enhanced then everybody would profit, including the wealthier people in society (Scheuerle et al. 2016b: 35, 172).

An important international network in social housing was the Garden City Movement that spread across Europe at the beginning of the twentieth century. It was influenced by the ideas of Ebenezer Howard and emerged in the wake of the Industrial Revolution when the issue of overcrowding became increasingly apparent (Kampffmeyer 1908). The core idea was to create decentralized independent entities instead of mere suburbs that were located in the countryside and contained housing estates, industrial, business, and cultural facilities. Howard also connected social reform thinking to his Garden City idea. Not only should the Garden City cope with the socio-economic, hygiene, aesthetic, and infrastructural problems of urbanization, but also with a lack of citizen control, participation, and city management (Fishman 1977: 30). A key problem for the creation of real garden cities was the access to work in such new settlements, although the influence of the movement and its principles is still visible today in some Garden City settlements (e.g. in Letchworth in the United Kingdom or Dresden-Hellerau in Germany). Financing of a model project was to be obtained by what would nowadays be coined as an 'impact investing' approach: for building the city, like-minded wealthy individuals would be convinced to invest funds that would pay a modest rate of return (Fishman 1977: 30). Once cheap agricultural land had been turned into an attractive Garden City, land prices would rise and investors would be paid off (Fishman 1977: 46).

Still, today, one can observe the formation of international movements that not only focus on providing accommodation, but also support more general principles for sustainable living and working. For example, the members of the global ecovillage movement try to practise a sustainable lifestyle, to live in resilient communities, and to offer education to group members and others.[16] Other examples include national initiatives such as the Mietshäuser Syndikate in Germany[17] and other self-help approaches that share knowledge about financing options, project development, and give assistance in accessing capital.

Institutions

According to the ESGM approach, cognitive frames directly and indirectly affect the institutions in a given Social Grid. Cognitive frames 'provide legitimation and can shape the wider perceptions of institutions' just as institutions 'can make values socially relevant' for cognitive frames (Nicholls and Ziegler 2015: 10). The big changes in institutions relevant for social housing reflect many of the elements already identified when discussing cognitive frames above. In many countries a strong emphasis on market solutions was institutionalized in laws; these were often the reason for the bad living conditions of labourers in the early phases of industrialization. The unregulated market and lack of building codes created high rents and low standards of building (Scheuerle et al. 2016b: 27).

The first noteworthy changes in institutions were regulations that focused on living conditions, especially security and hygiene. The British Public Health Act (1848) was a hallmark for such legislation. It allowed, for example, local boards of health to determine a maximum number of lodgers permitted per house.

[16] https://ecovillage.org/, last accessed 2 February 2018.
[17] https://www.syndikat.org/en/, last accessed 2 February 2018.

Until the First World War most regulations reflected a wider expectation that private provision would be the main source of social housing. The 'housing acts' that emerged in many European states around the end of the nineteenth century focused on leveraging more private resources and greater private sector involvement in the co-ordination and provision of social housing. Direct housing provision through municipalities remained at a minimum level before the First World War. After the First World War various housing programmes were launched and—more importantly—rent controls and compulsory billeting were introduced. In many countries, the state provided low-cost loans or some favourable taxation for actors providing social housing.

Self-Help and Technological Innovation

Further institutionalization of the Vienna Settlers' Movement during and after the First World War emerged with new guilds founded for constructing settlements, apartments, and infrastructure. Some observers called this 'guild socialism', a combination of state socialism and syndicalism and an important basis for the corporatism establishing at that time. It was the expression of an attempt to put parts of the economy under the control of the proletariat and the principle of local community government was transferred to different parts of the economy (Novy 1981: 34; Novy and Förster 1991: 89; Hoffmann 1982: 145).

Changes in the legal framework for construction facilitated organizational and technological innovation. Changes in building codes opened up new paths for thought and experimentation. The reform of several provisions in Vienna building regulations helped reduce the costs of settlements dramatically (see Box 5.5). This was also a field of further institutionalization on the basis of changed construction norms and rules, made possible directly or indirectly through the increased political influence of the Social Democrats.

Moreover, scarcity of materials and the need to reduce costs led to the use of alternative construction materials such as clay bricks or slag masonry—settlers increasingly produced them themselves. Many of the new settlements were also located close to such production sites, which saved transport costs. One important

Box 5.5: Regulatory innovations

For example, fireproof partition walls were eliminated from regulations after the reforms of 1920. Furthermore, the minimum height of a building storey was reduced to 2.6 metres; the minimum width of a stair to 90 cm. It was permitted to use: hollow masonry; wooden ceilings without filling; wooden stairs without flush-mounting; and outdoor peat litter toilets (Förster 1980: 124; Posch 1981: 63).

innovation concerning substitute materials is the 'pax brick'. It is a masonry brick made of cement, slag, sand, and water, pressed by hand and filled with clay. This alternative—and cheaper construction—material saved up to 50 per cent of the building costs (Schacherl 1926). Pax bricks served as major construction material until 1923 when the economic situation improved and conventional bricks could be used again (Baaser 1960; Koch 1987: 5; Novy and Förster 1991: 155). This cheaper production method can be considered as a technological innovation, although it was not necessarily a result of technological progress, but rather of scarcity and need—an early type of frugal innovation.

Most settlement construction sites also included carpentry, locksmith, tinsmith, and glass workshops, where the building elements were produced in small batches. Building a home was not understood as an individual effort but as standardized community work to serve the masses where efficiency was needed. These workshops were community-owned and some became cooperatives. This form of cooperative working has been interpreted as a milestone in offering alternatives to the private market economy and its subsequent large-scale mass production (Schacherl 1926).

One additional important innovation was Adolf Loos' 'house with one wall'. This idea was also born out of the necessity of building large numbers of houses using scarce resources in an efficient way. The house with one wall gave more flexibility to the builders and the occupants of the housing: an inventive system to build row houses with only one load-bearing wall. Several similar inventions not only helped save building materials, but also reduced the need for labour because unskilled workers could increasingly do the work (Cremer 1992: 37).

The 'core house' was another technical innovation of that time. The idea emerged in the early 1920s. With this type of innovation one part of the house was immediately habitable and was constructed with simple means and materials. Later on, this type of house could be developed into a complete settlement house through further building activities and by the settlers' themselves (Förster 1980: 68; Neumann 1929: 23; Novy and Förster 1991: 76). Altogether, 198 core houses were built in Vienna.

Building Codes

Our historical analysis suggests that in times of crisis and resource scarcity, innovations are likely to develop. These innovations often solved an immediate problem, but also generated new problems in the longer term, due to problematic social contexts, questionable quality standards of the buildings, or the nature of the surrounding infrastructure.[18] Alternative solutions like the 'cluster' or quadruple house (like the Prince Albert houses noted above) or multigenerational and mixed housing concepts develop and survive in niches (Scheuerle et al. 2016b: 39).

[18] Historic experience seems to suggest: better satisfy urgent needs with temporary solutions and in parallel test which concepts make (most) sense in the long run.

In general, the social housing buildings and projects mentioned above gave prestige to the architects or developers, while other parts of society also benefitted from these developments—at least to a certain extent. Today social housing is still used for experimentation with new blueprints and building methods. The image of social housing has been improved by such innovative projects that are partly enabled by the adjustment of regulations, such as the separation of living and working areas.[19]

Co-evolution of Challenge-Driven Innovations

It is a widely used practice in the social innovation research community to juxtapose social and technological innovations.[20] Our historical analysis of social innovation shows that a different approach using different terminology is more fruitful. Various types of innovations are needed to tackle the challenge of providing affordable housing at an acceptable level of comfort, hygiene, and safety for those in need. More generally, social innovation—in most cases—can only be successful when it is coupled with several types of innovations including technological, organizational, financial, business model, and market innovations.[21] These

[19] A recent example is a social housing project in the Allerød Municipality, north of Copenhagen, Denmark, where the new settlement was fully integrated into the natural environment (Schimpf et al. 2017: 12).

[20] Several authors claim that there are well over a hundred definitions of social innovation (e.g. Edwards-Schachter and Wallace 2017) and, thus, one can find a huge variety in terms of the unit of analysis and the type and degree of change produced (Havas 2016). Instead of aiming to characterize this plethora of social innovation definitions from the angle of the perceived relationships between social and technological innovations, a bold claim is cited here first:

> The category [of social innovation] re-emerged (in a positive light) in the second half of the twentieth century as a reaction—a 'political' reaction—to technological innovation and to the hegemonic discourses on technological innovation. Social innovation came to mean alternatives to 'established' solutions to social problems or needs, namely to technological innovation and State or government-supported social reform. (Godin 2012: 6)

Furthermore, two observations proposed by a thorough literature review indicated a prevailing ambiguity:

> During the first decades SI was conceived as a process developed by and oriented to the third sector, not based on technological knowledge or R&D, and differentiated from institutionalized social practices and social inventions (a program, a model, a standard, a norm, a procedure) arising from technology-based innovations. But progressively... SI was used to name the development of products, processes and services mediated by technologies or closely linked to technological innovations with social purposes (i.e. with the explicit objective to produce benefits in terms of social impact)... After decades of marginalization, SI is starting to be recognized as part of the 'black box' of innovation to inquire which is the 'place' of social practices in innovation processes and how they take part of different activities and the building of *social, technological even cultural innovation systems* and their contribution to sociotechnical change.
>
> (Edwards-Schachter and Wallace 2017: 73–4; emphasis added)

[21] Technological innovations refer to new or significantly improved goods (products and services) and processes (e.g. production methods). Market innovations include opening up new markets—by definition, social housing itself constituted a new market—and offering new products to new customers as well as entering existing markets which an innovator has not previously used to source inputs or sell outputs (OECD 2005).

types of innovations can be introduced either by the social innovators themselves or by other actors whose main aim is to make profits. In other words, it is useful to distinguish between the underlying objectives of a given innovation (addressing a societal challenge versus making profits) and the nature of innovation itself (new or significantly modified products, services, production processes, organizational set-ups and managerial methods, business models, financial and marketing methods).

As for the nature of innovations, our case has clearly shown that building a large number of flats for social housing—as opposed to building palaces for the aristocrats, villas for well-off business people or just 'elegant' flats for the better-off clients in any city—required:

- New, cheaper, mass-produced building materials, including bricks, flooring, tiles, windows, doors, fittings for kitchens, bathrooms, and toilets
- New business models for companies producing building materials
- New modes of logistics to ship building materials in huge volumes
- New approaches when designing blocks of flats for social housing
- New or modified methods, tools, and equipment to build these blocks of flats
- A large number of semi-skilled workers, in some cases including would-be tenants
- New types of mass-produced furniture, lamps, kitchenware, carpets, curtains, and so on, to furnish these flats
- Setting up new companies or established companies introducing and following new business models to service these new demands.

In other words, we can think of a virtuous circle of business and social innovation. Again, these business innovations include technological (products and production processes), organizational, management, market, and business model innovations. A large number of these innovations have been discussed at some length above, including: the example of pax bricks; new types of glass, iron, and concrete as building materials; new processes and building techniques (e.g. steel casting, iron trellis construction, glass columns); the introduction of cooperative working methods at construction sites; new, more efficient heating technologies; improved infrastructure at various phases of social housing, including the broad-scale electrification allowing the widespread diffusion of electronic household devices after the Second World War; the adoption and adaptation of a set of new technologies originally developed for industrial buildings; new organizations for self-help (guilds in Vienna, other initiatives in Germany, as well as those offering technical expertise and advice); the new concepts of the 'house with one wall' and the 'core house'; new layout for the flats in different phases and different models of social housing; the so-called reform furniture; the emergence of new 'techno structures'; and new funding modes.

To sum up, social housing as a social innovation has co-evolved with a range of technological, organizational, business model, financial, and market innovations—each shaping each other. Social innovators themselves developed some of these innovations, profit-seeking business actors others—hence social and business innovations have co-evolved. Using modern terminology, social housing can be understood as a challenge-driven innovation and, thus, the policies supporting these processes as challenge-driven innovation policies (Foray et al. 2012; Mazzucato 2016; Mowery et al. 2010).

Power

This historical analysis of social housing across various phases of development shows dynamic variations in the basic concept, as well as in its implementation and financing. These changes can be interpreted in terms of the power dynamics across the Social Grid. Different powers influenced all elements of the Social Grid—the cognitive frames, social networks and institutions—in similar ways. As the three social forces operated in dialectic with one another, changes in one aspect of the Social Grid entailed changes in one or both of the other elements. These interconnections are demonstrated here by concentrating on the dominant powers in a given phase of social housing, stemming mostly from the artefactual, cultural, economic, and political dimensions (see further in chapter 2).[22]

During the first phase of social housing from the mid-nineteenth century to the beginning of the First World War, social housing was considered a normatively appropriate intervention (cognitive frame) to solve the problem of miserable housing conditions for the poor through private means (*cultural power*). Philanthropists (like Peabody) and industrialists (like Godin) began to act. Besides charitable motives the fear of riots and mass epidemics was an important trigger (*security-related power*). Another innovation was cooperative building societies (*social network*) founded in several European countries as part of the cooperative movement (*economic power*). The state was not among the leading actors at this time (cognitive frame and *cultural power*)—though this changed in the second half of this phase when the state started actively to frame normative expectations of housing and to regulate new developments (for example, with the first laws [institutions] on social housing in Belgium, the United Kingdom, or France after 1889 [*political power*]).

During the second phase (end of the First World War to 1929), things changed significantly and social housing became a central part of the emerging welfare state. This was due to the increasing organization of the working class (*political*

[22] The two other powers considered within the ESGM, that is, natural power and security-related power, were in most cases not significant.

power) on the one hand, and to the dysfunctional social housing structures after the war (*economic power*) on the other. Social housing became integrated into direct public provision (*political power*). The rise of private not-for-profit or limited dividend housing companies and cooperatives, however, were also important during the period (such as in Rochdale, United Kingdom [*economic power*]).

Market differentiation between private and public providers (*economic power*) was a common feature of the third phase of social housing—from 1929 to 1945—with public providers concentrating on the poorer households as a residual approach (*political power*). During this period, the welfare state developed a top-down welfare model (cognitive frame) and style of social welfare provision (*political power*).

The demolition of transport and productive capacities as well as the decimation of the bulk of social housing stock (*impact of military and political power; loss of economic power*) as a major outcome of the Second World War, forced governments to take a leading role in the social housing field in the fourth phase post-1945 until the 1970s (*political power*). Demographic changes through migration, the baby boom, and urbanization further increased demand. A new cognitive frame emerged focused on a universalistic model of social housing (*political power, cultural power*). A new 'techno structure' coalition consisting of local politicians, urban planners, architects, construction companies, and banks emerged—for example, in France, to address this challenge (*economic and political powers*).

In the fifth phase (mid-1970s to 2008) a substantial market transformation took place in the economy with the increasing weight of services at the expense of manufacturing industries (*economic power*). This led to higher levels of industrial unemployment and a consequent increase in demand for social housing. The rise of neo-liberalism resulted in the deregulation of the financial markets, put pressure on public spending and brought about the growing privatization of social housing and other welfare domains (*economic and political powers*). Social housing policy targeted (very) low-income households while mass ownership of private homes emerged as a new policy goal (*political power*). Responsibilities in the field of social housing became more and more decentralized and market-based, compared to earlier phases in the twentieth century (*political power*).

The most recent phase (since 2008) is still partly shaped by the financial and economic crisis of 2008–9 with decreasing income for the middle class and rising unemployment rates (*economic powers*). The demand for social housing has been further boosted by demographic changes (a growing number of single or single-parent households plus more widespread gentrification) as well as by voluntary and forced migration (*economic, cultural, and political power*). The policy agenda is also framed by government cuts and austerity politics. Thus, social housing has once again become an important political issue. The need for more investment in social housing is increasingly under discussion (*political and economic power*).

Box 5.6: Cross-sector innovation

The PAAVO programme in Finland is an example of a so-called re-let system. Between 2008 and 2015, this programme helped the Finnish Government acquire decentralized supported accommodation for homeless people in rented accommodation from private owner-occupied housing companies. Foundations and other similar organizations let small flats to local authority social services, which then re-let them to those in need of accommodation while also trying to prevent social segregation. As a result, around 30,000 apartments became available in 2009 (Tainio and Fredriksson 2009: 184; for a more detailed description see Aro 2016).

The field has been characterized by private–public partnerships and different provision schemes (*political and economic power*), but more specialist stakeholders have increasingly been working in partnership with providers and cooperative solutions are resurfacing (*economic power*) (see Box 5.6).

Shared Facilities and Community Life

During the first phase of the Settlers' Movement in Vienna several additional social innovations increased the functions of the social networks of the rising working class and also catalysed the evolution of a class identity as part of a new cognitive frame, these included: kindergartens; playgrounds; new sports activities; day-care; youth clubs; theatre and music groups, and so on. The settlers themselves supported these social innovations financially, sometimes with the additional support of the city of Vienna. In some cases the Social Democratic Party had its own representations in the settlements (Novy and Förster 1991: 90).

Further social innovations during this phase evolved at the organizational level. The settlers' notion that their joint undertaking could only work if they formed a functioning community led to several initiatives and artefacts, for instance a type of community house known as the *Genossenschaftshaus*. Every larger settlement owned one of these houses and the settlers themselves built them or remodelled existing buildings. They were usually located at the centre of the settlement. These community houses typically included a meeting room, administrative offices of the cooperative, a cooperative store, a library, and a restaurant or cafeteria (Novy and Förster 1991: 92). The promoters of the Settlers' Movement regarded the community houses as the hearts and minds of the settlements: they were places of cultural activity that, at times, were also used for secondary education for adults and for festivities. This was seen as a formal expression of community life (Max Ermers, as cited in Novy 1981: 134).

There were social innovations on the economic side as well. Due to high unemployment, settlers depended on collective self-sustainability. They set up their own workshops, nurseries, and provisions for health care in a collective and cooperative manner to generate economies of scale, work more efficiently, and reduce prices. The entire food supply and retail sector was organized through the cooperative that ran the stores in the settlements (Novy and Förster 1991: 90; Kampffmeyer 1926: 135). The settlements were run and administered by their own members with outside experts brought in where necessary (working on a voluntary basis). Settlement boards of arbitration resolved conflicts (Novy and Förster 1991: 56, 91).

Capabilities

At the beginning of the development of social housing in the nineteenth century, marginalized people in need of affordable housing were deprived of various capabilities and opportunities to flourish. Along with personal conversion factors (gender, age, ethnicity) that made them vulnerable, they lacked access to affordable, private, and secure accommodation. It was impossible for them to find a healthy living environment. On top of a lack of social recognition and political participation, they were deprived of their freedom of settlement for themselves and their families (Scheuerle et al. 2016b: 30).

In the first phase of social housing, the situation improved for the few who were able to find secure, clean, and affordable accommodation. Family prospects improved. It has to be stressed, though, that quite often the picture is mixed with regard to their capabilities: in many instances, parts of the marginalized population experienced improvements while the situation of other groups stayed the same or even became worse.[23] In some cases, the political activities of marginalized people were suppressed and repressive measures were also taken against those who were seen as having unsuitable lifestyles (Scheuerle et al. 2016b: 41).

The second phase—after the First World War—saw improvements in terms of privacy, cleanliness, and security (for example, the *Neues Bauen*). Moreover, the political capabilities of marginalized people improved through membership of trade unions or political parties. However, their economic capabilities remained underdeveloped. The high risk of unemployment and/or homelessness in that period resulted in extreme marginalization. Also, slum clearance programmes limited their freedom to choose a place for living. Furthermore, an enforced paternalistic control system was still in effect (Scheuerle et al. 2016b: 50f.).

Interestingly, while such a control system is completely opposite to the core values of the capabilities approach, this was perceived differently amongst social

[23] For a more detailed treatment of this issue see chapter 10 in this book.

groups at the time. Thus, any ESGM analysis needs to be cognizant of any normative values that might differ from those in the past—this represents a challenge to this sort of historical analysis (Scheuerle et al. 2016b: 50).

Social segregation through slum clearance grew further in the third phase and social recognition remained constrained. In many cases hygiene capabilities were still compromised, and freedom of choice over a place to live was largely non-existent (Scheuerle et al. 2016b: 57).

After the Second World War, in the fourth phase, the capabilities of marginalized people improved due to large-scale building activities. However, restrictions on their autonomy remained or emerged anew. Marginalized people had no freedom to choose where to live (often re-settled against their will). Capabilities such as individual mobility, access to labour markets, or cultural living were severely constrained. Towards the end of this period, personal security was also negatively affected in many cases (Scheuerle et al. 2016b: 66).

The fifth phase shows a Janus face. Access to social housing became easier, at the same time as overall standards of housing worsened. Stigmatization increased, especially framed by the dominant neo-liberal discourse, so social recognition was still compromised. On the other hand, the first examples of co-decision making and co-management can be found here, where tenants were seen more as 'clients' than as passive welfare recipients (Scheuerle et al. 2016b: 75).

In the sixth phase, one important aim of social housing has been to improve educational levels, social inclusion, and individual opportunities for participation. Also, new building regulations have emerged that are tailored to people with special needs (such as physical or mental disabilities). However, there remains a real risk that these standards will again be lowered in social housing dwellings due to the stress put on the sector through the 2008 economic crisis and migration. Forced migrants and refugees, especially, are often still not free to choose their place of living. Thus, social recognition is often still missing and chances for social upward mobility for this group are rare (Schimpf et al. 2017: 10).

Conclusion

In conclusion, based upon our in-depth analysis of social housing in Europe, several general observations can be made.

Social Innovation as a Complex and Continuous Process

The long-term, historical, perspective on social innovation taken here reveals that its success often depends on the involvement of multiple actors and social networks in developing and implementing these new solutions. Most often these actors do not come from marginalized groups, rather they have a different socio-economic background. Their multi-faceted interests and mixed motives for engagement typically range from benevolence to economic self-interest and political goals. A simplistic understanding of social innovation as being produced by individuals or small groups of 'change agents' is, therefore, misleading.

Business innovation—as analysed by evolutionary economics of innovation, SHOT (social history of technology) or SCOT (social construction of technology)—is formed by a complex set of diverging ideas and proposals. After some time, a hegemonic new solution may emerge. But it will not stay forever. It is constantly contested and there will always be opposing forces waiting for a change in circumstance to restart the dynamic process of change. This applies to social innovation a fortiori.

Our case suggests that successful social innovations keep evolving and adjusting to their ever-changing contexts. The specific ecosystem in which they are embedded and upon which they are dependent is shaped and re-shaped by new discourses, emerging demands, and changing cognitive frames. The social context of the original social innovation becomes visible again, when the basic questions at issue are posed anew. These processes reopening the debate reveal normative decisions.

Coalitions as Condition for Success

The historical analysis here illustrates that the success of a social innovation is derived from a range of actors and innovators with various backgrounds, accumulated knowledge, and expertise. As they have different resources and are part of different social networks they can forge coalitions with a high potential for success. This is further facilitated if an innovative approach can be shown to enhance the lives of many in material or immaterial ways. Social innovators often succeed when they offer grand visions of change relevant to a majority (see Edwin Chadwick in mid-nineteenth century Britain, chapter 6 in this volume; in contrast see chapter 7 on the Kiútprogram in Hungary). That way, all have a chance to benefit; our study shows that often other groups in society profit, too, when the position of marginalized people improves. This may go so far that the originally intended target group drops out and the innovation changes its overall focus. In some instances, however, the cost of widespread diffusion might be the creation of a new form of marginalization elsewhere in society.

Supporting Conditions

Access to social networks proved here to be important for the ongoing viability of a social innovation, especially networks including policy-makers, decision-makers, and potential funders. A pluralism of providers of housing seems to enlarge the variety of approaches to finding a solution, lessening the dependence of all actors.

Our long-term analysis has shown that it pays to leave room for different approaches. Diverse solutions and variants develop in niches, which can be understood as a reservoir of elaborate ideas ready to be implemented in situations of change or crisis. They may also provide insights for others.

An advantage of social housing as a social innovation is that decentralized and local solutions can be used. These can be constructed by using elements that have been successfully employed in other places. Multiple combinations of blueprints, ways of financing and management are, therefore, possible. The knowledge created and experiences accumulated elsewhere, however, have to be adapted to the local situation, its demands and resources. Standardization (e.g. building codes, building materials, floor plans, organizational structures, and so on) makes sense to lower costs, but if it narrows down options, it may become a barrier for future innovation.

Co-Evolution of Social and Business Innovation

The diffusion of social housing has been connected to a different way of building houses since the beginning of this social innovation. The early promoters often intended to create both affordable housing and new styles of living. Their innovations were often combined with new approaches to architecture. This brought forward a demand not only for new designs and layouts, but also for new materials, new modes of building, new furniture, kitchenware, home appliances, and textiles for these flats. The style of the big buildings enabled and—for reasons of financing—required cheap, standardized semi-manufactured and prefabricated elements for their buildings. In reaction to the problems brought about by industrialization—such as massive migration to cities—an industrialized way of building houses for a large number of tenants was needed. Only this could lower the costs of buildings.

The widely used dichotomy of social versus technological innovations thus needs to be re-evaluated. It is more instructive and productive—both for social innovation practitioners and policy-makers—to analyse social housing as a co-evolutionary process of social innovation with business innovations, including technological, organizational, financial, business model and market innovations.

This chapter has set out a long-term, historical, case study of social housing in Europe. As noted above this empirical approach is unique to research on social innovation. The case has been analysed using the ESGM, set out in chapter 1, to reveal the dynamic ebbs and flows of actors, institutions, social networks, and cognitive frames that drove forward social housing across several phases of growth and change. Above all, this analysis reveals how episodic and complex the trajectories towards systems change are and how dependent on patterns of politics and power they are too.

References

Acker, S. v., M. Koomoen, and H. de Boer. 2008. 'De Toolbox voor huurders en huurdersorganisaties'. Amsterdam. http://www.huurdersvereniging-amsterdam.nl/toolbox/compleet.pdf, accessed 4 March 2015.

Adam, T. 2002. 'Transatlantic Trading: The Transfer of Philanthropic Models between European and North American Cities during the Nineteenth and Early Twentieth Centuries'. *Journal of Urban History* 28(3): 328–51.

Adam, T. 2004. *Philanthropy, Patronage, and Civil Society: Experiences from Germany, Great Britain, and North America*. Philanthropic and Nonprofit Studies. Bloomington, IN: Indiana University Press.

Aro, J. 2016. 'The Paavo Housing Programmes in Finland'. In 'Public Policy, Social Innovation and Marginalisation in Europe. A Comparative Analysis of Three Case Studies'. For 'Creating Economic Space for Social Innovation' (CrESSI), edited by D. Edmiston, and J. Aro, pp. 11–31. Brussels: European Commission.

Baaser, F. 1960. 'Gründung der Genossenschaft—eine Idee wird Wirklichkeit'. In *40 Jahre Gemeinnützige Kleingarten- und Siedlungsgenossenschaft Altmannsdorf-Hetzendorf Wien*, edited by H. Bauer, Vienna.

Blau, E. 1999. *The Architecture of Red Vienna, 1919–1934*. Cambridge, MA: MIT Press.

Blau, E. 2012. 'Das Neue Wohnen: Der Gemeindebau und die Entstehung einer proletarischen Wohnkultur'. In *Living Rooms—Politik der Zugehörigkeiten im Wiener Gemeindebau*, edited by F. Bettl, J. Mouraõ Permoser, and S. Rosenberger, pp. 165–96. Vienna: Springer.

Boccardo, N. 2008. 'The Impact of EU Rules on the Definition of Social Housing'. In *Social Housing in Europe II: A Review of Policies and Outcomes*, edited by C. M. E. Whitehead and K. Scanlon, pp. 261–70. London: London School of Economics and Political Science.

Brahams, E. 1987. *Der Wiener Gemeindebau. Vom Karl Marx-Hof zum Hundertwasserhaus* (Architectur im zusammenhang). Basel: Birkhäuser Verlag.

Cremer, U. 1992. *Wohnbau zwischen Dauer und Veränderung. Konzepte und Erscheinungsformen baulicher Entwicklungsfähigkeit*. Stuttgart: Karl Krämer Verlag.

Denby, E. 1938. *Europe Re-housed*. Studies in International Planning History. London: George Allen and Unwin.

Edwards-Schachter, M., and M. L. Wallace. 2017. '"Shaken, But Not Stirred": Sixty Years of Defining Social Innovation'. *Technological Forecasting and Social Change* 119: 64–79.

Eger, A. O. 2010. 'Evolutionary Product Development in Working-Class Housing'. http://doc.utwente.nl/72533/1/2010_02_03_EPD_in_Working-Class_Housing_Essay.pdf, accessed 3 July 2019.

Eigner, P., H. Matis, and A. Resch. 1999. 'Sozialer Wohnbau in Wien. Eine historische Bestandsaufnahme'. In *Jahrbuch des Vereins für die Geschichte der Stadt Wien*, edited by Verein für die Geschichte der Stadt Wien, Vienna.

Fishman, R. 1977. *Urban Utopias in the Twentieth Century: Ebenezer Howard, Frank Lloyd Wright, and Le Corbusier*. New York: Basic Books.

Foray, D., D. C. Mowery, and R. R. Nelson. 2012. 'Public R&D and Social Challenges: What Lessons from Mission R&D Programs?' *Research Policy* 41(10): 1697–702.

Förster, W. 1980. 'Die Wiener Arbeitersiedlungsbewegung vor dem Zweiten Weltkrieg—Eine Alternative zum kommunalen Wohnbauprogramm?' *der Aufbau* 35(12): 405ff.

Frampton, K. 2002. *Labour, Work and Architecture: Collected Essays on Architecture and Design*. London: Phaidon.

Frei, A. G. 1991. *Die Arbeiterbewegung und die 'Graswurzeln' am Beispiel der Wiener Wohnungspolitik 1919–1934* (Vergleichende Gesellschaftsgeschichte und politische Ideengeschichte der Neuzeit, 7). Vienna: Braumüller.

Ghékière, L. 2007. *Le développement du logement social dans l'Union Européenne. Quand l'intérêt général rencontre l'intérêt communautaire*. Paris: Dexia Editions.

Ghékière, L. 2008. 'Social Housing as a Service of General Interest'. In *Social Housing in Europe II: A Review of Policies and Outcomes*, edited by C. M. E. Whitehead, and K. Scanlon, pp. 271–86. London: London School of Economics and Political Science.

Giesecke, S. 2015. 'Community Housing in the City of Vienna—100 Years of Social Transformation'. In 'Evidence Base of Three Comprehensive Case Studies Following a Common Template'. For 'Creating Economic Space for Social Innovation' (CrESSI), edited by T. Scheuerle, G.-C. Schimpf, G. Mildenberger, and G. Glänzel, pp. 155–96. Brussels: European Commission.

Giesecke, S. 2016. 'Financing Social Housing'. In 'Theoretical Foundations of Social Innovation in Finance'. For 'Creating Economic Space for Social Innovation' (CrESSI), edited by C. Houghton Budd, and C. W. M. Naastepad, pp. 35–50. Brussels: European Commission.

Godin, B. 2012. 'Social Innovation: Utopias of Innovation from *c.*1830 to the Present'. Project on the Intellectual History of Innovation, Working Paper No. 11, Montreal. http://www.csiic.ca/PDF/SocialInnovation_2012.pdf.

Haindlmaier, G. 2017. 'The Relation between Social and Technological Innovation in Housing Projects: The Example of "Rosa Zukunft", Austria'. In 'Comparative Report on Historic Examples and Similar Recent Social Innovations in an Early Stage'. For 'Creating Economic Space for Social Innovation' (CrESSI), edited by G.-C. Schimpf, pp. 36–46. Brussels: European Commission.

Harloe, M. 1995. *The People's Home? Social Rented Housing in Europe & America*. Studies in Urban and Social Change. Oxford: Blackwell.

Havas, A. 2016. 'Recent Economic Theorising on Innovation: Lessons for Analysing Social Innovation'. For 'Creating Economic Space for Social Innovation' CrESSI Working Paper No. 27. Brussels: European Commission.

Hegedüs, J. 2008. 'Social Housing in Transitional Countries—The Case of Hungary'. In *Social Housing in Europe II: A Review of Policies and Outcomes*, edited by

C. M. E. Whitehead and K. Scanlon, pp. 145–62. London: London School of Economics and Political Science.

Hegedüs, J., and I. Tosics. 1996. 'Disintegration of the East-European Housing Model'. In *Housing Privatization in Eastern Europe*. Contributions in Sociology, 117, edited by D. Clapham, J. Hegedüs, K. Kintrea, and I. Tosics., pp. 15ff. Westport, CT: Greenwood Press.

Hoffmann, R. 1982. 'Proletarisches Siedeln—Otto Neuraths Engagement für die Wiener Siedlerbewegung und den Gildensozialismus von 1920 bis 1925'. In *Arbeiterbildung in der Zwischenkriegszeit. Otto Neurath und sein Gesellschafts- und Wirtschaftsmuseum in Wien 1925–1934. Politische Graphik von Gerd Arnitz und den Konstruktivisten*, edited by F. Stadler, pp. 140–8. Vienna: Löcker.

IZA—Institute for the Study of Labor (ed.). 2013. 'Social Housing in the EU: Report for European Parliament's Committee on Employment and Social Affairs'. Brussels. http://www.europarl.europa.eu/RegData/etudes/note/join/2013/492469/IPOL-EMPL_NT%282013%29492469_EN.pdf.

Kampffmeyer, H. 1908. 'Die Gartenstadtbewegung'. *Abhandlungen. Jahrbücher für Nationalökonomie und Statistik*: 577–609.

Kampffmeyer, H. 1926. 'Aus der Wiener Siedlungsbewegung'. *der Aufbau* 1/8/9: 130–5.

Kernbauer, H., and F. Weber. 1984. 'Von der Inflation zur Depression. Österreichs Wirtschaft 1918–1934'. In *"Austrofaschismus". Beiträge über Politik, Ökonomie und Kultur 1934–1938. Österreichische Texte zur Gesellschaftskritik*, edited by E. Talos and W. Neugebauer, pp. 1–30. Vienna: Verlag für Gesellschaftskritik.

Kieß, W. 1991. *Urbanismus im Industriezeitalter. Von der klassizistischen Stadt zur Garden City*. Berlin: Ernst.

Koch, R. 1987. *Die Pioniere vom Rosenhügel. Der zweite Aufbruch*. Eine Dokumentation der gemeinnützigen Siedlungs-Genossenschaften Altmannsdorf und Hetzendorf. Vienna.

Krämer, S. 2013. *Deutsche Unternehmer und ihre Arbeiterkolonien im 19. und frühen 20. Jahrhundert*. Schriftenreihe der Winckelmann Akademie für Kunstgeschichte München, Textbeitrag 4. Munich: Akademie für Kunstgeschichte.

Lévy-Vroelant, C., C. Reinprecht, and F. Wassenberg. 2008. 'Learning from Histories: Changes and Path Dependency in the Social Housing Sector in Austria, France and the Netherlands (1889—2008)'. In *Social Housing in Europe II: A Review of Policies and Outcomes*, edited by C. M. E. Whitehead, and K. Scanlon, pp. 31–47. London: London School of Economics and Political Science.

Malpass, P. 1986. 'The Development of Public Housing Policy in Britain' PhD thesis, University of Bristol.

Mazzucato, M. 2016. 'From Market Fixing to Market-Creating: A New Framework for Innovation Policy'. *Industry and Innovation* 23(2): 140–56.

Morgan, K. O. 1984. *Labour in Power 1945–51*. Oxford: Clarendon Press.

Mowery, D. C., R. R. Nelson, and B. R. Martin. 2010. 'Technology Policy and Global Warming: Why New Policy Models Are Needed (Or Why Putting New Wine in Old Bottles Won't Work)'. *Research Policy* 39(8): 1011–23.

Neumann, L. 1929. 'Österreichische Wohnungspolitik'. In *Das Wohnungswesen in Österreich*, edited by L. Neumann, pp. 21–33. Vienna: Gewista.

Nicholls, A., and R. Ziegler. 2015. 'An Extended Social Grid Model for the Study of Marginalization Processes and Social Innovation'. In 'Report on Institutions, Social Innovation and System Dynamics from the Perspective of the Marginalised'. CrESSI Working Paper No. 2. Brussels: European Commission, DG Research.

Novy, K. 1981. 'Selbsthilfe als Reformbewegung. Der Kampf der Wiener Siedler nach dem 1. Weltkrieg'. *arch+* 55: 26–46.

Novy, K., and W. Förster. 1991. *Einfach bauen. Genossenschaftliche Selbsthilfe nach der Jahrhundertwende: zur Rekonstruktion der Wiener Siedlerbewegung*. Vienna: Picus.

OECD. 2005. *Oslo Manual: Guidelines for Collecting and Interpreting Innovation Data*, 3rd edition. Paris: OECD Publishing.

Ottillinger, E. B. 2015. 'Küchenmöbel—Kochräume'. In *Küchen/Möbel. Design und Geschichte; [... erscheint zur Ausstellung 'Küchen/Möbel. Design und Geschichte' im Hofmobiliendepot—Möbelmuseum Wien, 4. März—26. Juli 2015]*. Publikationsreihe der Museen des Mobiliendepots, 32, edited by E. B. Ottillinger, pp. 29–80. Vienna: Böhlau.

Peltonen, M. 1992. *Talolliset ja torpparit. Vuosisadan vaihteen maatalouskysymys Suomessa*. Historiallisia tutkimuksia, 164. Helsinki: SHS.

Pirhofer, G. 1982. 'Ansichten zum Wiener Kommunalen Wohnbau der zwanziger und frühen dreißiger Jahre'. In *Die andere Kultur. Volkskunde, Sozialwissenschaften und Arbeiterkultur: ein Tagungsbericht*, edited by H. Fielhauer and O. Bockhorn, pp. 217–41. Vienna: Europaverlag.

Pirhofer, G., and R. Sieder. 1982. 'Zur Konstitution der Arbeiterfamilie im Roten Wien. Familienpolitik, Kulturreform, Alltag und Ästhetik'. In *Historische Familienforschung*. Suhrkamp-Taschenbuch Wissenschaft, 387, edited by M. Mitterauer and R. Sieder, pp. 326–68. Frankfurt am Main: Suhrkamp.

Pittini, A., and E. Laino. 2011. 'Housing Europe Review 2012: The Nuts and Bolts of European Social Housing Systems'. Brussels. http://www.housingeurope.eu/resource-105/the-housing-europe-review-2012.

Posch, W. 1981. *Die Wiener Gartenstadtbewegung. Reformversuch zwischen erster und zweiter Gründerzeit*. Tusch-Urbanistica, 1. Vienna: Edition Tusch.

Reinprecht, C. 2007. 'Social Housing in Austria'. In *Social Housing in Europe*, edited by C. M. E. Whitehead and K. Scanlon, pp. 35–42. London: London School of Economics and Political Science.

Reinprecht, C. 2012. 'Die Zukunft des Wiener Gemeindebaus und die Transformation des Sozialen'. In *Living Rooms—Politik der Zugehörigkeiten im Wiener Gemeindebau*, edited by F. Bettl, J. Mouraõ Permoser, and S. Rosenberger, pp. 205–20. Vienna: Springer.

Roberts, H. 1850. *The Dwellings of the Labouring Classes*. London: The Society for Improving the Condition of Labouring Classes.

Roberts, H. 1859. *The Improvement of the Dwellings of the Labouring Classes through the Operation of Government Measures*. London: Nabu Press.

Roberts, H. 1862. *The Essentials of a Healthy Dwelling and the Extension of its Benefits to the Labouring Population*. London.

Schacherl, F. 1926. 'Die Städtebauer der ganzen Welt'. *Arbeiterzeitung*, 12 September.

Scheuerle, T., and G. Glänzel. 2016. 'Five Per Cent Philanthropy as an Early Form of Social Impact Investing: Differences, Parallels, and What Can Be Learned for Today'. In 'Theoretical Foundations of Social Innovation in Finance'. For 'Creating Economic Space for Social Innovation' (CrESSI), edited by C. Houghton Budd and C. W. M. Naastepad, pp. 7–34. Brussels: European Commission.

Scheuerle, T., G.-C. Schimpf, G. Glänzel, and G. Mildenberger (eds). 2016a. 'Report on Relevant Actors in Historic Examples and an Empirically Driven Typology on Types of Social Innovation'. For 'Creating Economic Space for Social Innovation'. CrESSI Working Paper No. 29. Brussels: European Commission, DG Research.

Scheuerle, T., G.-C. Schimpf, G. Glänzel, G. Mildenberger, and R. Ziegler. 2016b. 'Three Major Social Innovations as Viewed through the Lens of the Extended Social Grid Model'. In 'Report on Relevant Actors in Historic Examples and an Empirically Driven Typology on Types of Social Innovation'. For 'Creating Economic Space for Social Innovation' (CrESSI), edited by T. Scheuerle, G.-C. Schimpf, G. Glänzel, and G. Mildenberger, pp. 1–224. Brussels: European Commission.

Schimpf, G.-C. (ed.). 2017. 'Comparative Report on Historic Examples and Similar Recent Social Innovations in an Early Stage'. For 'Creating Economic Space for Social Innovation'. CrESSI Working Paper No. 35. Brussels: European Commission, DG Research.

Schimpf, G.-C., T. Scheuerle, and G. Mildenberger. 2017. 'Comparative Case Analysis: Learning from Historic Case Studies for Current Social Innovations in Social Housing, Fresh Water Supply, and Beyond'. In 'Comparative Report on Historic Examples and Similar Recent Social Innovations in an Early Stage'. For 'Creating Economic Space for Social Innovation' (CrESSI), edited by G.-C. Schimpf, pp. 1–35. Brussels: European Commission.

Schwan, B. 1935. *Town Planning and Housing throughout the World*. Berlin: Verlag Ernst Wasmuth.

Tainio, H., and P. Fredriksson. 2009. 'The Finnish Homelessness Strategy: From a "Staircase" Model to a "Housing First" Approach to Tackling Long-Term Homelessness'. *European Journal of Homelessness*, 3. http://www.asuntoensin.fi/files/1199/Fredriksson_Tainio_2009.pdf, accessed 12 October 2016.

Viehhauser, M. 2016. *Reformierung des Menschen durch Stadtraumgestaltung. Eine Studie zur moralerzieherischen Strategie in Städtebau und Architektur um 1900*, Weilerswist: Velbrück Wissenschaft.

Weber, F. 1981. 'Hauptprobleme der wirtschaftlichen und sozialen Entwicklung Österreichs in der Zwischenkriegszeit'. In *Aufbruch und Untergang. Österreichische Kultur zwischen 1918 und 1983*, edited by F. Kadrnoska, pp. 593–621. Vienna: Europaverlag.

Whitehead, C. M. E., and K. Scanlon (eds). 2007. *Social Housing in Europe*, London: London School of Economics and Political Science. http://www.lse.ac.uk/geographyAndEnvironment/research/London/pdf/SocialHousingInEurope.pdf.

Wiener Magistrat. 2015. 'Growth of the City—History of Vienna'. https://www.wien.gv.at/english/history/overview/growth.html, accessed 19 March 2015.

Wiener Wohnen. 2015. 'Mitbestimmungsstatut'. https://www.wien.gv.at/english/history/overview/growth.html, accessed 19 March 2015.

Zimmerl, U. 1998. 'Wiener Siedlerbewegung und Siedlungswesen in der Zwischenkriegszeit'. Vienna: Universität Wien.

6

Trajectories of Social Innovation

Water for All?

Gudrun-Christine Schimpf and Rafael Ziegler

Introduction

In 2006, the UNDP published a report that starkly concluded: 'the crisis in water and sanitation is—above all—a crisis for the poor' (UNDP 2006: 7). This UNDP report backed up its claim with numerous facts: more than 660 million people without sanitation live on less than $2 a day accounting for almost two-thirds of all the people lacking access to clean water. The report documented global water inequalities between countries, but also, within countries and, even, cities, noting that people living in the slums of Jakarta (Indonesia), Manila (the Philippines) and Nairobi (Kenya) typically pay five–ten times more for water per unit than those in high-income parts of their own cities and more, even, than consumers in London or New York. One reason for these astonishing differences is the lack of water and sewage infrastructure in slums. The absence or insufficiency of water-supply pipes and of wastewater removal makes it very costly to supply households with water and, beyond contributing to economic inequality, also creates numerous health challenges in these densely populated areas.

While the UNDP report called for public financing to overcome these issues, it also raises important questions: why are such problems hardly known in the large, urban centres of 'developed' countries and what needs to be done so that high-quality, affordable drinking water becomes and remains a public good for all? From a historical perspective, these questions remind us that access to clean water is a social innovation long since institutionalized and taken for granted in rich countries. The consequence is that we tend to know little about its origins, about the actions needed to maintain and adapt it, or about lessons from this history of how best to provide universal access to clean and affordable water. Such a historical perspective reminds us that social innovation is not only a recent phenomenon. Rather, 'it is helpful to perceive the history of welfare and the welfare state as a history of social innovations taken up or rejected, marginalized or mainstreamed' (Evers et al. 2014). Urban freshwater supply as a social innovation even precedes the history of the welfare state by some time if Bismarck's social policies are taken as a starting point for the welfare state.

Gudrun-Christine Schimpf and Rafael Ziegler, *Trajectories of Social Innovation: Water for All?*
In: *Creating Economic Space for Social Innovation.* Edited by: Alex Nicholls and Rafael Ziegler,
Oxford University Press (2019).
DOI: 10.1093/oso/9780198830511.003.0006

This chapter examines the introduction and diffusion in nineteenth-century Europe of urban freshwater supply as a social innovation.[1] The story begins with the confluence of rapid urbanization in industrializing Britain and the critical evaluation of this process by utilitarian social reformers. Modern urban freshwater supply emerged in response to the social needs arising from these dramatic changes. There was nothing inevitable about these responses: the slums of the twenty-first century vividly illustrate alternative trajectories of rapid urbanization. A social-innovation focus allows us to examine in detail the ways networks of actors, institutions, and cognitive frames of thinking created the urban water supply we know today and critically to track its diffusion as a mainstream, institutionalized solution.[2]

The material used for our freshwater case study was collected through desktop research (historical sources and literature, statistics) and, for the most recent part of the trajectory, interviews.[3] We analysed the qualitative material using the Extended Social Grid Model (ESGM). In this way, we sorted through the complex reality of social innovation in history and explored the utility of the ESGM for social innovation research.

Our ESGM analysis revealed that the seemingly linear development of this social innovation was, in fact, rife with controversy. Modern freshwater supply is a centrally provided good requiring significant infrastructure. Its water works, piping, and pumping stations are, therefore, conducive to path-dependency. This artefactual power (see chapter 2) creates space for debate regarding economic and political power, especially in terms of private versus public provision of fresh water and rural versus urban diffusion.

This chapter is divided into four parts. The next section introduces the history of modern urban freshwater provision in Europe. The following three sections turn to the specifics of the development of urban freshwater provision: the non-trivial matter of establishing urban freshwater supply *as a social issue*; the controversy of private versus public modes of providing fresh water; and the role of knowledge and professional power in the prevailing solutions, as well as in alternative solutions for freshwater provision. The final section offers some conclusions.

Historical Phases of Freshwater Provision

A literature survey on freshwater supply suggests five phases of development in modern Europe (Sedlak 2014; Juuti and Katko 2005: 237–8; Prasad 2008b) that are

[1] We would like to thank Amelia Pope for her editorial work and suggestions. The chapter also has benefitted from prior presentations, notably in Budapest (April 2016) and the comments of our CrESSI colleagues there.

[2] 'Mainstream' here refers not to the most preferred solution but to the most widely used.

[3] To learn about research design and methodology in more detail, see the chapters 1 and 4.

briefly outlined below. We should stress that this is a rough sketch that seeks to highlight the major developments of interest to our analysis of the emergence and diffusion of modern urban freshwater supply as a social innovation. It is also possible to focus in each city and town in each country in Europe to discover further complexities and countervailing trends.[4]

The first phase begins in the early nineteenth century, when the prevailing cognitive frame presented the growing problems of access to safe drinking and domestic water as *private* issues that would naturally be resolved over time. In this context, private entrepreneurs typically set up the first water systems. An emerging network of social reformers, engineers, and parliamentarians subsequently reframed the challenge as a *social* issue: it was not the poor morals of the labouring class that caused the drinking-water access and hygiene problems, but a lack of sufficient public infrastructure. This change in cognitive frames represents the starting point for modern urban freshwater supply as a social innovation. The aim was to provide freshwater supply at the urban level of industrialized or industrializing countries so as to ensure safe living and working conditions for all, including the poor and marginalized in the rapidly growing cities.[5] The emerging infrastructural vision was of a central, piped supply of treated fresh water to all houses and their water closets linked to a sewage system that moved waste water from domestic and industrial uses to sewage treatment plants. The famous Chadwick report in 1842 (Chadwick 1842) is a good example of this change in cognitive frames that built new social networks of action. As a self-conscious attempt in applied science, it illustrates an emphasis on the importance of knowledge in terms of a medical, social, and infrastructural study of the challenge. It is of little surprise, then, that John Snow's discovery of a causal relation between a (contaminated) water pump in Soho, London, and a cholera outbreak in this neighbourhood in 1854 is widely cited as the beginning of modern epidemiology (Snow 1965; Johnson 2006; Hempel 2007; Prasad 2008b: 7). The emerging epidemiology provided arguments to make water filtration and chlorine disinfection standard practices—with a tremendous impact on health and life expectancy. Figures for England and Wales show that life expectancy increased with the improved freshwater supply: by 1912 the average lifespan had increased by twenty years. Likewise, infant mortality went down after a rise in investment in sanitation shortly before the turn of the nineteenth century (UNDP 2006: 29 f.).

[4] For more details, see the CrESSI report in Scheuerle et al. (2016a).

[5] In Roman cities and, later, in some medieval European ones there were public supply systems for water. However, there are important differences: the Romans did not have the modern conception of water as H_20 and for this reason transported different waters in separate aqueducts to their cities (Linton 2010: 81ff.). They lacked a systematic insight into the relation of water quality and health (as afforded by the emerging epidemiology of the nineteenth century) and, most importantly, the goal of safe health and working conditions for all citizens including the poor and marginalized. The latter is a distinctive feature linked to the rise of the industrializing states of the nineteenth century and indeed of the 'social' itself (Arendt 1998).

In the second phase, from the mid-nineteenth century to the early twentieth century, there was a marked change from private to public provision. While in the first phase private operators typically built urban freshwater provision, in the second phase municipalities increasingly assumed responsibility for supply. In countries like the United Kingdom, Germany, or Italy, municipalities started to build their own waterworks or took them over from private operators (Lenger 2012: 148; Lobina 2005: 107). The need to extend the freshwater network was one important reason to set up public freshwater provision. Experience showed that when provision was in the hands of a private company the network was not extended consistently, quality was not regularly improved, and charges were disproportionately high as private profits were maximized. Unprofitable areas where the number of expected customers was low were not supplied. Public providers, by contrast, usually invested in extending the freshwater network to everyone. Public bodies decided which areas required development first, and city governments exerted greater pressure to meet social criteria when setting up prices (Prasad 2008b: 19–20). These pro-active municipalities benefitted from networks of social reformers, doctors, engineers, and politicians who were driven, at least in part, by the conviction that states should meet the essential needs of all their citizens. The emerging public-health movement lifted these efforts from the local to the national and international levels by arranging lectures, conferences, and study tours (Schott and Skroblies 1987: 83–4, 87; Simson 1983: 22–5). Robert Koch's discovery of the bacteria responsible for tuberculosis (1882) and cholera (1883)—along with the growing field of bacteriology—pushed this trajectory further (Grüntzig and Mehlhorn 2010) and underlined the importance of scientific knowledge for shaping and diffusing modern freshwater supply. Laws on public health and water regulation were introduced, enabling municipalities to build and operate large water-supply systems. The availability of newly codified knowledge on building large-scale supply and disposal systems was also a significant driver.

The third phase of modern freshwater supply lasted from the early twentieth century to the 1980s. This phase saw the diffusion of centralized public water provision to many municipalities and subsequently, rural areas. During this phase, more than 99 per cent of the EU population became connected to the water network (WHO 2015). Safe and affordable drinking water for all became institutionalized and drinking-water quality standards became increasingly sophisticated. These institutional developments were also important from a social network perspective as their increasing knowledge requirements grew the demand for water professionals and other relevant experts. Expanding and maintaining water infrastructure became a major economic investment that attracted planners and engineers and created economic opportunities for professionals around water-quality treatment. The normative goal of providing fresh water, thus, also was accompanied by economic interests. Yet, with the extension to the countryside—to small villages, hamlets, or even single farms and houses—the model of centrally provided fresh water became increasingly expensive and began to meet resistance.

In the fourth phase, from the 1980s to the early 2000s, a private-provision perspective regained prominence. This time the new cognitive frame originated less from specific concerns around water management in towns. Rather, it came from a neo-liberal vision of the economy driven by a backlash against post-Second-World-War Keynesianism and its difficulties dealing with stagflation that combined high inflation and high unemployment (Mann 2013). Neo-liberalism had been gaining ground since the 1970s. Its ideal of unconstrained markets (Okereke 2008) made the privatization of publicly owned companies an obvious goal. Water was no longer framed as a public good, but as a commodity that should be treated as an 'economic good in all its uses', as the 1992 Dublin Principles noted (Conca 2006: 141–3). A focus on 'efficiency' (associated with market provision) was given priority over issues of universal distribution and equality of access. This policy agenda for the privatization of services, market provision, and a rolling back of the state began in the United Kingdom in the mid 1980s. In England and Wales, a change in government regulatory policies gave economic efficiency priority over social equity (Bakker 2001). Later, other European countries and cities followed (Prasad 2008b: 12). In this neo-liberal phase, water professionals became more closely associated with managers of private companies, as well as other financial actors—not least the World Bank—that pushed for further investment from private water companies in both 'developed' and 'developing' countries.

However, outside the United Kingdom, this agenda also encountered much more resistance than expected (Prasad 2008a). In Berlin, for example, the municipal Berlin Water Works were responsible for drinking water and waste water after the reunification of Germany. In 1999, a public–private partnership was set up between the Berlin Water Works, Veolia, and RWE. It was the biggest municipal public–private partnership in Germany. The relevant contract stipulated that, while only 49 per cent of the shares were private, the private actors had 100 per cent of the management rights (including pricing rights) and a guaranteed profit margin. However, due to popular resistance initiated by a citizens' initiative—the Berlin Water Table—the contract was made public, and Berlin Water Works were re-municipalized in 2012/13 (Härlin 2017). Thus, a social network of civil-society associations and trade unions—sharing a social justice and sustainability agenda—successfully made the case for water as a public good (Barlow 2008) resulting in the re-municipalization of the water supply. A 2014 report observed 180 cases of re-municipalization, 136 of which were in high-income countries: of these, forty-nine were in France, the country with historically the most powerful private water suppliers (Lobina et al. 2014). Importantly, those arguing for re-municipalization stressed the need to think beyond the private–public dichotomy so as to take into account new challenges including climate change adaption and new developments in ICT (such as 'smart' water metering).

A fifth phase can be seen today that started around the turn of the millennium. In the last few years, we can see an increasing reorientation towards public provision of fresh water and a new awareness of a diversity of supply solutions. Freshwater supply in some major European cities such as Berlin and Paris was re-municipalized.[6] This trend has been enforced by new associations supporting public water supply—such as Aqua Publica Europea, the association of European public water operators and civic-society networks as well as social movements such as Right2water. As growing technological sophistication and privatization processes made democratic accountability difficult, participation—meaning more than just representation in municipalities—became an important issue (Scheuerle et al. 2016b: 151–2, see also Juuti and Katko 2005: 238). These new social networks call for democratic accountability and improved social, as well as ecological, standards of universal freshwater provision. They aim to share and provide information and look for dialogue and participation in policy change processes. An important motive is to bring water back to the people and keep it affordable for all. These social networks have been bolstered by a UN General Assembly declaration that access to clean water is a human right in 2010.

However, the mode of market provision continues to play an important role. While some countries, like Finland, changed their provision, in many cases, from public to market, others (e.g. Italy, Hungary, and the United Kingdom) hold on to varieties of private–public partnerships. All in all, though, scepticism about handing over public resources to business has grown in many European countries. With pressure coming both from top-down (such as EU directives for drinking water, waste water, and the Water Framework Directive for rivers, lakes, and groundwater) and bottom-up (via citizens' initiatives), a more holistic and integrated freshwater management system has been called for. Considering the challenges ahead—such as global warming and changes in patterns of population and demography—longer-term perspectives, stakeholder participation, 'smart' coordination across sectors, and knowledge-intensive innovation have become essential (Koop and van Leeuwen 2016). However, the path-dependencies of urban water infrastructure pose considerable challenges to innovation around adaptation to climate change with increasingly extreme weather influencing both water resources as well as sewage treatment.

[6] For a list of all re-nationalizations see Lobina and Hall (2013), see also https://www.tni.org/en/publication/here-to-stay-water-remunicipalisation-as-a-global-trend (accessed 23 June 2017). On the re-municipalization in Paris and its social-impact focus see: http://www.aquapublica.eu/?Celia-Blauel-puts-forward-social&lang=en (accessed 20 April 2016); http://www.eaudanslaville.fr/spip.php?article883 (accessed 23 June 2017); http://www.eaudeparis.fr/lespace-culture/actualites/actualite/news/un-nouveau-contrat-dobjectifs-pour-eau-de-paris/?L=0&cHash=b4d8cedac3a10a77fd59807806ffc7b0 (accessed 23 June 2017).

In summary, economic and political power predominated in the nineteenth century (Mann 1993) and significant social change occurred as a result of the entwining of these powers. In response to the Industrial Revolution and rapidly growing urban centres, political power responded with the development of the welfare state. In our case, this drove social innovation in safe and affordable freshwater provision for all. The motivations were various. There was a clear moral utilitarian case for improving the social circumstances of the poor, but there were also instrumental reasons for such action to reduce outbreaks of epidemics to ensure a healthy workforce and to contain the social tensions created by the working-class population acquiring more collective power.[7] Social reformers drew on both moral and instrumental arguments. From an historical perspective, they largely succeeded.

Modes of Freshwater Provision and Wastewater Treatment

As introduced in detail in chapter 3 of this book, the economic space for social innovation is by no means limited to markets and money-based exchange mechanisms. Rather, it is clear that there are a variety of modes of provision with which to provide a public good or service. Indeed, this variety of modes and their dynamic combinations are central for social innovation. This section examines this point in detail with respect to modern freshwater supply and its modes of provision. Five modes are set out below: self-provision; informal provision; market provision; public provision; and professional provision (see chapter 3).

Self-Provision. While the development of urban freshwater provision is truly astonishing in its impact, this should not lead us to overlook self-provision. Especially in the countryside, to this day, self-provision from domestic wells and house fountains is the main source of fresh water. For this model, no exchange with others is required. This mode of provision became increasingly marginalized in the twentieth century, but still exists in many places across the world to this day.

Informal Provision. Closely related to self-provision, informal providers can be small units of freshwater supply—such as entire communities or associations of houses organizing their water supply together. These small-scale providers have been under intense pressure due to the expansion of central water supply as well as to the increased use of fertilizers and pesticides following the Second World War that have affected the purity of the water table. Networks have formed to resist such pressure and adapt to the new challenges—an example is the IKT Network in Bavaria (Ziegler 2017). While participants typically have to pay a membership fee

[7] Perhaps unsurprisingly, Friedrich Engels belonged to the early readers of Chadwick's report.

to a communal association, much of the work providing water and maintaining good quality is done on a voluntary basis. Somewhere in the grey zone between informal provision and market provision lie cooperatives. They are a specific organizational type, yet they typically do not sell their product to a water market but only provide water to their members (Steuer 1912: 57; Feldkamp 2009: 28; Katko 2004, 2013: 230–1; Scheuerle et al. 2016b: 113).

Market Provision. In this mode, private companies supply water, selling it to customers. The leader in private water provision is France, with a private water-supply history dating back to the nineteenth century. During this time drinking water became an industrial and commercial product (Hassan 1996: 122). Throughout the twentieth century water provision remained largely a public–private arrangement in most other 'developed' countries (Hassan 1996: 125). Yet, at the end of the twentieth century, about 80 per cent of France's water supply remained in private hands (Reynaud 2008: 38, 47–8; Hassan 1996: 121, 123). Importantly, private provision does not mean there is no public regulation: national, regional, and municipal governments regulate via quality standards and link provision with wider social policies. Due to the increasing expertise required for water provision, however, effective control of private investments and pricing is very difficult for the public sector to manage.

Public Provision: Public drinking-water provision is typically in the hands of municipally owned water works or inter-communal associations (e.g. the German 'Zweckverband'). Political processes of decision-making typically manage the provisioning modes, though maintaining democratic accountability can be challenging.

Professional Provision: Provision is based on the expert knowledge of the provider and is supplied to paying clients directly or indirectly linked to public or private subsidies. As noted above, the increase in engineering and health knowledge in water supply has been associated with an increase in water professionals. Water professionals, inter alia, take water samples and analyse them in laboratories, help orient planning, acceptance, and inspection of wastewater plants and are involved in the standardization of regulation and the definition of terms. In short, even where water supply is in public, private, or communal/self-providing hands, professional provision likely contributes significantly to the final 'water product'.

Historically, modern urban freshwater provision frequently started with private operators, but in the second half of the nineteenth century public provision largely became the norm. Both modes marginalized self- and informal provision in cities and towns and, later, also in rural areas. Public policy drove this, as policies increasingly set the goal that every household, regardless of geographical location, social class, or income, should have access to treated piped fresh water and later, should be part of an increasingly sophisticated wastewater treatment system. This was achieved for most urban regions in Europe by the early twentieth century (Prasad 2008b: 23; Juuti and Katko 2005: 41; De La Motte 2005: 205; Feldkamp 2009: 25).

This brief survey shows considerable diversity and dynamics in water provision in Europe over time. Analysing freshwater supply as a social innovation focused on equity raises several questions concerning the access to provision for the poorest and most marginalized populations. Are all modes of freshwater supply equally effective for the poor? What about the agency of citizens as an end and as a mean of social innovation—as beneficiaries of freshwater supply and as agents in water management? Finally, what can we learn from the historical dynamics for the ongoing development of this social innovation today? Table 6.1 sets out the five modes of provision set out above in relation to cognitive frames and the role of citizens. The content of the table is discussed next.

Table 6.1. Modes of provision

Mode of provision	Cognitive frames	Active role of citizens	Passive role of citizens
Self and informal provision (family, community)	Subsidiarity, autarky and self-determination Water as a commons Water as a natural good	Involved in provision Direct control of management	Passive community members due to group hierarchies, free riding etc.
Market provision	Efficiency Competition Profit-maximization Water as an economic good	Watchdog role Holding private providers to social and environmental standards	Customer paying for a service
Public provision	Safe and affordable freshwater access for all Water as a commons	Advocacy in problem formulation Watch-dog role Involved in set-up and/or controlling provision of services	Citizens with a basic entitlement to sufficient fresh water
Professional provision	Water as an epistemic expert good: H_2O with associated maximum permissible values (health) Water as artefactually mediated: 'Water is God's gift . . . but He forgot to lay the pipes' (Mann 2009).	Layperson controlling or cooperating with experts (for example citizen science)	Citizens as end users (health, household connections etc.)

Source: Authors' own compilation.

Establishing Water Provision as Social Challenge

For many people today public provision is arguably the best mode of water provision. Historically, however, this was not obvious and it was even less clear that the role of citizens should be considered. This section explores this notion of 'participation' and, then, moves on to the important issue of recognizing urban water provision as a social challenge in European history.

Citizen participation played a central role in the early twenty-first-century European discourse on social innovation (BEPA 2010). From a capabilities approach (see chapter 3), this is not surprising as participation is a key aspect of citizen empowerment in which they are treated not only as passive recipients of services but, instead, as engaged actors in the policies and decisions that govern their lives. There are various benefits of participation, including: improvement in social capital and social cohesion; empowerment and improvement in realizing individual capabilities; and greater confidence and skills (Davies et al. 2012: 9–18). However, these are potential rather than automatic benefits. Moreover, the term 'participation' needs to be specified further to assess such claims fully.

Nussbaum (2006) specified 'being able to participate effectively in political choices that govern one's life; having the right of political participation, protections of free speech and association' as a central capability category in her theory of basic justice. As access to fresh water is an issue centrally concerning 'one's life', the issue of participation is obviously germane. In contrast to participation defined as only 'getting informed', 'being consulted', or more actively 'getting involved' in the development of policies and their alternatives, Nussbaum's sense of participation requires individuals having an actual say in key decision-making. The focus is on 'top of the ladder of participation'—a metaphor made famous by Arnstein (1969)—and moves beyond manipulated or 'token' participation to partnership, delegated power, and citizen control. The capabilities approach suggests that while citizens are not required to exercise their power to 'say', they should still have a real opportunity to do so. The focus on the individual and her 'freedom to' (not just 'freedom from') reflects a liberal egalitarian (Nussbaum 2006; Sen 2009) or republican (Pettit 2014) political philosophy. What then about such participation in the history of fresh water?

A Glass of Water Provokes Mortal Questions

> My attention was first directed to this matter in London ten years ago, when a glass of water handed to me at a hotel, in another district, presented a peculiar film on its surface, which led me to set it aside; and after numerous inquiries, I was fully satisfied that the appearance which had attracted my attention arose from the coffins in a church-yard immediately adjoining the well where the water had been.
>
> (Chadwick 1843: 30)

Edwin Chadwick made this recollection in his *Report on the Sanitary Condition of the Labouring Population in Britain*. The 'other' district in this quote is significant for our discussion, as Chadwick's research on the poor took places in an institutional context that only gave full citizenry to men owning property.[8] At this point, the 'poor' did not have any formal rights to political participation, let alone real opportunity to participate.[9] Participation and political power (in Mann's sense) was limited to a select group of middle- and upper-class men, and their discussion in parliament and in the public sphere of nineteenth-century parliamentary democracy.

The district in the quote above is the district of the Houses of Parliament in London. Chadwick was an active citizen whose voice contributed to public discussion and decision-making. He was a lawyer by training and worked, from 1832 onwards, for the *Royal Commission into the Operation of the Poor Laws*. The Commission's reports directly influenced policymaking in parliament.

Two further aspects are noteworthy here. Chadwick—like other social reformers of the time—developed an interest early on in the role of science for social improvement. His 1843 report is packed with observations, materials, and interviews about hygiene in the growing cities of industrializing countries, especially London:

> In the poorer districts, in what state is the surface cleansing of the streets? Even the best streets are very badly cleansed, but in the poorer streets of the city the cleansing is very bad indeed, horribly bad! Take Duke's Place, for example; you will see cabbage stalks and rotten oranges that have been thrown away, and they often remain there for several days. We do not get our streets swept oftener than once a-week. (Chadwick 1843: 225)
>
> The great difficulty with the poor people is commonly how to get the water. There is a court in Cornhill which a man was cleansing the other day by applying a hose to the water-cock (which is used in case of fire), in order to cleanse the pavement. An officer belonging to the water company coming by, said, 'If I see you doing that again, I shall indict you.' (Chadwick 1843: 228)
>
> I do not remember an instance where water is properly laid on in any house of the labouring classes. (Chadwick 1843: 230)

His collection of observations about public hygiene conditions contributed to a detailed reframing of the issue of freshwater provision for the poor. He reported on the densely packed housing of the 'labouring population' and their

[8] The British Reform Act of 1832 introduced this limited suffrage.

[9] The Third Reform Act of 1884 introduced suffrage for all adult males. So-called 'universal' suffrage—including women older than 30—was only introduced in 1918. See http://www.nationalarchives.gov.uk/pathways/citizenship/struggle_democracy/getting_vote.htm, last checked 3 July 2017.

'over-packed' cemeteries—indeed, the role of coffins and churchyards for health was a central concern throughout the report. He argued that poor health, low life expectancy, and poor morals could not be attributed to the personal character and morality of the poor. Rather, they were (re)produced by the social circumstances:

> If there were a perfect system of drainage and cleansing in the city, do you think that the health and the duration of life of the inhabitants would be extended? I think there would be a considerable extension. The children born and bred up in London are more frequently of small stature and have slender limbs, are deficient in stamina and powers of endurance, are of irritable frames and prone to inflammatory attack, than children born and bred up in the country... When children are weakly, what is the effect on the temper and character? The temper and character of weakly children are generally found to correspond with, and are most probably derived from, the character of their constitution: their temper is quick and irritable, their passions ardent, their perception keen, and their imagination predominant over their judgment. (Chadwick 1843: 225)

This new cognitive frame underpinned the case for the development of an urban freshwater system that we know today:

> If all cesspools were removed, and water-closets substituted; if water were introduced into the houses of the poorest classes; if the sewers were regularly flushed weekly, or oftener, so as to prevent accumulations of deposit and the escape of miasma, such as you have described; if the carriage and foot pavements were more frequently and completely cleansed; if these several *public* duties were performed with practicable efficiency... I am quite confident that the adoption of such measures would not only diminish disease of every kind, but greatly improve the moral as well as the physical condition of the inhabitants.
>
> (Chadwick 1843: 225 f., italics added).

The second aspect of this new cognitive framing focused on practicable means of diminishing the number of deaths and burials in urban districts. Chadwick's philosophical outlook was utilitarian and he was concerned with increasing the overall utility of society—here in terms of life expectancy and improved health—as the ultimate moral and political task. Chadwick, who was in direct contact with other utilitarians such as Jeremy Bentham and John Stuart Mill, explored 'practicable means' of this philosophical doctrine. This philosophy legitimized a focus on maximizing utility and drove the statistical focus on 'numbers of deaths'. While in hindsight, and from our normative perspective today, improved health and life expectancy might improve the potential for the political participation of the poor, this was not the focus of Chadwick and his social reformer friends. There is a sense in Chadwick's report of what Williams would much later call 'Government house utilitarianism' (Williams 1985)—namely, the view that the educated and knowledgeable know best what should be done on behalf of the poor and for the general public good. Accordingly, hygiene and water management were increasingly seen as public duties, but without a focus on empowerment. Rather, there was a call for public officers qualified as experts (Williams 1985: 122) to administer an effective solution (Chadwick 1843: 122 ff.). Likewise, John Stuart Mill—in his discussion of utilitarianism—located ethical judgement with expert judges rather than with an appeal for increased political participation of those affected (Mill 1879). This is a first sign of the artefactual and professional power we encounter in the later phases of the development of freshwater provision.

We see in the early stages of modern urban freshwater provision a network of social reformers, doctors (and later epidemiologists), and engineers advocating the expansion of a universal urban freshwater supply and removal system. In terms of our discussion of participation and social innovation, this illustrates a public action that could be called *advocacy* or *vicarious* citizen participation. These reformers saw themselves as acting on behalf of marginalized populations, who were not directly included in systems of political participation. In this system of representative democracy and its attendant public sphere—Chadwick and the utilitarians actively contributed to newspapers and journals of the time—a paternalistic approach to citizen participation rested on an appeal to facts and science as well as a vision of welfare and the public good that did not require any political participation from those directly affected by policy decisions.

Such an approach to social innovation remains relevant today, in three ways. First, the Chadwick Report is an outstanding example of the importance of deliberative cognitive framing of an issue. The detailed evidence in the Report established that poor health and reduced life expectancy cannot be attributed plausibly to the 'morality' or 'character' of the poor. In terms of the capabilities approach, the Report shifted the focus on conversion factors from internal personal ones to external social ones—here urban planning and water management. Thus the case for public provision emerged, as did the conceptual foundation for urban freshwater supply as a social innovation providing water to all, including the most marginalized populations. Arguably, the case was so successful that it now requires some work to see the efforts required at the origins of this social innovation. The fundamental point Chadwick's Report demonstrated was that active engagement was required to reframe a problem as social (in contrast, say, to a regrettable but natural fact about the world). Arguably, this created the economic space—perhaps unintended at the time—within which to view the working-class population as active empowered citizens. The way this change was achieved—drawing on a detailed report linked to a new social network of doctors and engineers with the applied science, professional and technical know-how of the day—embodied the artefactual power of water professionals in the further diffusion and institutionalization of universal freshwater supply.[10] This artefactual power entwined with a typically Victorian view of political power that leaned more towards paternalism than laissez-faire (Mann 1993, 102). From this perspective, the regulation and provision of fresh water was framed as a necessary public good to be administered by experts.

Second, in addition to political participation, another major trend in the modern state is relevant today: *social* participation and citizenship. Marshall (quoted in Mann 1993: 19) defined this as 'the right to a modicum of economic welfare and security to . . . share to the full in the social heritage and to live the life of a civilized being according to the standards prevailing in the time.' The quote above concerning the cleansing of a pavement offers a 'pedestrian' example of such social standards and the difficulties of meeting them. Our case demonstrates how vicarious citizen participation created pressure to improve social citizenship and, with it, the pre-requisites of universal political participation.

Third, vicarious citizen participation was not only motivated by a moral consideration of the poor. Rather, instrumental reasoning of the 'middling' classes (as they were called at the time)—as well as of the political and economic elites—are also part of the case. In 1851, Chadwick's collaborator the engineer William Lindley, who built water supply and sewage systems in Germany, Switzerland, Hungary, and Russia (Scheuerle et al. 2016b: 88–9), put it this way:

> Lack of bodily cleanliness soon leads to lack of self-respect, roughness, and vice . . . An unclean population will suffer comparatively high rates of sickness and death, and since the poorer inhabitants of the city will be thrown onto the state finances to cover the costs in all such cases, this tax burden will for the most correspond to the cleanliness of the population. A dirty population degenerates and so commits all the more offences against the laws of the state, thus contributing to the continued need and expansion of our costly prisons . . . Lack of cleanliness makes the population all the more receptive to devastating epidemics such as cholera, smallpox, fever, etc., and encourages such diseases to become endemic or to return again. Experience shows that when these epidemics have reached a certain degree of severity they also reach the dwellings of the well off.
>
> (Quoted in Evans 1987: 118–19)

In summary, we argue that at the origins of our urban freshwater case we find an instance of vicarious citizen participation that remains relevant today as a mechanism for framing this problem as primarily *social*. This points to the advocacy

[10] Of course, Chadwick himself was an expert. He was one of the key figures that contributed to the creation of the economic space for new domains of expertise, especially in public health. However, it would seem anachronistic to label him as an expert for a specialized field that only fully emerged later. Therefore, we view his contribution mainly as a civic contribution to the public sphere. We would like to thank Attila Havas for pointing out this issue.

role of social innovators at the early stages of development and the discursive, normative aspects of claiming an issue as social (Schmitz 2015: 34–6). The freshwater case adds the epistemic novelty of reframing an issue via applied science and professional expertise in combination with a utilitarian vision of the public good. While this approach to urban freshwater provision has been successfully adopted across Europe and elsewhere, in the informal settlements and slums of rapidly growing urban centres worldwide much still needs to be done.

For new infrastructure development, for example linked to IT (Schimpf 2017), the freshwater case is also instructive. The value of vicarious citizen participation remains ambivalent and this ambivalence has accompanied the history of the welfare state from the beginning. The freshwater case noted an epidemiological-engineering perspective on urban freshwater provision that replaced the former, more diverse, place-based provision (Linton 2010). The new provision centred upon a vision of fresh water as a resource to be channelled to the citizen/welfare beneficiary and sluiced away again for sewage treatment. The prevailing standards (to use Marshall's phrasing) were increasingly complex. First national, then European, quality standards for drinking water and hygiene as well as for wastewater treatment were introduced. These would have been impossible to achieve without significant engineering knowledge and epistemic power. Moreover, standardized freshwater provision was conducive to a vision of water as 'H_2O' that was managed and circulated through the urban infrastructure.

Market versus Public Provision

The last few decades have seen a lively debate on the topic of privatizing or (re-)municipalizing the centralized freshwater supply. Our historical perspective shows that this debate is as old as the institutionalization of modern urban freshwater supply.

Early on, proponents of public provision of fresh water argued their case specifically with a view to supplying the whole population, and not just the rich, at affordable rates (Meyer 2011: 329). In 1866, Ludwig Hammers, the mayor of Düsseldorf in Germany, argued for public water provision: 'If only on account of the poorer classes, meeting such an indispensable need should not be left to the private sphere but should be met by the community' (quoted in Lenger 2012: 148). In the United Kingdom, in 1884, Joseph Chamberlain, a prominent Liberal Party politician, provided a classic argument in support of Hammers' view: 'It is difficult, if not impossible to combine the citizen's rights and interests and the private enterprise's interest, because the private enterprise aims at its natural and justified objective, the biggest possible profit' (quoted in Juuti and Katko 2005: 41). These views suggested that the state should take over responsibility for freshwater supply and sanitation services. In view of the enormous profits to be made from such services, universal freshwater supply was always threatened by the risk of profit maximization overriding social priorities.

During the peak of municipalization of the water supply in Italy, between 1903 and 1914, the hope was that effective local public management would finally represent 'a desired source of fair profits, and a relief for taxpayers' (Fazioli et al. 1999). However, the lure of profits also attracted the treasuries of the public sector since water pricing could be used to create cross-subsidies for other public expenditures or to reduce public debt. Opponents of public provision claimed that public administrative structures had counter-productive effects when running an enterprise. Bureaucracy was said to be inefficient, lacking in innovation, and to be incapable of effectively managing such a large organization or adjusting to changing economic situations (Meyer 2011: 88; Jellinghaus 2006: 218–19; Steuer 1912: 61).

Underlying the public-versus-private provision debate is one over alternative cognitive frames. These focus on whether freshwater provision is primarily a commons, a public or a private good. Some scholars have argued that this difference in framing draws from a further difference in framing: water as a natural resource versus water as a manufactured 'product'. They argue that in German-speaking and Nordic countries water has been regarded as 'a natural resource, which should ideally be supplied unpolluted and untreated, when possible'. As a consequence, publicly run freshwater provision has been maintained. However, countries like France or the United Kingdom have been more likely to regard drinking water 'as a "manufactured good" which regularly needs treatment before consumption'—this links more clearly to a greater acceptance of market provision (all quotes from Juuti and Katko 2005: 237).

Several lessons can be drawn from these longstanding debates over public versus private provision. First, when drinking water and sanitation are framed as a human right, the public regulation of freshwater is always part of the solution. Even in the case of private provision, public regulations for water quality and other water policies (with a view to affordability and access to all) are part of the approach.

Second, as the 'blue gold' will continue to attract the interest of private companies and public treasuries as a source of profit maximization, we also expect the public–private debate to continue. Regulation—and with it social and environmental standards—are important to hold organizations, private or public, accountable. In dense industrial and post-industrial environments, the regulatory control of water quality for human health and environment reasons is necessary. Water professionals who test water quality and standardize infrastructure exercise knowledge power beyond the public–private dichotomy. In practice, much of the accountability for safe and affordable freshwater provision and treatment depends on the work of these professionals ensuring water quality and anticipating new risks.

Third, in terms of freshwater supply as a social innovation providing water to all at an affordable price, the structural risk of the profit motive together with the difficulty of ensuring the democratic accountability of knowledge-intensive 'modern water' suggest that it is better to keep freshwater provision in public hands (Prasad 2008a). However, the various roles played by freshwater provision need to be considered—not just economic, but also social, environmental, and cultural roles (Juuti and Katko 2005: 242–3). As the European Water Framework Directive (European Parliament and European Council 2000) put it: 'Water is not a commercial product like any other but, rather, a heritage which must be protected, defended and treated as such.'

Knowledge, Path Dependency, and Niches

While at the beginning of modern freshwater supply many different approaches were discussed on the local or regional level, a standard approach eventually emerged (Vincenti 1990). Over time, this model was further enhanced with innovations and new technical norms. Path-dependencies developed with regard to the technical infrastructure and network character of urban water supply (Juuti and Katko 2005: 234, 239).[11] This is not necessarily a disadvantage from a social innovation perspective and the goal of providing everyone with fresh water. It still permits many innovative advancements in the organization of fresh water. However, adaptive innovation to tackle new challenges becomes more difficult as change entails high costs. For example, a system using the same treated fresh water for drinking and sanitation is not open to new experiments in sanitation—as the difficulty of experimenting with waterless closets demonstrates (DWA 2010). Additionally, there is the well-known innovation challenge that a solution in one place might turn out to be problematic elsewhere. Even within the mainstream solution approach there might be a 'mission shift' that can put social goals at risk. The next two sections discuss these challenges and their relation to social innovation further.

Self and Informal Modes of Provision

As rural areas became connected to central freshwater supply during the twentieth century—especially after the Second World War (Feldkamp 2009: 130)—this

[11] Juuti and Katko discussed path-dependency as present forms of operations and infrastructure binding future decisions: 'A *minor* or fleeting advantage, or a seemingly inconsequential lead, for some technology, product, or standard can have *important and irreversible influences* on the ultimate market allocation of resources, even in a world characterised by voluntary decisions and individuals' maximizing behaviour' (Juuti and Katko 2005: 22). They further pointed out that decisions regarding the form of water management (e.g. concessions given to private companies limited the possibilities for a certain time), decisions on (not) introducing metering, on combined or separated sewers, on water closets all set future agendas and are difficult or even impossible to revise (cf. Juuti and Katko 2005: 232).

diffusion process clashed with two alternative modes of provision: self and informal provision.

In many cases the connection of individual farms and hamlets to long-distance provision grids has improved water quality and quantity (though with significant investment costs to lay pipes for long-distance connection and to supply the energy for water transportation, especially for wastewater removal to central plants). In other cases, the existing self and informal provision might have been fine or only required some marginal improvements to meet the new standards. In both cases it is a question of political participation: do citizens have a choice regarding the water management systems that govern this aspect of their life?

The Interest Community for Drinking Water Provision (IKT)—that emerged in the 1980s in Southern Germany—is an example of a rural social innovation network countering the imposed expansion of long-distance water connection and putting forward their own concept of ecological restoration (Ziegler 2017). Historically, hamlets, typically subunits of recently merged larger villages, struggled to keep their fountains and sources. Their struggle shows that alternative modes of provision were easily delegitimized. Their call for ecological restoration of modes of self and informal provision was framed by their opponents as an obstacle to modern development, their forms of self-management were ridiculed and framed as dangerous in contrast to the expert knowledge of water professionals. Materially, their refusal to connect to the main pipeline grid meant missed investment opportunities for planners and construction companies. The restoration of their niche[12] required new network creation (the IKT) and alternative ways of framing the challenge in relation to protecting homes and cultural heritage, ecology, saving costs, and offering greater political self-determination. Additionally, lobbying by the network was required so that institutions, not least water standard and the public finances available for meeting these, were implemented in such a way that alternative modes of provision could survive.

The technical aspect of water infrastructure implies that adaption to changing circumstances is difficult and in many cases almost impossible: path-dependency makes it difficult to explore innovation. However, our rural case shows this does not mean that one solution 'fits all'—there are alternative modes. Policy agendas aimed at fostering greater citizen participation with respect to management choices governing basic aspects of citizens' lives should be sensitive to a variety of modes of provision and the choices they create.

[12] It is the *restoration* of a niche—or 'Sanierung' as the IKT network calls it—because the changing environmental, economic, and political conditions usually make the mere preservation of the status quo impossible (for a detailed discussion see: Ziegler 2017).

Centrally Provided Water Reconsidered

As noted above, while private entrepreneurs played a role in the initial set-up of urban fresh water, the business perspective became transnationally more significant only much later, when centrally provided urban fresh water became institutionalized across Europe. In the modern, neo-liberal period, private actors were partly successful in changing the mode of provision from public to private in the late twentieth century.

For example, the UK Thames Water Authority was partly privatized in 1989 as Thames Water and in 2001, the German energy company RWE fully acquired it. In Berlin in 1999, RWE—in partnership with Veolia, a transnational company originating from France—signed a public–private partnership with the city that gave the private companies a 49 per cent share in the *Berliner Wasserbetriebe* (see further above). As in other examples of privatization, this dynamic was contentious from the beginning, not least due to the tensions between profit maximization and the provision of a basic social need. This dynamic can threaten the prioritization of universal affordable provision of a public good. Such a 'mission-drift' is all the more likely as the considerable expert knowledge in urban water provision makes it difficult to hold management—public or private—accountable for their decisions.

At this stage of a social innovation having become an institution, there may be a new role for citizen participation as a watchdog and value guardian.[13] This was the case with the Berlin Water Table—founded by Berlin citizens in response to the privatization of freshwater provision who forced a referendum to make the PPP contract public and, subsequently, led to the re-municipalization of water provision. However, as was the case during Chadwick's time, the most marginalized populations were not directly involved in this civic action. Unlike the earlier phase, however, the marginalized were less directly affected by the struggle over public versus private provision. At least in the European welfare states, social policies tend to ensure universal access to fresh water for this group. For example, in Berlin the costs of freshwater provision for the long-term unemployed are covered by the state.

However, increasing water prices, lower water quality and insufficient/misdirected investment in infrastructure ultimately affect all citizens. The long-term challenge is, therefore, to keep this institutionalized social innovation consistently focused on ensuring clean and affordable water for all. The technical competencies required for operating a public utility at this scale are demanding and, in turn, the effective control of the operation by citizens is a challenging task. As in the rural case, citizens are likely to be 'ridiculed' as outsiders who do not really understand the complexity of the challenges. This raises an important challenge as to how to

[13] For this functional role see Schmitz (2015); our addition: the role is not only important initially when claims and problems are framed but also at a much later stage as discussed in the present section.

promote citizen participation and democratic accountability. There does not seem to be blueprint for this; however, the Berlin Water Table example suggests various issues to consider:

- *Cultural power and global civil society*: The Berlin Water Table saw itself as part of a global water justice movement, originally adopting the idea of a water table from Latin America (Härlin 2017). Further ideas promoted by the Table included a call for a more participatory approach to budgeting of the public utility, as well as the idea of a 'Blue Community' (including, inter alia, a ban on municipal procurement or sale of bottled, commercially sold drinking water). These are all ideas that had 'travelled' to Berlin out of wider discussions in global civil society. They suggest that 'discuss globally, act locally' might invigorate the citizen *watchdog role* with ideas as well as validate the role of being part of a bigger movement.
- *Political power and direct democracy*: Urban water provision, in both its public and private modes, is regulated and, thus, subject to the rules that representative democracy can design and impose. However, the complexity and expertise required for the maintenance of such water management makes democratic accountability challenging. It is noteworthy that the Berlin Water Table saw itself as an initiative of individuals, not a coalition of organizations. This increased the credibility of the Table as an expression of direct citizen participation. The Table—and in a similar way the IKT in rural areas—was very interested in direct democracy tools complementing representative democracy. It initiated a referendum to make the PPP contract public and pushed for a debate on the participatory budgeting of water investment. While referenda are unlikely to deliver much in terms of technical insights, they do help to make an issue publicly transparent, sometimes all that is needed to keep universal provision on track.
- *Preconditions:* The approach of the Table prevented it from directly developing organizational competencies in light of demanding technical issues. The Table needed to draw on the individual competencies of its members, provided on a volunteer basis as citizens. A practical implication is that the economically and educationally better-off are likely to play this watchdog role—similar to the Chadwick case. This point suggests that the state should provide good education and ensure economic security as a social investment strategy to foster social innovation.

Conclusion

Looking back on our analyses above, we can draw some conclusions from our case for the ESGM and social innovation more generally. For the collection and analysis of our water case, the ESGM proved helpful. In particular, it directed us to the importance of cognitive frames pushed for by social networks as a precondition of establishing the case for this social innovation. The shift in cognitive framing that freshwater provision is not a private problem of urbanites but a structural problem of public services was fundamental to get the social innovation going. Once this case was made, innovation and institutionalization followed. We highlighted this point as the advocacy role of social innovation and further characterized it as *vicarious* as the marginalized did not play an active role.

Using the ESGM, incorporating Heiskala's addition to Mann's sources of power, was also helpful in our case analysis due to the important role played by artefactual power in the development of freshwater provision. The power of water professionals (engineers, doctors, and other experts) shaped the key institutions and their expansion.

Welfare-state innovations can be overlooked as sites for social innovation. The historical, long-term perspective suggested by the ESGM proves helpful to counter this tendency. Our study also indicates a characteristic in the trajectory of this social innovation: social problems cannot be entirely 'solved'. Social innovations need to adapt continuously to be effective over time (Scheuerle et al. 2016b: 12). Part of the challenge is to keep the 'social' in focus—in our case this was exhibited by the danger of profit maximization limiting the reach and quality of water provision. Our case points to the need for new and innovative civic actors playing a watchdog role to keep institutionalized social innovations on track. Another part of this challenge is to recognize that solutions developed for a welfare institution do not fit equally well everywhere, as the rural case from the margins made clear. Our case suggests there is a need to be attentive to niches and alternative modes of provision.

The case also suggests that there is a need to address both the needs of the marginalized and the motives of others to frame and secure a social innovation that addresses a basic social need. To forge effective coalitions, it is useful to argue and show the solution will work to the advantage of different social groups—as Chadwick and his contemporary reformers did in mid-nineteenth-century Britain (Scheuerle et al. 2016b: 97). They addressed multi-faceted interests and mixed motives. These ranged from duty and benevolence to political and economic interests: if the social innovation helps to improve the position of marginalized people, others will profit as well (Schimpf 2017).

We used the modes of provision typology to track the variety of ways in which fresh water can be provided. We found that even though market provision frequently played a developmental role early on, this social innovation ultimately established a case for the public provision of fresh water (and of wastewater treatment) in the urban context. This solution was interwoven with professional provision. The emerging accountability challenge is how to use all this knowledge *with* and *for* citizens. This is an interesting and difficult challenge beyond the traditional public–private controversy in the water sector.

Additionally, we highlighted that there are other modes of provision that should not be ignored, especially if the participation of citizens in issues governing their lives is taken seriously. We illustrated this point with self and informal provision in the rural context, where citizens actively defended and restored alternative modes. This observation led us to consider the role of niches in ensuring diversity in solution approaches and, possibly, in generating more effective solutions. Niches offer a reservoir of ideas and alternative ways of doing things. Even if they are marginal today, they might have implications relevant in the future. In our case, the self and informal providers were sensitive early on to the value of ecological land use due to the direct impact of pesticides and fertilizers on their fountains and wells. The solutions they developed have, today, become mainstream with even big public providers struggling with the costs of technical, end-of-pipe solutions (such as nitrate removal). Moreover, alternative approaches serve as a constant challenge to examine the value and impact of mainstream institutions, arguably encouraging the continuous innovation that effective social innovation requires.

References

Arendt, H. 1998. *The Human Condition*, 2nd edition. Chicago, IL: University of Chicago Press.

Arnstein, S. R. 1969. 'A Ladder of Citizen Participation'. *Journal of the American Planning Association* 35(4): 216–24. https://www.planning.org/pas/memo/2007/mar/pdf/JAPA35No4.pdf.

Bakker, K. J. 2001. 'Paying for Water: Water Pricing and Equity in England and Wales'. *Transactions of the Institute of British Geographers* 26(2): 143–64.

Barlow, M. 2008. *Blue Covenant: The Global Water Crisis and the Coming Battle for the Right to Water*. New York: The New Press.

BEPA. 2010. 'Empowering People, Driving Change: Social Innovation in the European Union'. Luxembourg: Publications Office of the European Union.

Chadwick, E. 1842. *Report on the Sanitary Condition of the Labouring Populations of Gt. Britain*. London: University of London.

Chadwick, E. 1843. *Report on the Sanitary Condition of the Labouring Population of Great Britain: A Supplementary Report on the Results of a Special Inquiry into the Practice of Internment in Towns. Made at the Request of her Majesty's Principal Secretary of State for the Home Department*. London: W. Clowes and Sons. https://books.google.de/books?id=2IYIAAAAQAAJ&pg=PA224&hl=de&source=gbs_toc_r&cad>, accessed 31 May 2017.

Conca, K. 2006. *Governing Water: Contentious Transnational Politics and Global Institution Building*. Global Environmental Accords. Cambridge, MA: MIT Press.

Davies, A., J. Simon, R. Patrick, and W. Norman. 2012. 'Mapping Citizen Engagement in the Process of Social Innovation'. For 'The Theoretical, Empirical and Policy Foundations for Building Social Innovation in Europe' (TEPSIE). Brussels: European Commission, DG Research.

De La Motte, Robin. 2005. 'Netherlands'. In *Water, Time and European Cities: Histories Matter for the Futures*, edited by P. S. Juuti and T. S. Katko, pp. 134–45. Tampere: Tampere University Press.

DWA. 2010. *Brauchen wir neuartige Sanitärsysteme?* Hennef: DWA.

European Parliament and European Council. 2000. 'European Water Framework Directive. Directive 2000/60/EC'. http://eur-lex.europa.eu/legal-content/EN/TXT/HTML/?uri=CELEX:32000L0060&from=EN, accessed 26 April 2016.

Evans, R. J. 1987. *Death in Hamburg: Society and Politics in the Cholera Years, 1830–1910.* Oxford: Clarendon Press.

Evers, A., B. Ewert, and T. Brandsen (eds). 2014. 'Social Innovations for Social Cohesion: Transnational Patterns and Approaches from 20 European Cities', WILCO Consortium, Liège: EMES European Research Network. http://www.wilcoproject.eu/downloads/WILCO-project-eReader.pdf, accessed 15 May 2014.

Fazioli, R., B. Da Rin, L. Tiraoro, D. Donati, and C. Badon. 1999. 'Rapporto sui Servizi Pubblici Locali in Italia'. Report by Enea and Nomisma. Rome: Enea.

Feldkamp, M. F. 2009. 'Elemente die bewegen: Mensch und Technik im Gas- und Wasserfach: die Geschichte des DVGW von 1859 bis 2009 [und] eine Fotodokumentation' [Text für den historischen Teil: Michael F. Feldkamp]. Bonn: Deutsche Vereinigung des Gas- und Wasserfaches.

Grüntzig, J., and H. Mehlhorn. 2010. *Robert Koch: Seuchenjäger und Nobelpreisträger*, Heidelberg: Spektrum Akademischer Verlag.

Härlin, D. 2017. 'The Berlin Water Charter: Water Ethics from an Activist's Viewpoint'. In *Global Water Ethics: Towards a Global Ethics Charter*, edited by R. Ziegler and D. Groenfeldt, pp. 267–80. Abingdon: Routledge, 267–80.

Hassan, J. 1996. 'France: Public Responsibility—Private Execution'. In *The European Water Environment in a Period of Transformation*, edited by J. Hassan, P. Nunn, J. Tomkins, and Fraser Iain, pp. 121–35. Manchester: Manchester University Press.

Hempel, S. 2007. *The Strange Case of the Broad Street Pump: John Snow and the Mystery of Cholera.* Berkeley, CA: University of California Press.

Jellinghaus, L. 2006. *Zwischen Daseinsvorsorge und Infrastruktur*. Recht in der Industriellen Revolution, 3. Frankfurt am Main: Klostermann.

Johnson, S. 2006. *The Ghost Map: The Story of London's Most Terrifying Epidemic—and How It Changed Science, Cities, and the Modern World.* New York: Riverhead Books.

Juuti, P. S., and T. S. Katko (eds). 2005. *Water, Time and European Cities: Histories Matter for the Future*, Tampere: Tampere University Press.

Katko, T. S. 2004. 'Long-Term Development of Water and Sewage Services in Finland'. In *From a Few to All: Long-Term Development of Water and Sanitation Services in Finland*, edited by P. S. Juuti, and T. S. Katko, pp. 17–36. Tampere: Tampere University Press.

Katko, T. S. (ed.). 2013. *Hanaa! Suomen vesihuolto—kehitys ja yhteiskunnallinen merkitys*. Helsinki: Suomen Vesilaitosyhdistys.

Koop, S. H. A., and van Leeuwen, C. J. 2016. 'The Challenges of Water, Waste and Climate Change in Cities'. *Environment, Development and Sustainability* 19(2): 385–418.

Lenger, F. 2012. *European Cities in the Modern Era, 1850–1914*. Studies in Central European Histories, 57. Leiden: Brill.

Linton, J. 2010. *What Is Water? The History of a Modern Abstraction*. Vancouver: UBC Press.

Lobina, E. 2005. 'Italy'. In *Water, Time and European Cities: Histories Matter for the Futures*, edited by P. S. Juuti and T. S. Katko, pp. 106–22. Tampere: Tampere University Press.

Lobina, E., and D. Hall. 2013. 'List of Water Remunicipalisations Worldwide: As of November 2013'. London: Public Services International Research Unit.

Lobina, E., S. Kishimoto, and O. Petitjean. 2014. 'Here To Stay: Water Remunicipalisation as a Global Trend'. London: Public Services International Research Unit (PSIRU); Transnational Institute (TNI); Multinational Observatory).

Mann, C. C. 2009. 'The Rise of Big Water'. *Vanity Fair*, September. http://www.vanityfair.com/news/2007/05/bigwater200705, accessed 18 Dec 2017.

Mann, M. 1993. *The Sources of Social Power, Volume II: The Rise of classes and Nation States, 1760–1914*. New York: Cambridge University Press.

Mann, M. 2013. *The Sources of Social Power, Volume IV: Globalizations, 1945–2011*. Cambridge: Cambridge University Press.

Meyer, L. 2011. *Die Entwicklung Oldenburgs zur modernen Stadt. Wasser, Gas und Elektrizität 1850–1930*. Veröffentlichungen des Stadtmuseums Oldenburg, 62. Bremen: Ed. Temmen.

Mill, J. S. 1879. *Utilitarianism. Reprinted from 'Fraser's Magazine'*, 7th edition. London: Longmans, Green, and Co. http://www.gutenberg.org/files/11224/11224-h/11224-h.htm, accessed 21 Jun 2017.

Nussbaum, M. 2006. *Frontiers of Justice: Disability, Nationality, Species Membership*, Cambridge, MA: Harvard University Press.

Okereke, C. 2008. *Global Justice and Neoliberal Environmental Governance: Ethics, Sustainable Development and International Co-Operation*. Environmental Politics. London: Routledge.

Pettit, P. 2014. *Just Freedom: A Moral Compass for a Complex World*. New York: Norton & Company.

Prasad, N. (ed.). 2008a. *Social Policies and Private Sector Participation in Water Supply: Beyond Regulation*. Social Policy in a Development Context. Basingstoke: Palgrave Macmillan.

Prasad, N. 2008b. 'Overview: Social Policies and Private Sector Participation in Water Supply'. In *Social Policies and Private Sector Participation in Water Supply: Beyond Regulation*, edited by N. Prasad, pp. 1–36. Basingstoke: Palgrave Macmillan.

Reynaud, A. 2008. 'France'. In *Social Policies and Private Sector Participation in Water Supply: Beyond Regulation*, edited by N. Prasad, pp. 37–69. Basingstoke: Palgrave Macmillan.

Scheuerle, T., G.-C. Schimpf, G. Glänzel, and G. Mildenberger (eds). 2016a. 'Report on Relevant Actors in Historic Examples and an Empirically Driven Typology on Types of Social Innovation'. CrESSI Working Paper No. 29. Brussels: European Commission, DG Research.

Scheuerle, T., G.-C. Schimpf, G. Glänzel, G. Mildenberger, and R. Ziegler. 2016a. 'Three Major Social Innovations as Viewed through the Lens of the Extended Social Grid model'. In 'Report on Relevant Actors in Historic Examples and an Empirically Driven Typology on Types of Social Innovation'. For 'Creating Economic Space for Social Innovation' (CrESSI), edited by T. Scheuerle, G.-C. Schimpf, G. Glänzel, and G. Mildenberger, pp. 1–224. Brussels: European Commission.

Schimpf, G.-C. (ed.). 2017. 'Comparative Report on Historic Examples and Similar Recent Social Innovations in an Early Stage'. CrESSI Working Paper No. 35. Brussels: European Commission, DG Research.

Social Innovation, and Social Mission Organizations: Toward a Conceptualization'. In *Cases in Innovative Nonprofits: Organizations That Make a Difference*, edited by R. A. Cnaan and D. Vinokur-Kaplan, pp. 17–42. Los Angeles, CA: Sage Publications.

Schott, D., and H. Skroblies. 1987. 'Die ursprüngliche Vernetzung. Die Industrialisierung der Städte durch Infrastruktur-Technologien und ihre Auswirkung auf Stadtentwicklung und Städtebau. Eine Forschungsskizze'. *Die alte Stadt* 14(1): 72–99.

Sedlak, D. L. 2014. *Water 4.0: The Past, Present, and Future of the World's Most Vital Resource*. New Haven, CT: Yale University Press.

Sen, A. 2009. *The Idea of Justice*. London: Penguin.

Simson, J. v. 1983. *Kanalisation und Städtehygiene im 19. Jahrhundert*. Technikgeschichte in Einzeldarstellungen, 39. Düsseldorf: VDI-Verlag.

Snow, J. 1965. *Snow on Cholera: A Reprint of Two Papers*, B. W. Richardson and W. H. Frost, New York, London: Hafner Publishing Company.

Steuer, P. 1912. *Die Wasserversorgung der Städte und Ortschaften. Ihre wirtschaftliche Entwicklung und Analyse*. Berlin: Siemenroth.

UNDP. 2006. *Beyond Scarcity: Power, Poverty and the Global Water Crisis*. New York: Palgrave Macmillan.

Vincenti, W. G. 1990. *What Engineers Know and How They Know It: Analytical Studies from Aeronautical History*. Johns Hopkins Studies in the History of Technology, (new. ser., no. 11). Baltimore, MD: Johns Hopkins University Press.

WHO. 2015. 'European Health for All Database'. http://data.euro.who.int/hfadb/, accessed 26 April 2016.

Williams, B. 1985. *Ethics and the Limits of Philosophy*. London: Routledge.

Ziegler, R. 2017. 'Citizen Innovation as Niche Restoration: A Type of Social Innovation and its Relevance for Political Participation and Sustainability'. *Journal of Social Entrepreneurship* 8(3): 338–50.

7

Trajectories of Social Innovation

Tackling Marginalization with a Complex Approach

György Molnár and Attila Havas

Introduction

The Roma people have faced social exclusion in many European societies for centuries. This remains an unresolved problem: 'Many of the estimated 10–12 million Roma in Europe face prejudice, intolerance, discrimination, and social exclusion in their daily lives. They are marginalized and live in very poor socio-economic conditions' (EC 2011: 2). In Hungary, the marginalization of the Roma has a particularly long history. The last two fundamental transitions—the introduction of central planning and a one-party system in the late 1940s and, then, the transition to a market economy and parliamentary democracy in the early 1990s—only changed the causes and mechanisms of their marginalization, but not its severity to any significant extent. These issues of exclusion and marginalization remain key political, societal, and economic challenges. The various—half-hearted or sometimes dishonest—government strategies launched in the last seven decades have not tackled the root of the problem at all.

Hence, there is an urgent need for fundamentally different approaches. Kiútprogram,[1] a non-profit corporation, provides unsecured loans and mentoring primarily to socially excluded Roma in Hungary to alleviate their marginalization by enabling them to set up their own businesses or to become self-employed vegetable producers. This is a specific form of social innovation: social innovation for the marginalized (SIM). In this chapter, we analyse the Kiútprogram with the main objectives of drawing propositions for further theory building to better understand both marginalization and SIM processes. We also aim to distil from our case practical implications for underpinning more effective SIM-promoting policies and improving SIM practices more broadly. The Kiútprogram can only have limited socio-economic impacts given its narrow geographical scope and restricted financial resources. One also needs to be cautious when attempting

[1] The Hungarian name 'Kiútprogram' means 'Way Out Programme'. The sound 'ú' is pronounced as 'oo' in the word 'good'. György Molnár participated in the design and operation of the programme and is still a voluntary member of its Board.

György Molnár and Attila Havas, *Trajectories of Social Innovation: Tackling Marginalization with a Complex Approach*. In: *Creating Economic Space for Social Innovation*. Edited by: Alex Nicholls and Rafael Ziegler, Oxford University Press (2019).
DOI: 10.1093/oso/9780198830511.003.0007

generalizations from case studies, especially from a single one. Nevertheless, we believe the lessons learnt from this case—especially those focused on the processes that cause and reproduce marginalization, as well as the dilemmas and trade-offs faced by practitioners—are also relevant for SIM practitioners, policy analysts, and policy-makers working in other contexts.

To guide our analysis we apply the Extended Social Grid Model (ESGM) discussed in chapter 1—comprising Beckert's Social Grid, Mann's theory of the social sources of power and Sen's capability approach—as well as the analytical toolkit of evolutionary economics of innovation, in particular the multi-channel interactive learning model of innovation (Caraça et al. 2009). While these conceptual frameworks do not aim to provide a descriptive model of social innovation processes per se, they are all useful tools to explore and analyse SIMs.

This chapter is structured as follows.[2] First, we offer a brief history of the marginalization of the Roma in Hungary since the early twentieth century, considering the major factors driving their marginalization as well as the processes reproducing it. This section stresses the impacts of interactions between institutions (education, labour markets, social and regional development polices), social networks (social ties), and cognitive frames (prejudices, self-esteem), as well as the decisive influence of national and local power structures. Then we describe the Kiútprogram in overview: how it has been devised and implemented; why and in which important respects it differs from the 'prototype' of microcredit (the Grameen model); the two major phases of the programme and its outcomes. We also highlight the relevance of the multi-channel interactive learning model of innovation for analysing SIMs. This is followed by a more detailed exploration of the Kiútprogram, focusing on: the personal traits and conversion factors of participants; the issue of learned helplessness; the drawbacks of applying social collateral (a distinctive feature of the Grameen model); and the roles and impacts of various actors, such as fieldworkers, leaders, internal sponsors, external funders, and local political leaders. In the concluding section we distil theoretical propositions and highlight several policy and practical implications of the case including: the trade-offs requiring consideration when planning and implementing SIMs and/or devising policies aimed at supporting social innovation: in particular, those between exact targeting in a SIM versus building inter-community connections; the type and degree of assistance provided (a potentially paternalistic approach) versus short-term empowerment effects; and the degree of marginalization of the participants versus the costs of a given SIM.

[2] We are grateful for the comments and suggestions on earlier versions offered by the CrESSI team members, in particular Lara Maestripieri, Georg Mildenberger, Gudrun Schimpf, and Rafael Ziegler, as well as for those by Amelia Pope.

The Marginalization of the Roma in Hungary

The majority of Roma across Europe are disadvantaged in almost all aspects of life: education, employment, income, housing, land ownership, and health. Four-fifths of Roma live at risk of poverty (compared to less than one-fifth of the general population); one-third of Roma children are at risk of going to bed hungry at least once a month; more than three-fifths of young Roma are neither employed nor in the education system; two-fifths of Roma feel they have been discriminated against in schools, workplaces, housing, or hospitals.[3] Prejudices against the Roma are visible in everyday life and in the media. There is also much covert prejudice. All these factors of marginalization are closely connected and mutually reinforce each other.

Without a thorough understanding of a given marginalization process it is impossible to identify the appropriate intervention points for a social innovation that aims to find a way to halt the mechanisms leading to mutually reinforcing negative effects. Our aim is to highlight the main features of processes of marginalization for the Roma in Hungary by applying the theoretical framework of the ESGM.[4]

The Process of Marginalization

For centuries the Roma were at the periphery of the predominantly agrarian society of Hungary, with some inter-community connections, for example as musicians, pedlars, horse traders, or handcraft producers. They were isolated in their everyday life from the rest of society, governed by their own strong internal rules. Their separation, unique culture, and language created a special cognitive frame of the non-Roma majority on the Roma. Historically, the Roma had no ideological, economic, military, or political power in the Hungarian society.

In the 1930s the combined effects of political and economic power structures had a very negative effect on the Roma. Military preparations sped up industrialization, thereby excluding many traditional Roma products and services from the market. The Nazi genocide during the Second World War further undermined the social fabric of Roma society.

The introduction of a one-party system and central planning, imposed by the Soviet Union after the Second World War, fundamentally restructured Hungarian society. Political, ideological, and economic powers played a crucial role in the

[3] EU MIDIS II survey, European Union Agency for Fundamental Rights (2016).

[4] For detailed analyses see, e.g. Bernát (2014), Bernáth and Messing (2013), Hegedüs (2008), Karsai (1992), Kemény and Havas (1996), Kemény et al. (2004), Kertesi and Kézdi (2011), Ladányi and Szelényi (2004), Majtényi and Majtényi (2016).

further marginalization of the Roma. Forced industrialization put an end to the significance of their traditional products. Despite general land reforms, they were not given any land. Extensive industrialization required a large number of unskilled workers and that became the only employment option for most Roma.

Education of the poor was better supported, offering an escape from marginalization via learning, thereby making upward social mobility a possibility for those with adequate personal traits. Yet, due to the extreme nature of their marginalization and disadvantage, the majority of Roma still underperformed at school and most of them only finished primary school. Although the egalitarian ideology of the new regime had some positive effects, prejudices against the Roma did not diminish to a noteworthy extent.

In summary, the vast majority of Roma integrated into the Hungarian society only in a very limited way via employment in state-owned enterprises and—to a lesser extent—via education. Certain types of networks comprised of both Roma and non-Roma members did evolve in workplaces. These connections influenced the cognitive frames of both sides as learning about the other through direct, interpersonal communication reduced prejudice. However, Roma employees were typically at the bottom of the employment hierarchy, which had strongly negative effects on their self-esteem.

Hungary's transition to a parliamentary democracy and market economy in the 1990s radically changed the political and economic power relations, as well as the ideological landscape. The emerging democracy and entrepreneurial freedom opened up brand new opportunities for certain social groups, such as highly educated people—especially those with managerial experience—and dynamic, ambitious members of the urban youth. Yet, for a large number of people the regime change meant mass unemployment. Within months hundreds of thousands had lost their jobs, mostly poorly educated workers of unviable state-owned firms. The Roma constituted the highest proportion of this group. Rocketing unemployment was an inevitable repercussion of the transition to a market economy, but its extent was increased by the elite's ideology claiming that loss-making factories should be closed down as soon as possible. That also changed the framing of mass unemployment as an unavoidable sacrifice for the sake of future development. This is a prime example of ideological power in action.

These systemic changes in the labour market resulted in the transformation of cognitive frames; prejudice against the Roma became stronger. The fast and large drop in demand for unskilled workers created strong competition within this group. Prejudice against the Roma was used to create a competitive advantage for the non-Roma.[5] For the Roma, losing jobs meant losing their existing social

[5] In this way, a social problem and the related material interest were transformed into the moral problem of the Roma's 'bad working ethics'. The underlying mechanism is analogous to 'the positive functions of poverty', described in Gans (1972).

networks with non-Roma. Further, trust within Roma communities was severely undermined.

The transition process to a market economy aggravated existing regional inequalities too. As the Roma mainly lived in less developed regions, their social marginalization was further strengthened by regional segregation.

Changes in the education system also contributed to more excessive marginalization. The newly introduced right to choose a school in practice became the right for schools to select students, leading to early separation of middle-class children from those of poor families. Along with increasing regional inequalities, this separation led effectively to segregated education for most Roma. Schools with many disadvantaged children suffered from poor funding; hence better qualified, more ambitious teachers left these schools, further increasing the marginalization of the poor—to a large extent Roma—students.

The interest rate on favourable loans earmarked for new housing had been below 3.5 per cent throughout the 1980s. Then it was raised drastically: first to 18.5 per cent in 1989 and then to 24.5 per cent in 1990. A new type of subsidy was introduced in 1991: for those who paid back their mortgage immediately, half of the capital component of their outstanding loan was waived. Better-off families gained considerably this way, while the financial burden of the poorer families, among them the Roma, increased dramatically. Quite a few of them, mainly those who had become unemployed, lost their homes. Moreover, for them, renting was not an easy solution because of the mass privatization of flats.

Upper-middle-class tenants, living in better quality rental apartments, exerted pressure on municipalities to sell them these flats at a favourable price. Local municipalities, in turn, perceived privatization as an easy solution to get rid of the burden of social housing maintenance.[6] As a result, the share of social housing shrank from almost 20 per cent to below 3 per cent of the total dwellings.[7] These changes significantly limited the possibility of regional mobility, particularly for those attempting to move from the disadvantaged countryside to cities in order to find jobs. Urban private rental became prohibitively expensive, and hence out of reach for the poor. Moreover, landlords did not want to rent properties to Roma because of their prejudice.

In summary, all the important changes in power structures after the regime change in 1990 proved detrimental to the Roma. Lacking appropriate social networks and with poor collective self-esteem—their own internal organizing power—most of the Roma could not find a way out of the marginalization trap.

[6] Privatization of municipal flats was strongly advocated by experts of international organizations, including The World Bank (Buckley et al. 1994).

[7] Central Statistical Office census data, http://www.ksh.hu/nepszamlalas/docs/tablak/teruleti/00/00_1_3_2_1.xls.

The Reproduction of Marginalization

The marginalization of the Roma—and, more generally, of poor people—has been persistently reproduced in Hungary and other Central and Eastern European countries. Beckert's Social Grid (extended beyond the market) offers a useful focusing device to analyse these processes. Most of our observations here concerning the Roma—with the exception of ethnic discrimination—would also apply to other marginalized populations (poor, unemployed, undereducated). Ethnic discrimination, however, can turn marginalization into complete social exclusion.

First, let us consider the *interactions between institutions and social networks.* Several institutions have had a major impact on the social networks of the Roma in Hungary, of which education, labour market and employment policies are considered here briefly.[8] Segregated schooling prevents the formation of social ties between children coming from different family backgrounds. It creates a severe disadvantage in the long run as relationships among former schoolmates can be an important source of social ties and a lack of diverse relationships can carry through to adulthood. In turn, a lack of social connections with non-Roma—missing *weak ties* (Granovetter 1973)—significantly reduces the chances of finding a job. The loss of jobs due to the closure of unviable state-owned companies has also had long-lasting effects: once someone is forced out of the labour market, it is becoming increasingly difficult to re-enter it due the loss of former weak ties.

Insufficient school funding in less developed regions, where the Roma tend to live, leads to poor quality education, causing a further negative long-term effect: poorly educated people are excluded from the labour market which confines their social connections to other marginalized people. Furthermore, the lack of appropriate policies to reduce regional inequalities diminishes the chances of establishing social ties between Roma and non-Roma.

A major employment policy tool in Hungary is the extensive and massively expensive public works programme, aimed at replacing unemployment benefits, with questionable efficacy (Cseres-Gergely and Molnár 2015). The average number of people participating in these schemes reached 230,000 in 2017—5 per cent

[8] Other relevant policies include: regulations on social care; the self-government system; the housing market and social housing; launching and setting up businesses; as well as taxation and social contributions policies. By policies we not only mean policy documents, but policy practices as well, because implementation is certainly more important from the point of view of impacts than ideas presented in a document. For instance, segregated education is not part of any official policy agenda—quite the opposite—but in practice the Hungarian government has encouraged segregated education in various ways, e.g. by defending schools following this practice in court cases, with the minister giving a testimony in support of 'loving' segregation. See https://budapestbeacon.com/minister-balog-suggests-officially-segregating-roma-schools/?_sf_s=segregation; and http://www.europarl.europa.eu/sides/getDoc.do?pubRef=-//EP//TEXT+WQ+E-2014-010881+0+DOC+XML+V0//EN.

of the economically active population.[9] Participants in public works schemes belong to the same social group, that is, to the unemployed. This specific form of employment, therefore, cannot make up for lost work ties. Instead of integrating the unemployed, among them the Roma, into socially diverse networks, they have become clients in a feudal-style system of relations, where the mayor and a few other key figures are the patrons.[10] Moreover, the lack of alternative job opportunities turn the long-term unemployed in the same village into rivals competing for a limited number of posts financed by the public works scheme. This is detrimental to the relationships within Roma populations and further limits their social ties.

Inter-community bridges as social ties are also crucial in tackling marginalization: when a marginalized group is segregated from non-marginalized communities, it is practically impossible to alleviate their marginalized status (Csermely et al. 2014). The policies described above trigger and perpetuate mechanisms eroding the weak ties of the marginalized Roma in Hungary.

A vicious circle can be observed. The public works system has created a secondary labour market, insulated from the primary labour market,[11] with a different set of 'rules of the game'. Some of these emerged from hierarchical patron–client networks: the patron has an interest in tying the best workers to the system by creating and applying formal and informal rules to hinder their employment in the primary labour market.

Turning to the *interactions between institutions and cognitive frames*, when analysing marginalization, it is crucial to distinguish two types of the latter: the cognitive frame of the environment within which the marginalized group sits and the cognitive frame of the marginalized people about themselves.

The regulations on establishing and setting up businesses are much more burdensome in Hungary than in most advanced countries.[12] These rules are demanding even for educated people, let alone the marginalized Roma with poor education, who—as a result—would not even attempt to launch a business on their own. Additionally, the rules of the public works and social welfare systems—reinforced by the informal rules of the feudal-type hierarchical systems mentioned above—reduce the Roma's motivations to search for primary labour market jobs. Rules governing the education system also have important bearings on the Roma's cognitive frames. The curriculum contains hardly any relevant knowledge for solving everyday problems. Hence disadvantaged students,

[9] http://kozfoglalkoztatas.kormany.hu/havi-tajekoztatas-a-kozfoglalkoztatasrol and http://www.ksh.hu/docs/hun/xstadat/xstadat_eves/i_qlf002.html.

[10] These strongly hierarchical networks resemble the ones described by Eisenstadt and Roniger (1981).

[11] On day 180, after leaving a position financed by a public works scheme, a mere 13 per cent of these people had a job in the primary labour market in 2011–13 (Cseres-Gergely and Molnár 2015).

[12] http://www.doingbusiness.org.

especially the Roma, have hostile feelings about school. Furthermore, there are no elements in the curriculum to enhance positive self-identification for the Roma; teachers are not trained to use pedagogical methods developed for integrated education. Consequently, hostility is strongest in schools where segregation has started but is not yet complete.

The above institutions governing these three important domains—setting up businesses, welfare and workfare, education—lead to *learned helplessness* (Peterson et al. 1993), or even self-hatred in some cases. The feeling of 'no matter what I do, it will get worse in the end' has become ingrained among most of the marginalized.

A vicious circle can be detected here, too. As described above, several institutions, including education and regional development policies, together with the regulations on creating businesses, play a decisive role in creating unemployment among the Roma and keeping the level persistently high. This leads to false presumptions regarding the causes of unemployment. Many people think that the Roma are lazy and want to live off state benefits. This cognitive frame has underpinned major changes in social and employment policies: welfare tools—such as social transfers to the poor and unemployment benefits—have increasingly been replaced in Hungary by tax holidays—that by definition are only advantageous for those with a certain level of income—and by a 'workfare' type public works system. These policy changes, induced by a cognitive frame shared by most non-Roma, caused further institutional changes, creating specific rules for the secondary labour market, which, in turn, reproduced the Roma's marginalization.

Finally, there are also important *interactions between cognitive frames and social networks*. A lack of positive connections with other social groups has had a negative effect on the attitudes of parents with low educational attainment towards their children's education: they are less likely to support their children learning at home or taking up secondary school education compared to parents in better-off non-marginalized social groups. Lacking social networks leads to feeling unvalued and undermines self-esteem and collective self-respect to a large extent, contributing to the formation of learned helplessness. This lack of individual and collective self-esteem has destroyed the mutual respect and trust within Roma communities, negatively influencing their internal networks. The patron–client relations created by the public works schemes (mentioned earlier) have also strengthened the acceptance of—or even the perceived need for—paternalism, further increasing dependency.

The absence of inter-community social ties (friendships, accepting the Roma as 'good neighbours', casual communications among Roma and non-Roma) has led to a lack of knowledge about the Roma; a perfect breeding ground for prejudices among non-Roma. Vice versa, prejudices against the Roma hinder the formation of inter-community ties. Prejudices and racism have played a big role in the emergence, expansion, and increasing acceptance of far-right networks in Hungary.

Having considered the interactions between the three possible 'pairs' of the three major social forces of the ESGM, it should be stressed that this type of analysis can only provide a partial picture. In several important processes leading to the reproduction of marginalization, the interplay among all three social forces is crucial. For example, the persistently high unemployment rate of the Roma and their permanent exclusion from the labour market can be explained by the interactions between institutions and social networks. This situation, in turn, has created and constantly reinforces prejudices against the Roma: 'the Roma do not want to work' (Bernát et al. 2013: 2). This cognitive frame leads to changes in social and employment policies—welfare replaced by workfare—and the emergence of new rules governing the secondary labour market, insulated from the primary one.

Implications for Social Innovation

We have shown that the ESGM is relevant when analysing the formation and reproduction of marginalization of the Roma in Hungary. The concept of power sources (Mann) has assisted us in understanding the formation of marginalization when systemic social changes occur, while the interactions of the three social forces (Beckert) has helped in explaining the reproduction of marginalization. Paying attention to power structures and the interactions of the three social forces, thus, has pragmatic utility when devising a SIM. Thus, in the case of severe marginalization it is neither sufficient nor effective to innovate by modifying just a single social force and leaving the other two untouched. If a social innovation aims at changing only one component of the Social Grid, then the other two social forces are likely to reproduce the initial power structures and therefore marginalization, too, with somewhat different features.

An example of such a failed intervention is profit-seeking, or at least financially sustainable microcredit projects aimed at the poor. This type of social innovation intervenes at one point only by changing the rules of lending (institutional change). Accumulated experience shows that these projects do not reduce poverty over time and can even increase marginalization in quite a few cases (Bateman 2010; Ghosh 2013). A recent Hungarian case confirms that changing only one social force does not address marginalization. An NGO sued the local government for school segregation in one of the disadvantaged regions. Following the court ruling, an important change was introduced: the municipality closed the school attended only by Roma students and those students were reassigned to neighbouring schools. However, neither the teachers, the Roma students, their parents, nor the students and parents in the receiving schools were prepared for this change—no attempts were made to modify their cognitive frames. As a result, the Roma parents themselves asked to restore the original situation, re-establishing de facto segregation.

The Kiútprogram

The primary mission of the Kiútprogram is to promote social mobility and facilitate Roma inclusion by *assisting clients to establish sustainable formal businesses* (Kiútprogram 2012). The less explicit mission of the programme is to reduce negative stereotypes about poor and vulnerable groups, especially the Roma (Budapest Institute 2014: 1).[13]

The Polgár Foundation for Opportunities, a Hungarian civil foundation, initiated the programme in 2009. The concept of the Kiútprogram was inspired by Muhammad Yunus' social innovation, the Grameen microcredit model (Yunus 1999). Yunus launched his model in 1976 in Bangladesh, providing financial services—mainly unsecured loans of relatively small amounts—to people living in deep poverty to enable income generation. He established the Grameen Bank in 1983 after processing and assessing the results of early initiatives. Since then, a multitude of microfinance organizations have been set up globally.

The Grameen Model

The major characteristics of the Grameen model are summarized here.[14] At the core of this type of lending activity there is a voluntary group of five loan recipients that replaces standard banking collateral by the mutual sharing of risk as a moral commitment. In case of non-payment two types of sanctions are applied on the other group members. Firstly, loans are *sequential*: initially given to two members, if the first recipients make the weekly payments for six weeks, loans are granted to another two; after another six weeks, the group leader elected by the members is also granted a loan. If during these twelve weeks a member fails to service her loan as agreed, she is excluded from the group and the others have to find someone to replace this member. Further loans are not granted until the excluded member is replaced.

After this initial period, when all group members have received a loan, another type of sanction is used in case of default. Irrespective of the cause of the default no member of this group ever receives a new loan. This feature of the model is called contingent renewal. This is a tough measure: without a follow-up loan, businesses started with the help of microcredit can struggle, as the loan is usually granted only for one year and, moreover, the first loan is usually small.

To sum up, when a group member is unable to overcome difficulties with the new business, refuses to make payments, or uses the loan for other purposes, the remaining members are punished. The moral pressure is often even harsher: at the

[13] This section draws partially on Molnár (2017).
[14] Armendáriz and Morduch (2010) offers a thorough summary on microfinance.

joint meeting of local groups they are held morally responsible (even reprehended) for not being able to persuade the non-compliant member to repay the loan. Poor borrowers act as guarantors for each other: the usual banking collateral is replaced by social collateral (Karlan et al. 2009).

Kiútprogram Adaptations

The Kiútprogram targets people living in deep poverty, who are mainly of Roma origin. The programme is active in the least developed regions of Hungary, where the share of Roma is relatively high, but there is still an ethnically mixed population. The beneficiaries are not selected on ethnic grounds, but given the place-based approach of the Kiútprogram, 80 per cent of the beneficiaries identify themselves as Roma.

When planning the Kiútprogram, its architects realized that the complex nature of the reproduction of marginalization required complex interventions: non-market tools are also indispensable to help long-term unemployed people return to, or enter, the labour market. Unlike the original Grameen model, the Kiútprogram also offers business development and support services to its participants free of charge. Well-trained fieldworkers, as well as external business and professional consultants, paid by the programme, provide this assistance. Fieldworkers organize community meetings in areas with a higher density of the Roma, visit interested candidates, organize and facilitate group meetings, provide personal counselling for the clients, support business plan development, assist in registering businesses, accounting, and dealing with other administrative tasks such as settling former debts, building business connections, and establishing communication with municipal leaders (Kiútprogram 2012).

The Kiútprogram is a not-for-profit corporation owned jointly by the Polgár Foundation and private sponsors. It is not a standard microfinance organization: the focus of the programme is on participants' self-employment[15] and empowerment rather than profitability for the lender. Given the costs of the support services provided, the programme cannot be financially self-sufficient, let alone profitable. Moreover, external funding is continuously needed.

During the first phase of the programme (2010–12) sequential lending was applied to groups consisting of four to six members. Participants were given the option to realize their own entrepreneurial vision. This phase was financed by the Pan-European Coordination of Roma Integration Methods—Roma Inclusion EU pilot project.[16] In the first few months, the recruitment of clients took much longer than expected and the programme faced increasing late or non-payments of loans.

[15] Self-employment took two different forms in the two phases of the Kiútprogram as already mentioned in the introduction; see further below.

[16] http://www.welcomeurope.com/europe-funding-opportunities/pilot-project-pan-european-coordination-of-roma-integration-methods-roma-inclusion-2770+2670.html#tab=onglet_documents.

Drawing on this experience, Kiútprogram had to adjust its operating model in spring 2011. Fieldworkers started putting *a bigger emphasis on personality traits, capabilities, motivation, and credit history.* Furthermore, the rules of providing loans and forming groups were eased; the selection of fieldworkers and their training improved. *Network-building activities* were also started to connect clients with existing business networks (Audy et al. 2013). Client feedback—via surveys, face-to-face interviews, and everyday communication with fieldworkers—was systematically collected and it strongly influenced the revamp of the programme.

Peer lending group meetings, held weekly, were crucial. Groups discussed business ideas (the group members were not typically rivals in the market) and members had to convince their peers about the feasibility of their business plans. These debates developed participants' communication skills. Group meetings also provided a forum to discuss local community problems.

In 2012, the Kiútprogram implemented further operational changes, shifting toward integrated business solutions. Initiated by a group of clients, trilateral agreements were entered into with the Kiútprogram, a professional cucumber buyer (the production integrator), and more than twenty clients. The Kiútprogram provided loans for the investment necessary for cucumber growing, as well as free training for clients who had neither skills, nor experience in agricultural production. The production integrator provided the seedlings and chemicals needed for growing, likewise through loans. These costs were deducted from the revenues. This kind of cucumber production system is widespread in the region among non-Roma; due to lack of trust, however, no buyer would have entered into contracts with Roma partners without the participation of the Kiútprogram. The original model of sequential lending, underwritten by social collateral was then abandoned. We will return to this issue later.

Pilot Programme

Between 2010 and 2012 loans with an average value of EUR 1,800 were granted to 138 clients (see Table 7.1).[17] In this period fifteen clients also received a second loan. Depending on whether their groups were formed before or after the beginning of 2011, the clients are divided into a first or second batch and clients of the cucumber-growing subproject represent a third batch. The average duration of the loans was strongly influenced by the very short duration of the pilot programme: approaching the end date, the duration of the loans had to be shortened, also implying smaller loans.

[17] Survey-based client data are available only for the 2010–12 period, the lack of available funds hindered the continuation of systematic data collection. The detailed quantitative analysis of the 2010–12 period is presented in Molnár (2017); in this chapter we only refer to a few data points to illustrate the size and progress of the programme.

Table 7.1. Number of clients and loan repayments, 2010–12

	Persons	Still active as entrepreneurs*	Average loan per person (EUR)	Arrears per payments due* (%)
First batch	41	4	2,500	62
Second batch	74	37	1,800	45
Third batch	23	22	550	22
Total/average	138	63	1,800	51

Note: *As of May 2013

Source: Audy et al. (2013: 18–19).

Although the EU pilot project ended in September 2012, the Kiútprogram staff kept track of the clients. Repayment indicators are also presented in Table 7.1. Due to the fieldworkers' inexperience, the share of 'strategic' defaulters—those who had decided not to pay back the loan when joining the programme—was relatively high in the first batch. As a result of model corrections and accumulated experience, loan repayment performance improved over time. However, the average ratio of unpaid loans remained high.

Operating costs (including lending losses) were also high during the pilot period: the total cost of issuing EUR 1,800 (the average loan per person) was almost EUR 6,000 (Audy et al. 2013). The largest share of costs was the fieldworkers' wages and other field expenditures. According to rough calculations by Kiútprogram staff, for continuous operation at full capacity with well-trained and experienced fieldworkers, the ratio of total costs to loan could be reduced significantly, that is, to below two.[18]

The Second Phase

When the pilot project ended, the Hungarian government decided not to support the programme. Since then, it has been financed solely from private resources. Consequently, available financial resources have shrunk significantly, forcing the programme to scale down. From 2013 onwards, the Kiútprogram only continued the cucumber-growing project, with around one hundred clients a year (see Table 7.2). While the costs of this scheme per beneficiary are much lower compared to setting up a new business, it has also limits: a piece of land is needed with the right quality of soil and it can secure work and income only for five months a year.

Compared to 2012, both 2013 and 2014 were unfavourable years for cucumber growing; production results—and hence, the loan repayment ratio—were lower than before. Some of the production integrators misused their local monopoly too,

[18] These calculations assume 30 per cent average lending losses (Kiútprogram 2012: 26).

Table 7.2. Number of clients and loan repayments in the cucumber project, 2016

Year	New loan recipients	Old clients	Total clients	Average loan per person (EUR)		Arrears per payment due (%)
				Investment	Current assets	Investment
2013	87	22	109	310	—	66
2014	31	56	87	360	—	68
2015	58	22	80	560	700	50
2016	56	42	98	470	930	21

Source: Kiútprogram communication.

cheating clients in several ways (Molnár 2015). Based on these experiences, in 2015 the programme took over financing the current assets of the producers, contracting directly with a food industry plant as a buyer. The Kiútprogram's 2015 model offered:

- Interest-free loans for the investment costs (drilling a well, establishing a watering system with a pump, etc.) with a duration of two years. In the first year 25 per cent must be repaid, while the remaining 75 per cent in the second year. The size of the loan depended mainly on the costs of drilling a well.
- Necessary pesticides for the seedlings and production at regular market prices in the form of consumer loans. Costs were deducted up to a maximum of 50 per cent from the revenues.
- Winter training and availability of a production consultant.
- Direct trade contract with the final user (the food preserving plant).

Changes in the model structure and improvements in training increased the loan repayment ratio significantly. By 2016 the average yield of the Kiútprogram's clients reached that of other local producers.

Interactive Learning

The evolutionary economics of innovation theory posits that innovation is a cumulative, path-dependent, and interactive process, involving different types of actors whose knowledge and accumulated experience are crucial for the successful introduction of new solutions. These can include new or significantly improved products, processes, organizational, managerial, financial, or marketing methods, or new markets (Dosi 1988 and 2013; Dosi and Nelson 2010, Fagerberg et al. 2005). This process requires not only codified scientific and technical knowledge, stemming from R&D projects, but also practical knowledge, including its tacit elements.[19] Given the dynamic nature of innovation processes, learning capabilities are also of major importance.

These features are neatly captured in the Interactive Model of Learning and Innovation (Caraça et al. 2009).[20] This model is a useful analytic device that highlights:

- The types of actors who can be involved in actual innovation processes, playing diverse roles
- The types and forms of knowledge, which are needed for success
- The importance of interactions and exchanges among the actors, including the flow of information, knowledge, and money
- The role played by the formal and informal rules that govern these interactions and flows and the key role of the actors who set and shape these rules
- The other elements of the macro environment, including the education system, the information infrastructure, and the availability of private and public funds for innovation.

The Kiútprogram can be explored using this analytic device. Its major actors include: private funders with a variety of business knowledge and experience; advisors with social science analytical skills; fieldworkers with capability and social capital building experience. The Kiútprogram broadened its knowledge base by commissioning external experts to analyse: the Grameen model; foreign and other Hungarian attempts to fight poverty; marginalization dynamics and exclusion processes—both their generation and reproduction—with a special attention on the Roma minority in Hungary, including anthropological and sociological field research; and the role of relevant institutions. Other experts provided business and technological advice.

As in the case of most innovation, the programme implementation was a *trial and error* process: accumulated experience was analysed continuously and internal rules and methods modified accordingly. Client feedback was systematically collected and considered. The programme also had to be modified due to changes in external circumstances, especially the regulatory environment. The programme, therefore, had to be managed in a flexible way and managers had to constantly learn. Support schemes, however, are usually rather rigid given the

[19] Drawing on a major innovation survey among Danish companies, Jensen et al. (2007) identified two types of innovation activities: the so-called ST mode, in which innovators mainly exploit scientific and technological knowledge, and the DUI mode, in which innovation is based on learning by doing, using, and interacting. The survey showed that the most successful companies were the ones that combined both modes.

[20] Other models of innovation developed to analyse business innovations—the science-push, the market-pull, as well as the so-called chain-linked ones—are reviewed in Havas (2016) by focusing on their (ir)relevance to the study of social innovation.

strict rules introduced to prevent misuse of public funds. In quite a few cases it is fairly hard to amend a social innovation project, even when necessitated by internal learning and/or changes in the external environment.

The Kiútprogram and the Extended Social Grid Model

Personal Traits and Conversion Factors

This section applies the capability approach to describe the programme participants' situation (Sen 1999). Their *initial endowment* can be broadly characterized as follows: they have a low level of educational attainment; dropped out of the primary labour market a long time ago; have no savings and live in permanent poverty mainly in underdeveloped regions.

There are two *social conversion factors* that differ noticeably from village to village. First, local political leaders' attitudes towards marginalized groups, especially the Roma; using ESGM terminology, this is the way in which political power is applied. Some mayors tried their best to improve the status of the poorest in the village. In contrast, there were political leaders who aimed at maximizing the dependency of the poor in an attempt to win the support of the non-Roma residents. Many other examples were situated between these two extremes.

The second conversion factor was the existence and density of social connections, especially inter-community ties. Connections with local communities were crucial for enterprises to succeed in the programme's first phase. Clients who had more intense community connections before being involved in the programme were more likely to be successful (Molnár 2017). In certain cases a lack of inter-community connections caused failure because the effective demand within the Roma community was insufficient. The second phase of the Kiútprogram (cucumber production only) was different in this respect. It offered the possibility of joining an existing production network and, consequently the lack of inter-community connections was not an issue here. This structure, however, could contribute less to the development of inter-community connections than the model applied in the first phase.

Although the target group of the Kiútprogram was the Roma, ethnic origin was not a precondition for eligibility. Ethnic selection would have had negative effects on the cognitive frame of the non-Roma for several reasons. First, it would have increased the hostility against the Roma because many people would think they were getting special support yet again, while other Hungarians did not.[21] Second, it would have caused distrust in the programme itself, adding to the usual

[21] Three quarters of respondents in a survey did not agree with the statement that the Roma need more social help than the non-Roma populations (Publicus Research 2009).

suspicion against something new and unknown. These would have significantly hampered the strengthening of inter-community connections.[22] There is, thus, *a trade-off between exact targeting and building inter-community connections.*[23] While both are key components of an effective programme aimed at alleviating marginalization, the latter seems indispensable.

The *determination* of participants to change their circumstances was a prerequisite for success in the Kiútprogram. Equally crucial was their *willingness to take some risk.* The level of (actual and perceived) risk was influenced by the behaviour of local political leaders and their approach to exercising power, as well as the overall economic dynamics in a given micro-region. Higher risk tolerance was needed to start a new business than to join the cucumber project. Even in the latter case, when the programme was launched in a new village, the first clients were typically very committed and strongly motivated people with relatively low levels of risk aversion and who would take any opportunity to improve their family's situation. The risk-averse majority usually waited for the results of the first season of crops.

Learned Helplessness

Determination and willingness to take risk were necessary but not sufficient success factors for the programme: *learned helplessness also needed to be overcome.* Long-term deprivation can often lead to learned helplessness (Peterson et al. 1993), further aggravated by feeling constantly discriminated against. There were quite a few individuals in the Kiútprogram's target group without learned helplessness due to their personal traits, natural optimism, and dynamic personalities. For the majority, however, this was not the case. Various programmes targeting the marginalized often find that the marginalized do not want to take advantage of opportunities and, even when they get involved, often give up after the first severe problem. In these cases, the cognitive frame of the—actual or potential—participants needs to be modified: participants need to free themselves from their learned helplessness.

Providing unsecured loans proved to be a suitable tool to achieve these objectives. Such a loan served a dual purpose: it provided the missing financial capital as an initial endowment and, thus, helped overcome learned helplessness. These impacts evolved through the mechanism of building trust: unsecured loans

[22] In this case, inter-community connections refer to inter-ethnic connections, but in a general sense we mean connections between marginalized and non- (or less) marginalized groups.

[23] Similar problems can be observed in social housing, where a strict concentration on the most marginalized produces segregation. See chapter five in this volume, as well as Huttman et al. (1991).

strongly signal that the lender trusts both the honesty of the client and her capability in creating a successful business. As a Roma client said:

> I think the most important thing for the Roma is the fact that we get a loan. Because it means that they are not afraid that we would not repay it. For us, it was crucial that they give a loan and that they give it to us. This raised our attention: they give a loan to us. (Interview conducted by Molnár, 5 June 2015)

This emphasizes the important role of giving a loan instead of a grant (as in the case of some other EU-financed projects). *Free funds neither build trust nor create motivation to do everything for the business.* Thus, it can be generalized for SIMs as follows: *building trust between participants and leaders of a social innovation project is a prerequisite for maintaining participants' determination, building and reinforcing their self-esteem and eventually making the project a success.* Trust can be built in several ways, depending on the specific features of a given project and its context. A few basic rules apply, though: to sustain trust, promises must be kept, while rules must be made clear in advance and followed consistently.

Drawbacks of the Grameen Model

Using the mechanism of social collateral (sequential lending, joint liability, contingent renewal) is likely to undermine trust between the clients and the programme. It can be illustrated by the case of a Kiútprogram client, who was a role model for most people in his local Roma community. He misjudged two families, although he had known them since childhood. In one case he thought they would be intentional defaulters, in the other case he was convinced that they would pay back their loan. He was wrong in both cases. His level of identification with the programme was shown by the fact he felt as if those clients who had defaulted on the Kiútprogram had actually cheated him: 'I tell you that I trusted the people who tricked me most. We were good friends. They would not do it to me' (interview conducted by Molnár, 5 June 2015). According to the original Grameen model he should have been punished. Besides being unfair to punish somebody for someone else's fault, such a measure would have destroyed the credibility of the programme in the eyes of the fellow Roma.

Another consequence of the social collateral mechanism was the lack of freedom to leave the programme. This fundamentally hindered empowerment. To remove this obstacle, participants of Kiútprogram were not only given the freedom to join the programme in a well-informed way but, after 2012, they could also leave the programme without sanctions.

The experience of the Kiútprogram also refutes Yunus' conviction that there is no need for capability development when trying to tackle deep poverty. As he argued:

> From the very beginning, Grameen has gone against traditional methods of poverty alleviation by handing out cash without any attempt to first provide skills training... The fact that the poor are alive is clear proof of their ability. They do not need us to teach them how to survive. (Yunus 1999: 140)

However, the experience of Kiútprogram demonstrated that surviving and breaking out from a marginalized position required entirely different skills. The most important causes of entrepreneurial failure among the Kiútprogram's clients were insufficient business knowledge together with lack of practical experience and business connections (Molnár 2017).

Skills Development versus Paternalism

Within the Kiútprogram, participants also learn additional skills such as how to deal with administrative duties and how to solve basic financial and other business tasks. In the first phase some participants had—often very limited—vocational skills. In the second phase (cucumber growing) only a few participants had prior agricultural knowledge. As most participants had strongly adverse feelings towards formal education, the Kiútprogram applied two, practical, forms of skills development: group consultations and on-the-job training. Clients learnt about production processes while working. At the end of their first season, clients were able to follow instructions on pesticide packages and to calculate the dilution ratio by themselves.

The lesser the initial skills endowment project participants had, the more efforts and resources were needed to enable them to run their own business or successfully take part in the cucumber production project. As the programme provided sales—and later—supply channels, another trade-off emerged: the more the programme supported the integration of participants into production and sales networks, the less it contributed to developing their agency in the short run. A similar effect happens when support was provided to develop business plans or deal with administrative tasks. We can, therefore, infer that there was *a trade-off between the type and degree of help and the short-term empowerment effects.*

In conclusion, certain personal traits were prerequisites for the participants' success while other skills could be learnt during the social innovation project. However, participants' personal traits were not a static set of abilities: these traits changed during the social innovation processes. In SIM, one of the main objectives can be the modification of the participants' personal traits, through overcoming learned helplessness and providing help in building cultural and social capital.[24]

[24] Cultural and social capital is used here as in Bourdieu (1986).

Yet, this objective may entail a serious risk of unintended paternalism.[25] Here the short- and long-term effects can be different: a seemingly more paternalistic approach in the short run can increase the chance of starting an independent business at a later stage, which then leads to a very strong empowerment effect. In a follow-up survey, a large majority of the Kiútprogram clients (even those whose businesses were unsuccessful) reported an increase in their self-esteem, self-confidence, self-awareness, and overall sense of fulfilment in life (Molnár 2017).

The Role of Actors

Fieldworkers

The variety of fieldworkers' tasks can be summarized overall as building inter-community bridges. Through them, external knowledge 'travelled' to the participants, directly during daily communication, group meetings, or trainings, or indirectly via commissioning external experts with the relevant knowledge or by finding business partners.

Bridging is needed in both ways. For administrative duties, fieldworkers were present in various offices not only to help in complying with complicated requirements, but also to alleviate prejudices and protect against discrimination. The role of fieldworkers was similar when establishing contacts with potential business partners: they passed on information about the lives, ambitions, and efforts of the marginalized Roma to non-marginalized people who may not have been aware of this information. As a result, clients established new relationships with bank employees, suppliers, buyers, production system integrators, and other business people, who would not have otherwise contracted with poor Roma people. As a result, the participants in the programme became connected to existing business and societal networks. In the long run, these new connections enabled participants to achieve independence and business success after leaving the programme. Thus, *the activity and continuous presence of fieldworkers was crucial for reducing the chances of reproducing marginalization linked to normative prejudices (cognitive frames) and lack of access to social networks.*

Founders and Sponsors

The Kiútprogram was a specific SIM in the sense that those who launched and sponsored it were the same persons. They also led the main decision-making body of the programme since its very beginning. This allowed for innovation and flexibility in planning and implementing the programme. The main motivation

[25] Yunus has stood against skills training exactly because of this risk.

of the founders and sponsors was their strong repulsion against social injustice.[26] While the professional background of the decision-making body was varied, its members showed a common personality trait: they all strove for innovative solutions in their day-to-day jobs.

The primary objective of the programme was to be socially beneficial. Its 'outcomes' were the creation of new entrepreneurs and agricultural producers, as well as building their agency and cultural and social capital. The founders understood that overall financial sustainability for the programme could not be achieved even in the long run: they realized that their social goals could not be achieved within the framework of a sustainable social enterprise and that external financing would be continuously required. This was not because of low productivity, but rather it was due to the fact that the intangible outcomes of the programme—such as increased individual agency and enhanced cultural and social capital—are not monetizable. As a consequence, the programme aimed at a more modest but feasible objective: the financial benefits at a social level—the sum of taxes paid by the programme businesses plus the welfare benefits not needed to be paid to programme participants—should exceed the costs of the programme. This objective was met in the first phase (Audy et al. 2013).[27]

The most important dilemma for the founders of the programme was *the trade-off between the degree of marginalization of the participants and the attendant costs incurred.* If the programme worked with extremely marginalized participants only, then both the financial costs and the probability of failure would increase. This would significantly damage the public perception of the programme and reduce the likelihood of obtaining further financial and intellectual resources.

Yet, if the programme only accepted less marginalized participants, then overall costs could be reduced in the long run, the main social goals would not be met. This approach could also increase the social exclusion of the most disadvantaged, whose position in the local power structures would likely worsen.[28] This dilemma—typical in the case of bottom-of-the-pyramid interventions—has no 'optimal' solution that works in all contexts; it requires continuous analysis and discussion to achieve a good balance. This issue also highlights from a specific angle that effective social innovation is a continuous learning and adjustment process.

[26] Molnár (2018) provides a detailed, interview-based description of this issue, especially in sections 2.2.1 and 2.2.3.

[27] There are no sufficient data available for a thorough assessment of the second phase. Further, the evaluation criteria are not clear, either, as cucumber growing would not exclude employment in a public works scheme, financed by the state.

[28] Similar conclusions can be found in Geleta (2014: 122): 'Because some of the poor, especially the poorest of the poor, are excluded from gaining access to loans . . . the system of group-based MF [microfinance] contributes to the intensification of social differentiations and inequality among the poor.'

However, the biggest barrier to Kiútprogram's overall approach was the availability of financial resources. We review three types of—actual or potential—sponsors below: the European Commission, the Hungarian government, and private sponsors.

Funders: The European Commission

Between 2010 and 2012, the Kiútprogram's main source of finance was a Roma pilot programme managed directly by the European Commission (EC). The administrative requirements of this scheme were more straightforward and less demanding when compared to EU-funded schemes administered by the Hungarian government, while internal flexibility was greater. However, the programme suffered from a major weakness. It was obvious to all stakeholders that its two-year time span was not only unrealistically short, but also harmful to social innovation: it forced faster than optimal initial growth and an unrealistically short loan repayment period. The flexibility needed for social innovation to work effectively clashed with the fixed time span of this support scheme. Indeed, it became clear that *more flexibility in terms of the timing of the support would have ensured greater efficiency and efficacy using the same amount of money.* Learning by doing is essential for all interested actors—social innovation practitioners, beneficiaries, and policy-makers—and it is, therefore, crucial to allow some changes in a given support scheme or project without compromising the original, fundamental objectives.

According to an EC assessment, the Kiútprogram was successful in its first two years. Yet, there was no EU scheme available to finance its continuation. The EU programme for supporting microfinance[29] was not suitable for an atypical social microcredit programme like the Kiútprogram that provided very small loans with a high rate of failure. Giving priority to financial sustainability as a policy requirement for microcredit presented an obstacle to the implementation of inclusive and innovative social microcredit projects. Several EU documents set out this priority: 'Self-sustainability is a major issue for a microcredit fund. One way of achieving this goal can be to charge an above market interest rate. An above market rate is acceptable where the risk is higher' (EC 2003: 29).

As shown above, this approach is likely to lead to serious mission drift, not only in the case of microcredit, but also for all social innovations targeting the most marginalized groups. However, the removal of financial sustainability as a requirement may lead to irresponsible spending of external financial resources. A good solution to reduce this risk would be to involve private donors, given their strong interest—often coupled with appropriate expertise—to make sure that spending is

[29] Progress Microfinance, a formerly independent programme, now integrated into the EaSI framework. See http://ec.europa.eu/social/main.jsp?catId=836&langId=en.

efficient and responsible. An obvious further advantage of their involvement would be the extra funding obtained.

It is worth noting that the case of Social Impact Bonds (SIB: see chapter 12) is different. Those, who invest in a SIB, do so because they expect a financial return. In contrast, the private donors' motivation in the solution proposed above is to act against social exclusion while clearly understanding that it cannot be financially sustainable, let alone profitable.

The Kiútprogram revealed another problem in financing Roma programmes. The EU decision-making bodies presumed that the Operational Programmes of member states, co-financed by the EU Structural Funds, would fund the continuation of a successful pilot. While this makes sense in general, it is questionable if this is the right approach for the inclusion of permanently socially excluded groups, especially the Roma.

We have argued that national, regional, and local authorities are, in part, responsible actors in the processes of reproducing marginalization (see above). Schools and municipalities, as well as the education and social welfare systems, together with employment, housing, and regional development policies and business regulations all potentially contribute to its persistence. As a recent European Parliament resolution stated:

> Different forms of anti-Gypsyism can be identified in the work and workings of public authorities and institutions[30] in almost all spheres and at all levels in the Member States, manifesting itself most commonly in the failure to provide Roma with equal access or any access to public utilities and services, their denial of equal rights and equal treatment, the omission of Roma people from policy-making and knowledge-production processes, their underrepresentation in official bodies at all levels of society, the creation of discriminative programmes and the misuse of funding opportunities for improving the lives of Roma.
>
> (European Parliament 2017: 4).

Under such conditions, even the utilization of EU funds for the inclusion of the most deprived social groups can be ineffective and inefficient if administered by national authorities. What needs to be considered is whether the EU could create an economic space for social innovation aimed at alleviating marginalization by introducing new funding schemes.[31] An alternative model would see funds directly transferred to the NGOs supporting marginalized communities, bypassing the national and local administrations completely. This direct investment

[30] Please note that 'institutions' in this sentence refer to various organizations (e.g. service providers) and not the 'rules of the game' (as in the ESGM).

[31] The mid-term review of the EU framework for national Roma integration strategies lists the ongoing pilot programmes under its direct management (EC 2017: 6).

proposal faces objections from those who argue that issues should be dealt with via local political systems. Our analysis, however, suggests that entrenched marginalization and exclusion makes it unlikely that these issues will be solved via local politicians in every case—in such cases direct payments to frontline organizations may be more effective (Ziegler et al. 2017).

Funders: The Hungarian Government

In spite of the positive external evaluation of the Kiútprogram after the pilot phase,[32] the Hungarian government refused to support its continuation, let alone its wider application—although the first version of the Hungarian National Social Inclusion Strategy (Hungarian Government 2011) did mention the programme specifically.

The reasons were twofold. The first reason was political: since the previous government had supported the Kiútprogram in 2010, the incoming one reversed this decision.[33] It was relatively easy because it was a governmental decree on providing a one-off subsidy instead of rectifying a discriminative regulation against the self-employed entrepreneurs.[34] A policy implication can be drawn from this choice. Creating economic space for social innovation has a non-economic condition: it needs a thorough public discussion leading to wide acceptance and strong public support.[35]

The second reason was ideological: the Hungarian government had committed itself to the public works programme. The government aims at the 'social catching-up' of the Roma instead of social inclusion. The Hungarian term 'catching-up' suggests that those who need to catch up are somehow inferior to others—their social inclusion can only take place if they have reached the level of other less marginalized populations in society. This is the ideology behind the practice of segregated education.[36] The biggest theoretical difference between the Kiútprogram and the public works scheme is that, while the latter was fundamentally paternalistic, the main objective of the Kiútprogram was to strengthen the *independence* and *agency* of its participants.

The Hungarian government could have supported the social innovation of the Kiútprogram not only financially but also by modifying relevant institutions. This could have been achieved with a variety of policy tools, including:

[32] See the press release of the final conference: http://www.worldbank.org/en/news/press-release/2012/09/04/self-employment-through-social-microcredit or the World Bank's evaluation: Audy et al. (2013).

[33] For a detailed description see Molnár (2018).

[34] This is not unique to Hungary: Lodemann and Ziegler (2014) described a similar situation in case of the 'New Water Paradigm' in Slovakia.

[35] On the possible adverse effects of one-off subsidies see chapter 16, this volume.

[36] As has already been stressed, policy documents and practices do not always coincide. Sometimes even the official English and Hungarian versions of the same document differ in important details. In the Hungarian title of the National Social Inclusion Strategy the term is not 'inclusion' but 'catching-up'.

- Introducing specific regulations for microcredit and non-business lending by adapting good practices of other countries
- Establishing appropriate financial guarantee funds
- Reducing the social contributions to be paid by newly set up businesses and cutting the red tape they face
- Supporting the entry of micro- and small businesses into the market in disadvantaged regions
- Changing the system of adult education, implementing integrated training-on-the-job.

While none of these measures are directly connected to the Kiútprogram's social innovation or integration of the Roma, any improvements along these lines would be very impactful. The public works programme, however, has eclipsed all other active labour market programmes in recent years without reducing the marginalization of the Roma.

Further Private Sponsors

Fundraising was very difficult for the Kiútprogram due to its complex nature. Moreover, the culture of helping people in need has weak roots in Hungary. Potential donors who are willing to support charities are reluctant to contribute to a programme whose aim is to support marginalized people in becoming entrepreneurs or self-employed. They are typically sceptical about combining a business rationale with supporting the poor. Conversely, potential contributors from the business sector cannot accept that a microcredit programme offers costly services free of charge: they expect financial sustainability as opposed to 'planned' loss making. Moreover, the founder of the Kiútprogram made some mistakes when presenting the programme to the public through the media. They let the journalists overemphasize the banking aspects and that resulted in a misleading framing of the programme. An important conclusion is that social innovation should aim not only at shaping the cognitive frame about its target group but also concerning the perception of the social innovation itself.

Local Political Power and Empowerment

The most prominent representation of local political power was the local government: mainly the mayor, councillors, and office staff. Further government bodies—not necessarily in the same place—also had political power. These include employment centres, tax agencies, and authorities in charge of licensing and overseeing businesses. Local officials had various attitudes towards poor Roma clients: some of them were deliberately discriminative, while others were prejudiced and/or distrustful (this attitude seems the most common), a third group were supportive. Fieldworkers reported that—when interacting with these bodies—clients had faced discrimination in about half of the cases. Without the fieldworkers' intervention, this could have resulted in failed procedures. Discriminatory behaviour is technically illegal in Hungary, but this legislation is not enforced in practice. Hence officials showing this behaviour are not afraid of being held responsible for their misconduct. In the majority of cases the intervention of fieldworkers were able to defy discrimination and generate some sort of learning process for local officials. This experience supports a more general claim that a *devoted and coherent policy agenda against discrimination* could significantly improve the situation of the Roma.

The programme had a positive effect on the prejudiced and/or distrustful local politicians. In spite of negative expectations, many Roma people living in deep poverty still repaid their unsecured loans. This fact influenced opinions on the Roma and led to improved cooperation with local leadership in several villages. It also helped extend the territorial coverage of the programme during its second phase.[37]

In those villages, however, where the politically influential people felt their 'feudal' power threatened by the Kiútprogram, no positive changes occurred in their behaviour and ways of thinking. In a village, however, the participants of the cucumber project were able to play a role in getting a new mayor elected who promised cooperation with them during the campaign. This brought a remarkable change in the life of the village, where Roma were in the minority. This was the first time they had influenced local public life. Moreover, the candidate was not deterred by a concern that support from the Roma would alienate non-Roma voters.

There was no possibility for collective interest representation in the first phase of the programme as all clients had their own unrelated businesses. In contrast, the second phase provided much less decision-making freedom for the participants, but did enable collective action and a more empowered collective agency rather than individual agency.

Other Stakeholders

Other stakeholders included business partners, customers of the micro businesses, as well as others in the community. Due to lack of trust, quite a few business partners would not have contracted with the Roma without the cooperation of the Kiútprogram. Positive experiences lessened anti-Gypsyism to some extent, that is, changed the cognitive frames of the people who interacted with programme participants. A telling example was observed in a village with several grocery shops: one of the shop owners tried to attract more customers by providing interest-free consumer loans until the next harvest to Kiútprogram participants who had repaid their loans. The fact that the loan had been repaid has become

[37] The number of villages where the Kiútprogram had actual or former clients increased from six to twenty-six between 2013 and 2016.

moral collateral for other local lending transactions. These positive cases also opened the doors for Kiútprogram participants to join other existing business networks.

Although the media and other socially oriented NGOs are not direct stakeholders, they can contribute to amending the cognitive frames of people without entrenched anti-Gypsyism by disseminating the results of the Kiútprogram. The press coverage has been largely positive, except for some media outlets voicing government propaganda against the poor. The programme has been regularly mentioned in public debates as an example of Roma people, living in deep poverty, are capable of successfully running businesses or producing agricultural products when the necessary framework conditions are put in place.

Conclusion

Having analysed the marginalization of the Roma in Hungary we conclude that Mann's sources of power model is mainly useful for analysing the formation of marginalization during deep structural changes in society, while Beckert's Social Grid model helps us understand a given socio-structural status quo, as well as the processes reproducing marginalization.

When marginalization is persistently reproduced, practitioners and policymakers need to take into account power structures and the interactions of the three social forces: only those social innovations that target all three social forces and change the power structures at the level of the targeted community (be it a neighbourhood, a village, a city, a region, or a country) can ease marginalization. Otherwise, the 'untouched' social forces and power relations are likely to reproduce marginalization in a modified form.

In all societies we can observe complex power structures rather than simple dichotomies: the division of society into the powerful and the powerless is oversimplified. Regarding the severity of marginalization, socially excluded people are of utmost importance for SIMs. If a social innovation only targets the most disadvantaged, the probability of failure is higher, and this SIM is, thus, less appealing to practitioners and potential clients, reducing its potential for diffusion. If only less disadvantaged groups are assisted, the social exclusion of the most disadvantaged may, actually, be made worse. A particular form of this tension is the issue of ethnic targeting, namely the trade-off between exact targeting and building inter-community connections. Although socially excluded Roma were the explicit target group of the Kiútprogram, ethnic selection would have hampered, or even completely prevented, the strengthening of inter-community connections overall. As the latter is an essential component of social inclusion, this would have been a grave mistake.

In the case of SIMs, it is helpful to separate three types[38] of cognitive frames:

- The cognitive frame of the environment in which the marginalized group sits
- The cognitive frame of the members of the marginalized group about themselves
- The cognitive frame of the environment about the social innovation.

The experience gained from the Kiútprogram can be generalized as follows: changing the cognitive frame of the participants about themselves, namely reinforcing their agency and independence, is a necessary condition for a successful SIM. It is as important as changing the cognitive frame of the environment about the marginalized people. Building trust between participants and SIM practitioners is a prerequisite for maintaining participants' self-determination, reinforcing their self-esteem, and overcoming the problem of learned helplessness. Providing unsecured loans can be a very strong and effective signal of trust, but this method has significant cost implications too.

The Kiútprogram clearly shows that in the case of socially excluded groups a loan by itself is not sufficient to support the establishment of viable businesses in the formal economy. The main causes of entrepreneurial failure among the Kiútprogram's clients were insufficient knowledge and weak business connections and networks. The less initial individual capability endowments that the project participants had, the more efforts and resources were needed to enable them to run their own business. Consequently, different forms of capability building are indispensable for a successful SIM.

Following Sen's capability approach, knowledge, together with networks and inter-community bridges are especially crucial social conversion factors in the empowerment process. From a different angle, social ties and knowledge are also important power resources, as well as the ones identified by Mann. Yet, the more a given SIM supports the integration of participants into production and sales networks, facilitates knowledge absorption, and assists them in meeting administrative and regulatory requirements, the less it contributes to developing agency in the short run. Hence, there is a trade-off between the type and degree of support given and short-term empowerment effects. It is important to fully understand the differences between the short and long-term effects: a seemingly more paternalistic approach in the short run can increase the chances of starting a viable business at a later stage, which then leads to a very strong empowerment effect later on.

Another trade-off can be identified between the degree of marginalization of the participants and the costs of the SIM. In cases of highly marginalized target

[38] As our discussion on the Grameen model has indicated, in some cases it would be useful to consider a fourth type as well, the cognitive frame of the social innovation practitioners.

groups the quest for profitability—or at least financial sustainability—of a given social innovation project can lead to serious mission drift and even to the deterioration of the relative position of the most marginalized. Thus, a strict focus on financial sustainability can hamper the implementation of SIMs, endangering their empowering effects over time. Conversely, the removal of financial sustainability as a requirement may lead to irresponsible spending of external funds. This danger can be reduced by involving private donors who are likely to have a strong interest—in most cases coupled with the necessary experience and expertise—to check if resources are being used in a sensible, effective, and efficient way.

Social innovation—like business innovation—is a cumulative, path-dependent, and interactive process involving different types of actors whose knowledge and accumulated experience are crucial for the successful introduction of new solutions. Implementing—especially diffusing—these new solutions are learning and adjustment processes. Accumulating experience of a SIM—including systematically sought feedback from participants—needs to be analysed and reflected upon continuously, most likely leading to changes in internal rules and methods. The inevitable changes in external circumstances over time, especially the regulatory environment, also require flexibility from SIM practitioners.

Social innovation policymaking also needs to be understood as a learning process. The usually rigid public support schemes need to be eased to allow for more flexible implementation of SIMs without compromising the original fundamental policy objectives. National authorities are often responsible actors in the process of reproducing marginalization, either knowingly or unknowingly. Bypassing the national policy level to focus on more direct investment at the local level may offer a more effective option for EU funding. In some cases, it seems that EU-level bodies could best create an economic space for social innovation for the most marginalized, such as the Roma, without involving the national administrations at all.

References

Armendáriz, Beatriz, and Jonathan Morduch. 2010. *The Economics of Microfinance*. 2nd edition. Cambridge, MA: MIT Press.

Audy, Robin, Sandor Karacsony, Barbara Kits, Joost de Laat, György Molnár, and Lea Tan. 2013. 'Kiútprogram Social Microcredit Program: Case Study'. Washington, DC: The World Bank. http://documents.worldbank.org/curated/en/2013/06/18605991/kiutprogram-social-microcredit-program-case-study.

Bateman, Milford. 2010. *Why Doesn't Microfinance Work?* London: Zed Books.

Bernát, Anikó. 2014. 'Leszakadóban: a romák társadalmi helyzete a mai Magyarországon' [Falling behind: the social status of the Roma in Hungary today]. In *Társadalmi*

Riport [Social Report] 2014, edited by Tamás Kolosi and István György Tóth, pp. 246–64. Budapest: TÁRKI.

Bernát, Anikó, Attila Juhász, Péter Krekó, and Csaba Molnár. 2013. 'The Roots of Radicalism and Anti-Roma Attitudes on the Far Right'. Budapest: TÁRKI. http://www.tarki.hu/en/news/2013/items/20130305_bernat_juhasz_kreko_molnar.pdf.

Bernáth, Gábor and Vera Messing 2013. 'Pushed to the Edge: Research Report on the Representation of Roma Communities in the Hungarian Mainstream Media, 2011'. Working Paper Series, 2013/1. Center for Policy Studies, Central European University. http://publications.ceu.edu/sites/default/files/publications/cps-working-paper-pushed-to-the-edge-2013_0.pdf.

Bourdieu, Pierre. 1986. 'The Forms of Capital'. In *Handbook of Theory and Research for the Sociology of Education*, edited by John G. Richardson, pp. 241–58. New York: Greenwood Press.

Buckley, Robert M., Patric H. Hendershott, and Kevin Villani. 1994. 'Rapid Housing Privatization in Reforming Economies: Pay the Special Dividend Now'. Working Paper, Urban Development Division, The World Bank. http://siteresources.worldbank.org/INTURBANDEVELOPMENT/Resources/336387-1169585750379/twurdwp12.pdf .

Budapest Institute. 2014. 'Country Note--Hungary: Kiút ('Way-out') Social Microcredit Program, 2010–2012'. Contribution to the Local Economic and Employment Development programme of the OECD. http://budapestinstitute.eu/index.php/projektek/adatlap/lessons_learnt_from_kiut_microfinance_programme/en.

Caraça, João, Bengt-Åke Lundvall, and Sandro Mendonça. 2009. 'The Changing Role of Science in the Innovation Process: From Queen to Cinderella?'. *Technological Forecasting and Social Change* 76(6): 861–7.

Cseres-Gergely, Zsombor, and György Molnár. 2015. 'Labour Market Situation Following Exit from Public Works'. In *The Hungarian Labour Market 2015*, edited by Károly Fazekas and Júlia Varga, pp. 148–59. Budapest: Institute of Economics, Centre for Economic and Regional Studies, Hungarian Academy of Sciences.

Csermely, Péter, Ágoston Michalik, Zsolt Vassy, and András London. 2014. 'Crisis Responses and Crisis Management: What Can We Learn from Biological Networks'. *Systema* 2(1): 23–7.

Dosi, Giovanni. 1988. 'Sources, Procedures and Microeconomic Effects of Innovation'. *Journal of Economic Literature* 24(4): 1120–71.

Dosi, Giovanni. 2013. 'Innovation, Evolution, and Economics: Where We Are and Where We Should Go'. In *Innovation Studies: Evolution and Future Challenges*, edited by Jan Fagerberg, Ben R. Martin, and Esben Sloth Andersen, pp. 111–33. Oxford: Oxford University Press.

Dosi, Giovanni, and Richard R. Nelson. 2010. 'Technical Change and Industrial Dynamics as Evolutionary Processes'. In *Economics of Innovation*, edited by Bronwyn H. Hall and Nathan Rosenberg, pp. 51–127. Amsterdam: North-Holland.

Eisenstadt, Shmuel Noah and Luis Roniger. 1981. 'The Study of Patron–Client Relations and Recent Developments in Sociological Theory'. In *Political Clientelism, Patronage and Development*, edited by Shmuel Noah Eisenstadt and René Lemarchand, pp. 271–95. London: Sage.

European Commission. 2003. 'Microcredit for Small Businesses and Business Creation: Bridging a Market Gap'. Report. http://ec.europa.eu/growth/content/microcredit-small-businesses-and-business-creation-bridging-market-gap-0_en, accessed 19 January 2018.

European Commission. 2011. 'An EU Framework for National Roma Integration Strategies up to 2020'. Brussels: European Commission. https://ec.europa.eu/health//sites/health/files/social_determinants/docs/com2011_173_en.pdf, accessed 19 January 2018.

European Commission. 2017. 'Midterm Review of the EU Framework for National Roma Integration Strategies'. Brussels: European Commission. https://www.google.hu/url?sa=t&rct=j&q=&esrc=s&source=web&cd=2&ved=0ahUKEwj3rO-Do_XXAhWMbVAKHYbbAaMQFggvMAE&url=http%3A%2F%2Fec.europa.eu%2Fnewsroom%2Fjust%2Fdocument.cfm%3Faction%3Ddisplay%26doc_id%3D46282&usg=AOvVaw29svkijr0loCJgeq1CYDf2, accessed 19 January 2018.

European Parliament. 2017. 'European Parliament Resolution of 25 October 2017 on Fundamental Rights Aspects in Roma Integration in the EU: Fighting Anti-Gypsyism (2017/2038(INI))'. http://www.europarl.europa.eu/sides/getDoc.do?pubRef=-//EP//NONSGML+TA+P8-TA-2017-0413+0+DOC+PDF+V0//EN, accessed 19 January 2018.

European Union Agency for Fundamental Rights. 2016. 'Second European Union Minorities and Discrimination Survey (EU-MIDIS II) Roma—Selected Findings'. http://fra.europa.eu/en/publication/2016/eumidis-ii-roma-selected-findings, accessed 19 January 2018.

Fagerberg, Jan, David C. Mowery, and Richard R. Nelson (eds). 2005. *The Oxford Handbook of Innovation*. Oxford: Oxford University Press.

Gans, Herbert J. 1972. 'The Positive Functions of Poverty'. *American Journal of Sociology* 78(2): 275–89.

Geleta, Esayas Bekele. 2014. 'Social Capital as Collateral: Banking on the Poor'. *American Journal of Economics and Sociology* 73(1): 108–25.

Granovetter, Mark. 1973. 'The Strength of Weak Ties'. *American Journal of Sociology* 78(6): 1360–80.

Havas, Attila. (2016). 'Recent Economic Theorising on Innovation: Lessons for Analysing Social Innovation'. CrESSI Working Paper No. 27. Brussels: European Commission, DG Research.

Hegedüs, József. 2008. 'Social Housing in Transitional Countries: The Case of Hungary'. In *Social Housing in Europe II: A Review of Policies and Outcomes*, edited by Kathleen Scanlon and Christine M. E. Whitehead, pp. 145–62. London: LSE.

Hungarian Government. 2011. 'National Social Inclusion Strategy—Extreme Poverty, Child Poverty, the Roma (2011–2020)'. December. Budapest: Ministry of Public Administration and Justice, State Secretariat for Social Inclusion. http://ec.europa.eu/justice/discrimination/files/roma_hungary_strategy_en.pdf.

Huttman, ElizabethD., Wim Blauw, and Juliet Saltman (eds). 1991. *Housing Segregation of Minorities in Western Europe and the United States*. Durham, NC: Duke University Press.

Jensen, Morten Berg, Björn Johnson, Edward Lorenz, and Bengt-Åke Lundvall. 2007. 'Forms of Knowledge and Modes of Innovation'. *Research Policy* 36(5): 680–93.

Karlan, Dean, Markus Mobius, Tanya Rosenblat, and Adam Szeidl. 2009. 'Trust and Social Collateral'. *Quarterly Journal of Economics* 124(3): 1307–61.

Karsai, László. 1992. *A cigánykérdés Magyarországon 1919–1945* [The Roma question in Hungary 1919-1945]. Budapest: Cserépfalvi.

Kemény, István, and Gábor Havas. 1996. 'Cigánynak lenni' [To be Roma] In *Társadalmi riport 1996* [Social Report 1996], edited by Rudolf Andorka, Tamás Kolosi, and György Vukovics, pp. 352–80. Budapest: TÁRKI. http://www.tarki.hu/adatbank-h/kutjel/pdf/a894.pdf.

Kemény, István, Béla Janky, and Gabriella Lengyel. 2004. *A magyarországi cigányság 1971–2003* [The Roma in Hungary 1971–2003]. Budapest: Gondolat.

Kertesi, Gábor. 2005. *A társadalom peremén: Romák a munkaerőpiacon és az iskolában* [At the Periphery of the Society: The Roma on the Labour Market and in the School]. Budapest: Osiris.

Kertesi, Gábor, and Gábor Kézdi. 2011. 'Roma Employment in Hungary after the Post-Communist Transition'. *Economics of Transition* 19(3): 563–610.

Kiútprogram. 2012. 'Social Microcredit, Self-Employment and Roma Inclusion: Lessons of Kiútprogram, A Social Microcredit Pilot and Policy Recommendations for the New Structural Funds Period'. Budapest. http://kiutprogram.hu/wp-content/uploads/2018/06/kiut_policy_paper_final.pdf, accessed 29 June 2019.

Ladányi, János, and Iván Szelényi. 2004. *A kirekesztettség változó formái* [The Changing Forms of Social Exclusion]. Budapest: Napvilág Kiadó.

Lodemann, Justus, and Rafael Ziegler. 2014. 'A New Water Paradigm: Michal Kravčik and People and Water'. In *Social Entrepreneurship in the Water Sector: Getting Things Done Sustainably*, edited by Rafael Ziegler, Lena Partzsch, Jana Gebauer, Marianne Henkel, JustusLodemann, and Franziska Mohaupt, pp. 78–105. Cheltenham: Edward Elgar.

Majtényi, Balázs, and György Majtényi. 2016. *A Contemporary History of Exclusion: The Roma Issue in Hungary from 1945 to 2015*. Budapest: Central European University Press.

Molnár, György. 2017. 'Capability Building Combined with Microcredit: The Loan Alone Is Insufficient'. *Journal of Social Entrepreneurship* 8(3): 354–74.

Molnár, György. 2018. 'A Way out of Poverty? A Social Microcredit Programme Generating Self-Employment for the Roma in Hungary'. In 'Four Individual Case Studies Following a Common Template', edited by Gudrun Schimpf, Thomas Scheuerle, and Georg Mildenberger, pp. 5–76. CrESSI Working Paper No. 47. Brussels: European Commission, DG Research.

Peterson, Christopher, Steven F. Maier, and Martin E. P. Seligman. 1993. *Learned Helplessness: A Theory for the Age of Personal Control.* New York: Oxford University Press.

Publicus Research. 2009. 'Cigányellenesség a norma' [Being Anti-Gypsy Is the Norm]. http://www.publicus.hu/blog/ciganyellenesseg_norma/.

Sen, Amartya. 1999. *Development as Freedom.* Oxford: Oxford University Press.

Yunus, Muhammad. 1999. *Banker to the Poor: Micro-Lending and the Battle against World Poverty.* New York: Public Affairs.

Ziegler, Rafael, György Molnár, Enrica Chiappero-Martinetti, and Nadia von Jacobi. 2017. 'Creating (Economic) Space for Social Innovation'. *Journal of Human Development and Capabilities* 18(2): 293–8.

8

Trajectories of Social Innovation

Education

Martijn Jeroen van der Linden

> A general state education is a mere contrivance for moulding people to be exactly like one another; and as the mould in which it casts them is that which pleases the predominant power in government—whether this be a monarch, a priesthood, an aristocracy, or the majority of the existing generation—in proportion as it is efficient and successful, it establishes a despotism over the mind, leading by natural tendency to one over the body. An education established and controlled by the State should only exist, if it exists at all, as one among many competing experiments, carried on for the purpose of example and stimulus, to keep the others up to a certain standard of excellence.
>
> (John Stuart Mill 2001 [1859]: 97)

Introduction

Education's growing dependence on politics and, increasingly also on the market, reverses a major cultural innovation of the past: the struggle for freedom of education.[1] Such freedom was a prominent concern in Europe in the past—represented especially in the writings on self-development by John Stuart Mill (1806–73) and on *Bildung* by Wilhelm von Humboldt (1767–1835), as well as by the history of the Dutch School Struggle (*Schoolstrijd*) (1806–1920). This chapter investigates the implications for freedom of education when three important aspects of education are centralized with the state, in denial of educational freedom. These three aspects are: guaranteeing equitable *access* to education;

[1] The author is grateful to C. W. M. (Ro) Naastepad for co-authoring a first version of this chapter. This does not, however, necessarily imply her agreement with any views or interpretations expressed in this chapter. Additional thanks go to Amelia Pope for her language edits.

Martijn Jeroen van der Linden, *Trajectories of Social Innovation: Education*. In: *Creating Economic Space for Social Innovation*. Edited by: Alex Nicholls and Rafael Ziegler, Oxford University Press (2019). © Oxford University Press.
DOI: 10.1093/oso/9780198830511.003.0008

equitable *funding for* education; controlling the overall *quality* of education. The empirical focus of the chapter is on the Dutch history.[2]

In terms of the definition of social innovation used in this book (see chapter 1), this chapter is concerned with 'the development of a new idea' that 'intentionally seek[s] to... improve human capabilities'. Regarding the Extended Social Grid Model (ESGM), the social powers (per Michael Mann; see Heiskala 2014 and also chapter 2) relevant to this case study are *cultural* (referring to ideas about education, including ideas regarding how it is to be funded and what constitutes the right to education), *political* (the right to education), and *economic* (the funding of education). In terms of social forces (Beckert 2010, see also chapter 1), the Dutch School Struggle shows that changes in cognitive frames (ideas about education) can lead to changes in institutions (how education is legally organized) and social networks (the particular constellation that emerges with regards to the funding of education). With respect to the capability approach, Sen (1997) distinguished between the accumulation of human capital (a neoclassical concept that treats human qualities as factors to be used to augment production) and the expansion of human capabilities. For Sen (1997), the two are related as means and ends: the productive capabilities that lead to economic growth are linked to the expansion of human freedom to live the kind of lives that people have reason to value. Therefore, the role of economic growth in expanding these opportunities has to be integrated into a more fundamental understanding of the process of development and the expansion of human capabilities to lead freer and more worthwhile lives. However, Sen does not explain how economic growth is, or can be, used to expand human capabilities. The Dutch case discussed here provides an illustration of how the expansion of human freedoms and the growth of finance can be historically in opposition and how, especially, political-economic goals can interfere with the free expansion of human capabilities.

First, this chapter revisits the historical struggle for freedom of education—more generally, freedom of thought—which in the Netherlands has a precursor in William of Orange's quest for freedom of conscience enshrined in the 1576 Pacification of Ghent. In the first phase of the Dutch School Struggle, the focus was on this quest for cultural freedom—advocates argued that there was an indissoluble connection between freedom of conscience, freedom of worship, and freedom of education. In the second phase, the focus shifted to equal funding of all types of education. The Dutch School Struggle resulted in a centralization of the cultural, political, and economic aspects of education in the hands of the state that still exists today.

After this section, the chapter discusses implications for the freedom of education when the three key elements noted above are controlled by the state. This analysis suggests that the role of the state is to guarantee equitable *access* to

[2] For the more general European context see the comprehensive report in Scheuerle et al. (2016).

education as a normative feature of legal-political life. This can be achieved by ensuring that education is adequately funded. The state should, however, not control the *quality* of education since this is an aspect of cultural life.[3] If the state controls all three aspects, the funding of education is often made conditional on the quality of education, whereby norms for quality tend to be influenced by political goals that, in turn, are often driven by economic and financial interests.

According to John Stuart Mill (2001 [1859]: 15), human liberty 'comprises, first, the inward domain of consciousness; demanding liberty of conscience in the most comprehensive sense; liberty of thought and feeling; absolute freedom of opinion and sentiment on all subjects, practical or speculative, scientific, moral, or theological.' For Mill, freedom of thought included freedom to act on such thought too. Arguably, the latter includes freedom to teach, to establish a school, and to choose a school for one's children according to one's worldview—including one's pedagogical view. As regards practical implementation, Mill (2001 [1859]: 97) suggested leaving it 'to parents to obtain the education [for their children] where and how they pleased', while the government or society should 'content itself with helping to pay the school fees of poorer classes of children, and defraying the entire school expenses of those who have no one else to pay for them'. In line with Mill, von Humboldt, and Dutch proponents of freedom of education, this chapter develops an approach with which to disentangle the cultural, legal-political, and economic aspects of education. The key argument is that free education should be led by those whose profession it is—that is, teachers and researchers rather than politicians or owners of capital.[4]

The Dutch School Struggle (1806–1920)

From 1806 until 1920 the Dutch struggled with the implementation of the idea of freedom of education and its unconditional funding. The purpose of the Dutch

[3] Including with respect to pedagogy. Mill and Von Humboldt (1993 [1854]: 15) considered self-development (per Mill) or *Bildung* (per von Humboldt) as 'the end of man'. The developed person has, according to Mill (2001 [1859]: 15), an active character and expressions of his own nature. According to both there are two prerequisites for self-development: freedom and a variety of situations. Von Humboldt (1993 [1854]: 18) rejected state action aimed at improving 'the positive welfare of the nation' because state interference decreased variety (diversity) and produced uniformity—thus weakening the character of the individual and the nation as a whole. State interference also changed the direction of development from inward (one's own character) towards outward conditions (Valls 1999: 257–8)—in von Humboldt's (1993 [1854]: 41–2) words, 'Now all systems of national education, inasmuch as they afford room for the manifestation of a governmental spirit, tend to impose a definite form on civic development, and therefore to repress those vital energies of the nation.' Mill (2001 [1859]: 97) was also concerned that state action lead to uniformity and passivity, and argued that education established by the state 'should only exist, if it exists at all... for the purpose of example and stimulus.'

[4] Namely, this chapter makes a case for a professional mode of provision as in the typology of chapter 3.

School Struggle was to achieve equal treatment for private schools, which fell under the responsibility of school boards and parents, and public schools, which fell under the responsibility of the government. The first phase of the Dutch School Struggle (1806–57) focused on the right to establish private schools—the quest for freedom. In the second phase (1857–1920) the focus shifted to equal funding for private and public schools—the quest for equality.

Today the ideas of those who once defended freedom of thought and education—such as Guillaume Groen van Prinsterer, Johan Rudolf Thorbecke, Abraham Kuyper, John Stuart Mill, and Wilhelm von Humboldt—seem to have been lost, as standardization and uniformity have become the norm. Another factor contributing to this narrowing down of the scope of education has been the debt funding of post-secondary education. In a debt-based education system, students are more likely to choose (perceived) 'profitable' courses of study that prepare them for 'marketable' high-paying jobs, because they have to pay off their student loans.

It may be important to recall and make explicit what is lost in this process. To this end, we revisit the main arguments put forward in the Dutch School Struggle. By revisiting the theoretical arguments this chapter explores what freedom in education means, why it is important and what it requires. In addition to enshrinement in law (political space), freedom of education requires a type of funding (economic space) that respects the autonomy of education (cultural space).

The First Phase (1806–57)

The Dutch School Struggle was prompted by the enactment of the Education Law in 1806. An important preceding development was the invasion of the Republic of the Seven United Netherlands by the French in 1795. With French support, the Batavian Republic was proclaimed and a centralized federal government was established. The Batavian Republic became a client state of the revolutionary French Republic and subsequently, as the Kingdom of Holland,[5] part of the French Empire of Napoleon Bonaparte. Subsequently, this led to important changes in the law and the legal-political system[6] with a new emphasis on uniformity and centralization.

The new central government enacted national laws and implemented a system of state-subsidized 'neutral' primary public schools. The Education Law of 1806 formalized a public education system under the control of the government and distinguished two types of elementary schools: public schools funded by the state

[5] Taking the name of the province Holland for the whole country.
[6] The introduction of French revolutionary ideas and law and subsequently the *Code Napoléon*.

that promoted 'the development of all civic and Christian virtues'[7] (a definition of 'neutral'); private schools funded by private individuals or what would now be called non-governmental organizations (such as churches). To establish and run a private school, permission from the local municipality was required—in practice, however, this was rarely granted. The outcome of the Education Law was 'a *de facto* State monopoly on education' (Hooker 2009: viii). According to Van Essen (1990: 56), the Law was 'clearly a result of the principles of the French Revolution—the state could establish schools and determine the character of education: the child belonged to the state'.

This distinction between public and private schools and a 'neutral' worldview of education would dominate Dutch politics for over a century and become the heart of the Dutch School Struggle. The subject of the debate was the implicit assumption that knowledge is objective and this underpinned the entire system of centralized, state-funded, and 'neutral' public schools. According to historian Adriaan Goslinga (1884–1961), 'the [Dutch] School Struggle was really an effort to control the soul of youth; basically it was a conflict between different views of life' (Goslinga 1925, quoted in Valk 1995: 161).

However, supporters of freedom of education defended the right to determine the religious or philosophical worldview underlying children's education. They argued that freedom of religion, freedom of conscience, and freedom of education were inseparably connected. According to them, neutral education did not exist because, in the end, all knowledge is rooted in and, to some extent directed by, normative religious, philosophical, or scientific perspectives. As a result, the state's endorsement of one particular—so-called neutral—worldview was not only unjust, but also dangerous.

On the other hand, opponents of freedom of education argued that the state had a duty to support children to challenge normative religious or philosophical convictions—even if these reflected their parents' worldview. In the nineteenth century, these opponents argued that the state was the only supra-religious institution that could ensure that the Netherlands would develop as a modern state. Freedom of education with a diversity of doctrinal approaches was, in their opinion, a danger that could eventually destroy the unity of the Netherlands.

Initially, it was a relatively small group of 'enlightened', mostly upper-class, citizens and 'enlightened' pastors of the reformed and dissident Protestant Church that proposed the Education Law. Subsequently, the government decided to support it too (Boekholt and de Booy 1987: 132). However, it was clear that the average Dutch citizen did not understand why a change in education was needed. From the beginning, large parts of the population resisted an education based upon civic and Christian virtues. As a result, the education reforms were

[7] In Dutch: '*de opvoeding tot maatschappelijke en christelijke deugden.*' Available at: http://www.denederlandsegrondwet.nl/9353000/1/j9vvihlf299q0sr/vi9fk3zv7nq4.

implemented slowly and, in some cases, not at all. For example, the Catholics in the South of the Netherlands did not implement the proposed reforms. Over the years protests against the 'neutral' Christian schools took different forms, such as the establishment of illegal schools and keeping children at home. Although resistance took place all over the Netherlands, the discontent did not reach the Dutch parliament until the second quarter of the nineteenth century. According to Hooker (2009: viii): 'the first verbal shot in the *Schoolstrijd* was fired in 1825 by a Catholic Member of Parliament, Leopold van Sasse van Ysselt (1778–1844)'. In a speech, Sasse van Ysselt called for freedom of education, by which 'he meant the freedom to teach not just Christian principles, but Catholic principles to Catholic children in Catholic schools' (Hooker 2009: viii).

In 1830, the southern provinces separated from the Kingdom of the Netherlands and Belgium was established. After the secession of Belgium, 'political awareness [of freedom of education] slowly began to emerge in the Netherlands' (Hooker 2009: 9). In 1837, politician and publicist Guillaume Groen van Prinsterer (1801–76) wrote a pamphlet entitled 'Measures Used against the Dissenters Held against Constitutional Law'. Groen van Prinsterer argued that 'the Dutch public school system, far from being neutral, had fallen under the influence of the French revolution, which understood children to be property of the state and was imposing on children a deistic religion that was foreign to Christianity and to the Netherlands' (Naylor 2012: 251). Moreover, Groen van Prinsterer stated that Dutch parents should have the right to determine the religious worldview of their children's education. He argued that there existed an indissoluble connection between freedom of conscience, freedom of worship, and freedom of education (Groen van Prinsterer 1903: 18).[8]

In 1840, the king appointed a Commission on Elementary Education—composed of six members including Groen van Prinsterer—to review the complaints voiced in various petitions, to study the school system, and to make recommendations. Immediately after its establishment, the commission became divided over its task and, subsequently, over the issue of establishing schools based on an individual's personal worldview. Like many members of parliament, three members of the commission feared fanaticism and argued that state schools were needed to secure individual development and national unity. Groen van Prinsterer published a dissenting note accompanying the commission's report in which he defended freedom of education as a right—not a privilege—closely tied to freedom of religion. In Groen van Prinsterer's view, the state should not be allowed to monopolize education but, rather, should only support equal opportunities and uphold the rights of individuals:

[8] In Dutch: 'Vrijheid van geweten, vrijheid van Godsdienstoefening, vrijheid van onderwijs, hiertusschen is een onverbreekbare band.'

> Decisions should not be made on the basis of a numerical majority. If there are a hundred people who oppose removing the restrictions on Freedom of Education because they are neither helped nor hurt by them, and one who supports removing them, it is the duty of the Crown to defend the right of the one against the arbitrary decision of many. Asking the approval of the many, cases like this can effectively be used to countenance any form of discrimination.
>
> (cited in Hooker 2009: 12)

In 1840, Johan Rudolf Thorbecke (1798–1872)—a professor of diplomacy and political history who later became prime minister—wrote *Ideas on an Amendment to the Constitution.*[9] In it, he stated:

> One should not regret the special [private] school but, rather, consider them as a contribution of private individuals to the common good that would otherwise have to be organized by the government. A country with only special [private] schools could find itself doing very well. Education is not a task for the government. The government must only provide public education when private persons fail to do so. I, thus, do not share the opinion . . . that a special [private] school should be a rare exception. In contrast, I am of the view that the attempts by private persons to expand education deserve encouragement in every way possible.[10] (Author's translation)

Thorbecke considered the role of the state in education as one of *supervision* (providing certification of teachers, standard examinations, and inspections) and argued that the private sector should organize the rest. When the Liberals came to power in 1848, Thorbecke became prime minister and championed the principle of freedom of education into his constitutional reforms. After two amendments-- 'Public education is an object of abiding concern to the government' and 'Everywhere in the Kingdom sufficient public primary education shall be provided by the government'—Article 194 of the constitution of 1848 was ratified with the support of the Catholics and read as follows:

> Public education is an object of abiding concern to the government. Public education shall be organized, with respect for everyone's religious views, by

[9] In Dutch: 'Proeve van herziening der grondwet volgens de Aanteekening'.

[10] In Dutch: 'Men moet de bijzondere scholen niet betreuren; maar die integendeel beschouwen als eene bijdrage van particulieren aan de gemeene zaak, waarvoor anders het Bestuur moet zorgen. Een land waar enkel bijzondere scholen zijn, zou zich zeer wel kunnen bevinden. Het onderwijzen is geene taak van Regering. De Regering moet alleen voor een publiek onderwijs zorgen, omdat de bijzondere personen gemeenlijk te kort schieten. Ik ben dus niet van de meening van den geachten spreker (Gevers Deynoot), dat eene bijzondere school eene zeldzame uitzondering moet zijn. Integendeel meen ik, dat de pogingen van particulieren om het onderwijs uit te breiden allezins aanmoediging verdienen.' (quoted in De Savornin Lohman and Frederik 1889: 102).

> law. Everywhere in the Kingdom, government shall provide sufficient public primary. The provision of education is *free*, subject to supervision by the government and, insofar as secondary and primary education are concerned, subject to examination of the ability and morality of the teachers; these matters are to be regulated by law.[11] (Own translation, emphasis added)

The Constitution of 1848 did not change the purpose of public elementary education (the development of civic and Christian values), but it did secure freedom of education with the exception of the supervision and the examination of the competence and morality of teachers, both of which remained issues for the government. However, for freedom of education to be realized, a new Education Law had to be designed and ratified by the government. In 1857 this finally happened (Boekholt and de Booy 1987: 145). The long period between the new Article in the Constitution (1848) and the new Education Law (1857) shows how divided the parliament was on this issue (Hooker 2009: 15). Indeed, one of the main advocates of freedom of education, Groen van Prinsterer, resigned his seat in parliament when the new Education Law was enacted in 1857.

The Second Phase (1857–1920)

With the implementation of the new Education Law, the second phase of the Dutch School Struggle began. The focus shifted from the right to establish private (special) schools to equal rights for state funding of public *and* private schools.

Although a clear definition of freedom of education was not formulated and different interpretations existed at the time, many supporters of freedom of education thought that the Dutch School Struggle was now over, since anyone was now officially allowed to establish and operate schools based on their own religious or philosophical worldview. However, in an environment with public schools funded by the state, it was hard to establish private schools. One of the reasons was the interpretation of the First Amendment that stated that public education is an object of abiding concern to the government. This was interpreted as de facto excluding private schools from government support. Moreover, as Naylor (2012: 253)[12] explained: 'because the Constitution mandated that public schools be established everywhere [in the Second Amendment], all parents (except

[11] In Dutch: 'Het openbaar onderwijs is een voorwerp van de aanhoudende zorg der Regering. De inrigting van het openbaar onderwijs wordt, met eerbiediging van ieders godsdienstige begrippen, door de wet geregeld. Er wordt overal in het Rijk van overheidswege voldoend openbaar lager onderwijs gegeven. Het geven van onderwijs is vrij, behoudens het toezigt der overheid, en bovendien, voor zoover het middelbaar en lager onderwijs betreft, behoudens het onderzoek naar de bekwaamheid en zedelijkheid des onderwijzers; het een en ander door de wet te regelen.' Available at: http://www.denederlandsegrondwet.nl/9353000/1/j9vvihlf299q0sr/via0istdc4zt.

[12] In her PhD thesis on the role of Dutch politician Abraham Kuyper in the Dutch School Struggle.

for the indigent) were levied a substantial tax to establish and maintain public schools.'

This meant that free-school supporters had to pay taxes for public schools as well as additional fees for private schools. Some public schools also reduced their fees to attract more children. The result was that plenty of free-school supporters lacked the means to fund their own school. The funding of public and special schools was, therefore, fundamentally unequal and this lack of finance—effectively a restricted economic space[13]—made it almost impossible for the free-school movement to take advantage of their legal right to freedom of education. Consequently, the next step in the Dutch School Struggle focused on equal access to funding for all types of schools. In 1860, the lawyer and professor Joannes Theodorus Buys (1826–93) expressed the new purpose clearly:

> I believe that an unlimited right to establish special [private] schools is not enough to realize freedom of education; that the artificial protection of state schools, be it by providing tuition-free education to other than the needy, or through the provision of other advantages, renders the establishment of special [private] schools practically impossible and the granted right illusionary.... The modern state must be the conservative institution par excellence; all streams of thought and parties that can exist within the law, it must support equally and simultaneously. Should it [the state], on the other hand, become a tool of the majority or of a minority, destined not to preserve but to destroy everything that the ruling stream of thought disapproves of, then we return to the abuses of the old, medieval political spirit, and justice for all is no longer the principle of life, the actual raison d'être of the modern state. The state is not a moral exploitation company of someone or for someone, whoever it may be! That is my motto, and the truth of this motto is even dearer to me even than the mixed school.[14]
>
> (Author's translation)

[13] In my view, 'economic space' has two aspects. Theoretically, it points to the freedom to have, develop, and act upon different views regarding which concepts and ruling principles are essential to economic life. Empirically or practically, it refers to the financial means (money and capital) one needs to use and develop one's capabilities.

[14] In Dutch: 'Ik geloof, dat een onbeperkt regt om bijzondere scholen op te rigten nog niet genoeg is om de vrijheid van onderwijs te vestigen; dat kunstmatige bescherming van de staatsschool, 't zij door het verstrekken van kosteloos onderwijs anders dan aan behoeftigen, 't zij door het toekennen van andere voordeelen, de bijzondere school feitelijk onmogelijk en dus het gegeven regt illusoir maakt.... De moderne staat moet zijn de conservatieve instelling bij uitnemendheid; alle rigtingen en partijen, die bestaanbaar zijn met het regt, moet hij gelijkelijk en gelijktijdig steunen. Wordt hij daarentegen een werktuig van de meerderheid of van de minderheid, bestemd niet om te bewaren maar om te vernietigen alles wat de heerschende rigting niet is toegedaan, dan keeren wij terug tot de misbruiken van het oude en middeneeuwsche staatswezen, en is regt voor allen niet langer het levensbeginsel, het eigenlijke *raison d'être* van den modernen Staat. De Staat geen zedelijke exploitatie-maatschappij van wie of voor wie het dan ook zijn moge! Ziedaar mijne leus, en de waarheid van die leuze is mij liever, zelfs dan de gemengde school' (quoted in De Savornin Lohman and Frederik 1889: 102–3).

The journalist and statesman Abraham Kuyper (1837–1920) questioned the unequal access to funding of education in the following way:

> Do the poor, the less well-to-do, have no heart, no convictions, no desires concerning their offspring? And is it acceptable to dare to use the word 'freedom' in a program that offers us: freedom for the rich, but coercion for the poor?
> (Kuyper 1890: 243, cited in Naylor 2012: 264)

In the words of the proponents of freedom of education quoted above one may hear the echo of the British philosopher and political economist John Stuart Mill who, inspired by the German philosopher and government functionary Wilhelm von Humboldt, expressed similar objections against state education in *On Liberty*:

> A general State education is a mere contrivance for moulding people to be exactly like one another; and as the mould in which it casts them is that which pleases the dominant power in the government, whether this be a monarch, an aristocracy, or a majority of the existing generation; in proportion as it is efficient and successful, it establishes a despotism over the mind, leading by a natural tendency to one over the body. (Mill 2001 [1859], 97)

According to the advocates of freedom of education, the state should never be allowed to become an institution of moral exploitation for or against any worldview. Kuyper explained that schools should be based on answers to the most important questions in human life, answers about which consensus is impossible: 'questions of anthropology and psychology, of religion, and sociology, of pedagogy and morality' (Kuyper 1875, quoted in Naylor 2012: 261).

Instead of a state-based school system, a school system based on the *responsibility and governance of local school boards* would better respond to the education needs of children and better harmonize with the moral convictions at home. Kuyper was convinced that the Education Law of 1857 had led to a system based on unjust competition 'by arming the 'sect school of the modernist' with the monies and diplomas of the state, and denying that support of free schools' (Naylor 2012: 262). Kuyper considered public schools a *means* to promote and to spread the worldview of modernism.

Opponents of Kuyper and the free education movement argued that religion should not have a place in elementary schools; the best way to accommodate a diversity of worldviews was to offer general and rational Christianity-based teachings at school, while allowing parents to teach a worldview of their choice at home and in the churches. They asserted that the 'neutral' teaching of 'universally acknowledged facts' is not only possible, but also the only ethical option and is a necessity to protect the freedom of conscience in a country with a diversity of worldviews.

Kuyper disagreed and argued that when the state is responsible for the teaching of all children, it would then also determine its moral education and morality, and 'the school would become a de facto state church' (Kuyper 1875, 1890: 241–2 cited in Naylor 2012: 264). Kuyper attempted to convince the supporters of freedom of education that the Dutch School Struggle, after the enactment of the Education Law in 1857, had moved from what was a power struggle to what had become a debate about, and engagement, with a fundamental principle. According to him, freedom of education was the basis of freedom of thought and freedom of development and its funding was a necessary condition for a free society.

In Kuyper's view, society consisted of distinct spheres, 'each of which could only thrive according to its own God-given life dynamic and norms . . . He believed that God delegated His authority to each of these spheres in different ways' (Naylor 2012: 256). According to Kuyper: 'the state was not equipped to govern life in the social spheres (education, the arts, science, and the media) . . . This social doctrine of 'sphere sovereignty' provided him with a theoretical grounding for limited government very different from classical liberalism' (Naylor 2012: 256).[15]

In Kuyper's view schools could only flourish under the direct control of associations of parents—free from politics, the state, and the church—and competition between schools would lead to better education. Naylor summarized this argument:

> For 40 years Kuyper consistently argued for an education system whereby the state should equally fund no schools rather than equally funding all schools. While recognizing that indigent parents should receive state financial aid in order to provide their children's education, he also insisted that such provisions fall under the welfare laws, not the education laws. (Naylor 2012: 257)

In 1913, the Liberal prime minister Cort van der Linden (1846–1935) established a 'pacification' committee to resolve the issue of education. The Liberal Dirk Bos (1862–1916) chaired the committee and the vice-chairman was Alexander de Savornin Lohman (1837–1924) of the Anti-Revolutionaire Partij. The latter's view encompassed both sides of the debate: de Savornin Lohman argued that public and private schools were not competitors, but two complimentary parts of the education system and, therefore, fiscal equality for both types of schools was important to guarantee freedom of choice (Hooker 2009: 26, 92). The committee's final report came out in 1916 and 'recommended the fiscal equality of both Public and *Bijzondere* [special or private] Schools and proposed an amendment to the

[15] Namely, a pluralism of social spheres that is, today, often associated with a communitarian perspective (see chapter 3).

constitution' (Hooker 2009: 26). In 1917, the Constitution was amended. Article 192 of the Constitution now stated:

> Special primary education that fulfils the requirements set by the law will be funded from the public budget by the same measure as public [i.e. state] education. The law determines the conditions on which the public budget will fund special secondary education.[16] (Author's translation)

After more than a century, the Dutch School Struggle ended with this new amendment to the Dutch Constitution and the subsequent enactment of a new Elementary Education Law in 1920. The new Constitution recognized:

- The right to establish, manage and operate a school regardless of religious or philosophical worldview
- Equal access to public funding for all schools
- That 'all schools are accountable to the government regarding education quality and standards of hygiene and safety.' (Wolf and Maceto 2004, in Naylor 2012: 246)

Naylor (2012: 245) concluded that the Dutch finally 'recognised that most, if not all knowledge (curriculum) and behaviour (pedagogy) is embedded in core beliefs about the nature of God, humanity, and the world'.

According to different authors (James 1984; Naylor 2012) the amendment to the Dutch Constitution 'was unique in the history of Europe and remains unique in the world today' (Naylor 2012: 246)--unique because Article 23 not only regulates the *right* to establish a school but also the *means* of funding as well as *quality* standards.

However, a law specifying (minimum) standards of quality--that applies to all schools--was never established. The government was left to establish these standards and, as a consequence, the government simply applied its own legal instructions for public schools to all schools. Towards the end of the Dutch School Struggle—after the amendment to the Constitution—Cort van der Linden, then Minister of Education, stated: 'Now we are waiting for a pedagogical stream claiming their rights.'[17] This can be seen as a sad end to an highly contested struggle for educational freedom.

[16] In Dutch: 'Het bijzonder algemeen vormend lager onderwijs, dat aan de bij de wet te stellen voorwaarden voldoet, wordt naar denzelfden maatstaf als het openbaar onderwijs uit de openbare kas bekostigd. De wet stelt de voorwaarden vast, waarop voor het bijzonder algemeen vormend middelbaar en voorbereidend hooger onderwijs bijdragen uit de openbare kas worden verleend.' Available at: http://www.denederlandsegrondwet.nl/9353000/1/j9vvihlf299q0sr/vi7df7j09vx8.

[17] Information provided to C. W. M. (Ro) Naastepad in an interview with Dutch lawyer Mouringh Boeke.

After the Dutch School Struggle

In the first decades after the Dutch School Struggle (1921–45), the government monitored the implementation of freedom of education and restricted its activities in education to administrative, financial, and juridical tasks. Schools were heavily regulated on inputs (such as costs, wages) and less so on outputs (curriculum and degree requirements—that is, content and method). This has been called the period of 'distributive policy', during which citizens decided the direction of education and the national government and municipalities played a limited role.

After the Second World War, the role of the government in education changed gradually. This has been called the period of 'constructive policy'. In addition to administrative, financial, and juridical tasks, the government increasingly developed and took on responsibility for the content and methods of education. In particular, since the end of the 1960s, the government itself, through the Ministry of Education, has developed educational reforms. The idea that education and society are *maakbaar* (makeable or designable) became increasingly accepted, and, following this reasoning, the government increasingly used education as a means to create a better society. The most important manifestation of the development towards a 'constructive policy'—according to Bronneman-Helmers (2011: 14)—was the 1975 discussion paper 'Contours of a Future Education System'.[18] In this paper, minister of education Jos van Kemenade argued that the education system could be used to distribute knowledge, power, and income in the long term.[19]

Since the 1980s, while the government continued to expand its role in the determination of the contents of education, it increasingly withdrew from the funding task given to it by the Constitution. Debt funding increasingly supplemented state funding of education and, today, many students have to borrow money to fund their higher education studies.

Conclusion

The struggle for freedom of education—of which the Dutch School Struggle is a good example—is a struggle about *relationships* amongst the cultural, legal-political, and economic-financial spheres. The innovation sought by the proponents of

[18] In Dutch: 'Contouren van een toekomsting onderwijsbestel'.

[19] According to Mouringh Boeke (in an interview by C. W. M. (Ro) Naastepad) Van Kemenade's note consisted of two parts. Part 1 was sent to all schools with the question to respond to the proposals within three months with any responses taken into account in Part 2. However, Part 2 appeared before the three months had passed. The minister's behaviour was later investigated through a parliamentary inquiry. In one of his notes, Van Kemenade posed the question: 'What is to be understood by the autonomy of a teacher?' His answer was the autonomy of a teacher consisted of the freedom to choose examples that clarify or illustrate the contents of education decided upon by the government.

freedom of education--freedom of thought or of conscience—had not been achieved due to a failure to prevent the encroachment into the cultural sphere of the legal-political and the economic-financial spheres.

Despite their long history and international reputation as defenders of freedom of conscience and supporters of cultural liberalism, the Dutch failed to complete their struggle because they themselves failed to recognize its very essence. This was succinctly summarized by Abraham Kuyper as 'sphere sovereignty' and by Groen van Prinsterer as refraining from the appropriation of one sphere by another. This accords with John Stuart Mill (2001 [1859]) (writing about the 'tyranny of the magistrate' and the 'tyranny of the majority') when he emphasized that there needed to be:

> Protection also against the tyranny of the prevailing opinion and feeling; against the tendency of society to impose, by other means than civil penalties, its own ideas and practices as rules of conduct on those who dissent from them; to fetter the development, and, if possible, prevent the formation, of any individuality not in harmony with its ways, and compels all characters to fashion themselves upon the model of its own. (Mill 2001 [1859]: 9)

Society can implement (via the government) certain minimum standards for education—such as upon leaving primary school all children must be able to read and write—and all schools will then be subject to these standards. But the government (or the share of the population it represents) cannot comprehensively determine the 'ideas and practices' employed in education. According to the above, an independent cultural domain is as crucial for democracy and society as it is for the development of the individual—because the two are linked.[20]

However, the failure to take this cultural innovation to its completion is not unique to the Netherlands. Modern thinkers such as Sen (1999), Nussbaum (2010), and Higgins (see O'Brien 2016) speak of a 'silent crisis' in education. Instead of completing the journey towards cultural freedom, education is increasingly aimed not at the free development of the capabilities of the young, but, rather, is subordinated to political and, increasingly, financial demands. Thus, preparing young people for specific tasks in government or in the economy becomes the key purpose of schooling. Paraphrasing Beckert and Streeck (2008) and Beckert (2011), the cultural sphere is politically and economically constructed. In Mann's terminology, political power and economic power dominate cultural power.

[20] At the risk of stating the obvious, freedom of education does not imply freedom to act as one wishes. All citizens are subject to the laws and rules established by citizens collectively or by their representation in parliament.

So, is there a conceivable solution? Possibly, freedom of education requires 'sphere sovereignty'. Legally or politically, this would imply a separation of three tasks, which today are concentrated in the hands of the state alone (Boeke 1987):

- Guaranteeing equitable access to education
- Ensuring unconditional funding of education
- Controlling the quality of education.

As von Humboldt and Mill argued, the role of the state is to ensure equitable access to education for all, but not to direct the moral development of its citizens. Economically and financially, sphere sovereignty implies that the funding of education should be on its own terms—that is, unconditional funding. In this scenario, the government can help in channelling funds towards education via mechanisms such as a voucher system[21] that redistributes tax money to parents who can then choose the school that is most appropriate for their children.

Culturally it also implies that the potentially diverse criteria that define the quality of education—as well as the methods that ensure this quality—are to be established within the cultural sphere. This requires teachers to self-declare their rationales, missions, and methods, rather than have them defined by the state or market. It is ultimately because a vacuum has grown up within the cultural sphere that it is increasingly overpowered. Counteracting this trend requires teachers define and acknowledge the contents of their education, their pedagogical methods, and their concepts of assessment. Just as with other professions (such as accounting or health care) the criteria for quality are best set by the professionals who also have the task of maintaining that quality. The state can then provide the rights and the finance commensurate with a free cultural life.

Such a free cultural life would create the diversity that—according to Mill and von Humboldt—is so crucial for the successful development of individual:

> All that has been said of the importance of individuality of character, and diversity in opinions and modes of conduct involves, as of the same unspeakable importance, diversity of education. (Mill 2001 [1859], 97)

> The grand, leading principle, towards which every argument hitherto unfolded in these pages directly converges, is the absolute and essential importance of human development in its richest diversity; but national education, since at least it presupposes the selection and appointment of some one instructor, must always promote a definite form of development, however careful to avoid such an error.
> (von Humboldt 1993 [1854]: 41)

[21] As described in Houghton Budd, Naastepad, and Van der Linden (2015).

To conclude, in terms of the ESGM, the history of the Dutch School Struggle suggests that freedom of education (and the development of capabilities) requires *cultural* innovation (the recognition of freedom of education), *legal-political* innovation (equal rights to education), and *economic* innovation (the unconditional funding of education).

References

Beckert, Jens. 2010. 'How Do Fields Change? The Interrelations of Institutions, Networks, and Cognition in the Dynamics of Markets'. *Organization Studies* 31(5): 605–27.

Beckert, Jens. 2011. 'Die Sittlichkeit der Wirtschaft. Von Effizienz- und Differenzierungstheorien zu einer Theorie wirtschaftlicher Felder'. *MPIfG Working Paper* 11/8. Köln: Max Planck Institut für Gesellschaftsforschung.

Beckert, Jens, and Wolfgang Streeck. 2008. 'Economic Sociology and Political Economy: A Programmatic Perspective'. *MPIfG Working Paper* 08/4. Köln: Max Planck Institut für Gesellschaftsforschung.

Boeke, Mouringh. 1987. 'Wat in de Onderwijspolitiek Nu Gebeuren Moet'. In *Vrijheid van onderwijs?*, edited by Fred Beekers. Nijmegen: SSN.

Boekholt, P. Th. F. M., and E. P. de Booy. 1987. *Geschiedenis van de School in Nederland.* Assen/Maastricht: Van Gorcum.

O'Brien, Carl. 2016. 'President Higgins: Universities Facing "Intellectual Crisis"'. *Irish Times*, 8 April. http://www.irishtimes.com/news/education/president-higgins-universities-facing-intellectual-crisis-1.2602607.

Bronneman-Helmers, Ria. 2011. 'Overheid en Onderwijsbestel. Beleidsvorming Rond het Nederlandse Onderwijsstelsel (1990–2010)'. SCP-publicatie 2011–31. https://www.scp.nl/Publicaties/Alle_publicaties/Publicaties_2011/Overheid_en_onderwijsbestel.

De Savornin, Lohman, and Alexander Frederik. 1889. *De Pacificatie.* Amsterdam: J. A. Wormser.

Essen, J. L.,van. 1990. 'The Struggle for Freedom of Education in the Netherlands in the Nineteenth Century'. In *Guillaume Groen van Prinsterer: Selected Studies*, edited by J. L. van Essen and H. D. Morton, pp. 55–78. Jordan Station: Wedge Publishing Foundation.

Groen van Prinsterer, Guillaume. 1903. *De Maatregelen tegen de Afgescheidenen aan het Staatsregt Getoetst.* Baarn: Hollandia-Drukkerij.

Heiskala, Risto. 2014. 'Relating Mann's Conception to CrESSI'. CrESSI Working Paper No. 9. Brussels: European Commission, DG Research.

Hooker, Mark T. 2009. *Freedom of Education: The Dutch Political Battle for State Funding of All Schools Both Public and Private (1801–1920).* CreateSpace Independent Publishing Platform.

Houghton Budd, C., C. W. M. Naastepad, and M. J. van der Linden. 2015. 'Financial and Monetary Innovations for Overcoming Social Exclusion: The Financing of Generalised Education (as Instanced in the Netherlands and England).' Brussels: European Commission, DG Research.

Humboldt, Wilhelm von. 1993 [1854]. *The Limits of State Action.* Indianapolis, IN: Liberty Fund.

James, Estelle. 1984. 'Benefits and Costs of Privatised Public Services: Lessons from the Dutch Educational System'. *Comparative Education Review* 28(4): 605–24.

Kuyper, Abraham. 1875. *De Schoolkwestie I. Naar Aanleiding van het Onderwijs-debat in de Kamer.* Amsterdam: J. H. Kruyt.

Kuyper, Abraham. 1890. *Eenige Kameradviezen uit de Jaren 1874 en 1875.* Amsterdam: Wormser.

Mill, John Stuart. 2001 [1859]. *On Liberty.* Kitchener: Batoche Books.

Naylor, Wendy. 2012. 'School Choice and Religious Liberty in the Netherlands: Reconsidering the Dutch School Struggle and the Influence of Abraham Kuyper in its Resolution'. In *International Handbook of Protestant Education,* edited by W. Jeynes and D. W. Robinsin, pp. 245–74. Dordrecht: Springer.

Nussbaum, Martha C. 2010. *Not for Profit: Why Democracy Needs the Humanities.* Princeton, NJ: Princeton University Press.

Scheuerle, Thomas, Gudrun-Christine Schimpf, Gunnar Glänzel, and Georg Mildenberger (2016). 'Report on Relevant Actors in Historic Examples and an Empirically Driven Typology on Types of Social Innovation'. CrESSI Working Paper No. 29. Brussels: European Commission, DG Research.

Sen, Amartya.1997. 'Human Capital and Human Capability'. *World Development* 25(12): 1959–61.

Sen, Amartya. 1999. *Development as Freedom.* Oxford: Oxford University Press.

Valls, Andrew. 1999. 'Self-development and the Liberal State: The Cases of John Stuart Mill and Wilhelm von Humboldt'. *The Review of Politics* 61(2): 251–74.

Valk, John. 1995. 'Religion and the Schools: The Case of Utrecht'. *History of Education Quarterly* 35(2): 159–177.

Wolf, Patrick. J. and Stephen Maceto. 2004. *Educating Citizens: International Perspectives on Civic Values and School Choice.* Washington, DC: Brookings Institution Press.

9

Creating Alternative Economic Spaces

The Socially Innovative Practices of Solidarity Purchasing Groups

Lara Maestripieri

Introduction

Solidarity Purchasing Groups (SPGs)[1] have been defined as:

> Groups of individuals that decide to organise themselves in order to buy collectively food or any other everyday good, selecting suppliers on the basis of solidarity and critical consumption. (*Altreconomia* 2015: 14)

The main goal of their activities is to align their purchasing practices with the ethical principles of critical consumption, including: ensuring fair gate prices for producers; prioritizing local products; ensuring sustainability in the production and transportation of goods. The peculiarity of the Italian SPG movement can be better understood in the light of the social and economic history of cooperation (both secular and Catholic) and Fair Trade (Nicholls and Opal 2005) in this country. Starting in the 1990s, SPGs began to apply these two models to local producers: they avoided long supply chains by contacting suppliers directly, agreeing upon a fair price and (usually) preferring small units or social cooperatives as suppliers (an explicit reference to solidarity). Like Fair Trade, SPGs volunteer to distribute goods among their members; unlike Fair Trade, their activities happen mostly in informal groups or associations, not in shops open to the public.

Applying the definition of social innovation used by BEPA (2010), SPGs are innovations that are social in their ends *and* their means, specifically:

- They have an explicit social goal focused on integrating marginalized suppliers into economic systems by connecting them to new end markets.

[1] Solidarity Purchasing Group is the English translation of *gruppo di acquisto solidale*, commonly shortened in Italian to GAS. In Italian, a SPG member is called *gasista* (derived from the Italian acronym).

Lara Maestripieri, *Creating Alternative Economic Spaces: The Socially Innovative Practices of Solidarity Purchasing Groups*. In: *Creating Economic Space for Social Innovation*. Edited by: Alex Nicholls and Rafael Ziegler,
Oxford University Press (2019). © Oxford University Press.
DOI: 10.1093/oso/9780198830511.003.0009

- They change economic relations by innovating consumer-producer relations.
- The entire process is intentionally made explicit by SPGs members who frame it as innovative political action (von Jacobi et al. 2017).

Their success relies on the establishment of strong personal relations across members and producers that overcome the impersonal relations that characterize the market. Additionally, the goals of their activities are oriented to enhance the quality of life for consumers (favouring access to organic food) and to advance the economic inclusion of producers (by creating a direct relation with consumers). The SPG movement aims, particularly, at fighting the hegemony of big supply chains in the basic goods sector (such as food, clothes, or hygiene products). This hegemony typically excludes small family producers from accessing the markets in basic household goods.

In Italy in the 1990s, access to organic food was difficult and small organic producers were marginalized. As a consequence, the issue of reforming traditional market relations was of great importance in the preliminary phase of the SPG movement. More recently, as organic and local goods have become more accessible via supermarkets and organic shops, the principles of ethical consumption have progressively become more important as the main motivation for SPGs. Groups report that the main objective of their work is increasingly the promotion of new consumption practices that demonstrate responsibly towards the environment, humans, and animals. Unlike supermarkets, SPG members question market economic relations by proposing *solidarity* as an alternative model. SPGs fit into a wider set of institutional innovations around alternative food networks that have been developing in affluent countries in recent years (Maestripieri et al. 2018). These include farmers' markets and community-supported agriculture. *Gasistas* argue that thanks to the function of SPGs, their consumption choices have supported a growth in the sustainable production of primary goods and have helped producers who would otherwise be marginalized from mainstream markets.

This chapter investigates to what extent the actions of SPGs are able to tackle the marginalization of the producers with whom they engage by assessing how much SPGs foster the social and economic participation of small family farmers and to what extent they innovate economic relations along the food supply chain by introducing the principles of solidarity rather than competition. Several forms of solidarity—that occur internally among group participants—guide consumption in SPGs by ensuring that it is externally oriented to small local family producers. In what proportions the benefits of these social innovation activities' are distributed between SPG members (considered as social innovators) and their beneficiaries (SPG suppliers) is not entirely clear—although solidarity represents the most important rhetorical lever by which groups identify themselves.

The analysis proposed in this chapter is twofold: on the one hand it offers a detailed analysis of how socio-economic structures marginalize small family producers, while on the other, it proposes an assessment of the potential role of social innovation to address such structures. The chapter's ultimate goal is to assess to what extent SPGs are effective in their socially innovative activities aimed at fostering the economic inclusion of their suppliers. After a brief presentation of the empirical material for analysis in the second section, the third section discusses why SPGs can be considered a form of social innovation in the domain of agriculture and food. The subsequent section is devoted to an in-depth analysis of solidarity, the main concept lying behind the socially innovative activities of SPGs. The analysis demonstrates that SPG actions are only partially altruistic as benefits can be unequally distributed between consumers and producers. The final section provides evidence of how, and to what extent, groups are still able to tackle the marginalization of producers.

The analysis here applies the Extended Social Grid Model (ESGM, see chapter 1) with a focus on the interaction of three social forces (Beckert 2010): cognitive frames, institutions, and social networks. Using the ESGM in the analysis was particularly useful as the three social forces all proved to be important in the effective functioning of SPGs as a social innovation. Instead of separating the analysis with regards to the social forces, the chapter uses the ESGM holistically to inform the reader of the relevant transversal combinations of social forces that drove the case of SPGs. The analysis presented in this chapter is based on forty interviews aimed at investigating the activities of social innovators in light of the ESGM (see further chapter 4). The sample comprised five interviews with key informants—local and national representatives of the SPG movement and scholars who have investigated the phenomenon—and thirty-five interviews with social innovators, representatives of thirty-five SPGs distributed over the whole territory of Italy (see chapter Appendix).

SPGs as Social Innovation

The SPG movement can be considered a social innovation in the domain of agriculture and food supply as it promotes new processes that open up the market for their suppliers (for example, small organic producers, local artisans, or social cooperatives that employ vulnerable individuals). SPGs also have the declared goal of advancing their suppliers' inclusion into society and enhancing their proximity to the end customers. Central to this are trusted and long-term relations. SPGs challenge the mainstream logics of economic relations: from the maximization of profit to the definition of a fair price agreed between producers and consumers without any intermediating actor(s). A collaborative system of bargaining is at the basis of SPG model of economic relations. Producers are not (solely) selected on the basis of best price (as in the traditional economic model), but on several criteria pertaining to a 'critical' consumption model. This model prioritizes the shortest production chain—to favour local products—and specific projects considered socially relevant (e.g. that help in the integration of people at risk or that focus on organic production) to protect the environment and to increase the sustainability of food supply chains. SPGs, therefore, innovate in the processes of consumption as such groups help consumers disintermediate global supply chains by dealing directly with producers. In turn, this promotes critical consumption principles by choosing suppliers on the basis of social and ethical, rather than purely economic, principles.

The activities of SPGs can be framed in economic sociology in relation to the debate about *political consumerism* (Stolle et al. 2005). This is a concept that indicates the political awareness of a consumer as expressed via their consumption choices—namely, by preferring certain products or services on the basis of his or her political principles. In this way, the individual action of consumption becomes political and collective. SPGs mediate this action in which consumption principles are shared and put into practice as organized political action. The process is based on *voicing* that is, giving voice to actors such as consumers, who are usually considered powerless compared to other more powerful economic actors, such as corporations or mass retailers. SPGs show a strong conformity to common ideological principles—which is, perhaps, surprising considering the lack of any national coordination of this movement. Political consumerism can be seen as a social innovation, since its actions are based on the active participation of consumers to foster change in the dominant socio-economic system.

'Political consumerism' is the most comprehensive definition for the complex of cognitive frames characterizing the actions of SPGs (Maestripieri 2017). It rests on active opposition to the dominant system of mass retailers creating intermediation structures that deprive producers of the added value of their work. However, this critique of the mainstream economic system occurs entirely within the capitalist market model. In our empirical case study material, different respondents offered varying levels of critique of the dominant system within which SPGs operate. For some of them, the system was problematized in terms of the way primary goods such as food are produced and sold. For the most radical activist, the focus was problematizing the entire capitalist system as a focus for change, starting with a bottom-up transformation to be triggered by SPGs. The innovation SPGs propose lies in the process of consumption—groups allow consumers to avoid commercial intermediation by transacting directly with producers and promote critical consumption principles by choosing suppliers primarily on the basis of ethical principles:

> We try to be aware in the choices we make, product is important, price is important, but it is far more important the choice behind it, the political choice behind it, basically what we eat, also what we eat is a political choice [he laughs]. (SPG 4)

However, participants in SPGs are not, typically, fully aware of their role as social innovators: almost half of the interviewed groups did not link social innovation with their activities. When asked directly, respondents thought their group did not promote social innovation in a strict sense by promoting new processes (only seventeen groups agreed on the prompt). Instead they recognized their innovation in terms of recovering old-style processes that had disappeared from the mainstream food supply chains, such as building close relations with producers and small-scale production. Rather, respondents seemed more likely to agree on other characteristics usually associated in literature with social innovation such as focusing on the participation and sociality of SPGs members (such as creating new social relations and opening up participation).

Furthermore, interviewees perceived SPGs as a mature initiative that had moved into a period of critical reflection that was driving social innovation. The SPG movement was officially born in 1994 with the constitution of the GAS Fidenza association[2]—autonomous groups had started activities earlier but without any coordination. Looking back, it is possible to identify a series of steps in the evolution of SPGs:

- *Pre-1994: the precursor phase.* Scattered groups formed in order to buy organic food or Fair Trade products collectively. There was neither coordination nor a defined model at this point.
- *1994: the constitution phase.* The Fidenza Group—that had started its activities before 1994 but without formalizing them—formed as an association. It created the name Solidarity Purchasing Groups and set up a template that was used in the following years to create new groups.
- *1994–2001: the pioneering phase.* The number of groups grew, although at a relatively slow pace (from two to fifty-four groups: Forno and Graziano 2016). The first article about SPGs appeared in *Altreconomia* (the main journal for alternative economy in Italy) in 1999.
- *2001–7: the sustaining phase.* The pace of diffusion increased (from fifty-four to 358 groups: Forno and Graziano 2016). Mainstream media began to publish and broadcast on the phenomena. In this phase, the majority of

[2] It is one of the first SPGs founded in Italy. Their act of constitution as an association (1994) became the main model from which the subsequent groups developed using their name *Gruppo di Acquisto Solidale*. The founders were a group of families living in and around Fidenza, a medium-sized town located in Emilia-Romagna, an area particularly well known for its cooperative tradition and left-wing political orientation. Their initial main aim was access to locally produced organic food, but their activism evolved in tandem with the increasing awareness of the role of consumers as political actors. They are still active today and are one of the biggest and most important SPGs (Maestripieri 2016).

participants were also activists in social movements, focused on anti-globalization or the alternative economy. Other associated initiatives also arose at this point. Trade fairs such as *Fà la cosa giusta* began (2003), the main SPG website went online (2004) and meetings on the national level started. Also, the Italian government recognized the possibility for SPGs to operate without incurring any fiscal problems.

- *2007–13: the scaling phase.* The number of groups increased rapidly (from 358 to 977: Forno and Graziano 2016), thanks to the increasing attention of the mainstream media. According to our data, this led to a perception that this social innovation was now opened up to the general public. However, the growth of the movement put into question the uniformity of the SPG identity, with many groups joining only to access products rather than for any engagement in political activism against the mainstream economic system.

Since 2013, the movement has entered a phase of stagnation, which might result in either a systemic change or a progressive decline. While SPG growth has slowed down and groups have started to lose members a multiplicity of new entrants in the SPG market has started to appear, especially in the most affluent areas. For example, a number of private shops selling products from SPG suppliers have started up such as organic or short-production chain shops. Some of these shops emerged directly from SPGs that took on the role of a shop or social cooperative selling products directly to consumers, in parallel with offering logistic and distribution services to suppliers. Furthermore, farmers' markets have multiplied around many cities, easing direct relations between consumers and producers partly promoted by civil society, partly by farmers' associations (such as Coldiretti) and partly by public bodies. Finally, some of the biggest SPGs—Aequos near Como, RiMaflow, and Buonmercato near Milan—have implemented 'easy access' SPGs, comparable to online shops, that allow consumers to access SPG purchasing without having to volunteer and with a minimum mark-up to cover running costs and wages. From the farmers' point of view this evolution might sound positive as it multiplies their end markets—however, key informants reported that these new entrants were considered betrayers by the most radical fringes of the movement, as they reproduced the market intermediation practices that SPGs have always resisted.

This crisis is connected to the difficulty that working-class and low-income individuals have in accessing this type of consumption, which hinders the movement's expansion beyond an inner circle of activists and urban elites. The higher costs of SPG products compared to discount retailers makes accessibility difficult for those with a limited income, while principles of political consumerism require awareness and knowledge that is less common among the less-educated population:

> I have the impression that there is . . . I don't know how to explain myself, I would not do either a racist discourse, but certain characteristics . . . an indispensable grade of culture, I would not dare to say . . . of social level, but culture is indispensable to become a member of a SPG. At least in our group, maybe in other groups it is different, but to me it seems that . . . but I tell you because I can see the reality: the fact of seeing all those who entered the SPG and that participate in it are people with a certain level of culture, if not a tertiary degree almost . . . it makes me think that maybe there is a relation between the two things.
>
> (SPG 14)

The perception of a moment of entropy and fatigue currently characterizing the movement was evident across many SPG groups. Interviewees often reported a decrease in all activities promoted by their groups over the past few years. SPGs were less keen on communicating with the public or interacting with producers, increasing the impression of stagnation and an increased individualism within the movement:

> It is innovative for sure, in my opinion yes, although as with all the things that today are innovative after ten years they are . . . they are less innovative, that is, it will be likely that at a certain moment a need for overcoming the model will arrive . . . being innovative means also being able to transform the model you have started, at the time we began with a SPG group it was an absolute novelty, now we are still carrying on the SPG discourse at it is, as we started in 2008, we're . . . perpetuating rituals, so much so that participants don't even feel the necessity to meet because in any case now . . . the system is defined, it works, orders arrive, why do we have to meet? There is a strong risk of sclerotizing in the system, in my opinion. (SPG 27)

One of the main strong points of the SPG movement is its capacity to build up a network of local groups that are extremely adaptable and geographically dispersed. The added value of these organizations is the informality and bottom-up character of their meso-level organizing structures—called Districts of the Solidarity Economy—that works mostly at the provincial level. This operates by putting local groups in contact and organizing purchasing structures that are more efficient and effective at district scale, particularly, oranges, detergents, and pasta. A District of the Solidarity Economy is not a level of intermediation, but one of coordination: there is no mark-up on the final price and there are only volunteers who take care of the organization of shipping towards an area. Districts of the Solidarity Economy usually also promote working groups and informative exchange between the SPGs and civil society at the local level. Although SPGs offer a very effective mechanism for participation and intervention in local politics, they are restricted by the fundamental principle of volunteering that relies on individuals devoting part of their free time to the cause. SPGs also suffer from a general suspicion of the usual models of political action, which the movement has always been opposed to at local and national levels. Taking this position has hindered the use of Districts of the Solidarity Economy as consulting bodies for the development of new policies of relevance to the SPG movement.

In fact, SPGs activists often treat more traditional political activities with suspicion and this has hindered the transformation of SPGs into a political movement in the traditional sense. Most of the laws or public calls for funds, public spaces, or simply public recognition require a formal institutionalization process that many SPGs resist, which affects their capacity to be accepted as interlocutors by public entities or to access public money. This situation affects their capacity to tackle marginalization—they can typically only intervene on an individual case-by-case basis. Resistance to institutionalization further inhibits the capacity of SPGs to act as a lobby group at the local level. This situation is rarely seen as problematic, however, as most groups prefer to preserve their autonomy from all other actors instead of acquiring power and influence with public policies. Conversely, collaboration with public actors is limited as well:

> We have a cultural impact for sure, that is in fact when there are the municipal elections they look for us to know what we think about and so on, but we always turn down [she laughs], because *gasistas* don't want to be involved in politics.
>
> (SPG 0)

To conclude, SPGs can be considered as a social innovation in theoretical terms, although the innovators that animate them are more willing to see the social aspect of their contribution than the innovative character. This could be interpreted as a consequence of the wider sense of entropy and crisis common among many activists after twenty years of activity. Also, reports indicated a declining role of SPGs as mediators for accessing organic food since it had become more easily available in mainstream food supply by several new entrants. However, the category of political consumerism still retains its importance for understanding the complex sub-culture that characterizes the movement. The next section investigates the role of solidarity in SPGs so as to comprehend better what political consumerism implies in practice and to understand the role of this cognitive frame in the definition of actions characterizing this social innovation.

Solidarity: A Tool for Social Innovation

What makes the central cognitive frame of SPGs distinctive is its active promotion of solidarity: interviewees expressed the explicit goal of making economic relations as *personal* as possible, focusing on bringing social embeddedness into market exchange via creating new social networks. SPG participants did not only want to obtain better prices by supply chain disintermediation and by purchasing directly from producers, they also wanted to establish new economic processes that could disrupt traditional power economic hierarchies and pre-existing socio-economic settlements within the food supply chain. Their model was to build new and significant personal relationships between consumers and producers. In this sense, they perceived several potential beneficiaries of their actions beyond reducing prices for themselves. Despite the many different actors involved, the type of solidarity proposed by the SPGs was principally focused at the individual level: this excluded collective entities such as communities or private/public organizations from the reach of SPG activities.

Tuomela (2007) classified solidarity in a typology comprising three main orientations of actions: the I-perspective; the I/We-perspective; and the We-perspective. The I-perspective solidarity is oriented directly to benefit the person involved in the social innovation activity: in the case of SPGs members, this consists of accessing organic and high-quality food at lower prices compared to traditional food supply chains. This advantage can be spread across several social networks including relatives, friends, and neighbours. However, only certain categories of consumers are interested in accessing this type of product: even via SPGs, these products are still more expensive than buying food produced from industrial farming at supermarkets:

> But certainly, in this case the solidarity aspect is oriented to *gasistas* because we can have prices [she laughs] that otherwise we would not have, because in some cases we have discounts of about 40 per cent mostly because we buy in group, which is certainly more convenient compared to being a single consumer.
>
> (SPG 3)

An intermediate level of solidarity, the I/We-perspective, occurs in relations within groups and between social innovators. Although the most established groups have built significant social capital amongst their members—within a SPG each member benefits from the help and support of others without, necessarily, having any direct personal relationship with the other members. However, the limited number of people within each group is a guarantee that reciprocity underpins all interactions. SPG members receive emotional and practical support from the group: they organize social events like lunches in farmsteads or visits to producers, bake bread together, cook sauces or prepare preserves. Groups can be seen as a communal and informal mode of provisioning that concretize the call for non-market principles to be at the heart of SPGs:

> There's also someone who gave up having their own car once theirs broke down . . . the other cars are shared, for instance our car is often . . . popular. For

> example, in our SPG on Thursday morning there are two members that do food shopping first at the farmstead and then in the supermarket, and they do it not only for themselves. If I need something from this farmstead or from the supermarket I just call. (SPG 2)

Tensions can nevertheless occur among members. Ideally all the members of the group share its tasks: however, in practice, the principle of equal contribution is not always respected. Different types of groups can be identified in this regard:

- Centralized groups, in which core members manage purchasing (including organizing distribution or shipping) for the passive members (who do not actively volunteer)
- Groups in which general tasks (distribution, management, or secretarial) are periodically shared across different members
- Fully horizontal groups, where all members have an active role and make decisions together, without an executive committee.

In cases where the group opts for creating an association, the most active members tend to occupy positions such as president, public relations coordinator or treasurer. In cases where the group remains informal, individuals usually refuse to lay claim to a specific position in the group ('We are all referents', 'I'm not the spokesperson', 'I'm just a member'). Core members usually do more volunteer work for the group, but this sometimes creates resentment towards apparent free riders, who do not actively contribute to the SPG yet enjoy its benefits. This breaks the implicit reciprocity of the group that is the basis of the I/We perspective. As they usually rely on part-time volunteers, the success of SPGs' activities depends largely on the goodwill of their members. Moreover, the size of groups is often restricted since the volunteer model must always cover the costs of the logistics and distribution of goods:

> The main condition is having time. SPG is not a supermarket, we always repeat it and . . . therefore it's not like just going there and then you just collect your goods and you're done, absolutely not. (SPG 33)

The We-Perspective comprises all those solidarity actions that are characterized by a fully altruistic orientation—where the giver neither expects a direct benefit for herself nor any reciprocity from the receiver. In this category are locally oriented actions towards the community or for the preservation of the environment in which the person lives or universalistic oriented actions towards society as a whole. This orientation is less frequent in SPGs and is evidenced mostly via the organization of informative meetings, the organization or participation in events like farmers' markets or town festivals, support in organizing fairs that reinforce the principles of political consumerism. In this case, making the transformation from informal group to an association is critical: this process of institutionalization makes SPGs more visible, which enables them to become interlocutors for local public bodies and other actors within civil society.

Finally, another form of the We-perspective solidarity is evidenced by actions specifically oriented towards the producers framed as the main beneficiaries of SPGs activities. Interviewees suggested that their actions focused on producers were entirely altruistic offering them benefits like fair prices, new end markets, and personal relationships with consumers. However, in these SPGs, the reciprocity may be weaker between consumers and producers. In these cases, solidarity is based upon personal relations that are mediated by a single referent who is usually the only person directly in contact with and personally known by the producers for each SPG. Moreover, here solidarity is not typically oriented towards a social group or open to the general public, instead occurring between personal contacts directed to a single producer. Furthermore, power relations are usually asymmetrical: the consumer is still the one with the bargaining power, the one who may opt to change producers if they are dissatisfied with the product offered, the production, or the gate price.

Consumers may also risk succumbing to the paternalism typical of wealthier individuals that intrude on the agency of poor and vulnerable populations. Paternalism can occur when external actors deprive individuals of the right to decide what is best for improving their own life (Deneulin 2002). Thus, SPGs may claim the rights to decide what type of production and working practices their suppliers have to sustain, using the leverage of their purchasing power. More radical groups refuse to accept producers if they have any commercial relations outside of the SPGs. In certain cases, groups require new suppliers to complete a form in which they must declare the channels through which they sell their products and what type of production they have:

> For producers, on the contrary, they improve a lot because they sell... their products at a price which is far superior to the one they could normally sell their products for plus they can learn in a viral way as you... as you say, with word of mouth, because we Italians in practice learn by word of mouth for everything and... when producers become suppliers of SPGs they make a jump... decisively positive, as long as they don't disappoint them, because when they disappoint them, they are abandoned [she laughs]. (SPG 0)

An interesting example of this is one of the longstanding producers of the northern part of Italy, who collaborated with the SPG movement from the very beginning. Several SPGs decided to stop collaborating with the producer after he ran for mayor in his small town for the Lega Nord party.[3] Although producer's political activities were not directly related to SPGs economic actions, many *gasistas* stopped buying from him as retaliation for his party's unacceptable ideology (although interviewees declared, broadly, that SPGs do not get involved in politics):

> For example, you heard that several SPGs have decided to cut their relations with *** because has declared in favour of Lega Nord but now on this matter I don't feel like I followed them, in the sense that now if you tell me that the producer *** exploit minors or unregistered workers or hence he has non-ethical attitudes, I agree let's cut him out, but if he has expressed ideas that I don't share, I don't feel like... if he produces ethically anyway and if his political ideas are not shared by me I will still buy from him. (SPG 14)

In conclusion, apart from self-interested reasons, interviewed members of the SPGs viewed their activities as 'other-regarding' and, specifically, oriented towards suppliers—while other categories of potential beneficiaries were less relevant (such as local communities, other not-for-profit organizations, or socially excluded individuals). This might be interpreted as a legacy of the type of solidarity enacted by SPGs, which happens mostly through personal relations. Furthermore, as noted above, the solidarity of SPG action has often been limited in terms of a fully altruistic rationale (the We-perspective)—typically SPGs are more oriented towards forms of solidarity that are self-interested or that are guaranteed by reciprocity mechanisms across SPG members.

Thus, in SPGs, altruistic solidarity is mainly oriented towards the producers—who are the core of their socially innovative activities. However, relationships with producers are inherently characterized by power disparities and SPGs, perhaps inevitably, used their economic relationships with producers to shape their activities in alignment with their own principles. As a consequence, it is usually inappropriate to define the relationships between producers and consumers as 'reciprocal'. Indeed, reciprocity in Polanyi's terms (1944) only occurs when exchange is horizontal and bidirectional. In our case here, the relations between the SPG social innovators and their beneficiaries were characterized by asymmetrical relations in terms of bargaining power. SPG consumers typically chose to use their spending power as a tool to shape and control suppliers' behaviours rather than as a mechanism by which to address their economic marginalization. The next section follows this line of reasoning to understand better the ways in which SPGs *do* aim to tackle marginalization and to evaluate to what extent they are successful.

[3] Lega Nord is an extreme right-wing party, which is hegemonic in several small municipalities in the northern part of Italy.

SPGs: Reducing the Economic Marginalization of Suppliers

The small family farms that constitute the main targets of SPG activities are marginalized mostly because of their farming practices and their small size—factors that come together to create several layers of disadvantage in the market. Intermediaries and mass retailers often use their strong position of power to reduce the input prices of primary goods, concentrating their revenues at the intermediation level—instead of at the production level—of the food supply chain. Pursuing organic production also increases producer costs and decreases productivity as well, while small farm sizes impede access to regular markets unless farmers form cooperatives or other consortia. Additionally, small farm sizes hinder access to organic certification, which is important to reach high-end markets. Finally, small and micro- enterprises are typically owned and managed by a family and this may lead to inefficiencies and a lack of robust business planning. As a consequence, small organic producers are usually less competitive than traditional production that is driven by price competition alone.

However, despite these structural issues, our interviewees were hesitant to define their producer suppliers as 'disadvantaged'—they were more inclined to see them simply as being an alternative to the traditional supply chain. Only sixteen respondents out of thirty-five considered their suppliers to be marginalized. Moreover, this perception of marginalization was largely based upon the vulnerable biographies and personal traits (such as health problems or disabilities) of the suppliers: their marginalized position in the food supply chain was not automatically considered as a source of disadvantage. While interviewees generally saw the suppliers' disconnection with mainstream markets as a problem, only ten respondents (out of thirty-five) considered beneficiaries as potentially marginalized by this fact:

> Oh my God, I don't know. I'm not able to imagine them as a 'disadvantaged' group, then we are all disadvantaged [we laugh], that is, I don't know, there are producers that love to be sorry for themselves, but... I don't know, it doesn't seem to me, if you do your job well, then you're not disadvantaged. (SPG 2)

An exception to this was the smallest farms among the producers—for these the farm sizes were so small that interviewees thought that SPG involvement in their end markets was essential to sustain their basic economic activities. Quite often, however, small farming activities did not constitute the main income or revenue of the people involved. A second exception was those social cooperatives whose main goal was to foster the employment of vulnerable individuals. In this case, the cognitive frame of marginalization was not associated with the cooperatives' position in the food supply chain, but with the social traits of those employed by them:

> When he started selling eggs to us, he was working in *** and he had lost his job, his wife told me that he was in deep crisis, not because he had economic constraints but because he felt humiliated... having lost his job and not having one anymore, he was ashamed of going out of his home, the fact that he has this small task with us, of bringing eggs, now he is a pensioner and he is quite relaxed now, but he was helped very much by that, then he also went to the SPG of ***, that is having the thing of... I have this task and I supply eggs to *gasistas*.
>
> (SPG 25)

Interviewees confirmed that they aimed to tackle the economic marginalization of their producers by offering an alternative end market characterized by fair prices that were negotiated in a horizontal relationship with the final consumers. Their model also aimed to cut out intermediaries and to offer risk protection in the case of difficulties such as a bad harvest or economic downtown (by offering pre-financing support, for example). However, they did not think that any of the SPGs support was intended specifically to protect producers from vulnerability. Rather, they thought that it was only the coordinated actions of several SPGs that could uplift a producer from poverty and protect him/her against economic downturns—this tended to happen mainly with producers big enough to mobilize the entire local community of SPGs. However, such coordination was difficult to achieve, as there was typically no formalized and institutionalized structure connecting groups locally and nationally. As a result, any coordination tended to occur informally following a petition from well-known producers to mobilize dispersed groups for a specific project, for example. This suggests that coordination involving several SPGs usually came about as a response to an emergency or to the pleas from the most popular producers. For example, several interviewees reported the well-known case of the Tomasoni factory that was saved by coordinated pre-financing by the SPGs of Northern Italy at the beginning of the 2000s:

> In my opinion, our experience is so small that... let's say I don't believe that producers could have, let's say, big advantages from our purchases, so, that is when you have orders of something like 150 euros every month, therefore it's not that it changes your life in that sense. (SPG 1)

This limited social impact of SPGs' economic activity can be seen as strongly linked to their choice of being small, self-organized groups that rely mostly on the voluntary support of their members. Again, their resistance to formal institutionalization plays a fundamental role. This incapacitates their ability to grow, thereby hindering their capacity to change existing macro-level economic relationships:

> Now as it is organized, [the SPG experience] does something, but... I've spoken a lot with... some producers, I went visiting the producers and I know them and

> I know that many of them complain about the fact that the SPG group is a very informal experience and this informality makes . . . the thing, makes everything so variable that we cannot be a stable point of reference . . . in part because . . . in truth we would like to succeed in establishing a contract and a stable trusted relationship, but we don't have too much time to do it, we don't have too much energy to do it, sometimes we don't have either the competencies to understand whom we have in front of us or what he does and with what type of techniques he does to assess it . . . And, therefore, yes you should have an experience, more stability, to give them a guarantee . . . to have a ongoing purchase relationship, to have a purchase relationship that grows and instead we depend on our energy, on our strengths and therefore . . . those are subjected to losses. (SPG 30)

Along with reducing the economic marginalization of suppliers, a second important goal of social innovation is fostering the social participation of beneficiaries (in this case, suppliers) (von Jacobi et al. 2017). Although the main aim of SPGs is to create direct relationships with producers, only a couple of SPGs in our sample succeeded in having strong and systematic partnerships with producers or associations of producers, while the rest were mostly limited to the usual commercial exchange. Each member of a SPG is usually responsible for one (or more) type(s) of products: the person (called the referent) corresponds with a producer (usually a local family farmer), organizes purchasing and shipping, and distributes the items to the other members. Each producer is in contact only with their assigned referent and is usually not directly involved in other group activities.

Given this, SPGs struggle to foster greater participation for their beneficiaries (suppliers). In fact, most relations with producers occur at the commercial level, although interviewees do often recall friendships over the years between a referent and a producer as a signal of being distinct from normal economic exchange. None of the groups involve suppliers in defining goals and priorities; and relations between producers and members of the group (other than the referent) occur only occasionally (e.g. farmstead visits or product presentations). This cannot be regarded as systematic involvement for producers in the functioning of the social innovation.

Additionally, practices such as visits and controls of production can be regarded as a potentially paternalistic issue; for example, the organic certification that SPGs have promoted in the last few years. One of the biggest obstacles for the diffusion of organic production lies in the costs of organic certification, which in Italy is covered by private entities. Even though some regions do subsidize farmers, it is still quite difficult (especially for the smallest farms) to have a production that sustains the costs of third-party certifications. In response to this problem, single groups or a local coalition of groups promote what they call *participated organic certification,* a control mechanism on production—operated directly by *gasistas* or by experts on behalf of *gasistas*—to check if producers respect the rules of environmental sustainability that characterize the philosophy of the SPG movement. While this system enables the conversion of producers towards organic farming, it is questionable when SPG members—who might not have the necessary competencies to assess the work of suppliers—oversee it. Paternalism is also more implicit in terms of the different power relations that can occur between buyer and seller, especially given the different social positions members and suppliers typically have:

> We force the producers to give us the invoices and when this is possible to account for... for those who produce fruits and vegetables or anyway similar products, they have to account for how they produce, who they hire, who works for them and how the person works for them, which type of contract and things like that. We don't ask the signature of a contract or necessary a table, but we usually control who does what and how. In the case of meat or other things like that, it has already occurred to us... if we had to assess a new supplier maybe we should go to see where they live... where they reared the animals, what were their conditions, and things like that. We're not expert clearly, but we can get an idea. (SPG 15)

Despite this more negative dimension, two best-practice examples can be found in the areas of Bologna and Milan. These are a result of the local activation of informal networks of SPGs promoted by the Districts of the Solidarity Economy. In the first case, local groups were trying to promote the engagement of producers via an established network of daily farmers' markets (SPGs in Bologna supply fresh fruit and vegetables through the Campi Aperti project) and the promotion of a community-supported agriculture initiative that was supported by the municipality. The municipality of Bologna allocated to the Arvaia Association—the first Italian community-supported agriculture initiative—the fields surrounding the town that were mostly public property. The association of producers were entitled to manage these areas, while SPGs supported them by pre-financing their activities and buying their products. In the Milan area, it was the agricultural production chain that was privileged: SPGs sustained projects by acquiring their final products such as bread or flour[4] while different producers cooperated all along the production chain.

The most organized and coordinated initiatives avoided the risk of paternalism best—typically a committee of experts, *gasistas*, and suppliers took control, instead of self-organized SPGs members. However, such examples constitute an exception to the norm and are active only in the most populated and affluent regions of Italy. Local Districts of the Solidarity Economy act as coordinators for

[4] Spiga and Madia for the local DESBRI in the northern area; the wheat production chain for DES Parco Agricolo Sud in the southern area.

the producers involved, confirming the idea that to be effective in reducing the marginalization of beneficiaries, single-group activities are not enough—coordinated action is required.

In conclusion, SPG activists are reluctant to consider their suppliers marginalized on the basis of their positioning in the food supply chain alone. Marginalization was associated more so with individuals employed by the suppliers who had vulnerable biographies or with the producers owning the smallest farms. In this latter case, however, farming activities were often not the main income of suppliers, which puts in question the value of the SPGs' role in addressing suppliers' overall economic marginalization. SPG action mainly consisted of offering producers end markets characterized by fair prices. However, these markets were often quite limited in capacity and erratic in their continuity of demand. Additionally, the will to intrude on the suppliers' practices might leave SPGs open to paternalistic practices. A resistance to formalization also reduced the potential impact of SPG activities and also reduced their capacity to grow. Some interesting practices were observed at the local and national levels, when it was possible to coordinate the activities of several groups. However, only in the most affluent urban localities were these practices sustained with a degree of continuity.

Conclusion

This chapter investigated the experiences of Solidarity Purchasing Groups in Italy in terms of their contribution to reducing the economic marginalization of the producers with which collaborate. After more than twenty years, the SPG movement is now in a mature phase of development. As such, SPGs are one of the main social innovations in the domain of agriculture and food in Italy.

It is interesting to recognize how SPGs follow an ideology that is transversally shared across their local groups, in line with what is theorized as *political consumerism* in the sociological debate about alternative food networks (Stolle et al. 2005). Despite being inherently critical of mainstream economic relations, SPG activities question fundamental market relations. Consumers still retain a stronger bargaining power compared to producers and they are willing to use this to influence producers' behaviour to suit their own ends. Furthermore, an inherent risk arises from the social origins of these social innovators: SPGs are part of a social movement promoted by an educated and affluent middle class, whose actions are oriented towards beneficiaries—such as farmers and artisans—who might not have the same economic, social, and cultural capital. This unequal power relation risks producing and sustaining paternalistic practices embedded in the SPG social innovation model.

A second strong element in the ideological construct of SPGs is the concept of *solidarity*, which may be understood across three theoretical dimensions (Tuomela (2007): I-perspective, I/We-perspective, We-perspective. SPGs are a social innovation in which the benefit goes mostly to the consumer (I-perspective), to the inner circle of those participating in the social innovation (I/We-perspective), and, to a lesser extent, to their suppliers (We-Perspective). SPGs are not oriented to the general welfare of society nor do they help a particular social group. Rather, SPGs represent political action based on solidarity that remains mostly confined to the personal networks of the individuals involved. Producers tend to be involved in the activities of groups mostly on an individual basis. The type of relations that SPG groups put in place with their beneficiaries of their actions mostly occurs on the commercial level—which calls into question the effectiveness of their actions for reducing producers' overall marginalization. However, their emphasis on solidarity still puts SPGs into the category of a hybrid system of provision, as the market relations are also embedded in communal forms of provision based on reciprocity and volunteer work (see chapter 3).

Additionally, our interviewees were not keen to define themselves as social innovators nor did they consider the beneficiaries of their actions as marginalized individuals. In their opinion, SPG suppliers were simply an alternative to the mainstream economy. However, while they did recognize the inherent risk of the suppliers' market position, this was not seen as sufficient in itself to define them as marginalized. A single group was also rarely able to offer significant help to a marginalized producer—it was only the coordinated actions of multiple groups that made a difference. SPG groups' resistance to formalize themselves also hindered their capacity to access finance and grow.

In conclusion, the positive impact of SPG activities lies largely in offering market access, fair prices, and rich social networks to marginalized producers. As long as this is accompanied by a respect for labour laws and taxation, this social innovation also positively impacts the working conditions of producers. The negative impact lies in the limited extent of their overall effectiveness: SPG members help beneficiaries, yet they rarely involve them in the management of the group—contrary to the alternative food networks that are established elsewhere in affluent countries (e.g. community-supported agriculture). This research shows that a social innovation works best when it focuses on creating systematic and meaningful participation for its beneficiaries (Cruz et al. 2017). Thus, aiming for effective solidarity requires a reflexive criticism of their own actions by the SPG groups themselves as well their being attentive to wider policy agendas of relevance to their key beneficiaries.

Appendix: List of SPGs investigated in CrESSI and their main characteristics

Code	Region	Vulnerability of the context*	No. of members	Type of group
SPG0	Lombardia	Prevailing	40	Informal group
SPG1	Abruzzo	Vulnerable	30	Informal group
SPG2	Lombardia	Affluent	25	Formal association
SPG3	Lombardia	Affluent	45	Informal group
SPG4	Abruzzo	Vulnerable	7	Informal group
SPG5	Abruzzo	Vulnerable		
SPG6	Trentino-Alto Adige	Prevailing	38	Informal group
SPG7	Emilia-Romagna	Affluent	21	Informal group
SPG8	Emilia-Romagna	Affluent	130	Informal group
SPG9	Emilia-Romagna	Affluent	20	Formal association
SPG10	Emilia-Romagna	Affluent	91	Formal association
SPG11	Piemonte	Prevailing	30	Informal group
SPG12	Piemonte	Prevailing	20	Formal association
SPG13	Lazio	Prevailing	39	Formal association
SPG14	Liguria	Vulnerable	28	Formal association
SPG15	Lombardia	Affluent	18	Formal association
SPG16	Toscana	Affluent	30	Informal group
SPG17	Toscana	Affluent	25	Informal group
SPG18	Veneto	Affluent	25	Informal group
SPG19	Lombardia	Affluent	25	Formal association
SPG20	Veneto	Prevailing	203	Informal group
SPG21	Veneto	Prevailing	43	Formal association
SPG22	Veneto	Prevailing	28	Formal association
SPG23	Liguria	Vulnerable	75	Formal association
SPG24	Liguria	Vulnerable	80	Formal association
SPG25	Marche	Prevailing	49	Informal group
SPG26	Lombardia	Affluent	23	Informal group
SPG27	Lombardia	Prevailing	30	Informal group
SPG28	Piemonte	Prevailing	65	Informal group
SPG29	Piemonte	Prevailing	30	Informal group
SPG30	Veneto	Prevailing	20	Informal group
SPG31	Campania	Vulnerable	85	Formal association
SPG32	Campania	Vulnerable	15	Informal group
SPG33	Puglia	Vulnerable	15	Informal group
SPG34	Sardegna	Vulnerable	30	Formal association

Note: * The range of the analysis covered the entire Italian area to ensure that an equivalent proportion of SPGs in affluent contexts, prevailing contexts, and at-risk contexts, on the basis of an index of vulnerability (Chiappero Martinetti et al. 2017), were surveyed. This was determined using a combination of three different indicators: the at-risk-of-poverty rate (NUTS2), occupational level (NUTS3), and GPD per person (NUTS3).

References

Altreconomia. 2015. *Il libro dei GAS. Gruppi di acquisto solidali: come fare la spesa giusta, dalla 'A' al KM Zero*. Milano: edizioni Altreconomia.

Beckert, Jens. 2010. 'How Do Fields Change? The Interrelations of Institutions, Networks, and Cognition in the Dynamics of Markets'. *Organization Studies* 31(5): 605–27.

BEPA (Bureau of European Policy Advisers). 2010. 'Empowering People, Driving Change: Social Innovation in the European Union'. https://goo.gl/OvVnFV, accessed 22 February 2017.

Cruz H., R. Martínez Moreno, and I. Blanco. 2017. 'Crisis, Urban Segregation and Social Innovation in Catalonia'. *PACO* 10(1): 221–45.

Deneulin, Severine. 2002. 'Perfectionism, Paternalism and Liberalism in Sen and Nussbaum's Capability Approach'. *Review of Political Economy* 14(4): 497–518.

Forno, Francesca, and Paolo Graziano. 2016. *Il consumo critico. Una relazione solidale tra chi acquista e chi produce*. Bologna: Il Mulino editore.

von Jacobi, Nadia, Ziegler Rafael, and Edmiston Daniel. 2017. 'Tackling Marginalisation through Social Innovation? Examining the EU Social Innovation Policy Agenda from a Capabilities Perspective'. *Journal of Human Development and Capabilities* 18(2): 148–62.

Maestripieri, L. 2016. 'Part IV: Individual Case Study "Solidarity Purchasing Groups". In T. Scheuerle, G-C. Schimpf, G. Glänzel, G. Mildenberger, and R. Ziegler (eds) 'Report on Relevant Actors in Historic Examples and an Empirically Driven Typology on Types of Social Innovation'. CrESSI Working Paper No. 29: 335–68. Brussels: European Commission, DG Research.

Maestripieri Lara (2017) 'Are Solidarity Purchasing Groups a Social Innovation? A Study Inspired by Social Forces'. *PArtecipazione e COnflitto* 10(3): 955–82.

Maestripieri, Lara, Toa Giroletti, and Antonello Podda. 2018. 'Solidarity Purchasing Groups in Italy: A Critical Assessment of Effects on the Marginalisation of their Suppliers'. *International Journal of Sociology of Agriculture and Food* 24(3): 393–412.

Nicholls, Alex, and Charlotte Opal. 2005. *Fair Trade: Market-Driven Ethical Consumption*. London: Sage.

Polanyi, Karl. 1944. *The Great Transformation: The Political and Economic Origins of our Time*. Boston, MA: Beacon Press.

Stolle, Dietlind, Marc Hooghe, and Michele Micheletti. 2005. 'Politics in the Supermarket: Political Consumerism as a Form of Political Participation'. *International Political Science Review/Revue Internationale de Science Politique* 26(3): 245–69.

Tuomela, Raimo. 2007. 'Cooperation and the We-perspective'. In *Rationality and Commitment*, edited by Fabienne Peter and Hans Bernhard Schmid, pp. 227–57. Oxford: Oxford University Press.

10
Social Innovation and Agency

Nadia von Jacobi, Enrica Chiappero-Martinetti, Rafael Ziegler, Martijn van der Linden, and Cees van Beers

Introduction

In chapter 1 we suggested that social innovation can alter the structural factors that (re)produce marginalization. In this chapter we explore this proposition further via an empirical analysis that compares three different cases of social innovation.[1] As a common denominator for the quite different manifestations of marginalization, we focus on individual empowerment. Yet this too poses empirical challenges, in particular in terms of how to measure the empowerment of single individuals and how to detect any changes. To conceptually underpin our notion of empowerment we refer to agency, specifically framed within the capability approach (Sen 1999). For our empirical investigation we start with the hypothesis that empowerment—particularly of marginalized groups—is of key significance when it comes to investigating the impacts of social innovation.

While the concept of social innovation is becoming increasingly popular in the social sciences, empirical evidence for it is still scarce and fragmented and there is, as yet, no common methodology regarding the measurement of social innovation impact (see chapters 4 and 15). The aim of this chapter is to contribute to this research gap with an empirical analysis of three different ongoing social innovation projects in Europe. Our investigation is based on a mixed-method strategy that capitalizes on primary data discussed in chapter 4.

The three cases investigated here are very different from each other in many respects (their aims, characteristics, target groups). These diverse examples are examined through the lens of a common conceptual framework—the Extended Social Grid Model (see chapter 1)—that helps identify common mechanisms in the way these processes operate. As discussed in the earlier chapters, social

[1] The authors would like to thank Lara Maestripieri and Toa Giroletti for their contributions during primary-data collection for the SPG case; Mara Nothers, Hendrik Sönnichsen, and Justus Lodemann for the IKT case. We would also like to thank René Kemp for comments on a prior draft of this chapter, and Alex Nicholls for his editorial work.

Nadia von Jacobi, Enrica Chiappero-Martinetti, Rafael Ziegler, Martijn van der Linden, and Cees van Beers, *Social Innovation and Agency.* In: *Creating Economic Space for Social Innovation.* Edited by: Alex Nicholls and Rafael Ziegler, Oxford University Press (2019).
DOI: 10.1093/oso/9780198830511.003.0010

innovation can affect the structuration of marginalization by transforming the configuration of social forces (Beckert 2010) and their interactions. A principal aim of this chapter is to assess to what extent the three case studies examined here have enhanced the empowerment and agency of the given social innovation's beneficiaries, thereby reducing their marginalization.

Comparing different social innovation cases is difficult. One of the main contributions this chapter offers is to highlight the problems with which researchers are confronted when doing empirical research on social innovation at the micro-level. The central issue that the Extended Social Grid Model tries to capture is a very complex one, including tangible and intangible effects and composite concepts such as institutions, cognitive frames, power dimensions, and so on. The comparison of social innovations is even more challenging than is the case with technological innovations. In spite of robust survey data—such as the bi-annual Community Innovation Survey (CIS) in the EU—the comparison of technological innovations remains subject to debate (Mairesse and Mohnen 2010). The *Oslo Manual* helped improve and fine-tune such methodological approaches, but it took extraordinary efforts and time to achieve an appropriate framework for such comparisons (OECD 2005). Our attempts in this chapter should be viewed as the first methodological steps on a long journey. While our data collection and analytical strategy will undoubtedly benefit from future improvements, the results presented here may help to set up more articulated and standardized approaches for comparing social innovation and its impact.

The focus of this chapter is on the challenge of tracking, quantitatively, the impact of social innovation on individual agency. In the preparation of this chapter, we collected rich material on the stories and cognitive frames animating our three cases, their institutional context, and their respective networks. However, in this chapter, the primary focus is on agency and what we can learn from it about empowerment and, ultimately, about the mechanisms driving (dis) empowerment.[2]

The chapter is structured as follows: the next section briefly introduces the three cases we investigated. After this, we discuss the potential role played by social innovation in empowering people, particularly the marginalized, linking the notions of empowerment, agency and autonomy. Next, we describe the methodology adopted for our primary-data collection. Then, we illustrate the main findings and, finally, conclude by highlighting the lessons learnt.

[2] Readers interested in a thicker description of these cases and their stories are referred to chapter 9 (for Solidarity Purchasing Groups), to van der Linden and van Beers (2017) (for complementary currencies) and to Ziegler (2017) (for the IKT) and, in addition, to the further material in Chiappero-Martinetti et al. (2016) as well as von Jacobi and Chiappero Martinetti (2017).

The Three Cases

The case studies comprise Solidarity Purchasing Groups (Gruppi di Acquisto Solidale—SPG) in Italy,[3] interest communities that fight for decentralized drinking-water supply and wastewater removal (Interessengemeinschaft Kommunale Trinkwasserversorgung—IKT) in Germany, and complementary currencies (Complementair geld—CC) in The Netherlands.[4]

Solidarity Purchasing Groups (SPG) are 'groups of individuals that decide to organize themselves in order to buy collectively food or any other everyday good, selecting suppliers on the basis of solidarity and ethical consumption' (*Altreconomia* 2015: 14). This social innovation reduces marginalization when SPGs promote new processes that open up the market for marginalized suppliers (e.g. for small organic producers, local artisans, or social cooperatives that employ vulnerable workers). Its novelty lies in its focus on the *process* of consumption: SPGs link consumers directly to suppliers and promote ethical consumption in their choices of suppliers (Chiappero-Martinetti et al. 2017). In terms of capabilities, SPGs promote the ability of their consumers to access healthy food.[5] However, in the analysis here, the focus is on enhancing the capabilities of suppliers by offering access to more opportunities for engaging with the market.

The IKT[6] is a network for the promotion of decentralized drinking-water supply and wastewater treatment. It was established in Bavaria (Germany) in 1986 out of a concern that the new threshold value for nitrate would provoke a push towards large freshwater supply systems and gradually eliminate communal freshwater supply in towns and villages, especially hamlets as their subunits. The IKT was founded to lobby for the restoration and maintenance of such communal freshwater supply (IKT 1986) and, subsequently, of decentralized wastewater treatment (since 2002). This social innovation emerged from the need to find new ways of locally managing drinking water and wastewater. It also aims to support the development of a civic network that would empower citizens locally by improving their real choice between decentralized and centralized ways of managing water (Ziegler 2017). In terms of the capabilities approach, the IKT promotes citizen control of their environment (via decentralized water management) and their health (via safe water supply), while also enhancing sensitivity around environmental sustainability.

[3] Within the alternative food networks literature, Solidarity Purchasing Groups are typically abbreviated as SPGs. The Italian acronym is GAS and stands for *Gruppi di Acquisto Solidale*.

[4] For a more in-depth description of the three cases and additional empirical results, see Chiappero-Martinetti et al. (2017) and von Jacobi et al. (2017).

[5] For greater details on SPGs in Italy, see chapter 9 and Maestripieri (2017).

[6] *Interessengemeinschaft Kommunale Trinkwasserversorgung* translates as Interest Community for Communal Drinking Water Supply.

Complementary currencies (CCs)[7] are private media of exchange that function alongside the official national currency (the legal tender) in this case, the euro (see Naqvi and Southgate 2013). CCs are generally used as tools to stimulate change in economic, social, and environmental domains. Examples of CCs are local exchange trading systems (LETS), regional money, time banks, commercial barter systems, and, depending on the definition of CCs, also cryptocurrencies. Seyfang and Longhurst (2013) found a total of 3,418 CCs globally (excluding cryptocurrencies) and argued that 'CCs are developed with the aim of achieving a range of "new-economics"—inspired sustainable development objectives, principally community-building and social capital creation, boosting local economies and valuing marginalized labour, enabling collaborative consumptions to reduce environmental impacts of current life-styles' (Seyfang and Longhurst 2013: 75). After the introduction of the first cryptocurrency in 2009 (Bitcoin), the number of cryptocurrencies increased to 4,076 by 2017.[8] The innovativeness of CCs lies, particularly, in the fact that social innovators and CC members themselves organize the money and not institutions like central banks and commercial banks backed by the state. The Dutch CC case here aligns with the capability approach with regard to how individuals can act as agents of change in an intentional attempt to run and control their monetary system and local environment to improve social relations (van der Linden and van Beers 2017; Chiappero-Martinetti et al. 2016).

Despite the distinctiveness of each of these three cases, taken together they open up important new perspectives on the structuring of marginalization. Marginalization is here understood as the 'result of a social process through which personal, social, or environmental traits are transformed into actual or potential factors of disadvantage' (von Jacobi et al. 2017: 4, building upon Chiappero-Martinetti and von Jacobi 2015: 2). This conceptualization suggests that there is typically no single cause of marginalization, but, rather, it is the combination of personal and contextual traits in a *social process* that causes disadvantage and with it, marginalization and social exclusion. Marginalization itself is not an inherent characteristic: it emerges in connection with other social phenomena. Where personal traits or characteristics of the socio-environmental context in which a person lives result in marginalization, people are increasingly exposed to socio-economic vulnerability.

The actual or potential factors of disadvantage—embedded within existing social processes—that (may) lead to marginalization are different in the three cases investigated. In Italy, where the focus of analysis is on farmers, the trait that tends to expose them to marginalization is the small size of their enterprises—typically family businesses—combined with their choices regarding the processes of their production (for example, organic and ethical production). These choices can be contrasted with national (and global) systems of farming that focus on

[7] Studied in the Netherlands in this chapter, where they refer to *Complementair Geld.*

[8] https://www.cryptocoincharts.info/coins/info, accessed 22 March 2017.

increasing economies of scale within the food distribution system that tends to penalize alternative production mechanisms that are less cost-effective.

In Germany, communities organized in small, rural units—such as hamlets that are smaller than the administrative level of the municipality—are often exposed to potential marginalization in terms of their real opportunity to have voice in decisions that affect their lives. The fact that geographical location can represent a factor of marginalization has to be viewed within the context of historical developments in agriculture (e.g. more fertilizers and pesticides used after the Second World War) and the expansion of an urban freshwater model that does not necessarily 'fit' with hamlets, which often seek to preserve their own local water sources. This clash can create costly non-ecological outcomes and disempower citizens into marginalization.

In the Dutch CC case, the preference for alternative systems of economic exchange represents a potential factor of disadvantage. The organizers of these systems are not driven by a focus on efficiency or profit-maximization—as is typical in financial markets—but, instead, attempt to incorporate values related to tackling social inclusion and other non-financial values within the exchange thesis. As complementary currencies are private currencies, they are automatically relegated to a marginal position within the public monetary system (in this case the dominant euro system) and within the more general mechanism of market exchange.

Although they differ across our cases, each case has potential factors of marginalization that are dependent on social structures and social processes. To explore this further, we next investigate if the respective social innovations succeed in addressing social processes that (re)produce marginalization patterns.

Social Innovation and Empowerment

As Amartya Sen put it, an agent is 'someone who acts and brings about change, and whose achievement can be judged in terms of her own values and objectives, whether or not we assess them in terms of some external criteria as well' (Sen 1999: 18). From this point of view, empowerment can be understood as the *process* by which the capacity of an individual (or group) to make effective choices and to transform these choices into desired actions is created or improved (Alsop et al. 2006). This capacity is affected by the wider socio-structural environment, within which the interplay of institutions, social networks, and cognitive frames may set preconditions for exerting agency effectively--in line with our focus on the Extended Social Grid Model.[9]

[9] For an extensive account of definitions and measures of agency and empowerment see Ibrahim and Alkire (2007) and Alkire (2008).

In the empirical work presented here agency is measured in terms of *autonomy* that reveals an individual's freedom to reflect on, assert, and achieve her own ends. The framing of how to measure autonomy used follows Ibrahim and Alkire (2007) and other related empirical work,[10] referring to Self-Determination Theory as initially formulated by Deci (1971) and subsequently specified in its measurement aspects by Ryan and Deci (2000) in the Relative Autonomy Index. According to Ryan and Deci, an individual's motivation varies along a *continuum* of perceived self-determination, ranging from non-self-determined (controlled and with a lack of agency) to self-determined (autonomous with full agency) forms of behavioural regulation (Wilson et al. 2012). Autonomy, thus, serves as proxy for agency and empowerment (von Jacobi et al. 2015; von Jacobi and Chiappero-Martinetti 2017) and is here used as a key variable to capture the potential impact social innovation may have on individual marginalization.

In the cases investigated here, the Relative Autonomy Index is further elaborated with respect to its initial design and used to track the participants' *perceived* ability to act autonomously across six dimensions. These dimensions relate to Heiskala's and Mann's CESPNA account of the social sources of power: culture, economic, security-related, natural, artefactual and political (see chapter 2, and Heiskala 2015 and 2016). Such a multidimensional setting serves to help identify the potential dimensions within which a lack of power—and hence marginalization—can occur.

An individual's perceived ability to act autonomously is a subjective measure that seeks to capture aspects of the impact social innovation has on marginalization—namely, the subjective perception that individuals have of their own (dis)empowerment. While objective data are based upon observations of measurable facts and conducted by an independent assessment, subjective data relate to personal evaluations, perceptions, feelings, or opinions directly expressed by individuals. A growing literature considers the objective approach necessary but insufficient to evaluate individual living conditions such as poverty or well-being (Ravallion and Lokshin 2002; Biswas-Diener and Diener 2006; Stiglitz et al. 2009; Ravallion et al. 2013). While some individual achievements can be defined using objective methods (e.g. years of schooling), objective measurement does not necessarily reflect to what extent the observable achievement corresponds to that person's goals—something better captured by subjective evaluations.

Considering whether individual achievements relate to one's own goals is a crucial aspect of assessing agency. For comparative investigations of agency and empowerment, the use of subjective measures is key. We propose here that an increase in individual perceived autonomy indicates an increase of agency and empowerment across our different cases. The research presented in this chapter

[10] See Chirkov (2009), Alkire et al. (2013) and Vaz et al. (2015).

tests to what extent the social innovations explored here enhance the perceived autonomy of beneficiaries/participants. Thus, our empirical analysis focuses on whether the participation in three social innovations increases individual perceived autonomy across the six dimensions noted above.

Primary-Data Collection

To properly investigate our three European cases of social innovation an ad hoc primary-data collection strategy was implemented, in which a multi-layered methodology was adopted (see chapter 4). The primary-data collection process was subdivided into two major phases: one centred on social innovators and one centred on their beneficiaries. All data were, from the start, conceived of as being nested: each beneficiary belonged to a particular social innovation context. Interviews with social innovators provided information on a social innovation's emergence, the difficulties and challenges faced, as well as the types of support experienced. Information collected among beneficiaries allowed for the recognition of perceived impact of the key social innovation process. While the social-innovator phase of analysis predominantly made use of qualitative tools, the beneficiary phase was mainly centred on the questionnaire tool, which required quantitative analysis. Elements collected during the qualitative phases of data collection provided guidance for the precise formulation of questions inserted in the quantitative phase (the survey). This approach allowed fine-tuning of the specific information collected on a social innovation's characteristics, its perceived benefits and the relevant social forces that may interplay with it.

The use of a mixed-method approach (see chapter 4) facilitated the gathering of context-specific information for each social innovation that were also comparable within and across the different countries investigated through the use of a common template for the three case studies involved. Semi-structured interviews with social innovators were implemented following a brief—'pre-qualitative'—questionnaire, which was sent to interviewees beforehand in order to gather more standardized information (number of members, year of constitution, and so on). For the selection of social innovation contexts, a stratified sampling approach was used. This developed three samples each covering different local degrees of vulnerability (see Table 10.1). For greater detail on the tools used for data collection, and the technicalities of the sample selection, see chapter 4 and Chiappero-Martinetti et al. (2016).

Once the details of the scope, activities, and intended beneficiaries of the three social innovations were gathered, a second phase of data collection followed in which beneficiaries were the key focus of the analysis. An obstacle at this stage was the missing availability of a list of potential individuals involved in the respective social innovation processes. In order to create a database of beneficiaries' contacts,

Table 10.1. Social innovation groups interviewed for each case

	IKT Case	SPG Case	CC Case
Total number of SI contexts	58	990	44
Sampling selection	30 units	35 units	30 units
Units in low-vulnerability contexts	10	12	10
Units in medium-vulnerability contexts	11	13	14
Units in high-vulnerability contexts	9	10	6
Total number of interviews with social innovators	**30**	**35**	**30**

Note: In Italy, the researchers randomly selected about a hundred cases (corresponding to 10 per cent of the total population of the social innovation groups), divided into thirty units for groups with low vulnerability, thirty units for the group with medium vulnerability and forty units for the one with highest vulnerability. The thirty-five interviews represented those who agreed to participate in the study at the end of this selection process.

Source: Elaboration by the authors.

several strategies were implemented including the collection of primary contacts through relevant social innovators on the ground and, additionally, country-specific data strategies based on networking with relevant associations.[11] Two different tools were used to collect data from the beneficiaries: focus groups[12] and surveys (see chapter 4). This methodological approach allowed for some comparative analysis enhanced by nuanced case details concerning each social innovation.

The first step in data analysis was to organize focus groups for each of the cases investigated: this involved gathering between six and ten beneficiaries for each. The aim of the discussion was to identify the ways in which beneficiaries' participation and exposure to the social innovation processes affected their autonomy. This exercise aimed to identify the concrete, everyday manifestations of different levels of autonomy among beneficiaries. The structure of the focus groups allowed beneficiaries to concentrate on the actual benefits they experienced as a result of each social innovation. Suggestions were gathered in the first phase of the discussion and, subsequently, with the help of a moderator they were attributed to the six pre-determined dimensions mentioned above. The practical, everyday aspects of life mentioned by the beneficiaries constituted the main resource for specifying the self-assessment questions that measured the perceived autonomy of all beneficiaries in the surveys (see Table 10.2).

[11] For further details see chapter 4 and von Jacobi and Chiappero-Martinetti (2017).

[12] The technique used in this phase was 'brainstorming' (Bezzi and Baldini 2006): this was a group discussion with interviewees aimed at creating data by using a bottom-up approach in which data is co-constructed. This technique is usually employed for bottom-up definitions of indicators for assessing a specific process or outcome. For simplicity we refer to 'focus groups' and not to 'brainstorming' in this chapter.

Table 10.2. Dimensions of social (em)power(ment)

Dimension	IKT Case	SPG Case	CC Case
Cultural	Relationship to public administrations	Relationship between producers and consumers	Meeting people with the same interests and values
Economic	Financial aspects linked to water provision/ treatment, e.g. price paid for water	Choice of products to produce and their quality	Financial aspects such as the ability to save and/or access more goods and services
Security-related	Guarantee of water provision/treatment in terms of quantity and quality	Ability to enhance worker protection, e.g. through safe and health-preserving production methods	Assistance and protection in case of emergency by social network
Natural	Participation in protecting the resource 'water', also for the next generations	Ability to contribute to the care and quality of the territory	Contribution to environmental care by sharing, reusing, and exchanging local products
Artefactual	Use of technologies to guarantee water provision and treatment	Choice of preferred production techniques	Knowledge about the financial system and financial skills
Political	Participation in decision-making regarding water provision and treatment	Choice of the productive model, such as sustainability, transparency, ethics, and solidarity	Practical implementation of a new way of thinking (local economy, other money)

Source: Elaboration by the authors, based on focus groups, 2016.

The second tool represented the heart of the data collection: a survey questionnaire was implemented via an online platform that combined a common core set of questions with a set of questions adapted to the case-specificities based on the information gathered in the first phase.[13]

Table 10.3 presents the participant numbers of the three coordinated survey data collections implemented. Numbers refer to those observations for which the information on their participation in the social innovation is available (yes for beneficiaries, no for control group).

[13] Where the online tool was deemed inadequate to capture the entire population of beneficiaries (e.g. due to insufficient ICT capacities) or where response rates were low for other reasons, additional data collection strategies were used. In some cases, a paper version of the questionnaire was sent out via post (Germany and Italy), in others additional data was collected via phone (Italy) to increase the number of completed surveys.

Table 10.3. Participation in Survey Data Collection

	IKT Case	SPG Case	CC Case
Number of social innovation contexts	16	32	28
Sample population	236	2,965	240
Current beneficiaries	72	750	185
Past beneficiaries	29	175	16
Control group	135	2,040	39

Source: Elaboration by the authors based on CrESSI Survey Data, 2016.

The design of the data collection allowed for subsequent impact analysis. This involved interviewing beneficiaries and comparable control groups and identifying a dependent variable with which effects of different social innovations could be compared. Control groups—defined here as potential beneficiaries—were distinguished by the research design from *actual* beneficiaries. They were case-specific and tended to be social groups similar in characteristics to the social innovation beneficiaries, but who, at the time of the data collection, had not participated in the social innovation itself.

To estimate the impact of the social innovation processes on participants, changes in the autonomy of the beneficiaries compared to their respective control groups were compared at two different times and across all the dimensions of the CESPNA model. The two time periods were simply the present and the past (i.e. retrospectively). Respondents were asked if and how their current level of autonomy had changed across each dimension with respect to the 'beginning of the social innovation' (if the respondent belonged to the beneficiary group) or 'three years ago' (if the respondents belonged to the control group). To guarantee comparison, the beneficiaries were also asked this latter question. While the exposure to the social innovation may date back several years, the comparison with the control group kept a constant time frame of three years.

The time frame for the retrospective exercise was chosen as a pragmatic methodology given that longer periods of retrospective data risk reflecting confounding memories due to effects of life-changing events, while shorter time periods may not be sufficient to capture the full effects produced by social innovation initiatives.

The beneficiaries' subjective level of autonomy was evaluated by using two self-assessment questions. In both cases, the respondents were invited to rate their level of autonomy from zero to ten along a Likert scale. The first question aimed at evaluating their actual level of autonomy, whereas the second one asked them to compare their present level of autonomy with that of 'three years ago' (control group) or 'before getting in touch with the social innovation' (beneficiaries).

Findings

What is the perceived change in autonomy of beneficiaries? In the survey both beneficiaries and control groups were asked to evaluate their autonomy in the six dimensions comprised by the CESPNA model. As mentioned, the questionnaire requested the same information twice, once for their current situation and once referring to the time before they started participating in the social innovation (beneficiaries) or with reference to three years ago (control group, beneficiaries). Table 10.4 summarizes differences in perceived autonomy levels and their change between the two timeframes.

As can be seen in Table 10.4, the average rating of their own autonomy tended to be slightly higher among beneficiaries than among the respective control groups, but the results lack statistical significance.[14] This may be to be due to the reduced sample size of data in the German and Dutch cases, but also suggests that the beneficiary and control groups were not significantly different in terms of their post-intervention perceived autonomy. This result applies to all three of the cases. When comparing participants and their control groups in terms of their autonomy in the past, similar results were obtained: with respect to three years ago, beneficiaries again tended to self-assess their autonomy at slightly higher level, but without statistical significance.

Table 10.4. Differences in perceived autonomy across time

Sub-group in sample	After (current perception)	Before (three years ago)	Before (first involvement in SI)	% Change (in three years)	% Change (different time moments)
IKT beneficiaries	7.5	7.2	5.65**	4.17	32.74**
IKT control group	6.95	6.7	—	3.73	3.73
SPG beneficiaries	7.58	6.87	6.38***	10.33	18.81
SPG control group	6.56	6.06	—	8.25	8.25
CC beneficiaries	7.95	7.35	6.9	8.16	15.22
CC control group	6.91	6.14	—	12.54	12.54

Note: Statistical significance: * p-value of 0.10 or below; ** p-value of 0.05 or below; *** p-value of 0.01 or below.

Source: Elaboration by the authors based on CrESSI Survey Data, 2016.

[14] Tests were run to check for statistical significance in the difference of average values of beneficiaries against those of their respective control group.

As a second step, the effect of participation in the social innovation was separated out: a specific question asked beneficiaries to report their autonomy levels before getting involved in the social innovation. This deliberately blurred temporal issues, as different individuals might have been participating for different lengths of time. The past autonomy levels of the control group on the other hand were constant, set at three years before the data collection. In this scenario, the comparison in autonomy levels produces statistically significant results: beneficiaries tend to report lower values of autonomy before getting involved in the social innovation in comparison to later reports. An analysis of percentage changes in perceived autonomy shows that improvements in the last three years tended to be comparable between beneficiaries and control groups (there is no statistically significant difference between the two groups). The improvements among beneficiaries since their participation in the social innovation are higher on average than those among the control groups, but only in the German case is such difference statistically significant.

In a further question, the survey directly investigated the changes in perceived autonomy between the two time periods. The questions used in the three surveys asked interviewees to reflect on the changes in their autonomy across the dimensions previously presented in Table 10.2, which were case-specific. The overarching dimensions of the CESPNA model were used to facilitate comparison across the cases. Again, while the time reference period for beneficiaries was set at any point when the relevant social innovation intervention began, for the control group the reference period was set at three years before data collection. Figure 10.1 summarizes the distributions of replies to the question:

Considering the [specification in Table 10.2] dimension has your participation in the social innovation contributed to your autonomy and how do you feel about this compared to three years ago?

Figure 10.1 maps the replies to this question for each of the dimensions of the CESPNA model. For each of the six sub-figures, the upper line reports the replies of beneficiaries, the lower line those of the respective control groups. The sequence of cases from left to right is IKT, SPG, and CC.[15]

As can be seen in Figure 10.1, within the cultural dimension beneficiaries perceived more positive autonomy changes than their respective control groups across all cases. Figure 10.1 also suggests that autonomy within the economic dimension did not seem to be particularly influenced by participation in the social

[15] As the reply options constituted a categorical variable, no statistical tests were reported since the sample size was insufficient to test the single reply options of beneficiaries against their respective control groups.

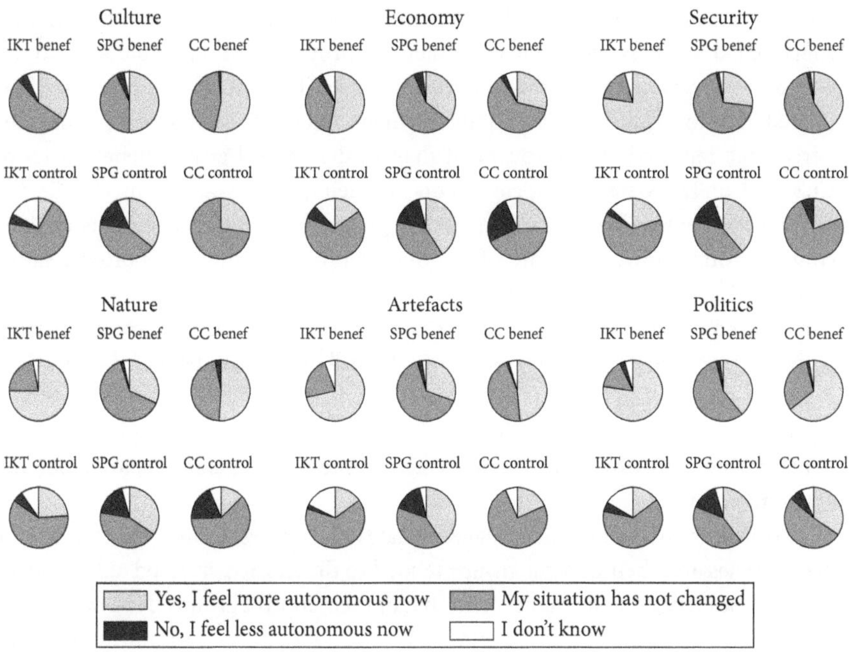

10.1 Differences in perceived autonomy change in six different dimensions of (em)power(ment), comparison between beneficiaries (higher rows) and their control groups (lower rows), all cases

Source: Elaboration by the authors based on CrESSI Survey Data, 2016.

innovation for the beneficiaries of SPGs and CCs. Among beneficiaries of IKTs, a clear improvement in autonomy was perceived.

The segment of people perceiving improvement in their autonomy in the natural dimension tended to be bigger among beneficiaries than among the control group. From the latter, the most frequent reply was that their 'situation has not changed', although some also reported that it worsened. However, a worsening of the situation was almost never reported among the beneficiary groups, hinting that the social innovations managed to buffer factors that could affect the perceived ability to act autonomously in the natural dimension, which enshrines some sort of control (or at least concern) over one's environment.

Within the artefactual dimension, the contrast between control groups and beneficiaries was stark for the IKT and the CC cases, suggesting that these social innovations somehow contributed to the beneficiaries' control over key technologies. However, for the SPG case, improved autonomy was more often perceived among the control group. In this group, however, perceived autonomy was also reported as having deteriorated more often.

Similarly, it is in the IKT case that the biggest segment of beneficiaries perceived an improvement in their security-related autonomy. Participants in CCs also reported greater autonomy in this dimension than their control group. The data suggested that SPGs were not really able to provide a more stable and secure economic environment for their beneficiaries (see Table 10.2). Suppliers to SPGs tended not to report deteriorations in their autonomy, but overall a smaller percentage reported an improvement than in the control group. Beneficiaries of CCs and of IKTs stated improvements in their political autonomy, while the farmers supplying SPGs described similar proportions of improvements as their control group. However, some of the SPG control group also reported relative deterioration in their autonomy—in contrast to the beneficiaries.

When comparing the three cases it is noticeable that the smallest differences between beneficiaries and their respective control groups can be found in the SPG case. The starkest can be seen in the IKT case, where beneficiaries overwhelmingly reported improvements. The CC case is somewhere in the middle—with more beneficiaries reporting improvements across most dimensions, apart from the economic one.

In summary, overall the data suggests that the self-assessments of autonomy for beneficiaries and their control groups tended to differ: the perceived autonomy of beneficiaries tended to be higher than that of their control groups. However, when prompted specifically about the effects that the relevant social innovation might have had on their autonomy levels, the evidence became blurred. For the SPG case, the beneficiaries—mainly small enterprises in the agricultural sector—did not demonstrate any significant differences from their control group apart from within the cultural dimension, where SPG beneficiaries tended to experience an improvement in autonomy more often. Moreover, across the other dimensions, SPG beneficiaries tended to report some deterioration in autonomy *less often*; this hints at a 'safety-net' effect with respect to their control group, which perceived deterioration in autonomy more often.

For the CC case, improvements in autonomy were more prevalent among beneficiaries across the natural, technological, cultural, and political dimensions. Again, the social dimension seemed to play a 'safety-net' role in the economic dimension, where beneficiaries reported deterioration less frequently. Yet, the limited amount of observations in the CC control group calls for caution in the interpretation of these results.

For the IKT case, there was clear evidence of improvement in perceived autonomy across most of the dimensions with the exception of culture with beneficiaries reporting improvements between 50 per cent and 75 per cent. This may be due to the fact that the IKT dated back further in time, thereby allowing for a greater manifestation of improvements and of greater perceived effects among beneficiaries. A qualitative explanation would be that the IKT strategy was centrally focused on the empowerment of local groups. From this perspective, the results suggested this was successful. Additionally, the data suggests that this strategy was holistic in that it covered the environmental, economic, and political aspects of empowerment (rather than narrowing down on one domain of 'expertise'). Such a holistic approach was quite typical for the citizen initiatives emerging in Germany from the 1960s onwards (Engels 2016).

These changes in perceived autonomy can provide useful insights into the channels through which participation in social innovation can foster the empowerment of marginalized individuals. The fact that overall levels of perceived autonomy across the cases were higher among beneficiaries may hint that more marginalized individuals have been reached by the social innovation activities. Yet, it may also reveal an underlying sample bias as self-selection mechanisms lead more enthusiastic people (with greater inclination for autonomous action) to participate in a social innovation.

The results discussed so far provide some interesting evidence of the effects of three very different social innovations on the perceived autonomy of marginalized people. However, our survey included further questions aimed to test these results. First, interviewees were asked to endorse the classifications used to identify the prior beneficiaries of the social innovation: this tested the validity of our research design.

As can be seen in Table 10.5, in the IKT and CC case the majority of the interviewed sample agreed with the definition of beneficiaries adopted by the

Table 10.5. 'In your view, are [see table for categories] prior beneficiaries of the social innovation?'

	'To a large extent'%
IKT	
Local citizens	92.7
Farmers	36.6
Citizens of neighbouring hamlets	4.8
The environment	74.4
The local administration	26.2
(1) SPG	
Consumers in SPG and their families	80.8
Suppliers of SPG	34.6
Small producers	46.4
Special projects of the solidarity economy	14.6
The environment	40.3
(2) CC	
All participants	69.0
Organisations/companies	23.3
Core team members/directors	51.9
The whole society	45.0
Monetary reformers and innovators	36.0

Note: Reply options were: 'not at all'; 'to a small extent'; 'to some extent'; 'to a large extent'; 'not anymore now'; 'I don't know'. Typologies of beneficiaries were derived from qualitative interviews carried out with social innovators.

Source: Elaboration by the authors based on CrESSI Survey Data.

research design. However, in the SPG case, the suppliers interviewed tend to perceive consumers—rather than themselves—as the main beneficiaries of the social innovation.

Second, the survey tested to what extent beneficiaries felt that they had *personally benefitted* from the social innovation (Table 10.6): 80.8 per cent (across all cases) were positive about receiving some sort of benefit from their participation in the social innovation. It is also notable that only a minority of respondents felt they had *not* benefitted: 6.5 per cent (CC case); 12.7 per cent (SPG case); 17.2 per cent (IKT case).

Third, we asked what *kind* of perceived benefits did the social innovations achieve. Figure 10.2 compares the perceived benefits across the three cases and shows that creating friendship—an element of one's personal social network—seemed to be one of the predominant ways through which social innovations benefitted their participants. This benefit was perceived as

Table 10.6. 'Are you personally benefitting or have you personally benefitted from this social innovation?'

Social innovation case	No%	Yes%	I don't know%	N
IKT	17.2	77.4	5.4	93
SPG	12.7	79.2	8.0	756
CC	6.5	88.7	4.8	186

Note: Current and past beneficiaries combined.
Source: Elaboration by the authors based on CrESSI Survey Data, 2016.

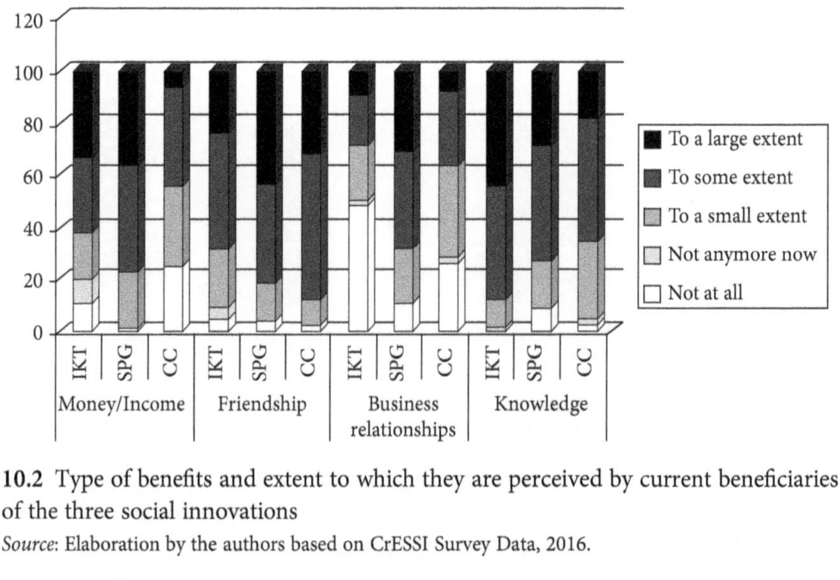

10.2 Type of benefits and extent to which they are perceived by current beneficiaries of the three social innovations
Source: Elaboration by the authors based on CrESSI Survey Data, 2016.

significant by 68 per cent of the IKT's, 82 per cent of the SPG's, and 88 per cent of the CC's beneficiaries.

Of equal relevance seems to be new knowledge, underlining a potential for social innovation to be altering cognitive frames and what informs them. Eighty-eight per cent of the IKT, 73 per cent of the SPG, and 66 per cent of the CC beneficiaries perceived new knowledge as a benefit. Benefits in terms of money and income also played a role (61 per cent IKT; 77 per cent SPG; 45 per cent CC). This was more than was the case with new business relationships, which were important in the SPG case but not elsewhere (78 per cent of SPG beneficiaries reporting the benefit). Somewhat surprisingly, perhaps, the CC social innovation—centred on economic transactions—did not produce perceived economic benefits. When re-running this analysis on marginalized subgroups—in this case, identified as people with the two lowest levels of education or that report having difficulty in making ends meet—the results did not change. This suggests that there is no clear separate distribution of benefits among the most marginalized in this case.[16]

Beyond the benefits reported in Figure 10.2, Table 10.7 provides further detailed information on the case-specific benefits that were identified during the qualitative phase of data collection in which social innovators were interviewed.

Table 10.7. Other benefits perceived by participants

Degree the benefit is perceived (row %)								
Type of benefit	**Country**	**Not at all**	**Not anymore**	**To a small extent**	**To some extent**	**To a large extent**	**Total (observations and row %)**	
Local way of managing water	GER	0	1.47	7.35	23.53	67.65	68	100
Fair price	ITA	1.47	0.21	11.16	40	47.16	475	100
Social inclusion	NL	14.17	1.67	20.83	50	13.33	120	100
Improved empowerment	GER	4.35	2.9	4.35	23.19	65.22	69	100
Possibility to stay on market	ITA	11.02	1.08	22.46	33.26	32.18	463	100
More employment (work)	NL	23.89	5.31	35.4	27.43	7.96	113	100

Source: Elaboration by the authors based on CrESSI Survey Data.

[16] Results are not included in this chapter but are available upon request.

Such benefits differed in their nature and also in the kind of effects they may have on the social structures that (re)produce marginalization.

The SPG case-specific benefits 'earning a fair price' and 'having the possibility to stay in the market' were widely acknowledged by the beneficiaries: 87 per cent and 65 per cent, respectively, reported that they perceived such benefits 'to a large' or 'to some extent' (see Table 10.7). Access to a fair price for products characterized the economic context in which the farmers were embedded. Moreover, since the SPG social innovation aimed to drive changes in the hierarchical position of small farmers in the supply chain the broader effects would challenge the stasis of market institutions and could alter the cognitive frames of consumers across the cultural power dimension. From a capability perspective this would affect the conversion processes of farmers to increase the opportunity for the capabilities of this marginalized group to flourish. In the IKT case, the improved ability and know-how to locally manage water systems was a widely perceived benefit (more than 90 per cent) and represented a way to change the kinds of knowledge citizens could access. This could drive empowerment across the cultural and technological/artefactual dimensions and can be seen as a means but also as an end in capability terms.

Another example was social inclusion, which was mentioned in the CC case. In the qualitative interviews in this case study, eighteen out of thirty social innovators explicitly mentioned social objectives such as 'improving social cohesion' and 'promoting neighbourliness'. This benefit was perceived by 63 per cent of beneficiaries and would suggest a need to change existing networking patterns. This, in turn, would offer the opportunity for an improvement in the capabilities of beneficiaries by constituting a new positive social conversion factor.

Beyond this micro (individual-centred) analysis of impacts, our survey also asked beneficiaries what kind of impact they expected from the social innovation in which they were participating. The questionnaire provided a list of tentative expected impacts and required the respondents to select the three most important ones. With specific reference to the Social Grid, our data suggest that respondents expected social innovations, primarily, to affect *cognitive frames*. Across all cases at least a quarter and up to a third of respondents foresaw an impact on people's worldview. No other category gathered a similar consensus and differences tended to be associated with the specificities of the cases studied (von Jacobi and Chiappero-Martinetti 2017). However, there was also evidence for an expectation of dynamic change in existing *institutions*—though this was only explicitly relevant in the IKT case—here the political battle for the decentralization of water was central (an expected impact for less than 30 per cent of respondents). New relationships and *network* change were not key expected outcomes across our cases, with the exception of new friendships noted above.

In summary, the results suggest that across the three social forces within the Social Grid, the perceived benefits of the social innovations focused, primarily, on changing dominant cognitive frames to benefit the marginalized. However, beneficiaries also recognized the personal value of new knowledge to themselves as a benefit—in this context the social innovations may also change the cognitive frames of their beneficiaries too. This assumption is supported by the evidence of beneficiaries reporting positive perceived changes in their autonomy across the cultural dimension when compared to their respective control groups. Thus, acquiring new knowledge and contributing to changing other people's worldviews seems to have been perceived a vehicle for cultural empowerment. The knowledge benefits generated by the social innovations may also have effects across other power dimensions, as in the IKT case where the social innovation contributed to acquiring new technical know-how that led to greater empowerment in the artefactual dimension.

While such empowerment does not modify the potential factors of disadvantage (such as the size of enterprises or their geographical remoteness), it can contribute to changing the social processes that transform such traits into systematic (dis)advantage. If citizens in rural hamlets acquire greater skills and self-consciousness about their potential role in local water management (IKT case), they may cease to be passive marginalized observers of centralized decision-making and, instead, move towards greater empowerment. Equally, if customers increasingly value products that enshrine solidarity values (SPG and CC cases), the traits that characterize their producers may cease to produce systematic marginalization.

A final observation from our data is that *perceived* empowerment can apparently be quite high even in the absence of *systemic* societal change. For example, neither IKT nor CCs actually changed the central water supply or the mainstream monetary system, but they were still perceived as having delivered important benefits.

Conclusion

The findings presented here are the results of a first exploratory study. Nevertheless, they offer some insights into the effects social innovations may have on marginalization and its social structuration. The data analysis presented here is preliminary and offers a foundation for future research that can test and extend our work to refine and add new insights. Despite the obvious difficulties of comparing different social innovation cases in different countries, the analysis above captured some common elements across all three. Although our analysis shows the inherent difficulties that quantitative research on intangible outcomes faces (cf. chapter 4, chapter 15, and von Jacobi and Chiappero-Martinetti 2017), the data suggests that an analytic focus on agency and autonomy offers a pathway to connecting individual capabilities to social structure and, consequently, a theoretical framework to explore how social innovation may bring about change for marginalized groups.

Our results support the proposal that social innovation can increase the agency and autonomy of beneficiaries, although precise and statistically significant quantifications of this effect were hard to find for a series of reasons. Self-selection may lead to more motivated and enthusiastic individuals choosing to participate in a social innovation, whereas less motivated people may simply not do so. In the attempt to quantify the impact of social innovation on agency, the use of control groups encounters limitations: as individuals participate in social innovations for different lengths of time, it is almost impossible to construct a completely comparable control group in which time lags are equivalent. Future collection of panel data could improve the reliability of data in this sense.

There appear to be further effects of social innovation beyond enhancing agency directly. Our second group of findings seems to suggest concrete ways through which such agency improvements may be taking place in an indirect manner. Knowledge is empowering and so are personal relationships. Information, technical know-how and the ability to share it with like-minded people represent key elements through which social innovation seems to be spurring perceived autonomy in the three cases investigated. For instance, in the SPG case the engagement in the social innovation helped farmers acquire the technical know-how needed for increasing productivity in organic farming. In the IKT case, a different kind of knowledge contributed to the ability to restore alternative, local water management systems. The CC case showed how individuals that pursue a radical new way of thinking succeeded in getting in touch with each other, thereby supporting their local economy. Social innovators observe the need for local social cohesion in today's globalized world and it appears that meeting on a regular basis with individuals who strive for the same values (sharing cognitive frames) in the local community empowers individuals.

In conclusion, these results suggest that the development and fostering of social ties as well as knowledge might be general mechanisms of empowerment for social innovation projects. Acquiring and diffusing knowledge can be further differentiated into the skills and practical know-how that participants experience as empowering and into new ways of thinking (i.e. cognitive frames) that afford more empowering ways of seeing, talking about, and sharing an issue.

People participating in social innovations mainly perceive intangible benefits, which seem to contribute to improvements in their perceived autonomy but to different degrees in different dimensions. These qualifiers also point to a further challenge: different social innovations have different objectives and thematic foci. It is to be expected that they will also have differential views of perceived autonomy (see chapter 15). In this light, it is surprising that in all three cases perceived autonomy gains were reported across several dimensions of power. This seems to point to a tendency of social innovation to produce holistic empowering effects. Empowerment is multi-dimensional. At the same time, this point also implies that people empowered in one or several dimensions are not necessarily empowered in other dimensions and that some inequalities may be inadvertently reproduced within the social innovation initiatives.[17]

Our research suggests that the construction and diffusion of knowledge and friendship as meta-themes cutting across the power dimensions receives new importance. Within the capability approach, knowledge can be viewed as an achievement in itself, but—importantly—also as a means to achieve other capabilities. Personal relationships, on the other hand, and the density of the network to which one may belong through the social innovation, emerge as those social conversion factors that may facilitate the conversion of means/resources into those ends that the single person *values*. In terms of the ESGM, our cases show clear examples through which social innovation can, indeed, contribute to reducing marginalization. By putting pressure on—and altering—social forces (here meant mainly as cognitive frames and networks), the benefits connected to acquiring and accessing knowledge and building new personal relationships and networks are redistributed in different ways. Potentially marginalized individuals benefit from better inputs/resources or conversion factors through which they are empowered and can enact their agency.

References

Alkire, Sabina. 2008. 'Concepts and Measures of Agency'. In *Arguments for a Better World: Essays in Honor of Amartya Sen, Volume I: Ethics, Welfare, and Measurement*, edited by Kaushik Basu and Ravi Kanbur, pp. 455–74. Oxford: Oxford University Press.

Alkire, Sabina, Ruth Meinzen-Dick, Amber Peterman, Agnes Quisumbing, Greg Seymour, and Ana Vaz. 2013. 'The Women's Empowerment in Agriculture Index'. *World Development* 52: 71–91.

Alsop, Ruth, Mette Bertelsen, and Jeremy Holland. 2006, *Empowerment in Practice: From Analysis to Implementation*. Direction in Development. Washington, DC: World Bank Publications.

Altreconomia. 2015. 'Il libro dei GAS. Gruppi di Acquisto Solidali. Come Fare la Spesa Giusta, dalla 'A' al KM Zero'. Milano: Edizioni Altreconomia.

Avelino, Flor, Julia M. Wittmayer, Bonno Pel, Paul Weaver, et al. 2017. 'Transformative Social Innovation and (Dis)Empowerment.' *Technological Forecasting and Social Change*. https://doi.org/10.1016/j.techfore.2017.05.002.

[17] See for example the further study by Maestripieri (2017), which finds that SPGs are not specifically empowering as far as gender inequality is concerned. For a qualitative discussion of empowerment and disempowerment in social innovation see also Avelino et al. (2017).

Beckert, Jens. 2010. 'How Do Fields Change? The Interrelations of Institutions, Networks, and Cognition in the Dynamics of Markets'. *Organization Studies* 31: 605–27.

Bezzi, Claudio, and Irene Baldini. 2006. *Il Brainstorming. Pratica e Teoria*. Milano: Franco Angeli Editore.

Biswas-Diener, Robert, and Ed Diener. 2006. 'The Subjective Well-being of the Homeless, and Lessons for Happiness'. *Social Indicators Research* 76: 185–205.

Chiappero-Martinetti, Enrica, and Nadia von Jacobi. 2015. 'How Can Sen's Capability Approach Contribute to Understanding the Role for Social Innovations for the Marginalised?' CrESSI Working Paper No. 3. Brussels: European Commission, DG Research.

Chiappero-Martinetti, Enrica, Nadia von Jacobi, Lara Maestripieri, Rafael Ziegler et al. 2016. 'Comparison of Four Cases of Social Innovation in Europe'. CrESSI Working Paper No. 34. Brussels: European Commission, DG Research and Innovation.

Chirkov, Valerie. 2009. 'A Cross-Cultural Analysis of Autonomy in Education: A Self-Determination Theory Perspective'. *Theory and Research in Education* 7: 253–62.

Deci, Edward. 1971. Effects of Externally Mediated Rewards on Intrinsic Motivation'. *Journal of Personality and Social Psychology* 18: 105–15.

Engels, Jens Ivo. 2016. 'Ökologiebewegung'. In *Handbuch Umweltethik*, edited by Konrad Ott, Jan Dierks, and Lieske Voget-Kleschin, pp. 94–9. Stuttgart: J.B. Metzler.

Heiskala, Risto. 2015. 'Relating Mann's Conception'. CrESSI Working Paper No. 9. Brussels: European Commission, DG Research.

Heiskala, Risto. 2016. 'Forms of Power, European Empires, and Globalizations: Michael Mann's The Sources of Social Power and Beyond'. CrESSI Working Paper No. 28. Brussels: European Commission, DG Research.

Ibrahim Solava, and Sabina Alkire. 2007. 'Agency and Empowerment: A Proposal for Internationally Comparable Indicators'. *Oxford Development Studies* 35(4): 379–403.

IKT. 1986. Resolution der Interessengemeinschaft zur Erhaltung der kommunalen Trinkwasserversorgung (IKT): An das Bayrische Innenministerium, z. H. Staatsminister Dr Hillermeier, Sebastian Schönauer.

von Jacobi, Nadia, Enrica Chiappero-Martinetti, Toa Giroletti, Lara Maestripieri, and Flavio Ceravolo. 2015. 'Toolkit (Methodology)'. CrESSI Working Paper No. 16. Brussels: European Commission, DG Research.

von Jacobi, Nadia, Daniel Edmiston, and Rafael Ziegler. 2017. 'Tackling Marginalisation through Social Innovation? Examining the EU Social Innovation Policy Agenda from a Capabilities Perspective'. *Journal of Human Development and Capabilities* 18 (2): 148–62.

von Jacobi, Nadia, and Enrica Chiappero-Martinetti. 2017. 'Social Innovation, Individuals and Societies: An Empirical Investigation of Multi-layered Effects'. *Journal of Social Entrepreneurship* 8(3): 271–301.

van der Linden, Martijn, and van Beers, Cees. 2017. 'Are Private (Digital) Moneys (Disruptive) Social Innovations? An Exploration of Different Designs'. *Journal of Social Entrepreneurship* 8(3): 302–19.

Maestripieri, Lara. 2017. 'Does Social Innovation Reduce the Economic Marginalisation of Women? Insights from the Case of Solidarity Purchasing Groups'. *Journal of Social Entrepreneurship* 8(3): 320–37.

Mairesse, Jacques and Pierre Mohnen. 2010. 'Using Innovations Surveys for Econometric Analysis'. In *Handbook of the Economics of Innovation, Volume 2*, edited by H. Bronwyn H. Hall, and Nathan Rosenberg, pp. 1129–55. Amsterdam: Elsevier Publishers.

Naqvi, Mona, and James Southgate. 2013. 'Banknotes, Local Currencies and Central Bank Objectives'. *Bank of England Quarterly Bulletin* 4: 317–25.

OECD. 2005. *Oslo Manual*, 3rd edition. Paris: OECD.

Ravallion, Martin, Kristen Himelein, and Kathleen Beegle. 2013. 'Can Subjective Questions on Economic Welfare Be Trusted? Evidence for Three Developing Countries'. Policy Research Working Paper No. 6726. Washington D.C.: World Bank.

Ravallion, Martin, and Michael Lokshin. 2002. 'Self-Rated Economic Welfare in Russia'. *European Economic Review* 46: 1453–73.

Ryan, Richard, and Edward Deci. 2000. 'Self-Determination Theory and the Facilitation of Intrinsic Motivation: Social Development, and Well-Being'. *American Psychologist* 55(1): 68–78.

Sen, Amartya. 1999. *Development as Freedom*. Oxford: Oxford University Press.

Seyfang, Gill, and Noel Longhurst. 2013. 'Growing Green Money? Mapping Community Currencies for Sustainable Development'. *Ecological Economics* 86: 65–77.

Stiglitz, Joseph, Amartya Sen, and Jean-Paul Fitoussi. 2009. 'Report of the Commission on the Measurement of Economic Performance and Social Progress'. https://ec.europa.eu/eurostat/documents/118025/118123/Fitoussi+Commission+report.

Vaz, Ana, Pierre Pratley, and Sabina Alkire. 2015. 'Measuring Women's Autonomy in Chad and its Associations with Breastfeeding Practices Using the Relative Autonomy Index'. OPHI Research in progress series 44a. Oxford.

Wilson, Philip, Catherine Sabiston, Diane Mack, and Chris Blanchard. 2012. 'On the Nature and Function of Scoring Protocols Used in Exercise Motivation Research: An Empirical Study of the Behavioral Regulation in Exercise Questionnaire'. *Psychology of Sport and Exercise* 13: 614–22.

Ziegler, Rafael. 2017. 'Citizen Innovation as Niche Restoration: A Type of Social Innovation and its Relevance for Political Participation and Sustainability'. *Journal of Social Entrepreneurship* 8(3): 338–53.

11
Social Innovation Policy in the European Union

Alex Nicholls and Daniel Edmiston

Introduction

In the last two decades, a focus on social innovation (Nicholls and Murdock 2011; Nicholls et al. 2015) has become an important element in European Union (EU) policymaking (Borzaga and Bodini 2014; Pol and Ville 2009; Grisolia and Ferragina 2015). In the EU, social innovation has been posited as a solution to both old and new social risks under conditions of increased pressure on government finances (Bonoli 2005; OECD 2011; Sinclair and Baglioni 2014). Moreover, social innovation has also been presented as a mechanism by which existing policy agendas can be implemented more efficiently and effectively to tackle social exclusion and marginalization. Indeed, a key feature of the Europe 2020 strategy was to facilitate and embed social innovation across Europe to 'deliver the kind of inclusive and sustainable social market economy we all want to live in' (BEPA 2010: 16).

The sustained interest in social innovation as a focus of EU policy has a range of drivers depending on specific nation contexts. However, there appear to be two overarching and interlinked policy objectives:

- To increase policy *efficiency* under conditions of austerity and reduced public expenditure. However, social innovation policy of this sort has also been critiqued as being too constrained by the dominant normative economic order (broadly speaking meritocratic market liberalism) to offer any systemic solutions to issues such as poverty (Grisolia and Ferragina 2015).
- To increase policy *effectiveness* often by means of rethinking the relationships between the state, the market, and civil society via new hybrid political arrangements (Caulier-Grice et al. 2012)—this type of social innovation conforms to the EU agenda of reducing social exclusion and marginalization as a part of an inclusive and sustainable social market economy (Langergaard 2014; Green and Hay 2015). This policy agenda has also been critiqued in a similar way because of its inherent inability to create the economic space outside of neo-liberalism that is required to deliver innovation addressing

Alex Nicholls and Daniel Edmiston, *Social Innovation Policy in the European Union*. In: *Creating Economic Space for Social Innovation*. Edited by: Alex Nicholls and Rafael Ziegler, Oxford University Press (2019). © Oxford University Press.
DOI: 10.1093/oso/9780198830511.003.0011

systemic issues such as inequality, structural unemployment, and wider health and demographic challenges (Nolan and Whelan 2011).

In the context of these two policy agendas, not only has social innovation been understood as a *means* to achieve an end in this regard, it has also been recognized as an *end* in itself. Social innovation has been cited by the European Commission as 'another way to produce value, with less focus on financial profit and more on real demands or needs . . . for reconsidering production and redistribution systems' (European Commission 2014a: 8). Moreover, there have been a series of flagship initiatives and process innovations developed to encourage EU member states to engage with social innovation. These activities have been informed and supported by the EU's largest public research funding programme, Horizon 2020 (European Commission 2013b), which has had a key research focus on establishing the origins and effects of social innovation as well as the efficacy of related policy instruments.

However, despite this sustained interest in Brussels and across the EU, social innovation as a concept and phenomenon has remained essentially (and perhaps necessarily) emergent and contested (Nicholls and Murdock 2011; Ayob et al. 2016). Policy-makers and practitioners, at the EU and domestic level, regularly differ in what they understand social innovation to be. Some have argued that social innovation is defined by its processes, methods, and socio-structural functions; others have defined social innovation according to preceding approaches and organizational forms; while others believed social innovation is characterized by its outcomes and objectives. Many of the most influential definitions have conflated these different dimensions to describe the essence of social innovation. For example, the European Commission has defined social innovation as:

> The development and implementation of new ideas (products, services, and models) to meet social needs and create new social relationships or collaborations. It represents new responses to pressing social demands, which affect the process of social interactions. It is aimed at improving human wellbeing. Social innovations are innovations that are social in both their ends and their means. They are innovations that are not only good for society but also enhance individuals' capacity to act. (European Commission 2013a: 6)

Very often, however, it is less clear which characteristics (or even outcomes) are seen as necessary and/or sufficient conditions. Some have suggested that the 'uses and definitions of the concept are so disparate that it is becoming increasingly difficult to assess whether social innovation is in fact a helpful construct or just another fad that will soon be forgotten' (Borzaga and Bodini 2014: 411). Indeed, Jenson (2012, 2015) argued that social innovation is effectively a 'quasi concept' that has a reputable intellectual basis but is equally exposed to theoretical, analytical, and empirical criticism. The conceptual malleability of the term and phenomenon make it particularly susceptible to modification and reinterpretation by policy actors. With its character so loosely and inconsistently defined, social innovation can be understood as: 'a hybrid. It builds on empirical analysis and thereby benefits from the legitimising area of the scientific method. But it is simultaneously characterised by an indeterminate quality that makes it adaptable to a variety of situations and flexible enough to follow the twists and turns of policy that everyday politics sometimes make necessary' (European Commission 2013b: 13).

This ambiguity and fluidity of meaning may well explain why social innovation has gained such popularity and apparent policy momentum over recent years. Beyond its capacity to affect social change in an innovative manner, there is little agreement as to the nature, role, and purpose of social innovation. Due to the conceptual and empirical malleability of the term, social innovation has the capacity to 'be many things to many people' (Grimm et al. 2013). Indeed, apparently bi-partisan, cross-sectoral interest in social innovation does not necessarily reflect a re-alignment of values, practices, and interests. Rather, it may well be that the indefinite character of social innovation is able to accommodate a plurality of applications and motivations:

> This is also a part of the explanation of why social innovation is gaining speed. Today, there is no definite consensus about the term 'social innovation'. There is a range of definitions and interpretations around, in which linguistic nuances and different social, economic, cultural, and administrative traditions play a role.
> (European Commission 2013b: 5)

Social innovation appears, then, as a bundle of ideas and models that are politically malleable and that can operate as a convenient consensus-building bridging concept through which widespread policy support for ostensibly progressive or 'social' projects can be built. In this sense, social innovation policy is at once politically malleable and strangely apolitical with crucial questions of power and governance regularly sidestepped.

This chapter has two objectives. First, it will establish how the concept of social innovation has been understood, applied, and managed in pan-European policy agendas over recent years. Second, the chapter will examine the key policy agendas from the perspective of institutions, cognitive frames, and networks.

Conceptualizing Social Innovation Policy

There are a number of conceptual and empirical challenges in seeking to map differences and commonalities between social innovation policy agendas at the domestic and pan-European level. This chapter serves partly as a data collection exercise to identify how social innovation is understood and supported at the EU level. This is a necessary step to identify the different contextual factors that give rise to marginalization, social innovation, and particular policy responses. However, the diversity of the social, economic, and institutional environments considered in this research makes it difficult to track systematically, let alone compare, how social innovation operates and the conditions under which it flourishes.

However, a distinction can be drawn between 'policies for social innovation' and 'policies as social innovation'. 'Policies for social innovation' include those designed to support social institutional entrepreneurship, social service entrepreneurship, and social change entrepreneurship. 'Policies as social innovation' denote measures fostering public-sector innovation through social policy entrepreneurship and social entrepreneurship policymaking via regulations, fiscal policy, and public procurement.

This, perhaps, goes some way to explaining why the popularity of, and interest in the term have gained such momentum in recent years. The conception of social innovation and its potential within the EU was largely shaped by the definition of social innovation employed by the European Commission. At first, the European Commission was reluctant to commit to one definition because it was believed that 'social innovation, as a new and emerging concept, cannot be encapsulated within a tight definition with strictly designated objectives and means' (BEPA 2010: 30). The Bureau of European Policy Advisers (BEPA) argued that there were a number of facets to social innovation that needed to be attended to or accommodated within a common working definition employed by the European Union:

> Social Innovation relates to the development of new forms of organisation and interactions to respond to social issues (the process dimension). It aims at addressing (the outcome dimension):
>
> 1. Social demands that are traditionally not addressed by the market or existing institutions and are directed towards vulnerable groups in society.
> 2. Societal challenges in which the boundary between 'social' and 'economic' blurs, and which are directed towards society as a whole.
> 3. The need to reform society in the direction of a more participative arena where empowerment and learning are sources and outcomes of wellbeing (BEPA 2010).

According to BEPA, these objectives of social innovation were not mutually exclusive. Meeting social demands, societal challenges, and encouraging empowerment as a source and outcome of wellbeing were understood as interdependent and mutually reinforcing objectives of social innovation. Innovations that addressed social needs were able to address societal challenges, and through the development of new forms of organization and social interaction it was possible to facilitate empowerment and active participation.

European Union Policy Frameworks

The EU has supported a range of measures designed to instigate, embed, and support social innovation. These measures are generally considered 'rich but scattered' (BEPA 2010: 46), operating across diverse policy domains and different socio-structural levels. Nonetheless, there were three core policy frameworks that underpinned and gave cohesion to these activities. These were the Europe 2020 strategy (2010–20), the Social Business Initiative and the Social Investment Package. These policy frameworks provided an overall logic and organizational structure to the social innovation policy in practice. Significantly, they also articulated the broader social, political, and economic objectives of the EU towards which social innovation policies were intended to contribute. However, social innovation policies have to be viewed within their broader setting to appreciate how public bodies and actors mediate countervailing priorities, interests, and challenges.

Europe 2020

Europe 2020 was the European Union's jobs and growth strategy, which ran from 2010 to 2020 and was conceived as the 'overarching framework for a range of policies at the EU and national level. In particular, the strategy has served as a guide for the design and programming of the European Structural and Investment Funds over 2014–2020' (European Commission 2015a: 1). The primary objective of the strategy was to create the conditions and environment for 'smart, inclusive, and sustainable economic growth'. The overall priorities of Europe 2020 included significant investments in education, research, development and innovation, sustainable energy consumption, and a strong focus on job creation and poverty reduction. These priorities were operationalized in the following targets to be met by 2020, which aimed to:

- Increase the proportion of the working-age population in employment to 75 per cent
- Invest 3 per cent of the EU's GDP in research and development
- Reduce greenhouse gas emissions by 20 per cent compared to the 1990 level
- Increase the share of renewables in final energy consumption to 20 per cent
- Increase energy efficiency by 20 per cent
- Reduce the proportion of early school-leavers to below 10 per cent

- Increase the proportion of 30 to 34 year olds who have completed tertiary education to at least 40 per cent
- Lift at least 20 million people out of the risk of poverty or social exclusion.

Seven flagship initiatives were conceived to realize the objectives of Europe 2020: Digital Agenda for Europe; Innovation Union; Youth on the Move; Resource Efficient Europe; Industrial Policy for the Globalisation Era; an Agenda for New Skills and Jobs; and the European Platform against Poverty and Social Exclusion. Despite the claim that 'social innovation is often reflected in the provisions of these initiatives' (European Commission 2014a: 60), not all of the seven flagship initiatives engendered a commitment to social innovation. In addition, the Digital Agenda for Europe purported to deliver sustainable economic and social benefits, but the legislative actions within it do not pay adequate attention to social, cultural, or economic dimensions for tackling marginalization and facilitating social innovation.

The Innovation Union Initiative aimed to create an environment in which innovation could flourish, so that ideas could be turned into products and services. While this initiative articulated a more explicit commitment to the social dimensions of innovation, social innovation only featured in one of its ten substantive objectives. The majority of the Innovation Union objectives focus on enhancing the capacity of research, development, and innovation, and translating this into economic benefits and growth for Europe. By contrast, the one objective concerning social innovation emphasized its capacity and potential to instigate economic growth but *also* to address social problems. To realize this latter objective, a number of measures and actions were taken that focused on social innovation specifically in the context of public-sector innovation:

- Establishing the Social Innovation Europe virtual hub (SIE) for social entrepreneurs, policy-makers and the third sector
- Piloting a European Public-Sector Innovation Scoreboard to measure, but also champion the extent of innovation in the design and delivery of public services within member states. This was also intended to open up opportunities for dialogue and policy transfer
- Strong promotion of social innovation as a focus and objective through key funding instruments such as the European Social Fund, the Progress Programme (2007–13) and the EU Programme for Employment and Social Innovation (2014–20)
- Investment in a significant research programme on social innovation and public-sector innovation to explore measurement, evaluation, finance, and barriers to scaling up and development
- Piloting a network of social innovation incubators to assess, support, and scale up (TRANSITION)

- Supporting innovative social experiments through the European Social Fund and the European Platform against Poverty and Social Exclusion
- Introducing five European Innovation Partnerships which bring together EU, national, and regional actors for joint investment and to collaborate on challenges and issues facing Europe. Two of these partnerships focus on active and healthy ageing, and smart cities and communities.

Another flagship initiative, Youth on the Move, aimed to increase labour market integration and mobility, while also improving the rate and quality of education and training received by the young working-age population of Europe. A range of actions was introduced focusing on lifelong learning, higher education, learning mobility, vocational education, and training. The value of innovation was principally understood as a vector of growth in the knowledge economy that needed to be supported through increased education, training, research, and development. However, at the *strategic* level, there was little, if any, substantive demonstration that social innovation featured as part of the Youth on the Move initiative.

An Agenda for New Skills and Jobs came closer to specifying how 'inclusive growth' might be achieved. The initiative outlined a number of priorities to address the challenges of structural unemployment, global competitive pressures, and a shrinking working-age population. These included better functioning labour markets supported by job creation and 'flexicurity' policies, a more skilled workforce and better quality jobs and working conditions. The European Commission suggested that these priorities were 'essential for the scaling up of social innovation' or indirectly contributed to 'wider social innovation' (European Commission 2014a: 65). However, the actions and instruments underpinning the initiative did not clearly represent 'new responses to pressing social demands' (European Commission 2013b: 6).

The final flagship initiative was the European Platform against Poverty and Social Exclusion. The Platform was established to reduce the share of the total population at risk of poverty or social exclusion (AROPE) in the European Union. It aimed to tackle poverty and social exclusion by delivering actions across the policy spectrum; protecting and making better use of funds to support social inclusion; promoting evidence-based innovations in social policy and incorporating civil-society actors and organizations into the design and delivery of inclusion strategies. The European Commission also proposed that 20 per cent of the European Social Fund be earmarked to tackle poverty and social exclusion, and called for greater policy coordination between EU countries through the open method of coordination for social protection and social inclusion, and through the Social Protection Committee.

Both the European Commission and a number of its Directorates-General considered the Europe 2020 policy agenda to be the most explicit commitment to the idea, practice, means, and ends of social innovation in the EU. Europe 2020 has been said to encapsulate a social innovation approach and ideal (European Commission 2014a). However, upon closer inspection, there was, on occasion, little in the way of social innovation in the detail of the strategy. The overall priority was to 'move decisively beyond the crisis and create the conditions for a more competitive economy with higher employment'. The relative *separation* of the social and economic objectives of Europe 2020 belied the integrated social market economy model espoused by political and policy leaders, and somewhat contradicted the Bureau of European Policy Advisers' (BEPA) suggestion that a 'social innovation culture has spread in support of the Europe 2020 strategy and its implementation' (European Commission 2014a: 9).

Social Business Initiative

The second policy framework that established social innovation on the EU's policy agenda was the Social Business Initiative (SBI). Launched in 2011, the SBI was a product of the Single Market Act I. The Act outlined a series of structural reforms to integrate the European market economy, boost growth, and strengthen confidence in the economic and monetary union. In addition, though, the Single Market Act I also encouraged the European Commission to 'continue to improve its coverage of the social dimension of the impact assessments which accompany legislative proposals concerning the internal market' (European Commission 2011b: 5). As part of this, the European Commission developed twelve key actions that included mobility for citizens, intellectual property rights, taxation reform, and consumer empowerment (European Commission 2011a). A number of other actions were also launched that had the capacity to support social innovation:

- *Access to finance for SMEs*: making it easier for venture capital funds established in a member state to invest freely in any other member state, without obstacles or additional requirements.
- *Public procurement*: revising and modernizing public procurement legislative frameworks, with a view to underpinning a balanced policy which fosters demand for environmentally sustainable, socially responsible, and innovative foods, services, and works. It was hoped this revision would result in simpler and more flexible procurement procedures for contracting authorities.
- *Social cohesion*: improving and reinforcing the EU Posted Workers Directive by enforcing and sanctioning any circumvention of the applicable rules, to protect freedom of establishment and freedom of association, alongside other fundamental social rights. The rationale for this action was to realize the ambitions of a 'social market economy by ensuring, with no race to the

bottom, that businesses are able to provide their services . . . while at the same time providing more high quality jobs and a high level of protection for workers and their social rights' (European Commission 2011: 17).
- *Social entrepreneurship*: creating a level playing field for 'social purpose' organizations in terms of their mobility, the economic environment within which they operate, their legal status, and the regulations to which they are subject.

By supporting businesses motivated by social, cultural, and environmental commitments, the European Commission argued it should be possible 'to introduce more fairness in the economy and contribute to the fight against social exclusion' (European Commission 2011a: 14). To help organizations realize their objectives relating to social, ethical, or environmental development, the European Commission proposed to develop legal models better adapted to their needs, set up a European framework facilitating the development of social investment funds a,nd establish the Social Business Initiative.

The Act also announced a new Commission on corporate social responsibility that led to a new EU strategy encouraging businesses to pursue actions with social or environmental objectives as part of their daily activities: the Social Business Initiative. The SBI was designed to create a favourable climate for social enterprises and key stakeholders in the social economy. Outlining the rationale for the initiative, the European Commission stated that the 'single market needs new, inclusive growth, focused on employment for all, underpinning the growing desire of Europeans for their work, consumption, savings and investments to be more closely attuned to and aligned with ethical and social principles' (European Commission 2011b: 2). As part of the SBI, social enterprises were championed as a key mechanism for inclusive economic growth that contributed to social cohesion and responded to unmet need through social innovation. The European Commission defined a 'social enterprise' as the following types of business: those for which the social or societal objective of the common good is the reason for their commercial activity, often in the form of a high level of social innovation; those where profits are mainly reinvested with a view to achieving this social objective; and those where the method of organization or ownership system reflects their mission, using democratic or participatory principles or focusing on social justice.

Such definitions captured the potential for a social enterprise or 'social business' to contribute towards social and economic transformation. As part of the SBI, a range of measures sought to:

- Improve access to financial markets, private funding mechanisms, and social investment funds through favourable regulation

- Improve analysis, promotion, and development of the legal and institutional environment for micro-finance
- Encourage micro-finance by issuing guarantees for lending to social enterprises
- Mobilize European Union funds through the European Regional Development Fund and European Social Fund to prioritize the capacity-building, activities, and impact of social entrepreneurship
- Develop tools to gain a better understanding of the sector and increase the visibility of social entrepreneurship
- Reinforce the managerial capacities, professionalism, and networking of social business
- Develop appropriate legal forms which could be used in European social entrepreneurship
- Enhance the element of quality in awarding contracts in the context of the reform of public procurement, especially in the case of social and health services
- Simplify the implementation of rules concerning state aid to social and local services.

In January 2014, the Strasbourg Declaration was signed as a follow-up to the SBI. The Declaration outlined a series of agreed recommendations to continue developing the potential of social entrepreneurship across the EU. The European Economic and Social Committee established a working group to implement a set of substantive actions stemming from the declaration (European Commission 2014e).

In sum, the SBI demonstrated a sustained strategic commitment to the actors and organizations engaged in features of social innovation. These commitments ranged broadly from light-touch regulation encouraging corporate social responsibility amongst for-profit businesses to more heavy-handed regulative frameworks, funding mechanisms and knowledge creation to enhance the capacity of social enterprises and social purpose organizations.

Social Investment Package

The third policy agenda was the Social Investment Package (SIP). While social protection and stabilization of the economy have been recognized as core functions of the welfare state, the EU also emphasized the value and potential of the third function of the welfare state: *social* investment. As a response to the economic crisis of 2008/9, the European Parliament launched the SIP in 2013 as an integrated framework designed to help European public authorities modernize and reform their social and public services.

The SIP encouraged member states to 'use their social budgets more efficiently and more effectively and to tackle the social consequences of the crisis by identifying best practices and providing guidance on the use of EU funds for social investment' (European Commission 2013c: 3). The European Commission argued that public policies and finances should focus more on preventative measures and actions. As part of this strategy, the European Commission claimed that member states should be investing in people or 'human capital', so that public authorities would be able to reap the maximum social and economic 'dividends' on their 'social investment'. The implementation of the SIP included measures to tackle childhood inequality; improve the sustainability and provision of healthcare; enhance personalized social services; tackle gender inequality; modernize pension systems; reduce poverty and improve employment and activation services (European Commission 2014d).

The European Commission identified social issues principally as a threat to the sustainability of EU welfare regimes, and they were understood as functionally disruptive (European Commission 2015b). The SIP was seen as a key strategy to make the best use of limited financial resources to address these issues—notably growing poverty and social exclusion (European Commission 2013c). The ambition to move from a 'welfare state model' to a 'social investment state model' was understood as a key means by which to cope with the social effects of macroeconomic shifts, demographic changes, and globalization (European Commission 2013c).

According to the SIP, 'social innovation (and social policy experimentation), need to be embedded in mainstream policymaking and connected to social priorities' (European Commission 2014e: 72). The SIP shaped member states' policy reforms in the framework of the European Semester. Moreover, the performance of member states was monitored through indicators underpinning the employment and poverty targets of the Europe 2020 strategy. The reforms set out in the SIP were wide-ranging and focused on the social dimensions of the European Semester.

Member states were expected to realize key objectives by making use of EU financial and non-financial support services for social policy experimentation, testing new approaches to social policies and scaling the most effective innovations, exchanging experiences and expertise and exploring new financing mechanisms such as Social Impact Bonds.

Crucially, the SIP approach focused on methods of activation that prioritized individual solutions and interventions to socio-structural causes of marginalization and resource scarcity. Indeed, a great deal of the SIP focused on reforming public services and social policies in a way that better equipped people with the knowledge, skills, resilience, and resources to adapt to social risks. This end goal of 'adaptation' was particularly interesting given the European Commission's focus on the structural factors propagating marginalization and resource scarcity

(European Commission 2013c). Rather than addressing the structural causes of social exclusion, the SIP advocated a 'preventative' strategy based on 'activating and enabling policies' that improve social inclusion through access to the labour market.

Regulatory Frameworks

To improve the regulatory environment for actors and organizations engaged in social innovation, the European Commission introduced a number of measures to instigate a change in public procurement practices, state aid regulations, and the legal status of organizations engaged in social innovation. In fact, some of the primary actions of the SBI were designed to improve legal and regulatory frameworks so that actors and organizations could more effectively produce or execute social innovations. Governance and reporting mechanisms, such as the open method of coordination for social protection and social inclusion, and the Social Protection Committee, helped monitor the extent to which EU member states were supporting social innovation or public-sector innovation. A variety of impact assessments examined the economic, social, and environmental impact of regulations. However, the European Commission has also made a number of efforts to affect the regulatory and legal frameworks that have a bearing on the capacity for socially innovative activities. These actions principally focused on facilitating cross-border activity as part of the wider project of EU integration.

Privileged Legal Status

Introduced in 2006, the European Cooperative Society was a legal entity in company law that enabled cooperatives to bypass the need to establish a subsidiary in each EU member state within which they operated. A study on the implementation of the European Cooperative Society found that the regulation had only limited success. This was due, in part, to the fact that there has been low uptake (only seventeen organizations), but it was also due to a lack of harmonization. More recently, the European Commission also funded data collection, organized events, and ran a consultation process on the need to amend the existing legislation.

In 2012, the European Commission published a proposal for a new regulation for a 'European Foundation'. Designed to support public benefit purpose foundations undertaking cross-border activity, it was hoped that the legal status of the 'European Foundation' would reduce the bureaucratic and administrative burden of operating across EU member states. Very often, foundations engaged in activities in more than one country were faced with legal and administrative obstacles that meant they were compelled to commit financial and non-financial resources to navigating these challenges. By creating a single European legal form, the European Commission hoped it would be possible to overcome some of these challenges. Organizations taking this new legal status would operate alongside domestic foundations.

In 2013, the European Parliament adopted a specific resolution with recommendations on the Statute for a European Mutual Society. This statute was principally motivated by a desire to reduce the legal and administrative burden for mutual societies undertaking cross-border activities. The European Commission aimed to support cooperatives across Europe by guaranteeing 'that enterprises of this type, independently of their size, can continue to operate in the market by preserving their social role, particular style of functioning, and ethics' (European Commission 2014a: 100).

Favourable Procurement and Commissioning Guidelines

One of the key actions of the SBI was to emphasize social value metrics in public-sector procurement and commissioning guidelines. This led to the adoption of new regulations on public procurement in several sectors (European Commission 2014b), utilities (European Commission 2014c), and a new directive on specific concessions (European Commission 2014c). The aims of the new public procurement rules included contributing to the implementation of environmental, social inclusion, and innovation policies.

These new regulations enhanced the competitiveness of actors and organizations engaged in social innovation—specifically in terms of their ability to bid for public-sector contracts and deliver public services. This included reducing the administrative and financial burden incurred by organizations engaged in public-sector procurement and bidding, providing clear and simple rules awarding concession contracts, and eliminating price as the sole award criteria for the procurement of social and health services. This enhanced the competitive advantage of smaller organizations engaged in social innovation.

The regulations also enabled public authorities to consider the long-term social value of certain contracts, such that they could factor into their consideration how public services or goods might be delivered, purchased, or produced if a particular provider were to be awarded the contract. In addition, for some social services it was possible to reserve contracts for not-for-profit organizations that had a public service remit based on employee participation. Reserved procurement procedures enabled 'sheltered workshops' or social enterprises to participate provided that 30 per cent of their workforce was deemed 'disadvantaged'. Previously, social enterprises working for the inclusion of disadvantaged groups were required to be able to define at least 50 per cent of their workforce as 'disadvantaged'. This possibly enabled social enterprises to compete for contracts on a more competitive basis due to their lower—social—operating costs.

Social Innovation Funding and Finance

European Regional Development Fund

The principal objective of the European Regional Development Fund (ERDF) was to address the key regional imbalances within the European Union. The fund was, therefore, concerned with economic regeneration and development, territorial cooperation, and increasing competitiveness. There was also a particular focus on reducing economic, environmental, and social problems in urban areas. For the period from 2007 to 2013, the overall budget totalled €210 billion. For the period from 2014 to 2020, the budget fell to €183 billion. While the EU allocated the funds, member states and managing authorities controlled the funding and were able to exercise some degree of discretion in how the funds were used. This was borne out by the variation across the regions and territories in terms of how these funds were used. While the majority of the investment priorities did not formally focus on social innovation, the regulations outlined for the European Regional Development Fund stated that:

> It is necessary to promote innovation and the development of SMEs, in emerging fields linked to European and regional challenges such as creative and cultural industries and innovative services, reflecting new societal demands, or to products and services linked to an ageing population, care and health, eco-innovation, the low-carbon economy and resource efficiency.
>
> (European Commission 2013a: 290)

In addition, one investment priority focused on supporting social enterprises to promote social inclusion and combat poverty and discrimination. This opened up the opportunity for significant investments which could scale the capacity and impact of social innovation. However, there was little substantive specification of what this support could and should entail.

Perhaps in an attempt to ensure social innovation featured in funding outcomes, a number of changes were made to the regulations surrounding ERDF 2014–2020.

European Social Fund

The European Social Fund (ESF) was designed to reduce inequalities across and within EU member states, and promote economic and social cohesion (SIE 2011).

Between 2007 and 2013, around €75 billion were distributed to member states—representing around a tenth of the total EU budget. During this period, the proportion of funds allocated to social innovation varied across member states, but generally ranged from between 1 per cent to 5 per cent of the total funding received by the country in question (European Commission 2013c). It is estimated that more than €2 billion of these funds were dedicated to public-sector innovation, and more than €1 billion were dedicated to innovative activities designed to support the development of skills and combat unemployment (European Commission 2013c).

For the period 2014 to 2020, member states negotiated the funds they received from the ESF. Member states partially matched the funding received through the ESF, and managing authorities in member states then distributed these funds to operational programmes. These programmes aimed to support local and specialist organizations to deliver a range of employment-related projects. While member states and managing authorities were, to some extent, able to interpret the strategic priorities of the ESF, the funding priorities were principally negotiated and agreed at the EU level. The strategic priorities of the ESF from 2014 to 2020 focused on 'getting people into jobs' by providing opportunities to obtain training, qualifications, and skills with a view to finding gainful employment, promoting social inclusion, enhancing the educational outcomes, skills, and training received by young people, and improving the quality of public administration and governance. According to the European Commission, the ESF represented the EU's biggest 'human capital investment', with almost €80 billion committed between 2014 and 2020.

The ESF was committed to promoting social innovation within all areas falling under its scope. This commitment was aimed at 'testing, evaluating, and scaling up innovative solutions, including at the local or regional level, in order to address social needs in partnership with the relevant partners and in particular, social partners' (European Commission 2013d: 477). Across policy areas, the ESF intended to ensure social innovation contributed towards the headline targets of Europe 2020. As a condition of their funding, member states were required to identify fields of social innovation that corresponded to their specific needs. This could be undertaken during the development of operational programmes or at a later stage. Each operational programme co-financed by the ESF would have to demonstrate how planned actions contributed towards social innovation (European Commission 2013b).

A particular aim of the ESF was to support innovation and experimentation by measuring evidence-based solutions and selecting the most effective ideas before scaling them on a larger level. In addition to a dedicated social innovation facility in the new ESF regulations, the European Commission also proposed support for innovative policies and public services that were responsive to social change.

Through the ESF, social innovation was only officially recognized and supported in a way that reproduced existing social relations. While it may have been innovatively social in its *means*, the activities and objectives funded were not innovatively social in their *ends*. That is, the existing funding structures limited the capacity for social innovation significantly in terms of disrupting or altering 'the process of social interactions' (European Commission 2013b). While social innovation did occur that was genuinely transformative as a result of the ESF, this was largely a by-product rather than an explicit objective of operational programmes. This limitation was, perhaps, propagated by the lack of systematic evidence collected on how the funds were used to support social innovation (TEPSIE 2014).

European Union Programme for Employment and Social Innovation

The Employment and Social Innovation Programme (EaSI) was a much smaller financing instrument designed to support employment, social policy, and EU labour mobility. The European Commission claimed that 'the concept of social innovation, which has a special focus on youth, is at the heart of EaSI' (European Commission 2013a: 7).

This integrated programme was originally going to be called the Programme for Social Change and Innovation, but was later renamed to reflect its changing focus. With a total budget of €919.5 million, the Programme for Employment and Social Innovation, which ran from 2014 to 2020, focused on:

- Supporting the development of adequate social protection systems and labour market policies, and promoting good governance, mutual learning, and social innovation by modernizing employment and social policies with the PROGRESS axis (61 per cent of the total budget)
- Promoting geographical mobility and boosting employment opportunities through the development an open labour market with the EURES axis (18 per cent of the total budget), increasing the availability and accessibility of microfinance for vulnerable groups and micro-enterprises, and increasing access to finance for social enterprises through the Microfinance and Social Entrepreneurship axis (21 per cent of the total budget).

The PROGRESS axis, or the Programme for Employment and Social Solidarity, was the EU's main instrument for promoting welfare reforms through employment and social policy experimentation. The programme aimed to contribute towards fulfilling the targets of the Europe 2020 strategy by identifying innovative methods of designing and delivering public services so that these were more responsive to the social and economic needs of EU member states. Between

2009 and 2013, PROGRESS funded twenty-three projects on social policy experimentation, with a total budget of €21.4 million (European Commission 2014e).

Between 2014 and 2020, PROGRESS committed between €10 and €14 million each year to test labour market policy innovations and social policy experimentation, looking at methods, processes, and finances. Overall, PROGRESS aimed to:

- Increase the capacity of organizations to contribute towards the implementation of European Union strategies
- Finance labour market and social policy innovations
- Support the development of an analytical and comparative evidence base that could lead to effective information-sharing, mutual learning, and dialogue, to share and learn from best practice in social innovation.

Once again, innovation (social or otherwise) was only accommodated and supported in a way that was financially and strategically valued by EU public bodies and activities.

Beyond the funding programmes already discussed in this section, various EU bodies were also involved in a range of other regulatory and funding initiatives that, in some measure, were designed to create economic space for actors and organizations engaged in social innovation. These initiatives focused on financial operations that ranged broadly from increasing the availability of microcredit and microfinance to supporting infrastructure projects which could grant access to larger capital markets for social businesses or organizations engaged in social innovation.

In 2011, the European Commission published a European Code of Good Conduct for Microcredit Provision, which outlined a set of recommendations and standards to encourage and foster good practice in the microcredit sector. Developed in collaboration with stakeholders and practitioners across the small but growing European microcredit market, the Code of Good Conduct sought to address some of the main challenges facing the sector.

Developed during the programming period between 2007 and 2013, the European Commission provided technical assistance to microcredit institutions through a range of special support instruments. These included:

- JEREMIE (Joint European Resources for Micro to Medium Enterprises): promotes the use of financial engineering instruments to improve access to finance for small to medium-sized enterprises through European Structural and Investment Fund interventions.
- JESSICA (Joint European Support for Sustainable Investment in City Areas): supports sustainable urban development and regeneration through financial engineering mechanisms.

- JASMINE (Joint Actions to Support Micro-finance Institutions in Europe): seeks to improve access to finance for small businesses.
- JASPERS (Joint Assistance to Support Projects in European Regions): offers technical assistance to twelve member states that joined the European Union between 2004 and 2007.

In 2013, the Regulation on European Social Entrepreneurship Funds (EuSEF) was established to create a label so that investors were easily able to identify funds which invest in European social businesses. Provided funds met certain criteria, social enterprise funds would be able to use the new label and market their funds across Europe. In order to use the label, social enterprise funds had to ensure that at least 70 per cent of their funds were 'invested in businesses whose primary aim is to provide goods and services to vulnerable, marginalized, disadvantaged, or excluded people, use a method of production of goods and services that embodies its social objectives or provide financial support only to social businesses that are trying to achieve those ends' (European Commission 2014e: 106).

Under these new regulations, organizations using the European Social Entrepreneurship Fund label were required to measure the social impact of their funds and ensure profits distributed to investors did not undermine the objectives of the social businesses supported. European Social Entrepreneurship Funds could also only invest in social businesses that did not currently have access to capital markets to fund their operations or growth.

Following the launch of a Taskforce for a European Social Investment Facility, the European Investment Fund also established the Social Impact Accelerator—the first public–private partnership supporting social enterprises. The Social Impact Accelerator invested in social impact funds targeting social enterprises across Europe. The aim of the initiative was to address the emerging need for social enterprises to access equity finance.

The European Investment Fund rationalized this initiative by highlighting the increasingly prevalent role of social enterprises in tackling social exclusion and promoting alternative forms of employment for 'disadvantaged' groups. The Social Impact Accelerator was considered to be the first step in cultivating a sustainable funding market for social enterprises across Europe. It was hoped that this would be achieved by developing a financial market infrastructure that supported the operation of organizations seeking a social impact.

The Social Impact Accelerator sought to support funds that, in addition to financial return targets, also pursued explicit social impact targets through their portfolio of investments. The European Investment Bank managed the fund, and Crédit Coopératif and Deutsche Bank also funded the scheme. Fifty-three million euros were dedicated to the accelerator. For the purposes of the scheme, the European Investment Bank also developed its own specific definition of social enterprises and a methodological approach to measuring social impact.

The European Commission also undertook public consultation on crowdfunding to identify opportunities and costs associated with this emerging form of finance. As well as a form of social innovation in itself, this funding model also opens up economic space for social innovation projects. In 2014, the European Commission published a Communication that set out a number of measures to encourage growth of this form of finance. This included establishing an expert group on crowdfunding to provide advice and expertise to the Commission, raising awareness of crowdfunding and its benefits and mapping national regulatory developments to support, where possible, optimal functioning of the internal market (European Commission 2014f). The European Commission also supported a number of crowdfunding stakeholder fora.

As awareness around the needs, opportunities, and challenges facing social innovation organizations increased, the European Commission responded accordingly. The European Commission has, via research and public consultation, explored the changing financial needs of the social economy, and either provided funds for capacity-building and social innovation projects, or opened up access to private and larger capital markets for organizations engaged in social innovation through new regulation or market infrastructure.

In addition to the policy measures outlined above, the European Commission has also supported a wide-ranging body of research that has sought to identify barriers to social innovation as well as identify measures and instances of best practice. This body of research has aimed to act as an evidence base to make the case for future interventions as well as to inform future policy direction. The Commission has also supported applied networks, capacity building, incubation, peer learning, knowledge exchange, and networking. These efforts were not only intended to support private actors and organizations engaged in social innovation, but also to encourage public-sector innovation so that public authorities were better able to meet the evolving needs and expectations of public service users. The definition of social innovation endorsed by the European Commission promoted the active participation and empowerment of European citizens as a source and outcome of well-being.

There has, on occasion, been a mismatch between the strategic objectives of the EU and the measures taken to realize these ambitions. This mismatch arose from the tensions and limitations inherent in any social innovation which is supported by existing institutions that are the product of, or have a significant bearing on, socio-structural dynamics, power relations, and cognitive frames. Within this context, the EU has often only supported social innovation within the parameters deemed strategically and financially valuable by other policy priorities. Where the ideals and ends of social innovation have competed too strongly with other priorities of the EU, it appears that the underlying ideals have either been lost in translation or sacrificed to countervailing concerns. The blurring of the boundary between the social and economic against the backdrop of fiscal austerity has been particularly troubling in this regard.

EU policy documentation and rhetoric has used the term social innovation interchangeably to refer to a very broad range of activities, processes, and outcomes. Very often, the term social innovation has been used in a way that does not accurately represent the phenomenon or definition endorsed by the European Commission. Moreover, post hoc identification and justification of initiatives has made it particularly difficult to track social innovation, and in particular, the effect of EU public policy purportedly designed to support it.

Having surveyed the key policy instruments enacting social innovation policy agendas across the EU, this chapter will now turn to an analysis of these policies from an institutionalist perspective.

Social Innovation Policy and the Extended Social Grid Model

As was discussed in chapter 1, the Extended Social Grid Model (ESGM) is made up of three interrelated social forces: institutions, social networks, and cognitive frames (Beckert 2010; Nicholls and Ziegler 2014). According to the model, these three social forces do not exist in isolation—they operate in dialectic with one another. Thus, the social dynamics between institutions, social networks, and cognitive frames will have some bearing on the prevalence of marginalization within a given society and the capacity for social innovation to address this.

The ESGM sensitizes policy analysis to the multi-level realities of policy development and implementation. From the international to the local level, institutions profoundly affect social relations and the capabilities of EU citizens. Policies, laws, and regulations control the (re-)distribution of resources and services. This influences the extent to which individuals are marginalized from common experiences and opportunities available across the EU. Political, economic, and social institutions reproduce rules and norms that can constrain or enhance social innovation to address these phenomena. Social networks existing between and within EU member states determine the structure of social divisions. Patterned relations between individuals, groups, and communities will dictate whether a particular social innovation is suitable, how it might work and what its effects could be. Finally, dominant attitudes (or cognitive frames) inform how socio-economic phenomena are understood and explained by the general public and policy-makers. Shared or common interpretations of societal challenges frame what solutions are conceived as possible or appropriate. For example, established ways of thinking and assumptions about the causes of poverty and social exclusion inform policy responses to marginalization and the extent to which social innovation is seen as a solution. This has four important implications for social innovation policy agendas.

First, attending to the dynamics of the ESGM as opportunities for social innovation requires policy-makers to conceptualize issues such as marginalization as the product of macro-level socio-economic structures. To date, such conceptualizations have been poorly attended to in the policymaking process at both the domestic and European level. For example, a policy initiative may attempt to challenge public perceptions of Roma communities (cognitive frames) or increase civic engagement (social networks) but may not address the institutional factors and social dynamics that have such a bearing on its success.

Second, the implementation of social innovation policy has often occurred without a wide and deep consideration of the factors that may affect its potential and effects. Very often, social innovation initiatives or funding have not fully accounted for external costs and constraints.

Third, ex ante and ex post evaluations of social innovation policy have often overlooked the reflexive and, thus, diffuse effects of policy on the three social forces within the ESGM.

Finally, while public policies have the capacity to disrupt social relations and alter the dynamics of the ESGM, the model also shapes and constrains the development and implementation of policy itself. This process of institutional structuration is iterative and constant and has significant effects on how public policy conceptualizes and responds to the causes and effects of marginalization, as well as how social innovation might be seen as a policy solution and in what contexts.

Therefore, marginalization and social innovation can be seen as embedded within a set of co-dependent relationships. Social innovation will inevitably have some bearing (positive or negative) on marginalization, but equally, marginalization shapes the capacity and character of social innovation processes. Once understood as such, analysis of social innovation takes on a novel form requiring a clear understanding of the patterns of institutional dominance and hierarchies of power that shape and sustain policy issues.

This process has two elements. First, policy-makers must recognize and overcome their own institutional dominance. As Edmiston (2016: 2) noted:

> In seeking to identify how policy might best foster disruptive social innovation, public bodies are faced with a perennial challenge: how to unsettle and destabilise the institutional dominance upon which, thus far, publicly-sponsored social innovation has been so greatly dependent. That is, how to mobilise resource and activity that is essentially systemic without compromising the means and ends from which social innovation derives its value.

Reducing the institutional dominance of policy-makers within the policy process is, of course, difficult. This involves both self-reflexivity and institutional entrepreneurship. It may also involve significant courage. As Baumgartner et al. (2006: 961) wrote:

> As new participants with fresh ideas break into the inner circle of policy-making, the system is jolted . . . the common core of policy agenda research is attention to the dynamics of how new ideas, new policy proposals, and new understandings of problems may or may not be accepted in the political system.

A major barrier to such self-reflexivity and change has been the apparently apolitical character of social innovation policy in the EU. Absent a conceptualization of the power dynamics of political systems, revisions of hierarchies and dominance within policy development and implementation becomes literally inconceivable. As a result, public policy directed at social innovation has often been open to institutional and cognitive capture by the current dominant policy discourses that limits its transformative potential. Moreover, despite a plurality of applications and motivations, public policy agendas supporting social innovation rely upon and exploit hybrid networks of power that risk reproducing, rather than altering existing socio-structural relations (Mann 1986)—this is most clearly evidenced by the centralization of policymaking power within Brussels. To unlock the full transformative potential of social innovation policy, therefore, both a reassessment of the dominance of normative ideological frames and a relaxing of centralized policy control are needed. Each issue is considered in turn next.

The second key issue concerns policy centralization. Edmiston (2016) identified a tendency within social innovation policymaking to avoid questions concerning the redistribution of power and resources, while placing much greater emphasis on micro-level questions concerning individual well-being. Thus, within EU social innovation policymaking, the exercise of marginalized agency tends only to be supported and recognized in ways that consolidate the position of the existing decision-making centre. This distracts from the broader and more fundamental question of systemic and socio-structural change that could more effectively address the causes and effects of marginalization. Capabilities associated with individual and collective political action and that could contribute towards a transformation of the decision-making centre rarely receive policy backing or support in EU social innovation policy.

Within the policymaking process, not only ideological dominance but also the power to identify, define, and address societal challenges tends to lie at the political centre within the EU. An examination of EU and domestic social innovation policy suggests this has significant implications (and limitations) for addressing socio-structural disadvantage (Edmiston 2015; Aro and Heiskala 2015; Ziegler et al. 2016). For example, work integration social enterprises that bring excluded populations into the labour market are often presented as a public policy initiative to foster social innovation. Policies and funding to support work integration social enterprises give legitimacy to and shape wider perceptions of institutions while also shifting cognitive frames associated with unemployment and disadvantage. In addition, social innovation policymaking tends to encourage and support stronger networks of coordination between the public, private, and third sectors. As an ancillary objective, these networks of collaboration are put towards a variety of ends. Central to these policy initiatives is an attempt to influence the structure, perceptions an,d capacity of social networks within the social economy. Overall, EU and domestic public policies have supported social networks in a way that contributes towards *incremental*—rather than disruptive—social innovation through the fulfilment of (usually) pre-defined policy objectives. According to Mann (2013: 1), power entails the 'capacity to get others to do things that otherwise they would not do'. In this regard, a transference or realignment of power towards the powerless is central to the political project of social innovation in the EU. Within such a setting, social innovation policy runs the risk of depoliticizing the causes of and solutions to marginalization.

Multi-Level Analysis

From an ESGM perspective, social innovation must always engage with power and politics to achieve systemic change. Furthermore, the dynamics of power and politics will have multiple meanings and engage different actors in different contexts and at different socio-structural levels. Thus, the relationships between social innovation political actors will be significant factors in achieving overall systemic change. There are two formal domains of public policy that are of relevance here (see Nicholls and Edmiston 2015). First, there is policy *for* social innovation that is specifically designed to have a direct bearing on the capacity of agents and organizations to affect structural change through social innovation. Second, there is social innovation in the policymaking process that offers novel approaches to the design and delivery of assistance, services and initiatives that have some bearing on structural relations and/or the well-being of citizens.

However, it is suggested here that the effective development and implementation of social innovation is contingent on a wider coordination of actors at different levels of political action beyond government alone. This has significant implications for the design, delivery, and evaluation of public policies that seek to facilitate social innovation tackling marginalization. However, the irreducibility of the ESGM requires a further level of analysis to be developed if its explanatory value is to be fully realized in terms of power dynamics and socio-structural change around systems and how social innovation can address them. Nicholls and Edmiston (2015) noted that the non-reductive approach taken in the ESGM explained the reflexive relationships that exist between institutions, social networks and cognitive frames, while also seeking to capture the power networks that affect these relationships in terms of their impact on marginalization. In this analysis of the complexity of socio-structural relations, it becomes particularly difficult to anticipate how and which policies might be able to address power imbalances and social forces when the relationships between them are inherently dynamic. To achieve this, therefore, it is necessary to take into account a wider set of power relations at multiple levels to articulate effective social innovation policy agendas. While this appears to have been acknowledged at the centre of the EU, it has been less well implemented. As Edmiston noted (2015: 3):

> The definition of social innovation endorsed by the European Commission promotes the active participation and empowerment of European citizens as a source of and outcome of wellbeing. The European Union has attempted to encourage participatory methods as an approach to domestic policymaking and embed it in networks and organizations engaged in social innovation. However, consultations on existing strategies tend to be more commonplace than initiatives that enable citizens to actually set the social and economic agenda themselves. As such, activities and measures designed to support social innovation tend to be imposed rather than co-constructed by stakeholders at different socio-structural levels. While it is clear that EU public authorities encourage the means of social innovation, there is less cognitive space and institutional support for the ends of social innovation.

As a consequence, the political and power particularities of the institutional, social network, and cognitive elements of the ESGM—in any given case—will be key, as will their dynamic relationships. Furthermore, they can be reclassified in terms of a multi-level schema of power to allow this dimension of analysis to be integrated in the model. Thus, in terms of a political analysis, the three constituent elements of the ESGM can be mapped against specific political loci of action in society (see Table 11.1). *Institutions* map against formal government action and structures as rule-setting bodies. Within this two types of social innovation can be observed: external that focuses on social policy to encourage social innovation outside of government; internal that introduces social innovation into the policymaking process within government. *Social networks* map against a political locus of action linked to power dynamics in and around market structures. Within this, two levels of social innovation are also present: macro-level (social dynamic innovation) action that aims to (re)shape market structures and dynamics; micro-level (social service innovation) action that responds to market as it is. Finally, *cognitive frames* map against a political locus of action that reframes perceptions of issues and solutions typical of social movements and community-led grassroots initiatives. Here too, two types of social innovation can be seen: formal and (semi-)

Table 11.1. A typology of politics in social innovation

Type of social innovation	ESGM referent	Political locus of action	Example
Policy for social Innovation	institutions	government departments (external policy)	Community Interest Company legislation
Social innovation in policymaking	institutions	government departments (internal policy)	Social Impact Bonds
Social dynamic innovation	social networks	social enterprises (systems focus)	Fair Trade
Social service innovation	social networks	social enterprises (welfare focus)	Work Integration Models
Formal social change innovation	cognitive frames	formal social movements	Greenpeace
Informal social change innovation	cognitive frames	informal collective action	Occupy Wall Street

Source: Authors.

permanent organized collective action around a political grievance; informal and impermanent grass-roots clusters of actors around a new idea for change.

This structuralist analysis of politics and power allows the inter-relations of political actors and their agendas to be considered at, and across, different levels of action. It reveals where the drivers of social innovation policy lie and how well or badly they align with related agendas at other socio-structural levels. Such an analysis also helps explain why policy agendas encounter resistance and may fail at the implementation phase. This typology also underlines the observations made above concerning the dangers of institutional dominance and centralization in terms of the effective articulation of social innovation policy agendas.

A second feature of the typology is that it facilitates a granular analysis of the strategic tools employed at different socio-structural levels within the policy process (see Table 11.2). It also demonstrates how these tools relate to strategic objectives. For example, in terms of macro-level government policy to encourage social innovation, the strategic tools will primarily be regulation, fiscal policy, and direct commissioning or investment. The strategic objectives will relate to the successful implementation of desired policy outcomes. In contrast, for social innovation within the policymaking process the strategic tools will be reform-based, typically around new commissioning practices such as the introduction of quasi-markets or outcomes based contracts. The strategic objectives will be the articulation of new policy discourses and frameworks as institutional 'rules of the game' that frame, shape, and constrain the actions of government itself.

Table 11.2. Strategic processes in social innovation

Type of social innovation	ESGM referent	Strategic tools	Strategic objectives
Policy for social innovation	institutions	regulation fiscal policy direct commissioning and investment	policy implementation and outcomes
Social innovation policymaking	institutions	reforms to commissioning practices	policy discourses and frameworks
Social dynamic innovation	social networks	hybridity boundary blurring	new market structures
Social service innovation	social networks	innovative public goods (outputs) new social relations (process)	new markets
Formal social change innovation	cognitive frames	advocacy and protest	cognitive/normative frame shifts
Informal social change innovation	cognitive frames	collective action	localized solidarity and mobilization

Source: Authors.

For social enterprises operating at the meso-level to shape and respond to market environments the strategic tools and objectives will also differ. Social enterprises engaged in social dynamic innovation often focus on boundary-blurring activities by creating new hybrid organizations in order to achieve strategic objectives based on reshaping existing market structures. For example, microcredit represents a new bottom-of-the-pyramid market that links the traditions of development aid to the commercial logics of retail lending and debt in hybrid market format. The consequence is both to give access to finance to poorer borrowers and to reshape how capital markets conceive of the poor as customers—primarily by correcting inaccurate risk assumptions in terms of repayment rates. Social enterprises working on social service innovation, on the other hand, usually focus on strategic objectives that aim to create new markets within existing market structures. The strategic tools employed are often either the creation of innovative public goods (an outputs focus) or forming new social relations (a process focus). An example of the former is Project Impact that offers a new low cost foot-pump to improve irrigation and crop yields for the poorest farmers. An example of the latter is Fair Trade—a new model of the supply chain that passes more of the total value chain to the (poor) producer than in existing practice.

Finally, at the micro- or grass-roots level, organizations engaged in formal social change use the strategic tools of advocacy and protest to shift normative and cognitive frames around a key issue such as Climate Change to a new (in this case more sustainable) equilibrium. For informal social change organizations collective action offers a strategic tool by which to achieve strategic objectives around new localized solidarity and mobilization.

An additional insight from this typology is that to achieve social innovation policy outcomes it may be necessary to achieve consensus and objective alignment across the three levels of action set out here. But this has its hazards too. The multiple framing and pursuit of social innovation in public policy makes it possible to encourage collective action *for* a particular outcome or activity, but this equally detracts from mobilizing resources and individuals *against* the structural determinants of exclusion. For example, if utility maximizing approaches—as enshrined in the dominant neo-liberal policy paradigm in the EU—are presented as *complementary* to, rather than in conflict with, more grass-roots and radical approaches to social innovation, then this runs the risk of presenting both approaches as compatible or mutually conceivable. At a stroke this removes the potential of bottom-up social innovation as a driver of policy reform, disempowering many of the most marginalized communities.

The typology above suggests that, on the contrary, the political subjectivity, local embeddedness, and collective action of marginalized groups may be a key resource for ensuring social innovation policy is able to tackle the structural determinants of marginalization and, thereby, contribute towards systemic and 'positive' social change. This presents a particular challenge for public policy in trying to overcome the paradox of embedded agency that characterizes both institutional entrepreneurship and social innovation. As noted above, it requires, first, a process of self-reflection to recognize institutional dominance and, then, a process of reform to develop new participatory structures by which individuals at different socio-structural levels can engage meaningfully in policy development and implementation. This would be, of course, in itself a social innovation in policymaking.

To achieve this, social innovation policy-makers seeking to improve the human capabilities and empowerment of marginalized individuals would focus on fostering localized and collective action with measures that encourage self-organization. These measures would aim to develop individual and collective competencies to recognize—and advocate for change—in the socio-structural position of marginalized communities via new mechanisms of participation and voice. Moreover, the typology of politics suggests that to foster systemic social innovation, public policy must go further not only to engender collective identification amongst marginalized individuals but also to identify how their individual disadvantages are shared and connected to broader regimes of production, consumption, inequality, welfare, and power. This process brings in the meso-level of market analysis highlighted above and connects marginalized populations with market actors and structures that can mediate the socio-structural space between grass roots and government via social innovation.

In doing so, it would be possible to foster collective material and post-material transformations that effectively resource and politicize—in the sense of revealing otherwise hidden power structures—social innovation as a policy concept. This would advance a social innovation paradigm that entails collective action *for* measures that seek to fulfil human capabilities and social needs. However, it would also encourage measures that venerate and foster collective action *against* those institutions, networks, and cognitive frames that structure social disadvantage. Without a policy approach that offers systemic solutions to overcoming marginality (through problematizing its structuration), social innovation policy runs the risk of being co-opted as another tool of oppression that distracts from, and thereby legitimizes persistent inequalities of resource, power, and opportunity.

Conclusion

This chapter has taken stock of the public policy agendas associated with social innovation in the EU. This analysis shows that social innovation has generally been inconsistently defined and has been a fluid and contested policy space. Moreover, social innovation policy across the EU has often reflected a more generalized disaffection with the existing socio-economic order, and has been positioned as a mechanism by which to affect economic, social, or institutional change. Across the EU, the specified objectives of social innovation have typically differed according to the political priorities and socio-economic challenges faced by individual member countries. Furthermore, the nature, goals, and effectiveness of public policy agendas supporting social innovation vary significantly according to the social macro-structures in operation within a given country context. Furthermore, the fluidity and adaptability of the meanings associated with social innovation have made it very attractive to policy-makers as something of a panacea for complex and contingent social problems. With this in mind, despite its transformative potential and ideals, social innovation has only tended to be recognized and supported by public institutions when it does not compete too strongly with the *existing* socio-economic and political settlements.

Social innovation has frequently been articulated in policy as offering new, novel, or disruptive solutions that depart from the prevailing dominant paradigms and models. However, if public policy is a manifestation of existing power relations, then social innovation is likely only to be supported in a way that reproduces such power relations. An ESGM analysis of EU social innovation policy suggests that the minimal recognition of the significance of politics and power in social innovation policymaking has rendered it susceptible to institutional or ideological capture by prevailing institutional and cognitive norms—quite the opposite of what many policy proponents have claimed. By failing to problematize or attend to the social structuration of marginalization—as revealed by the ESGM—social innovation policy may prove incapable of displacing the patterns of institutional dominance or sites of power that sustain marginalization.

In this context, several policy recommendations can be made for policy-makers focused on developing and implementing effective social innovation in the EU:

- Pay attention to the constellations of power that go beyond government and map out key actors and their social-structural positions in terms of social innovation development lifecycles. Understand that a wide variety of stakeholders can play different roles at different points in the social innovation process to optimize its impact.
- Be prepared to surrender institutional dominance and develop more participatory models of policy development and implementation across stakeholder groups. Consider supporting localism and empowering grassroots action as a constituent part of social innovation policy. However, recognize that grassroots-based solutions that actively involve the disadvantaged or marginalized rely on a capability to associate that may need nurture and support. To involve service users in social innovation processes as active co-producers demands approaches that actively foster the capacity to associate.
- Conceive of social innovations as long-term strategies for social change rather than as short-term welfare programmes. Reflect on history to note previous social innovation lifecycles and learn how to shape ecosystems to maximize and embed social innovation impact.
- Encourage ideological plurality and frame market actors in terms of wider systems of collective action. Acknowledge alternate perspectives and cognitive frames and use discourse dissonance as a source of innovation and hybridity.

With these recommendations in mind, effective social innovation policy needs not only to extend beyond its existing confines to focus on the social forces affecting marginalization and social innovation, but also to consider the social dynamics that exist therein. This would, arguably, be a social innovation in itself. However, importantly, this would also provide a deeper understanding of the potential scope of social innovation policy, the conditions under which it may thrive, and the extent to which it may address marginalization through systemic, structural, change.

References

Aro, J., and Heiskala, R. T. 2015. 'The Finnish Innovation System and Innovation Policy'. CrESSI Working Paper No. 22. Brussels: European Commission, DG Research.

Ayob. N., S. Teasdale, and K. Fagan. 2016. 'How Social Innovation "Came to Be": Tracing the Evolution of a Contested Concept'. *Journal of Social Policy* 45(4): 635–53.

Baumgartner, F., C. Green-Pedersen, and B. Jones. 2006. 'Comparative Studies of Policy Agendas'. *Journal of European Public Policy* 13(7): 959–74.

Beckert, J. 2010. 'How Do Fields Change? The Interrelations of Institutions, Networks, and Cognition in the Dynamics of Markets'. *Organization Studies* 31(5): 605–27.

BEPA 2010. *Empowering People, Driving Change: Social Innovation in the European Union*. Brussels: Bureau of European Policy Advisers.

Bonoli, G. 2005. 'The Politics of the New Social Policies: Providing Coverage against New Social Risks in Mature Welfare States'. *Policy and Politics* 33: 431–49.

Borzaga, C. and R. Bodini. 2014. 'What to Make of Social Innovation? Towards a Framework for Policy Development'. *Social Policy and Society* 13: 411–21.

Caulier-Grice, J., A. Davies, R. Patrick, and W. Norman. 2012. 'Defining Social Innovation'. London: TEPSIE.

Edmiston, D. 2015. 'Executive Summary of an EU Social Innovation Policy Survey'. CrESSI Working Paper No. 17. Brussels: European Commission, DG Research.

Edmiston, D. 2016. 'The (A)Politics of Social Innovation Policy in Europe: Implications for Socio-structural Change and Power Relations'. CrESSI Working Paper No. 32. Brussels: European Commission, DG Research.

European Commission. 2011a. 'Social Business Initiative: Creating a Favourable Climate for Social Enterprises, Key Stakeholders in the Social Economy and Innovation'. Communication from the Commission to the European Parliament, the Council, the European Economic and Social Committee, and the Committee of the Regions. Brussels: European Commission.

European Commission. 2011b. 'Single Market Act: Twelve Levers to Boost Growth and Strengthen Confidence "Working Together to Create New Growth"' (SEC(2011) 467 final). Communication from the Commission to the European Parliament, the Council, the European Economic and Social Committee, and the Committee of the Regions. Brussels: European Commission.

European Commission. 2013a. *EaSI: New EU Umbrella Programme for Employment and Social Policy*. Brussels: European Commission, Directorate-General for Employment, Social Affairs and Inclusion.

European Commission. 2013b. *Guide to Social Innovation*. Brussels: Regional and Urban Policy Publications, Office of the European Union.

European Commission. 2013c. *Investing in Social Europe*. Brussels: Directorate-General for Employment, Social Affairs and Inclusion.

European Commission. 2013d. 'Regulation (EU) No 1304/2013 of the European Parliament of the Council of 17 December 2013 on the European Social Fund and Repealing Council Regulation (EC) No 1081/2006'. *Official Journal of the European Union*. Brussels: European Commission.

European Commission. 2014a. *Community-Led Local Development: Cohesion Policy 2014–2020*. Brussels: European Commission.

European Commission. 2014b. 'Directive 2014/24/EU of the European Parliament and of the Council on 26 February 2014 on Public Procurement and Repealing Directive 2004/18/EC'. *Office Journal of the European Union* L 94/65.

European Commission. 2014c. 'Directive 2014/25/EU of the European Parliament and of the Council on 26 February 2014 on Procurement by Entities Operating in the Water, Energy, Transport and Postal Services Sectors and Repealing Directive 2004/17/EC'. *Official Journal of the European Union* L 94/243.

European Commission. 2014d. *Policy Roadmap for the 2014 Implementation of the Social Investment Package*. Brussels: Directorate-General for Employment, Social Affairs and Inclusion.

European Commission. 2014e. *Social Innovation: A Decade of Changes*. Luxembourg: Publications Office of the European Union.

European Commission. 2014f. 'Unleashing the Potential of Crowdfunding in the European Union'. Communication from the Commission to the European Parliament, the Council, the European Economic and Social Committee, and the Committee of the Regions. Brussels: European Commission.

European Commission. 2015a. 'Results of the Public Consultation on the Europe 2020 Strategy for Smart, Sustainable and Inclusive growth'. COM(2015) 100 Final. Communication from the Commission to the European Parliament, the Council, the European Economic and Social Committee, and the Committee of the Regions. Brussels: European Commission.

European Commission. 2015b. *Social Policy Innovation: Meeting the Social Needs of Citizens*. Brussels: Directorate-General for Employment, Social Affairs and Inclusion.

Green, J., and C. Hay. 2015. 'Towards a New Political Economy of the Crisis: Getting What Went Wrong Right'. *New Political Economy* 20: 331–41.

Grimm, Robert et al. 2013. 'Social Innovation, an Answer to Contemporary Societal Challenges? Locating the Concept in Theory and Practice'. *Innovation: The European Journal of Social Science Research* 26(4): 436–55.

Grisolia, F., and E. Ferragina. 2015. 'Social Innovation on the Rise: Yet Another Buzzword in Times of Austerity?' *Salute e Società* 1: 169–79.

Jenson, Jane. 2012. 'Social Innovation: Gadget, Concept or Mobilizing Idea?' RC19 Annual Conference. Oslo, Norway.

Jenson, Jane. 2015 'Social Innovation: Redesigning the Welfare Diamond'. In *New Frontiers in Social Innovation Research*, edited by Alex Nicholls, Julie Simon, and Madeleine Gabriel, pp. 89–106. London: Palgrave Macmillan.

Langergaard, L. L. 2014. 'Social Entrepreneurship and Capitalist Crisis'. *Nordicum-Mediterraneum* 9(3). https://nome.unak.is/wordpress/09-3/c73-conference-paper/social-entrepreneurship-and-capitalist-crisis/.

Mann, M. 1986. *The Sources of Social Power, Volume 1: A History of Power from the Beginning to AD 1760*. New York: Cambridge University Press.

Mann, M. 2013. *The Sources of Social Power, Volume 4: Globalizations, 1945–2011*. Cambridge: Cambridge University Press.

Nicholls, A., and D. Edmiston. 2015. 'Policy Brief D1.2 Re-assessing Social Innovation to Tackle Marginalization'. CrESSI Working Paper No. 11. Brussels: European Commission, DG Research.

Nicholls, A., J. Simon, and M. Gabriel (eds). 2015. *New Frontiers of Social Innovation*. Basingstoke: Palgrave Macmillan.

Nicholls, A., and A. Murdock (eds). 2011. *Social Innovation: Blurring Boundaries to Reconfigure Markets*. London: Palgrave Macmillan.

Nicholls, A., and R. Ziegler. 2014. 'An Extended Social Grid Model for the Study of Marginalization Processes and Social Innovation'. In 'Report on Institutions, Social Innovation and System Dynamics from the Perspective of the Marginalized'. CrESSI Working Paper No. 2. Brussels: European Commission, DG Research.

Nolan, B., and C. T. Whelan. 2011. *Poverty and Deprivation in Europe*. Oxford: Oxford University Press.

OECD. 2011. 'Fostering Innovation to Address Social Challenges'. http://www.oecd.org/science/inno/47861327.pdf OECD.

Pol, E., and S. Ville. 2009. 'Social Innovation: Buzz Word or Enduring Term?' *The Journal of Socio-Economics* 38: 878–85.

SIE. 2011. *Financing Social Impact Funding Social Innovation in Europe—Mapping the Way Forward*. Brussels: Social Innovation Europe Initiative.

Sinclair, S., and Baglioni, S. 2014. 'Social Innovation and Social Policy—Promises and Risks'. *Social Policy and Society* 13: 469–76.

TEPSIE. 2014. 'Growing the Field of Social Innovation in Europe'. For 'The Theoretical, Empirical and Policy Foundations for Building Social Innovation in Europe' (TEPSIE). Brussels: European Commission.

Ziegler, R., G. Molnar, E. Chiappero-Martinetti, and N. von Jacobi. 2016. 'Creating (Economic) Space for Social Innovation'. CrESSI Working Paper No. 31. Brussels: European Commission, DG Research.

12

Public Policy as Social Innovation

Social Impact Bonds

Alex Nicholls and Daniel Edmiston

Introduction

This chapter explores a significant structural innovation in the provision of public services—Social Impact Bonds (SIBs). SIBs not only represent a public policy instrument designed to promote public service reform, but also aim to scale social investment and tackle social exclusion (Edmiston and Nicholls 2017). SIBs represent an example of policy *as* social innovation within government in contrast to other policy agendas that aimed to encourage social innovation outside of the public sector (policy *for* social innovation). SIBs began in the United Kingdom in 2010, but have since proliferated across the world with examples in over twenty countries with more under development (Nicholls and Tomkinson 2015). By 2016, there were eighty-nine SIBs operational globally, accounting for over £300m of investment (Social Finance 2017). Moreover, it seems likely that by the end of 2018 more than 150 SIBs will be operational around the world, including examples across Continental Europe in Belgium, Germany, Italy, and elsewhere.

SIBs are essentially 'payment-by-results' contracts that leverage private social investment to cover the up-front expenditure associated with costly social and welfare services. Capitalizing on the expertise and skills of civil-society organizations and social enterprises, service interventions tend to be preventative in nature and focus on achieving one or more specified social outcome. These outcomes are often intended to focus on reducing long-term public expenditure in key policy domains by early intervention in costly (and sometimes failing) areas of social service provision. The (theoretical) cost-savings accrued by the public sector are then used to pay back private social investors' capital plus a 'dividend' calibrated to the level of outcomes achieved (see Figure 12.1). Rather than paying for service inputs or outputs, SIB contracts pay for pre-defined outcomes associated with a range of objective and subjective metrics that dictate both the amount received by service providers, but also the rate of return received by private social investors (Warner 2013; Hughes and Scherer 2014).

To date SIBs have been the subject of intense policy interest and no little hyperbole—the rapid expansion of SIBs across the world has occurred with only

Alex Nicholls and Daniel Edmiston, *Public Policy as Social Innovation: Social Impact Bonds.*
In: *Creating Economic Space for Social Innovation.* Edited by: Alex Nicholls and Rafael Ziegler,
Oxford University Press (2019).
DOI: 10.1093/oso/9780198830511.003.0012

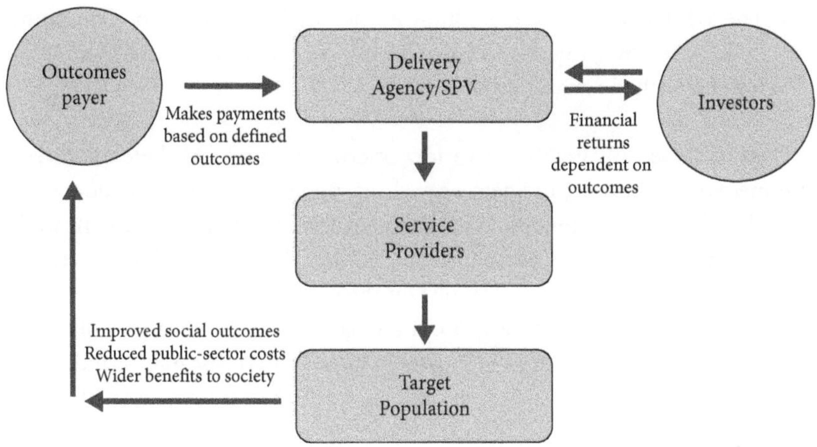

12.1 The SIB model
Source: Authors.

very limited evidence of success. As a consequence, more rigorous analysis is overdue. This chapter draws together the emerging literature in the field with new documentary analysis and qualitative fieldwork undertaken in relation to three distinct UK SIBs. From this, it is possible to observe a number of common and divergent experiences and patterns and thereby make some broader inferences about how and why particular social innovation policy agendas succeed or fail in tackling marginalization. SIBs tend to be specifically targeted at populations with highly complex needs, most vulnerable to social exclusion and policy failure. The empirical evidence gathered from this research can be brought to bear on the speculated opportunities and challenges SIBs pose for social innovation tackling marginalization across the wider European Union (EU).

The three SIBs under consideration here were all part of the first cohort of UK SIBs established—so they have some track record. As such, it is possible more fully to explore their development and impact. In this sense, this research not only explores the immediate effects but also the 'legacy' of interventions that have sought to foster social innovation capable of tackling marginalization. The three SIBS under consideration are as follows:

- The Children's Support Services Programme commissioned by Essex County Council designed to improve the situation and outcomes of children on the edge of residential care
- The 'New Horizons' Programme commissioned by Department for Work and Pensions designed to improve educational and employment prospects for vulnerable young people in Greater Merseyside area

- The SIB for rough sleepers commissioned by Department for Communities and Local Government and Greater London Authority to improve outcomes for entrenched rough sleepers.

Each of these SIBs involves a variety of cross-sectoral stakeholders: investors, intermediaries, service providers as well as public-sector commissioners from central and local government. With different funding models, payment metrics, and systems of impact measurement, these SIBs demonstrate how internal and external power dynamics can impinge on the development of SIBs as means and end of social innovation. Table 12.1 outlines some of the key features of each SIB.

Examination of these three SIBs entailed desk-based research of independent and stakeholder documentation as well as qualitative interviews with EU and domestic policy-makers, public sector commissioners, social financial intermediaries, service providers, and service users. Notably, a great deal of the existing literature 'is from sources that have an interest in promoting the benefits of SIBs' so critical care needs to be taken in reviewing the evidence and documentation available (Ronicle et al. 2014: 24). A total of forty-one interviews were undertaken to explore stakeholder experiences of and perspectives on SIBs. Research findings were also disseminated as part of a practitioner seminar, policy roundtable, and conference symposium and the feedback received during these events has informed the research process. The following organizations and individuals contributed towards the research:

- European Investment Fund
- Cabinet Office
- Department for Work and Pensions
- Department for Communities and Local Government
- Greater London Authority
- Essex County Council
- Cambridgeshire County Council
- Bridges Ventures Fund
- Triodos Bank
- Social Finance
- Big Society Capital
- Action for Children
- Thames Reach
- St Mungo's Broadway
- Greater Merseyside Connexions Partnership
- CAF Venturesome
- Social Investment Business Group
- Individual (social) investors
- Service users.

Table 12.1. Key features of the Social Impact Bonds

	Essex: Children on the Edge of Care	Merseyside: New Horizons	London: Rough Sleepers
Target population	Young people (11–16) on the edge of care or custody	Disadvantaged young people (14–19) who are, or are at risk of becoming, not in education, employment, or training (NEET)	Individuals that have been observed 'bedded down' at least six times in the past two years. Identified through Combined Homeless and Information Network (CHAIN) database.
Intervention	2 Multi Systemic Therapy (MST) Teams	Interventions include group sessions, 1-2-1 coaching, mental toughness training, signposting to provision, access to ring-fenced job interviews, and links to employers. Carried out on partner premises and in schools.	Tailored interventions plans based delivered by personal navigators who develop a programme of support based on the circumstances of the individual. Longer-term interaction and support between individual and personal navigator.
Public-sector commissioner	Essex County Council	Department for Work and Pensions (via Innovation Fund)	Greater London Authority and (Department for Communities and Local Government)
Service provider	Action for Children	Greater Merseyside Connexions Partnership	1) St Mungo's Broadway (Street Impact) and 2) Thames Reach (Thames Reach Ace)
SIB intermediary	Social Finance Ltd	Triodos Bank	1) Triodos Bank 2) N/A
Special purpose vehicle	Children's Support Services Ltd	Triodos New Horizons Limited	1) Street Impact Ltd 2) N/A
Investors	Bridges Ventures Social Entrepreneurs Fund (27%), Big Society Capital (27%), Barrow Cadbury Trust, Tudor Trust, Esmee Fairbairn Foundation, King Baudouin Foundation, Charities Aid Foundation, Social Venture Fund (8%), David Burnett	Bridges Ventures, Big Society Capital, Esmee Fairbairn Foundation, Charities Aid Foundation, Knowsley Housing Trust, Helena Partnerships, Liverpool Mutual Homes, Wirral Partnership Homes	1) CAF Venturesome, the Orp Foundation, St Mungo's Broadway and other individuals 2) Big Issue Invest, Department of Health Social Enterprise Fund, Thames Reach and other individuals

(*Continued*)

Table 12.1. *Continued*

	Essex: Children on the Edge of Care	Merseyside: New Horizons	London: Rough Sleepers
Contract	Five-year service delivery period and a 2.5-year period for tracking of final outcomes	Three-year service delivery contract	Three-year service delivery period and a further year for tracking of final outcomes
Social investment	Initial investment of £3.1 million growing to around £5.9 million	Initial investment of £1.5 million growing up to £4.5 million	1) Initial investment of £887,000 growing up to £2.4 million, 2) Unknown initial investment: TR says £850K growing up to £2.4 million
Payment metric(s)	Total days adolescents from a treated cohort spend in residential care, measured over 30-day time periods.	Re-engagement with education, achieving educational qualifications, starting and sustaining employment and/or training.	Transition into accommodation, initial and sustained reconnection (move to another country), training and education outcomes, starting and sustaining employment.

Source: Authors.

While the specificities of each SIB affect its performance, operation, and impact, the findings from this analysis are presented thematically to draw out broader lessons that can be learnt about SIBs as a manifestation of social innovation policy.

Policy Context

The Extended Social Grid Model (see further chapter 1) suggests that, at the macro-level, the dynamic relationships between cognitive frames, institutions, and networks shape social structures and constrain individual action. This section explores the distinctive conditions under which SIBs have emerged as a defining feature of social innovation policy in the United Kingdom. Public policy can be seen as the complex manifestation of social processes and power relations that give rise to institutional dominance, as well as prevailing networks of action and cognitive norms and modes of thinking. In this sense, public policy is both 'structured' and 'structuring'—it is a manifestation of social and political relations as well as a mechanism by which to affect these relations. The 'institutional, cultural, and social embeddedness' (Beckert 2009: 264) of public policy makes it particularly important to consider policy agendas within their historical context. Arguably, there are a number of institutional conditions that have contributed towards the development of UK SIBs. Similar conditions also apply (though contextually shaped) across many of the countries that have been early adopters of SIBs globally—including in the EU.

First, as a liberal welfare regime, the United Kingdom is traditionally characterized by a system of residual means-tested provision, low levels of de-commodification, and higher levels of social stratification (Esping-Andersen 1990; Raffass 2016). Within this context, policy measures designed to tackle social exclusion tend to pursue strategies of labour market integration (Levitas 1996). Notably, a significant majority of the UK SIBs base at least one of their outcome payment metrics on education, training, or employment outcomes (cf. Gustafsson-Wright et al. 2015). While over half prioritize employment as a key social outcome and payment metric, others treat labour market integration as a key condition that contributes towards overcoming marginalization. These SIBs pay for social outcomes that move individuals closer towards the paid labour market. In this regard, SIBs are a symptomatic feature of prevailing liberal welfare arrangements in the UK context.

Second, the development and implementation of SIBs can largely be seen as a continuation of policies designed to embed *welfare pluralism* within public services. Beyond its well-rehearsed ideological motivations, welfare pluralism seeks to increase the efficiency and effectiveness of welfare services by drawing on the expertise and skills of civil-society organizations and the market logics of private actors. Since the 1980s, there has been a concerted commitment to embed entrepreneurial and 'enterprising' approaches into the management, organization, and delivery of welfare provision. As a policy instrument, SIBs involve private actors in the delivery, control, and finance of welfare services and represent the next phase towards an increasingly mixed economy of welfare.

Alongside the quasi-marketization of welfare, successive rounds of public-service reform have sought to encourage *outcome-based commissioning* and *payment-by-results* contracts. Attempts to modernize public services have been characterized by a move away from paying for service *outputs* and towards paying for service and social *outcomes*. In this respect, SIBs are part of 'a new ideational landscape that has emerged for the third sectors in the Anglo-Saxon cluster dominated by a focus on transparency, impact, and social innovation' (Phillips and Smith 2014: 1158). As a contract and financing model that depends on the fulfilment of pre-defined social outcomes and payment metrics, SIBs represent a key instrument (or rather product) of public-sector reform and innovation.

The persistence of old social problems and the emergence of new social risks have raised questions about the operation and function of the contemporary welfare state in the United Kingdom. Since the 1990s, there has been an increasing preoccupation with the capacity for the welfare state to facilitate policy of *social investment* (quite distinct from *social impact investment*—the allocation of investment capital for impact, see Nicholls et al. 2015). Social investment is intended to address the causes, rather than the effects of social problems and disadvantage. The rise of third way politics in the United Kingdom stimulated an increasing interest in welfare services that invested in the human capital of service users, but also contributed towards economic growth and development. In keeping with the social investment approach to welfare provision, SIBs are often understood as an opportunity to address intractable social problems that inhibit 'economic and human development, leading to the persistence of social inequities' (Gustafsson-Wright et al. 2015: 1). In this vein, SIBs are based on a principle of preventative service intervention that seeks to tackle the root causes of social disadvantage, reduce the cost of welfare and maximize its economic contribution.

In light of the 'austerity consensus' (Farnsworth and Irving 2012) that emerged post 2008, the increasing pressure to cut public social spending stimulated interest in public-sector innovation and social impact investment. Essentially, a lack of economic space has cultivated a mandate and case for social innovation in public policy. In an attempt to leverage new forms of capital, SIBs 'represent the continuation of a trend by successive UK governments to reduce direct public investment in social services while simultaneously encouraging increased investment from private sector financial and other intermediaries' (McHugh et al. 2013: 252). The public sector has sought to leverage these alternative forms of finance in a way that increases the effectiveness and efficiency of social services (Big Lottery Fund 2010). As such, SIBs are the latest policy instrument that aims to marketize, modernize, and reduce the fiscal burden of costly welfare interventions (see Nicholls and Teasdale 2016).

Having moved away from an initial period of social democratic welfarism, ideological and political shifts have challenged the role and function of welfare in the United Kingdom. Since the 1980s, conflicting ideologies have brought the social democratic principle of welfarism into contestation and dispute. Successive rounds of public service and welfare reform in the United Kingdom have sought to constraint an increasing financial and social commitment to welfare provision. Subsequent to the introduction of the world's first SIB under the New Labour government in 2010, the opposition Conservative Party included SIBs within their manifesto platform 'Big Society, Not Big Government' during the May 2010 general election. As a part of this, the party promoted 'Social Impact Bonds, that offer a blend of social and financial return that is attractive to socially responsible, mainstream investors' (Conservative Party 2010). Since the consolidation of their political position, the Conservatives have demonstrated a political, administrative, and financial commitment to SIBs. In many respects, SIBs characterized an 'ideological shift which favours removing delivery of social and welfare services from conventional public or third sector providers... and they mark a significant challenge to the traditional ethos and operation of the voluntary and community sector' (McHugh et al. 2013: 253).

The cognitive/institutional conditions outlined above are intimately linked to the development of SIBs as a social innovation policy agenda in the United Kingdom. These conditions were, in many ways, discrete and independently significant. However, their dynamic interrelations help explain the distinctive modes of thinking and action that characterized UK social innovation policy. Invariably 'new ideas and solutions' or, at least, the motivations behind them are not conceptually pure. Arguably, these features of social innovation are a transmutation of (or indeed, against) previous approaches and paradigms. Within any setting, this transmutation is instigated by certain socio-economic, cognitive, and institutional processes. While many EU member states have observed conditions similar to those outlined above; their particular configuration in the UK context has given rise to a social innovation policy agenda that is relatively distinctive in Europe but also has points of overlap. Indeed, the European Investment Fund has, through intermediaries, partly funded a number of UK SIBs via its Social Impact Accelerator (Edmiston 2015). This reflects a general alignment between the European Commission's strategic commitment to social impact investment and the United Kingdom's relatively advanced social investment market (e.g. European Commission 2014; European Parliament 2014).

Policy Implementation

Since 2010, the UK government has committed more than £266 million to the development of SIBs and outcome-based commissioning so that these might be taken up more widely across central and local government. The Social Outcomes Fund (£20 million) and Commissioning Better Outcomes Fund (£40 million) were conceived to tackle some of the primary barriers inhibiting the growth of SIBs. They provided a 'top-up' contribution to outcomes-based commissioning designed to deal with complex and expensive social issues. According to the Big Lottery Fund, the Commissioning Better Outcomes Fund was specifically designed to support the development of 'more innovative approaches to improving social outcomes. This is to enable more people, particularly those most in need, to lead fulfilling lives, in enriching places, and as part of successful communities'. The Department of Work and Pensions Innovation Fund (£30 million), the Youth Engagement Fund (£16 million), and the Fair Chance Fund (£15 million) supported SIBs focused on disadvantaged young people aged between fourteen and twenty-four. In 2015, the UK government committed a further £80 million to capitalize a Life Chances Fund designed to support outcome-based contracting and SIBs. In March 2016, this lead to the establishment of a five-year partnership between the Blavatnik School of Government at the University of Oxford and the Cabinet Office Centre for SIBs to establish a 'Government Outcomes (GO) Lab' that aimed to develop 'world-leading research in this field and provides practical, on the ground support to local commissioners'. In response to the announcement, Minister for Civil Society Rob Wilson stated that:

> Social Impact Bonds represent a revolution in the way government can deliver public services. They generate huge potential savings for the taxpayer, the prospect of increased revenues for charities and social enterprises, and returns to social investors.

In addition to this, £40 million has also been ring-fenced to support NHS England in commissioning innovative interventions that seek to improve health and work outcomes.

While SIBs should be recognized as a distinct type of payment-by-results model, they can be seen as part of a broader movement towards outcome-based commissioning in the United Kingdom. According to the National Audit Office, in 2015, there were fifty-two schemes with an element of payment-by-results contracting across six central government departments and their affiliated bodies (NAO 2015: 13–15). These schemes were worth a total of over £15 billion. This included the consolidation of all welfare-to-work schemes into the Work Programme which was worth between £3 and £5 billion (NAO 2015) and the introduction and extension of the Troubled Families programme which was worth up to £668 million. In addition, the Transforming Rehabilitation scheme, run by the Ministry of Justice was worth up to £3.1 billion and DFIDs international payment-by-results aid schemes were worth up to £2.2 billion.

Social Impact Bonds as Social Innovation

SIBs aim to facilitate innovative welfare interventions designed to improve the outcomes and opportunities of target service users, often through early intervention and novel partnerships. To this extent, SIBs are a mechanism through which to facilitate social innovation. However, beyond this, SIBs can also be seen as a social innovation *in themselves* that seek to build new cognitive norms around commissioning for outcomes, to create new institutional models to mobilize private finance for public good, and to build new partnerships and develop effective social networks, often with a view towards tackling marginalization.

If an instance of social innovation is both a source and outcome of well-being (European Commission 2013), it is important to consider what role and value it has relative to existing approaches and paradigms of need provision. Any number of policy instruments and measures may effectively support new forms of finance, partnerships, and networks, but whether these are capable of improving human capabilities through social innovation is another matter entirely. With this in mind, this section examines the role and value of SIBs with respect to their capacity to develop finance, partnerships, and networks for social innovation that are capable of improving human capabilities.

Financing Social Innovation

A key argument for SIBs is that they mobilize private-sector capital in a way that fosters social innovation (e.g. Big Lottery Fund 2010; Hughes and Scherer 2014). According to Social Finance, SIBs exhibit the 'potential to unlock an unprecedented flow of finance for social sector organizations. By focusing returns on outcomes, these organizations will be incentivized to develop innovative interventions to tackle ingrained social problems which weigh heavily on our society and national purse.' These forms of capital investment, and the dividends expected based on service performance have been argued to encourage an outcome-centred approach to welfare interventions.

While service outcomes are ultimately paid for by the public sector, SIBs are understood as a key mechanism to foster social impact investment capable of addressing social need. This view was shared by a number of policy-makers, and social finance stakeholders interviewed for this chapter. SIBs, and the development of social impact investment more generally, was seen as a way to tap resources that would otherwise remain unused or inaccessible to organizations capable of generating significant social value through these ventures. An interviewee stated:

> Yes there's a lot of money in the world and there's a lot of rich people in the world and yes there will be a certain amount of rich people who will want to give a certain proportion of their wealth away but there's also a large proportion of people with money that don't want to give it away and actually what social investment gives you is an opportunity for money to be accessed and recycled.

For some, SIBs were seen as a 'financial product' that was at the more extreme end of the social impact investment market compared to more traditional and 'vanilla' vehicles such as charitable loans. Stakeholders across the board felt that the introduction of private capital opened up economic space for flexible, innovative, and experimental service interventions. Many stated that these 'small-scale and experimental' projects were only possible because private investors were taking on, either all or part of, the financial and reputational risk in return for a prospective financial reward (Warner 2013: 6). In this respect, SIBs can be understood as transferring at least some of the 'financial risk away from government and small providers and onto social investors' (Kohli 2010; Disley et al. 2011: 16). As one interviewee noted:

> There is no expectation of making money, any super-normal profits at all, yet the investor stood to lose all their money.

This opens up opportunities for policy experimentation and innovation that would otherwise not be possible or, perhaps, even justifiable within the context of government budgetary constraints. The involvement of private capital minimizes certain reputational risks in the event that service outcomes are not met. However, certain forms of reputational risk are also introduced with public sector commissioners open to the accusation of privatizing public goods and allowing social investors to profit from poverty.

Social innovation was clearly an important objective to many SIB investors who were concerned about increasing the efficiency and effectiveness of public services. Others were interested in encouraging charities and social purpose organizations to act more transparently and effectively. For one individual, SIBs were seen as a 'powerful way of reducing the involvement of government' in the delivery of welfare services. This was based on a belief that organizations outside the public sector could more effectively deliver social and welfare services—especially if they drew upon social impact investment.

For many stakeholders, SIBs—and social impact investment more generally—represented a structural market-level innovation that offered an opportunity to move beyond an individual profit-maximizing model of income-generation towards a blended model that may generate economic *and* social returns:

> It's about the opportunity to use their money to do good without them losing it if you like and I think that's a win-win situation.
>
> You're really taking a sub-normal return on your investment—you're risking your capital but you're a getting really good moral return on your buck.

Moreover, for some, SIBs were more about a 'proof of concept' than necessarily about addressing a specific social problem. These individuals stated that they were not particularly interested in the service intervention or social outcome in question. Instead, they were principally concerned with the potential for SIBs to drive more social impact investment along with the operational and efficiency benefits that it purports to engender. This represents an attempt to shift the cognitive frames around the purpose and structure of financial markets more generally:

> If the early SIBs could work, work well, and be seen to work well then it would encourage more money to come into the sector, encourage more charitable and social welfare organizations to be funded though that mechanism—which I think is a very good thing.
>
> I would say I'm definitely more motivated by the model. I mean did look at the particular project but my core interest was the model.

However, SIBs are, to some extent, challenged by the institutional and cognitive conventions around financial risk and return in investment markets. Namely, while SIBs are supposed to transfer service innovation and performance risk onto private investors, 'these very market features have made SIBs unattractive to private investors without substantial guarantees' (Warner 2013: 6). This perhaps goes some way to explain why, despite significant interest surrounding SIBs, the supply of private social investment has been relatively slow. In light of the risk and uncertainty associated with SIBs as a contract model, a number of those interviewed stated that SIBs were only suitable for investors 'who can afford to lose' their investment. Furthermore, some of the social impact investment stakeholders interviewed for this chapter suggested that investors were still concerned about losing money and that there was a lack of 'investment-ready' organizations that had a 'demonstrable track record of social impact':

> Big Society Capital coming online is a great opportunity for the sector in many ways but you need people to give that money to and you need organizations that are ready to take that money on.
>
> The biggest challenge going forward is that we've been principally government funded... the biggest challenge is going to be bringing in different types of money from private sources.

One potential mechanism by which it would be possible to overcome the high uncertainty associated with SIBs would be to compensate risk-taking with a higher rate of return for social outcomes achieved. However, there is some doubt as to whether this could or would be justifiable in light of the high transaction costs already associated with SIBs. Some have suggested that the need to encourage private social impact investment has meant 'private investors in SIBs (to date) have required substantial loan guarantees or subordinated debt' (Warner 2013: 6). Crucially, this raises an important question about the relative value of involving private investors rather than just drawing on direct 'investment' and funding from the public sector. Again this innovation presents a challenge both to existing institutional structures (as a hybrid model) and to cognitive norms concerning the distinctive roles of public and private capital as well as the purpose of markets.

The high transaction costs associated with putting a SIB together (up to three years of work in the most extreme case) was also cited as a policy issue potentially detracting from the relative value of the SIB model when compared to other more conventional commissioning mechanisms. From this perspective, it was felt that the social outcomes achieved through SIBs would have significantly to exceed those achieved through conventional service interventions to justify the involvement of private investors and the 'extra costs' they incur:

> There is quite a cost attached to setting up an individual SIB. I think that's probably one of the biggest barriers to them being more widely deployed.
>
> If it wasn't for certain logistical difficulties, you would probably want to do it directly because it adds to the costs--very high transactions costs.

While some expressed concern about the costs and sustainability of SIBs, one interviewee felt that SIBs were inevitably 'expensive' in their nascent phase but this was not something to be concerned about in the long run:

> The way new financial instruments tend to work is that someone invents them. They're quite costly to build. They're quite costly to execute as a result in pure hard-nosed business. The margins are very high but then over a period of time they become more accepted and more people can create them, issue them, the margin goes down—the appeal goes up and they seep their way slowly into broader ownership.

By and large, UK third-sector organizations tended to view social impact investment as a necessary endeavour in light of cuts to public social services: 'this type of social investment is going to keep growing... as it provides a source of additional funding when public spending is constrained' (Ronicle et al. 2014: 35). Taking this into consideration, the extent to which SIBs can be characterized as an effective mechanism by which to finance social innovation largely depends on whether they are viewed within their narrower or broader context. To the extent that SIBs 'allow for the commissioning of services that would otherwise not be commissioned', they can be understood as financing social innovation. For example, a number of service providers felt that the principle innovation of the SIB was the length of the contract and the extended time it allowed practitioners to work with service users (Nicholls and Tomkinson 2015). The value of contractual longevity has also been highlighted by a number of stakeholders across evaluations of the SIB model (e.g. OPM 2015). On the other hand, the capacity of SIBs to facilitate social innovation may well be inhibited by broader budgetary constraints on public social services and third-sector organizations. In this sense, the SIB model may not in itself be a tool to finance social innovation but rather presents a vehicle to facilitate it under the right conditions.

Building New Partnerships

According to the UK Cabinet Office, a SIB is a 'contractual arrangement between at least three separate parties, including a commissioner, an investor, and a service provider, where payments are dependent on the achievement of specified social outcomes'. Thus far, SIBs have had varying levels of success in building public–private partnerships and aligning the interests of these three sectoral stakeholders. Over the past twenty years, a variety of collaborations between the private, public, and third sectors have been developed aiming to maximize the efficiency and effectiveness of public services (and, some argue, to dilute government and open up lucrative new private markets). The hybridity model present within much social innovation (Molina 2010) means organizations and actors involved operate across 'over-lapping landscapes rather than distinct fields' (Alcock 2009: 3). The claimed benefits of an effective partnership (or compact even) between the public and third sector have been well rehearsed (Hopkins 2010; Somers 2013).

In addition to this, many have claimed SIBs present an opportunity to foster effective partnerships between both the private sector and the public sector, and the private sector and the third sector. In both instances, it has been repeatedly claimed that the organizational culture, skills, and expertise of the private sector can offer something of unique value to organizations and authorities operating within the public and third sectors (Social Finance 2009; Deloitte 2012; UK Cabinet Office 2012). Drawing on data from policy documentation and stakeholder interviews, this chapter critically considers the extent to which SIBs can be seen as an effective instrument through which to build new public–private partnerships and networks and whether this represents a challenge or opportunity for fostering social innovation to tackle marginalization.

As previously stated, in the SIB model the introduction of actors and capital from the private social impact investment market is intended to cover the up-front costs and working capital associated with welfare interventions and to transfer some of the risk of experimentation (and failure) away from public authorities (Cooper 2013). To this end, the partnerships created through SIBs have the capacity to be mutually beneficial where all parties have a vested interest in the pre-defined outcomes being achieved. For the respective parties, this may result in a financial saving, a financial reward, a positive social impact, or a mixture thereof. While this may constitute an alignment of interests, it may equally function to accommodate a plurality of interests and motivations around a common social outcome:

> Every stakeholder has their own objectives that they're using this to fulfil and they're very different and that's fine.

It could, therefore, be argued that the SIB policy agenda is an effective instrument through which to foster public–private partnerships capable of fostering social innovation. However, it seems that an alignment of cross-sectoral interests is a necessary condition of a SIB rather than a product of its operation.

Partnerships between the Public Sector and the Private Social Impact Investment Market

According to some of public-sector commissioners, policy-makers, and civil servants interviewed, the presence of private capital and actors in outcome-based commissioning is intended to encourage 'a more rigorous approach towards assessing and evaluating specific sets of interventions'. It was also seen as a way of adding 'discipline' to payment-by-results contracts to support public service reform. Where service interventions were seen as being particularly costly or ineffective at improving the outcomes of a target population, a number suggested that the role of private-sector actors and methods had the capacity to improve the effectiveness and efficiency of service provision:

> The potential for using commercial business approaches to improve the efficacy of projects and I think there is a role for bringing together some of those more commercial aspects to these projects, and I think it does have the potential to deliver better results.

In this respect, the public–private partnerships created through SIBs were seen to be beneficial because they introduced a 'profit motive' into the design and delivery of 'public services' and thereby fostered new capacity for social innovation. This was seen as a way of 'testing contract models' and 'securing value for money' for commissioners and taxpayers. Whether these perceptions hold true remains to be seen. Crucially though, it was widely recognized that the state of public finance was crucial to making these partnerships work:

> I think that private capital which has some element of profit motive, is on balance probably, with lots of caveats, going to be a better deliverer than the state sector but obviously it needs the state to put up some money because there's no profit to be made from just improving the outcomes of disenfranchised people.

With regards to the economic underpinnings of social innovation, this latter observation about SIBS is particularly interesting. The SIB model highlights the fact that social innovations that are principally designed to improve the outcomes of marginalized groups and whose principal operations centre on this objective, may require some degree of charitable or public-sector involvement and support. Without it, there may not be any sources of funding available because 'there's no profit to be made from *just* improving the outcomes of disenfranchised people'.

Beyond this, the introduction of actors from the social impact investment market is intended to transfer some of the burden of oversight and performance management away from the public sector. It has been said that SIBs have the capacity dramatically to alter 'the entire arrangement of responsibility and accountability between public and private entities for the provision of public services' (Cooper 2013: 2). By drawing on new mechanisms of performance management, accounting and accountability, public sector commissioners are able 'to ensure that partners are on track to deliver the outcomes sought' without being directly responsible for the day-to-day oversight of the service (Goodall 2014: 12). A commissioner noted:

> We have very little influence over what the delivery bodies are doing and how successful their sub-contractors are so in terms of that element I think that's down to investors and intermediaries and how they manage their delivery bodies.

Some of those interviewed were positive about the 'opportunity' for public authorities to delegate their role and relationship with service providers to an intermediary (Disley et al. 2011). Performance management undertaken by private-sector actors and organizations was seen as an effective way of increasing the oversight and accountability of service interventions. On the other hand, some were less positive about the role of private-sector involvement. These interviewees felt that public-sector commissioners could lose too much control over the operation and evaluation of service provision and these partnerships may principally benefit actors in the social impact investment market.

Some were also sceptical about the extent to which the involvement of private actors reduced the administrative and logistical burden on public-sector commissioners. A number of stakeholders noted how 'time-consuming', 'complicated', and 'demanding' the development of SIBs could be. At least in the design phase, it appears that the time it takes to compose a SIB is a significant barrier to their wider appeal and take-up by public authorities.[1] For many of the relevant stakeholders, SIBs were seen as placing significant administrative burden and pressure on public-sector commissioners. These public authorities were not only required to assist in the development of an experimental contract model, they also needed to put measures in place to ensure they were sufficiently prepared to address strategic and practical issues concerning finance, cross-departmental coordination, and legal challenges.

Despite claims that these public–private partnerships reduce the burden placed on public authorities in managing outcome-based commissioning, a number of interviewees felt that SIBs placed an *additional* pressure on public authorities at a time of particular strain and budgetary constraint on statutory services. It may be more accurate to conclude, then, that SIBs can *increase* the administrative burden on all parties involved with a view to ensuring the *effective* and *efficient* operation of outcome-based commissioning.

Partnerships between Civil Society and the Private Social Impact Investment Market

In large part, the utility of the partnerships between the private and public sector created through SIBs depends on the nature and extent of the partnership between service delivery organizations and private-sector actors. The partnerships, or rather, working relationships created between actors across these two sectors can have a number of intended and unintended effects on the capacity and service delivery of third-sector organizations.

Perhaps the most commonplace argument advanced by advocates of SIBs is that 'they promote innovation in social services and bring market forces to bear on service providers previously funded by traditional government grants' (Cooper 2013: 2) Underlying this argument is the belief that third-sector organizations delivering particular service interventions would benefit from a more 'entrepreneurial', 'commercial', 'business-minded' approach to their operations. This view was expressed particularly strongly by some of the social impact investment stakeholders interviewed for this chapter. While, they recognized the social value and expertise of third-sector organizations, many of these individuals suggested that third-sector organizations lacked the skills, know-how, and strategic vision to safeguard their own sustainability and the capacity of their operations. Some felt that a partnership between private- and third-sector actors would foster a positive degree of *corporatization* within the operation of civil-society

[1] These negative effects of these high transaction costs led to the development of, first, the Centre for SIBs within government and, second, the launch of the GO Lab at Oxford. Both aim to help reduce these costs for commissioners.

organizations. Ultimately, it was felt this would enable service providers to 'adapt their culture' and 'become more professional' and, thereby, encourage service innovation:

> They have to be able to talk to the private world and to investor-minded fund providers and be able to cope with that and adapt their culture to that. The ultimate objective is to being able to keep on delivering those services to the poor or to underprivileged populations.

In certain instances, this was justified on the basis of safeguarding the sustainability of third-sector service providers in a challenging funding and commissioning landscape (NCVO 2015). In other instances, it was justified as an opportunity to increase the capacity and impact of civil-society organizations. As several civil servants observed:

> All of the actors working in the social field have to change a little bit of their mindset otherwise they will simply die and no longer be able to offer a service because the public budgets are scarcer and scarcer.
>
> The main driver was around thinking that the voluntary and community sector are often best placed to deliver the innovative and very localized services to whatever group you want to target and SIBs traditionally have suffered in perhaps not being able to take on the risk of payment by results. So this was a way of actually building their capability and capacity to ensuring that their up-front costs were covered by a range of one or more investors.

At least from the perspective of the social impact investment stakeholders interviewed, there appeared to be numerous improvements in the practices, capacity, and impact of third-sector providers. The partnerships created through SIBs were seen as instrumental in this process. Interestingly, the nature and tone of these partnerships differed quite dramatically from SIB to SIB. Some viewed this as a collaborative partnership whereas others saw it as more of a confrontational endeavour where the 'bending of wills' was deemed a necessary feature of the process of organizational learning and improvement:

> I don't think that the project would have concluded as successfully were it not for the interventions of the sort of SIB-related stuff if that makes sense. I think that, in the end, the project was much better managed and that helped the delivery partner to deliver effectively to the [service beneficiary group] and therefore they got much better results.
>
> They [the service provider] feel like dealing with government employees. They're very, very fixed in their ways. They've got a very long tradition and it makes them inflexible and very process driven and we're struck by it again and

> again and again . . . If we talk about innovation, [the service provider] will naturally be suspicious and resistant.

Contrary to the typical relationship between a third-sector organization and a public-sector commissioner, a SIB requires service providers to engage with actors and organizations from the private social impact investment market (though sometimes this is intermediated by a third party such as Social Finance, Instiglio, or Numbers4Good). Third-sector organizations interviewed for this chapter felt that there was a greater degree of oversight and accountability to their private-sector partners compared to government commissioners. Requirements to report on social outcomes, rather than service inputs and outputs compelled these organizations to alter their data collection and data management processes. In turn, this appeared to produce a number of beneficial outcomes for their 'investment-readiness':

> Collecting that data can be time consuming and can be difficult . . . But actually I think it's a challenge that the sector can rise to and I think the better the sector rises to it, the more it's just gonna reap more and more rewards because if you can show to somebody what impact you're having it makes investing in you or just supporting you a no-brainer.

In certain instances, this increased oversight and accountability was felt to have induced a behavioural change in how front-line practitioners assisted target service users and how 'back-office' staff sought to realize their social mission (DWP 2014). While some did not feel it had altered their organizational practice, others were positive about the frequency of oversight from investors and felt that their criticisms carried more weight and utility. In certain instances, it did, indeed, appear that the partnerships arising from SIBs helped improve the capacity and operation of third-sector providers.

Through a series of pre-defined payment metrics, a SIB intends to open up space for service innovation and flexibility. Rather than fulfilling a range of service inputs and outputs, a SIB is designed to grant third-sector providers the flexibility to provide tailored intensive provision according to the requirements of the service user rather than the requirements of the contract and to adapt and change service provision models mid-contract if necessary (Disley et al. 2015). However, in practice some of the social impact investors required data, information, and updates on much more than the pre-defined payment metrics. In certain instances, third-sector providers were required to collect substantial amounts of information on what was working, under what conditions, and by what means. While intended to foster dynamic and responsive service provision, this actually created a significant data, administrative, and organizational burden for some service providers. On occasion, it was felt that the SIB actually *inhibited* their discretion and capacity to innovate around their social mission. Some felt that the burdensome nature of oversight and micro-management by investors was diverting resources that could be better spent on broadening and intensifying service provision:

> We underestimated the amount of management time that was required to run a SIB and we radically underestimated the kind of information demand there would be from investors there would on a daily basis about how things were going and what conversion rates were and progress reports and forecasts and re-forecasts.
>
> No absolutely not. If anything I would say less, there was less flexibility. Because the amount of management structures that are placed on a SIB mean that you have less manoeuvrability, you have to clear everything with this board to get permission to do anything. The board has investors and they very rarely see the world in the same light as you.
>
> It isn't the commissioner that's requiring the burdensome and time-intensive reporting—it's the investors really—it's like nothing we've ever experienced before.

As a result, a number of third-sector organizations talked quite negatively about the degree of micro-management that came with a SIB and, particularly, their interaction with social impact investors. In a number of instances, a difference was noted between different types of investors. Organizations principally involved in grant-making activities tended to have a much more collaborative relationship with service providers. By contrast, some social impact investment organizations and individual 'high net worth' investors were perceived as not fully trusting service providers and having 'little understanding of what we do and why we do it'. On a number of occasions, social impact investors exhibited a lack of awareness and understanding of the factors that inhibited or slowed the take-up or impact of service provision—perhaps explained by them interpreting the role of the intermediary and the contract in purely legalistic and financial terms:

> The social [impact] investors who saw themselves as being more commercial, interpreted everything from a legal perspective. So they wanted to go to the contract all the time.
>
> The chairman is charged with ensuring that the board is fit for purpose and operates well and that it achieves the outcomes that it sets itself.

At times, service providers felt pressured to secure outcomes to such an extent that they took measures to 'insulate' their front-line staff from the influence of certain social investors. The 'marketization' exerted by the influence of social impact investors had the capacity to encourage outcome-focused service provision but, equally, ran the risk of promoting dysfunctional practice such as 'creaming' and 'parking' in payment-by-results contracts (Carter and Whitworth 2015). Rather than resisting attempts to improve responsiveness and innovation, some organizations responded by seeking to safeguard the professional practice and integrity of their services. One service provided noted:

> I think you've got to be careful you don't contaminate your professional practice by erm . . . I have to fend off the investors and have the financially focused discussion . . . otherwise you start to get into some quite questionable practices and run the risk of people starting to do things because of financial pressures . . . The whole reason for doing this is to help the hardest to reach [target beneficiary group] and to help them make a or realize an outcome so we tend to be the firewall around investor pressure around quick return and professional practice of our staff and I don't think we had any inkling about how fine a line it would be to secure and operate like that but I think we've done it successfully.

In these instances, tensions arose between service providers and social impact investors. While these tensions were usually accommodated and managed, the lack of understanding and awareness exhibited by the investors sometimes discouraged service providers from engaging in similar contracts in the future:

> We wouldn't engage in those sorts of contracts or with those investors in future. We would engage in future SIBs, we are developing a new one in Manchester. We want to ensure that future social investment contains a much stronger partnership between the parties, and less an element of private-sector contracting which can be bullying.

These experiences belie the collaborative ideal and transformative potential of a partnership between third-sector service providers and actors from the social impact investment market. As a contract model, SIBs seek to embed an entrepreneurial and innovative approach to the operations and service delivery of third-sector organizations. However, one interviewee went as far as to suggest that 'there aren't any lessons being learnt' within their own organization. They were 'walking the walk and talking the talk' but, ultimately, were doing what they knew was best for their client group. Another third-sector stakeholder wanted 'less micro-management, more partnership, more trust' from social impact investors.

Overall, new cross-sectoral partnerships and networks in SIBs seem to have the capacity to innovate and encourage 'discipline' and 'rigour' in the measurement, commissioning, and evaluation of public services. In addition, they have the capacity to increase the flexibility, responsiveness, and autonomy of service providers. In certain cases, these benefits were observable. However, in other instances, the profit motive and pressures exerted by social impact investors threatened the autonomy and integrity of service provision so that practitioners were not able fully to capitalize on their own expertise and skills. It seems, then, that under different conditions, SIBs and the increased exposure to social investment market forces have the capacity either to foster or to stifle social innovation.

Building Effective Networks to Support Social Innovation

SIBs and their successful operation rely on a series of networks to coordinate cross-sectoral finance and skills towards pre-defined social outcomes. This section examines the extent to which SIBs, as a policy instrument, have the capacity to facilitate and foster new networks for social innovation. More specifically, this section considers what features of the SIB model support the development of effective networks and what bearing this has on the character and extent of the resultant social innovation.

SIBs have received considerable policy support globally based on the assumption that holistic and preventative service interventions will, in due course, lead to cost-savings for the public sector (Mulgan et al. 2010). As previously stated, the projected savings and effects of interventions are often diffuse and may well fall across a number of departments within and across different public authorities (and, in some cases, actually lead to increased public sector costs as in the GLA homelessness SIB). With this in mind, SIBs both demand and encourage networks of cross-departmental collaboration. As one interviewee noted, 'a lot of the time the fiscal savings are attributable to other government departments and areas so ideally they would act as co-commissioners'. As commissioners public authorities have the capacity to create networks of action that transcend the existing parameters of public service administration and governance. Indeed, this is repeatedly cited as a key source of public service reform and a necessary characteristic of public-sector innovation (HM Government 2011). One policy-maker stated:

> Co-commissioning is certainly a key source of the innovation.

In terms of public-sector commissioning, SIBs present a number of challenges for public authorities. The legal and accounting mechanisms by which contracts and cost-savings are conceived and service provision evaluated requires effective networks of communication and collaboration between governmental departments. On a number of occasions, public-sector commissioners found that:

> It is really hard to get people to get past their fiefdoms and get them to see the bigger picture.

In certain instances, overcoming 'territorial attitudes' and approaches within and across public authorities appeared to have been a key challenge for the development and operation of SIBs. Several interviewees highlighted an institutional culture within local public authorities that inhibited the development of networks to share knowledge and further the development of SIB contracts (e.g. Thames Reach 2015: 6). In particular, they highlighted a culture of secrecy and competition, which inhibited information sharing. Despite initiatives and funding from central government, a number of interviewees felt that this, coupled with the administrative burden of SIBs, had inhibited their wider take-up across public authorities. However, going forward, some were more optimistic about the prospects of SIBs in the longer term:

> The inefficiency of this and the layers of management is just huge but as time goes on that management will be needed less and less and to the extent that there is management, it can be spread over a greater network of actors.

In this regard, it is not entirely clear whether SIBs *rely* on effective networks of social innovation or whether SIBs *foster* effective networks for social innovation. It is possible, that both interpretations are valid. However, it remains to be seen whether some of the newly formed networks arising from SIBs will facilitate any institutional learning or enduring effect on public service administration and social innovation.

In addition to the systems of action and change emerging across public authorities, SIBs support the creation of networks that extend well beyond the public sector. On a number of occasions, the establishment and operation of SIBs appeared to foster operational networks that transcend sectoral boundaries. For some interviewees, SIBs had led to the creation of working relationships and networks that would not otherwise have come about. Through this sort of cross-agency co-ordination, these individuals were able to develop innovative solutions to shared challenges and organizational problems. For one service provider, they were able to initiate a working relationship with a key strategic partner as a result of the SIB. Based on this, the service provider went on to consolidate its relationship with this organization and, thereby, extend and enhance its operational activities (Thames Reach 2015: 4). The novelty and value of these networks appeared to reside in their hybrid character where third-sector providers were able to capitalize on the skills, finance, or expertise available in other sectors.

For many SIBs, their establishment greatly depended on leveraging existing contacts and networks of support. This was particularly the case for drawing together a syndicate of social impact investors, or for identifying a group of ancillary organizations to assist third-sector service providers fulfil the terms of their SIB contract. Local stakeholder involvement and collaboration was a particularly important factor in fostering a degree of service innovation. Depending on the context, this was both a product and condition of the social innovation.

While many exploited existing networks, others were able to develop and consolidate new networks of actions to realize their social mission:

> SIBs have definitely consolidated that relationship we have with schools and other stakeholders.

Some of the public-sector commissioners and policy-makers interviewed were keen to emphasize the importance of local stakeholder involvement. In addition to this, a number of interviewees stated that local stakeholder investment was a key source of, and opportunity for, social innovation and public service modernization.

Social impact investment has been repeatedly framed as a *blended* activity that has a social and economic return. At the very least, this means there is a financial return for the investor and a social return for the investee. However, there are varying degrees to which investors can also benefit from a social return. Where an individual or organization is fulfilling their specified social mission by investing in an organization or activity, it could be argued that this represents a genuine blend of social and economic return for both the investor and investee. Beyond the basic premise of 'doing good' or 'making a change', this represents a genuine alignment of specified interests and values shared by the investor and the investee. Where such alignment occurs, this may foster effective networks for social innovation. Local stakeholder investment in SIBs is one such example of this. Thus far, there are a number of examples of local authorities and housing associations co-investing in SIBs. In these instances, public-sector and third-sector agencies are able to pool their resources in a sustainable manner that may disrupt existing power relations and meet social need in innovative ways:

> But that's healthy in terms of sharing interest and commitment to the programme so local authorities sort of stood at the side of these programmes first time round but are now actively involved as co-investors.

Local stakeholder organizations that did decide to co-invest greatly depended on the expertise and oversight of national social investment organizations who were much more familiar with the SIB contract model. In large part, these local stakeholders deferred to national social investors to undertake the necessary due process and diligence as a part of the development of a SIB. This proved crucial to their buy-in and involvement.

Perhaps at the most extreme end of a social impact investment with social and economic returns, a third-sector service provider may elect to become a co-investor in a SIB. In this scenario, a co-investing service provider is paid up-front for the delivery of a service but is also paid a dividend based on the social outcomes it achieves. In many respects, this represents a typical payment-by-results contract but has the capacity to significantly alter the way in which third-sector organizations go about achieving and measuring the impact of their social mission. If done successfully, it may enhance the capacity of third-sector organizations; allowing them the freedom to engage in more innovative and experimental forms of service provision. On the other hand, if social outcomes are not achieved, it may expose the service provider to significant financial risk. For one of the SIBs under consideration, the service provider elected to co-invest and found this a broadly positive experience for their operations as well as financially beneficial.

Across all of the SIBs examined here, the national intermediary and social investment organizations played a pivotal role in establishing and maintaining networks of action and innovation. As outlined above, there are a number of beneficial outcomes to the establishment of these networks. However, these networks did tend to be orchestrated and managed by those with vested interests in the SIB model succeeding. This makes it particularly difficult to establish the role networks play and whether they facilitate a continuation, exploitation, or disruption of power relations.

Tackling Marginalization

Thus far, a great deal of attention has been paid to the ways in which SIBs affect the processes and organizational practices that have a bearing on the capacity for social innovation. This section examines the extent to which SIBs, as a policy instrument, effectively support social innovation that is capable of addressing social inclusion for marginalized and vulnerable populations—the key focus of this book. Arguably, the central consideration that determines whether a SIB is considered suitable is its capacity to produce *improved* social outcomes compared to the outcomes achieved through other service interventions. Ultimately, such evidenced effects are necessary to justify the extra costs, time, and effort associated with SIBs to establish whether they are financially viable and sustainable as an economic model for social innovation. In this sense, the 'litmus test' for a SIB is whether it improves the social outcomes for target populations that have, too often, been subject to policy failure.

To assess the effectiveness of SIBs in this respect, it is necessary to look at and beyond the outcome metrics that seek to capture their social impact. Despite the number and range of SIBs currently in operation, there is still relatively little systematic or methodologically rigorous evidence that is publicly available. As a result, the claimed or perceived potential of SIBs is largely inconclusive at this stage (Ronicle et al. 2014).

One example of a completed SIB is the world's first, established in 2010 at Peterborough Prison SIB. The results for the first cohort of one thousand prisoners were released in 2015 and suggested the service intervention has successfully reduced reoffending by 8.4 per cent (Jolliffe and Hedderman 2015). This was below the 10 per cent reduction required to trigger investor payments per cohort, but above the 7.5 per cent average reduction required to trigger final payments across all cohorts. In 2017, the results for the second cohort were made public demonstrating a 9.7 per cent reduction. This meant that the final result—for both cohorts—was an overall reduction in reoffending events of 9 per cent. This average result was well above the minimum required to trigger investor payments. As a consequence, seventeen investors were paid back in full with an additional return 'just over 3 per cent per annum for the period of investment' (Social Finance 2017). The SIB was, as a result, widely considered to be a success. Moreover, for the service providers brought together in the One Service, the Peterborough SIB also enabled service learning, innovation, flexibility and outcome-focused provision (Disley et al. 2011; Disley and Rubin 2014).

In addition, a number of qualitative evaluations of SIBs have been undertaken and there is anecdotal evidence to suggest that positive social outcomes have been achieved. However, there is comparatively little evidence on whether SIB services are performing any better than conventional service interventions or less complicated alternatives. Where evidence is available, it is mixed. For example, a survey found that just over half of commissioners and just over a third of service providers felt that the 'SIB they were involved in was leading to a greater level of impact with beneficiaries than would otherwise have been achieved' (Ronicle et al. 2014: vii).

To establish whether SIBs are performing comparatively better, it is necessary to refer to the comparative baselines and thresholds that dictate the extent and level of payment received by social investors. For the three SIBs under detailed consideration in this chapter, the payment metrics and comparative baselines are outlined in Table 12.2.

Reviewing the available quantitative and qualitative evidence on these three SIBs, there is some uncertainty as to whether SIBs are producing the social outcomes they set out to. In part, this is due to the poor availability of data or because a genuine comparison is not possible. On other occasions, it is simply because a service intervention has failed to deliver on pre-defined social outcomes. Each of the three SIBs is now considered in turn.

As of 2016, the evaluations of the Essex SIB suggested that it had exceeded the majority of its targets and was performing at a rate above the national average (OPM 2015). However, it was hard to disassociate the relative impact of the SIB model from the Multi-Systemic Therapy (MST) introduced as part of the Essex Children Support Services Programme (Social Finance 2014a). In its own right, MST was a relatively innovative service intervention for Essex County Council and the comparison of its effect against a historical baseline can prove problematic. In addition, the programme of children support services was restructured at the same time as the Essex SIB was established. As a result, it was hard to identify and attribute the cause of any improvement, or indeed deterioration, to the SIB

Table 12.2. Social outcome metrics

	Outcome payment metric(s)	Comparison group
Essex: Children on the Edge of Care	Total days adolescents from a treated cohort spend in residential care, measured over 30-day time periods.	Baseline historical comparison group
Merseyside: New Horizons	For Years 10 and 11: • Improved behaviour at school (£800) • Stop persistent truancy (£1,300) • Achievement of NVQ level 1 (£700) • Achievement of NVQ level 2 (£2,200)	Counterfactual group established using a matched area comparison design
London: Rough Sleepers	• 12 months accommodation (£7,000) • 18 months accommodation (£3,000) • Initial reconnection (move to another country) (£800) • 6 months reconnection (£6,100) • Achievement of NQF level 2 equivalent qualification (£400) • Volunteering/self-employment 13 weeks (£200), 26 weeks (£600) • Part-time employment 13 weeks (£500), 26 weeks (£1,500) • Full-time employment 13 weeks (£1,300), 26 weeks (£4,000) • Payment per individual above given baseline not seen rough sleeping in given quarter (£3,800 for first four quarters and £2,400 thereafter) • Payment per accident and emergency service use avoided beyond baseline per year (£100). Initial accommodation (£700)	Comparative baselines on a historical virtual cohort for rough sleeping and A&E usage. Other metrics do not use a baseline but evidence needs to be provided for payments

Source: Authors.

model. As many have noted, the benefits and risks of SIBs have to be considered within a broader system of service provision and socio-structural change. At best, the Essex SIB could be seen as helping improve the outcomes of the service users 'indirectly' (OPM 2015).

The New Horizons SIB was part of the Innovation Fund pilot programme commissioned by the Department for Work and Pensions. The objectives of the Innovation Fund were to grow the social investment market and support young people who are disadvantaged, or at risk of disadvantage, by helping them succeed in education or training and, thereby, improve their employability and reduce their long-term 'dependency on benefits'. As a senior policy-maker noted:

> Ian Duncan Smith [Minister for DWP at the time of fieldwork] was interested in exploring SIBs as a way of supporting some of our most disadvantaged groups in society.

Quarterly published statistics confirmed that, through the New Horizons SIB, at least 4,700 positive outcomes were achieved by 2016 (DWP 2016). While it was not possible to establish whether the service intervention would prevent service users from becoming NEETs, an interim qualitative evaluation found that 'virtually all young people interviewed were positive about the project interventions they were participating in' (DWP 2014: 28). Furthermore, a number of reports suggested that the New Horizons programme far exceeded its targets and expectations. For example, 24 per cent of its service users achieved 5 A*–C GCSEs against a target of 5 per cent (BSC 2013). This confirmed that, in many respects, the SIB achieved its intended social outcomes. Whether this would translate into a reduction in the overall rate of NEETs in the Merseyside area remained to be seen. Difficulty in producing outcomes for those service users already classified as NEETs suggested that service interventions would not always prove successful in this regard. However, despite the lack of any official data, information available suggested that there was some positive progress achieved through the Innovation Fund pilots (Ronicle et al. 2014).

Overall, the performance of the London Homelessness SIB was mixed. While the final evaluation had not been released as of 2016, the latest available data suggested that its service interventions had struggled to fulfil targets (DCLG 2015). Performance improved over the course of the SIB but the service intervention consistently underperformed in a number of areas (Ronicle et al. 2014). For example, rough sleeping was not reduced below the modelled baseline and both service providers struggled to meet their initial and sustained reconnection targets. By contrast, it appears service providers exceeded their targets for securing stable accommodation and its maintenance. It is important to note that 'providers were pleased with their achievement of this outcome, which accounts for 40 per cent of the available payments' (DCLG 2015: 32). This is particularly significant as this ensured the financial viability of the London Homelessness SIB—particularly for Thames Reach as a co-investor. In addition, the service exceeded its targets on sustainable full-time employment but did not achieve targets on attainment of qualifications, volunteering, or part-time work.

As noted by the evaluations and stakeholders involved in the establishment of the SIB, service providers were working with a target population with highly complex needs and challenges (DCLG 2014; Ronicle et al. 2014; DCLG 2015).

In this instance, it appears that the SIB model was neither successful in producing a number of its desired social outcomes nor in improving outcomes compared to a baseline. On the only *comparable* baseline (rough sleeping), the London Homeless SIB did not produce sufficient social outcomes. While there is no doubt that the SIB produced positive social outcomes for many service users (DCLG 2014: 93), there is no evidence to suggest that this worked any more effectively or efficiently than other services. In key documentation, both service providers confirmed the value and difference that the SIB model had offered. However, while the SIB model facilitated the opportunity to work with clients in a different way (St Mungo's Broadway 2015; Thames Reach 2015), it did not appear to lead to improved social outcomes when compared to other services.

Overall, an analysis of the three SIBs discussed above suggests that there is little definitive evidence that these examples tackled marginalization more successfully than possible alternatives. That is to say, while service interventions offered through the SIB model were producing a range of valuable social outcomes, it remains unclear whether these outcomes were any better than the existing service offer to service users. Put another way, there is little evidence to suggest that the extra costs, time, and effort associated with these SIBs translated into superior outcomes. In these instances, it seems that conventional funding mechanisms may be better placed to deliver and produce social outcomes for a greater number of service users.[2] As one social investor commented:

> I have mixed opinions about SIBs if I'm honest... I wanna pay for stuff that makes a difference so on that hand I think SIBs have got a lot of potential. The difficulty though with SIBs is that I don't think they can apply to everything and they need to be set up right because the risk is that you don't want them to be set up in such a way that the outcomes don't get paid for—or worse the outcomes don't actually get achieved. What is being paid for is success but it needs to be that.

Of course, this is not to say that, the SIBs examined here, as a policy instrument, do not have the capacity effectively to achieve pre-defined social outcomes—as evidenced in Peterborough. For example, the Merseyside SIB successfully met and exceeded some of its key outcome targets. However, overall, it seems that there are a number of challenges that arose in seeking to establish the impact and effect of these SIBs on fostering social innovation capable of tackling marginalization.

At least within the UK context, SIBs can be seen as part of broader actuarial approach to public services and welfare provision in recent years (Cameron 2013; HM Government, 2016). Within this context, social problems and their resolution

[2] This was, to some extent, the argument for introducing the statutory probation service Transforming Rehabilitation following on from the Peterborough Pilot SIB. That this had the effect of ending the SIB early was not considered to be a problem by policy-makers.

have been considered with respect to their cost and prospective savings to 'taxpayers'. SIB outcomes and payment metrics have been similarly constructed based on the prospective financial savings that they may eventually produce for the public sector. According to Mulgan et al. (2010), for SIBs to be an appropriate funding model the specific impacts of the intervention need to be quantifiable, enough people need to benefit from the intervention to enable robust impact measurement, and savings for government stakeholders need to be greater than the costs of an intervention. Based on the premise of preventative service provision, this funding model has many prospective benefits for increasing (social impact) investment in public services and social outcomes.

However, there are many outcomes, particularly those associated with tackling marginalization that may not necessarily be 'bankable' or marketizable. That is to say, their social value is not always of financial value to social impact investors or public finances. This poses a particular challenge for ensuring outcomes are financially justifiable while also being grounded in a commitment to tackling the causes and effects of social exclusion. There is a potential for slippage in this regard, where the democratic imperative for government to address social problems is rendered secondary to the objective of reducing public social expenditure against a backdrop budgetary restraint. For example, the reconnection of non-UK rough sleepers through the London Homelessness SIB could certainly be seen as motivated by financial savings to the public sector. This is particularly the case given that service provider guidance highlighted 'the very harsh approach' to rough sleepers in many of the settings in which they sought to achieve a reconnection.

Despite attempts to create and measure against a comparable counterfactual, the shifting social and policy landscape within any setting makes a systematic evaluation of impact methodologically challenging. For example, it is hard to establish the specific impact of the London Homelessness SIB in light of housing benefit and welfare reforms implemented over the course of the service intervention. Indeed, an evaluation of the SIB acknowledged how such changes inhibited and assisted the attainment of pre-defined social outcomes (DCLG 2015). Within such a context, articulating and ascribing the cause of a SIBs 'success' or 'failure' can be highly problematic (cf. McHugh et al. 2013). This is due, in large part, to the focus on siloed inputs and outcomes that acknowledge little relation to the broader setting within which SIBs operate. On a number of occasions, service providers and practitioners pointed to factors that might obscure the impact of service interventions on marginalization. In certain instances, the broader policy context may actually serve to over-exaggerate the relative value of social innovation policy instruments such as SIBs. A service provider noted:

> A slightly perverse response I know but the amount of disinvestment through local authorities has really helped us. There used to be funding routes that many of these [service beneficiaries] could of accessed and programmes they could of

> used and due to the kind of austerity cost-cutting they are just not there anymore so there are swathes of [service beneficiaries] who have been abandoned by some of the national policy decisions so that's really helped this programme in that the eligible cohort is huge and the need is bigger than ever so there was never any scarcity of participants... perversely cuts have made this programme more popular and more necessary and more likely to succeed I think.

Arguably, not enough attention has been paid to the substantial implications this has for making *relative* conclusions about how SIBs affect marginalization and the long-term opportunities and outcomes for marginalized and vulnerable populations.

Rather than a static condition, marginalization is essentially a social process through which personal, social, or environmental traits are transformed into actual or potential factors of disadvantage (see further chapters 1 and 3). If a social outcome is achieved through a SIB, there is sometimes an assumption about the permanency of its effect. In reality, service users are subject to dynamic conditions within and beyond the SIB intervention. This raises an important question about the legacy of SIBs and the extent to which it is reasonable to assume their lasting effect on marginalization, particularly with regard to payment metrics constructed on the basis of prospective future savings to the public sector. This 'exit' problem only becomes a pressing policy issue as SIBs come to their conclusion (see Nicholls and Tomkinson 2015).

With respect to the three SIBs considered here, it is clear that the tailored and intensive support received by many service users greatly improved their immediate situation and opportunities. Based on interviews with a number of service users, interventions were clearly transformative to their current and future prospects. Intense and tailored support helped service users identify and realize their goals within particular settings, as interviewees made clear:

> Through the SIB and all that, I ended up getting some volunteering and a part-time job in a hostel for about six months. It's given me the confidence to go further than what I, er, have done in the past.
>
> If it weren't for [practitioner name], I wouldn't be here. And that's actually the truth... If I wouldn't have worked with him I wouldn't be here now. Everyone I knew thought that I probably wouldn't make it until the end of the year and I surprised myself how long I've lasted.
>
> I'd say it's helped quite a bit in terms of helping me get to where I want to be. I'm not there yet but I will be. If they didn't help me I suppose I'd still be homeless.
>
> Helping me get my grades because otherwise I wouldn't have been getting my grades or nothing. Because I'm achieving my goals, my Bs and Cs.

Service interventions helped equip service users with the resources and skills they needed to overcome factors that contributed towards their marginalization or social exclusion. In doing so, these interventions helped tackle 'actual or potential factors of disadvantage' for many service users:

> I feel more positive now because I'm learning more--I'm getting the work done what I've got to and I know where to aim and what grades to hit.
>
> It's given me opportunities plus money in my own pocket, which means I don't gotta rely on the government supporting me. That's important to me because it gives me a sense of self-worth and it means that I'm contributing.
>
> It's given me confidence to keep my accommodation and pay my rent.

Very often the intensity and regularity of support proved particularly important to securing social outcomes. Without this kind of support, a number of service users felt that they would not have been able to overcome the challenges they faced. The holistic assessment and sensitive treatment of a service user's situation was considered especially important:

> I was being excluded all the time and being naughty and all that, and it come to the point where [practitioner name] came to see me near enough every other day in Maccy's or something.
>
> [Service provider's name] filled out loads of forms for me to go to the housing team which I'm not sure how that works but... and just took it from there... he took me through the different panels who assess me. He did all the paperwork for that—if he hadn't of done that I've probably still be in the hostel now. They were constantly on the phone with me and I needed that—just that little bit of guidance... you know more hands on—just to get me in the door sort of thing.

Undoubtedly, these services were of immense value to service users. However, through the course of interviews it became clear that their highly complex needs threatened the sustainability of particular outcomes. By virtue of the SIB model, services focused on achieving social outcomes, rather than the continuity of service outputs characteristic of some conventional public sector commissioning. As a result, a number of service users felt that there needed to be 'more of a transition period' between the intense support they received through the SIB and their subsequent 'independence'. Following receipt of services through the SIB, one service user felt that they lacked the resources and information to operate independently and effectively. They attributed their recent drug abuse and social isolation to feeling somewhat 'abandoned' after outcomes had been achieved:

> I'm surprised the way it's just been ended so suddenly—it's meant I'm not doing so well now.
>
> I'm struggling at the moment... I've moved so far away from everybody that hasn't helped and it's something I've got to sort out. I've relapsed and I'm hoping it's not permanent.

This points to the fact that SIBs have the capacity effectively to tackle marginalization but only if they exist alongside continued service and support systems made available to service users at the exit point (alternatively the SIB may be recommissioned as was the case with the New Horizons SIB). While service users were overwhelmingly positive about service interventions, there still remained concerns regarding their future prospects and opportunities. For example, many of the young people receiving support through the Merseyside New Horizons SIB felt that the service had helped improve their educational attainment but were worried about their employment prospects and living arrangements in the future. Despite significant help, these individuals were still confronted with broader structural factors such as localized unemployment and disadvantage. Therefore, while SIBs can demonstrate some success in tackling certain 'factors of disadvantage', they also need to feature as part of a wider policy agenda committed to addressing the broader structuration processes through which marginalization and vulnerability arise and are maintained.

Conclusion

This chapter has examined the evidence to date to explore how far Social Impact Bonds can generate social innovation to address social exclusion and marginalization. By means of three detailed case analyses this chapter has also used new empirical data to delineate the complex drivers and effects of the SIB model in action. This work suggests that SIBs can have positive effects on the social outcomes for key service user groups but that this cannot be considered in isolation from other contextual factors. It has also proposed a number of lines of critical enquiry into the utility and appropriateness of the payment-by-results approach to service provision more generally and the specifics of the SIB model in particular (see also Cooper et al. 2015; Child et al. 2016).

For example, the significant amount of public attention and investment in SIBs noted above has occurred alongside substantial cuts to state funding for the voluntary and community sector. The National Council for Voluntary Organisations (NCVO) estimated that statutory income for civil-society and third-sector organizations fell by 9.4 per cent between 2010/11 and 2015/16 (Bhati and Heywood 2013). Moreover, grants from government fell by two thirds between 2000 and 2013 (NCVO 2015). This posed considerable challenges for the capacity of third-sector organizations to realize their social mission (NCVO 2015). In tandem, policy support and interest in social impact investment has grown substantially over the same period as evidenced by increased interest in SIBs: 'at a time of tight public finances, Social Impact Bonds represent a new and innovative way of attracting investment from outside the public sector' (Big Lottery Fund 2010). While some have viewed this as an opportunity, others have seen social impact investment as a tool 'of last resort' within the context of limited funding sources. Third-sector service providers made this clear on several occasions:

> In an ideal world we (charities and voluntary and community groups) wouldn't have to resort to social investment.
>
> I could mount an argument that the role of the state should be to use public expenditure to properly support [service beneficiary] as part of the welfare state. Given that we live in a country where the welfare state has withdrawn from that level of intervention, then social investment is an effective alternative.
>
> The wider agenda is about the withdrawal of the state and the reduction of its responsibilities. If we were in a time with a government that was investing more in public spending no one would go to social investment.

Furthermore, SIBs have attracted wider criticism as representing a neo-liberal model of welfare that places the responsibility for a social exclusion on the individual service user (Cooper 2013) rather than on more systemic issues in society. This is evidenced in the outcomes metrics typically focusing on changes in *individual* service-user behaviour or actions rather than addressing their context or circumstances. As such, this critique suggests that SIBs can never have long-term impact or any effects beyond their immediate cohort or target group. Such an analysis, while valid in terms of its individualized focus, ignores the more experimental models of SIBs (such as the Rykers Island SIB in New York City) where the SIB offers an untried service delivery innovation that—if successful—could scale.

With respect to the Extended Social Grid Model, these critiques also remind us that SIBs offer innovation (and, at times, controversy) across institutions, cognitive norms, and networks. As noted above, SIBs drive new institutional arrangements around the financing of social outcomes bringing together private and public capital in contracts predicated on social outcomes. SIBs also challenge cognitive norms around the process of service delivery and the most effective and efficient models of such provision. Finally, SIBs are predicated on building new (successful) partnerships and networks across the private, public, and third sectors around common impact objectives and incentives. As such, SIBs stand as an example of the model of social innovation proposed by the Extended Social Grid Model—where social innovation resides in changing the dynamics within each of its three constituent elements to drive broader socio-structural change. Thus, while the body of robust evidence on the overall *effectiveness* of SIBs is yet to be established, there is already good reason to believe that SIBs offer examples of innovation around service provision for the marginalized both within and without government. However, future research will need to determine whether this has been for the better or the worse of society as a whole.

References

Alcock, P. 2009. 'Devolution or Divergence? Third Sector Policy across the UK since 2000'. TSRC Working Paper No. 2. Birmingham: Third Sector Research Centre.

Beckert, J. 2009. 'The Social Order of Markets'. *Theory and Societ,* 38: 245–69.

Bhati, N., and J. Heywood. 2013. 'Counting the Cuts: The Impact of Spending Cuts on the UK Voluntary and Community Sector, 2013 Update'. London: NCVO.

Big Lottery Fund. 2010. 'BIG Paves Way forward through Social Investment'. London: BIG.

BSC. 2013. 'Strong Uplift in GCSE Results for Young People Benefiting from Social Impact Bond Scheme: Pilot Project to Address Youth Unemployment Could Save the Taxpayer over £88,800 per Young Person'. London: Big Society Capital.

Cameron, D. 2013. 'Social Investment Can Be a Great Force for Social Change'. Social Impact Investment Forum. London.

Carter, E. and A. Whitworth. 2015. 'Creaming and Parking in Quasi-Marketised Welfare-to-Work Schemes: Designed out of or Designed in to the UK Work Programme?' *Journal of Social Policy* 44: 277–96.

Child, C., B. Gibbs, and K. Rowley. 2016. 'Paying for Success: An Appraisal of Social Impact Bonds'. *Global Economics and Management Review* 21(1–2): 36–45.

Conservative Party. (2010). 'Big Society Not Big Government: Building a Big Society'. London: Conservative Party.

Cooper, Trudi. 2013. 'Institutional Context and Youth Work Professionalization in Post-welfare Societies'. *Child and Youth Services* 34(2): 112–24.

Cooper, C., C. Graham, and B. O'Dwyer. 2015. 'Social Impact Bonds: Can Private Finance Rescue Public Programs? *Accounting, Organizations and Society* 55: 63–82.

DCLG. 2014. 'Qualitative Evaluation of the London Homeless Social Impact Bond: First Interim Report'. London: Department for Communities and Local Government.

DCLG. 2015. 'Qualitative Evaluation of the London Homelessness Social Impact Bond: Second Interim Report'. London: Department for Communities and Local Government.

Deloitte. 2012. 'Paying for Outcomes: Solving Complex Societal Issues through Social Impact Bonds'. London: Deloitte and Touche LLP.

Disley, E., J. Rubin, E. Scraggs, N. Burrowes, and D. Culley. 2011. 'Lessons Learned from the Planning and Early Implementation of the Social Impact Bond at HMP Peterborough'. London: RAND Europe and Ministry of Justice.

Disley, E. and J. Rubin, J. 2014. 'Phase 2 Report from the Payment by Results Social Impact Bond Pilot at HMP Peterborough'. London: RAND Europe and Ministry of Justice.

Disley, E., C. Giacomantonio, K. Kruithof, and M. Sim. 2015. 'The Payment by Results Social Impact Bond Pilot at HMP Peterborough'. London: RAND Europe and Ministry of Justice.

DWP. 2014. 'Innovation Fund Pilots Qualitative Evaluation'. Research Report No. 880: A report of research carried out by Insite Research and Consulting on behalf of the Department for Work and Pensions. Sheffield: Department for Work and Pensions.

DWP. 2016. 'Youth Unemployment Innovation Fund Pilot: Starts and Outcomes'. Sheffield: Department for Work and Pensions.

Edmiston, D. 2015. 'EU Public Policy, Social Innovation and Marginalisation: Reconciling Ambitions with Policy Instruments'. CrESSI Working Paper No. 18. Brussels: European Commission, DG Research.

Edmiston, D., and A. Nicholls. 2017. 'Social Impact Bonds: The Role of Private Capital in Outcomes Based Commissioning'. *Journal of Social Policy* 46(1): 1–20.

Esping-Andersen, G. 1990. *The Three Worlds of Welfare Capitalism*. Cambridge: Polity.

European Commission. 2013. *Guide to Social Innovation*. Brussels: Regional and Urban Policy Publications, Office of the European Union.

European Commission. 2014. *Proposed Approaches to Social Impact Measurement in European Commission Legislation and in Practice Relating to EuSEFs and the EaSI*. Brussels: GECES Sub-group on Impact Measurement, European Commission.

European Parliament. 2014. 'Social Impact Bonds: Private Finance That Generates Social Returns'. Brussels: European Union.

Farnsworth, K., and Z. Irving. 2012. 'Varieties of Crisis, Varieties of Austerity: Social Policy in Challenging Times'. *Journal of Poverty and Social Justice* 20: 133–47.

Goodall, E. 2014. 'Choosing Social Impact Bonds: A Practitioner's Guide'. London: Bridges Ventures LLP.

Gustafsson-Wright, E., S. Gardiner, and V. Putcha. 2015. 'The Potential and Limitations of Impact Bonds: Lessons from the First Five Years of Experience Worldwide'. Global Economy and Development. Washington, DC: Brookings Institute.

HM Government. 2011. 'Scaling up Innovation in the Public Sector'. London: HMSO.

HM Government. 2016. 'Social Investment: A Force for Social Change: 2016 Strategy'. London: HMSO.

Hopkins, L. 2010. 'Mapping the Third Sector: A Context for Social Leadership'. London: The Work Foundation.

Hughes, J. and J. Scherer. 2014. 'Foundations for Social Impact Bonds: How and Why Philanthropy Is Catalyzing the Development of a New Market'. New York: Social Finance US.

Jolliffe, D., and C. Hedderman. 2015. 'Peterborough Social Impact Bond: Final Report on Cohort 1 Analysis'. Prepared for Ministry of Justice by QinetiQ Ltd and University of Leicester. https://www.gov.uk/government/uploads/system/uploads/attachment_data/file/341684/peterborough-social-impact-bond-report.pdf.

Kohli, J. 2010. 'Financing What Works: Social Impact Bonds Hold Promise'. Washington, DC: Center for American Progress.

Levitas, R. 1996. 'The Concept of Social Exclusion and the New Durkheimian Hegemony'. *Critical Social Policy* 16(46): 5–20.

McHugh, N., S. Sinclair, M. Roy, L. Huckfield, and C. Donaldson. 2013. 'Social Impact Bonds: A Wolf in Sheep's Clothing?' *Journal of Poverty and Social Justice* 21: 247–57.

Molina, A. H. 2010. *Hybridity in Social Innovation and Entrepreneurship: State of the Art and Theoretical Challenge*. Edinburgh: University of Edinburgh.

Mulgan, G., N. Reeder, M. Aylott, and L. Bo'sher. 2010. 'Social Impact Investment: the Challenge and Opportunity of Social Impact Bonds'. London: The Young Foundation.

NAO. 2015. 'Outcome-Based Payment Schemes: Government's Use of Payment by Results. London: HMSO.

NCVO. 2015. 'UK Civil Society Almanac 2015'. London: National Council for Voluntary Organisations.

Nicholls, A., R. Paton, and J. Emerson (eds). 2015. *Social Finance*. Oxford: Oxford University Press.

Nicholls, A., and S. Teasdale. 2016. 'Neoliberalism by Stealth? Exploring Continuity and Change within the UK Social Enterprise Policy Paradigm'. *Policy and Politics* 45 (3): 323–41.

Nicholls, A., and E. Tomkinson. 2015. 'The Peterborough Pilot Social Impact Bond'. In *Social Finance*, edited by A. Nicholls, R. Paton, and J. Emerson, pp. 335–82. Oxford: Oxford University Press.

OPM. 2015. 'Evaluation of the Essex MST SIB'. London: OPM: Helping to Improve Social Outcomes.

Phillips, S. D., and S. R. Smith. 2014. 'A Dawn of Convergence? Third Sector Policy Regimes in the "Anglo-Saxon" Cluster'. *Public Management Review* 16: 1141–63.

Raffass, T. 2016. 'Work Enforcement in Liberal Democracies'. *Journal of Social Policy* 45(3): 417–34.

Ronicle, J., N. Stanworth, H. Edward, and T. Fox. 2014. 'Social Impact Bonds: The State of Play: Full Report'. Commissioning Better Outcomes Evaluation. London: Big Lottery Fund.

Social Finance. 2009. 'Social Impact Bonds: Rethinking Finance for Social Outcomes'. https://www.socialfinance.org.uk/resources/publications/social-impact-bonds-rethinking-finance-social-outcomes, accessed 21 June 2019.

Social Finance. 2014a. 'The Essex Social Impact Bond: A Year in Review'. Social Impact Bonds: Supporting Adolescents on the Edge of Care. London: Social Finance.

Somers, A. 2013. 'The Emergence of Social Enterprise Policy in New Labour's Second Term'. PhD thesis, University of London.

St Mungo's Broadway. 2015. 'Street Impact: Stories from the Street—Holistic Approaches to Lasting Recovery'. London: St Mungo Community Housing Association.

Thames Reach. 2015. 'Social Impact Bond for Entrenched Rough Sleepers—Key Areas of Learning'. London: Thames Reach.

UK Cabinet Office. 2012. 'Social Impact Bonds. https://www.gov.uk/social-impact-bonds, accessed 12 February 2013.

Warner, M. E. 2013. 'Private Finance for Public Goods: Social Impact Bonds'. *Journal of Economic Policy Reform* 16: 303–19.

PART III

IMPLICATIONS FOR THEORY AND PRACTICE

13

The Extended Social Grid Model Revisited

Rafael Ziegler, Alex Nicholls, Jari Aro, Cees van Beers, Enrica Chiappero-Martinetti, Daniel Edmiston, Attila Havas, Risto Heiskala, Nadia von Jacobi, Klaus Kubeczko, Martijn Jeroen van der Linden, Lara Maestripieri, Georg Mildenberger, György Molnár, and Gudrun-Christine Schimpf

Introduction

The preceding chapters drew on the Extended Social Grid Model (ESGM) to offer new insights into the contexts and applications of social innovation. In terms of an analysis of social innovation and marginalization the model sets out a plural focus on social sources of power—cultural, economic, security-related, natural, artefactual, and political—and how these relate to a dynamic triumvirate of social forces represented by the interactions of cognitive frames, social networks, and institutions across time and space.

The ESGM does not attempt to represent quantitative relations in the social world, let alone model or visualize precise causal or spatial relations, as more linear and positivistic models do. Rather, it draws together a number of theoretical strands of work to offer a novel heuristic of the complexities of the social world. Drawing especially from Beckert (2010) and Mann (Mann 1986; Heiskala 2016), taken together these theories offer explanatory pluralism and with it a thesis that the explanation of social change is irreducible to a single source of power (Mann) or to a single social force (Beckert). The ESGM serves as a discovery mechanism for 'spaces of innovation' (Beckert 2010: 605) that lie in the interplay of the sources of power and their expression in social forces. Drawing on the capabilities approach (Sen 1999; Nussbaum 2000), a further, theoretic commitment evinced here is ethical individualism used to help us evaluate the effects of social power and of social innovation at the level of individuals. Put together, these strands of theory offer a new integrated approach with which to examine social innovation that is sufficiently sophisticated—does not define issues away at the outset—while also grounding itself in a normatively explicit ethical vocabulary.

The ESGM is deliberatively interdisciplinary drawing upon work in economics, philosophy, and sociology, especially at the intersection of economic sociology

Rafael Ziegler, Alex Nicholls, Jari Aro, Cees van Beers, Enrica Chiappero-Martinetti, Daniel Edmiston, Attila Havas, Risto Heiskala, Nadia von Jacobi, Klaus Kubeczko, Martijn Jeroen van der Linden, Lara Maestripieri, Georg Mildenberger, György Molnár, and Gudrun-Christine Schimpf, *The Extended Social Grid Model Revisited*. In: *Creating Economic Space for Social Innovation*. Edited by: Alex Nicholls and Rafael Ziegler, Oxford University Press (2019).
DOI: 10.1093/oso/9780198830511.003.0013

and ethics. As such it aims to offer new research insights into social innovation. By locating the capabilities approach within a broader social sciences framework, the emancipatory ethical contribution of the capabilities approach for human development is enhanced (Otto et al. 2017). Inversely, social innovation research drawing only upon the main social science disciplines has been limited by a failure to engage with ethics (Jenson and Harrison 2013: 8), often producing an overly economistic perspective that may lose sight of key questions of power and social structure in favour of narrow conceptions of agency and market dynamics (Jessop et al. 2013: 110–20).

Revisiting the chapters in Part II of this book (as well as the accompanying reports and papers within the CrESSI project),[1] we are now in a position to summarize our main observations (sections one to three) and to reconsider the model and its relevance for social innovation research (section four). Section five critically revisits the ESGM and the final section summarizes the main conclusions.[2]

Economic Space for Social Innovation

Discussions of 'economic space' or the 'economic underpinnings' of social innovation share the conceptual malleability of the concept of social innovation (Ayob et al. 2016), not least due to the diverse set of actors that the concept attracts both in theory and practice, and that in turn co-shapes its use and potential as a concept for social change (Ziegler 2017a). Still, this does not mean that 'anything goes' (Jenson and Harrison 2013: 15). Economic power, according to Mann, derives 'from the human need to extract, transform, distribute, and consume the produce of nature' (Mann 2013: 1–2). We have explored this point via a typology of modes of the provision of goods and services—public, self, informal, public, market, and professional modes of provision—and the reconfiguration and blurring of these modes throughout history and different regimes and contexts. In this way, a narrow focus on market action alone—focusing only on business organizations—is avoided and the complex diversity of our conceptualization of economic space is made visible for analysis.

Moreover, the ESGM situates our discussion of economic space in relation to the widely used social ontology of state, business, civil society, and family, and its variations in several theoretical traditions.[3] Public provision refers to the state,

[1] See the various CrESSI reports available from: https://www.sbs.ox.ac.uk/creating-economic-space-social-innovation.

[2] This chapter has benefitted from editorial work by Amelia Pope, as well as discussions at ISIRC 2015 and 2016 and at the Social Innovation Conference in Vienna 2015 where the ESGM was presented for discussion.

[3] Hegel (1821–2), in his lectures on the *Philosophy of Right*, discusses a threefold structure of family, the state, and civil society (the latter referring to self-interested actions today commonly associated with capitalist markets); in the twentieth century, Jürgen Habermas (1981), in his *Theory of Communicative*

market provision to business, self and informal provision to civil society and family (see chapter 3). Intriguingly, professional provision based on expert knowledge cannot be situated in this way—and, yet, knowledge is very important for social innovation according to the case studies presented. We will specifically return to this question of knowledge further below in section four. The historical perspectives within our case studies suggest that there are a dynamic variety of such configurations (see also Scheuerle et al. 2016: 177–8). For social housing, Lévy-Vroelant et al. (2008: 42) capture this diversity well:

> Social housing was never dominated by one actor for a long period. Private and public interests, central governments and local authorities, left-wing and right-wing ideologies, individualism and collectivism, big estates and single family units, renting and ownership—all could be found in social housing. The heterogeneous (patchwork) character of the system may explain its exceptional capacity for adaptation and innovation. It is also the source of its remarkable pluralism—the actors are continuously reconfiguring, establishing new alliances and 'techno-structures' to adapt the fundamental ideas to new needs and circumstances and the structural characteristics given by path dependency.

Our historical observations—based on studies in a European context—are confirmed elsewhere by work mapping the global actors involved in social innovation (e.g. Howaldt et al. 2018: 12): 'We can say that cross-sectoral collaboration of the public sector, civil society, and the private sector is playing a key role.' In areas such as social housing, freshwater supply or education, the historical perspective shows a continuous variety and reconfiguration of modes of provision, including heated controversies when one mode gains strength or threatens to eliminate others.

However, this last observation requires two important qualifications. First, observing a variety of configurations of the state, the market, civil society, and the family does not mean that there are no crosscutting phenomena. While a variety of welfare regimes can be seen to co-create social innovation policies, a distinct cognitive frame has had a systemic impact since the 1970s: neo-liberalism. It proposes the idea that market exchange is and should be the primary framework for the allocation of all resources including welfare and public goods. This ideological turn brought with it an agenda of privatization, fiscal austerity, liberalization, and the monetization of all goods and services.[4] For social policy this

Action, distinguishes the political and economy systems from a lifeworld of everyday action and communication. See the contributions in Nicholls, Simon, and Gabriel 2015 for various uses of such social ontology in social innovation research.

[4] We cannot go into the details of an extended discussion of neo-liberalism here. See Brown (2015), and Heiskala and Aro (2018) for an analysis of neo-liberalism in the EU in terms of the ordoliberalism

often means, more subtly, a push to improve, complement, or enhance activities of the state via the introduction of various private actors from business and civil society (such as charities or social enterprises). However, a primary focus on market provision and market actors has reduced the former pluralism of provision of social goods and its capacity to provide users with a variety of options adaptive to their respective (local) contexts. Unsurprisingly, then, there has been a concern in some social innovation research when the term (and its actions) is reduced to a narrow definition drawing upon models of social business in markets (Jessop et al. 2013). With respect to those least advantaged in society, such a reductive conceptualization introduces a tension between the social goals of supporting the most marginalized and a business focus on the financial sustainability (equated with profitability) of attendant projects and programmes. For example, the quest for financial sustainability in micro-credit has sometimes been an obstacle to addressing extreme poverty (see chapter 7). Similarly, a primary focus on profitability incentivizes social enterprises to 'cream' their service user populations—for example, in some Social Impact Bonds programmes (see chapter 12).

Molnár and Havas (see chapter 7) proposed abandoning the dogma of financial sustainability with its focus on loans and their repayment, and to focus instead on providing sufficient power to community-focused private-sector funders who can make sure that financial support in the form of loans, grants, and combinations of both is used in an effective and efficient way while keeping the needs and capacities of those supported in primary focus. Arguably, this was also one of the initial motivations behind Social Impact Bonds; so far, however, this has proven far from straightforward (see chapter 10). Thus, there is a need for a deep but difficult shift, or at least rebalancing, in the cognitive frame of social innovation finance from returns to investors and profitability to social freedom returns to service users in the sense of paying attention to advancing the capabilities of beneficiaries as a primary strategic objective (see chapter 14).

Furthermore, offering a pluralism of configurations of provision (and their reconfigurations) does not imply that social innovation is 'good' or 'just' and necessarily helps the marginalized. Rather, the task is to evaluate how various configurations and their interactions advance (or hinder) the opportunities and well-being of their respective target groups. There are numerous challenges in this balancing and there is often a tension between a focus on those most marginalized and the success of social innovation itself:

> If a social innovation only targets the most disadvantaged, the probability of failure is higher, and this SIM is, thus, less appealing to practitioners and

in evidence in primary EU-strategies such as the Lisbon Strategy and Euro 2020. See also Dardot and Laval (2013), who particularly emphasize the impact of these developments on what we here call cognitive frames, more precisely on self-understanding and governing in terms of competition.

> potential clients, reducing its potential for diffusion. If only less disadvantaged groups are assisted, the social exclusion of the most disadvantaged may, actually, be made worse. A particular form of this tension is the issue of ethnic targeting, namely the trade-off between exact targeting and building inter-community connections. Although socially excluded Roma were the explicit target group of the Kiútprogram, ethnic selection would have hampered, or even completely prevented, the strengthening of inter-community connections overall. As the latter is an essential component of social inclusion, this would have been a grave mistake. (Molnár and Havas in chapter 7)

These qualifications and tensions within even an internally diverse economic space for social innovation point to a central finding of the CrESSI research project: a focus on economic space for social innovation alone is insufficient, especially if marginalized populations are to be prioritized. Put differently, for a better understanding of the contours of the economic space for social innovation, we need to consider further sources of power and how these interact with economic power. Of these sources, political power is especially important. It creates much of the context within which social innovations evolve. Our perspective on social innovation specifically underlines the influence of the state and, more recently, of supranational entities such as the European Union (EU: see especially chapter 11). This influence is varied, not least due to the variety of states and their socio-economic structures and welfare regimes (Esping-Andersen 1990).[5] Such regimes and their historical trajectories strongly influence the development of the economic space for social innovation. For example, in the social democratic tradition, much social innovation can be initiated and carried out via the government policy administered by state actors. As the example of the Finnish Housing programme PAAVO shows, there might be market-related elements, but the public sector dominates (Edmiston and Aro 2016). By contrast, Social Impact Bonds as a manifestation of the encroachment of private capital into the welfare state emerge first in the liberal-welfarist capitalism of the United Kingdom (see chapter 11).

The central role of the state and its regimes leads to a second point that emerges from our use of an historical empirical perspective. While the dominant social business framing of social innovation focuses on new enterprises and firms, a normative focus on marginalization first calls for a consideration of basic needs and capabilities in domains such as health, housing, and education (and, more recently, access to information and communication technology—for example, via broadband internet). Our historical case studies suggest that meeting such needs tends to be strongly associated with public provision: the set-up and maintenance of infrastructure by towns, regions, and states. Public provision is more likely to

[5] For new member states in relation to social innovation see Saman and Kaderabkova (2015).

advance secure housing, clean water, and education for all, not just the affluent. Private actors are usually ill suited to provide generally accessible goods or services since universal provision is both costly and, typically, not profit-maximizing (Scheuerle et al. 2016: 182f.). Therefore, social innovation theory and research, especially if focused on those least advantaged in society, would be enhanced by focusing more attention on the history of the welfare state, its failures and achievements (Evers et al. 2014: 49) as well as the challenges of maintaining and renewing already existing infrastructures. Looking ahead requires looking back. This point, however, is not to be confused with the idea that the state is a neutral actor. On the contrary, it frequently also reproduces marginalization. Therefore, business and civil society are required as critical correctives in a collaborative pluralism of configurations of actors to improve citizen choice and the availability of alternatives modes of provision.[6]

Of specific interest in these dynamics framing economic space is the role of cognitive frames. Cognitive frames held by dominant political actors are typically reified as concrete policies legitimated by these frames. As a consequence, changing such frames can be a primary focus of effective social innovation. Quantitative research conducted here on the basis of the ESGM suggests that the primary outcomes of social innovation for beneficiaries may not so much be products and services but rather changes in the dominant cognitive frames and social ties (see chapter 10).

Such changes are not limited or reducible to economic space only. On the contrary, an exclusive focus on economic space might hamper the diffusion and success of a social innovation (Scheuerle et al. 2016: 176). The interests of different stakeholder groups beyond the main beneficiaries are important too and these are likely to include politicians, thematically related professionals (such as the epidemiologists and engineers in the freshwater supply case) and businesses interested in the well-being of their workforce.

Cognitive frames are also important methodologically. Rather than assuming a given social reality, with specified actors and their rationalities, the focus on cognitive frames sheds light on the 'social imaginaries' (Jessop et al. 2013: 124) and 'visions' (Schumpeter 1949) that orient the interpretation of institutions and the formation of networks in discursive processes. We will further discuss this point in the next section.

Power and the Politics of Social Innovation

Social innovation policy in the EU has followed the goal of increased efficiency and effectiveness in times of austerity by means of rethinking the collaborations

[6] Recent research suggests that civil society's role in this cannot be taken for granted, as space for it appears to be shrinking in international perspectives (Anheier 2017).

and reconfigurations of state, market, and civil society (see chapter 11). As such approaches seek to go beyond government and to include business and civil society, it is appropriate to speak here in terms of innovations in governance. Still, governments and intergovernmental relations play an important role. To date, the EU has launched three core policy frameworks in relation to social innovation: the Europe 2020 Strategy, the Social Business Initiative, and the Social Investment Package (see chapter 11; Sabato et al. 2017).

Social innovation policy not only has a bearing (positive or negative) on the marginalization it seeks to tackle, but is itself a process already co-determined by marginalization and the social forces that (re)produce marginalization. In spite of transformative and empowering ambitions, social innovation policy so far has been mainly carried out in a way that is incremental and not in conflict with prevailing political and economic power (Edmiston 2016; von Jacobi et al. 2017). As the EU social innovation platform puts it: 'The European Commission's objective is to encourage market uptake of innovative solutions and stimulate employment.'[7] EU social innovation policy, so far, has only minimally recognized this structural issue and the reproduction of political and economic power it implies (see chapter 11). Full recognition calls for the difficult task of surrendering institutional dominance and for more participatory modes of policy development. This task is especially difficult as those marginalized are especially unlikely to participate unless specific actions are taken to increase their capability to associate (Ziegler et al. 2017).

This challenge for a more reflexive use of power also applies to levels of power. While the ethically relevant impact of social innovation takes place primarily at the level of individuals, social innovation initiatives mostly operate at the micro- and meso-level of communities, organizations, and networks. The cognitive frames these initiatives propose tend to challenge assumptions about how to view a problem, as well as their attendant policies, laws, and other rules. This point is evidenced, for example, in initiatives such as the de-growth movement calling for alternative ways of regulating economic space where macro-level cognitive frames are challenged, such as economic growth and international competitiveness, as are the associated institutions. Conversely, macro-level frames can be used to manipulate and co-opt social innovation. This is most obvious where the call for transformative social innovation in response to the financial crisis turned into the idea of 'getting people into jobs' and inserting them into a vision of the neo-liberal economy that produced the crisis.

[7] See https://ec.europa.eu/growth/industry/innovation/policy/social_en, accessed 17 October 2017. Such an exclusive focus on markets fits quite well with the analysis of an economically driven EU that has no problems postulating and organizing the EU as 'an economy' (Aro and Heiskala 2018) but struggles to offer substance to 'political union'.

Social innovators can also draw strategically on macro-level cognitive frames that support their vision and mission, such as the emergent climate change discourse (Smith and Raven 2012). However, our research here suggests that social innovation itself is not an alternative macro-frame; rather, it refers to an ensemble of micro- and meso-level initiatives and developments that, in heterogeneous ways, provide substance to alternative visions of human and sustainable development (Nicholls and Teasdale 2017). This point suggests that a reflexive use of power is valuable to advance systemic social innovation and should:

- Pay attention to alternative cognitive frames at the micro- and meso-levels and the different interpretations of institutions and policy implementation they might provide. For example, different modes of implementing social housing and freshwater supply according to the respective contexts (Ziegler 2017b). If such local experience feeds back into the further development of institutions and policies, 'democratic experimentalism' (Sabel 2012, see also chapter 1) may be fostered.
- Reject the assumption of a homogeneous social innovation discourse as a macro-frame for the more efficient and effective provision of goods and services in times of austerity, and leave space for social innovation as an approach suggesting a variety of social imaginaries and adjacent possibilities.

A reflexive perspective on political power in a multi-level governance system such as the EU also provides opportunities for social innovation in and of itself. Miquel et al. (2013: 158) noted that the EU has made a commitment to more decentralization and increased opportunities to participate for non-state actors. They also observed, however, that in most policy fields redistributive mechanisms are missing that could make this participation possible (Miquel et al. 2013: 158). In this context, a focus on social innovation for the most marginalized groups suggests a specific opportunity for reflexive social innovation policy: where marginalization is reproduced via the state at the regional and national level, the more detached supranational level has an opportunity to encourage social innovation through the policy levers of government.

An example of the potential impact of reflexive social innovation policy can be seen in the case of the marginalized Roma population in in Central and Eastern Europe (Ziegler et al. 2017: 296). In this case, the systemic configuration of institutions, networks, and cognitive frames constantly serves to reproduce their marginalization. Seeking to change this systemic power structure requires social innovation to target all three of these social forces. National authorities are not a neutral, long-term finance provider for marginalization problems, but in part are responsible actors in the process of its reproduction. Schools and municipalities, employment and regional development policies all potentially contribute to the persistence of marginalization in certain populations. Under such conditions, even the utilization of EU funds for the inclusion of the most deprived social groups can be ineffective and inefficient if facilitated via national authorities that are an integral part of the social process from which marginalization results. In such a case, to address the marginalization of the Roma requires the EU to invest directly into the social inclusion of the most marginalized, leapfrogging national government actors. In this way, funds could directly (and meaningfully) reach the NGOs supporting marginalized communities, bypassing the national and local administrations. This is an existing but very rare practice in the case of some Roma pilot projects. Such direct investment faces objections from those who argue that it breaks the EU conventions of subsidiarity. However, our analysis suggests that entrenched marginalization makes it unlikely for some issues to be solved at the national level. The reflexive use of power at that level helps national administrations recognize its own limitations and emphasizes the legitimacy of direct investment from an alternative policy level (here the EU) to local-level actors. Enlightened political power agrees to such a 'Ulysses pact,' designed to willingly disempower itself to break the cycle of the reproduction of systemic marginalization.

A reflexive perspective on power also considers problems with social innovation. In particular, social innovation itself might be conducive to (reconfigurations of) modes of provision that perpetuate inequality and marginalization (sometimes as unexpected consequence). Therefore, preventing some innovations and overcoming questionable practices as well as technologies ('ex-novation') is an important topic for balanced social innovation research. Our case studies suggest that one critical domain are innovations of the welfare state that address a universal need (water, housing, education), which have a potentially large market and are accordingly under pressure for privatization even in the absence of any serious malfunctioning: for example, the privatization of municipal waters that only get privatized because they work well and make money (see chapter 6). Again we stress the utility of an historical and contextual analysis of such cases: what might be true for the context of the Western European states need not hold for the new members of the EU from Central and Eastern Europe.

Participation, Paternalism, and Social Innovation for the Most Marginalized

In this book we have defined marginalization as a social process through which personal, social, or environmental traits are transformed into actual or potential factors of disadvantage (von Jacobi et al. 2017; see also chapters 1 and 3). In this context, therefore, effective social innovation changes social processes in such a way that individuals are no longer disadvantaged and have a choice as to how their individual traits emerge as capabilities. Such an effect on agency is best understood as a process of empowerment. The public and academic discourses on social innovation tend to assume that social innovation empowers actors to deal with societal challenges, but what is the evidence?

Our quantitative survey suggests that social innovation has some empowering effects (see chapter 10). This result corresponds to findings from qualitative research that social innovation initiatives are experienced as empowering (Avelino et al. 2017: 9). However, in our survey, there was only a weak effect across all case studies and power dimensions. This latter result may point to the complex and contingent nature of social innovations addressing messy, multi-dimensional wicked problems and challenges. In this context, even though it was not an expected benefit from the point of view of the beneficiaries, new knowledge and friendships/social ties seem to play an important transversal empowering role in social innovation. Molnár and Havas (chapter 7) refine this point, arguing that knowledge and social ties, such as inter-community ties, are an important conversion factor (to use the capability terminology): namely, they affect the capabilities of the beneficiaries.

Our analyses of social innovation and marginalization also suggest that the empowerment aspect of social innovation is not to be confused with *participation*. Participation, in the sense of having a voice in decisions that govern one's life (Nussbaum's formulation of a central capability, Nussbaum 2000) is rarely directly present in the cases we examined. The marginalized tend not to be the initiators of social innovation, are usually not involved in the decision-making of public administrators (see PAAVO case, Edmiston and Aro 2016), might only be superficially included by civil-society actors seeking to support them (see chapter 9), and are not typically conceived of as *participants* but, rather, as clients whose feedback might be welcome (see chapter 7). To be sure, there are exceptions of citizen innovation with much stronger participatory elements (Ziegler 2017b). Still, the basic point seems valid that even if social innovation seeks to empower its beneficiaries, this is not to be confused with participation. Rather, participation is a medium- or long-term goal for some social innovation projects, and not a goal at all for some others.

This finding of our empirical work means that we have to focus on the 'targets' or 'beneficiaries' of social innovations both as agents and as patients, and that it is important to consider the possibility and limits of paternalism in social innovation. 'Patients' (or 'subjects') refers here to the intended beneficiaries of social innovation who permanently or contingently are not able to voice their interests for themselves.[8] The ideal of agency notwithstanding, the marginalized tend not to be participants in social innovation processes, or at least not in the early stages. Other beneficiaries are in principle unable to participate unless there are advocates

[8] See chapter 3, where this terminology is introduced.

or trustees acting on their behalf: for example, infants, animals, and, for some green social innovations, also plants and ecosystems.

Paternalism refers to the actions and associated social structures where one actor 'undertakes to supply needs or regulate the conduct of those under its control in matters affecting them as individuals as well as in their relations to authority and to each other'.[9] Such paternalism is typically justified to prevent the harm of individuals who would otherwise voluntarily or involuntarily harm themselves (Claassen 2014). Prima facie, the ESGM seems to account well for the challenge of paternalism at the level of theory, as the capability approach explicitly aims to preserve the opportunities of individuals. For example, chapter 9 reports on Solidarity Purchasing Groups, whose participants belong to an urban, well-educated, and affluent group with the main declared aim to improve the conditions of the producers with whom they collaborate. However, a closer look at the Solidarity Purchasing Groups suggests that, in spite of this goal, there is also space for paternalistic practices, not least due to unequal power relations between consumers and producers. Producers come from a rural, typically poorly educated and socially disconnected group, which tends to have less bargaining power than the rich and educated consumers. As a result, the Solidarity Purchasing Groups do not, specifically, need to listen to the opinions of the producers and there is a risk of paternalism. The capabilities approach offers one way to identify such paternalism.

Our research suggests it is not enough to focus only on issues where there is a risk of paternalism due to power hierarchies. We also need to consider the case of potentially justified paternalism, of *functioning* promotion or even enforcement, for example by:

- Respecting subjects: in the case of beneficiaries who are not able to make choices for themselves, paternalism is not a relevant issue. Nevertheless, it is evidently important that social innovators consider the well-being of these patients sensitively. It is a semantic issue if appropriate consideration in this category is still discussed as an issue of paternalism (potentially violating the well-being of the subjects) or not (due to the absence of liberty in the sense of participation possibilities). At any rate, the substantive challenge is clear and there is a rich literature from animal rights to environmental ethics that can be drawn from on this matter (Kymlicka and Donaldson 2011; Gorke 2010).
- Moving to agency: in the case of contingent patients the matter is more complicated. Promoting functioning seems justified where it serves the goal of fostering their capabilities, thus bringing them into a position of choice. The education of children is an important instance of this. This category also

[9] Source: 'Paternalism' in *Merriam-Webster*, accessed online 23 August 2017.

applies to the socially marginalized, who likewise might not be in a position of choice (Molnár 2017). It seems justifiable for a social innovator to only support a marginalized group on the condition that they accept various implementation parameters, for example in the effort for improved sanitation and drinking water, as long as it results, at least in the medium term, in the enhanced capability of participation with respect to this issue (Ziegler 2012: 248ff.). Evidently, this case for capability promotion depends on a scrutiny of the actual development of the programme and the associated 'capability training' (Claassen 2014) and its outcomes. The multi-dimensional character of social innovation and the many inter-linkages and mutual strengthening between different capabilities and functionings suggest that such promotion is unlikely to be limited to one domain or sector. For example, in the water and sanitation case, a key step for the social innovator might not just be in developing the technical infrastructure for water and sanitation, but the gradual setting up of local governance groups that eventually will be in a position to further implement and control the management of the infrastructure themselves. Thus, this category includes both the direct targeting of the respective core problem (say the provision of clean water and sanitation) and indirectly strengthening participation by 'supporting capabilities' (Claassen 2014) development.

- Guarding agency: there is also the case of diminishing capabilities that is relevant for our analysis of social innovation. According to the sociologist Blühdorn (2013), there is a tendency for citizens to emancipate themselves from emancipation, including the associated empowerment. In light of the achievements of the social state, people 'emancipate' themselves from participating so as to have more time for individual well-being, lifestyle management, and so on. Why not delegate issues to experts and avoid messy and time-consuming participation in 'rigged' power politics (Hibbing and Theiss-Morse 2002)? Such a generalized emancipation from empowerment may undermine the goals of social innovations such as urban freshwater supply and social housing since citizens may cease to monitor the development of the associated institutions and infrastructures in terms of the public goods, solidarity, and social justice they provide. Without some level of civic engagement, the risk of losing effective civic control seems very real. If the sociological analysis of a widespread economistic *self*-governance in terms of the competition that *homo economicus* faces in all spheres of life is valid (see footnote 4), then civic engagement and vigilance is itself at risk. Countering such a trend, social innovation has a role of guarding the role of civic agency.[10]

[10] Here too it is a semantic question if paternalism is the right label. Civil-society organizations demanding participation from their citizens do not act paternalistically in the way that a state can

In terms of effective social innovation for the marginalized, the second category of moving beneficiaries into a position of agency, seems of the utmost importance. While there are many ways to achieve this, our empirical survey points to a change in cognitive frames as an especially important aspect of this process (see chapter 10). In short, conversion in the old religious-cultural sense of 'converting' to a different way of thinking about a problem (and one's own power in relation to it) is central. However, the success of such conversions critically depends on social networks and the establishment of social ties that provide assurance, knowledge, and support. In turn, this point suggests that the 'capability to associate', defined as the real opportunity individuals have to engage in social relations that enable them to act together, plays an important role for social innovation aiming at agency and empowerment.[11] Finally, while social innovations sometimes succeed in creating new institutions (see especially the chapters on fresh water, social housing, education), it is important to note that for many social innovations the interpretation of institutions and their implementation is just as important as creating new rules and new institutions. Cognitive frames and social networks together can support the application of existing formal and informal rules in a way that also benefits and recognizes marginalized groups.

Transformation and Structural Change

Social innovation is frequently associated with systemic, transformative change. Westley, for example, defined social innovation as:

> Any initiative, product, process, program, project, or platform that challenges and over time contributes to changing the defining routes, resources and authority flows of beliefs of the broader social system in which it is introduced; successful social innovations have durability, scale and transformative impact.
>
> (Westley 2013: 72)

Transformative impact has been defined in the social innovation literature as 'irreversible, persistent adjustment in societal values, outlooks and behaviours' implying 'a systemic perspective' (Avelino et al. 2017: 2).

Our research suggests some caution is wise with respect to social innovation and structural change. In social innovation, gains in autonomy often seem relatively weak in the sense that power relations tend to be changed only partially.

enforce policies (for example, in education). Still, they have soft power and it is, moreover, conceivable that social innovation policy develops in the future to promote active participation.

[11] See Ibrahim (2017) for a discussion of collective capability in relation to social innovation.

While there is evidence of some improvements, the larger inequalities frequently persist because of the interrelated nature of power dimensions and the corrosive effect (Wolff and de-Shalit 2007) of disadvantage in one domain (say, capability of health) on other domains and their capabilities (say, the capability to participate).[12]

In historical perspective, the strongest evidence of social innovation driving systemic, structural change, are those innovations that include the state as part of welfarist or rights-based social state provision. These cases—in Part II of this book—focus on infrastructure that provides universal access: fresh water, housing, education. In all these cases the social state can point to major outcome achievements over time. There is, however, an important qualification to these achievements: the state also creates marginalization if policies are implemented without regard for the context. Examples of this include public education that not only regulates equal access and funding but also exclusively seeks to provide education, thereby undermining the possibilities of parents and teachers to co-determine the process and content of education (see chapter 8); and the infrastructure extension of urban water supply to rural areas, where this is both costly and against the will of local communities (see chapter 6).

This points to the risks that emerge if the state or other powerful organizations seek to push through systemic change by 'scaling' of one 'solution' approach. Alternatively, diversity of provision allows alternatives to emerge and can provide a reservoir of socially innovative ideas (Scheuerle et al. 2016). They increase the options for citizens due to a diversity of ways in which needs and capabilities are framed and addressed.[13] They are places of innovation where citizens are able to restore what they value in response to societal changes (Ziegler 2017b).

In our empirical survey, perceived gains in autonomy were present even in the absence of major societal structural change (chapter 10). This result could be interpreted as an adaptive yet illusionary self-assessment in the absence of societal change—people believing that change is happening even if this is not the case. There is also another interpretation: the beneficiaries might value their context and improvements in it more than expected. Accordingly, level-analysis is important again here: we should not identify social innovation only with macro-level change, thereby ignoring or defining away social innovation at the local, meso-, or micro-level. Put differently, the dominant focus of social innovation research on systemic change should not lead one to overlook the value of diverse micro-contexts and their cumulative importance for transformative societal change. Recognition of this point further refines the reflexive use of power discussed above.

[12] On the macro-level it has been frequently observed that the financial and economic crisis of 2008–9 has not lead to a radical change of economic and social policies; rather, via austerity policy, has reinforced the focus on markets.

[13] A commitment to entitlement and rights is compatible with a variety of approaches for implementing them.

The Extended Social Grid Model Revisited

The ESGM offers a comprehensive approach to social innovation and social change that reflects the integrative and adaptive potential of social innovation initiatives to tackle issues across multiple dimensions of power. Yet, the explanatory role of the model is not to prescribe/predict outcomes or test causal mechanisms: rather, in keeping with our commitment to explanatory pluralism, the ESGM seeks to guide us towards more nuanced explanations in specific contexts and to discover explanatory patterns there.

We have used two major approaches for the implementation of the model: a comprehensive case-study approach and a mixed-method approach focused specifically on agency and empowerment (see chapter 4). Our comprehensive case studies suggest caution with respect to linear, staged, or phased concepts of social innovation. Linear or staged models all suggest a specific order of things, but our historical case studies did not find evidence for such orders (Scheuerle et al. 2016: 193–9).

The ESGM is one way of adopting some major insights from the wider world of innovation studies specifically to social innovation. For example, the innovation systems approach emphasizes the need to pay attention to the parts and interlinkages of systems and their specific characteristics in historical context (Lundvall and Borrás 2005: 612f.). Likewise, the ESGM seeks to follow the trajectories of social innovation in their historical institutional contexts, with their cultural framings and traditions as well as the social networks that maintain and change both institutions and ways of thinking about them. From this perspective, neither social innovators nor those studying them can be expected to follow a linear pattern. Sterne captured this point well in a reflection on historiography more generally (1980: 26):

> Could a historiographer drive on his history, as a muleteer drives on his mule, straight-forward; for instance, from Rome all the way to Loretto, without ever once turning his head aside either to the right hand or to the left, he might venture to foretell you an hour when he should get to his journey's end. But the thing is, morally speaking, impossible. For if he is a man of the least spirit, he will have fifty deviations from a straight line to make.

For 'spirited' social innovation research, we found the social sources of power (in the Mann–Heiskala sense, see chapters 1 and 2) particularly useful for studying the structural drivers of marginalization, as well as for a more nuanced study of the effects of empowerment, beyond agency and autonomy across heterogeneous levels of power. It is also analytically useful to draw the larger historical picture that is so important for social innovation from a long-term perspective. Beckert's social forces schema provides a useful tool for the analysis of social innovation for marginalized groups, and the interrelation between forces it puts forward is evidenced in our case studies. While the ESGM does not claim any explanatory priority of one single force, our case studies suggest that a change in cognitive frames might be a frequent starting point for effective and systemic social innovation. There has typically been no effective social innovation aimed at addressing marginalization without a reframing of the fundamental issues involved. Even the legitimacy of a social issue can be difficult to grasp. For example, why invest in urban freshwater infrastructure if one thinks that hygiene and health issues are primarily a matter of the moral failure of the marginalized? As we saw in chapter 6, Chadwick and the social reformers had to reframe the issue as a wider societal one. For social innovation, reframing a problem as societal may be of central importance, i.e. as one structured by society and its rules rather than as a problem of specific individuals who have failed to take responsibility for their own destiny. However, for such changes in cognitive frames to be effective—and this confirms Beckert's point—they need to be linked to institutions that can adapt the normative rules and to networks that can diffuse them.

The capabilities approach and its focus on individuals sensitizes us to the role of agents and subjects in social innovation processes. Rather than offering a prescriptive judgement regarding 'good' and 'bad' social innovation, its strength is to highlight the heterogeneous ways in which social innovation affects those benefitted as agents and patients and to create space for a discussion of both empowerment as well as justified paternalism.

This being said, we also encountered major theoretical challenges in our work. In chapter 1, we introduced institutions as the constraining and enabling rules and norms of a given social context, and cognitive frames as providing the shared meanings and interpretations with which to make sense of society and its actions. However, in our empirical work the distinctions between institutions and cognitive frames often became blurred. In a related way, the social sources of power can be readily grasped as theoretical ideal-types, whereas in any specific context the distinction of sources of power tends to be difficult and controversial to establish.[14]

While social sources of power provide a useful way to move beyond a focus on markets and business alone, a topic emerged that appeared as both substantively important yet difficult to capture within the ESGM: knowledge. Knowledge is not one of the sources of social power in our model. There is, however, one direct link: cognitive frames and with them the way a problem or challenge is perceived. As was noted above, such a framing is arguably one of the key ways in which social innovation may create impact. Framing is also a well-known aspect in the

[14] This also applies to the theory discussion of institutions. See inter alia Scott (2014), Schmidt (2008), and Heiskala (2007).

discussion of power. For example, in Lukes' (2005) discussion of power, controlling the framing of an issue is an exercise in power distinct from coercion and force and with a more subtle effect. Such power is typically articulated in a 'thick' way including both descriptive and evaluative aspects of an issue.

Yet it is insufficient to represent knowledge only in terms of cognitive frames. Especially in social innovation for the marginalized, knowledge is also about skills: the practical and theoretical knowledge necessary to facilitate agency. For example, the case for micro-credit for marginalized groups in Europe is insufficient if conceived of only as a mechanism for money transfer; rather, education and with it knowledge transfer, plays a crucial role in empowerment (Molnár 2017). This observation makes it tempting to classify knowledge as an important aspect of 'cultural power': for example, education and science. Via education (in a wide sense) marginalized populations can learn practical skills and, most importantly, critical tools for overcoming 'learned helplessness' (Peterson et al. 1993). Yet culture is essentially about meaning (see chapter 2) and does not seem fully to capture this point, especially as practical knowledge can be just as relevant in relation to economic power (for example, as financial literacy), political power (as civic literacy), and so forth. It seems more appropriate to locate knowledge in all sources of power: from expert knowledge to less developed forms of power that are sufficient to get by (if only by knowing the right experts); from cognitive frames to skills and practical know-how.

Assuming, then, that knowledge is a transversal topic across dimensions of power, a social innovation challenge emerges for our model: social innovators, their organizations, and networks themselves inevitably exercise power over marginalized groups. Effective social innovators have the capacity to get them to do things that otherwise they would not do (to emphasize the Weberian heritage of Mann's power formulation): it is power over others.[15] And yet, its ideal telos is a kind of anti-power: if subjects become agents, the exercise of power becomes self-effacing. It is a power-over that reduces itself so as to create power-to (the agency of marginalized groups) or space for well-being and flourishing (in subjects). Alternatively, we would need a stronger counter-factual, normative sense to argue that there was no power-over to begin with: in promoting agency, the social innovators promote what the beneficiaries would have chosen if only they had been in a position of choice. Either way, social innovation challenges power-over via knowledge and reflection as anti-power, and, thus, the prevalence of power-over in any analysis of the social sources of power. This observation, however, manifestly does not mean that there are no power-over issues—after all, a

[15] Mann distinguishes two aspects of social power (Mann 1986: 6f.). Distributive power, citing Weber, as the ability to carry out one's will despite resistance; collective power as the jointly exercised power of two parties over a third party. He says that in most social relations both aspects tend to 'operate simultaneously and are intertwined' (Mann 1986).

successful social innovation empowering an individual to gain new agency in practice is effectively a change in overall distributive and collective power.

Conclusion

In this chapter, we have revisited the ESGM based on our empirical work in Part II of this book. We can summarize our main findings around four main themes:

- The need to move beyond a narrow analysis of economic space as markets if social innovation for the marginalized is to be understood in its full complexity and its impacts recognized beyond a reductive focus on business
- The importance of a reflexive use of power in recognition of the reproduction of marginalization (as well as the multi-level opportunities that emerge once this move is made)
- The role of beneficiaries in social innovation not only as participants but also as patients or subjects and, hence, the need to consider the role of (justified) paternalism in social innovation
- A note of caution regarding systemic structural change in favour of the value of local niche action.

Exploring the ESGM with our comprehensive case studies and a mixed-method approach allowed us to navigate the complex trajectories of social innovation in practice. Moreover, the social sources of power theory proved helpful as a heuristic to move out of the 'box' of narrow and linear ways of thinking about social innovation. However, we would like to stress their role as a heuristic rather than as a social ontology, not least due to the considerable overlap of attributing sources of power in the complexity of empirical reality.

While this research has compiled a considerable amount of qualitative and quantitative data, the long view suggests a note of humility in closing this chapter: our empirical focus was evidently limited both in terms of the types of cases and the geographical scope of our analyses. Accordingly, it would be interesting to see the ESGM applied and interrogated further both in other and non-European contexts and also from a global perspective.

References

Anheier, Helmut K. 2017. Civil Society Challenged: Towards an Enabling Policy Environment'. Economics Discussion Paper No. 2017-45, 13 July. http://www.economics-ejournal.org/economics/discussionpapers/2017-45.

Aro, Jari, and Heiskala, Risto. 2018. 'A Promoter of Values or a Shopkeepers' Empire? Economy and Society in the Europe 2020 Strategy and the Trade Policy of the EU.' In *Policy Design in the European Union: An Empire of Shopkeepers in the Making?* edited by Risto Heiskala and Jari Aro, pp. 67–86. London: Palgrave.

Avelino, Flor, Julia M. Wittmayer, Bonno Pel, Paul Weaver et al. 2017. 'Transformative Social Innovation and (Dis)Empowerment'. *Technological Forecasting and Social Change* 145: 195–206.

Ayob, Noorshea, Simon Teasdale, and Kylie Fagan. 2016. 'How Social Innovation "Came to Be": Tracing the Evolution of a Contested Concept'. *Journal of Social Policy* 45(4): 635–53.

Beckert, Jens. 2010. 'How Do Fields Change? The Interrelations of Institutions, Networks, and Cognition in the Dynamics of Markets'. *Organization Studies* 31 (5): 605–27.

Blühdorn, Ingolfur. 2013. *Simulative Demokratie: Neue Politik nach der postdemokratischen Wende*. Berlin: Suhrkamp.

Brown, Wendy. 2015. *Undoing the Demos: Neoliberalism's Stealth Revolution*. Cambridge, MA: MIT Press.

Claassen, Rutger. 2014. 'Capability Paternalism.' *Economics and Philosophy* 30(1): 57–73.

Dardot, Pierre, and Christian Laval. 2013. *The New Way of the World: On Neo-Liberal Society*. London: Verso.

Edmiston, Daniel. 2016. 'The (A)Politics of Social Innovation Policy in Europe: Implications for Socio-structural Change and Power Relations'. CrESSI Working Paper No. 32. Brussels: European Commission, DG Research.

Edmiston, Daniel, and Jari Aro. 2016.'Public Policy, Social Innovation and Marginalisation in Europe: A Comparative Analysis of Three Cases'. CrESSI Working Paper No. 33. Brussels: European Commission, DG Research.

Esping Andersen, Gøsta. 1990. *The Three Worlds of Welfare Capitalism*. Princeton, NJ: Princeton University Press.

Evers, Adalbert, Benjamin Ewers, and Taco Brandsen. 2014. *Social Innovations for Social Cohesion: Transnational Patterns and Approaches from 20 European Cities*. Liege: EMES European Research Network.

Gorke, Martin. 2010. *Eigenwert der Natur*. Stuttgart: Hirzel.

Habermas, Jürgen. 1981. *Theorie des kommunikativen Handelns*. Frankfurt am Main: Suhrkamp.

Hegel, Georg F. W. 1822/2004. *Die Philosophie des Rechts: Vorlesung von 1821/22*. Frankfurt am Main: Suhrkamp.

Heiskala, Risto. 2007. 'Social Innovations: Structural and Power Perspectives'. In *Social Innovations, Institutional Change, and Economic Performance: Making Sense of Structural Adjustment Processes in Industrial Sectors, Regions, and Societies*, edited by Timo Hämäläinen and Risto Heiskala, pp. 52–79. Cheltenham: Edward Elgar.

Heiskala, Risto. 2016. 'The Evolution of the Sources of Social Power, and Some Extensions.' In *Global Powers: Michael Mann's Anatomy of the Twentieth Century and Beyond*, edited by Ralph Schroeder, pp. 11–37. Cambridge: Cambridge University Press.

Heiskala, Risto, and Jari Aro (eds). 2018. *Policy Design in the European Union: An Empire of Shopkeepers in the Making?* London: Palgrave.

Hibbing, John, and Elizabeth Theiss-Morse. 2002. *Stealth Democracy: Americans' Beliefs about How Government Should Work*. Cambridge: Cambridge University Press.

Howaldt, Jürgen, Christoph Kaletka, and Antonious Schröder. 2018. 'Social Innovation on the Rise Worldwide: What Over 1,000 Initiatives and Projects Worldwide Reveal about the Potential of Social Innovation to Address the Great Societal Challenges'. Dortmund: Atlas of Social Innovation.

Ibrahim, Solava. 2017. 'How to Build Collective Capabilities: The 3C-Model for Grassroots-Led Development'. *Journal of Human Development and Capabilities* 22(2): 1–26.

Jacobi, Nadia von, Daniel Edmiston, and Rafael Ziegler. 2017. 'Tackling Marginalisation through Social Innovation? Examining the EU Social Innovation Policy Agenda from a Capabilities Perspective'. *Journal of Human Development and Capabilities* 18 (2): 148–62.

Jenson, Jane, and Denis Harrisson. 2013. *Social Innovation Research in the European Union: Approaches, Findings and Future Directions*. Brussels: EU Publications.

Jessop, Bob, Frank Moulaert, Lars Hulgard, and Abdelillah Hamdouch. 2013. 'Social Innovation Research: A New State in Innovation Research?' In *The International Handbook on Social Innovation: Collective Action, Social Learning and Transdisciplinary Research*, edited by Frank Moulaert, Diane Maccallum, Abdid Mehmood, and Abdelillah Hamdouch, pp. 110–30. Cheltenham: Edward Elgar.

Kymlicka, Will, and Sue Donaldson. 2011. *Zoopolis: A Political Theory of Animal Rights*. Oxford: Oxford University Press.

Levy-Vroelant, Claire, Christoph Reinprecht, and Frank Wassenberg. 2008. 'Learning from Histories: Changes and Path Dependency in the Social Housing Sector in Austria, France, and the Netherlands (1889–2008)'. In *Social Housing in Europe II: A Review of Policies and Outcomes*, edited by Christine Whitehead and Kathleen Scanlon, pp 123–42. Chichester: John Wiley.

Lukes, Steven. 2005. *Power: A Radical View*. 2nd edition. London: Palgrave.

Lundvall, Bengt-Åke, and Susanna Borrás. 2005. 'Science, Technology, and Innovation Policy'. In *The Oxford Handbook of Innovation*, edited by Jan Fagerberg, David C. Mowery, and Richard R. Nelson, pp. 599–631. Oxford: Oxford University Press.

Mann, Michael. 1986/2012. *A History of Power from the Beginning to AD 1760*. Cambridge: Cambridge University Press.

Mann, Michael. 2013. *Globalizations, 1945–2011*. Cambridge: Cambridge University Press.

Miquel, Marc P., Marisol Garcia Cabeza, and Santiago Eizaguirre Anglada. 2013. 'Theorizing Multi-Level Governance in Social Innovation Dynamics'. In *The International Handbook on Social Innovation: Collective Action, Social Learning and Transdisciplinary Research*, edited by Frank Moulaert, Diane Maccallum, Abdid Mehmood, and Abdelillah Hamdouch, pp. 155–68. Cheltenham: Edward Elgar.

Molnár, György. 2017. 'Capability Building Combined with Microcredit: The Loan Alone Is Insufficient'. *Journal of Social Entrepreneurship* 8(3): 354–74.

Nicholls, Alex, and Simon Teasdale. 2017. 'Neoliberalism by Stealth? Exploring Continuity and Change within the UK Social Enterprise Policy Paradigm.' *Policy and Politics* 45(3): 323–41.

Nussbaum, Martha. 2000. *Women and Human Development: The Capabilities Approach*. Cambridge: Cambridge University Press.

Otto, H., P. Spyridon, H. Ziegler, and A. Potsi (eds). 2017. *Human Development in Times of Crisis: Renegotiating Social Justice*. London: Palgrave.

Peterson, C., S. Maier, and M. E. P. Seligman. 1993. *Learned Helplessness: A Theory for the Age of Personal Control*. Oxford: Oxford University Press.

Sabato, Sebastiano, Bart Vanhercke, and Gert Verschraegen. 2017.'Connecting Entrepreneurship with Policy Experimentation? The EU Framework for Social Innovation'. *Innovation: The European Journal of Social Science Research* 30(2): 147–67.

Sabel, Charles. 2012. 'Dewey, Democracy, and Democratic Experimentalism'. *Contemporary Pragmatism* 9(2): 35–55.

Saman, Saeed, and Anna Kaderabkova. 2015. 'Social Innovation in New Member States, Part II: Survey of Expert Panel'. SIMPACT Working Paper No. 2.

Scheuerle, Thomas, Gudrun Schimpf, Gunnar Gänzel, and Georg Mildenberger. 2016. 'Report on Relevant Actors in Historic Examples and an Empirically Driven Typology on Types of Social Innovation'. CrESSI Working Paper No. 29. Brussels: European Commission, DG Research.

Schmidt, Vivien A. 2008. 'Discursive Institutionalism'. *Annual Review of Political Science* 11: 303–26.

Schumpeter, Joseph. 1949. 'Science and Ideology.' *American Economic Review* 39: 345–59.

Scott, Richard W. 2014. *Institutions and Organizations*. 5th edition. London: Sage.

Sen, Amartya. 1999. *Development as Freedom*. Oxford: Oxford University Press.

Smith, Adrian, and Rob Raven. 2012. 'What Is Protective Space? Reconsidering Niches in Transitions to Sustainability'. *Research Policy* 41(6): 1025–36.

Sterne, Laurence. 1980. *The Life and Opinions of Tristram Shandy, Gentleman*. New York: W. W. Norton.

Westley, Frances. 2013. 'The History of Social Innovation'. 14–15 November 2013, London. Keynote at NESTA Conference Social Frontiers: The Next Edge of Social Science Research. https://uwaterloo.ca/waterloo-institute-for-social-innovation-and-resilience/about/what-social-innovation, accessed August 2017.

Wolff, Jonathan, and Avner de-Shalit. 2007. *Disadvantage*. Oxford: Oxford University Press.

Ziegler, Rafael. 2012. 'Capability Innovation and the (Re)Making of Social Order'. In *The Capability Approach on Social Order*, edited by Bilal Hawa, Yanti Martina Hölzchen, and Niels Weidtmann, pp. 232–51. Münster: LIT Verlag.

Ziegler, Rafael. 2017a. 'Social Innovation as a Collaborative Concept'. *Innovation: The European Journal of Social Science Research* 30(4): 388–405.

Ziegler, Rafael. 2017b. 'Citizen Innovation as Niche Restoration—A Type of Social Innovation and its Relevance for Political Participation and Sustainability'. *Journal of Social Entrepreneurship* 3: 338–53.

Ziegler, Rafael, György Molnár, Enrica Chiappero-Martinetti, and Nadia von Jacobi. 2017. 'Creating (Economic) Space for Social Innovation'. *Journal of Human Development and Capabilities* 18(2): 293–8.

14

Capital and Capacities

Using Capital to Create Economic Space for Capacities

C. W. M. (Ro) Naastepad

Introduction

A major part of human existence concerns the development and fulfilment of capacities (Houghton Budd 2011) or, *per* Sen (2001) and Nussbaum (2011), the promotion of capabilities, the freedom and opportunity to get educated, to be included and to live in dignity ('functionings').[1] However, while Sen (2001) does relate capabilities to economic development—viewing the latter as a '*means* to expanding the freedoms enjoyed by the members of the society'—he does not, to our knowledge, explicitly address the question, taken up in this chapter, of how capabilities are funded.[2] As we explain in this chapter, capital[3] plays a crucial role as an enabler of capacities, or promoter of capabilities, for unless they are funded, individuals cannot develop and unfold their capacities.

The success of capital in terms of furthering the capacities of people depends on whether and on which conditions it is made available to individuals seeking funding for their initiatives. Indeed, it is here that social innovation is most needed if the development and unfolding of capacities is to be taken seriously. Such innovation—which we have called *social innovation in finance*, or *creating*

[1] This chapter is based on joint work with Christopher Houghton Budd in the EU PF7 project Creating Economic Space for Social Innovation (CrESSI). The author gratefully acknowledges Christopher Houghton Budd's contribution in the preparation of this chapter, especially in terms of conceptual and linguistic nuances and of many valuable discussions and joint work in the CrESSI project. The expression 'linking capital and capacities' is also due to Christopher Houghton Budd. Responsibility for views and interpretations expressed in this chapter remains with the author.

[2] For an explanation of 'capacities' in relation to 'capabilities', see Houghton Budd and Naastepad (2014), Section 4.6: 'Of Capacities, Capabilities, and Credit'. Briefly, we conceive capacities as the counterpart to capital, and capital as the enabler of capacities.

[3] The word 'capital' is used in many ways in the social sciences. In this chapter, depending on the context, 'capital' is used in the accounting sense of the debt and equity that finances the fixed and current assets used by an entrepreneur; in the economic sense of the physical means of production ('*K*', 'capital goods'); in the metaphysical sense of the ideas, knowledge, and ingenuity which, when 'embodied' in production processes, become the source of productivity growth; and in the sense (explained in this chapter) of the savings that arise as a consequence of productivity growth and end up as 'freed capital' on the business's balance sheet.

C. W. M. (Ro) Naastepad, *Capital and Capacities: Using Capital to Create Economic Space for Capacities.*
In: *Creating Economic Space for Social Innovation.* Edited by: Alex Nicholls and Rafael Ziegler,
Oxford University Press (2019). © Oxford University Press.
DOI: 10.1093/oso/9780198830511.003.0014

economic space for capacities[4]—depends first of all on how we conceive capital and its role in society.

The urgency of social innovation in finance is underscored by recent predictions regarding an acceleration of technological un(der)employment in the near future, which have led to images of a future society that does not need the capacities of the majority of the population.[5] Yet, the obviation of labour by ICT and other 'new technologies' does not necessarily imply that technology creates un (der)employment. It does so only if those whose labour is obviated cannot find a meaningful new role in society for lack of funding—which is a matter not of technology but of the allocation of capital.

As we argue in this chapter, the binding constraint on the free and general development and unfolding of people's capacities is neither technology, nor 'the economy' or capital per se, but how we *think* about capital and the purpose(s) it serves—meaning that our first problem is one of 'cognitive frames' (per Jens Beckert) and 'ideology' (per Michael Mann) or, more plainly, culture.[6] We point to an approach that views capital *itself* as inherently social and fair, because by its nature emancipatory (see section 'The Emancipatory Nature of Capital').[7] However, this emancipation has tended to be confined to a narrow group of capital owners and has focused on progress primarily in the material sense.

We suggest that capital could support the emancipation of every individual if it were linked to non-material as well as material progress, because the source of emancipation increasingly lies in the former. For capital to take on this role, the principle currently guiding it would need to be reconsidered. With Hirschman (1997), Houghton Budd (2011), Beckert (2011), and others,[8] one can ask whether the pursuit of individual self-interest as the principle for guiding capital[9] deserves the same moral ranking today as when it rose to prominence in seventeenth- and eighteenth-century England. How widely or generally effective capital can be as enabler of human capacities depends on humanity's readiness to allow self-interest

[4] Ideas originally expressed in Deliverables 1.1 and 1.3 of the CrESSI project (Houghton Budd and Naastepad 2014; Houghton Budd 2014; Naastepad and Houghton Budd 2015) and subsequently in, for example, Houghton Budd 2015a, 2015b, 2015c, 2016a; Houghton Budd and Naastepad 2016a, 2016b.

[5] See Houghton Budd and Naastepad 2016a, Naastepad and Mulder 2018, and the references therein.

[6] Understood as the domain of knowledge, consciousness and ideas, science, education, art and all sorts of reflection.

[7] A clue to what we mean by 'inherently social' is given by the word 'fair', another word for 'market'. We mean that 'true' economic life is naturally fair to all parties; it only ceases to be so when we act egotistically, for our own gain without thought for the rest of the world. Similarly, *mutatis mutandis*, for capital.

[8] e.g. Naastepad and Houghton Budd (2015, 2019).

[9] With its theoretical underpinnings in Renaissance 'pleasure-pain psychology'—e.g. Bacon (1605), Hobbes (1651), Locke (1689 [1690]), on whose ideas Bentham (1781) built his version of utilitarian moral philosophy (today's dominant 'microeconomic foundation').

as the predicate of social life to give way to taking others' interests into account in addition to one's own.[10]

We set out the wider framework within which we investigate these questions (see section 'Is Capital Today Predicated on Capacities?'). In terms of the realms of social life perceived by, for example, certain well-known macro-sociologists,[11] there appears to exist confusion regarding the principle or value that should guide behaviour, and especially capital, in the economic realm. Although the pursuit of self-interest, when it was assigned the role of guiding economic behaviour, was intended from the beginning as a *means* towards a social goal (overall welfare), the focus in practice often is on the means while the goal tends to disappear from sight. When, as part of 'economic imperialism' (Lazear 2000), this 'free-market'[12] approach is 'exported' to the cultural realm, so that self-interest becomes the organizing principle also in cultural activities such as education, research, health care, art (see section 'Overcoming Finance's Achilles' Heel'), the question regarding the implications for capacities becomes even more urgent.

Capital is unlikely to flow towards funding capacities on a sufficiently large scale unless we understand the nature of capital. As we explain (in section 'Freed Capital'), the growth of human knowledge and its application in production obviates labour and creates savings in the economy which end up as capital on businesses' balance sheets. Part of this capital used to be redistributed via taxation towards social and cultural activities. For those whose labour was obviated, this created new opportunities to use and develop their capacities. However, when governments withdraw from this task, as they have done in recent decades, the question arises how 'freed capital'—the capital freed by the working of human intelligence in production—is made available to support the further growth of human capacities.

New forms of funding such as 'social impact investing' have stepped in. We ask what this implies for capacities (see section '"Philanthropy Capital"'): does this capital support the capacities of individuals? Even if it does, is this in support of what individuals themselves aspire to develop? Linking capital and capacities requires 'Open Access Credit', that is, credit focused on the intentions and possibilities of the users of credit and the social and individual needs met through

[10] A theme explored in various contributions to the CrESSI project, including Sebastianelli, Chiappero, and von Jacobi (2015); Molnár (2015, 2016); Naastepad and Houghton Budd (2015) and subsequent papers by these authors.

[11] As explained by Risto Heiskala (in his lecture at the first CrESSI meeting at Said Business School, Oxford, 4–5 March 2014), Marx's distinction between 'superstructure' and 'material base' was succeeded by a perception of social life as taking place in three realms (cultural, political, and economic) by Weber and others. Mann's four and Heiskala's six 'social powers' (Heiskala 2014a, 2014b) as well as Nicholls and Ziegler's (2014) Extended Social Grid Model are further elaborations.

[12] Free in 'free market' refers to freedom from obstacles to the pursuit of self-interest (e.g. Berlin 1969; Naastepad and Mulder 2019).

their initiatives, rather than on demands of the providers. In a word, it is for the users or borrowers of capital to determine its 'terms of trade', determined out of the circumstances and profitability of their initiative, not the owners or lenders of it.

We point to a dual role for capital as the financier of production *and* the source of funding of capacities (see section 'Towards a Dual Role of Capital').[13] However, this dual role requires an evolution in the principle that currently guides capital. We bring forward 'other-interest'[14]—the allocation of capital according to the use made of it by its users—as a non-self-serving approach to economics and capital that allows capital to be emancipatory in terms of individual capacities (see section 'Capital and Character').

Finally, we suggest that financial literacy based on this wider understanding of capital can enhance individuals' and communities' resilience in the face of today's abstract and 'disassociated'[15] financial markets, enabling them to ensure that markets do what they are supposed to do—to create economic space for the developing and unfolding of capacities, the furtherance of capabilities (see section 'Financial Literacy Predicated on Character'). In a world where civil society is thrown back on itself, it is for citizens to decide what the world economy will be like. The outcome depends on financially literate individuals identifying their role in the economy especially as regards capital.

The Emancipatory Nature of Capital

Capital has always been emancipatory, as Beckert (2011: 9) reminds us; however, to continue in this role, the principle that has governed capital for several centuries needs to be reconsidered. As Beckert (2011) writes:[16]

> Historically, one would not do justice to modern economic theory, as it has developed since the eighteenth century, if one considered it as a theory that reduces the goal of the social order to economic efficiency.
>
> Albert Hirschman (1977) has shown, in his brilliant history of ideas, that the orientation towards self-interest and economic efficiency in those days had a moral attraction, since market freedom and free trade could be seen as a means towards the establishment of peace in a society plagued by wars and civil wars. In the nineteenth century, John Stuart Mill had praised the market economy as liberation from the fetters of a feudal and aristocratic society. And Karl Marx had

[13] Elaborated in a series of CrESSI papers and deliverables; see the papers by C. Houghton Budd and C. W. M. Naastepad in the list of references.
[14] Houghton Budd (2011: xvii); Naastepad and Houghton Budd (2015, 2019).
[15] See J. K. Galbraith (1991), Ch. 12: 'The Separate Personality of Money', p. 140–54.
[16] Translation by the author of this paper.

> celebrated the emancipatory working of unleashed markets, because the capitalist economy destroyed the feudal order and established equality before the law as a universal principle. Even in the theories of the Austrian school, and of the German Ordoliberalism of the inter-war period—also a time in which almost the whole of Europe was controlled by totalitarian regimes—one can find the motive of securing a free order as the central justification for strict limitations on state intervention (Röpke 1948).
>
> Even so, Hirschman (1977) points out in his work that the assumption of pacification of society through the market was contested at the time. It was, however, understood throughout as an emancipatory social theory. Today this interpretation would be accepted only by hard-core Libertarians. If the interpretation is right, one could wonder whether the normative content of this theory based on (unlimited) market freedom itself is subject to historical change in the form of a dialectics of the Enlightenment. Could it be that this theory, which was normatively indicative in the days in which it emerged, lost its moral adequacy as a result of its very success in the moulding of social life? Following this thought, it would follow that economic theory with its focus on individual pursuit of self-interest as the central coordinating mechanism is historically specific, in the sense that it assumed a different moral ranking in the eighteenth and nineteenth century than in contemporary society.[17]

The emancipatory motive underpinning neoclassical economic theory emerged in the historical context of an upcoming middle class and the growth of mercantile capital in eighteenth- and nineteenth-century Britain. This form of capital permitted middle-class individuals to stand on their own, free from the hierarchies of feudalism, church, and state. Their drive for independence transposed itself into an economic theory that regarded private ownership of capital and the freedom to pursue self-interest ('*laissez faire, laissez passer*') as the twin foundation on which the growth of welfare depended.

This economic model has tended to confine emancipation to a relatively narrow group of capital owners in a context where capital was relatively scarce. Today, however, there is no scarcity of capital, although there is still huge inequitable distribution of it. Though seldom recognized, driving the distributional problem is the relatively simple fact that the shift in emphasis from the material (goods) to

[17] Perhaps surprisingly, in much of his work Beckert appears to accept the pursuit of self-interest as the principle guiding economic behaviour. Beckert analyses markets 'from a Weberian viewpoint as arenas of social struggle in which actors confront each other *under conditions of competition*' (emphasis added; see http://www.mpifg.de/forschung/projdetails_en.asp?ProjektelD=113). According to Beckert (2011), the economy is 'embedded in morality'; morality is 'marktermöglichend' (market-enabling), 'marktbegleitend' (market-accompanying) and 'marktbegrenzend' (market-constraining), rather than a property of the market itself. At the same time, however, Beckert acknowledges that the economy is *culturally* and *politically* constructed in the sense that it reflects prevailing systems of *meaning* and the results of political debate over *regulation* (Beckert and Streeck 2008).

the non-material (the free development of ideas, knowledge, capacities) has yet to be mirrored in our understanding of capital.

The emancipatory nature of capital was first applied to material productivity, and mainstream economic theory has got stuck there. Even so, the world is gradually moving up Maslow's pyramid to its higher, non-material categories: creativity, morality, and self-actualization. In the sense of Amartya Sen (2001), as living standards improve, the source of happiness increasingly lies in the satisfaction of immaterial rather than material needs. Yet, economic theory has not yet recognized that capital could also be emancipatory, and much more so, in regard to our *non*-material existence—meaning that there is a need to finance individuals' creativity and capacities directly, for which the lack of appropriate capital for individuals seeking funding for their (often innovative) initiatives is both a conceptual proxy and practical example.

With their livelihood taken care of, people can focus on their creativity, each one in his or her own way. But for this they not only need food in their stomachs, shoes on their feet, and a roof over their heads; they also need their innovative activity as well as their education to be appropriately capitalized. Conversely, were capital to become linked to innovation—on *all* our parts—its current footlooseness would be overcome, or at least mitigated.

This, indeed, seems to be the import of comments made by Christine Lagarde, managing director of the IMF, when, in her Amartya Sen Lecture at London School of Economics on 6 June 2014, having equated capabilities with capacities[18], she said that 'too many people lack the basic tools to get ahead—decent nutrition, health care, education skills, *and finance*', a problem that could be remedied in her view by building 'a modern financial sector, so that people can empower themselves through *access to credit*' [19] (emphasis added).

One can ask, however, precisely what 'credit' means and on what conditions it is to be made available:

> It makes a difference, for example, if, instead of being secured against real assets (in order to protect the lenders from loss), loans are made 'to the person not the asset', as used to be the norm in banking. Loans then act like the air beneath the wings of borrowers—providing 'lift', they confirm them in their initiative, on the successful fulfilment of which fresh values (and therefore a true return to capital) depend.[20]

For education, it makes a difference whether those wishing to develop their capacities are funded through loans or gifts. As capital takes on the role of

[18] 'To use Amartya's Sen's language: if we want better *capability*, then we need better *capacity*' (Lagarde 2014).

[19] International Monetary Fund (IMF), http://www.imf.org/external/np/speeches/2014/060614.htm.

[20] Christopher Houghton Budd in Houghton Budd, Naastepad, and van der Linden (2015).

enabling the development and unfolding of capacities, access to it needs to become 'open', that is, based on the users' possibilities and intentions rather than demands of the providers.[21] Naturally, such a change in ideas or 'cognitive frames' as concerns economics, especially as regards capital allocation, will also entail significant change in institutions and social networks (per Jens Beckert 2010), and in power relations generally, as argued by Michael Mann.[22]

However, the main question, as suggested in this chapter, concerns humanity's readiness to allow self-interest as the predicate of social life to give way to taking others' interests into account in addition to one's own. In a word, can we enlarge our egoism from its narrow focus on oneself to embrace the entire human family? We start by explaining the wider framework within which we investigate this question.

Is Capital Today Predicated on Capacities?

A common understanding about society—reaching back through Comte and Montesquieu to Plato, and found among some of the most eminent macro-sociologists including Alfred Weber, Max Weber, Émile Durkheim, Jürgen Habermas—is that it is made up of three dimensions or spheres: the economy, political life (including law-giving and regulation, parliamentary democracy, etc.), and culture.[23] Adding the individual with his or her capacities to this understanding of social life, Figure 14.1 depicts the individual—the agent of all innovation—in relation to society.[24]

The idea Figure 14.1 seeks to illustrate is perhaps not controversial: the individual's capacities are influenced by the different dimensions of society which are co-created by each individual. More interesting and perhaps more challenging is the question *how*, precisely, the individual manages mutual relationships between the economic, political, and cultural spheres. Indeed, the individual is 'at one and the same time both perceiver and representative of each field and therefore the unifier of them' (Houghton Budd and Naastepad 2014). If any problem arises in the relationships between the three spheres—such as usurpation or crowding out

[21] The meaning of 'open' in 'open access credit' as proposed by Christopher Houghton Budd (2016a). See also the quote from Aristotle's *Nicomachean Ethics* in section 'Capital and Character'.

[22] Michael Mann (1986, 1993, 2012, 2013) *The Sources of Social Power* (four volumes).

[23] 'Lebenswelt' *per* Habermas (1981).

[24] To these three dimensions, some authors add nature, security, and technology. In our reading, nature is not part of social life (it is not created by human beings but given from outside), while security belongs to political life, and technology (a consequence of the growth of human knowledge, consciousness, and inventiveness) to cultural life. Nature is closely related to the economy since in production, materials taken from nature are transformed into goods by human labour with the help of capital. It is true that today, nature is manipulated and artificially synthesized in laboratories; in our view, such 'artefacts' belong to the sphere of technology/cultural life.

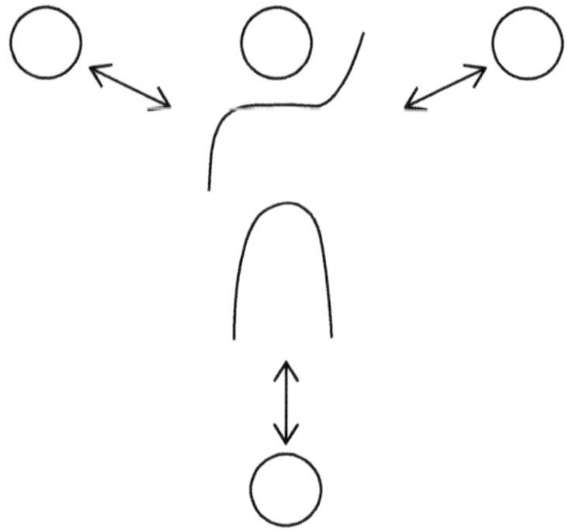

14.1 The individual in relation to society
Source: Houghton Budd and Naastepad (2014).

of one sphere by another[25]—it is the individual who can bring an end to this, 'both conceptually and in concrete circumstance', because (s)he 'recognises inter-determination and co-evolution and foreswears hegemony and field supremacy' (Houghton Budd and Naastepad 2014).

This (s)he can do only when (s)he is clear in his or her mind about the nature of each sphere and the relationships between them, and their impact on capacities. However, especially with respect to the economic sphere, both the economic and the sociological literature have created a paradox that has not been solved to date, on the solution of which (we suggest) the further growth of human capacities depends.

Of the three realms mentioned above, the cultural sphere has been associated with knowledge and emancipation by Habermas, and with values such as freedom of thought, freedom of conscience, freedom of education and *freischwebende Intelligenz* by Alfred Weber, Max Weber, Karl Mannheim,[26] John Stuart Mill, and others. In the course of history, many individuals have defended their freedom and attempted to protect that of others in this realm.[27] The legal-political sphere is commonly associated with equality before the law. In short, freedom has been identified as belonging to the cultural sphere, and equality as belonging to the law and political life.[28]

[25] Examples are dictatorship (where political life usurps cultural life) and 'economic imperialism' (Lazear 2000) or the 'colonization' of political and cultural life by demands coming from parties in the economy.

[26] See, for example, Hoeges (1994).

[27] See, for example, Nussbaum (1998, 2010); Houghton Budd, Naastepad, and van der Linden (2015); van der Linden (chapter 8, this volume).

[28] In terms of marginalization, this would imply that an individual is marginalized *culturally* when he or she is not free, for example, to pursue the education of his or her choice (see Houghton Budd, Naastepad and van der Linden 2015) or to think and speak freely (without insulting others, of course);

Less clarity exists as regards the values and tasks belonging to the economic sphere. On the one hand, the economic sphere is related almost unanimously to social values, in the sense that the economy is perceived as the domain where individuals (as producers) create the goods that people need to live and to take up their tasks in life. The task of the economy is, therefore, to generate welfare for all; in this sense, the economy is perceived as having a social or 'other-interested' task.

At the same time, while acknowledging this task, economists and especially neoclassical economic theory have placed 'freedom' rather than 'other-interest' centre-stage in economic life—where freedom is understood as 'the absence of obstacles to the fulfilment of a man's desires',[29] or freedom from constraints on the pursuit of personal gain. According to the moral philosophy underlying the neoclassical paradigm, Benthamite utilitarianism, not only are human beings inclined by nature to pursue self-interest; they *should* behave in a self-interested way because only then will overall output and hence welfare be maximized. This is the 'Orientierung an Eigeninteresse'[30] referred to by Beckert (2011).

At first sight, we are left with a paradox: How can one be self-interested and other-interested at the same time? However, the opposition disappears when one realizes that the pursuit of self-interest is advocated precisely to promote the social goal of welfare. Striving for personal gain is advocated as the *intermediate goal* towards the *ultimate* goal of social welfare. The social goal is primary; the pursuit of self-interest is the means towards this goal. Solving the paradox then depends on proof of the idea that welfare is best served *via* the pursuit of self-interest—especially in regard to the allocation of capital.

What does this mean for capacities? As mentioned above, capacities cannot unfold, and capabilities are not assured unless they are funded. But today capital is not predicated on capacities and capabilities, or on trying to see how individuals could develop unto themselves. Instead, it is guided by the principle of individual profit maximization—or its modern version, maximization of shareholder value (MSV)—on the (yet unproven) assumption that this maximizes overall welfare. Is this guiding principle adequate when capacities or emancipation are taken as the criterion of welfare?[31]

We suggest that the difficulties encountered in overcoming marginalization—especially in finding funding for the use and development of capacities or the securing of capabilities—are due to too narrow an understanding of capital and

and *politically-legally*, when the law does not treat individuals equally (think, for example, of the expensive lobbies for changes in laws and regulation). For a classification of different kinds of marginalization, see Table 1 in Houghton Budd, Naastepad and van Beers (2014, 2015).

[29] Berlin (1969) Preface (p. xxxviii); Naastepad and Mulder (2019).

[30] 'Orientation towards self-interest'.

[31] A question addressed in various deliverables of the CrESSI project including Houghton Budd, Naastepad, and van Beers (2014, 2015); Houghton Budd (2014, 2015a–2015c); Houghton Budd and Naastepad (2016a, 2016b).

the principle that should guide it. This too-narrow definition is in the end the Achilles' heel[32] of finance, in the sense that, paradoxically perhaps, a society dominated by it will continue to recreate the marginalization that it regards itself as addressing, thereby eroding the source of its own further progress (Houghton Budd and Naastepad 2016a).

To investigate this problem, let's look at how capital is currently used, and what this means for capacities.[33]

Overcoming Finance's Achilles' Heel

The aim of economic activity is traditionally said to be: to provide for the material livelihood of human beings. As a result of the working of human knowledge and intelligence in the production process, the goods that are needed by people are produced with progressively less labour. Thus a growing share of the hours that used to be required for producing goods are no longer needed for this purpose. As we take hold of the physical economy (the production of goods) by way of invention and innovation, we further the division of labour between human beings and machines, thereby lightening and eliminating human labour. A progressive saving of labour is taking place, reducing opportunities to use and develop capacities (or secure capabilities) through *labouring*.

However, the obviation of labour by capital (or rather by the human intelligence[34] embodied in it) *in production* does not necessarily imply that technology reduces work *overall* (creating unemployment). In the past, individuals whose labour was obviated by technology could often find new work. For example, when productivity growth started to rise in agriculture a few centuries ago, the labour that was no longer needed in agriculture was used for the expansion of industry. And when, over time, the hours of labour needed in industry also started to decline, many whose labour was obviated in manufacturing were able to find new occupations especially in domains such as education, health care, research, and the arts, in short, in the cultural realm.[35]

More recently, however, economists have pointed to the possibility of a sizeable increase in unemployment in the coming decades due to the displacement of work by technology; the 'ICT revolution' is expected to accelerate the loss of work through automation and robotization, this time especially in 'white collar' work

[32] The weakness in an argument. Foretold at birth that he would die, Achilles's mother dipped him in the River Styx, forgetting that the heel she held him by would not be protected. As a grown man and warrior he was killed by an arrow aimed at his heel.

[33] The title of the next section, 'Overcoming Finance's Achilles' Heel', is due to Christopher Houghton Budd (see Houghton Budd and Naastepad 2016a).

[34] Note that in Marx's view, in contrast, means of production are embodied labour.

[35] See Naastepad and Mulder (2018) for estimates regarding the countries of the Eurozone.

(e.g. Frey and Osborne 2013; Spence 2014; Vogel, Kratena, and Hranyai 2015; Acemoglu and Restrepo 2017; Chui, Manyika, and Miremadi 2017; Barton, Woetzel, Seong, and Tian 2017). On the other hand, others observe and predict an increase in what may be called technological un*der*employment: rather than becoming unemployed, those whose labour is no longer needed in production increasingly can only find new work in 'mindless' jobs shaped by a contemporary version of 'scientific management' empowered by information technology that dictates individual goals and judgement, trumping human abilities and expertise (e.g. Graeber 2013, 2015, 2018; Head 2014). This places society before a riddle: how to prevent mass technological un(der)employment?

Technological un(der)employment, we suggest, is not caused by technological progress per se, but by a failure to understand the significance of labour-saving technological progress in production. Such progress implies that the material values needed by people can be produced with progressively less labour. This is an advance in the human condition as, for example, John Maynard Keynes explained in 1930: it liberates humanity from the need to work full-time for material livelihood. This advance is also referred to by the term *productivity dividend* (e.g. Schor 1993) and it entails a choice: as productivity increases, one can either produce the same level of goods with less labour, using the hours that are no longer required in production to attend to other ends in life, or one can keep labour constant and produce more goods. Keynes (1930) referred to a point in the future (a hundred years from when he was writing) where 'the economic problem would be solved': due to centuries of accumulation, the economy would be sufficiently productive to provide a comfortable living for everyone. From then onwards, the hours liberated by further productivity growth would be free for the enjoyment of 'the real values of life'. In the rich parts of the world, at least, are we approaching this point?

Even where further *material* growth is needed, the advance in knowledge will make this growth increasingly 'jobless'. If an ever-growing share of the hours that used to be required for producing goods is no longer required for that purpose, what will humanity do with the abundance of time brought about by human intelligence, creativity, capacities? When hours of labour are reduced as a result of the working of human intelligence on labour in the production of goods, this does not mean that we will work less. Human beings long to learn and to be intellectually active;[36] *this* kind of work has the tendency to grow.

For many decades in many countries, the hours that were no longer required for the production of material values (goods) were used for the creation of non-material values in the cultural realm. Where this happens, those whose labour is no longer needed in the physical (goods-producing) economy will find

[36] Intelligence is perhaps too narrow a term for the metaphysical phenomena we refer to. Ideation, insight, imagination, inspiration, intuition, ingenuity, creativity... —the Germans say 'Geist'.

opportunities to use and develop their capacities in the creation of non-material values, and technological unemployment need not arise. However, values can only be created when those who create them are funded. Today, funding has become a problem, both in terms of whether it is made available and in terms of the conditions attached to it.

Until relatively recently, financing the growth of work in the cultural sphere was not a problem because governments took it upon themselves to siphon off, via taxation, (part of) the surpluses that are continually generated in the economy, and to redistribute them to the cultural sphere (schools, universities, hospitals, artists, etc.). However, as the validity of the state as the funder of private activities came to be questioned, the question arose how the cultural sphere would be funded. Individuals and institutions experiencing difficulties in finding money to fund their work in this field were advised to attract private capital. In many cases private capital owners were very willing to step in where governments withdrew, also because of reduced 'opportunities' for 'safe and high-yielding investments' in the economy proper (e.g. Bain and Company 2012a, 2012b). However, what entered was profit-maximizing capital rather than grants.[37]

Driven by 'old habits and instincts' (Keynes 1930)—the drive to accumulate—today's private funders of cultural activities demand financial returns comparable to those that can be obtained elsewhere. What will be the impact on capacities? In the sphere of production there exists a natural tendency to obviate labour, giving rise to profit. However, work in the cultural realm declines only when the natural tendency of this work to grow is distorted—for example by inviting the principle of profit maximization to govern the allocation of capital in this realm.

When the cultural sphere was 'opened up to the market' in order to attract funding, and private capital owners entered, the idea was that the profits that were demanded could be realized in a way analogous to the productivity growth that had taken place in the physical economy (agriculture, mining, industry), that is, by reducing hours of work. The main 'cost' in the cultural realm being hours of work, efforts were directed towards reducing the work of doctors, nurses, therapists, teachers, or increasing their 'productivity'. To this end, new 'markets' were created—such as the 'health care market', the 'market for higher education', the 'market university',[38] the 'market for well-being'—in fields that previously were acknowledged to belong to non-economic realms. In the competition and collusion between 'players' in these 'markets', original hitherto creative intellectual work and human relationships are being standardized, automated, and robotized (Pramudita 2015; Koshy 2015), with two main effects.

[37] For example, funding higher education through grants (redistributing surpluses via taxation), has given way to individual borrowing to fund higher education, thus creating a new financial market, yet another opportunity for people to lend rather than give their excess funds.

[38] Berman (2012).

Attempts to reduce 'cost' or 'increase efficiency' through automation and robotization reduce hours of work of creators of non-material value. At the same time, information technology is also used to control work through protocols and continuous monitoring, examination of dysfunction, and feedback (e.g. Head 2014), altering the nature of work. If technology is used to rule over how doctors diagnose and treat patients, what teachers teach, what researchers research etc., thus removing the demand for individual knowledge and experience and discouraging creative original thinking (Head 2014; Carr 2014), what will be the impact on capacities?

Concerns are mounting that the way we currently shape (albeit often unconsciously) economic and technological progress undermines human capacities and their further development, because the capital that is freed by productivity growth in the economy, or 'freed capital', is used to displace and discourage rather than support original creative work.

The future of human well-being depends, we suggest, on the role we assign to capital. The question is, how can the capital that is freed by productivity growth in the economy come to support the initiatives of individuals aspiring to unfold and develop their capacities while making themselves useful to others?

Freed Capital

Preventing or overcoming technological un(der)employment requires that the inventiveness of human beings is funded in an ongoing way so as to contribute to the further development of human capacities (on which, indeed, technological progress itself depends). But will this be possible with the principles that currently govern capital?

As explained in the previous sections and as most people would probably assert, apart from goods or material values, human beings also need non-material values (for example a class, a lecture, a sermon, a concert, a doctor's advice, nursing, etc.). However, like material values, non-material values can be created only when the person creating the value is funded. Where does the money to fund the creation of non-material values come from?

When human intelligence obviates labour in the physical economy (mining, agriculture, manufacturing), savings arise. In terms of accounting, a profit arises on the business's income-and-expenses account which is, at the end of the business year, transferred to 'own capital' on the balance sheet. In principle, the money that is freed from production by human intelligence—or 'freed capital'[39]—is free to fund

[39] How capital is freed in the economy by the growth of human knowledge and intelligence is explained more elaborately in Wilken (1982), Naastepad and Mulder (2018), Naastepad and Houghton Budd (2019).

the new initiatives of individuals whose labour is obviated in physical production. But will it be made available for this purpose, or be used mainly to benefit capital owners, by increasing their 'stock' of capital?

Corresponding to the reduction in public funding of social and cultural activities, there has been a rise of 'philanthropy capital' in these fields—but this amounts to the lending, rather than giving, of surplus capital to selected parts of health care, education, etc., on condition that they become marketized. Does 'philanthropy capital' support capacities?

'Philanthropy Capital'

The reduced scope of governments with regard to the funding of cultural activity has led to the emergence of various novel 'hybrid' (private–public) modes of funding including, for example, Social Impact Bonds (SIBs) and social impact investing (SII).[40] The relevant yet unanswered question is whether this has altered the way capital is allocated, meaning, in terms of the argument advanced here, is the allocation of capital determined by the user of capital and what (s)he is trying to achieve for society?[41]

A Social Impact Bond (SIB), for example, is a contract between a private capital owner and a government in which a public service (such as a programme for re-integration of presently unemployed persons, or an education programme targeted at improving the student's 'employability') is financed by private capital in exchange for a return that depends on the outcome of the service. The idea is that profit-maximizing owners of private capital will drive a service provider to bring about a specific measurable social outcome (such as a reduction in the number of people demanding an unemployment benefit), and the expectation that this way of funding will result in public savings. According to Edmiston and Nicholls (2018: 74), however, 'it remains unclear whether and under what circumstances SIBs might be considered appropriate or suitable within the broader context of public service reform.'

Likewise, social impact investing (SII) refers to private capital (equity, debt, or a combination of these) that finances businesses or organizations with the stated intention to generate social or environmental impact alongside a financial return. However, the measurement of the effects of SII is a problem, according to Scheuerle and Glänzel (2016), and their impact on capacities or capabilities remains unclear.

[40] According to the Global Impact Investing Network, 'impact investors' make investments 'into companies, organizations, and funds with the intention to generate measurable social and environmental impact alongside a financial return' (https:\\thegiin.org).

[41] For further explanation, see section 'Capital and Character'.

Although the literature on SIBs and SII emphasizes intended philanthropic aspects or 'social impact', their emergence is also related to stagnation in the physical economy,[42] which has prompted 'investors'[43] to search for new financial 'instruments'; and to the withdrawal of governments from some of their traditional tasks, thus offering new 'opportunities' for 'investment' in these areas.[44]

When taken up by the public sector, the funding of social and cultural activities (via taxation) tended to be focused on societal (social or cultural) benefit, not on financial return. It could be said that these activities were financed through a gift by society (qua tax payers) to itself on the understanding that the (non-material) benefits to the recipients (such as improved education or health care) ultimately benefit society as a whole.

When, on the other hand, SIBs and SII are used to fund social and cultural activity, it might be asked what they do 'other than deliver civil society into the hands of financial markets or at least the precepts that animate such markets' (Houghton Budd 2016a). SIBs benefit from the readiness of 'market-states' to contract out social welfare and cultural tasks on relatively attractive terms, effectively 'corporatising a previously tax-funded third sector'[45] (Houghton Budd 2016a). Are SIBs and SII more than 'a technique for displacing or crowding out the state, as is the averred philosophy and indeed aim of today's prevailing neo-liberal paradigm' (Houghton Budd 2016a), therefore?

SIBs and SII appear to pay 'no attention to what is arguably the real problem', namely 'the need for capital write-downs and even outright donations in the first place' (Houghton Budd 2016a). Unless capital is re-conceived and permitted to circulate and given away, rather than preserved and multiplied, it is hard to see how private capital can support capacities.

Even if 'philanthropy capital' does support capacities, is this in fact in support of what individuals themselves aspire to develop? Marginalization has many dimensions. A significant dimension can be characterized as 'credit marginalization'—understood as lack of access to capital on terms that derive from circumstances of the user of capital rather than the demands of the providers of capital.[46] For example, if 'philanthropy capital' funds educational projects, does it support what individuals themselves want to learn? Linking capital and capacities requires 'open access credit' (OAC)—or a change in the conditions on which capital is made available to individuals that is enabling in terms of capacities—with

[42] Related to such phenomena as the financial crisis, 'secular stagnation' (e.g. Storm 2017), or more generally 'demand saturation' (Naastepad and Houghton Budd 2015).

[43] Unfortunately, modern mainstream economics does not distinguish between the activity of investing in the means of production (a useful economic function) and the purchase of assets for financial gain—or between 'investors' and 'rentiers', a distinction made by Keynes and the classical economists.

[44] As explained in the section 'Financial Literacy Predicated on Character'.

[45] 'Third sector' or civil society (Houghton Budd 2016a).

[46] A concept inspired by Aristotle; see section 'Capital and Character'.

whatever consequences this may have in terms of the cultural, political, and economic aspects of social life.

The problem underlying credit marginalization, we suggest, is a failure to reconsider at a more fundamental level the role of capital in relation to the aspirations and initiatives of people seeking to use and develop their capacities or further their capabilities. Credit marginalization is due to a one-sided focus on material growth, the solution to which is to widen our understanding of capital as it relates to capabilities or capacities (i.e. non-material growth). Unless capital is linked to capacities as well as production—in theory as well as in practice—the kind of funding needed by those made jobless is unlikely to come forward in the required measure.

Towards a Dual Role of Capital

The capital that is freed by productivity growth could be used to fund the further development and unfolding of the capacities of those whose labour it has obviated. Accordingly, we have proposed[47] to link freed capital to capacities, arguably the source of all further progress and innovation.

To say this is to hint at the idea of a *dual role* of capital—the one linked to labour as it works on and transforms nature to produce goods with the help of technology, and the other linked to the creation of non-material values: the ideas, knowledge, intelligence that organize the production process, but that also have value of themselves. Based on the view of value creation referred to above, capital can be seen to serve two purposes: the production of goods and the creation of non-material value.

However, this change will not occur automatically. In the words of Keynes (1930), there may be a problem of 'readjustment of the habits and instincts of ordinary man, bred into him for countless generations' (Keynes 1963: 366). If our task at this point in history is to widen our orientation from self-interest to other-interest as the basis of capital allocation, 'must we not expect a general "nervous breakdown"?' asked Keynes (1963: 366).

A widespread pessimistic belief today is that human beings are unable, out of themselves, to engender characterful, other-interested conduct. A consequence is that the allocation of capital is left to *homo economicus* in the cultural realm as well as in the sphere of production. The view taken in this chapter is that the answer to the question how capital can come to support capacities lies in the free development of other-interest *within* the economy itself, especially with respect to the allocation of capital. This requires expanding *homo economicus* to include

[47] Naastepad and Houghton Budd (2015, 2019); Naastepad and Mulder (2018).

character or excellence in the Aristotelian sense or more specifically, responsibility for the welfare of others.

Capital and Character

Of course, placing character centre-stage in this way may be regarded as naïve. As Hirschman (1997) has lucidly described, many who consider themselves 'practical people' do not believe in 'such a miraculous transformation of mankind' (Hume 1752). With Francis Bacon we may be critical of 'holding out the examples of Good, Virtue, Duty, Felicity' while altogether passing over the question as to 'how to attain these excellent marks, and how to frame and subdue the will of man to become true and conformable to these pursuits' (Bacon 1605/2011: 418, quoted in Hirschmann 1997: 22). Bacon was one of the first to formulate the idea that the self-interested passions could be restrained by setting one against the other (Hirschman 1997).

But if, in a capitalist order based on self-interest and without character, capacities dwindle and capabilities are unfurthered, it might be worth considering what kind of economy character would give rise to. In particular, characterful individuals would take direct responsibility for providing the world's citizens with the means to use and develop their capacities, enabling them to reach their destination as human beings, so that financial life would become the field par excellence for enabling people to unfold and develop their capacities. The task of the economy would be to produce goods *and* to generate the capital required to fund the growth and unfolding of capacities.[48]

As already mentioned,[49] the pursuit of self-interest was selected as the basis of economic order in economic and institutional circumstances that differ substantially from the present ones. However useful Benthamite utilitarian morality may have been in promoting the accumulation of the capital required to raise living standards in eighteenth- and nineteenth-century Britain, does it provide an adequate answer to the problems in relation to capacities that we are facing in the twenty-first century? In his foreword to Hirschman's account of the history of the rise to dominance of the belief in self-interest as a 'civilizing medium' (Hirschman 1997), Amartya Sen questions the rationality of the pursuit of self-interest in the context of modern society (see also Sen 1977). Has the pursuit of personal gain become anachronistic, therefore?

[48] Before Milton Friedman's dictum of self-serving shareholding came to hold sway, Richard Eells, when CEO of General Electric, argued that corporations had two purposes—to meet clients' needs profitably and to use surpluses to fund culture (see Eells 1967).

[49] In section 'The Emancipatory Nature of Capital', and more elaborately in Naastepad and Houghton Budd (2015).

This is the direction in which Keynes appears to have been thinking when he described the 'love of money' as a 'distasteful and unjust' habit or instinct which may have been useful in the accumulation of capital required for raising living standards in centuries past but which, once 'the economic problem is solved', should be recognized for what it is—'a somewhat disgusting morbidity, one of those semi-criminal, semi-pathological propensities which one hands over with a shudder to the specialists in mental disease' (Keynes 1930: 366). For humanity to be able to enjoy and develop the 'real values of life', the 'love of money' would have to be resolutely discarded.

Regarding capital, in this event the conditions on which it is provided would become reversed.[50] Rather than being determined by the *provider* of capital, they would be determined by the circumstances of the *user* of capital—as, for example, Aristotle long ago proposed within the context of credit contracts:

> The law holds that it is more just that the person whom credit was given should fix the terms than that the person who gave credit should do so. For most things are not assessed at the same value by those who have them and those who want them; each class values highly what is its own and what it is offering; yet the return is made on the terms fixed by the receiver. But no doubt the receiver should assess a thing not at what it seems worth when he has it, but at what he assessed it at before he had it. (*Nichomachean Ethics* 1164b: 15–21)

Aristotle's reversal of terms on which credit is provided may be extended to capital in general. This is the meaning of what has been named 'Open Access Credit' (OAC).[51]

Financial Literacy Predicated on Character

The technique that will allow us to cross from capital preservation and accumulation to the circulation and giving away of capital—or from self-interest to 'character'—as suggested by Houghton Budd (2016a), is 'financial literacy predicated on accounting when the latter is understood as a means for perceiving and so managing economic life for all our benefit, not merely as a tool of tax avoidance or profit-maximising'.

The essential element in financial literacy, according to Houghton Budd (2015a, 2015b, 2016b, 2017) is its enabling effect, or 'the empowering experiences that financial literacy can engender' (Houghton Budd 2017). This does not refer to the

[50] As suggested by Houghton Budd in various publications mentioned in this chapter and in Naastepad and Houghton Budd (2015).

[51] Houghton Budd (2016a).

experience one may have from an expertise in accounting that is used as a medium for self-enrichment, but to the experience one may have when one realizes that one has the power to serve others 'through the uniqueness of one's gifts, talents and capacities, all the while supported by the capital of others as evidence of their belief in you—hence, "credit"' (Houghton Budd 2017).

Chances that students of financial literacy will have such experiences are low when accounting is taught in a context of economic or financial theories that argue that the purpose of a business is to maximize profit for shareholders, and when accounting is used mainly to avoid taxes and to compute equity and how much it increases. Interest in how a business can serve others is more likely to arise when accounting is taught in a way that explains and reinforces the inherently social and ethical nature of accounting, capital, and business. The empowering experience also derives from reflection on one's own activities, and from sharing one's accounts with one another, making visible what each is trying to achieve and how this may influence the attitude and conduct of others.

Central to such financial literacy, therefore, is not only a viable theoretical understanding of bookkeeping and accounting, but also the ability to apply this to one's own affairs (Houghton Budd 2017). The latter entails the ability to devise and navigate by a financial plan—based on the three precepts of adequate profit, appropriate capitalization, and positive cash-flow management—cast over the life of one's project. A financial plan enables one to envisage and achieve the level and type of capital one needs and to identify the type and amount of credit the project warrants. The latter is essential in rendering access to credit more open 'because the borrower develops the kind of awareness traditionally expected only of lenders or lending agencies' (Houghton Budd 2017), giving him or her financial and economic agency in relationships with lenders.

The accounting underlying this approach to financial literacy is nested in a paradigm that considers profit as a metric of the social validity of a business,[52] capital as the counterpart of capacities, and cash-flow as evidence of the ability of the users of capital to manage their own affairs, with accounting becoming in the process an instrument of economic perception rather than a tool for achieving or recording gain.[53] *Adequate profit* and *positive cash-flow management* are required for the continuation and normal operation of the business. *Appropriate* capitalization entails choosing the amounts and types of capital that fit the initiative. Profit arises on the income-and-expense account and is transferred to the balance sheet as internally generated capital, where the real question regarding this capital is not to whom it belongs, but to what use it is put, and whether that use is provider- or user-determined.[54]

[52] Rather than as something to be maximized.

[53] Houghton Budd (2015a, 2015b, 2015c, 2016a, 2017).

[54] Houghton Budd (2016a).

The pedagogical approach envisaged for teaching financial literacy is inspired by the methods used by Luca Pacioli to teach accounting, nowadays known as 'cognitive apprenticeship'. Through this approach, students learn to understand accounting as a mirror of human behaviour, and economic life as being about using one's skills and capacities to meet other people's needs through: trade/the production of goods; capitalizing capacities; and maintaining an overview of the economic process as a whole with an eye to contributing to all-round fairness. The main insight that is conveyed is that 'nothing is achieved in economic life unto oneself, but always in link with others. Recognising this and re-grounding economic life on a shared understanding of its essentially cooperative or mutual nature, as reflected in finance, is an important aspect of overcoming marginalisation' (Houghton Budd 2017: 39–40).

The focus of financial literacy in this sense is on those who are wanting for the kinds and amounts of credit that match their circumstances, as decided by them, as users of capital, rather than by the providers of it. In the sense explained above, financial literacy is the prerequisite for and corollary of 'Open Access Credit'.[55]

Conclusion

If the development and fulfilment of capacities is important for human beings individually and collectively, it becomes urgent to reconsider capital, for unless they are funded, individuals cannot unfold and develop their capacities or further their capabilities. Does capital today support capacities?

Capital is emancipatory in essence, but for many decades, the conventional societal configuration has been to leave the allocation of capital to be determined by the self-interested pursuit of personal gain, while any resulting gaps between the social goal of economics (overall welfare) and the actual economic outcome were left to the political sphere to repair or compensate.

However, the withdrawal by governments all over the world from this social task has brought the world to a point where civil society is thrown back on itself and today, it is for citizens individually and collectively, therefore—not 'the market' or 'the state'—to decide what the world economy will be like. The outcome will depend on individuals identifying their role in the economy especially as regards capital and that part of it which today arguably exists in excess.

Recent social innovations in finance reveal a growing awareness that for capital to be enabling for all world citizens, the chief innovation that is required is an evolution from the selfish to the social as the guiding principle with respect to capital. The consistency and effectiveness of such social innovation in finance

[55] Houghton Budd (2016a).

could be strengthened if it were given a solid theoretical basis, grounded on the recognition of the dual role of capital as financier of production *and* enabler of capacities, and of other-interest as the basis of economic order.

References

Acemoglu, Daron and Pascual Restrepo. 2017. 'Robots and Jobs: Evidence from U.S. labour Markets'. NBER Working Paper 23285. Cambridge, MA: National Bureau of Economic Research.

Bacon, Francis. 1605. 'The Advancement of Learning'. In Francis Bacon. 2011 [1857]. *The Works of Francis Bacon, Vol. III*, edited by James Spedding et al., pp. 253–492. Cambridge: Cambridge University Press.

Bain and Company, Macro Trends Group. 2012a. 'A World Awash in Money: Capital Trends through 2020'. http://www.bain.com.

Bain and Company. 2012b. 'Health Care 2020'. https://www.bain.com/contentassets/063d85be0237467fabe711835fb36e7d/bain_brief_healthcare_2020.pdf

Barton, Dominic, Jonathan Woetzel, Jeongmin Seong, and Qunzhen Tian. 2017. 'Artificial Intelligence: Implications for China', McKinsey Global Institute (MGI) Discussion Paper, April 2017, presented at the 2017 China Development Forum.

Beckert, Jens. 2010. 'How Do Fields Change? The Interrelations of Institutions, Networks, and Cognition in the Dynamics of Markets'. *Organization Studies* 31 (5): 605–27.

Beckert, Jens. 2011. 'Die Sittlichkeit der Wirtschaft. Von Effizienz- und Differenzierungstheorien zu einer Theorie wirtschaftlicher Felder'. MPIfG Working Paper 11/8. Köln: Max Planck Institut für Gesellschaftsforschung.

Beckert, Jens and Wolfgang Streeck. 2008. 'Economic Sociology and Political Economy: A Programmatic Perspective'. MPIfG Working Paper 08/4. Köln: Max Planck Institut für Gesellschaftsforschung.

Bentham, Jeremy. 1781. *An Introduction to the Principles of Morals and Legislation*. 2nd edition 1823. [1988 edition: Amherst, NY: Prometheus Books.]

Berlin, Isaiah. 1969. *Four Essays on Liberty*. Oxford: Oxford University Press.

Berman, Elizabeth P. 2012. *Creating the Market University: How Academic Science Became an Economic Engine*. Princeton, NJ: Princeton University Press.

Carr, Nicholas (2014) *The Glass Cage: Automation and Us*. New York: W.W. Norton.

Chui, Michael, James Manyika, and Mehdi Miremadi. 2017. 'The Countries Most (and Least) Likely to Be Affected by Automation'. *Harvard Business Review*, 12 April. https://hbr.org/2017/04/the-countries-most-and-least-likely-to-be-affected-by-automation.

Durkheim, Émile. 1893. *The Division of Labour in Society*.

Edmiston, Daniel and Alex Nicholls. 2018. 'Social Impact Bonds: The Role of Private Capital in Outcome-Based Commissioning'. *Journal of Social Policy* 47(1): 57–76.

Eells, Richard. 1967. *The Corporation and the Arts*. New York: Macmillan.

Frey, Carl Benedikt and Michael Osborne. 2013. 'The Future of Employment: How Susceptible Are Jobs to Computerisation?' OMS Working Paper 1. Oxford Martin School.

Galbraith, John Kenneth. 1991. *A History of Economics: The Past as the Present*. London: Hamish Hamilton.

Graeber, David. 2013. 'On the Phenomenon of Bull-Shit Jobs'. *Strike! Magazine*, 17 August.

Graeber, David. 2015. *The Utopia of Rules: On Technology, Stupidity, and the Secret Joys of Bureaucracy*. New York: Melville House.

Graeber, David. 2018. 'Are You in a BS Job? In Academe, You're Hardly Alone'. *The Chronicle of Higher Education*, 6 May.

Habermas, Jürgen.1981. *Theorie des kommunikativen Handelns*. Frankfurt am Main: Suhrkamp.

Head, Simon. 2014. *Mindless: Why Smarter Machines Are Making Dumber Humans*. New York: Basic Books.

Heiskala, Risto. 2014a. 'Forms of Power, European Empires and Globalisations: Michael Mann's *The Sources of Social Power and Beyond*'. In 'Report on Institutions, Social Innovation and System Dynamics from the Perspective of the Marginalised', edited by C. Houghton Budd, C. W. M. Naastepad, and C. P. van Beers, Chapter 8. CrESSI Working Paper No. 28. Brussels: European Commission, DG Research.

Heiskala, Risto. 2014b. 'Relating Mann's Conception to CrESSI'. In 'Report on Institutions, Social Innovation and System Dynamics from the Perspective of the Marginalised', edited by C. Houghton Budd, C. W. M. Naastepad and C. P. van Beers, Chapter 10. CrESSI Working Paper No. 9. Brussels: European Commission, DG Research.

Hirschman, Albert O. 1997 [1977]. *The Passions and the Interests: Political Arguments for Capitalism before its Triumph*. Princeton, NJ: Princeton University Press.

Hobbes, Thomas. 1651 [2016]. *Leviathan*. London: Penguin Classics.

Hoeges, Dirk. 1994. *Kontroverse am Abgrund: Ernst Robert Curtius und Karl Mannheim. Intellektuelle und freischwebende Intelligenz in der Weimarer Republik*. Frankfurt am Main: Fischer.

Houghton Budd, Christopher. 2011. *Finance at the Threshold: Rethinking the Real and Financial Economies*. Farnham: Gower.

Houghton Budd, Christopher. 2014. 'Resilience and Financial Literacy'. In 'Report on Institutions, Social Innovation and System Dynamics from the Perspective of the Marginalised', edited by C. Houghton Budd, C. W. M. Naastepad and C. P. van Beers, Chapter 7. CrESSI Working Paper No. 7. Brussels: European Commission, DG Research.

Houghton Budd, Christopher. 2015a. 'Entrepreneur Capital: Individual Case Study 4'. In 'Four Individual Case Studies Following a Common Template', edited by Gudrun Schimpf, Thomas Scheuerle, and Georg Mildenberger.

Houghton Budd, Christopher. 2015b. 'Accounting, Social Innovation, and Finance: Teaching Financial Literacy Using Double-Entry Bookkeeping'. In 'Training

Material on Accounting'. CrESSI Working Paper No. 15. Brussels: European Commission, DG Research.

Houghton Budd, Christopher. 2015c. 'Alternative or Deep Accounting'. Paper for Task 3.5 of the CrESSI project (unpublished).

Houghton Budd, Christopher. 2016a. 'Twin Value Theory as Reflected in Accounting, and its Consequences for our Understanding of Capital'. In 'Theoretical Foundations of Social Innovation in Finance', edited by C. Houghton Budd and C. W. M. Naastepad, Chapter 4. CrESSI Working Paper No. 30. Brussels: European Commission, DG Research.

Houghton Budd, Christopher. 2016b. 'In the Shoes of Luca Pacioli: Double-Entry Bookkeeping and Financial Literacy'. In *International Handbook of Financial Literacy*, edited by Carmela Aprea, Eveline Wuttke, Klaus Breuer, Noi Keng Koh, Peter Davies, Bettina Greimel-Fuhrmann, and Jane S. Lopus, pp, 621–38. Berlin: Springer.

Houghton Budd, Christopher. 2017. 'Financial Literacy Seminars Based on Private Finance'. In 'Financial Literacy Seminars and Financial Accounting Plans for Social Innovators', CrESSI Deliverable No. D10.6 and D10.7, edited by C. W. M. Naastepad.

Houghton Budd, Christopher, and C. W. M. Naastepad. 2014. 'Beckert, Sen and Finance: A Response to Marginalisation Mindful of Today's Prevailing Monetary and Financial Environment'. In 'Report on Institutions, Social Innovation and System Dynamics from the Perspective of the Marginalised', edited by C. Houghton Budd, C. W. M. Naastepad, and C. P. van Beers, Chapter 4. CrESSI Working Paper No. 4. Brussels: European Commission, DG Research.

Houghton Budd, Christopher, and C. W. M. Naastepad. 2016a. 'Linking Modern Finance to Social Innovation'. In 'On the Co-evolution of Technology, Economy and Society', edited by Klaus Kubeczko, Part 3 (unpublished).

Houghton Budd, Christopher, and C. W. M. Naastepad (eds). 2016b. 'Theoretical Foundations of Social Innovation in Finance'. CrESSI Working Paper No. 30. Brussels: European Commission, DG Research.

Houghton Budd, Christopher, and C. W. M. Naastepad. 2016c. 'Introduction'. In 'Theoretical Foundations of Social Innovation in Finance', edited by C. Houghton Budd and C. W. M. Naastepad, Chapter 1. CrESSI Working Paper No. 30. Brussels: European Commission, DG Research.

Houghton Budd, Christopher, C. W. M. Naastepad, and Cees P. van Beers. 2014. 'From Common Framework to Measurement and Analysis'. In 'Report on Institutions, Social Innovation and System Dynamics from the Perspective of the Marginalised', edited by C. Houghton Budd, C. W. M. Naastepad, and C. P. van Beers, Chapter 11. CrESSI Working Paper No. 10. Brussels: European Commission, DG Research.

Houghton Budd, Christopher, C. W. M. Naastepad, and Cees P. van Beers (eds). 2014. 'Report on Institutions, Social Innovation and System Dynamics from the Perspective of the Marginalised'. CrESSI Deliverable No. D1.1.

Houghton Budd, Christopher, C. W. M. Naastepad, and Cees P. van Beers. 2015. 'CrESSI's Common Framework'. In 'Report Contrasting CrESSI's Approach of Social Innovation with That of Neoclassical Economics', edited by C. Houghton

Budd, C. W. M. Naastepad, and C. P. van Beers, Chapter 10. CrESSI Working Paper No. 12. Brussels: European Commission, DG Research.

Houghton Budd, Christopher, C. W. M. Naastepad, and Martijn Jeroen van der Linden (eds). 2015. 'Report Contrasting CrESSI's Approach of Social Innovation with that of Neoclassical Economics'. CrESSI Working Paper No. 12. Brussels: European Commission, DG Research.

Houghton Budd, Christopher, C. W. M. Naastepad, and Martijn Jeroen van der Linden. 2015. 'Financial and Monetary Innovations for Overcoming Social Exclusion: The Financing of Generalised Education (as Instanced in the Netherlands and England)'. Comprehensive Case Study 2, CrESSI Deliverable No. D2.1.

Hume, David. 1752. 'Of Refinement in the Arts'. In *David Hume, Essays—Moral, Political and Literary*, edited by Eugene F. Miller, pp. 268–80. Indianapolis, IN: Liberty Fund, 1987.

Keynes, John Maynard. 1930. 'Economic Possibilities for our Grandchildren'. In J. M. Keynes, *Essays in Persuasion*, pp. 358–73. London: W. W. Norton, 1963.

Keynes, John Maynard. 1963. *Essays in Persuasion*. London: W. W. Norton.

Koshy, Mariam Asha. 2015. 'Is Health Care a Market? Does Turning Health Care into a Market Lower the Cost (and Increase the Quality) of Health Care?' MSc thesis, Delft University of Technology.

Lagarde, Christine. 2014. 'Empowerment', Amartya Sen Lecture given at the London School of Economics on 6 June. International Monetary Fund. http://www.imf.org/external/np/speeches/2014/060614.htm.

Lazear, Edward P. 2000. 'Economic Imperialism'. *The Quarterly Journal of Economics* 115(1): 99–146.

Locke, John. 1689 [1690]. *An Essay Concerning Human Understanding*. London: Thomas Bassett.

Molnár, György. 2015. 'The Role of Incentives versus Intrinsic Motivation in Relation to Micro-Credit Activities'. In 'Report Contrasting CrESSI's Approach of Social Innovation with that of Neoclassical Economics', edited by C. Houghton Budd, C. W. M. Naastepad, and C. P. van Beers, Chapter 10. CrESSI Working Paper No. 12. Brussels: European Commission, DG Research.

Molnár, György. 2016. 'The Problem of Social Collateral in Micro-Lending'. In 'Theoretical Foundations of Social Innovation in Finance', edited by C. Houghton Budd and C. W. M. Naastepad, Chapter 5. CrESSI Working Paper No. 30. Brussels: European Commission, DG Research.

Naastepad, C. W. M., and Christopher Houghton Budd (2015) 'Aristotelian Economics and Modern Finance: A Consideration of the True Counterpart to Today's Financial Markets'. In 'Report Contrasting CrESSI's Approach of Social Innovation with that of Neoclassical Economics', edited by C. Houghton Budd, C. W. M. Naastepad, and C. P. van Beers, Chapter 6. CrESSI Working Paper No. 12. Brussels: European Commission, DG Research.

Naastepad, C. W. M., and Christopher Houghton Budd. 2019. 'Preventing Technological Unemployment by Widening our Understanding of Capital and Progress: Making Robots Work for Us'. *Ethics and Social Welfare* 13(2): 115–32.

Naastepad, C. W. M. and Jesse M. Mulder. 2018. 'Robots and Us: Towards an Economics of the "Good Life"'. *Review of Social Economy* 76(3): 302–34.

Naastepad, C. W. M. and Jesse M. Mulder. 2019. 'How Do We Judge the Responsibility (or Otherwise) of Research and Innovation? Capital, Aristotle, and the Neglected Factor: Freedom'. In *New Perspectives on Responsible Innovation*, edited by Roland Ortt, Martijn Blaauw and Jeroen van den Hoven. (forthcoming.)

Nicholls, Alex and Rafael Ziegler. 2014. 'An Extended Social Grid Model for the Study of Marginalization Processes and Social Innovation'. In 'Report on Institutions, Social Innovation and System Dynamics from the Perspective of the Marginalised', edited by C. Houghton Budd, C. W. M. Naastepad, and C. P. van Beers, Chapter 2.

Nussbaum, Martha C. 1998. *Cultivating Humanity: A Classical Defence of Reform in Liberal Education*. Cambridge. MA: Harvard University Press.

Nussbaum, Martha C. 2010. *Not for Profit: Why Democracy Needs the Humanities*. Princeton, NJ: Princeton University Press.

Nussbaum, Martha C. 2011. *Creating Capabilities: The Human Development Approach*. Cambridge, MA: The Belknap Press.

Pramudita, Damar Aji. 2015. 'Impact of ICT on the Productivity–Compensation Gap: A Study of Technology, Work, and the Role of Capital'. MSc thesis. Delft: Delft University of Technology.

Röpke, Wilhelm. 1948. 'Die Gesellschaftskrisis der Gegenwart'. (5., durchgesehene Auflage.) Erlenbach-Zürich: Rentsch.

Scheuerle, Thomas, and Gunnar Glänzel. 2016. 'Five Per Cent Philanthropy as an Early Form of Social Impact Investing—Differences, Parallels, and What Can Be Learned for Today'. In 'Theoretical Foundations of Social Innovation in Finance', edited by C. Houghton Budd and C. W. M. Naastepad, Chapter 2. CrESSI Working Paper No. 30. Brussels: European Commission, DG Research.

Schor, Juliet B. 1993. *The Overworked American: The Unexpected Decline of Leisure*. New York: Basic Books.

Sebastianelli, Marco, Enrica Chiappero, and Nadia von Jacobi. 2015. 'From Rational Agents to Human Diversity'. In 'Report Contrasting CrESSI's Approach of Social Innovation with That of Neoclassical Economics', edited by C. Houghton Budd, C. W. M. Naastepad, and C. P. van Beers, Chapter 8. CrESSI Working Paper No. 12. Brussels: European Commission, DG Research.

Sen, Amartya. 1977. 'Rational Fools: A Critique of the Behavioral Foundations of Economic Theory'. *Philosophy and Public Affairs* 6(4): 317–44.

Sen, Amartya. 2001. *Development as Freedom*. Oxford: Oxford University Press.

Spence, Michael. 2014. 'Labor's Digital Displacement'. *Project Syndicate—The World's Opinion Page*. https://www.project-syndicate.org.

Storm, Servaas. 2017. 'The New Normal: Demand, Secular Stagnation and the Vanishing Middle Class'. INET Working Paper No. 55. New York: Institute for New Economic Thinking.

Vogel, Johanna, Kurt Kratena, and Kathrin Hranyai. 2015. 'The Bias of Technological Change in Europe'. Working Paper No. 98 of the EU FP7 project Welfare, Wealth, Work for Europe.

Wilken, Folkert. 1982. *The Liberation of Capital.* London: George Allen and Unwin.

15

The Impact of Social Innovation

Alex Nicholls, Nadia von Jacobi, Enrica Chiappero-Martinetti, and Georg Mildenberger

Introduction

Over the years, the question of how to establish whether organizations have achieved their intended social or environmental impact has been widely discussed across several disciplines including accounting, welfare economics, development studies, and NGO and not-for-profit sector research (Nicholls et al. 2015a; Ebrahim and Rangan 2010, 2014). For example, welfare economics has provided guidance via cost–benefit analyses of welfare outcomes to support policy decision-making for decades (see e.g. O'Connell 1982). Development finance institutions, charities, and other not-for-profits, have been capturing and reporting their social impact for an equally long time. More recently, corporations and other firms have used corporate social responsibility reporting and, in some cases, internal measures of their economic, social, and governance (ESG) as well as carbon intensity performance to highlight their social and/or environmental value creation (or destruction). As a consequence, today, there are many well-established methodologies for capturing social impact—often drawing upon tried and tested techniques from social science—including randomized control trials (common in development contexts), experimental methods such as revealed and expressed preference models, cost–benefit analyses and strategic dashboard methods.

More recently, the growing interest in hybrid organizations, such as social enterprises (Battilana and Dorado 2010), and blended value enterprises (Emerson 2003), has focused new attention on the complex set of relationships between social and financial value creation that has, in turn, generated new frameworks that do not treat these two streams of value as separate and unrelated. As a result, the last two decades have seen the emergence of a new and distinctive set of impact measurement methodologies focused on capturing the impact associated with innovations such as social entrepreneurship (Nicholls 2006) and social finance (Nicholls et al. 2015b; Ebrahim and Rangan 2014; Hall 2012; Patton 2011). Today, as Mulgan (2010) has noted, there is a multitude of impact metrics and methodologies available linked to a growing field of professional evaluators.

One question that this chapter seeks to address is whether the impact measurement and management of *social innovation processes* can be accommodated

Alex Nicholls, Nadia von Jacobi, Enrica Chiappero-Martinetti, and Georg Mildenberger,
The Impact of Social Innovation. In: *Creating Economic Space for Social Innovation*.
Edited by: Alex Nicholls and Rafael Ziegler, Oxford University Press (2019). © Oxford University Press.
DOI: 10.1093/oso/9780198830511.003.0015

within this broader trend of social impact measurement or whether it requires a new theoretical framework. As indicated elsewhere in this book, social innovation typically seeks to alter power structures and to promote human capabilities—particularly of the most marginalized and excluded from sources of power and welfare. For this reason, such social innovations tend to exert pressure on existing social structures and institutional arrangements as represented by our Extended Social Grid Model (ESGM)—theorized in this volume as the dynamic interaction of institutions, cognitive frames, and social networks. From this point of view, social innovation represents a dynamic process of developing institutional arrangements that can address marginalization as a socio-structural issue. In this sense, social innovation—defined here as new ideas, products, or processes that intentionally seek to change power structures to improve human capabilities—represents a driver of participatory and locally embedded institutional change (Pritchett 2013). Moreover, aligning with Sen's work on capabilities, the ESGM framing suggests that—for social innovation to succeed—marginalized actors must be directly involved in the construction of the institutional context that can (re)shape the opportunity landscape available to them and their communities. Citizen participation in co-creating the institutional context in which they live is, thus, a *sine qua non* of the development of institutions that can empower rather than oppress the most marginalized. However, disentangling the positive (and negative) social impacts of these processes is a complex analytic task and demands a range of metrical approaches. This chapter provides an overview of the landscape of measuring the impact of social innovation and develops a set of impact measurement and management principles to help capture the effects of these processes.

In this chapter, social impact is defined as follows:

Material changes in the lives of target populations in alignment with specific organizational/project objectives.

There are three particularly important features within this definition:

- *Material*: this refers to the established concept of *materiality* within financial accounting that describes any data without which an investor cannot make an informed decision concerning a firm. In the context of social impact measurement, materiality refers to any data without which the nature of the intended changes in the lives of key stakeholders cannot be fully understood. It will be further argued below that to achieve this involves participatory and empowering impact measurement design and implementation processes (see Nicholls 2018).
- *Target populations*: this refers to the specific groups of stakeholders/end-users that are in the focus of an organization or programme. The implication here is that effective social impact measurement must take stock of all potential stakeholders and make careful judgements over which groups are most significant for their work.

- *Alignment*: this refers to the issue of *intentionality*—namely how social impact connects to organizational/programme strategy and objectives. That is not to say that social *externalities* (best defined as either unintended social impacts on intended populations or intended impacts on unintended populations) may not also be included in measurement processes, but these lie outside the core definition of social impact. Capturing social externalities may be particularly important when they are negative.

Central to this chapter is the development of a *Critical Issues Framework* for social impact measurement to inform the development of the most appropriate and accurate evaluative space for data collection and analysis. As such it advocates standardization in the *process* of developing social impact indicators and methodologies, rather than in the metrics and units of analysis themselves.[1] This model pays careful attention to the three elements in Beckert's Social Grid, developed in chapter 1, in so far as they help to shape normative models of social impact measurement that may entrench marginalization and limit stakeholder voice. Special attention is also given to the delicate issue of how to measure human capabilities, in line with Sen's theoretical approach. In summary, this chapter offers a framework for thinking about optimizing measurement choices, one that identifies the main methods indicating when each will be more or less appropriate. This is similar in approach to the contingency framework developed by Ebrahim and Rangan (2014). Next we consider a central conceptual formulation of the social impact creation process: the Theory of Change model.

Theory of Change

A Theory of Change model (also known as a logic model) represents social impact creation as a linear process linking resource inputs to ultimate impact (Aguilera et al. 2007: see Figure 15.1).

[1] Standardized impact metrics (and attendant measurement processes) offer an attractive proposition—primarily because they offer the tantalizing prospect of allowing a comparative analysis of the impact of interventions. Moves towards standardization could be driven by one of three possible processes of institutionalization. First, standardized data could be regulated into being, as it has been the case for financial data via waves of accounting legislation. Second, such data could come about via various self-regulated methods or schemes such as the Social Return on Investment (SROI) approach (Nicholls 2004) or the Global Impact Investing Reporting System (GIIRS) metrics. In this context, the Impact Management Project (IMP) has built an international collaboration to agree a set of common over-arching principles for impact measurement and management. The IMP has subsequently agreed a partnership with the UNDP to align its principles with the metrics defined for the seventeen Sustainable Development Goals. In time, this may lead to a standardized set of metrics. Finally, standardization could come about in an entirely laissez-faire manner as the 'market' of social impact data coalesces around one favoured approach (Mulgan 2010). Whatever the pathway to standardization proves to be—if, indeed, consensus is ever established—it seems likely that this will remain an ongoing issue as society seeks the most effective ways of addressing social problems.

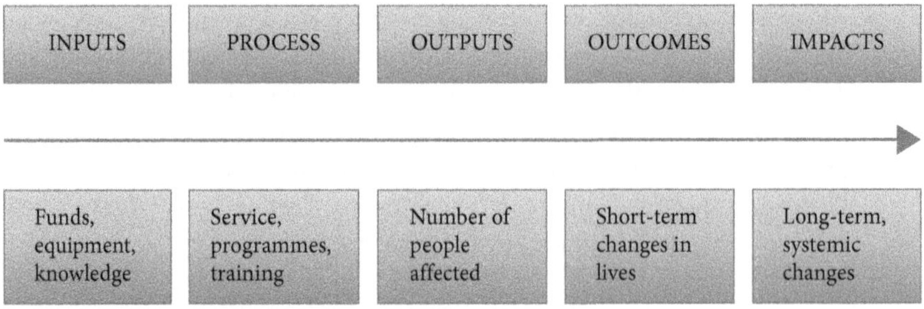

15.1 Theory of Change model
Source: Aguilera et al. (2007).

The model begins with *inputs* that encompass a range of material (e.g. money, programme officers) and immaterial (e.g. knowledge, social capital) resources. Key stakeholders may also be considered an *input* in this context (e.g. in the case of a literacy project, these would include children as well as teachers). Deliberative *processes* of action and operations—essentially programmes of work or projects—then transform these input resources to achieve particular strategic objectives (e.g. classroom activities to teach children to read). This, in turn, produces *outputs* that are typically quantified as the number of participants in a programme (e.g. the number of children who can now read). The Theory of Change model next proposes that certain social *outcomes* will typically follow from given outputs (e.g. the output of a number of children who can now read leads to the outcome of improved overall educational attainment for this group and better employment opportunities). Outcomes are typically identified and measured at a later stage than direct outputs that can usually be measured as soon as a target population has finished a given programme. Finally, the model suggests that—typically even further in the future from the programme processes and outputs—outcomes may lead to *impact* transformations that may go beyond the individual stakeholder participant or service user (e.g. the outcomes of improved educational attainment may lead to final impacts including increased economic resilience in a given community or, even, reduced crime). Another set of issues concerns whether the units of analysis across the model are chosen in terms of either breadth or depth of data. In this case, *breadth* refers to data that aims to catch the widest set of impacts that may credibly be connected to an intervention across multiple stakeholders while *depth* data aims to drill down within individual cases to account for the full scale of impact at this level of analysis.[2]

The Theory of Change model has been widely criticized for its linear determinism (e.g. Finger and Princen 2013)—in real life the relationships between its

[2] This issue of *attribution*—i.e. what impact can be credibly linked to a particular intervention—is considered further below.

constituent parts are likely to be more complex. As such, the model does not take into account any issues around social risk and return (Nicholls and Tomkinson 2015)—namely the likelihood that a given social outcome will actually happen. But it has, nevertheless, proved to be a very attractive—and widely used—method of modelling the intended impact effects of many service delivery organizations.

In terms of measuring social impact, each stage of the Theory of Change model will likely require a different unit of analysis and methodology. Moreover, the point in time when effective measurement will best be implemented will vary across the model—most obviously outputs and outcomes tend to be best measured some time after a programme has been completed since they typically involve changes that occur over time after an intervention. When considering the impacts of systemic social innovation, the focus will likely be on longer-term outcomes and impacts measures and data with all the attendant challenges this creates.

The relationships between macro-systemic impacts and micro-capabilities impacts also need careful consideration here. Each will likely require different measurement regimes. Moreover, as the Theory of Change model reminds us, social impact occurs across all elements of the social innovation process as well as in specific outputs and outcomes. In terms of measuring the effects of social innovation, Moulaert et al. (2005) differentiated between the content dimension (satisfaction of human needs), the empowerment dimension of social innovation (socio-political capabilities), and the process dimension (changes in social relations). Each of these dimensions will need distinctive analytic approaches—for example, capturing the impact of the state and the structure of the relationships and networks that enact social innovation (Krlev et al. 2014; Reeder and Colantonio 2013) will require network analysis methods and case studies that pay respect to the circumstance that social innovation is 'embedded in the "social fabric" of communities' (Reeder and Colantonio 2013: 11). Similarly, Nicholls (2018) pointed out the need to embed participatory action in the processes of social impact measurement both as refinement of the accuracy of the metric and as socially impactful process in and of itself. These themes are explored further later in this chapter. But first, let us consider the larger theoretical context of social impact measurement more generally.

Impact and Accounting Theory

As has already been noted, there is no shortage of methods with which to measure social impact. But every method has its subtext—the assumptions it makes, the uses expected of it, and so on. Making those assumptions explicit can provide a convenient way of grouping similar approaches and highlighting what may otherwise go unnoticed.

Table 15.1. Different logics of social impact measurement

Epistemology	Focus	Logic	Example
Positivist	Truth	Measurement captures empirical reality	Audited accounts
Critical Theorist	Power	Measurement enacts power mechanisms	Participatory methods
Interpretive	Dialogue	Measurement acts as a symbolic mediator for discussion between organizational practice and stakeholders	Stakeholder driven Data collection Design

Source: Authors.

To that end, it is useful to take three theories of accounting and apply them to the different approaches to impact measurement (Table 15.1). The first takes a positivist view of accounting: it assumes that accounting data is and should be a representation of financial realities (Whittington 1986). The second sees accounting from a critical theorist perspective suggesting that accounting processes are essentially about the enactment of power (Chua 1986; Power and Laughlin 1996; see also Lukes 1974). The key issue is who determines what data are captured and reported and for what purpose—since it is well understood that what is to be measured attracts more management attention than what is not. The third theory reconstructs accounting as, ultimately, an interpretive activity—one that provides shared symbolic mediators (terms, codes, conventions) and institutional spaces (practices, formal occasions) for a discussion among interested parties about the nature and extent of value creation, and how best to capture it (Ryan et al. 1992; Gambling et al. 1993).

These three approaches represent a spectrum of conceptualizations of accounting and reporting from being a scientific process to representing a set of framing principles for control and action. Taken together in relation to social impact measurement, the three perspectives throw further light on the challenges involved. These three frames are discussed in turn next.

Since these challenges are considerable, a fourth approach—one, which essentially tries to reduce the need for additional impact measurement by using audit and certification—is also outlined later.

Positivist Methods

Central to the positivist measurement approach is an assumption that social impact proceeds in a linear fashion from a set of inputs and processes to a set of outputs and outcomes. This is usually known as a logic model and in line with the engineering approach, typical of many evaluation studies. The idea underlying logic models is a set of 'if..., then...' causal propositions that set out the thinking behind a social, economic, or development intervention. The evaluator's task is to clarify these linkages and to establish cost-effective ways of gathering the information needed in order to track whether or not the intended interventions are working as intended and are leading to the hoped-for outcomes and social impact. The ways of gathering such information are many and varied—from operational records, interviews, surveys, observation, and official statistics. But however many and complicated these may be, the underpinning rationale is the same.

Two points concerning the logic model approach are worth noting. First, it may be argued that for an impact study, the only information that really matters is whether or not the impact is realized. This may be so, but generally, those involved want to understand their results: if there is some impact, but less (or otherwise different) than one hoped for, why is that? Could the results be improved by changing the way the scheme is run? Or was the intervention based on flawed thinking? Many evaluators will know this as the distinction between *formative* evaluation (aimed at improving a process) and *summative* evaluation (what has actually been achieved).

Secondly, if the organization wants to establish whether (say) some lasting community benefit has been achieved, the volumes of information required can become very large indeed. Moreover, the findings are often not clear-cut and thus evaluators may feel professionally obliged to report on the uncertainties and ambiguities involved. As a result, data-rich evaluations often gather dust because they do not provide the categorical conclusions after which time-poor decision-makers hanker. Such reports do not provide information in standardized form for comparisons and/or aggregation and use by others, either. Nor, normally, would they relate the benefits to all the costs involved in achieving them.

Most methods of social impact measurement and reporting are based, explicitly often, on a logic model, and so they fall into the positivist category. This suggests, above all, that interested parties favour an approach that appears to offer 'certainty', 'objectivity', or 'scientific rigour' with a strong focus on numerical abstractions. At its extreme, this approach also attempts to monetize and 'value' social impact in order to allow comparative analysis across projects and interventions by using financial value as a common unit of social impact.

Methods under this heading include: cost–benefit analyses or expected return models such as Acumen's Best Alternative Charitable Option (BACO); experimental methods of choice modelling and valuation such as randomized control trials (RCTs);[3] behavioural models, such as stated or revealed preferences tests;

[3] The use of RCTs in social impact evaluation has increased markedly in recent years (Bannerjee and Duflo 2010; Haynes et al. 2012). Nevertheless, controversy still abounds over the scope for using RCTs and their practical value, largely because science is a cumulative enterprise and so what can be

welfare economics models, such as public value assessments (judging how much the public values a service), value-added assessments (in education, judging how much a school adds value to a student), quality-adjusted-life-years (QALYs) in health, life satisfaction assessments (how much extra income people would need to achieve an equivalent gain in life satisfaction); government accounting measures that used standardized 'pricing' of welfare interventions to account for government spending.

Critical Theory Methods

While the range of methods currently used to capture social impact is dominated by those predicated on positivistic logics, alternative approaches are available. An important alterative approach is SROI. Over time, SROI has evolved from a positivistic focus on calculative accuracy (paying careful attention to discount rates and the best proxies to monetize impact) to a more general principles-based framework for how to choose the most appropriate sources of input data. The shift has been from technique to principles. Partly, this reflects a realization that the quest for ever-more accurate numerical models of social impact had not delivered robust, standardized, or comparable data sets. As a result, SROI models have not yet been shown to improve the quality or quantity of capital flows to social projects. Nevertheless, the principles of SROI have offered a credible way of advancing stakeholder engagement for better and more rounded measurement. So SROI now goes well beyond its logic model origins to highlight a set of principles that acknowledge power relations and locate judgements of materiality in stakeholder consultation. It combines this with a cost–benefit model that uses the principles of net present value discounting to monetize future *blended* value (financial plus social) outcomes. While controversial, this has the merit of embracing a central concept in accounting and finance and, thus, provides additional legitimacy to this approach with certain audiences (notably investors).

Other methods imbued with the sort of assumptions associated with Critical Theory are 'strategy approaches' (Ebrahim and Rangan 2010). Typically, these view decision-making in and around organizations as the outcome of pluralistic rather than monological processes, involving coalitions and alliances of internal and external stakeholders. For example, balanced scorecard approaches—whose origin was precisely to offer a way of resisting the dominance in the corporate domain of (usually short-term) financial concerns—aim to hold in tension the data and interpretations on performance arising from different stakeholder

established by a single RCT is often quite limited. Often, RCT results are puzzling, raising more and better questions to be sure, but not giving the clarity about 'what works' for which, understandably, busy investors and policy-makers long.

perspectives across the range of actors directly affected by a given social innovation. Other versions present 'dashboards' that attempt to provide managers and funders with manageable summaries of performance across important dimensions, however disparate (e.g. Paton 2003: chapter 8).

Interpretive Methods

Methods that prioritize stakeholder participation, voice, and dialogue also align closely with the interpretive theory of accounting practice. These relationship-based methods typically focus on outcome mapping based on deep engagement with relevant stakeholder or beneficiary groups—for example the 'outcomes star' model.[4] Such engagement often starts before an intervention begins and uses stakeholder consultation to design the intervention as well as to shape the appropriate units of performance measurement and the subsequent methodology used. Moreover, this approach usually has built-in feedback loops to test for the ongoing accuracy of data and the effectiveness of the method. It is, thus, iterative, dynamic, and adaptable. Interpretive methods work well to capture key social impacts in complex or integrative settings by embracing collaborative learning, inter-subjectivity, and dialogue among those directly involved. Thus, measurement systems that prioritize stakeholder judgement and build beneficiary voice can generate additional social impact through the very process of measurement. These issues are considered next in terms of agency and individual capabilities.

Social Innovation and Impact

As set out in chapter 1, social innovation is conceived of here as a set of actions designed to disrupt existing institutional structures and to shape new arrangements in order to diminish marginalization. The Extended Social Grid Model (ESGM) is designed to break this process down into an analysis of a set of dynamic relationships between institutions, cognitive frames, and networks. From this perspective, social innovation will be enacted via changes in these sets of relationships.

The ESGM is intrinsically complex (indeed, it is designed to study complexity) and aims to trace the various factors that—at different levels of analysis—may play a role in social innovation processes to create impact in terms of social change and the reduction of marginalization. Transforming this conceptual model into an actionable impact measurement methodology poses a series of challenges. The

[4] http://www.outcomesstar.org.uk.

main conceptual finding from an ESGM analysis of marginalization suggests that it is a consequence of disempowerment and is socio-structural. This conceptualization of marginalization leads, in turn, to three methodological issues with respect to measuring the impact of social innovation. Each is considered in turn next.

Agency

Although agency and well-being refer to individuals in much of social science research, the role of group action or of collective action is less well recognized or analysed (see chapter 10). While it is difficult to imagine that a single individual and her/his agency might be sufficient to change any given social structure alone, a group of individuals that get together (to form a network) and structure their goals (by developing a shared cognitive frame) can exert pressure for change at the societal level (in line with Beckert's view on social innovation processes). Therefore, collective agency takes place when individuals engage in a joint process that results in a common set of decisions and action (see Crocker and Robeyns 2009). Agency is here defined as an individual's freedom to act and to achieve one's potential.

Within the capability approach, individual agency is one of the components that enables individuals to be empowered and gives them the ability to realize their own life plans. More specifically, agency can assume two different, though related, dimensions: *agency achievement* or *agency freedom*. According to Sen, an individual's *agency achievement* 'refers to the *realization* of goals and values she has reason to pursue, whether or not they are connected with her own well-being' (Sen 1993: 37, emphasis added). *Agency freedom*, on the other hand, refers to the *potential* a person has in order to pursue 'whatever goals or values he or she regards as important' (Sen 1985: 206, emphasis added).

Both definitions are relevant here: agency achievements demonstrate impact data for completed actions, whereas agency freedom refers to process aspects and to impact that may occur in the future. While the definition of agency is rather intuitive, the assessment of what influences agency, namely what enables or restricts it is more problematic. Narayan (2005) argued that agency is constrained by the 'opportunity structure' that individuals face during their life comprising institutional as well as social and political elements. From this perspective, Beckert's Social Grid shapes the opportunity set perceived by individuals as the bounds of their individual and collective agency. By putting Sen's work on capabilities at the micro-level analytic focus of the ESGM, the link between the social structuration of opportunities and individual agency is partly resolved: even more so by putting the individual as the centre of the data collection process (see chapter 10 and also Nicholls 2018).

Agency can, in particular, be further qualified, extended, or constrained by the social, political, and economic opportunities available as well as by wider social arrangements (Robeyns 2007; Crocker 2008). These are captured in the three irreducible social forces of the Social Grid in the ESGM. To the extent that social innovation can contribute to enlarging agency achievements and—more importantly—agency freedom, it may directly reduce marginalization. For this reason, this book has put individual agency at the focus of the data collection process—as a useful proxy measure (see chapter 4) for the enlargement of freedom at the personal level. Agency achieves impact per se, as it can be—in combination with other socio-economic variables—a determinant of a range of final outcomes that an individual can achieve. In this sense, agency increases personal freedom and, thus, also grows the space for future agency. Agency is, therefore, a crucial factor in achieving self-realization and increasing the opportunities that an individual might have. However, agency not only has effects at the individual level, but also in terms of wider social innovation processes. Where individuals gather to change the environment that surrounds them, agency results in innovative collective approaches that exert pressure on the Social Grid.

In as much as the capability approach suggests focusing on individuals and putting 'human agency (rather than organizations such as markets or governments) at the centre of the stage' (Drèze and Sen 2002: 6), the ESGM proposes to use agency as a key metric for social innovation impact analysis. This requires on the one hand a careful account of people's well-being, on the other hand evaluation methodologies that measure how social innovation affects people's conditions and interacts with their individual levels of agency. Specifically, to quantify individual agency levels and the perceived impact that participation in social innovation activities has had, the research design made use of the Relative Autonomy Index (RAI), which builds upon self-determination theory, as proposed by Deci et al. (1989).

The emphasis given to the agency dimension and the people-centered view adopted by the capability approach suggest that it is of utmost importance to account for how conventions and practices contribute to enact and entrench power relations across interrelated stakeholder groups. In practice, this requires developing methodologies that give voice to the most marginalized or vulnerable stakeholders in an accounting system so that the consequent evaluative space allows for their materiality and performance judgements to have greatest weight. Such an approach not only has the power to *empower*, re-enfranchise, and enhance the capabilities of vulnerable beneficiaries, but also to generate a more reliable and accurate social impact evaluation, since it is these populations themselves who can most accurately assess the impact of programmes or innovations addressed at them.

Temporality

A second analytic issue in terms of effectively capturing social innovation impact is temporality. Systemic social innovation typically takes time, so paying attention to temporal issues is highly important in the process of metric design and data collection. One promising approach is to use long-timescale qualitative case studies (see chapter 4). A historical and longitudinal case analysis of social innovation processes allows a fuller understanding of its systemic outcomes and impacts over time (see chapters 5 to 9). Such a methodological approach can track societal changes at the macro-level, but may find it more difficult to account for the multi-dimensional impacts of specific innovative individuals, groups, or movements. As the ESGM suggests, systemic social innovation involves a number of factors working together to achieve change. Often, social innovation develops and grows in niches in society. But systemic change is not brought about by brilliant and innovative ideas alone, but also by entropy or institutional weaknesses in existing systems that lack effective solutions. At this point, the existing solutions lose their legitimacy and many people are willing to take the risk of something new.

McGowan and Westley (2015) and Blundel and Lyon (2015) used historically informed cases to explore the roots, growth, and development of various social innovations over time (2015: 52; Nicholls and Murdock 2011). This methodology was ideally suited to examine trends and dynamics of social innovation at different societal levels (McGowan and Westley 2015: 55). This was also connected to a lifecycle conceptualization of social innovation linked to network theory. One example they explored studied how the IQ test initially evolved as a means to prove white supremacy, but was later transformed into a tool to fostering equal opportunities in education (McGowan and Westley 2015: 60–4).

This book takes a long-term methodological view on five social innovations over time. These examples demonstrate that historical analysis allows us to discern the key phases of a social innovation's development (including periods of failure or retrenchment) and to map out the interrelations and interactions of different drivers, institutions, and actors over time. This approach also emphasizes the importance of context and helps us capture negative as well as positive impacts. Both these aspects of impact creation are largely ignored in many analyses of social innovation. While historical accounts of social innovation processes allow tracking their evolution, it is more difficult to disentangle the degree of participation of actors and to what extent these were inclusive. Effects of social innovation on agency are better captured in studies of ongoing innovation processes.[5]

[5] A further point about temporality and the social grid: the cognitive frame of 'innovation' in capitalist regimes introduce a perspective on the present from the future based, usually, on expected return (Beckert 2016). This in turn necessarily marginalizes innovations that does not follow this selection mechanism.

Levels of Analysis

A third important measurement issue with respect to social innovation impact concerns the level of analysis. At the macro-level of society as a whole, government data can be used to capture aggregated changes in the living standards of communities and regions. Other public data may also provide evidence of changes in patterns of employment, educational attainment, health and well-being. However, attributing robust causality to an organization or programme for such changes will always be problematic.

At the meso-level of organizations, methods such as process tracing may be used to analyse observed changes across identified actors. At this level, the impacts of social innovation processes may also be evidenced in analyses of changes across the elements within the ESGM. There will be institutions, cognitive frames, and social networks that are of specific relevance to a given social innovation process, as per Beckert's Social Grid. Activities and pressure exerted may put these social forces under pressure and induce (slow or fast) changes. Such changes in the way people think only materialize slowly, first in modified attitudes, then in behaviours. Over time these behaviours may reach the necessary diffusion and breadth to form new organizations—and eventually, fields and institutions. For this reason, the impacts only become visible after a considerable time and it is typically impossible to foresee the exact timeframe by which this may best be measured. Our research suggests that the impacts that social innovation produces in terms of the ESGM typically represent changes to the social *processes* through which marginalization is (re)produced. But the variable timeframes within which such impacts become apparent makes evaluation at this level complicated, even more so because the cumulative processes leading to impact may be different from context to context (see chapters 5–9).

At the micro-level, the impacts of social innovation can be captured in changes to well-being or human capabilities, as noted by Sen. However, it remains difficult to identify the constituent population without biases and to find a control group that has not been touched by the social innovation under analysis (see further chapter 4). Identifying the most appropriate timescale within which to measure individual impacts is also challenging. Moreover, while subjective perceptions on individual empowerment offer some potential metrics for social innovation impact, it is unclear how such perceptions may be affected by retrospective evaluations and may require repeated monitoring at different moments in time.

Considering the differences and interconnections between these levels of impact, a general conclusion is that measuring social innovation impacts requires attention to both short-term and long-term changes as well as a careful attention to the appropriate units of measurement at different levels of analysis. Broadly speaking, careful attention to participatory methods and the recognition of the importance of embedding beneficiary voice in measurement systems are also central to effective metrics. Having highlighted these three significant issues, we now move on to set out a principles-based framework to guide effective impact measurement decision-making for social innovation.

Critical Framework

Thus far this chapter has suggested that social innovation may require innovative approaches both to the development of metrics and of the methods that enact them. Moreover, we suggest here that being attendant to these issues will increase the reliability of the impact evidence base for investors and policy-makers and their comparability across different social innovation fields across society. In what follows, transversal questions are addressed that could underpin such future developments. It is argued here that effective impact measurement and management systems are built on a series of critical questions rather than on a standardized methodology only, namely (see Figure 15.2): why measure and for whom; who measures; when to measure; what to measure; how to measure (Nicholls 2009).

At the heart of these questions lies the recognition that accounting and reporting systems mobilize and articulate power structures (Chua 1986; Power and Laughlin 1996; see also Lukes 1974), as well as being mechanisms for a more positivistic capturing of organizational value creation (Hopwood and Miller 1994). This approach acknowledges a more interpretive framing of accounting as reporting data that acts as a symbolic mediator for discussion between organizational practice and key stakeholders (Ryan et al. 1992; Gambling et al. 1993; Nicholls 2009, 2018). Moreover, the use of a critical framework for establishing the optimal social impact measurement and reporting system demands a renewed attention to professional *judgement* in terms of the accounting process, since the answer to questions posed by the framework typically do not have clear-cut answers.

The critical issues framework of questions can be grouped under several headings. Each is now considered in turn together with principal learning that the two empirical investigations noted in chapters 4 and 10 produced.

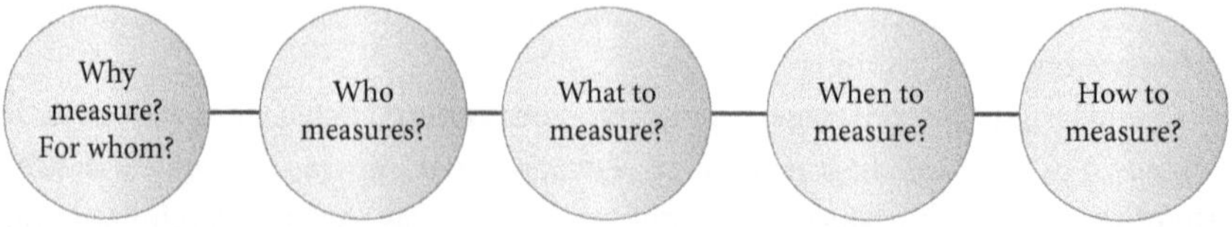

15.2 The Critical Framework
Source: Nicholls (2009).

Why Measure and for Whom?

There are three main—related—reasons for measuring and reporting the social impact of an organization: external accountability to stakeholders; internal strategic planning and decision-making to maximize the value created by an organization or project; assessing the holistic impact of the resources (financial, social, political) focused on the social outcome in the wider ecosystem. These three strategic approaches also highlight the variety of audiences for social impact data (managers, funders, other staff, beneficiaries, government, the media, society at large, and so on). The key question here is: who *cares* about the data? Given this variety of audiences and the likelihood that their perspectives on impact may differ, decisions need to be made concerning *whose opinion matters most* for a social innovation to thrive and impact data collection and reporting tailored accordingly.

Accurate and proportionate measurement of social impact provides both a measure of mission success and a guide to future activity. This may create some moral hazard since it often creates an incentive to be less than candid about shortcomings—'Campbell's law' comes into play (Campbell 1976). Nevertheless, there is both a moral and pragmatic argument that organizations that claim to create social value and that may attract additional support as a result (a tax break or government subsidy or wider public legitimacy and greater donations) have a duty to evidence their claims. Moreover, creating effective social impact metrics and reporting and sharing the resultant data can help create wider good practice and offer benchmarks for other investments (as may be an important externality of the Social Impact Bond model, for example).

The evidence from our primary data collection suggests that an important reason for measuring and reporting the impact of social innovation processes is related to the justification for scaling up. Where external support, for example, public funders, offered investment in order to scale activities, demonstrable impact was a crucial legitimating asset. However, the data set out in chapters 5 to 10, also demonstrated that impact evaluation in terms of accountability to external stakeholders was difficult. This was, partly, because three of the social innovations were cases in which no single external funder was present: the Italian Solidarity Purchasing Groups (see chapter 9), German decentralized water management, and Dutch complementary currencies were all initiatives pushed forward by citizens. A second issue was transaction costs or the *proportionality* of impact measurement. While the social innovators in the cases all reported an interest in capturing the systemic impacts of their initiatives, they sometimes lacked the resources and intentionality to create robust monitoring and measurement mechanisms with which accurately to capture their impact.

Having decided on the strategic purpose of impact measurement and reporting and having identified the key audience to whom this data should be reported, we can now move on to explore the unit of analysis of impact.

What to Measure?

The question of what to measure to get an accurate picture of the impact of a social innovation is more complex that it might first appear. First, is the focus solely on direct impacts or *all* impacts including externalities or accidental effects (which could be negative)? If the objective is only to capture direct impacts (which is often the most appropriate approach) there still remains the question of on what stage of the Theory of Change model will measurement focus—the input, process, output, outcome, or impact phase (or, even, across all phases). Each phase may need a different methodology to capture its impact. This question arises as a result of proportionality issues—as each phase of the Theory of Change typically gets more difficult and expensive accurately to measure. As a result, it may be decided only to measure inputs rather than, say, outcomes—despite the impact data of the latter usually being more meaningful for assessing impact performance.

Next, the specific unit(s) of analysis needs to be considered. This has two aspects to it: the level of analysis; the specificity of the analysis. With regard to the first issue, impact can be measured at the individual, family, community, organizational, sector, field, or societal level. Each level has a different set of epistemological logics and empirical methodologies. With regard to the second issue, the empirical focus can be narrowed to a specific individual or community and so on, or it can attempt to take account of a wider group of stakeholders who may not be the main target of the social innovation. Such an analysis is useful for determining wider impact externalities including unintended negative effects. Making decisions over these two issues is a managerial task that will be informed both by the strategic focus of 'why measure' and by a more general sense of what is *material* in terms of impact data measurement and reporting. Here, materiality is the same concept as in mainstream accounting—namely it is a question of professional judgement determining what data needs to be included or excluded from reporting in order for it to be fit for purpose (e.g. answering the 'why' question).

In terms of the historical cases in this book, the identification of *what* impact to look at has two interpretations. First, the analysis could focus on whether a social innovation really made a difference for key individuals over time—in which cases the measurement methodology would focus at the micro-level and look, for example, at participants in the social innovation process or people belonging to specific marginalized groups. In our research, this built upon the conceptual foundations of the capability approach and used measures of individual agency as data (see chapter 4). Second, the analysis could focus on the macro-level drivers of social change—in which case a (historical) case-study approach that reconstructs the trajectories of a social innovation and marks its crucial stages and key actors would be most useful. This was the method used in chapters 5–9. Once the most meaningful unit of analysis is established, we can consider the important question of who provides the impact data.[6]

Who Measures Social Impact?

Both users (external stakeholders) and producers (the organization itself) can generate social impact data. In addition, users can be co-producers. Users (and co-producers) can include the direct beneficiaries or clients of a project, but also other stakeholders including funders, employees, government, the wider community, partner organizations, employees, and even society at large. As noted above, different stakeholder groups may have very different perceptions of the impact of a social innovation, so professional judgement is needed to establish the materiality of these different points of view and involves two sets of issues: first, the strategic purpose and target audience of the impact data, as was discussed earlier; second, the accuracy and appropriateness of the data, with respect to impact objectives.

The involvement of beneficiaries throughout the impact measurement design and implementation process can also help mitigate the risk of the impact being misunderstood and misreported. A process that starts with the beneficiary and then mediates their involvement with professional judgement is likely to be more accurate than one that starts with managers' data collection and then checks that this is correct by considering selective stakeholder input. Moreover, from a process perspective, beneficiary participation in the methodological design and data collection itself becomes a source of social impact—offering empowerment, participation, and voice to often-marginalized beneficiary groups. Linked to key questions concerning stakeholder roles in generating impact data are temporal issues concerning when the data is collected. We consider this next.

Participatory Methods

Participatory processes require a certain amount of *process freedom* (Ferrero and Zepeda 2014) in which goals, methods, and solutions can gradually be adapted to the ongoing process of trial-and-error, as well as to the constant bargaining between different collective identities and their goals. This poses a challenge for impact evaluation, as it challenges the prevalent linear logic of most Theory of

[6] For issues around measuring climate change impact other scientific data may well be more useful and appropriate.

Change models—often tied to top-down-driven policy design—into question. Policy approaches that pursue a linear logic often apply command-and-control approaches, deciding on desired outcomes in a top-down manner. This is in stark contrast to co-creation, Design Thinking, models that actively embed ideas originated within civil society. They also subsume linear effects, expecting a specific intervention to deliver (positive, intended, direct) benefits. Limits to linear logic models include their inherent incapacity to empower local beneficiaries, deliver sustainable results, or support local institutionalization processes. Especially for social innovation that aims at tackling marginalization, empowering processes appear to be of utmost importance. This will also be true of any attempts to track their social impact, which may be crucially informed by empowerment and indirect or unintended effects.

Thus, the evaluation of the full range of impacts that social innovations produce requires a paradigm shift away from top-down project-cycle-management linear models that typically focus on the achievement of *ex ante* defined indicators. Yet, there are currently no established models that specifically account for the ambitions of beneficiaries and improvements in their agency due to an intervention or initiative. What seems to be necessary, therefore, is greater beneficiary involvement in the design of evaluation models and the implementation of real-time feedback loops that allow for constant re-adjusting of the methodology. This is in line with findings from complexity science that provides technical reasons for abandoning the engineering approach in policymaking in general. Command-and-control in policymaking often attempts to isolate a single action or policy target from other complementary or conditioning factors, whereas complexity science has highlighted the co-evolution of multiple interconnected relationships in the economy and society, jointly resembling a complex adaptive system (e.g. Waldrop 1993). Single elements interact and adapt to changes in a cumulative process. Such interactions are also a crucial element of the Extended Social Grid Model, in which time- and context-specific institutions, cognitive frames, and social networks are seen as interdependent and co-evolve. As social innovation develops to address the dynamics of the social forces that interact in the Social Grid, its inherent complexity becomes apparent.

With increasing process complexity, it becomes increasingly difficult to account for all interactions and effects and design for optimal performance. In this context, evolutionary processes—intended as trial and error with subsequent adjustment—will outperform engineered design (Barder and Levine 2012; Ramalingam et al. 2008). The evaluation and monitoring of social innovation will, therefore, equally need to be cautious about the validity of linear methodological approaches that are designed to capture the impact of a linear theory of change, focusing instead on capturing the success of experimentation, interdependencies, stakeholder voice, and the involvement of actors in the social innovation process. This requires shifting the analytic focus away from intermediate indicators focused on predetermined process variables to methodologies that capture the adaptability and dynamism of interventions, as well as stakeholder voice and engagement. Such a change of analytic focus is tied to the *conditionalities* used to support social innovation (see chapter 16), where the measurement of impact requires innovation in the *type* of accounting methodologies themselves.

When to Measure Social Impact?

In many examples of social innovation, impact performance will vary according to when it is measured and this may affect perceptions of success or failure. In a simple example, the impact of a literacy programme may be measured quickly in terms of the number of illiterate children who can now read, but this tells us little about the real impact of being able to read on these children's lives. To capture this takes time. Similarly, a project working with ex-offenders aiming to reintegrate them into society to reduce re-offending rates may only be considered a 'success' in terms of its impact after several years.

Conversely, early interventions may often have a far greater total social impact than several interventions over time: the logic is of prevention rather than cure. This idea provided the foundation for the contingent liability bond (Wood 2010) developed to provide upfront loan capital for clean-water projects. This model was subsequently adapted to develop the Vaccine Bond and also provided the basic logic of Social Impact Bonds and Development Impact Bonds (Nicholls and Tomkinson 2016). The principle here is of a *social* net present value calculation that values investment in social impact today as being of significantly greater *social* value than investment deferred to future years. However, while Social Impact Bonds have begun to establish methodologies for making this connection explicit in financial valuation (by linking investor payments for early prevention to improved social outcomes in the future), some issues such as climate change necessarily operate on such long timescales that hyperbolic discounting remains the norm in practice (how to calculate the value of an improved climate to future generations fifty years hence?).

On the other hand, another set of temporal issues concerns activities focused on immediate cure rather than on prevention. Here, early measurement makes sense and should provide useful managerial data as a project proceeds. However, in such cases, the impact of a social innovation may continue after a programme itself has finished—the question then is one of the *attrition rate* of the social innovation. This requires careful measurement to determine how long after an intervention has finished can subsequent social impact in a target population be demonstrated to be a direct consequence of its activities.

A further set of temporal issues emerged from the research set out in this volume. Within the impact measurement evaluation described in chapter 10, primary participant data would ideally have been collected *ex ante* (before beginning their participation in the social innovation) and *ex post* (either at the conclusion of their participation in the social innovation or at a defined subsequent moment in time). However, participants typically experience a social innovation at different moments in time. For this reason, the time span between *ex ante* and *ex post* is hard to standardize even *within* a single case—instead it is highly temporally individualized. One approach to this issue is to gather data on the basis of continuous observation with the appropriate data collection infrastructure. All of the examples set out in this section require careful impact measurement design and close attention to the validity of data within a temporal context defined by the social innovation's impact objectives, the context within which it operates, and the particular features of its target populations.

The ESGM developed in this book suggests that social innovation can exert pressure on the social forces that drive social problems. However, the cases presented in chapters 5–9 demonstrated that capturing *when* their effects occur is at least as difficult as predicting when broader institutional change will happen. Our research confirms that changes in socio-structural factors are typically the result of slow-moving cumulative effects. Eventually these will materialize in a sudden rupture of the previous status quo after a case- and context-specific *tipping point* is reached (Pierson 2004). These slow-moving and non-linear features of change in socio-structural factors are significant when trying to measure the effects of social innovation. Since the impact of social innovation is typically dependent on—and seeks to address—socio-structural factors, it can be seen as a function of the capacity to drive change in key social forces and the connections between them. But each social force and interconnection to other structural factors is likely to have different tipping points. For this reason, social innovation life-cycles—in particular their ability to affect the social context in which they are embedded—will be different and will require different times to have effect, which suggests that they will need a different amount of time for producing clearly measurable impact.

Having summarized the temporal issues around social impact measurement within the Critical Framework, next we consider methodologies.

How to Measure Social Impact?

The final step in the Critical Framework process is to consider methodologies for data collection to capture social impact. There are a multitude of methodologies available—this is not the managerial problem. The problem lies in selecting the right one to match the strategic focus of the impact measurement objectives established earlier in the Critical Framework process.

A range of different impact measurement methods have developed from within welfare economics to capture the impact of a given government policy or a programme. Based upon the logics of individual utility these approaches have also been widely used in development contexts. They have the advantage of aggregating individual utilities and, effectively, pricing them to allow policy-makers to do cost–benefit analyses of different programme choices. More recently, these models have been refined by a greater emphasis being placed on human happiness and well-being to provide more nuanced data on individual experience (see e.g. de Neve 2018).

Specific methodologies include: the use of available post intervention data without any comparator; historic baseline models that compare a population before and after an intervention against a series of criteria; matching methods, such as the propensity score matching that compares a population that has experienced an intervention against similar individuals that have not; regression discontinuity that is based on a comparison of those who are eligible for an intervention and those who are just below the cut-off; randomized control trials that compare a population that has experienced an intervention against a random group of individuals that has not.[7]

RCTs have witnessed increasing popularity for policy-analysis and have lately become the prevalent methodology for *ex post* evaluation. A part of the data collection implemented for this volume has therefore attempted to apply this technique to the ad hoc designed primary collection. The distinctive feature of RCTs is that separate *treatment* and *control* groups are designed from the beginning of the intervention as individuals are randomly assigned to either receiving the intervention or being in the control group. For this reason, it is considered to be a more rigorous method and less prone to estimation biases due to the difficult choice of the comparison group than the other options mentioned. The overall *validity* of impact measurement methods (and the data they produce) is usually correlated to the presence or absence of a valid *counterfactual* that can demonstrate what would have happened in the absence of the intervention. However, this is often very difficult (and expensive) to demonstrate, given the multiple—and often unknown/invisible—interdependencies between different social facts. As was mentioned, the key determinant of whether or not to strive for high levels of impact data validity will be *proportionality*—namely, what is the relative value (versus cost) of data validity in context. In some cases, it will not be necessary to 'prove' impact data validity to the *n*th degree for it still to be managerially relevant and useful. In others, such as Social Impact Bonds that explicitly link impact data to financial performance, data validity will be much more important. Indeed, many Social Impact Bonds employ external impact verification/audit

[7] For an extensive presentation and discussion of these techniques see Kekow et al. (2010). For a general overview see Pomerantz (2017). On RCT see Glennerster and Takavarasha (2013).

organizations for just this purpose—though there has yet to be any systematic analysis of such measures.

Non-experimental methods have the advantage that they can be used retrospectively whereas random assignment has, ideally, to be done before the programme is implemented and it is not possible to carry out retrospective randomized evaluations. This was the practical reason why a standard RCT approach was not viable for the empirical analysis conducted in our work (see, further, chapter 4).[8] In all of our case studies, the social innovation initiatives were already in progress and had begun in different moments in time before our evaluation began. Where so-called control groups were used, this was as proxies—namely they were groups that were *potential* but not *actual* participants. Another complexity of applying RCTs to social innovation impact evaluation is that in many social innovation processes, self-selection drives who participates in the social innovation or not. This may represent a key psychological difference between people that *do* get involved and those that do not. Such a variable is difficult to observe and may, therefore, make it impossible to identify an appropriate control group that is similar enough to the treatment group to be valid. This is problematic because complete comparability between a treatment and control group is a key assumption that underpins all effective experimental designs.

If these are mostly pragmatic reasons for not recommending experimental designs for social impact measurement, other more substantial factors may in general make researchers refrain from making use of RCTs when it comes to investigating the impacts of social innovation. If the research analysis is to be focused on the processes that are intrinsic to social innovation—such as how participating individuals are affected in a plurality of dimensions—there may be issues of subjectivity in terms of data collection from the perception of the individuals affected. Yet, the individual—as argued above—must be at the heart of the data collection. This is necessary to qualify the effect, but it cannot quantify it through the calculation of an average effect. While such an approach inherently gives more *voice* to the motivations, expectations, and perceptions of participants, it also automatically limits the validity of the *quantifiable* impact of the social innovation.

Our primary data collection (see chapter 4) was principally focused on developing methodologies through which different social innovation cases (in different contexts) could be compared. This approach paid less attention to the internal validity of the data informing each case study but, rather, emphasized the comparability of (external validity)—and potential learning from—a diverse group of social innovations in terms of their effects on individuals' agency and the changes

[8] Although the primary data collection did foresee the distinction between treatment and control group, defined *ex post*.

they brought to the social forces interacting within a complex system of actions, reactions and relations.[9]

Conclusion

This chapter has built upon the Critical Framework to set out a process and principles-based model of how best to measure the social impact of social innovation. It has also highlighted key learning from our own methodological and empirical work set out elsewhere in this book. Table 15.2 summarizes some of the main examples of social impact metrics mapped against the logics of social impact measurement discussed above in Table 15.1. Table 15.2 also groups its examples by the typology of methods first proposed by Ebrahim and Rangan (2010, 2014). Analytically, this table helps articulate how the Critical Framework can be used in managerial decision-making.

In summary, it is suggested here that asking six critical questions provides a useful grounding and orientation to inform key choices concerning impact data

Table 15.2. Mapping critical issues against approaches to social impact measurement

Approach	Positivist	Critical Theorist	Interpretive	Examples
Logic model	**How to measure?** Methodology			IRIS, GIIRS, EngagedX
Expected return			**What to measure?** Materiality	Outcomes Matrix, results Mark
Experimental methods	**How to measure?** Methodology			Social Impact Bonds RCTs
Systematic reviews			**Why measure?** Strategy	International initiative for impact evaluation
Participatory methods		**Who measures?** Empowerment		Outcomes star, patient voice
Integrative methods			**When to measure?** Variability	Social balanced scorecard

Source: Adapted from Ebrahim and Rangan (2014)

[9] For a critique on RCTs along these lines see Rodrik (2008) and Deaton (2010). These authors stress that results produced through RCTs have so-called interval validity—namely they are valid for the specific case and context, but cannot be generalized. They are, therefore, lacking so-called external validity.

collection design and implementation. Taken together, they offer a pathway to ensure that data collection and analysis will generate an accurate picture of the impact brought about by a social innovation. They also force us to consider key issues of proportionality, data validity, attrition, and attribution. It has also been suggested here that participatory methodology design and data collection processes are of significance in establishing data materiality and validity. They also empower beneficiaries and create a positive social impact that is additional to programme or project impacts.

From our analysis of the impact of social innovation, it appears that a mixed-methods approach is promising (see chapter 4). Qualitative elements, such as in-depth and open interviews, as well as focus groups or brainstorming, can both collect data concerning the case-specific inputs on the goals of social innovations and represent a viable tool to capture and include the voices and perceptions of participants in the measurement process. This is further enhanced if the quantitative data collection also makes use of subjective variables, which further deepen the contribution of beneficiary voice. As previously mentioned, subjective perceptions seem to be of fundamental empirical importance when impacts such as increases in agency or empowerment are to be measured. Yet, subjective perceptions are prone to biases that may, for example, be given by specific idiosyncratic situations that affect the evaluation of one's conditions (Ravallion 2010). Furthermore, the incomparability of subjective evaluations has often been named an intrinsic limit of such metrics. In the research examined here, a first attempt was made to use an anchoring methodology that effectively removed subjective perceptions from data in terms of potential interpersonal incomparability biases. Using anchoring vignettes allowed us to link individual answers to a self-assessment question on the one hand—to remove personal biases—to a shared and comparable situation of a hypothetical peer. The vignettes—which resemble such hypothetical peer situations—allow a construction of a common scale against which the subjectively reported evaluation of one's own situation can be compared. Our primary data collection only implemented this methodology for one case (the Italian SPGs), because it was costly in terms of preparation and implementation. Nevertheless, it appears that such anchoring methodologies are likely to become more important in a future in which subjective evaluations may be the key to the comparable impact measurement of social innovations (Kroeger and Weber 2014).

References

Aguilera, R. V., D. E. Rupp, C. A. Williams, and J. Ganapathi. 2007. 'Putting the S Back in Corporate Social Responsibility: A Multilevel Theory of Social Change in Organizations'. *Academy of Management Review* 32(3): 836–63.

Banerjee, Abhijit V. and Esther Duflo. 2010. 'Giving Credit Where It Is Due.' *Journal of Economic Perspectives* 24(3): 61–80.

Beckert, J. 2016. *Imagined Futures. Fictional Expectations and Capitalist Dynamics.* Cambridge, MA: Harvard University Press.

Barder, Alexander D. and Daniel J. Levine. '"The World Is Too Much with Us": Reification and the Depoliticising of Via Media Constructivist IR'. *Millennium* 40 (3): 585–604.

Battilana, J., and S. Dorado. 2010. 'Building Sustainable Hybrid Organizations: The Case of Commercial Microfinance Organizations'. *Academy of Management Journal,* 53(6): 1419–40.

Blundel, Richard K. and Fergus Lyon. 2015. 'Towards a "Long View": Historical Perspectives on the Scaling and Replication of Social Ventures'. *Journal of Social Entrepreneurship* 6(1): 80–102.

Campbell, D. T. 1976. 'Assessing the Impact of Planned Social Change'. The Public Affairs Center, Dartmouth College, Hanover, NH.

Chua, W. 1986. 'Radical Developments in Accounting Thought'. *The Accounting Review* LX1(4): 601–32.

Crocker, D. 2008. *Ethics of Global Development: Agency, Capability and Deliberative Democracy.* Cambridge: Cambridge University Press.

Crocker, David A. and Ingrid Robeyns. 2009. 'Capability and Agency'. In *Amartya Sen,* edited by Christopher W. Morris, pp. 60–90. Cambridge: Cambridge University Press.

Deaton, Angus. 'Instruments, Randomization, and Learning about Development'. *Journal of Economic Literature* 48(2): 424–55.

de Neve, J. (2018), 'Work and Well-being: A Global Perspective'. Global Happiness Policy Report, Global Happiness Council.

Deci, Edward L., James P. Connell, and Richard M. Ryan. 1989. 'Self-Determination in a Work Organization'. *Journal of Applied Psychology* 74(4): 580–90.

Drèze, Jean and Amartya Sen. 2002. *An Uncertain Glory: India and its Contradictions.* Princeton, NJ: Princeton University Press.

Ebrahim A. and V. K. Rangan. 2010. 'The Limits of Nonprofit Impact: A Contingency Framework for Measuring Social Performance'. Harvard Business School Working Paper 10–099, Boston, MA.

Ebrahim A. and V. K. Rangan. 2014. 'What Impact? A Framework for Measuring the Scale and Scope of Social Performance'. *California Management Review* 56(3): 118–41.

Emerson, J. 2003. 'The Blended Value Proposition: Integrating Social and Financial Returns'. *California Management Review* 45(4): 35–51.

Ferrero, Gabriel Y de Loma-Osorio and Carlos Salvador Zepeda. 2014. 'Rethinking Development Management Methodology: Towards a "Process Freedoms approach"'. *Journal of Human Development and Capabilities* 15(1): 28–46.

Finger, M. and T. Princen. 2013. 'NGOs and Transformation: Beyond Social Movement Theory'. In *Environmental NGOs in World Politics*, edited by Tomas Princen and Matthias Finger, 62–80. London: Routledge

Gambling, T., J. Jones, and R. Karim. 1993. 'Credible Organizations: Self Regulation vs. External Standard-setting in Islamic Banks and English Charities'. *Financial Accountability and Management* 9(3): 195–207.

Glennerster, Rachel and Kudzai Takavarasha. 2013. *Running Randomized Evaluations: A Practical Guide*. Princeton, NJ: Princeton University Press.

Hall, M. 2012. 'Evaluation Logics in the Third Sector'. *Voluntas* 25(2): 307–36.

Haynes, L., O. Service, B. Goldacre, and D. Torgerson. 2012. 'Test, Learn, Adapt: Developing Public Policy with Randomised Controlled Trials'. London: Cabinet Office Behavioural Insights Team.

Hopwood, A., and P. Miller. 1994. *Accounting as Social and Institutional Practice*. Cambridge: Cambridge Studies in Management.

Kekow, J. et al. (2010). 'Improvements in Patient-Reported Outcomes, Symptoms of Depression and Anxiety, and their Association with Clinical Remission among Patients with Moderate-to-Severe Active Early Rheumatoid Arthritis. *Rheumatology* 50(2): 401–9.

Kroeger, Arne, and Christiana Weber. 2014. 'Developing a Conceptual Framework for Comparing Social Value Creation'. *Academy of Management Review* 39(4): 513–40.

Krlev, G., E. Bund, and G. Mildenberger. 2014. 'Measuring What Matters—Indicators of Social Innovativeness on the National Level'. I*nformation Systems Management* 31(3): 200–24.

Lukes, S. 1974. *Power: A Radical View*. London: Macmillan.

McGowan, Katharine and Frances Westley. 2015. 'At the Root of Change: The History of Social Innovation'. In *New Frontiers in Social Innovation Research*, edited by Alex Nicholls, Julie Simon, and Madeleine Gabriel, pp. 52–68. London: Palgrave Macmillan.

Moulaert, F., F. Martinelli, E. Swyngedouw, and S. Gonzalez. 2005. 'Towards Alternative Model(s) of Local Innovation'. *Urban Studies* 42(11): 1969–90.

Mulgan, G. (2010). 'Measuring Social Value'. *Stanford Social Innovation Review* Summer 2010: 38–43.

Narayan, D. 2005. 'Measuring Empowerment: Cross Disciplinary Perspectives'. Washington, DC: World Bank.

Nicholls, J. 2004. *Social Return on Investment: Valuing What Matters*. London: New Economics Foundation.

Nicholls, A. (ed.) (2006). *Social Entrepreneurship: New Models of Sustainable Social Change*. Oxford: Oxford University Press.

Nicholls, A. 2009. 'We Do Good Things, Don't We?: "Blended Value Accounting" in Social Entrepreneurship'. *Accounting Organizations and Society* 34(6–7): 755–69.

Nicholls, A. 2018. 'A General Theory of Social Impact Accounting: Materiality, Uncertainty and Empowerment'. *Journal of Social Entrepreneurship* 9(2): 132–53.

Nicholls, A., and Murdock, A. (eds) (2011). Social Innovation: Blurring Boundaries to Reconfigure Markets. London: Palgrave Macmillan.

Nicholls, A., J. Nicholls, and R. Paton. 2015a. 'Measuring Social Impact'. In *Social Finance*, edited by Alex Nicholls, R. Paton, and J. Emerson, pp. 253–81. Oxford: Oxford University Press.

Nicholls, A., J. Nicholls, and R. Paton (eds). 2015b. *Social Finance*. Oxford: Oxford University Press.

Nicholls, A. and E. Tomkinson. 2015. 'Risk and Return in Social Finance: "I am the Market"'. In *Social Finance*, edited by Alex Nicholls, R. Paton, and J. Emerson, pp. 282–310. Oxford: Oxford University Press..

Paton, R. 2003. *Managing and Measuring Social Enterprises*. London: Sage.

Patton, M. Q. (2011). Developmental Evaluation: Applying Complexity Concepts to Enhance Innovation and Use. New York: Guildford Press.

Pierson, Chris. '"Late Industrializers" and the Development of the Welfare State'. In *Social Policy in a Development Context*, edited by Thandika Mkandawire, pp. 215–45. London: Palgrave Macmillan.

Pomerantz, James R. 2017. 'Perceptual Organization in Information Processing'. In *Perceptual Organization*, edited by Michael Kubovy and James R. Pomeranttz, pp. 141–80. London: Routledge.

Power, M., and R. Laughlin, R. (1996). 'Habermas, Law and Accounting'. *Accounting, Organisations, and Society* 21(5): 441–65.

Pritchett, L. 2013. *The Rebirth of Education: Schooling Ain't Learning*, Center for Global Development. Washington DC: Brookings Institution Press.

Ramalingam, Ben, et al. 2008. 'Exploring the Science of Complexity: Ideas and Implications for Development and Humanitarian Efforts'. ODI Working Paper No. 285. London: Overseas Development Institute.

Ravallion, Martin. 2010. 'Mashup Indices of Development'. Policy Research Working Paper No. 5432. Washington, DC: World Bank.

Reeder, N. and A. Colantonio. 2013. 'Measuring Impact and Non-financial Returns in Impact Investing: A Critical Overview of Concepts and Practice'. LSE Cities, London School of Economics and Political Science.

Robeyns, Ingrid. 2007. 'The Capability Approach: A Theoretical Survey'. *Journal of Human Development* 6(1): 93–113.

Rodrik, Dani. 2008. *One Economics, Many Recipes: Globalization, Institutions, and Economic Growth*. Princeton, NJ: Princeton University Press.

Ryan, B., R. Scapens, and M. Theobald. 1992. *Research Method and Methodology in Accounting*. London: Academic Press.

Sen, Amartya. 1985. *Commodities and Capabilities*. Cambridge, MA: Harvard University Press.

Sen, Amartya. 1993. 'Capabilities and Well-Being'. In *The Quality of Life*, edited by Martha Nussbaum and Amartya Sen, 30–53. Oxford: Clarendon Press.

Waldrop, M. M. 1993. *Complexity: The Emerging Science at the Edge of Order and Chaos*. New York: Simon and Schuster.

Whittington, G. 1986. 'Financial Accounting Theory: An Over-view'. *The British Accounting Review* 18(1): 4–41.

Wood, A. 2010. 'New Legal Structures to Address the Social Capital Famine'. *Vermont Law Review* 35: 045.

16
Social Innovation Policy

Nadia von Jacobi, Alex Nicholls, Daniel Edmiston, Attila Havas, Klaus Kubeczko, György Molnár, Georg Mildenberger, and Gudrun-Christine Schimpf

Introduction

What are the drivers that make government seek innovation, and social innovation in particular? Governments may not always be assumed to have the best for their citizens at heart, yet often policy discourses around social innovation assume a clearly benevolent and constructive narrative: policy agendas are designed to encourage, sustain, and scale innovative solutions to pressing social needs. Yet what are the concrete implications of such noble ambition?

The logic of the Extended Social Grid Model (ESGM: see chapter 1) suggests that in order to tackle marginalization, it is necessary to identify and address the structural processes that give rise to it. Similarly, the conditions under which social innovation flourishes or fails need fully to be understood to explore its potential as a driver of structural change. Our research proposes that marginalization and social innovation are shaped by the prevailing socio-economic and political system that articulates a specific institutional dominance via a Social Grid. The Social Grid conceptualizes a set of dynamic relationships between three social forces: institutions (rules or norms), cognitive frames (mental structures with which people process reality), and networks. Taken together in equilibrium, these forces constitute a specific institutional dominance, or in other words, the social reality of relationships, communications, and exchange between people, which also determine their social positioning (von Jacobi and Nicholls, 2017).

Within the Social Grid, the social dynamics between institutions, social networks, and cognitive frames will have some bearing on the prevalence and typology of marginalization within a given society, as well as on the capacity for social innovation to address this. From this perspective, social innovation emerges and acts within a framework of pre-existing institutional dominance, which also constitutes the institutional framework within which policy is made. The ESGM, therefore, highlights a crucial yet underlying paradox of social innovation policy: if social innovation aims to change systemic power structures to improve human capabilities, how can policy-makers reassess their own role in perpetuating the

Nadia von Jacobi, Alex Nicholls, Daniel Edmiston, Attila Havas, Klaus Kubeczko, György Molnár, Georg Mildenberger, and Gudrun-Christine Schimpf, *Social Innovation Policy*. In: *Creating Economic Space for Social Innovation*. Edited by: Alex Nicholls and Rafael Ziegler, Oxford University Press (2019). © Oxford University Press.
DOI: 10.1093/oso/9780198830511.003.0016

status quo of institutional dominance? Given this apparent paradox, the guiding principles for successful social innovation policymaking must entail heightened self-critique and self-awareness.

In a number of important respects, the way of thinking inherent in mainstream economics fails to capture accurately the operation and effects of the market and as a result cannot explain or remedy marginalization. From this perspective, the causes of marginalization are conceived on the basis of individual agency with little appreciation of the role of socio-structural dynamics that shape the individual factors of marginal productivity or exclusion (economic or otherwise). Within mainstream economics, individual motivation and incentive structures are narrowly conceived as a matter of self-interested rational choice. This poses a particular challenge for explaining and diffusing social innovation, which principally derives its purpose and character from incentive structures orientated towards the welfare of others (Sebastianelli et al 2015; Nicholls and Edmiston 2015b).

Social innovation policy analysis therefore needs to be informed by a framework that combines theory on individual preferences and choices with insights on structural mechanisms that (re)produce marginalization in a systematic way. The ESGM offers a useful analytic framework as it combines Beckert's (2010) Social Grid model with Sen's capabilities approach. The ESGM combines micro- and macro-levels of analysis that are able to capture motivations that go beyond pure market self-interest.

This chapter capitalizes on the key insights produced by the ESGM in order to derive policy implications. This research primarily focuses on findings that mainly reflect insights gathered in the institutionally multi-level reality of the European Union. Yet, many results of the research relate to more general and universal trends that characterize the difficulty of policymaking to promote truly transformative social innovation. Social innovation policy needs to be conceptualized as a broad array of possible policy instruments (see, further, chapters eleven and twelve). It is also in a constant dialectic with the institutional dominance within which it is nested.

Next, this chapter explores the key dimensions of social innovation policy. After this, a series of social innovation policy dilemmas are set out and analysed. Finally, conclusions make some key policy recommendations to maximize the effectiveness of social innovation policy agendas and policymaking and implementation.

Policy as Social Innovation: Policy for Social Innovation

When the returns to an innovation are social in nature (i.e. cannot be privately appropriated), how is the creation of this kind of innovation to be financed? This is an enduring challenge for any social innovation process which seeks to create and disseminate new social practices and solutions. This becomes particularly salient when knowledge supporting the development of products, services, and processes is of a non-exclusive kind. Namely, where the benefits of knowledge creation—and of social innovation—are diffuse (accruing, for example, to society generally) and so too are the financial and social returns. As in the case of goods with positive externalities, this can lead to an under-production of new knowledge that may be necessary for further social innovation. The benefits of social innovation are often long term, social, and non-monetized. Sourcing funds for social innovation designed to tackle marginalization is particularly difficult in this regard. For example, the fulfilment of capabilities—the expansion of substantive freedoms—is hard to quantify and the economic returns of such achievement are invariably spread among different beneficiaries (Nicholls and Edmiston 2015b). In welfare economics, the presence of positive externalities typically justifies public interventions, yet how can policies in support of social innovation overcome the related disincentives?

Social innovation includes forms of action, process, or changes that intend to affect the social and economic space within which marginalization occurs. These forms may arise within the realms of market economy, civil society, or the public sector itself. Consequently, different domains of public policy are of relevance in this regard, which can be grouped into three categories (see also chapter 11). First, there are social innovation policies that are specifically designed to have a direct bearing on the capacity for agents and organizations to affect structural change (e.g. in the Social Grid) through social innovation. Secondly, innovation-oriented social policies offer novel approaches to the design and delivery of assistance, services, and initiatives that have some bearing on structural relations and/or the outcomes for citizens. Of course, there are also other public policies that, while not directly targeting social innovation or marginalization, have indirect effects on both phenomena.

There is now a broad recognition that social innovation is contingent on effective coordination across the policy spectrum but particularly in the realm of social policy. This has significant implications for the design, delivery, and evaluation of public policies that seek to facilitate social innovation that is intended to tackle marginalization (Nicholls and Edmiston 2015a). There is a challenge for support to social innovation that is essentially tied to the fact that social innovation as a concept and phenomenon is essentially emergent and maybe even necessarily contested. Policy-makers, practitioners, and academics today have different understandings of social innovation (Edmiston 2015), which can represent an obstacle to coordination and collaboration. Furthermore, the benefits of social innovation are often intangible (von Jacobi and Chiappero-Martinetti 2017), which also increases the difficulties for policy design and evaluation.

In such cases where the social discount rate, or the present value of future—social—benefits, needs to be accounted for in present policymaking, politics enters as a key factor: who will take over responsibility for voicing the need, which *ex ante* legitimizes risk-taking and investment of resources for such future benefits? The working assumption here is that *all* social innovation is, to some degree, political, but that such 'politics' will have multiple meanings and engage different actors in different contexts and at different socio-structural levels (Nicholls and Edmiston 2017). Moreover, the relationships between the different political actors that support the social innovation system, will be significant factors in achieving overall systemic change.

Policymaking, therefore, can essentially be viewed from two different perspectives:

- While policy *for* social innovation is specifically designed to have a direct bearing on the capacity of agents and organizations to affect structural change through social innovation
- Social innovation in the policymaking process will offer novel approaches to the design and delivery of assistance, services, and initiatives that also have some bearing on structural relations and/or the degree of marginalization of citizens.

The distinction between the two domains helps identifying the kind of policies that will be of relevance for social innovation (and this chapter):

- 'Policies *for* social innovation' comprise support for social institutional entrepreneurship, social service entrepreneurship and social change entrepreneurship.
- 'Policies as social innovation' instead foster public sector innovation through social policy entrepreneurship and social entrepreneurship policymaking via regulations, fiscal policy, and public procurement (Edmiston 2015: 6).

Lessons from Business Innovation

In the realm of economic and industrial policies, business innovation—conducted by profit-oriented companies—has been a key field for policymaking since the 1970s. Therefore, a long tradition exists with respect to theorizing and justifying innovation policies, developing policy instruments, and policy learning.

Although most policy-makers, journalists, natural scientists, and other opinion leaders tend to think of innovation as a ground-breaking technological idea, the modern literature on business innovations is based on a different understanding. First, innovation is not an idea, but a solution introduced to the market—that is, an idea with a proven practical use. Second, not only 'world class' new solutions are defined as innovations, but these new solutions are distinguished by their degree of novelty: a solution can be new (i) to the firm introducing it, (ii) to a given market (that is, not only to the firm introducing it, but to a given country or region), and (iii) to the world. These results are relevant for social innovation practitioners and policy-makers, too.

The literature on business innovation stresses the need to identify the subject (or level) of change and has developed relevant notions to perform detailed analyses. From a social innovation policy point of view, it is also of crucial relevance to have a clear objective as to what sort of change is aimed at, at what level.

A further important lesson of business innovation studies is that innovation does not always bring positive changes. The obvious examples are lock-in in inferior technological trajectories (Arthur 1989; David 1985); the negative health and environmental consequences of widespread motorization (Barker 1987); planned obsolescence purposely limiting the life-span of particular consumer goods (Calvano 2007); and the so-called financial innovations introduced in the name of 'dispersing the risk', but in essence allowing a few well-informed and well-positioned actors to realize substantial profits while putting a huge burden on society as a whole. Social innovation may also have a 'dark side' (Nicholls et al. 2015: 5–6). Clearly, no society is homogenous, not even those members of it who are marginalized and disempowered: they still have their own values and views and, thus, might perceive a certain change process and its effects in different ways. Moreover, a particular measure/solution that improves the situation of some groups can, in fact, affect other groups negatively—and not because they perceive it that way, but as an actual (neutrally/objectively measurable) impact. This needs to be considered carefully by social innovation policy-makers when devising interventions and specific policy tools.

Various economics paradigms treat business innovation in diametrically different ways. They may consider different notions as crucial ones, offer diverse justifications (policy rationales) for state interventions, interpret the significance of various types of inputs, efforts, and results differently, and thus—implicitly—identify different 'targets' for measurement, monitoring, and analytical purposes: what phenomena, inputs, capacities, processes, outcomes, and impacts are to be measured and assessed.

Evolutionary economics is concerned with several key notions that are relevant when analysing social innovation: the importance of dynamics; uncertainty; differences across contexts; learning; various types, forms and sources of knowledge; path dependence; processes of generating variety; selection among diverse solutions; networking and cooperation among actors; and co-evolution of various types of changes (Dosi and Nelson 2010; Fagerberg et al. 2005).

Social innovations draw on various types (scientific and practical) and forms (codified and tacit) of knowledge, stemming from different sources (organized and systematic R&D activities, as well as other types of search processes, e.g. those 'informed' by practitioners). Diversity is, therefore, a key notion. To devise appropriate policy tools, policy-makers need to recognize the diversity of social innovations too, in terms of their nature, drivers, objectives, actors, knowledge bases, and process characteristics.

The market failure argument, advanced by mainstream economics, implies that a strong intellectual property rights (IPR) regime is a must. This policy approach is unlikely to be the most germane one to promote social innovation. Furthermore, gaining the recognition of being a creative social innovator is likely to be a stronger driver than protecting IPR. Overall, policies should rather promote the dissemination and exploitation of knowledge to foster social innovation than constrain these processes.

The system failure concept,[1] developed by evolutionary economics of innovation, can be extended to social innovation without any theoretical constraint. While it is a demanding task to establish what elements of a social innovation system are missing or fledgling, what institutions ('rules of the game') hamper social innovations and, thus, what policy actions would be appropriate to induce the necessary changes, these analytical efforts cannot be spared if social innovation policy-makers strive for devising effective policy measures.

In sum, those business innovation studies that are based on the theoretical underpinnings of institutional and evolutionary economics, are dealing with aspects that are compatible with the ESGM approach. Hence, several of their considerations and results are relevant—without or with some modifications—when analysing social innovation.

Another stream of the business innovation literature deals with the question of whether technology and the social sphere can be separated when analysing innovation. Three, somewhat different, schools in science and technology studies can be identified as sharing a common understanding and interpretation in that tradition: (i) the Social Construction of Technology approach in a narrow sense, as initially outlined by Pinch and Bijker (1984); (ii) Actor Network Theory (Callon 1987); and (iii) the Large Technological Systems models (Hughes 1987). These three theories have been developed as an answer to technological determinism that neglects the role of the social factors and forces in technological change. Thus, all three approaches share an ambition to move away from previous conceptualizations that emphasized the role of the individual inventor (or genius) and from

[1] System failure can be interpreted as 'the inability of a system of innovation to support the creation, absorption, retention, use, and dissemination of economically useful knowledge through interactive learning or in-house R&D investments' (Chaminade et al. 2009: 361). Policies in this approach are meant to intervene on specific problems/failures related to a process within the national innovation system (Capriati 2018: 149).

making distinctions between technical, social, economic, and political aspects of technological development, conceptualizing society and technology as a seamless web, in which different actors, social groups, or technological artefacts constantly interact (Bijker et al. 1987: 3). Bijker and colleagues have argued that frequently used distinctions—such as society/technology, technical/social, or pure/applied science—are socially constructed and can be misleading.

Thus, social and technological/artefactual (see chapter 2) aspects of innovation are equally important and relevant and, therefore, need to be considered in both social innovation research and social innovation policymaking. This becomes clear, for example, when looking at financial services for marginalized groups particularly in Africa, based on mobile communication technologies.

Our longitudinal analysis of social housing and freshwater supply (chapters 5 and 6 in this volume) has also shown that several types of social innovations can only be successful when supported by various types of business innovations (that is, technological, organizational, business model, financial, and market innovations). Social innovations, therefore, need to be considered within science, technology, and innovation (STI), as well as in social innovation policymaking. In line with this, three ways of looking at social innovation policy can be identified:

1. Social innovation policy can be considered as a separate policy domain related to social policy aiming at providing new solutions to societal challenges such as marginalization (policy as social innovation). For example, developing a solution to operationalize free or heavily subsidized Kindergartens would fall under this category.
2. Social innovation policy can be regarded as a sub-field of STI policies comprising policy measures in support of those involved in social innovation processes (policy for social innovation), independently of the actors (profit-oriented firms or non-for-profit organizations). An example could be funding social innovation projects that aim at co-creation and testing of new Kindergarten models by involving service providers, municipalities, parents, and social science researchers.
3. Social innovation policy can also assume the role of a sub-field of economic policymaking, in which only firms are being considered as solution providers to societal challenges when designing policy tools. For example, entrepreneurs might be offered tax incentives to introduce profitable models of Kindergartens, running at the lowest cost for municipalities and parents.

For policy *as* social innovation—or social innovation policy as part of social policy—key lessons from business innovation policymaking can be useful in several respects. First, lessons can be drawn in relation to the understanding of the functions and failures of innovation systems, and to the importance of getting users and customers engaged in the innovation process (user-led innovation).

Second, invention should not be confused with innovation: social innovation policy measures should be designed in a way that ideas meant to address societal challenges should become implemented through the social innovation process, that is, leading to the successful introduction and diffusion of social innovation.

In terms of policy *for* social innovation—or in the case in which social innovation may be considered as a sub-field of STI policies—policy-makers need to pay more attention to (a) the interactions between business and social innovations; (b) frugal innovation, which aims at solutions for poor customers; as well as (c) inclusive innovation, aimed at inclusive economic growth, and in the meantime at involving various stakeholders in the innovation processes, and thereby mobilizing a diverse set of knowledge and experience.

A new type of justification for STI policies is also emerging based on the bold ambition that besides correcting market and/or systemic failures, policies should also aim at creating new opportunities and new markets. The basic idea of challenge-driven and market-creating STI policies (Cagnin et al. 2012; Coenen et al. 2015; Foray et al. 2012; Mazzucato 2016; Mowery et al. 2010) might provide a useful starting point for social innovation policymaking on the one hand, and might also make it easier to accept that STI policies should consider social innovation too as a legitimate 'target' on the other.

The widely used dichotomy of social versus technological innovation thus needs to be reconsidered. It is more instructive and productive—both for social innovation practitioners and social innovation policy-makers—to understand social innovation as a co-evolutionary process of social innovation and all the necessary business innovations. It is also worth stressing that the concept of user-led innovation (von Hippel 1988) can be at least as relevant for social innovation policymaking as in the case of STI policies aimed at fostering business innovations.

The Courage for Disruption

For either of the typologies of targeted social innovation policy introduced above, the paradox of challenging institutional dominance from within which policies emerge is of relevance. The potential of social innovation to address/redress marginalization effectively is contingent on existing power relations enshrined in a given equilibrium between social forces—or the institutional status quo (von Jacobi and Nicholls 2017). To some extent, successful social innovation always needs to induce institutional change and, therefore, represents a threat to the current institutional dominance. This raises questions about the relationships between power, marginalization, and social innovation. For example, who decides the policy priorities and strategic framework of governments? How do institutions govern the behaviour and outcomes of citizens and, in particular, of those who are most marginalized? Who controls common or shared ways of thinking? What role can national and trans-national social networks play in instigating a realignment of power when they are concurrently subject to power relations? (Nicholls and Edmiston 2015a). Only the transference of power from the powerful to the powerless can help ensure that social innovations are enacted, but more importantly, that these are implemented in a way that maximally benefits the most disempowered citizens. Accordingly, if social innovation and innovative social policies intend to tackle marginalization through structural change, it is necessary to take account of and where possible address the power imbalances that exist at the individual, collective, and institutional levels of politics (Nicholls and Edmiston 2015a). The next section will try to shed light on this paradox of embedded versus transferred power.

One aspect of such transference of power may imply the absorbing of ideas and values into policymaking that emerge from citizens themselves. The inclusion of such values is intrinsic to the goals of social innovation to improve individual capabilities, in terms of people living the lives they have reason to value (Sen 1999: 87). Opening up the political decision-making process to new objectives and long-term goals constitutes a transference of power and *voice* itself, in as much as people's *agency* is directly connected to their ability to act and to bring about change in accordance with their own values and objectives (Sen 1999). The inclusion of the collective goals or values of groups that were previously excluded can be interpreted as a modification in the power relations that govern an institutional status quo (von Jacobi and Nicholls 2017). This is in line with BEPA's (2010: 12) conception of social innovation itself, as a process that:

> Aims to meet the social demands of vulnerable groups that are not currently met by the existing socio-economic settlement; address societal challenges in which the boundary between the 'social' and 'economic' blurs; and promote a participatory approach to social organization and interactions that centres on empowerment.

Second, innovations that meet previously neglected social needs may be able to address societal further challenges and—through the development of new forms of organization and social interaction—facilitate empowerment and participation, both as a source and outcome of well-being (von Jacobi, Edmiston, and Ziegler 2017). This ensures that an individual's power to pursue her own chosen ends assumes a central role in overcoming marginalization.

From this perspective, the transformative potential and effects of social innovation need to be seen as on the one hand directly addressing marginalization, but also on the other to be contributing towards structural change that, in turn, may alter the conditions and processes that lead to poverty and social exclusion in the first place (Nicholls and Edmiston 2015a). Marginalization can, in this sense, be conceived as 'the result of a social process through which personal, social, or environmental traits are transformed into actual or potential factors of disadvantage' (von Jacobi, Edmiston, and Ziegler 2017: 4). Social innovation targets such social processes and seeks to modify them. This mode of analysis has significant implications for policy design, implementation, and evaluation—not only within the arena of social innovation, but more broadly across other policy domains.

Ultimately, if policy-makers are to design and implement effective social innovation agendas to address marginalization, it is necessary to identify and address the complexities of the power hierarchies that frame their own policy objectives. Such a process requires policy-makers to recognize and overcome their own institutional dominance, requiring both self-reflexivity and institutional entrepreneurship. Importantly, this will require the introduction of careful analyses of power and politics into the largely apolitical realm of social innovation policymaking.

Issues for Policy-makers

Picking Winners versus Providing Horizontal Support

Chapter 7 explored the case of the Kiútprogram. The Hungarian private founders of the Kiútprogram had asked the government in 2009 to support the programme in the form of reduced social contribution and other pieces of favourable regulation. Finally, they reached an agreement with the government to obtain public support in the form of subsidies tied to the programme, as opposed to changing the regulation as a general rule for this type of social innovation. The incoming government overruled that agreement and did not fulfil the promise of the previous government.

Governments come and go in parliamentary democracies and it is not unusual that the incoming government does not respect the promises of the previous one. This case, therefore, points to a general dilemma: should social innovation practitioners try to obtain public support dedicated to a specific project or should they aim at changing the overall regulation and thus improve the framework conditions for social innovation (beyond a specific project)? That question, of course, can be raised from a different angle too: should policy-makers try to support specific social innovation projects (on a one-off basis, with tailored, individually negotiated subsidies, grants, and contracts) or would it be a more effective policy stance to create favourable framework conditions for social innovations in general and thus promote social innovation more broadly?

In the context of better understanding what constitutes successful social innovation policy, it is worth considering some of the lessons that can be learnt from the domains of innovation and industrial policies. A key point from these domains is the practice of 'picking winners': in other words, selecting and subsidizing 'national champions'. This was a dominant policy logic—especially in France and the United Kingdom—for decades. Very high costs typically accompanied such projects, for example, Concorde or the Alvey Programme for Advanced Information Technology.

Ergas (1987) introduced a typology of mission- versus diffusion-oriented technology policies. Mission-oriented technology policy is, in essence based on heavy subsidies provided to 'national champions' in various forms. His analysis confirmed that mission-oriented policies are costly and rarely pay off. The exception was in the United States due to the specific features of its national innovation system. This includes: a wide and fast diffusion of new technologies, due to a smooth transfer of knowledge between sectors (academia, business, policymaking) and across state borders as people are more mobile in the United States (more frequently cross sectoral and geographical borders) than in most other countries; the sheer size of the market; the hidden, but effective, innovation policy tools often in the form of targeted public procurement; the clever strategies to promote dual-use technologies (fast, and widespread use of military technologies in various economic sectors for civil use).

Given the failures of the 'picking winners' approach, a new policy rationale emerged in the late 1980s and early 1990s stressing the importance of favourable framework conditions for innovation and the need to avoid the mistake of offering substantial subsidies to 'national champions'. In other words, so-called 'horizontal policies' were favoured over vertical policies.[2]

Later on, cluster policies were invented as a compromise between horizontal and vertical policies. Firms form clusters as they pursue interconnected economic activities and, thus, represent a more promising target for public policy than conventional horizontal policymaking. Policies can, therefore, be better defined and more carefully directed to clusters. At the same time, clusters are looser than the usual targets of vertical policies, especially 'national champions'.

In addition, the notion of grand challenges was introduced in the early 2000s to stress the need to tackle major global problems (most notably, climate change, energy, environment, safety and security, and so on). Such an approach put the emphasis on devising and implementing challenge-driven (solution-oriented) STI policies.[3] A similar more general policy approach stresses the need for directionality when setting and implementing STI policies. Another approach proposes that besides correcting market or systemic failures, policies should also aim at creating new opportunities and new markets.

[2] 'National champions' were often almost as large as an entire economic sector due to high concentration of industries and the importance of a national champion in any given sector.

[3] Other policy tools, beyond the domain of STI policies, are also needed to tackle these grand challenges.

Seemingly, we can observe a 'policy pendulum' in operation here, swinging from picking winners to horizontal policies and then back again to more tailored support, albeit using different buzzwords. A closer look, however, reveals that the most recent approaches should not be mistaken as a resuscitated form of the previously discredited picking-winners approach. In summary, a promising policy to support social innovation aimed at tackling marginalization would rely on an appropriate combination of measures from a rich policy toolbox, as opposed to just one or two dominant policy tools. Policymaking is an art not a science or technology strictly following scientific theories and predictions or user manuals. The task is to strike a balance between too narrowly and too loosely set objectives and to apply an appropriate mix of policy measures, also devising and introducing new types of measures, when needed. Context does, indeed, matter.

The Relative Costs of Social Innovation Policy

While social innovation and innovative social policies often enhance capabilities at an aggregate level, they can at times fail to address the needs of the *most* marginalized and disempowered citizens. Individuals and groups suffering multiple forms of deprivation or exclusion are often the least able and likely to make use of services, initiatives, and goods. In addition, public agents and organizations are often better equipped to address minor aspects of marginalization, rather than, for example, chronic or absolute poverty. In the political economy of social policy and social innovation, policy-makers, practitioners, and social innovators need to be mindful of this and its repercussions for tackling poverty and social exclusion (Nicholls and Edmiston 2015a).

Usually, we can observe a complex power structure in society as opposed to a neat dichotomy—a division of society into powerful and powerless people is a rather oversimplified description. Thus, differentiating between more and less marginalized people is an important issue regarding social innovation for the marginalized. In this context *social exclusion* is regarded as an extreme form of marginalization, when different kinds of disadvantages (e.g. in education, employment, income, housing, land ownership, or health conditions) are exacerbated by discrimination and the lack or weakness of social ties with non-marginalized social groups are mutually reinforcing each other. The example of the Roma minority in several European countries illustrates this general description. The sudden drop in demand for unskilled workers during the transition to a market economy in the 2000s led to the marginalization of undereducated people in the labour market. However, within this group the Roma became even more socially excluded.

In the case of socially excluded target groups, social innovation should be multifaceted. It is not sufficient to intervene at one point only, social innovation must aim at improving institutions, building inter-community bridges, empowering beneficiaries through capability building, and influencing the dominant cognitive frames (in alignment with the Social Grid). This is a costly activity. An important condition of achieving empowerment is creating trust between the beneficiaries and the social innovators (Molnár 2017).

There is a trade-off between the degree of the participants' marginalization and the necessary costs of social innovation: the worse the beneficiaries' initial status, the larger the costs. There is a significant difference between the position of groups that are marginalized in some way and the genuinely socially excluded groups—in the case of socially excluded population the costs can be especially high. If, as a consequence of cost considerations, only less disadvantaged groups are included in a social innovation, the exclusion of the most disadvantaged may become even stronger. Some forms of increasing exclusion can be growing inequalities within the marginalized population, further deterioration of social ties, distrust between socially excluded people and social innovators, and strengthened learned helplessness. Looking at it from the other side, if a social innovation based on social action, that aims at reducing marginalization, only targets the most disadvantaged, the probability of failure is higher, given that the goal may be more difficult to achieve. Thus, this type of social innovation may be discredited as a failure—on top of losing the time, funds, and goodwill invested. This dilemma has no optimal solution in theory either—it requires continuous analysis and discussions.

Moreover, a quest for profitability or, at least, the financial self-sustainability of social innovations can *ab initio* create this dilemma—leading to discrimination against the most expensive possible beneficiaries. This phenomenon is analogous to the 'skimming' effect that selects the easiest/cheapest clients to serve in providing welfare services (Le Grand and Bartlett 1993). Given the importance of capability building and its ensuing costs, expecting financial sustainability from social innovation seems to be a major policy misconception, potentially leading to perverse outcomes, reduced funding, and even serious mission drift. However, on the contrary, the removal of financial sustainability as a requirement may lead to the irresponsible spending of external financial resources. Involving private funders who are likely to have a strong financial interest—in most cases coupled with the necessary experience and expertise—to check if spending is responsible reduces risk here. Again, this solution corresponds to the co-payment system suggested by Le Grand and Bartlett (1993).

Not only the degree of marginalization of the social group but also the extension of the support provided by the social innovation influences the costs of a given social action. There is a trade-off between the degree of help and the short-term empowerment effect, leading to another policy dilemma. The more a social innovation supports capability building and the integration of participants into different kinds of social networks, the less it contributes to developing agency in the short run. Here the short- and long-term effects may be different: a seemingly more paternalistic approach in the short run can increase the chance of social mobility, which leads later to a very strong empowerment effect over time. To find the balance between paternalism and empowerment is a critical question in the case of social innovation addressing the most socially excluded people.[4]

In line with efforts to reduce poverty more generally, social innovation for the marginalized requires an extensive policy debate on the desired extent and depth with which marginalization is to be reduced. Again, the issue of social long-term returns is of relevance. Often those kinds of marginalization that are more deeply rooted and more difficult to eradicate also bear the highest social costs for society. In such cases, greater amounts of investment are justified in order to tackle the *most* marginalized by the expected (high) social returns. An example of social innovation that has put this perspective at the centre of its model is Social Impact Bonds (see chapter 12). These new contracts between private capital, government, and service providers claim to offer reductions in public expenditure via social innovations in welfare projects. In such cases, the high costs of these integrated approaches targeting a small portion of the population are claimed to be well justified by their significant effect on ultimately reducing the overall social problem—thus combining high social benefits with reductions in public spending.[5]

The Capability to Associate

While more radical conceptions of social innovation have been partially adopted through the principle of co-production in social policymaking, these initiatives have on the whole been rather perfunctory and superficial. As the ESGM highlights, the role of social networks—their formation and ability to advance claims—should not be neglected. In the EU, for example, social innovation policy has had little regulatory or financial support given to the social networks that strengthen the collective political power of marginalized populations. Without these political networks of action, disadvantaged individuals and communities have little power to shape dominant institutions and cognitive frames that so profoundly affect the extent and character of their social exclusion. Unless a series of measures to encourage the incorporation of marginalized views and experiences into the policymaking process is put in place, the agenda-setting and decision-making centre may remain largely unchanged in terms of the solutions to marginalization deemed appropriate and necessary. If public policymaking neglects the political mobilization of those most negatively affected by structural inequalities (of power,

[4] With regard to the problems concerning the relationship between a capabilities approach and paternalism, see chapter 13 and Claassen (2014).

[5] There is, however, little robust evidence yet of public-sector savings from Social Impact Bonds. Indeed, they may actually *raise* overall costs (Edmiston and Nicholls 2018).

resource, and opportunity), social innovation is unlikely to fulfil its transformative promise for the marginalized (see chapter 11).

Finding bottom-up solutions that actively involve those disadvantaged or that ensure they have a say in the definition and implementation of social policy relies on the capability to associate. The empirical findings in chapters 5 to 9, however, suggest that this capability cannot be taken for granted. The disadvantaged do not necessarily organize themselves, either in formal and established organizations or in social innovation processes. They typically lack the access, frequency, and intensity of contacts in the right social networks. Moreover, the social innovator is frequently an actor external to the disadvantaged group. If the goal is to promote social innovation processes that, at least in the medium term, involve marginalized beneficiaries as active co-creators of the policy process, there is a need to focus on approaches that actively foster the capacity to associate (Ziegler, Molnár, Chiappero-Martinetti, and von Jacobi 2017).

Examples of approaches that may successfully contribute towards building such capacity include network approaches that start at the community level (neighbourhood, village, or hamlet) with activities that focus on information sharing and group formation. Investment and support are also crucial for the building of bridges to other similarly affected, as well as non-marginalized, groups and actors. Policy-makers have several opportunities here: education can, early on, lay important foundations in terms of civic education. Children and youngsters can acquire mental openness and the ability to grasp opportunities by being exposed to and learning from concrete involvement in civic organizations. The content of education can play an important role in fostering the capacity to aspire to an improved life via textbook examples, specific awards, or game-like competitions. The education system also exerts a fundamental mechanism of *social mixing* that may promote or hinder cross-pollinating of social networks. Enrolment rules—not based on residency—can also promote diversified social ties. Apart from education, policymaking in other areas of peoples' lives can have important effects on their ability, predisposition, and material opportunity to associate. Labour and unemployment policies can provide space and time for association and the exchange of thoughts, ideas, and solutions. Secure conditions further reduce the risks of associative action. Finally, policy that actively encourages the formation of associations, especially among the least advantaged is also very valuable (Ziegler, Molnár, Chiappero-Martinetti, and von Jacobi 2017). Equally relevant are tools and actions that reduce the economic, political, and administrative costs of the foundation and operation of such undertakings. These political instruments can be viewed as key horizontal supports to social innovation processes.

The implicit dilemma of supporting the capability to associate is complex. The associative patterns and the formation of networks are intangible processes that only become apparent when they reach a significant critical mass. Especially among those segments of the population where such networks are lacking, investments and projects may require more time and effort to achieve successful results. The efficiency of such investments may, therefore, be difficult to track, leading policy-makers to struggle to justify and *ex post* validate the rationale for their public spending. Furthermore, a blank cheque approach to promoting the capability to associate may end up supporting networks and groups that defend values that are quite incompatible with social democracies such as extreme right-wing groups, populists, or terrorists. Again, policy-makers face the difficulty of properly tracking how effectively spending reaches the intended marginalized groups. Care must be paid to effective monitoring and evaluation of key policy interactions if these two challenges are to be tackled. In particular, a paradigm shift seems to be necessary in which an outcome-oriented logic of evaluation, based on pre-determined indicators of achievement is replaced by more process-oriented mindsets that focus on participatory approaches (see chapter 15). Intended beneficiaries can stop being passive agents (see chapter 3) but instead can become active agents of their own change. Only by creating effective feedback mechanisms, in which their voice co-determines the design of impact evaluation and monitoring systems, can truly transformative policy inputs and their effect on the capability of individuals to associate be accurately assessed.

Subsidiarity versus Adverse National Conditions

Another crucial question for policy-makers is to which level of decision-making social innovation policy should refer. Clearly, this depends on the specific topic and the thematic and functional interactions between ministries, departments, and existing regulatory frameworks. For example, while EU policies are embedded in a multi-levelled form of governance, many other countries in the world are federated or adopt some logic of decentralization. In what follows, while the insights are largely informed by the reality of the EU, the findings can have equal relevance in other contexts.

Which is the appropriate level of governance at which social innovation for the marginalized should be financed? This depends on the factors that constitute the social processes in which the sources of marginalization lie. To be most effective, social innovation would be financed at those levels that have a bearing on the structural factors that play a role in perpetuating marginalization. What should be noted, however, is that the national level is not always and automatically the most appropriate one. The interactions between institutions, networks, and cognitive frames can reproduce marginalization at this level. In this process, national authorities are not a neutral, long-term finance provider for marginalization problems—rather, they may be responsible actors—in part—for the processes of reproducing marginalization (Ziegler, Molnár, Chiappero-Martinetti, and von Jacobi 2017). This phenomenon is especially strong and widespread in the case of the Roma minorities in Hungary where there is evidence of misuse of EU finance. Therefore, leaping over political levels from the national to the regional for direct investment into the social inclusion of the most marginalized may provide a more effective method of funding. In this way, funds could directly reach the NGOs best supporting marginalized communities, bypassing the national and local administrations and their political goals.

This solution, however, may contradict the EU subsidiarity principle (Moulaert et al. 2005). According to the Treaty on European Union there are three preconditions for intervention by the EU in accordance with the principles of subsidiarity:

1. The area concerned does not fall within the Union's exclusive competence (i.e. non-exclusive competence)
2. The objectives of the proposed action cannot be sufficiently achieved by the Member States (i.e. necessity)
3. The action can, therefore, by reason of its scale or effects, be implemented more successfully by the Union (i.e. added value).[6]

According to our argument above, the second condition holds. However, it is less clear as to whether condition three is also met. The experiences of Roma pilot projects financed directly by the EU may suggest a possible positive answer—funding at the regional level works.[7]

Interactions Matter

Policy interacts with the socio-structural processes that social innovation seeks to address in a complex way. Policy in support of transformative social innovation needs to recognize—and act on—the multiple direct and indirect effects it might generate. It has to comprehend, and contemporaneously address, different social forces and the way they interact with each other. Where the policy objective is the transference of power to the marginalized, such transference may not be easy because key social forces are interconnected and co-evolve in an interdependent way. Effective policy initiatives need to recognize such interconnections and act upon them in an integrated way. For example, where public perceptions of Roma communities (cognitive frames) or the increase of their civic engagement (social networks) is aimed for, not also paying attention to addressing institutional factors will undermine the overall likelihood of success.

[6] http://www.europarl.europa.eu/atyourservice/en/displayFtu.html?ftuId=FTU_1.2.2.html.

[7] Pan-European Coordination of Roma Integration Methods--Roma Inclusion EU pilot project, reference.

Moreover, public policy has many diffuse and unintended effects. As a result, it is often hard to anticipate how individuals are going to respond to legislative or distributive changes. As a result, it is equally, if not more, difficult to anticipate how the interconnected and co-evolutionary relationships between institutions, social networks, and cognitive frames may be affected by policy change. In acknowledging the complexity of socio-structural relations, it becomes particularly difficult to anticipate which policies might best be able to address power imbalances across the social forces when the relationships between them are inherently dynamic and co-dependent (Nicholls and Edmiston 2015a).

The irreducibility of socio-structural relationships also makes it difficult to assess the efficacy of social innovation—the latter always unfolds within a dense web of causal ties that make it difficult to identify one primary driver of change. However, assuming that it is possible to capture this process, if a social innovation does not lead to a positive change in social relations, can this still be considered a success? While it might directly address some of the effects of poverty and social exclusion, it may not directly address the *causes* of such marginalization. Should such an activity be considered a policy priority? Empirical evidence presented elsewhere in this book (see chapters 5 to 12) suggests that social innovations only rarely enact a transformation of society, and that this only happens when all links that tie together the social forces in the Social Grid are substantially modified (von Jacobi and Nicholls 2017).

While the institutionalist literature has often stressed the theoretical need to look at interdependencies (Seo and Creed 2002; Dacin et al. 2002; Bassanini and Duval 2009; Belloc and Bowles 2013; Hodgson and Stoelhorst 2014; Thévenon 2016; Langlois 2016), the contemporaneous investigation of multiple links is under-investigated. However, the literature on *institutional complementarities* has suggested that bipartite relationships between social structures matter, for:

- The functioning of a single institution or social structure
- The persistence of particular institutional landscapes
- The available policy options that seek to promote institutional change, conditioned by transition costs in and out of a particular institutional setup (von Jacobi 2018).

Moreover, North's work has highlighted the relevance of the interplay between formal rules and the informal constraints embodied in customs, traditions, and codes of conduct (1990: 6). Such relationships between institutions and cognitive frames form the cultural-institutional conventions (Belloc and Bowles 2013) that are likely to shape the available policy options, the costs of institutional change, and the overall integrity, inertia, and resilience of a complex institutional system. Social innovation—and the policies that seek to support it—operates in such a landscape of inter-dependent social forces. A crucial acknowledgement that policymaking needs to make is, therefore, not only to consider social forces in an isolated way but also to recognize and to disentangle the web of inter-connections that makes these forces interdependent on each other.

Social innovation will potentially (and in some cases, intentionally) address each of the six dynamic links (see chapter 1) across the three elements of the Social Grid. Policy actions may facilitate or impede such processes by facilitating or limiting access to public channels of promotion or by regulating the access and affiliation mechanisms of relevant networks (such as professional associations). Only a careful analysis of the wide-reaching effects of policies that relate to civic freedoms and an individual's capability to associate will enable the most effective policy mix that supports transformative social innovation to be identified.

Learning from the Past

As outlined in more detail in chapter 4, a historical analysis of social innovation cases can contribute to the understanding of how the complex interactions of a given institutional dominance have been put under pressure and modified by social innovation processes. The historical analysis of cases presented here across Europe (see chapters 5 to 9) produced some interesting insights for social innovation policymaking. First, there may not be a clearly identifiable target group for a social innovation. The beneficiaries of a social innovation can be multiple and very different. Indeed, in some cases, a social innovation may be valuable to society as a whole as a public good—meaning that everyone may benefit not just the key target groups, as was the case with social housing (see chapter 5). Access to clean water is a similar example (see chapter 6). When policy focuses on network goods that resemble public goods with a natural monopoly, public interventions can lead to a situation where society as a whole can profit from the social innovation, not just the marginalized, which were the immediate target (Scheuerle et al. 2016: 172). To policy-makers this means that wider social benefits (even if intangible and of long-term nature) need to be recognized, acknowledged, and possibly be put at a central position within the policy discourse. Where possible, advocating the spread of a social innovation to benefit all, therefore, seems sensible (as e.g. Edwin Chadwick in mid-nineteenth-century Britain, in Scheuerle et al. 2016: 97 and chapter 6). If the position of marginalized people improves through the social innovation, others will profit as well (Schimpf 2017: 34). The case of freshwater supply in Europe (chapter 6) made this clear: if all benefit, the support for the social innovation is stronger than if only a part of society is targeted. Moreover, marginalized groups will, in the long run, benefit more if actors from different backgrounds shape the social innovation (Schimpf 2017: 33), as this indirectly affects the cross-social strata nature of the networks of which they are a part.

Second, in the implementation of social innovation policy, multi-levelled interactions need to be accounted for. The more that policy-makers ignore the complexity and local specificity of social problems, the more likely the solutions will create costly problems in the long run (Scheuerle et al. 2016: 183). This is particularly true when decisions are taken under time pressure or using scarce resources, such as after or during economic crises. In such situations, the complexity of social problems is often not adequately understood with pernicious effects (Westley et al. 2007: 21–2; Neck et al. 2009; Rittel and Weber 1973). Historically, the more distant the service providers were from the local reality of the beneficiaries (e.g. major top-down programmes in social housing), the more likely were the unintended—negative—effects. Thus, local knowledge seems to be crucial properly to identify and understand the social forces and their interactions that have a bearing on the sources of marginalization. Yet, as previously mentioned, local knowledge alone may not be sufficient if there is a lack of political will to overcome the institutional dominance in which it is embedded. Yet, even so, the inclusion of multiple political levels may not always lead to satisfactory results. Privatization of the water sector, for example, created economic problems for marginalized people because of different levels of policymaking. While different suppliers (private companies or public entities) determined the pricing, the laws or regulations (e.g. concerning social benefits) were set at the national or supranational level. The more political levels that are acting within a complex field the more difficult it is to limit the unintended effects (Scheuerle et al. 2016: 183). Ideally, responsibilities and compensatory tools would be distributed according to the *subsidiarity* principle, to guarantee proper inclusion of local knowledge and maximize the likelihood for functioning real-time feedback loops. Yet, where marginalization is deeply embedded in local dynamics, such knowledge also needs higher-level policy responses with compensatory actions.

A historical investigation of social innovation processes shows that early achievements for the mainstream do not, necessarily, offer a solution for everyone in the long run. As in technology, in social innovation too there is no single best way. Depending on the resources available locally, constellations of interests and cultural preferences, solutions that work in one place might not be very useful somewhere else. For this reason, it is important to start valuing niches. Complex interactions between social forces, path dependencies, and lock-in effects make corrective changes difficult and costly. Therefore, collecting experience by thorough and locally relevant tests is typically needed. Niche activity—which may be social innovation attempts that failed or that persist at a very small scale, represent an archive of such tests or possible solutions that policy-makers can keep as a stock of possible future models. Niche activities can be kept as future options for divergent solutions and variants. These niche activities offer a reservoir of ideas, which can be drawn upon, especially in times of emergency or crisis, in which policymaking may lack the resources and focus for investing in new solution-finding. A particular social innovation may well remain in a niche and does not have to scale. It can be seen as an 'island solution', only relevant for a very specific and restricted context. In the best case, it may offer a solution for the problems of tomorrow and even if some social innovations never reach the stage in which they make it to the mainstream, they can still provide helpful insights for those that eventually will (Scheuerle et al. 2016: 199). Solutions do not all develop in the same way or with the same timeframe, but are, rather, dependent on their specific ecosystem and contextual conditions. Against this background, it seems to be a general rule-of-thumb for policymaking to stimulate exchange between solution developers on one hand, while also respecting the specifics of local circumstances in their attempts at scaling and transferring solutions on the other (Scheuerle et al. 2016: 199f.). Social innovation does not, typically, follow a linear trajectory, which often makes technocratic policy approaches to social innovation clumsy and inadequate.

Embracing the logic of limited knowledge, policy-makers should remember that social innovators need access to infrastructures and funding. Having a variety of providers of solutions increases the probability for the best solutions for future societal problems to emerge. It is impossible to know today which social innovation will cure the problems to come. Therefore, policy-makers should support the horizontal availability of funding. Policies and regulations should allow for different models of financing and organization. It is not only necessary to fund the creation of new ideas. It is also important to keep open the possibility to quickly implement good ideas in an emergency. This is an investment in the future, which supports societal stability and grows the innovation capacity of society in the future. Project funding is not an effective solution. It is more important to open up regular paths to funding that should, however, not be tied to a logic of short-term pay off. Just as in the case of start-ups, long-term mindsets are crucial to obtaining significant results. Moreover, policymaking should be careful to avoid the formulation of regulations that do not leave space for alternative approaches or that implicitly favour a certain standard implementation (Scheuerle et al. 2016: 200).

Providing Network Support

Social innovations that involve citizens in having a voice in decisions that govern basic aspects of their lives typically engage civic groups and networks for the coordination of this task. Any support for social innovation that takes this participatory aspect seriously should, therefore, not just support new ideas and innovations via project-based support and competitions. In addition, an alternative and viable support focus could be networks that have already established themselves and have a stable number of network members or have existed for more than a number of years. Such network support could focus on financial resources to be used for coordination work, as this is precisely the kind of work that is responsible for creating additional social value and that, at the same time, is often a blind-spot of project-focused innovation support. Coordination is also necessary when new networks are to be constructed that bridge across established and cohesive social groups. Especially for social innovation that targets the marginalized, the improbability of a capability to associate to be naturally emerging needs to be recognized. In view of the interactions across networks, cognitive frames, and the associated claims for new institutional solutions, it is important to create and support new mechanisms of affiliation that may break down previous stereotypes and segregation in social behaviour. However, in order to succeed in creating new networks of collective identity, careful coordination across relevant actors and organization will be necessary.

Networks are living social entities confronted with numerous organizational challenges. This raises several important questions. How are decisions made? How can knowledge be effectively documented and shared? How can rules that stabilize interactions and modes of action within a network be established? These questions require coordination, which is typical of public goods that have positive externalities of non-rival nature. However, coordination activities are typically underfunded. Yet, such funding is vital for promoting the capability to associate. Moreover, as such networks frequently emerge from local and regional struggles, they frequently require strong leaders—this character attribute can be selected for and strengthened too. Succession issues may emerge later, however, but these challenges are not new. As such, there is significant potential in public support for coaching and exchange between networks to deal with these issues and share lessons learnt (Ziegler 2017).

Keeping Partnerships Open

Networks represent the material reality in which social relations become manifest. If the transformative potential of social innovation is to be realized, then the reshaping of old networks and the formation of new ones represents a fundamental task. Policy-makers need to support both the reformation and creation of networks to redistribute tasks and responsibilities. Often, the formation of new networks creates new methods of sharing tasks (e.g. public–private partnerships) or assigning responsibilities to new type of actors (e.g. the provision of social services through the third sector). The creation of new partnerships to support emerging actors constitutes a key policy opportunity for the identification, experimentation, and testing of social innovative models.

The empirical work elsewhere in this book (see chapters 5 to 9) demonstrates that the existing rules or laws defining the eligibility criteria for working with government often hamper new partnerships. Legal frameworks that regulate public provision or the eligibility for public funding often create barriers to access for actors that may have blurred legal identities (informal associations not legally constituted as organizations) or that represent new typologies of actors (e.g. co-working spaces), not yet recognized by the current normative framework. In the case of the Italian Solidarity Purchasing Groups (SPGs: chapter 9), for example, the selection of consumption products based upon ethical and organic criteria was a mechanism by which Italian families could enact politicized consumption. However, the groups of families in SPGs tended to shy away from formally constituting as an organization. This was due to various reasons, from a sort of anarchic cultural tradition, to the perceived red-tape associated with the management of any kind of *formal* association in Italy. Although SPGs could potentially unlock a series of interesting innovations—such as collective investment into clean energy production—they often lack funding because of their ineligibility for public funds to scale their impact reach and depth. In Hungary, on the other hand, the legal framework regulating social enterprises hinders them from delivering social services unlike other cooperatives elsewhere. This is mainly due to the funding eligibility criteria defined by the Ministry of Finance in terms of setting its own budget. This has seriously hampered the development of social entrepreneurship in the country.

In such cases, the complex interactions between legal frameworks (institutions) and the perception of them (cognitive frames) shapes the kind of networks (type of eligible actors) that are either empowered or marginalized in terms of whether or not they can compete for funding contracts to provide services. To be more effective in terms of supporting social innovation, policy-makers should aim to dismantle the barriers and obstacles that tightly define the eligibility criteria for funding social impact. Such a process of dismantling requires some courage as it would be in opposition to the usual command-and-control model of welfare spending that is typical of top-down policymaking. However, if the objective is to allow for greater co-creation of social innovation policy by citizens, more trust and openness is needed, for example by funding initiatives the results of which cannot be easily modelled *ex ante*.

Rethinking the Conditionalities of Funding

There is an intrinsic *problematique* at the heart of policymaking that seeks to support social innovation. Policy approaches defined in line with the managerial approach of command-and-control are intrinsically in contrast with the principles of co-creation typical in social innovation processes, which actively search for ideas originated within civil society. Policy-makers should also avoid isolating a single action or policy target from other, complementary actions or conditioning factors. However, the interdependencies between social forces stressed by the

ESGM highlight the threat of underestimating the complex environment within which social innovations emerge and unfold.

For policymaking, this implies a recognition that it is basically impossible to know and foresee all interdependencies, which characterize a social innovation process. As in all forms of innovation, successful social innovation processes are unlikely to follow predictable trajectories and the possibility of identifying best practices and transferring or replicating them may seriously be hampered by the context-specific patterns asserted by the Social Grid. Interdependencies are often harder to disentangle than in the case of business innovation with quantifiable financial implications. This makes the exact identification of causal relationships and connected action more difficult. So, it is the way that the policy interlinks with other elements of the system that determine whether its outcomes are sustainable or not (von Jacobi and Bonan 2014).

Complexity science has contributed to our understanding of the co-existence of multiple interconnected relationships in the economy and society by proposing a view of them as complex adaptive systems (Arrow, Anderson, and Pines 1988; Waldrop 1992; Beinhocker 2007; Fontana 2010). This implies that single elements interact and adapt to changes in a cumulative process. Recognizing complexity has important consequences for policymaking, in particular that some old certainties may falter: for example, we might have to rethink the value of the technocratic, engineering, approach in which the purpose of analysis is to predict accurately and to design best solutions (von Jacobi and Bonan 2014). According to complexity studies, it is *evolutionary processes*—intended as trial and error with subsequent adjustment—that outperform engineered design (Barder 2012; Ramalingam 2014). From this perspective, it seems clear that policymaking that seeks to support transformative social innovation needs to refrain from engineering approaches and instead adopt a more cautious role in which experimentation is actively supported.

Experimentation has the advantage that interdependencies unfold in a natural way, with the actors involved acquiring and converting context-specific knowledge into the identification of the most apt solutions. For policymaking this implies several things:

- Refraining from using conditionalities of funding as much as possible—in as much as conditionalities shape the kind of results that need to be produced *ex ante*. Experimentation—and innovation—are crucially tied to the concept of trial and error and may be severely hampered by constraints on the results (and the timing by which these) need to be achieved.
- The tendency to believe in convergence and the attempt to transplant solutions that have worked in context A directly to context B is risky, as it tends to simplify and to flatten the mechanics that characterize the local and context-specific Social Grid.

- In general, the one-size-fits-all logic seeking to identify a single most relevant determinant in support of social innovation needs to be abandoned, giving way instead to the logic of best-fits (Ramalingam 2014), which highlights the context-specificity of solutions.
- Policy action needs to be recognized as single elements within an adaptive system. Public funding needs to be reframed in order to put diverse implementations and innovative approaches (experimentation) at the centre of intervention efforts, coupling them with the design of effective feedback loops that allow for the evaluation and the selection of the most appropriate solutions.
- The active participation of citizens in co-creation processes and a more structural reliance on local knowledge and resilience may play a major role in a successful adaptive process (von Jacobi and Bonan 2014).
- Letting go of the technocratic and engineering approach has important advantages too. The drivers of local implementation are embedded into the context and the local knowledge available within it. Therefore, more locally credible solution-finding processes automatically create a more holistic approach as complex interdependencies unfold in the trial-and-error process. Different problems are likely to be targeted jointly as a result of greater *process freedom* (Ferrero Y de Loma-Osorio and Zepeda 2014) that allows participants to develop their agency and to re-align the targets of the action with existing external conditions. Decentralized policy-design is also strengthened.

An open challenge for policymaking, however, is the construction and maintenance of functioning real-time feedback loops that allow the monitoring and evaluation of public programmes to take place. These are essentially tied to the ability to implement successful participatory approaches and to design mechanisms of co-creational accounting (see further chapter 15). What policy-makers should abandon, however, is the facile assumption that policy outcomes need to be certain and known *ex ante* (Dolphin and Nash 2012).

Conclusion

Social innovation and, particularly, its capacity to tackle marginalization, cannot be left to market forces alone. This model has demonstrably failed. For different reasons, unfettered market mechanisms will leave economically disadvantaged and politically disenfranchised societal groups in a marginal position without voice. Public intervention is crucial if social innovation is to be recognized and supported as a means *and* an end in which citizens contribute to the continuous transformation of their society. As obvious as this may seem, policy processes need to interiorize this insight by avoiding relying only on mainstream conceptions of market functioning and of socio-economic inequality. The following actions would come some way towards embedding social innovation in policy and practice.

Policy-makers need to support or even create intellectual, institutional, and economic space for social innovation to flourish. Public bodies and regulators need to create a new *intellectual space* for the assessment of social innovation by giving greater consideration to how policy design, implementation, and evaluation might better capture, assess, and reward the returns on social innovation. Embedding the recognition of interdependent social forces and their bearing on the production and resolution of marginalization is key. A major challenge in this regard is the fact that social innovation can be seen as a nested micro-paradigm within a hierarchically superior paradigm that is prevailing in wider mainstream economic thinking (such as neo-liberalism). Social innovation *must* challenge such paradigms, if it does not wish to become involved in mere conciliatory politics, in which a provision of 'pragmatic solutions' to 'political problems' regarding the redistribution of resource, power, and opportunity is at its centre. Relying on the market only for assessing whether an innovative solution is successful or not, as in the case of business innovation, may leave no space for an assessment of the more enduring effects of social innovation tackling marginalization. The social innovation policy concept itself depends on its nesting within other policy domains and paradigms, which constitutes the established institutional logics, ideas, and practices. This is profoundly relevant in mediating any significance, salience, and efficacy that social innovation policy may achieve (Edmiston 2016).

As effective measures to foster social innovation require political, economic, and social commitment (based on shared cognitive frames) to realign or displace existing power relations and dynamics in the Social Grid, *conflicts* between differing policy levels, their operational functions and ideological interests should acquire greater importance within the intellectual space of social innovation policymaking. Only such a *challenging* attitude can succeed in mobilizing networks of resource and actions to tackle marginalization without incurring the risk of 'capture' by those fundamental assumptions that shape the prevailing policy paradigms and policy options available (Béland 2005).

To date, there seems to be disinclination amongst policy-makers for such approaches leading to a tendency to treat social innovation and related policymaking as a-political (Edmiston 2016).[8] While this ultimately leads to the insufficient identification of *sources* of marginalization, including culpability, accountability, and responsibility for them, such an approach also maintains

[8] However, in some countries, social innovation policymaking is explicitly political.

and reinforces the vagueness of the social innovation concept, allowing for the accommodation of a plurality of social, political, and economic interests in mobilizing resources and action (Edmiston 2016). While openness to (potentially opposing and conflicting) actors and ideas may be beneficial for the process of social innovation itself, the specific risk that social innovation for the marginalized incurs, is to merely treat symptoms instead of curing the causes.

Institutional space should be created to increase the capacity for governance systems and processes to operate within a climate of uncertainty, experimentation, and risk. Given the non-monetary and diffuse nature of returns on social innovation, and its embeddedness into multi-level complex structural factors, significant public funding and support is needed to support it. Actions that address social processes may have initial—yet insufficient—effects to reach that tipping point (Pierson 2004) at which a social force *de facto* changes. Public finance is justified where the social discount rate highlights the value of future benefits. Where this is not possible, public bodies should only leverage private sector investment when the diffuse, long-term, and non-economic returns on an investment are valued and recognized as the principle objective of social innovation.

Public policies also need to challenge assumptions surrounding self-interested, so-called 'rational' choice. Social innovation is predominantly driven by a commitment to the social good of others, therefore, challenging the market assumptions about the 'rational' utility-maximizing motivations that underpin the actions of individuals (Sebastianelli, Chiappero-Martinetti, and von Jacobi 2015). A greater recognition of the values and objectives that go beyond self-interest and the maximization of individual utility is, therefore, needed in shaping policies effectively to support social innovation. Public deliberation and consultation, such as the public consultation on the Europe 2020 strategy, should be extended to identify and give credence to the social and economic commitments elsewhere that citizens value (Nicholls and Edmiston 2015b).

The functioning of the social economy needs to be understood as an intrinsic feature of social innovation—as both a means and an end that can give expression to social commitments. Economic growth and the function of this market are the means rather than the end—that is, a means to expanding the real freedoms enjoyed by the members of the society. Policy interventions should be framed as supportive of people-led and people-centred social innovations that intervene on market actors and institutions in real-time sustainably and meaningfully to address the socio-structural dynamics that lead to marginalization (Nicholls and Edmiston 2015b). As Edmiston (2016: 7) put it:

> One possible solution to addressing the apolitical nature of social innovation policymaking, and scaling the capacity and impact of projects funded through public institutions, would be to foster a greater degree of collective identification and political action amongst marginalized populations... To effectively scale

> social innovation and resist the instrumentalization of need provision, public policies must move beyond diffuse, isolated instances of self-organization and empowerment... To foster systemic social innovation, public policies must engender collective identification amongst marginalized individuals so that they are able to identify how their individual disadvantages are shared and connected to broader regimes of production, consumption, inequality, welfare. and power.

Creating new collective identities is the key to developing the cognitive frames and their institutionalization that social innovation drives forward. These are, however, culturally mediated too and not equally visible/powerful across all of society. Only through significant and deep support to build the capability to associate and by contemporaneously opening up channels through which collective claims can challenge, complement, and gradually substitute the prevailing institutional logics (Thornton and Ocasio 1999) will social innovation policy remain faithful to its transformative promise. In this way policy-makers can reap the benefits of both social policy *for* social innovation and social policy *as* social innovation.

References

Arrow K., P. Anderson, and D. Pines. 1988. *The Economy as an Evolving Complex System*. Reading, MA: Addison-Wesley.

Arthur, B. (1989): 'Competing Technologies, Increasing Returns and Lock-In by Historical Events'. *Economic Journal* 99(March): 116–31.

Barder O. (2012): 'Complexity and Development'. Kapuściński Lecture 2012, Center for Global Development.

Barker, T. C. (ed.). 1987. *Economic and Social Effects of the Spread of Motor Vehicles.* Basingstoke: Macmillan.

Bassanini, A., and R. Duval. 2009. 'Unemployment, Institutions, and Reform Complementarities: Re-assessing the Aggregate Evidence for OECD Countries'. *Oxford Review of Economic Policy* 25(1): 40–59.

Beckert, J. 2010. 'How Do Fields Change? The Interrelations of Institutions, Networks, and Cognition in the Dynamics of Markets'. *Organization Studies* 31(5): 605–27.

Beinhocker E. 2007. *The Origin of Wealth.* London: Random House.

Béland, D. 2005. "Ideas and Social Policy: An Institutionalist Perspective'. *Social Policy and Administration* 39(1): 1–18.

Belloc, M. and S. Bowles. 2013. 'The Persistence of Inferior Cultural-Institutional Conventions'. *American Economic Review* 103(3): 93–8.

BEPA. 2010. *Empowering People, Driving Change: Social Innovation in the European Union.* Brussels: Bureau of European Policy Advisers.

Bijker, W. E., T. P. Hughes, and T. Pinch (eds). 1987. *The Social Construction of Technological Systems: New Directions in the Sociology and History of Technology*. Cambridge, MA: MIT Press.

Cagnin, C., E. Amanatidou, and M. Keenan. 2012. 'Orienting European Innovation Systems towards Grand Challenges and the Roles That FTA Can Play'. *Science and Public Policy* 39(2): 140–52.

Callon, M. 1987. 'Society in the Making: The Study of Technology as a Tool for Sociological Analysis'. In *The Social Construction of Technological Systems: New Directions in the Sociology and History of Technology* edited by W. E. Bijker, T. P. Hughes, and T. Pinch, pp. 83–103. Cambridge, MA: MIT Press.

Calvano, E. 2007. 'Destructive Creation'. SSE/EFI Working Paper Series in Economics and Finance No. 653.

Capriati, M. (2018): *Capabilities, Innovation and Economic Growth*. London: Routledge.

Claassen, R. (2014): 'Capability Paternalism'. *Economics and Philosophy* 30(1): 57–73.

Chaminade, C., B-Å Lundvall, J. Vang, and K. J. Joseph. 2009. 'Designing Innovation Policies for Development: Towards a Systemic Experimentation-Based Approach'. In *Handbook of Innovation Systems and Developing Countries: Building Domestic Capabilities in a Global Setting*, edited by B-Å Lundvall, K. J. Joseph, C. Chaminade, and J. Vang, pp. 360–79. Cheltenham: Edward Elgar.

Coenen, L., T. Hansen, J. V. Rekers. 2015. 'Innovation Policy for Grand Challenges: An Economic Geography Perspective'. *Geography Compass* 9(9): 483–96.

Dacin, M. T., J. Goodstein, and W. R. Scott. 2002. 'Institutional Theory and Institutional Change: Introduction to the Special Research Forum'. *Academy of Management Journal* 45(1): 45–56.

David, P. A. 1985. 'Clio and the Economics of QWERTY'. *American Economic Review* 75(2): 332–7.

Dolphin T., and D. Nash (eds). 2012. 'Complex New World: Translating New Economic Thinking into Public Policy'. London: IPPR—Institute for Public Policy Research.

Dosi, G., and R. R. Nelson. 2010. 'Technical Change and Industrial Dynamics as Evolutionary Processes'. In *Economics of Innovation*, edited by B. H. Hall and N. Rosenberg, pp. 51–127. Amsterdam: North-Holland.

Edmiston, D. 2016. 'The (A)Politics of Social Innovation Policy in Europe: Implications for Socio-structural Change and Power Relations'. CrESSI Working Paper No. 32. Brussels: European Commission, DG Research.

Edmiston, D. 2015. 'Executive Summary of an EU Social Innovation Policy Survey'. CrESSI Working Paper No. 17. Brussels: European Commission, DG Research.

Edmiston, D., and A. Nicholls. 2018. 'Social Impact Bonds: The Role of Private Capital in Outcome-Based Commissioning'. *Journal of Social Policy* 47(1): 57–76.

Ergas, H. 1987. 'The Importance of Technology Policy'. In *Economic Policy and Technological Performance*, edited by P. Dasgupta and P. Stoneman, pp. 51–96. Cambridge: Cambridge University Press.

Fagerberg, J., D. C. Mowery, R. R. Nelson (eds). 2005. *The Oxford Handbook of Innovation*. Oxford: Oxford University Press.

Ferrero Y de Loma-Osorio, G., and C. S. Zepeda. 2014. 'Rethinking Development Management Methodology: Towards a "Process Freedoms Approach"'. *Journal of Human Development and Capabilities* 15(1): 28–46.

Fontana, M. 2010. 'Can Neoclassical Economics Handle Complexity? The Fallacy of the Oil Spot Dynamic'. *Journal of Economic Behaviour and Organization* 76: 584–96.

Foray, D., D. C. Mowery, and R. R. Nelson. 2012. 'Public R&D and Social Challenges: What Lessons from Mission R&D Programs?' *Research Policy* 41(10): 1697–702.

von Hippel, E. (1988): *The Sources of Innovation*. Oxford: Oxford University Press.

Hodgson, G. M., and J. W. Stoelhorst. 2014. 'Introduction to the Special Issue on the Future of Institutional and Evolutionary Economics'. *Journal of Institutional Economics* 10(4): 513–40.

Hughes, T. P. 1987 'The Evolution of Large Technological Systems'. In *The Social Construction of Technological Systems: New Directions in the Sociology and History of Technology* edited by W. E. Bijker, T. P. Hughes, and T. Pinch, pp. 51–82. Cambridge, MA: MIT Press.

von Jacobi, N., and J. Bonan. 2014 'Methodological Questions for the Post-2015 Development Agenda'. *Glocalism: Journal of Culture, Politics and Innovation*. http://www.glocalismjournal.net/issues/feeding-the-planet-energy-for-life/articles/methodological-questions-for-the-post-2015-development-agenda.kl.

von Jacobi, N., and E. Chiappero-Martinetti. 2017. 'Social Innovation, Individuals and Societies: An Empirical Investigation of Multi-layered Effects'. *Journal of Social Entrepreneurship* 8(3): 271–301.

von Jacobi, N., D. Edmiston, and R. Ziegler. 2017. 'Tackling Marginalisation through Social Innovation? Examining the EU Social Innovation Policy Agenda from a Capabilities Perspective'. *Journal of Human Development and Capabilities* 18(2): 148–62.

von Jacobi, N., and A. Nicholls. 2017. 'Social Innovation and Institutional Change: An Analysis of Micro-processes, their Transformative Potential and Constraints'. Presented at the IVth WINIR Conference, Utrecht, 14–16 September.

von Jacobi, N. 2018. 'Institutional Interconnections: Understanding Symbiotic Relationships'. *Journal of Institutional Economics* 14(5): 853–76.

Langlois, R. N. 2016. 'Institutions for Getting out of the Way'. *Journal of Institutional Economics* 12(1): 53–61.

Le Grand, J., and W. Bartlett. 1993. 'Quasi-Markets and Social Policy: The Way Forward?' In *Quasi-Markets and Social Policy*, edited by J. Le Grand and W. Bartlett, pp. 202–20. London: Palgrave Macmillan.

Mazzucato, M. 2016. 'From Market-Fixing to Market-Creating: A New Framework for Innovation Policy'. *Industry and Innovation* 23(2): 140–56.

Molnár, G. 2017. 'Capability Building Combined with Microcredit: The Loan Alone Is Insufficient'. *Journal of Social Entrepreneurship* 8(3): 354–74.

Mowery, D. C., R. R. Nelson, and B. R. Martin. 2010. 'Technology Policy and Global Warming: Why New Policy Models Are Needed (or Why Putting New Wine in Old Bottles Won't Work)'. *Research Policy* 39(8): 1011–23.

Moulaert, F., F. Martinelli, E. Swyngedouw, and S. Gonzalez. 2005. 'Towards Alternative Model(s) of Local Innovation'. *Urban Studies* 42(11): 1969–90.

Neck, H., C. Brush, and E. Allen. 2009. 'The Landscape of Social Entrepreneurship'. *Business Horizons* 52(1): 13–19.

Nicholls, A. and D. Edmiston. 2015a 'Policy Brief D1.2: Re-assessing Social Innovation to Tackle marginalization'. CrESSI Working Paper No. 11. Brussels: European Commission, DG Research.

Nicholls, A., and D. Edmiston. 2015b. 'Policy Brief D1.4: CrESSI's Approach to Social Innovation: Lessons for Europe 2020'. CrESSI Working Paper No. 13. Brussels: European Commission, DG Research.

Nicholls, A. and D. Edmiston. 2017. 'Policy Paper. How to Facilitate the Growth of Different Kinds of Social Innovation: The Politics of Social Innovation'. CrESSI Working Paper No. 37. Brussels: European Commission, DG Research.

Nicholls, A., M. Gabriel, and J. Simon (eds). 2015. *New Frontiers of Social Innovation*. Basingstoke: Palgrave Macmillan.

North, D. C. (1990): *Institutions, Institutional Change, and Economic Performance*. Cambridge: Cambridge University Press.

Pierson P. 2004. *Politics in Time: History, Institutions, and Social Analysis*. Princeton, NJ: Princeton University Press.

Pinch, T. J., and W. E. Bijker. 1984. 'The Social Construction of Facts and Artefacts: Or How the Sociology of Science and the Sociology of Technology Might Benefit Each Other'. *Social Studies of Science* 14(3): 399–441.

Ramalingam B. 2014. *Aid on the Edge of Chaos: Rethinking International Cooperation in a Complex World*. Oxford: Oxford University Press.

Rittel, H. W. J, and M. M. Weber. 1973. 'Dilemmas in a General Theory of Planning'. *Policy Sciences* 4(2): 155–69.

Scheuerle, T., G.-C. Schimpf, G. Glänzel, G. Mildenberger, and R. Ziegler. 2016. 'Three Major Social Innovations as Viewed through the Lens of the Extended Social Grid model'. In 'Report on Relevant Actors in Historic Examples and an Empirically Driven Typology on Types of Social Innovation'. In 'Creating Economic Space for

Social Innovation' (CrESSI), edited by T. Scheuerle, G.-C. Schimpf, G. Glänzel, and G. Mildenberger, pp. 1–224. Brussels: European Commission.

Schimpf, G.-C. (ed.). 2017. 'Comparative Report on Historic Examples and Similar Recent Social Innovations in an Early Stage'. In 'Creating Economic Space for Social Innovation' (CrESSI). CrESSI Working Paper No. 35. Brussels: European Commission, DG Research.

Sebastianelli, M., E. Chiappero-Martinetti, and N. von Jacobi. 2015. 'From Rational Agents to Human Diversity'. In 'Report Contrasting CrESSI's Approach of Social Innovation with that of Neoclassical Economics', edited by C. Houghton Budd, C. W. M. Naastepad, and C. P. van Beers. CrESSI Working Paper No. 12. Brussels: European Commission, DG Research.

Sen, A. 1999. *Development as Freedom*. Oxford: Oxford University Press.

Seo, M.-G., and W. D. Creed. 2002. 'Institutional Contradictions, Praxis, and Institutional Change: A Dialectical Perspective'. *Academy of Management Review* 27(2): 222–47.

Thévenon, O. 2016. 'Do Institutional Complementarities Foster Female Labour Force Participation?' *Journal of Institutional Economics* 12(2): 471–97.

Thornton, P. H. and W. Ocasio. 1999.' Institutional Logics and the Historical Contingency of Power in Organizations: Executive Succession in the Higher Education Publishing Industry, 1958–1990'. *American Journal of Sociology* 105(3): 801–43.

Waldrop, M. 1992. *Complexity*. New York: Simon and Schuster.

Westley, F., B. Zimmermann, and M. Q. Patton. 2007. *Getting to Maybe: How the World Is Changed*. Toronto: Vintage Canada.

Ziegler, Rafael, György Molnár, Enrica Chiappero-Martinetti, and Nadia von Jacobi. 2017. "Creating (Economic) Space for Social Innovation." *Journal of Human Development and Capabilities* 18 (2): 293–98.

Ziegler, R. 2017. *Wer zur Quelle will, muss gegen den Strom schwimmen: Innovation aus Bürgerhand für eine demokratisch-ökologische Wasserwirtschaft*. München: oekom Verlag.

Index

Note: Tables, Figures and boxes are indicated by an italic '*t*', '*f*' and '*b*', respectively, following the page number.